Civil Procedure

BY RICHARD L. MARCUS
University of California, Hastings

THOMAS D. ROWE, JR.
Duke University

Sixteenth Edition

THOMSON
BAR/BRI

EDITORIAL OFFICES: 111 W. Jackson Blvd., 7th Floor, Chicago, IL 60604
REGIONAL OFFICES: Chicago, Dallas, Los Angeles, New York, Washington, D.C.

PROJECT EDITOR
Steven J. Levin, B.A., J.D.
Attorney At Law

SERIES EDITOR
Elizabeth L. Snyder, B.A., J.D.

QUALITY CONTROL EDITOR
Sanetta M. Hister

Summary of Contents

Text Correlation Chart

Gilbert Law Summary Civil Procedure	Cound, Friedenthal, Miller, Sexton *Civil Procedure: Cases and Materials* 2001 (8th ed.)	Field, Kaplan, Clermont *Materials for a Basic Course in Civil Procedure* 1997 (7th ed.) 2000 Supp.	Hazard, Tait, Fletcher *Pleading and Procedure, State and Federal, Cases and Materials* 1999 (8th ed.) 2000 Supp.	Marcus, Redish, Sherman *Civil Procedure: A Modern Approach* 2000 (3rd ed.)	Rosenberg, Smit Dreyfuss *Elements of Civil Procedure: Cases and Materials* 1990 (5th ed.) 1997 Supp.	Yeazell, Landers, Martin *Civil Procedure* 2000 (5th ed.)
I. TERRITORIAL JURISDICTION AND RELATED MATTERS						
A. Introduction	Page 62-73	Page 923-932	Page 175-195; Supp. 4	Page 667-696	Page 178-179, 222-225	Page 77-118
B. Contemporary Constitutional Grounds for State Court Jurisdiction	73-80, 91-182	932-982, 995-1043	196-380; Supp. 4-6	706-804	225-248, 259-325; Supp. 91-94	119-184
C. Statutory Authorization for Jurisdiction	80-91, 182-185	982-995	266-285; Supp. 4-6	697-705	248-258, 325-329; Supp. 93-97	191-194
D. Litigating Jurisdiction	185-190		361-362	804-809	325	168-174
E. Venue	339-359	1052-1071	447-468; Supp. 10	825-832	335-350; Supp. 100-101	197-201
F. Forum Non Conveniens	359-370	1071-1083	469-481; Supp. 10-11	833-841	335-350; Supp. 100-101	203-211
G. Notice	191-254	1084-1111	317-338	815-824	330-335; Supp. 98-100	174-180
II. SUBJECT MATTER JURISDICTION OF THE FEDERAL COURTS						
A. Introduction	255-259, 333-338	858-862	381-384	846	178-181	213-215
B. Diversity Jurisdiction	259-277	191-199, 889-904	400-410; Supp. 7	846-856	181-189, 200-205; Supp. 68-72, 75-76	228-243
C. Federal Question Jurisdiction	277-298	188-191, 862-868	385-389	857-877	189-200; Supp. 73-75	215-227
D. Supplemental Jurisdiction	298-321	868-889	411-433; Supp. 7	878-904	206-219; Supp. 76-90	244-250
E. Removal	321-333	904-910; Supp. 129-130	434-446; Supp. 7-10	905-920	219-222; Supp. 90-91	251-256
III. RELATION BETWEEN STATE AND FEDERAL LAW						
A. State Law in the Federal Courts	371-431	222-284	482-575; Supp. 12-13	921-1005	351-389, 395-398; Supp. 102-114	261-300
B. Federal Common Law	431-455	284-291	576-580	1006-1031	389-395; Supp. 114-118	274-275
IV. PLEADING						
A. Introduction	463-466	502-504	582-583	118	543-545	383-384
B. History of Pleading	466-509	489-493	583-595	118-128	546-562	384-399
C. Complaint	511-544	32-44, 520-540	595-640; Supp. 14	128-137	575-588; Supp. 197-198	399-424, 436-452
D. Challenges to Complaint	544-555	44-52, 559-565	640-645	152-178	589-614; Supp. 197-198	452-456

Gilbert Law Summary Civil Procedure	Cound, Friedenthal, Miller, Sexton *Civil Procedure: Cases and Materials* 2001 (8th ed.)	Field, Kaplan, Clermont *Materials for a Basic Course in Civil Procedure* 1997 (7th ed.) 2000 Supp.	Hazard, Tait, Fletcher *Pleading and Procedure, State and Federal, Cases and Materials* 1999 (8th ed.) 2000 Supp.	Marcus, Redish, Sherman *Civil Procedure: A Modern Approach* 2000 (3rd ed.)	Rosenberg, Smit Dreyfuss *Elements of Civil Procedure: Cases and Materials* 1990 (5th ed.) 1997 Supp.	Yeazell, Landers, Martin *Civil Procedure* 2000 (5th ed.)
E. Attorney's Duty to Investigate Claims and Defenses	582-596	52-54, 540-546	685-708; Supp. 15	139-152, 178-182	563-574; Supp. 183-197	424-436
F. Answer	555-565	46-49, 565-568	655-666	184-199	32-33, 604-611	456-469
G. Counterclaims and Cross-Claims	597-622	55-60, 568-573	711-723	199-204, 226-227	417-426, 435-437; Supp. 119	891-904
H. Amended and Supplemental Pleadings	567-581	60-64, 507-512	666-685; Supp. 14	207-220	614-629; Supp. 198	470-483
I. Default Procedure	944-952	44, 1092	1003-1010	184-191	630-631, 941-942	565-571
J. Judgment on the Pleadings	545, 553	98-99, 530-531	1001-1002	182-183	558-562	453-455
K. Voluntary Dismissal by Plaintiff	943-944	703-705, 1145	1002-1003	204-207	650-654	573-576

V. PARTIES

A. Real Party in Interest Rule	622-625	1281-1282	783-789	220-225	400-405; Supp. 119	928-938
B. Capacity of Party to Sue or Be Sued	625	1281-1282	790-796	225-226	406-412	
C. Joinder of Parties	625-694	211-214, 1263-1281, 1371-1398	727-783; Supp. 16	227-281	412-483; Supp. 119-121	904-962
D. Class Actions	695-790	1283-1370; Supp. 132-153	796-896; Supp. 16	281-320	483-542; Supp. 121-182	962-1017

VI. DISCOVERY

A. Introduction	791-793	64-70; Supp. 1-2	897-901	320	658-665; Supp. 199-207	485-486
B. Basic Discovery Devices	813-846	70-90; Supp. 3-5	901-968	330-346	719-729	496-508, 515-524
C. Scope of Discovery	793-813, 849-875	67, 577-603; Supp. 2	913-916	346-360	665-719	486-496, 525-544
D. Protective Orders	810, 879	73-81, 603-612	911-913	391-394	729-748	508-512
E. Failure to Disclose or to Comply with Discovery	875-886	81-82, 603-607, 612-618	974-983	394-399	729-748	548-565
F. Appellate Review of Discovery Orders	1159	616-618	1366-1368, 904-905	1062-1064	1068-1070	881-887
G. Use of Discovery at Trial	846-849	85-87, 153	901-902, 1058-1061	391-393	719-735	485-487
H. Private Investigation		65	905	393-394	660-663	

VII. SUMMARY JUDGMENT

A. Introduction	913	99-107	8-9, 1045-1046	404-406	631-634	42-49
B. Standard for Grant of Summary Judgment	914-943	99-107, 650-667	1037-1058	427-444	634-644	627-642
C. Procedure	914-943	650-667	1020-1037	407-427	644-650	42-49, 627-642

Gilbert Law Summary Civil Procedure	Cound, Friedenthal, Miller, Sexton *Civil Procedure: Cases and Materials* 2001 (8th ed.)	Field, Kaplan, Clermont *Materials for a Basic Course in Civil Procedure* 1997 (7th ed.) 2000 Supp.	Hazard, Tait, Fletcher *Pleading and Procedure, State and Federal, Cases and Materials* 1999 (8th ed.) 2000 Supp.	Marcus, Redish, Sherman *Civil Procedure: A Modern Approach* 2000 (3rd ed.)	Rosenberg, Smit Dreyfuss *Elements of Civil Procedure: Cases and Materials* 1990 (5th ed.) 1997 Supp.	Yeazell, Landers, Martin *Civil Procedure* 2000 (5th ed.)
VIII. MANAGERIAL JUDGING, PRETRIAL CONFERENCE, AND SETTLEMENT PROMOTION						
A. Pretrial Conferences and Managerial Judging	887-912	619-650; Supp. 125-126	983-1001	444-462	781-827; Supp. 219-227	644-655
B. Court-Annexed Settlement Devices	1334-1376	98-107, 343-353	47-48	462-496	1111-1135; Supp. 266-296	576-626
IX. TRIAL						
A. Right to Trial by Jury	955-1008, 1010-1015	116-118, 808-855; Supp. 5-10	1058-1123; Supp. 53-54	506-556	753-754, 760-773; Supp. 208-218	666-696
B. Selection of the Jury	1015-1027	126-133	1123-1156	575-584	829-836; Supp. 228-240	697-710
C. Disqualification of Judge		132	1156-1172	15-20		655-666
D. Order of Trial	1028-1029	133-136	1058-1061	497-506	837-842	49-56
E. Presentation of Evidence	1032-1034	136-156; Supp. 10	9-12, 1229-1230	498-502	838-851	718-722
F. Motions at Close of Proof	1036-1061	157-159, 703-727	1186-1208; Supp. 54	584-620	895-918; Supp. 240-241	722-723
G. Argument to Jury	1034-1035	159-160, 763-766	1208-1217	502-503	41, 837	51
H. Instructions to Jury	1061-1070	735-740, 159-161	1217-1229	503-505	41-42, 838-842	732-733
I. Jury Deliberation and Verdict	1070-1081	156-159, 740-761	1230-1232	505-506	42-43, 851-872	744-751
J. Motions after Verdict or Judgment	1081-1115	161-164, 761-808; Supp. 127-128	1232-1248	620-665	43, 872-895, 911-915	733-743
X. APPEAL						
A. Right to Appeal	15-17	17-18, 179-185	1366-1368; Supp. 15-18	1032-1035	1031-1034, 1040-1045	64-68, 754-763
B. Courts of Review	1216-1222	179-185	1371-1379	1090-1091	1031-1034, 1081-1092	67-68
C. Appellate Procedure	1186-1192	182-183	1369-1379	1113-1115	43-45, 1034-1040	64-69
D. Rulings Subject to Appeal	1144-1186	1409-1423	1379-1408	1035-1069, 1075-1091	1046-1081; Supp. 251-265	763-785
E. Scope of Appellate Review	1193-1216	1398-1409	1366-1368	1091-1103	1092-1101	785-795
F. Appellate Review by Extraordinary Writ	1146, 1168-1174	1432-1445	1398-1401	1069-1075	1107-1110	781-785
XI. PRECLUSIVE EFFECTS OF JUDGMENTS						
A. Introduction	1223-1225	1111-1118	1285-1286	1114-1117	955-958; Supp. 242-248	797-798
B. Claim Preclusion	1225-1243	1118-1154	1286-1307	1117-1153	958-964, 974-977	798-834
C. Issue Preclusion	1243-1268	1154-1179	1307-1317	1153-1174	978-986, 1001-1021; Supp. 248-250	834-862

Gilbert Law Summary Civil Procedure	Cound, Friedenthal, Miller, Sexton *Civil Procedure: Cases and Materials* 2001 (8th ed.)	Field, Kaplan, Clermont *Materials for a Basic Course in Civil Procedure* 1997 (7th ed.) 2000 Supp.	Hazard, Tait, Fletcher *Pleading and Procedure, State and Federal, Cases and Materials* 1999 (8th ed.) 2000 Supp.	Marcus, Redish, Sherman *Civil Procedure: A Modern Approach* 2000 (3rd ed.)	Rosenberg, Smit Dreyfuss *Elements of Civil Procedure: Cases and Materials* 1990 (5th ed.) 1997 Supp.	Yeazell, Landers, Martin *Civil Procedure* 2000 (5th ed.)
D. Persons Precluded by Judgments	1280-1311	1179-1220	1317-1337	1174-1199	964-974, 986-1001	862-871
E. Interjurisdictional Preclusive Effects of Judgments	1312-1333	1220-1244	1343-1359		1021-1030	871-887

Capsule Summary

I. TERRITORIAL JURISDICTION AND RELATED MATTERS

A. INTRODUCTION

1. Types of Territorial Jurisdiction §1

Territorial jurisdiction is a state's power to hear a case and enforce its judgment.

   a. In personam jurisdiction §2

In personam jurisdiction permits a court to enter a judgment that is *personally binding* on defendant.

   b. In rem jurisdiction §3

In rem jurisdiction permits a court to adjudicate the rights of *all possible claimants in a specific piece of property*.

   c. Quasi in rem jurisdiction §4

There are two types of quasi in rem jurisdiction. The first type permits a court to determine rights of *particular parties* in property under its control. The second type permits a court having jurisdiction over defendant's property, but not over defendant personally, to use the property to satisfy plaintiff's personal claim against defendant. Use of this latter type as a basis for jurisdiction over nonresident defendants has been severely limited.

2. Traditional Power Theory §5

Under *Pennoyer v. Neff*, a state's jurisdiction was generally limited to persons or property served with process or seized in the state.

3. Shift to Minimum Contacts §21

With *International Shoe,* the Court shifted from an emphasis on in-state service to a requirement of *minimum contacts* with the forum state "such that the maintenance of the suit does not offend traditional notions of fair play and substantial justice."

B. CONTEMPORARY CONSTITUTIONAL GROUNDS FOR STATE COURT JURISDICTION

1. Contacts with Forum §26

International Shoe generated a two-stage approach to jurisdiction problems, looking first to whether the defendant *purposely availed* himself of the privilege of conducting activities in the forum and then at the *reasonableness* of permitting jurisdiction.

a. Minimum contacts—purposeful availment §27

Purposeful availment inquiry *focuses solely on activities of defendant*, looking for some voluntary action by defendant establishing a *beneficial relationship* with the forum state.

(1) Foreseeability §28

Mere foreseeability of contact with the forum is important but insufficient; defendant's conduct with respect to the forum state must be such that he should reasonably *anticipate being haled into court there* (e.g., long-term relationship with forum or seeking to serve forum market).

(2) Relation to claim §39

The Court assumes "specific" jurisdiction is proper with regard to claims that are related to forum contacts that satisfy the purposeful availment requirement, but jurisdiction may also be proper where the claim arises from contacts that do not satisfy the purposeful availment requirement, but is of the same type as claims that do. This might be rationalized by focusing on foreseeability of facing claims of this type in this state.

(3) Commercial vs. noncommercial §40

Purposeful availment is more easily found with regard to defendant's commercial activity.

(4) Choice of law distinguished §41

The fact that a particular state's law may apply under choice-of-law "center of gravity" principles does not alone satisfy the purposeful availment requirement as to that state.

(5) Reasonableness insufficient to satisfy purposeful availment requirement §44

Factors such as a lack of inconvenience to defendant cannot outweigh the requirement of purposeful availment.

b. Fair play and substantial justice—reasonableness §45

In the reasonableness inquiry, consideration of *plaintiff's interests* is proper.

(1) Factors §46

Reasonableness factors include the *state's interests* in providing a forum and regulating the activity, *relative burdens* on plaintiff and defendant, *nature of defendant's activities* in forum, and the *avoidance of multiple suits*.

c. Application to Internet activities §52

Although still an evolving area, the same minimum contacts analysis applies to Internet activities, but the *purposeful availment requirement* is emphasized and *the reasonableness requirements are probably relaxed*.

2. Presence of Defendant's Property in Forum §60

Presence of defendant's property in the forum will often establish a constitutionally sufficient contact between defendant and the forum, ordinarily because it establishes relevant contact between defendant and forum.

a. Location of property §61

Tangible property is located in a state if it is physically present there. Intangible property may be considered located in a jurisdiction if some transaction related to the property occurred there, but if embodied in an instrument, it is usually said to be located where the instrument is. This is usually governed by *state law*.

b. Presence of property supports jurisdiction §65

The presence of property in state may support jurisdiction by providing contacts among the forum, defendant, and litigation.

(1) True in rem §66

States continue to have power to exercise true in rem jurisdiction, as in condemnation proceedings.

(2) Claim related to rights and duties arising from ownership §69

Property provides sufficient contact if the claim is related to rights or duties related to the property (*e.g.,* absentee owner might be sued for injuries sustained on property located in the forum).

(3) Absence of other forum §73

The Court has not ruled on the scope of jurisdiction by necessity, which may exist in cases where defendant's property is located in the forum and no other forum is available to plaintiff.

c. Presence of property insufficient for jurisdiction §76

When property is completely *unrelated* to plaintiff's cause of action, its presence alone will not support jurisdiction.

3. General Jurisdiction §79

Some courts distinguish between *general jurisdiction*, which subjects defendant to suit on any claim in the forum; and *specific jurisdiction*, which confers jurisdiction only for claims related to defendant's contact with the forum.

a. Natural persons §81

General jurisdiction is available in the state of a natural person's *domicile*.

b. Corporations §82

A corporation is subject to general jurisdiction in the *state of incorporation*, the state in which its *headquarters* are located if different from state of incorporation, and in states in which it conducts *"substantial activity."*

4. Consent §93

Defendant may consent to jurisdiction in a forum.

a. Express consent §94

Defendant may expressly consent to jurisdiction, either before or after suit is filed.

b. How citizenship determined §314

For ***natural persons***, including ***permanent resident aliens***, citizenship is generally the same as ***domicile***. A ***corporation*** is a citizen of every state in which it is incorporated and of the state of its ***principal place of business***. Unincorporated associations are citizens of ***each state in which any member is a citizen***.

(1) Class actions §330

In class actions, only the citizenship of the ***named representatives*** is considered.

(2) Executors, guardians, and trustees §331

Legal representatives of decedents or incompetents are deemed citizens of the ***same state as the person represented***.

(3) Fictitious defendants §332

A 1988 federal statute permitted cases with fictitious defendants (John/Jane Doe cases) to be removed to federal court, but the diversity statute was not similarly amended. There is a split among federal courts as to whether such cases can be heard under diversity jurisdiction.

c. Time for determination §333

Diversity need exist only at the ***commencement of the action***.

(1) Partial exception—removal §337

For removed cases, diversity must exist ***both*** at the time of filing the suit and at the time the removal notice is filed.

d. Realigning parties §338

In considering diversity, the court looks to the ***real interests*** of the parties and may realign them accordingly as plaintiffs or defendants; *e.g.,* in shareholder derivative cases, the corporation may likely be realigned as a defendant.

e. Efforts to create diversity §339

Diversity cannot be created by collusively or improperly joining a party or by ***assigning a claim*** without sufficient consideration.

f. Efforts to defeat diversity §343

Plaintiffs are allowed some latitude in taking steps to defeat diversity (*e.g.,* adding bona fide claims against nondiverse defendants).

g. Effect of lack of diversity §348

A plaintiff may sometimes preserve diversity by dismissing a nondiverse defendant, but may not proceed in federal court without a necessary party, *infra*.

h. Jurisdictional amount §351

More than $75,000 must be in controversy in a diversity case, computed as of the date of ***commencement*** of the suit.

(1) Legal certainty test §353

The amount claimed by plaintiff is determinative unless defendant shows to a legal certainty that the minimum cannot be met. The fact judgment is ultimately entered for a lesser amount does not affect diversity jurisdiction. *Interest and costs are excluded* in computing the minimum amount.

(2) Aggregation of claims §361

Separate claims can be aggregated to satisfy the requirement in the following situations:

(i) *All claims of a single plaintiff against a single defendant*, even if the claims are unrelated;

(ii) The *claims of a single plaintiff against several defendants only if all defendants are jointly liable*;

(iii) Claims of *several plaintiffs against one defendant only* if plaintiffs have a *common undivided ownership interest* in the claims; and

(iv) *Counterclaims generally cannot be aggregated* with plaintiff's claim. (Note that compulsory counterclaims, *infra*, need not meet the amount in controversy requirement providing plaintiff's claim does.)

i. Exceptions to diversity jurisdiction §368

Courts decline to exercise diversity jurisdiction over cases involving domestic relations, probate actions, and local actions (*e.g.*, title to real property).

C. FEDERAL QUESTION JURISDICTION

1. Constitutional Grant §375

Article III, Section 2 extends the federal judicial power to cases *arising under* the Constitution, the laws of the U.S., and treaties; cases affecting ambassadors, consuls, etc.; admiralty cases; and cases to which the U.S. is a party. This power is viewed broadly.

2. Federal Question Statute

a. Statute interpreted more narrowly than Constitution §379

The language of the federal question statute is very similar to that in Article III, but has been interpreted more narrowly.

(1) State court jurisdiction over cases raising federal questions §381

State courts have *concurrent* jurisdiction over most federal question issues.

b. Standards for determining whether federal question is raised §383

A federal question may be raised when federal law has created the claim sued upon (inclusive of implied claims) or when a right under state law turns on construction of federal law if the federal law has a *substantial bearing* on the outcome.

c. Well-pleaded complaint rule §391

The federal question must appear in the properly pleaded allegations in the complaint. If federal law did not create the claim sued upon, this means the federal issue must be a *required element of the state law claim*.

hear nonfederal claims against a nondiverse defendant as long as the claims arose from the same event as the federal claim.

c. **Lack of statutory basis** §423

In 1989, the Supreme Court called the validity of ancillary and pendent jurisdiction into doubt, at least with regard to claims against added parties, because there was no statutory basis for such jurisdiction and all exercises of federal court jurisdiction have been said to require a statutory basis.

3. **Supplemental Jurisdiction Statute** §424

In 1990, Congress adopted the Supplemental Jurisdiction Statute, which grants federal courts that have original jurisdiction over a claim supplemental jurisdiction over all other claims that form *part of the same case or controversy* under Article III. Thus, any claim that is part of the same constitutional case may be added, including claims that involve the joinder or intervention of additional parties.

a. **Standard** §426

In determining whether supplemental jurisdiction is proper, the Court will ask whether:

(i) The *federal claim is sufficiently substantial*;

(ii) The federal and nonfederal claims arise from a *common nucleus of operative fact*; and

(iii) The federal and nonfederal claims are such that they would ordinarily be tried in *one judicial proceeding*.

b. **Limitation on diversity cases** §435

When federal subject matter jurisdiction is founded *solely* on diversity, there is no supplemental jurisdiction over claims *by plaintiffs* against persons made parties under Rule 14 (impleader), Rule 19 (necessary party joinder), or Rule 24 (intervention), or over claims *by persons proposed to be joined* under Rules 19 or 24.

(1) **Compare—class actions** §439

Lower courts disagree whether the statute still permits supplemental jurisdiction over class members' claims that do not satisfy the minimum amount in controversy requirement.

c. **Discretionary decline of jurisdiction** §442

A federal court can decline to exercise supplemental jurisdiction where: (i) a novel or complex issue of state law is involved; (ii) the nonfederal claim predominates; (iii) all original jurisdiction claims are dismissed; or (iv) in other extraordinary circumstances.

d. **Tolling of limitations** §451

The limitations period for claims asserted under supplemental jurisdiction, or for any other claim in the same action voluntarily dismissed, is tolled while the case is pending in federal court and for 30 days after dismissal by the federal court.

E. REMOVAL

1. Grounds for Removal   §454
In general, a state court action that plaintiff *could originally have filed in federal court* can be removed there by defendant.

a. Federal question   §455
The *well-pleaded complaint rule* governs the removal of a federal question case by defendant, *e.g.*, a federal defense in an answer is insufficient for removal. *Supplemental jurisdiction* permits a defendant to remove a federal claim case even if it also includes defendants against whom only state law claims are asserted.

b. Diversity of citizenship   §463
Complete diversity is required for removal of diversity cases. However, removal is *not* permitted if any defendant is a citizen of the state in which the action is brought, *i.e.*, a *local defendant*. *Fictitious defendants* are disregarded in determining complete diversity for removal purposes. The *jurisdictional amount* requirement applies to removed cases.

c. Separate and independent federal claim   §468
If the separate and independent federal question claim requirement is met, a court may retain jurisdiction over otherwise nonremovable claims or remand them to state court.

d. Special statutes   §473
Special removal statutes apply to certain types of cases, *e.g.*, *federal civil rights* regarding racial equality when protection in state court is inadequate.

2. Procedure for Removal   §475
Defendant removes by filing a notice of removal in the appropriate federal district court and notifying the other parties and the state court.

a. Only defendants can remove   §476
Plaintiff may not remove on the basis of defendant's assertion of a counterclaim.

b. All defendants must join   §477
Unless an individual defendant has a *separate and independent claim against him*, all defendants who have been served must join in filing for removal.

c. Timing   §478
Upon *service of process*, a defendant has 30 days to file a notice of removal unless the case becomes removable later, in which case the 30 days begins running from that point. The case is considered removed as soon as the notice is filed and served.

3. Remand   §483
The federal court should remand an improperly removed case to state court, or it may remand only *supplemental claims* if the other claims are

dismissed, or if it declines to exercise supplemental jurisdiction. Orders of remand based on lack of subject matter jurisdiction or for defects in the removal procedure are **not reviewable,** although a remand motion **erroneously denied** may be appealed.

4.   **No "Reverse" Removal**   §490
Presently, there is no method to remove a case originally filed in federal court to state court. However, federal courts may apply the **abstention** doctrine.

III. RELATION BETWEEN STATE AND FEDERAL LAW

A. STATE LAW IN THE FEDERAL COURTS

1.   **Rules of Decision Act**   §492
Under the Act, the **laws of the states** are the rules of decision in federal courts, except where the Constitution or federal laws or treaties provide otherwise.

2.   **Former Rule—*Swift v. Tyson***   §493
Under S*wift v. Tyson,* "laws" in the Rules of Decision Act was held not to include state common law. Thus federal courts followed their own view of what the "general" common law was or should be.

3.   **Overruling of *Swift* by *Erie***   §500
Erie held that state common law principles should govern where Congress had not provided otherwise.

   a.   **Reasoning of *Erie***   §501
The Court **found** that the Rules of Decision Act was not intended to exclude all state general common law and that *Swift* had led to a **lack of uniformity and resulting discrimination**. But more importantly, the Court **held** that the Constitution did **not** give federal courts the power to declare the substantive common law that would apply in a state.

   b.   ***Erie* as part of practice revolution**   §511
Erie coincided with adoption of the Federal Rules of Civil Procedure. Thus, at the same time federal courts increased **application of state substantive law**, they also began using **uniform federal procedural law**.

   c.   **Principal cases developing *Erie***   §512
Cases after *Erie* have attempted to implement the general guideline that **state substantive law** and **federal procedural law** should govern state law actions in the federal courts.

      (1)   ***Guaranty Trust Co. v. York***   §513
York, in holding that a state statute of limitations took precedence over a more flexible federal laches approach, articulated an "**outcome determination**" test; *i.e.,* a federal law is substantive if application of the federal law instead of the state law will **significantly affect the outcome of the litigation**. It was hard to

know where to stop in applying this rule, since almost any rule could qualify as substantive under the test, especially if disobeyed.

law expressed in one of the forms, resulting in numerous pleadings and counter pleadings in an effort to fashion a single issue. Amendments to change from one form to another were not permitted.

a. Compare—equity pleading §580
Equity courts were governed by different procedures. Equitable relief was available only where there was no right to recover under any forms of action at law, *i.e.,* no adequate remedy at law. In equity, a plaintiff went outside the forms of action and recited *facts* showing his grievance. This *fact pleading* was the basis of code pleading.

2. Code Pleading §581
The New York Code of 1848 (Field Code) originated code pleading. It was later adopted or adapted by a majority of the states and is still used in several today. Code pleading departed from common law pleading rules in several important ways.

a. Single form of action §582
The fundamental principle of code pleading is that plaintiff's claim is a *statement of facts showing a right to a remedy.* Code pleading abolished forms of action; a plaintiff could recover under any legal theory applicable to the facts he pleaded and proved.

b. Merger of law and equity §583
Code pleading generally eliminated separate courts of law and equity, a change persisting to modern practice. However, while procedural distinctions have been abolished, legal and equitable *remedies* remain distinct.

c. Limited number of pleadings §586
Far fewer pleadings are allowed under code pleading than under the common law, and no attempt is made to reduce a case to a single issue.

d. Fact pleading §588
A pleading under the codes must set forth the *ultimate facts* constituting the *cause of action* in ordinary and concise language.

3. Pleading Under the Federal Rules §591
The Federal Rules, now adopted by most states, *further liberalize* pleading rules and eliminate the technicalities of the Field Code.

a. Pleadings permitted §592
Fewer pleadings are permitted under the Federal Rules than in code states. A *motion to dismiss* is used instead of demurrer.

b. Notice pleading §593
The Federal Rules eliminate the requirement of "facts constituting a cause of action." Now, all that is needed is a *"short and plain statement of the claim showing the pleader is entitled to relief."*

C. COMPLAINT §594
In most jurisdictions, filing of the complaint commences a civil action.

1. **Form** §595
   The essential parts of the complaint are as follows.

   a. **Caption** §596
      The complaint must set forth the name of the court, the number assigned to the action, a designation of the pleading (*e.g.,* Complaint for Damages), and the names of the parties.

   b. **Jurisdictional allegations** §600
      In *federal court*, the complaint must allege the ground(s) upon which federal jurisdiction is invoked. Failure to do so results in a dismissal if the complaint is not amended to supply the ground(s). (This is *not* normally required in *state courts* because they are usually courts of general jurisdiction.)

   c. **Body** §602
      There must also be a statement of ultimate facts constituting the cause of action (code pleading) or a short and plain statement of the claim showing that the pleader is entitled to relief (Federal Rules). Each claim or cause of action should be set forth in a separate group of paragraphs, and each paragraph should be limited to a single set of facts.

      (1) **Allegations** §604
          The allegations should be simple, concise, and *direct*. A plaintiff who *lacks personal knowledge* as to some element of the claim may plead that "to the best of his knowledge, information, and belief," the claim is "well-grounded in fact," but in federal court, reasonable inquiry must first be made pursuant to Rule 11. Similarly, in code pleading states, allegations may be *denied* on lack of information and belief.

      (2) **Alternative and inconsistent allegations** §612
          A plaintiff may plead in the alternative by alleging facts based on *inconsistent legal theories*; he may also allege *inconsistent facts* if he has reason for not knowing which version is true. However, an *election of remedies* must be made *before* judgment.

      (3) **Defenses need not be anticipated** §617
          Ordinarily, plaintiff's complaint need not anticipate defendant's defenses.

   d. **Prayer for relief** §620
      The pleading must set forth a prayer for relief. If a defendant *defaults* by failing to defend, the relief granted cannot exceed what is requested. In *contested* cases, on the other hand, relief is *not* limited to that which is requested, with a few exceptions. In *federal court*, a prayer determines the *amount in controversy* for jurisdictional purposes. In *state court* (and state law actions in federal court), the prayer may determine the nature of the action (legal vs. equitable) on which the *right to jury trial* depends.

e. Subscription   §627

The complaint must be signed by the attorney, or by a party if she has no attorney. In federal practice, the signature certifies that: (i) to the best of the attorney's knowledge formed after reasonable inquiry, the evidentiary contentions have evidentiary support or are likely to have support after discovery, (ii) the claims or defenses are warranted by existing law or a good faith argument for change in existing law, and (iii) the complaint is not presented for any improper purpose.

(1) Verification   §630

A verified pleading contains an affidavit at its end averring that the pleading is true to the best of affiant's knowledge, information, or belief. Verification is not required in federal practice unless so specified by rule or statute, *e.g.*, shareholders' derivative suits.

2. Pleading Specific Claims   §635

The *elements* of the claim are specified by the applicable *substantive law*, *e.g.*, torts, contracts, etc. The responsibility to plead and prove various issues relevant to liability may be allocated to plaintiff or defendant. If plaintiff must plead an element, it is essential to stating a claim, *i.e.*, a *prima facie case*. Otherwise it is an *affirmative defense*, which must be raised by defendant.

a. Form complaints   §676

In many jurisdictions, complaint forms for specific types of claims are presumptively sufficient, *e.g.*, forms appended to the Federal Rules.

3. Splitting of Claims   §677

A pleader cannot split a single claim or cause of action into several parts and file separate suits on each. If suit is brought on only one part of a claim, *res judicata (infra)* bars later suit on the omitted claim(s).

4. Joinder of Claims   §680

Except for the effect of res judicata, there is *no compulsory* joinder of claims. Practically, however, plaintiffs usually join related claims because of the danger of res judicata, *infra*.

a. Permissive joinder   §681

At common law, joinder was permitted only if all claims were in the same form of action and there was complete identity of parties to each claim. Under the *Federal Rules*, adopted by most states, a single plaintiff may join *as many claims* as he has against a single defendant, *regardless of the subject matter*. However, in *multi-party* cases, *at least one* of the claims by or against each party must arise out of the same transaction *and* must involve a common question of law or fact.

5. Consolidation of Separate Actions   §688

A trial judge has power to order joint trials of separate lawsuits or may consolidate them if they involve a common question of law or fact. If such cases are pending in *different courts*, many jurisdictions permit *transfer*, in whole or in part, so the cases can be consolidated or joined.

D. CHALLENGES TO COMPLAINT §692

A defendant can challenge the legal sufficiency of the complaint *before* responding to the factual allegations in it.

1. Common Law §693

At common law, defects in the pleadings could be raised by two kinds of demurrer.

a. General demurrer §694

This challenged the *substantive sufficiency* of the causes in the complaint.

b. Special demurrer §695

This demurrer challenged *specific matters of form*.

2. State Practice §696

In the Field Code, the demurrer was preserved. Elsewhere, a motion to dismiss or a motion to make more definite and certain is used.

a. General vs. special demurrer §700

A general demurrer is used for a failure to plead facts sufficient to constitute a cause of action. A demurrer on any other ground is a special demurrer.

b. Rulings on demurrer §704

Rulings must be *based on grounds* raised by the demurring party. If a demurrer is overruled, defendant must answer within the time ordered by the court or take a default; if sustained, the court usually grants plaintiff leave to *amend* the complaint.

c. Effect of failure to raise §708

Grounds for demurrer are *waived* unless raised in the defendant's *initial pleading* (demurrer or answer). *Exceptions: Failure to state facts* sufficient to constitute a cause of action and the court's *lack of subject matter jurisdiction* are *never* waived.

d. Motion to strike §712

A motion to strike reaches defects not subject to demurrer (*e.g.,* irrelevant or redundant matter in the complaint) and *extends the time* to file an answer.

3. Federal Practice

a. Motion to dismiss §716

In federal practice, a motion to dismiss is the basic challenge to the legal sufficiency of adversary pleadings and is *always optional* with the defendant. It can be made on grounds such as lack of subject matter or personal jurisdiction, improper venue, or a failure to state a claim. If the motion is *granted*, a court has discretion to allow the plaintiff to *amend* the complaint [Fed. R. Civ. P. 12(b)].

materials, the court may treat it as a motion for summary judgment, *infra*.

b. Anticipatory defenses §766
A complaint need ***not*** anticipate affirmative defenses that might be raised. However, if it does so, it must plead facts to avoid the defenses.

E. ATTORNEY'S DUTY TO INVESTIGATE CLAIMS AND DEFENSES

1. Certification Requirement §769
Federal Rule 11 requires that every paper filed in court be signed by an attorney, or by the party himself if unrepresented.

2. Matter Certified by Signature §773
By signing, a person certifies that:

(i) She has made an ***inquiry reasonable under the circumstances*** to support the factual and legal positions taken;

(ii) The ***factual assertions have evidentiary support***; and

(iii) The paper was ***not filed for an improper purpose***.

3. Sanctions §798
Imposition of sanctions for violation of Rule 11 is ***discretionary***. Sanctions can be monetary or nonmonetary, but in any event are to be limited to what is necessary to ***deter repetition*** of such conduct. Law firms should be held ***jointly liable*** for sanctions along with the firm members who violate Rule 11.

4. Procedure §807
A party may move for sanctions, but must give the nonmoving party notice and 21 days to withdraw or correct the sanctionable paper. The court also has power to impose sanctions on its own initiative.

F. ANSWER

1. Denials §815
A defendant's answer must contain ***effective*** denials to put plaintiff's allegations at issue. Material allegations ***not denied*** are ***deemed admitted***.

a. General denials §817
A defendant may deny all the allegations of a complaint in a single denial. However, this is no longer good practice in most jurisdictions, because ***federal*** (and similar state) ***practice*** requires a basic pleading requirement of ***good faith***; thus, a general denial is ***rarely proper*** since there is usually something in a complaint (*e.g.*, allegations about plaintiff's identity) that defendant should admit.

b. Specific denials §821
Anything less than a general denial is a specific denial, *e.g.*, denial by ***parts*** (paragraphs or sentences in complaint); merely ***negating*** an allegation ("defendant was not drunk"); or alleging a ***lack of sufficient information*** to respond.

(1) Damages §831

In federal practice, damages are at issue even if not effectively denied. Most state jurisdictions are contra.

2. Affirmative Defenses §833

Any defense or objections constituting new matter or an affirmative defense must be pleaded in the answer; a simple denial is not sufficient to raise these. New matter is anything that the defendant must prove to **avoid** plaintiff's claim. The test usually is whether defendant would bear the **burden of proof** on the issue at trial; if so, it is new matter.

a. Application §835

The following new matter **must** be specially pleaded in most states and **in federal practice**.

(1) Tort cases §838

New matter includes the defenses of self-defense, consent, justification or other privilege, contributory negligence and assumption of risk, privilege or license (defense to trespass), and consent (defense to conversion). **Lack of proximate cause** is **not** new matter.

(2) Contract cases §839

Fraud, mistake, duress, incapacity, release, waiver, estoppel, condition subsequent, payment, Statute of Frauds (federal and most states), statute of limitations, and pleas in abatement (assert a reason why action should be put off or not heard) must usually be specially pleaded.

b. Effect of failure to plead new matter §854

If new matter is not pleaded in the answer, defendant **may not offer evidence** of such defenses **unless** plaintiff fails to object to the introduction of the evidence or the court allows leave to **amend**. A motion to amend **cannot revive** waiver of personal jurisdiction, venue, or manner of service.

3. Procedure in Answering Complaint §856

Requirements for allegations in a complaint also apply to allegations in an answer. Rule 11 requires a signature, and defendant may deny based on "a lack of information and belief." A federal defendant must file her answer within 20 days after service, absent a Rule 12(b) motion; if she waives service, defendant has 60 days after the waiver request was sent to answer.

4. Allegations of Answer Deemed Controverted §865

In federal practice, **no reply** to an answer is permitted unless the answer contains a counterclaim. However, some federal courts now require a reply when a defendant asserts a qualified immunity defense. Plaintiff may avoid any new matter in defendant's answer by the introduction of evidence without further pleading.

5. Challenges to Answer §867

Plaintiff may challenge the legal sufficiency of an affirmative defense by *demurrer* (state practice) or ***motion to strike*** (federal practice). A motion for summary judgment or judgment on the pleadings may also be used.

G. COUNTERCLAIMS AND CROSS-CLAIMS

1. Federal Practice

a. Counterclaims §868
A defendant may set forth as counterclaims in the answer any claims she has against plaintiff, even if ***not related*** to plaintiff's claims in the complaint.

(1) Subject matter jurisdiction §869
If a ***compulsory*** counterclaim is based on the same transaction or occurrence as plaintiff's claim, it falls within the court's supplemental jurisdiction. However, a ***permissive*** counterclaim must satisfy subject matter jurisdictional requirements, *i.e.*, must be based on some federal question or on diversity.

(2) Pleading §872
The sufficiency of a counterclaim is tested by the same rules used to test the sufficiency of a complaint.

(3) Joinder of other parties §876
Although a counterclaim is against the plaintiff, it can give rise to joinder of other parties. Joinder can be permissive, with an independent basis for subject matter jurisdiction, or the court may order joinder.

(a) Voluntary dismissal §881
The assertion of a counterclaim bars plaintiff's dismissal of the action without ***defendant's consent***.

(4) Permissive vs. compulsory §882
If defendant's counterclaim is ***unrelated*** to plaintiff's claims, it is ***permissive***. A ***compulsory*** counterclaim arises out of the ***same transactions*** as set forth in the complaint and must be asserted in the action or is barred in a later action.

(5) Statute of limitations §888
The majority view finds that if a counterclaim arises out of the ***same transaction***, it will not be barred if the complaint was timely filed.

b. Cross-claims in federal practice §893
A defendant may set forth in the answer any claims that she has against a ***co-defendant*** that relate to the ***transaction or occurrence*** (or to any property) that is the subject of plaintiff's complaint, *e.g.*, cross-claim for contribution or indemnification.

(1) Impleader §899
Impleaders are claims against a ***third person*** not a party to the original action and are limited to indemnification and contribution claims.

offered at trial is only a *partial* variance from the pleadings, leave to amend is usually granted if no prejudice will result.

  c. **Federal practice**   **§943**
    Since pleadings are now less important, amendments are liberally allowed; the doctrine of variance is effectively *abolished*.

 3. **Amendments After Trial**   **§952**
   In federal practice, pleadings can be amended to conform to the proof at any time, even after entry of judgment or on appeal.

 4. **Supplemental Pleadings**   **§953**
   The function of supplemental pleadings is to call attention of the court to material facts that have occurred *subsequent* to the filing of the complaint. The right to file a supplemental pleading is at the court's *discretion*, but is liberally given. A supplemental pleading *adds to*, but does not modify, the original pleading.

I. DEFAULT PROCEDURE

 1. **In General**   **§958**
   If a defendant fails to answer or otherwise timely plead, a default is entered.

 2. **Effect of Default Entry**   **§959**
   Defendant's failure to plead is considered an *admission* of the claim against her.

 3. **Obtaining Judgment**   **§960**
   After entry of a default, plaintiff must proceed to obtain a default judgment. *Relief is limited* to the amount or type that was sought in the prayer. The defendant is *not* entitled to appear in the proceeding.

 4. **Setting Aside Default**   **§963**
   Once a default is entered, defendant's remedy is to move the court to set it (and any judgment entered pursuant to it) aside. In *federal practice*, the motion can be made at any time before judgment is entered. Thereafter, the motion must be made within *one year* after entry of the judgment or order. The defendant must show that she has a *valid excuse* for the default *and* a *meritorious defense* to the action and that *plaintiff will not be prejudiced*.

J. JUDGMENT ON THE PLEADINGS

 1. **Purpose**   **§967**
   A motion for judgment on the pleadings is analogous to a demurrer or motion to dismiss, and challenges the adversary's pleadings on the ground that they are insufficient to establish any valid claim or defense.

 2. **Making the Motion**   **§968**
   Either party may move for judgment on the pleadings at any time after the pleadings have closed, but not so late as to delay trial.

assignments. If the assignment is of a *partial* interest, at common law the assignee could not enforce a claim; the modern rule is that partial assignees and the assignor are *necessary parties*.

b.	**Subrogation**	§1000

Subrogation is equitable and results in an assignment by operation of law so that one who pays another for loss or injury caused by an act of a third person becomes entitled to enforce (as subrogee) the claim that the injured person (subrogor) had against the third party.

c.	**Trusts**	§1002

The trustee, as holder of legal title, is the real party for redress of any wrong to the *trust estate*. But a beneficiary may sue the trustee to protect her beneficial rights.

d.	**Executors and administrators**	§1004

These are the proper parties to sue on behalf of decedents' estates.

e.	**Principal and agent**	§1007

If the obligation is owed to the *principal alone*, he is the only proper plaintiff. If the obligation is owed to both the agent and the principal, either may sue.

f.	**Third-party beneficiary**	§1008

A third-party beneficiary who has enforceable rights under a contract is a real party in interest. If a promise was given for the benefit of a third party, *both* the promisee and third party would have enforceable rights.

B. CAPACITY OF PARTY TO SUE OR BE SUED

1.	**Definition**	§1015

"Capacity" is the legal competence of a party to sue or be sued.

2.	**Individuals**	§1016

A person's capacity is determined by the law of her domicile. If she lacks capacity (*e.g.,* is a minor), suit must be filed by a guardian or conservator.

3.	**Corporations**	§1019

The capacity of a corporation to sue (or be sued) is determined by the law of the state in which it is organized.

4. **Partnerships**

a.	**Federal practice**	§1021

In federal court, a partnership can always sue or be sued as an *entity if the litigation involves a federal question.* However, in other actions, including diversity cases, the partnership's capacity is determined by the law of the state in which the court is located.

b.	**State law varies**	§1022

Some states permit a partnership to sue *or* be sued as an entity. Many states permit a partnership to be sued, but *not* to sue, as an entity (in the partnership name). In those states, an action on behalf of the partnership must be brought in the names of the individual partners.

5. Unincorporated Associations §1023

At common law, unincorporated associations lacked capacity to sue or be sued as entities.

a. State practice §1024

Many states now treat unincorporated associations like corporations.

b. Federal practice §1025

An unincorporated association has capacity to sue or be sued when a *federal right* is being enforced by or against the association. But when a *state* law is being enforced (*e.g.,* in a diversity action), the capacity of the unincorporated association is determined by the law of the state in which the federal action is brought.

C. JOINDER OF PARTIES

1. Permissive Joinder

a. Early approach §1032

Under the original codes, a plaintiff could join plaintiffs or defendants only if they *all* had an interest in the subject of the action *and* the relief sought.

b. Modern approach §1033

Today, a person may join or be joined if:

(i) A right to relief is asserted by (or against) her *jointly, severally, or in the alternative*;

(ii) The right to relief *arises out of the same transaction or series of transactions*; *and*

(iii) There is *at least one question of law or fact common to all parties* sought to be joined.

(1) Additional claims §1038

As long as the above requirements are met, a party may assert as many claims as she has against an opposing party, but the court has discretion to sever.

c. Subject matter jurisdiction §1041

In addition to the requirement of personal jurisdiction, federal subject matter jurisdiction requirements must be satisfied as to *all* parties.

2. Compulsory Joinder §1042

Joinder is required for any person who has a *material interest* in the case and whose absence would result in *substantial prejudice* to him or to other parties.

a. Traditional approach §1043

Traditionally, a distinction was made between *necessary* parties (those who ought to be joined *if possible*; interests are *severable*) and *indispensable* parties (interests are *nonseverable*; action would have to be dismissed without them).

being adversely affected by a judgment in the action. Whether intervention is allowed depends on a balancing of two conflicting policies: (i) plaintiff alone should generally be allowed to join parties, with or against him, as he wishes; and (ii) other interested parties and the court have an interest in avoiding multiplicity of litigation or inconsistency of results.

a. Types of intervention in federal cases

(1) Intervention of right §1091

Intervention is granted as a matter of right if the unconditional right to intervene is conferred by a federal statute, **or** where the **disposition** of the action without the applicant would likely **impair or impede** his ability to protect an interest relating to the subject of the action.

(2) Permissive intervention §1105

This is granted at a court's broad discretion where a **federal statute** gives a conditional right to intervene or where the applicant's claim or defense has a **question of law or fact in common** with the action.

b. Effect of intervention in federal cases

(1) Subject matter jurisdiction §1110

In actions based solely on diversity, there is no supplemental jurisdiction over claims by intervenors or by plaintiffs against persons who intervene. When jurisdiction is not based solely on diversity, there usually is supplemental jurisdiction over claims by or against intervenors of right.

(2) Judgment §1112

Judgment rendered after intervention is binding on the intervenor as though he had been an original party and he has a right to appeal.

5. Consolidation of Separate Actions §1116

Even if joinder rules do not permit addition of new parties, almost the same result may be achieved by consolidating suits pending in the same court. The court has broad discretion to consolidate actions with common issues.

6. Interpleader §1117

Interpleader enables a party against whom conflicting claims to the same debt or property are asserted (the "stakeholder") to join all adverse claimants in one action and to require them to litigate among themselves to determine who, if anyone, has a valid claim to the involved property. Once the stakeholder deposits the funds or property in the court, he can be discharged from the litigation, unless he also claims the asset.

a. Procedure §1119

The party against whom claims are made may: (i) institute an interpleader action, naming all claimants as defendants, or (ii) interplead in any action pending between the adverse claimants. If he is named as a defendant in such an action, he may interplead by filing a *counterclaim, infra*.

(1) Deposit with court §1120
In a statutory interpleader action, the stakeholder must *deposit with the court,* or give security for, the entire disputed amount in his possession. Rule 22 interpleader does not require deposit.

b. Types of federal interpleader actions

(1) Statutory §1125
Interpleader is permitted by 28 U.S.C. section 1335 if two or more *claimants of diverse citizenship* (minimal diversity) are making adverse claims to the same property, debt, or instrument and it has a *value of at least $500*.

(2) Rule 22 interpleader §1126
Rule 22 permits interpleader in an action that meets the normal jurisdictional requirements in federal court. Unlike statutory interpleader, there must be *complete diversity* between the stakeholder and *all* of the adverse claimants, and the jurisdictional amount must be in excess of $75,000, or a federal question must be involved.

(3) Limits of process §1133
In *statutory* interpleader, the reach of process is nationwide. Under *Rule 22*, service of process is the same as in other civil actions.

(4) Cross-claims and counterclaims §1134
Interpleaded claimants often cross-claim against each other, counterclaim against plaintiff, and implead third parties. Such additional claims must have an independent basis of jurisdiction unless they relate to the original impleaded claim (and thus fall within supplemental jurisdiction).

(5) Venue §1137
In statutory interpleader, proper venue is the district where *any* claimant resides. Under Rule 22, venue is the same as in any other civil action.

D. CLASS ACTIONS

1. In General §1139
One or more members of a class of persons similarly situated may *sue or be sued* on behalf of all members of that class if such action is justified by considerations of *necessity or convenience*.

2. Background §1140
Class actions were originally permitted *only in equity*, and then only if it was shown that joinder of all parties was *impractical* and a few members could fairly represent all of the class. Later, under *code pleading*, class

actions were allowed if there were "questions of common or general interest of many persons," or if the parties were so numerous as to make it impractical to join all of them.

3. **Prerequisites to Class Action**   §1148
    Under Fed. R. Civ. P. 23(a), *all four* of the following conditions must be met:

    a. **Numerous parties requirement**   §1149
        The trial court has considerable discretion in this issue since there is *no fixed minimum* needed to make a class. However, the class must be definitely *ascertainable* and it must be *manageable*. In some cases, all members must be given *individual notice* of the action.

    b. **Common question**   §1155
        There must be "questions of law or fact common to the class" and the common questions must *predominate*.

    c. **Typical claim requirement**   §1161
        The representative's claim must be typical of those of the class so that she will be motivated to protect the class interests.

    d. **Adequate representation**   §1165
        Similar to the typical claim requirement, this condition also focuses on whether there is any *actual or potential conflict of interest* between the representative and the class. To ensure adequate representation, a court may divide a class into *subclasses* based on divergent interests.

4. **Three Grounds for Class Actions**   §1173
    If the above *four conditions are met*, a class action may be based on *any one* of the following grounds.

    a. **Prejudice from separate actions**   §1174
        A class suit is permitted if the prosecution of separate actions would create the risk of *establishing incompatible standards of conduct* for defendant through inconsistent adjudications, or of *substantially impairing the interests* of other class members.

    b. **Equitable relief**   §1177
        A class action is also proper if the basis on which the opponent has acted is generally applicable to the class and *declaratory or injunctive* relief would benefit the class as a whole.

    c. **Common predominant question**   §1180
        The most common basis for a class action occurs when common questions of law or fact *predominate* over questions affecting only individual members, and, *on balance*, *a class action is superior* to other available methods for adjudication.

5. **Jurisdictional Requirements in Class Suits**

    a. **Diversity of citizenship**   §1198
        Only the citizenship of the *representative* is considered.

a. **Obtaining factual information** §1276

A party who has effectively used discovery can go to trial with the best evidence for his contentions and knowledge of his adversary's case, thus avoiding delay or surprise, and the chance of a judgment resting on an accurate finding of fact is enhanced.

b. **Narrowing and simplifying** §1277

Discovery eliminates fictitious issues, claims, and defenses. Additionally, since pleadings are no longer the sole source of information, pleadings are simplified.

2. **Problems in Discovery** §1282

Some concerns regarding discovery include **nonlitigation use** of discovery information, **harassing** an opponent into settlement, and **failure to respond** to requests in a timely or thorough manner.

B. **BASIC DISCOVERY DEVICES**

1. **Prediscovery Disclosure** §1286

Federal Rule 26(a) requires certain disclosures to be made **before** formal discovery begins.

a. **Early conference of counsel** §1287

Counsel are required to meet as soon as practicable to develop a proposed discovery plan that is then presented to the court. Generally formal discovery cannot commence until **after** this meeting.

(1) **"2000" amendment** §1291

Before amendments to the prediscovery disclosure rule, effective December 1, 2000, disclosure was limited to information relevant to facts **alleged with particularity**. The particularity requirement is **no longer applicable**.

b. **Material to be disclosed** §1297

Each party is required to disclose:

(i) The **names and, if known, addresses and phone numbers** of persons with discoverable information that the disclosing party may use to support its claim or defense;

(ii) Copies or descriptions of **all documents** that the party possesses which it may use to support its claim or defense;

(iii) A **computation of damages** and the **documents** on which the computation is based; and

(iv) Any insurance agreement that might cover the claim.

c. **Timing** §1301

These disclosures are to be made at or within 14 days after the early meeting of counsel and must be signed by an attorney.

d. **Sanctions** §1304

A party failing to disclose is subject to sanctions, such as a prohibition against using the undisclosed material as evidence.

3. Interrogatories §1349

Interrogatories are written questions *from one party to another* requiring written responses.

    a. Who must answer §1351

    Parties are obliged to answer; a nonparty witness is not subject to interrogatories.

    b. Numerical limit §1356

    Interrogatories are limited to 25 per party, including subparts, but that limit may be changed by stipulation or court order.

    c. Duty to respond §1357

    A party must respond (or object) to interrogatories within 30 days of their service with all the information under her control (*i.e.,* in her files or by questioning employees). A *motion to compel* is available for incomplete or evasive answers.

4. Requests for Admissions §1364

This is a device that imposes a duty on the party served to acknowledge facts not in doubt which thus need not be proved at trial. A request for admission may be served by any party *on any other party*.

    a. Subject of request §1366

    A request may ask for the admission of the *genuineness* of a document, the truth of factual allegations, or the applicability of legal concepts to facts. The admissions requested may include *conclusions of law*, *ultimate facts* (under Federal Rules), matters of opinion, or facts that are outside the responding party's knowledge.

    b. Appropriate responses §1373

    A requested admission, if made, binds the responding party in the present action. A party may always *deny*, but may be liable for full costs of proof if the denial is unjustified. Refusal to respond at all is rarely justified. If *no* timely response is made, the matter is deemed *admitted*.

    c. Withdrawal or amendment §1383

    A withdrawal or amendment of an admission is allowed when it would promote presentation of the merits.

5. Requests for Inspection of Documents and Other Things §1384

A party may inspect and copy real evidence in the possession of any other party (*e.g.,* documents, maps, records). Inspection may include testing and sampling of materials.

    a. Computerized information §1385

    This type of information is discoverable. Discovery of it may require access to and information about the possessor's computer system.

    b. Making request for inspection §1387

    A party may serve a request without prior court order or a showing of good cause unless the other party objects. In federal practice, a request may be served at any time after the Rule 26(f) conference;

some states are more restrictive. Some showing of *necessity* is generally required for *inspection of premises*.

c. **Designation of items** §1390

The description of the items to be produced must be clear enough to allow a person of ordinary intelligence to know what is sought. The request must also specify the *time, place, and manner* of making the inspection.

d. **Objection to requests** §1394

Written objections to requests must be filed within 30 days after service of a request.

e. **Organization of produced materials** §1397

In federal court and some state courts, the responding party is required to produce requested materials either as they are normally kept or organized to correspond to the request.

f. **Failure to respond** §1400

A failure to respond exposes a party to sanctions, including the striking of pleadings and a determination of the facts on the assumption that inspection would have provided the requesting party with persuasive evidence.

g. **Materials in possession of nonparty** §1401

Under the Federal Rules and in some states, a subpoena can order a nonparty to permit inspection and copying of documents in its control or inspection of premises. Some states require a showing of good cause as a condition precedent to issuance of the subpoena.

6. **Medical Examinations** §1403

In federal court a court order is required to examine a party whose physical or mental condition is in issue. The *condition in issue* must be raised directly by the pleadings or in discovery. A showing of *good cause* is required, and *only parties* (or persons in the custody or control of parties) are subject to examination.

a. **Qualifications of examiner** §1407

In federal court, examinations may be conducted by any *suitably licensed or certified examiner*, not always a medical doctor. The examiner is usually selected by the party requesting the examination. Upon objection, the court may choose an impartial examiner.

b. **Types of procedures** §1410

If the sought information is important, a novel or even uncomfortable procedure may be allowed, as long as it is reasonably safe.

c. **Presence of counsel** §1411

Absent compelling circumstances, a *majority of federal courts* do *not allow* the presence of counsel, a third party, or an unattended videotape machine. Other courts permit observers, while still others decide on a case-by-case basis.

d. Copies of reports §1412

Upon request an examinee has the right to receive a copy of the examiner's report. However, if such a request is made, the examinee **waives** the doctor-patient privilege as to any previous examination of the same condition by the patient's own physician. Remember that even without a request, a plaintiff in a personal injury case waives the privilege as to the injury at issue.

7. Duty to Supplement Discovery Responses

a. Federal practice §1414

Prior discovery disclosures or responses must be supplemented if in some **material respect they are incomplete** or incorrect or if **additional or corrective information** has been obtained since the disclosure or response was made.

b. State practice compared §1417

In states not following the Federal Rules, **supplemental interrogatories** or other procedures may be used to obtain the same information.

C. SCOPE OF DISCOVERY

1. Relation of Discovery to Proof §1420

Usually, discovery may inquire into all nonprivileged information **relevant** to the **claim or defense of any party** (whether or not admissible as proof) that is reasonably calculated to lead to discovery of admissible evidence, although a few courts limit discovery to admissible evidence. Federal courts, becoming increasingly uneasy with broad discovery, have moved to limit it.

a. Scope of discovery in federal court §1421

Note that the 2000 amendments changed the scope of relevancy to "the claim or defense of any party," thus prohibiting parties from using discovery to develop new claims or defenses. However, upon a showing of good cause, courts may **expand** the amended scope of relevancy to the prior standard of "any matter relevant to the subject matter of the action."

b. Judicial limitations on disproportionate discovery §1425

The court must limit discovery that it finds to be unreasonably **cumulative, delayed,** or **burdensome**.

2. Scope of Relevant Material

a. Meaning of relevance §1429

Information is relevant if it tends to make the existence of any fact that is of consequence to the determination of the action more probable or less probable than it would be without the evidence.

b. Relation to claims and defenses §1434

Although the scope of discovery has been narrowed by the amendments, it is clear that it need only relate to the claims and defenses and is not limited to information needed to satisfy a party's burden of proof.

c. Information about witnesses §1436

The identity and location of witnesses is discoverable, as is information relating to a witness's *credibility*.

d. Insurance coverage §1437

Although not admissible, such coverage is discoverable in most jurisdictions.

e. Financial status §1438

A defendant's ability to satisfy a judgment is usually not discoverable. However, in some cases, both a defendant's and plaintiff's financial conditions are pertinent and thus discoverable.

3. Privilege §1443

Privileged material is excluded from obligatory disclosure through discovery. The attorney-client privilege is the most frequently invoked.

a. Requirements for attorney-client privilege §1445

The privilege applies only to communications made *in confidence while seeking legal advice from a lawyer*, and it is *waivable* by the client.

b. Federal vs. state law §1461

In federal court, when a federal claim or defense is involved, the federal courts may make rules governing privileges; if a state law claim or defense is involved, privilege issues are determined in accordance with state law.

c. Corporate clients §1463

Questions as to which corporate employees are covered by the attorney-client privilege may be determined, depending on the jurisdiction, by the older *control group test* or by the newer *Upjohn test*, which potentially extends coverage to *any* employee if certain requirements are met.

d. Other communicational privileges §1470

Other privileges protect certain communications between spouses, doctors and patients, priests and penitents, and psychotherapists (even if not doctors) and patients.

4. Trial Preparation Materials

a. "Work product"—*Hickman v. Taylor* rule §1479

Materials prepared by or under the direction of a party or her attorney in anticipation of litigation are subject to discovery *only if* the seeker can show substantial need and an inability to obtain equivalent material by other means; *i.e.*, it is a *qualified privilege*.

(1) Matters protected §1481

The Federal Rule covers any materials prepared *in anticipation of litigation or for trial*. Materials such as accident reports might not be protected if they are regularly made and usable for purposes other than litigation.

(2) **Special protection for mental impressions of an attorney** §1487
Federal Rule 26(b)(3) and similar state provisions protect absolutely against disclosure of the mental impressions and legal theories of an attorney.

(3) **Other applications** §1492
The work product privilege also applies to the work product of claims agents, insurers, sureties, indemnitors, and some statements of witnesses to lawyers.

b. **Expert reports** §1505
Experts may help the lawyer prepare for trial, or may testify at trial to support the party's case.

(1) **Nontestifying experts** §1506
Facts known to and opinions held by nontestifying experts are discoverable only in exceptional circumstances. Where discovery is ordered, the discovering party must pay a portion of the expert's fee. District courts are split on whether the identity of nontestifying experts is discoverable.

(2) **Testifying experts** §1512
At least *90 days before trial*, each party must identify each person that the party will call as an expert witness and must provide a detailed report of the witness's testimony and the basis therefor, qualifications, and compensation.

(3) **Unaffiliated experts** §1528
On occasion, experts who have not consented to assist either side may be compelled by subpoena to testify, although they probably must be paid a fee.

D. **PROTECTIVE ORDERS**

1. **Purpose** §1531
The purpose of a protective order is to *prevent undue burdens* due to discovery.

2. **Requirement of Good Cause** §1532
A protective order should be granted only on a showing of good cause by the party seeking protection.

a. **Confidential information** §1533
A protective order may be entered to protect trade secrets or other confidential research, development, or commercial information.

(1) **Showing required** §1534
The party seeking protection must show that the information has in fact been held in confidence and that a specific harm is likely to flow from discovery of the information.

(2) **Format—umbrella orders** §1539
A common type of order allows the producing party to designate

material as confidential, and requires the other party to hold it in confidence and use it only for trial preparation.

b. Other uses of protective orders   §1558

Protective orders may be issued if a deposition has been scheduled at an inconvenient place; to prevent a litigant from conducting a deposition that is annoying, embarrassing, or oppressive; and to limit discovery that is burdensome in relation to the importance of the case.

E. FAILURE TO DISCLOSE OR TO COMPLY WITH DISCOVERY

1. Order Compelling Response—Necessary Prerequisite   §1567

Before discovery sanctions can be imposed, a party seeking discovery must usually obtain an order compelling it.

a. Exception—failure to respond or disclose   §1569

If a party *completely* fails to respond to a valid discovery request or to attend his deposition, sanctions can *immediately* be sought. Failure to make Rule 26(a) disclosures or to supplement them allows the court to *exclude undisclosed materials* in addition to imposing other sanctions.

b. Before motion   §1572

Before filing a motion to compel, a party must confer with the opposing party in an effort to secure compliance with discovery.

2. Sanctions for Failure to Comply with Order   §1573

The court has discretion in choosing from among a variety of options available as sanctions, including orders that establish facts in favor of the party seeking discovery, disallowance of claims or defenses, grant of dismissal or default, or a finding that a party is in contempt.

3. Culpability Necessary for Sanctions   §1581

Due process limits the power of the court to impose sanctions that affect the merits of a case. The court will ordinarily consider whether the party was guilty of willfulness, bad faith, or other fault. If a lawyer's misconduct is involved, most courts will consider the extent of the *client's involvement* in the litigation before imposing harsh sanctions on the client.

4. Contempt Power   §1591

Contempt is an appropriate sanction *only* if the party or witness refuses to make disclosure in *defiance of a prior court order*. The contempt sanction may be *civil* (party may purge himself of the contempt by providing the information) or *criminal*. *No* contempt sanction of either kind may be used to compel a *medical examination*.

5. Compare—Sanctions for Improper Certification   §1595

Federal Rule 26(f) makes the attorney's signature on a discovery paper a certification that the material in it *is supported by law, has a proper purpose,* and *is reasonable*. If a paper is signed in violation of the Rule, the court is to sanction the offending person.

F. APPELLATE REVIEW OF DISCOVERY ORDERS

1. Orders Usually Not Appealable §1599

Most discovery orders are not final, and thus in most jurisdictions are not appealable. Neither are discovery orders considered collateral to the main action, nor are they injunctions.

2. Modes of Review

a. Certified appeal §1603

In federal practice, a trial court may certify an important discovery question to the appellate court.

b. Mandamus or prohibition §1604

These writs may be issued by an appellate court (in both state and federal practice) in *extraordinary situations* to correct or prevent a trial judge's *abuse of discretion* in discovery.

c. Review after judgment §1605

Failure of the trial court to compel effective disclosure *may* be the basis for reversal if the ruling was *prejudicial*.

d. Review of contempt order §1607

A civil contempt order against a party is not final and appealable; a conviction of criminal contempt *is* final and appealable.

G. USE OF DISCOVERY AT TRIAL

1. Statements of Adversary §1608

Admissions by a party in a deposition or in response to interrogatories are admissible and, in some cases, are conclusive proof of facts admitted. The *right to object* is retained at all times by the party whose statement is used at trial.

2. Statements of Other Witnesses §1610

Prior inconsistent statements of a witness may be shown by a deposition admitted at trial. A *deponent's unavailability* also permits a deposition to be admitted. A *party's own deposition* may be used by the party if he is *genuinely* unavailable for trial.

H. PRIVATE INVESTIGATION §1613

Civil litigants may conduct their own private investigation of the facts; *i.e.,* they are *not* required to use formal discovery procedures. Such litigants may use proof obtained, even by tortious means, since they are not subject to Fourth Amendment limits on searches.

VII. SUMMARY JUDGMENT

A. INTRODUCTION

1. Purpose §1616

Summary judgment enables a court to look behind the pleadings to determine whether some *contentions are so lacking in substance* that judgment can be rendered against the party making them without the expense and delay of a full trial.

 2. **Impact on Right to Trial**   §1627
  Although the traditional belief is that a litigant has a right to test her claims at trial, there is no such right where there is no genuine factual dispute.

 3. **Trend Favoring Use of Summary Judgment** §1628
  The advent of notice pleading has helped the motion for summary judgment supplant the motion to dismiss.

B. **STANDARD FOR GRANT OF SUMMARY JUDGMENT** §1629
 The court is to grant summary judgment if there is *no genuine issue as to any material fact*.

 1. **Relation to Standard for Judgment as a Matter of Law** §1630
  The Supreme Court has stated that in federal court the standard is the same at the summary judgment stage as at the judgment as a matter of law stage.

  a. **Moving party with burden of proof** §1631
   If the moving party has the burden on the issue, summary judgment should be granted only if the jury could not reasonably disbelieve the moving party's evidence.

  b. **Opposing party with burden** §1632
   If the moving party does not have the burden, summary judgment should be granted only if the opposing party does not present sufficient evidence to permit a jury reasonably to find for her.

 2. **Case-by-Case Determination** §1633
  The evaluation of motions for summary judgment is done case-by-case, based not on specific rules but rather on general principles.

  a. **All reasonable inferences in favor of opposing party** §1634
   The court makes all reasonable inferences in favor of the opposing party, and views evidence in the light most favorable to that party.

  b. **Court may not "weigh" evidence** §1635
   The court may not judge the relative persuasiveness of conflicting versions of events.

  c. **Role of higher burden of proof** §1636
   The Supreme Court has held that when a party will bear a higher burden of proof at trial, that standard should be used in deciding the motion for summary judgment.

  d. **Witness credibility** §1637
   Witness credibility is not ordinarily assessed in deciding a motion for summary judgment.

   (1) **Uncontradicted interested witness** §1638
    Even if uncontradicted, an *interested* witness's testimony will

usually not be sufficient to support summary judgment because it might not be believed by the jury.

(2) Disinterested witness §1639
Some courts have held that an uncontradicted affidavit of a *disinterested* witness will support summary judgment for the party with the burden of proof.

e. Motive, intent, and state of mind §1642
When mental state is at issue, summary judgment is usually *inappropriate*.

f. "Slightest doubt" standard contrasted §1645
The notion that summary judgment should be avoided whenever there was the "slightest doubt" about the outcome at trial has been *repudiated*.

C. PROCEDURE

1. Initial Showing §1646
The court must first evaluate the moving party's showing to determine whether it justifies pretrial scrutiny of the evidence.

a. Moving party's burden §1647
The moving party must show that there is no factual issue and that he is entitled to judgment.

(1) Moving party with burden of proof §1648
If the moving party has the burden of proof, he must produce evidence such that *no reasonable jury* could find for the opponent.

(2) Moving party without burden of proof §1649
The Supreme Court has rejected the early view that a moving party without the burden of proof must make a showing of the same strength as a party with the burden. The exact requirements are not clear, but a bald assertion that the opposing party lacks sufficient evidence is not enough; and the moving party should at least point to portions of the record showing the absence of factual issues. In some cases, the content (or lack thereof) of the opposing party's required initial disclosures may be used to support the motion.

b. Opposing party's burden §1658
If the moving party has not made the required initial showing, the opposing party technically need not make any showing in response. If the moving party has made an initial showing, the opponent has the burden of *coming forward with sufficient evidence* to support a jury verdict in his favor.

2. Time for Motion §1666
In federal court, a plaintiff must wait 20 days after commencement of the action. The defendant can move for summary judgment anytime.

3. **Materials Considered on Motion** §1667
A court deciding a motion for summary judgment may consider *admissions* contained in the pleadings, *affidavits* made on personal knowledge, and *discovery materials*. Oral testimony is rarely used.

    a. **Admissibility** §1672
Materials considered in deciding a motion for summary judgment must generally be capable of admission as evidence, and the court will entertain objections to admissibility before considering the materials.

        (1) **Possible relaxation for opposing party** §1673
The opposing party might not be held to the requirement of admissibility if it can show that it will have admissible evidence at trial.

4. **Partial Summary Judgment** §1677
The court can grant summary judgment as to some but not all of the claims or defenses before it.

5. **Inability to Provide Responsive Materials** §1680
The court may *continue* the hearing on the motion for summary judgment to allow time for the opposing party to obtain evidence. The evidence with respect to which the continuance is sought must be *material* to the motion and reasonably *obtainable*.

6. **Appellate Review** §1686
The appellate court uses a *plenary standard* of review, giving no deference to the trial court decision.

    a. **Timing** §1687
If full summary judgment is not granted, review may be delayed until the final decision of the case.

    b. **Order denying motion** §1688
If summary judgment is mistakenly denied, the order is not reviewable until after trial, at which time it may be *harmless error* if the trial was properly conducted.

VIII. MANAGERIAL JUDGING, PRETRIAL CONFERENCE, AND SETTLEMENT PROMOTION

A. PRETRIAL CONFERENCES AND MANAGERIAL JUDGING

1. **Historical Background** §1689
The original Federal Rule 16 authorized a pretrial conference to be held shortly before trial for the purpose of organizing it. Amendments in the 1980s and 1990s provided for mandatory meet-and-confer sessions among the parties, more numerous pretrial conferences, discovery conferences, and a final pretrial conference.

2. **Scheduling** §1691
Federal district courts are required, after consulting the parties, to enter a *scheduling order* within 90 days after a defendant's appearance and

within 120 days after service of the complaint. This order sets time limits for joinder, amendments, discovery, and motions. A district may, by local rule, *exempt* certain types of cases inappropriate for the scheduling rule.

3. **Discovery Control**
Judges are required to limit discovery that is unduly cumulative, delayed, or burdensome.

   a. **Conference by parties**
   At least 14 days before the Rule 16 scheduling conference or order, the parties are to hold a conference regarding the nature and basis of their claims and defenses and to develop a discovery plan. Within 10 days after the meeting, they are to submit a written report to the court. Cases exempted from the initial disclosure requirements are also exempt from the conference rule.

   b. **Court's pretrial order**
   Based on the parties' submission, the court is to enter an order limiting the time to complete discovery.

4. **Issue Simplification**
By the time a pretrial conference is held, the parties know more about their case and are in a better position to simplify the issues for trial. The court may not compel admissions, but may pressure parties to abandon unsupportable positions.

5. **Settlement Promotion**
Judges were once reluctant to become involved in settlement discussions, but Rule 16 now explicitly authorizes it.

   a. **No power to dictate terms of settlement**
   The court may suggest but not dictate the terms of settlement.

   b. **Ambiguity of judicial role**
   It is unclear how the judge's role in settlement comports with her usual role of deciding disputed matters according to legal standards. It is also unclear what role her pretrial opinion of the relative strengths of the cases should play.

   c. **Promotion of alternative dispute resolution**
   The judge may discuss special procedures to assist in resolving the dispute at a pretrial conference.

6. **Final Pretrial Conference—Purpose**
The final pretrial conference seeks to resolve as much as possible before trial and to give notice of the subjects to be covered at trial.

   a. **Required pretrial disclosures**
   At least 30 days before trial, each party is to: (i) *disclose the names of witnesses* the party expects to present, (ii) *designate witnesses whose testimony will be presented by deposition*, and (iii) *identify documents and other exhibits* the party expects to offer.

   b. **Topics covered**
   The *final pretrial order* encompasses the matters covered at the

pretrial conference. It controls at trial and can be **modified only to prevent manifest injustice**.

7. Sanctions §1721
Federal courts have explicit authority to use sanctions with regard to their pretrial supervision of cases.

B. COURT-ANNEXED SETTLEMENT DEVICES §1727
To promote settlement, courts began experimenting with other ways of facilitating settlement.

1. Mandated Alternative Dispute Resolution §1728
Under 1998 legislation, **federal district courts** must devise and implement an ADR program that all **civil** litigants must consider using in promoting a settlement. Each district must maintain a **panel of neutrals** to serve in ADR proceedings.

2. Mediation §1733
This involves a neutral third party who attempts to find a common ground on which the **parties can reach an agreement.** Since **formal legal rules are not binding** in mediation, the mediator can devise a solution that would not be available in litigation. Mediation procedures are also available in state courts.

3. Early Neutral Evaluation §1739
This is an ADR device, used early in a case, that relies on an experienced neutral lawyer to advise the parties on their prospects after both sides have presented their positions.

4. Summary Jury Trial §1744
Generally held after normal pretrial activities have concluded, an SJT is an abbreviated trial held before a jury summoned in the usual manner. Lawyers present summaries of the evidence at the SJT, which is usually **held in secret**. Occasionally, parties can stipulate an SJT will be binding. Courts are split on the issue of compulsory participation.

5. Court-Annexed Arbitration §1758
With consent of the parties, a federal court can refer any **civil** action for **nonbinding arbitration**, **except** cases involving **civil rights claims**, alleged **violations of constitutional rights**, or **damages exceeding $150,000**. Some states have also set up arbitration programs.

a. Hearing §1766
The arbitration decision is based on a hearing at which the rules of evidence and procedure may be relaxed.

b. Award §1769
The arbitrator's award **becomes the judgment unless a trial de novo** is demanded. The party who demands a trial may be required to **reimburse** the opposing party for certain costs if the party demanding trial does not receive a result more favorable than the award.

IX. TRIAL

A. RIGHT TO TRIAL BY JURY

1. Source of Right §1772

In federal courts, the right to a jury trial in civil actions at law is derived from the **Seventh Amendment** and, if that does not apply, the right may be provided by **Congress**. In **state courts**, the right to a jury trial in civil cases is **not** a due process right protected by the Fourteenth Amendment. However, there may be a federal statutory right to jury trial in state court actions that are governed by federal law. Note that most **state constitutions** have provisions similar to the Seventh Amendment of the U.S. Constitution.

2. Cases Where Right Exists

a. Basic historical test §1777

The historical test used to determine whether a right to jury trial exists in civil cases in federal court is whether the claim involved is **legal or equitable** as those terms were understood in 1791 (when the Seventh Amendment became effective).

b. Present standards for right to jury trial §1780

The right was observed in English law courts but not in Chancery (equity). Modern actions that are **counterparts to actions at law** (e.g., personal injury claims) are triable to a jury. Actions that are **counterparts to equity suits** (e.g., injunctions) do **not** give rise to a jury trial. Proceedings to enforce statutory rights in federal court are triable to a jury when the relief sought is a **legal remedy**.

c. Declaratory relief §1787

As a **statutorily created right**, declaratory relief is historically neither law nor equity. Generally, federal courts examine the underlying non-declaratory claim and permit a jury trial if that claim was triable.

3. Proceedings in Which Right to Jury Applies in Part

a. Actions joining legal and equitable claims §1788

In federal court, actions involving both legal and equitable claims are to be structured to preserve a jury trial on issues common to the legal and equitable aspects of the case, even if the equitable aspects predominate. Some states are contra and allow nonjury disposition of minor legal matters under the equitable "clean-up" doctrine.

(1) Priority of issues at trial §1789

The order in which issues are tried can be important because it may determine the outcome. In **federal** court, issues respecting a claim for legal relief ordinarily must be tried **first**. In **state** courts, the order is often within the **discretion** of the trial judge.

b. Equitable proceedings seeking legal relief §1793

Federal courts focus on the **nature of the underlying claim** in determining the right to jury trial.

c. Issues of law and fact for same claim

§1796

Even when a right to jury trial exists, some *issues* may be questions of law for the judge while others are issues of fact for the jury. If the legal issue is dispositive, there is no jury trial.

4. Right to Jury Trial Depends on Timely Demand

a. State practice

§1797

The right to jury trial usually must be exercised by a written demand at the time the case is set for trial; if demand is not timely made, the right is waived.

b. Federal practice

§1799

In federal court, a jury must be demanded in writing not later than 10 days after service of the last pleading directed to the issue for which the jury is demanded.

5. Jury Trials Discretionary with Court

§1801

A court may order a jury trial on any or all issues where the right *has been waived*, where a claim is not jury triable (with both parties' *consent*), and for the purpose of taking an *advisory verdict*.

B. SELECTION OF THE JURY

1. Summons of the Venire

§1804

Prospective jurors ("veniremen") are summoned by the court. The venire must be selected by a method that does not systematically exclude any religious, racial, ethnic, or political group.

2. Number of Jurors Required

§1822

The venire is usually at least two to three times larger than the number of jurors needed. Common law required a jury of 12. However, today *12 is not required* by either due process or the Seventh Amendment. In federal civil cases, there must be at least six. Due process *does* require at least six jurors in a *criminal* case, and some local district rules also require six jurors in *state civil trials*, but this depends entirely on state law.

3. Voir Dire Examination of Jurors

§1829

The examination of prospective jurors as to possible biases is known as voir dire.

a. Challenge for cause

§1830

A prospective juror may be challenged if it appears that he or a member of his family has a financial interest in the litigation, or for other reasons indicating he will not be an impartial juror. There is *no limit* to the number of challenges for cause.

b. Peremptory challenge

§1831

Each party is entitled to a limited number of challenges *without* a showing of cause, but peremptory challenges cannot be based on the juror's race or sex.

C. DISQUALIFICATION OF JUDGE

1. Grounds for Disqualification §1841

Grounds include any basis that may affect a judge's impartiality; *e.g.,* personal bias, personal knowledge of facts, previous involvement as a lawyer, financial interest, or family relationship. The disqualifying reason must be based on *matters outside the courtroom.* A judge must disqualify herself if adequate grounds exist.

2. Procedure for Disqualification

a. Federal practice §1849

A party seeking disqualification files an affidavit of bias setting forth the necessary facts. If the facts are legally sufficient to disqualify the judge, she *must* excuse herself and reassign the case.

b. State practice §1852

Most states require an actual showing by affidavit on grounds for disqualification. In some states, each party has an absolute right to disqualify *one* judge by simply stating in an affidavit that a fair trial cannot be obtained before that judge.

D. ORDER OF TRIAL

1. Right to Speak First and Last §1853

The general rule is that the party that has the *burden of proof* as to the principal issues (usually plaintiff) speaks first and last. However, the trial judge usually has the discretion whether to accord that right.

2. Stages of Jury Trial §1855

The normal sequence in a civil trial is plaintiff's opening statement; defendant's opening statement; presentation of direct evidence by plaintiff, with cross-examination of each witness by defendant, followed by re-direct and re-cross, whereupon *plaintiff rests*; presentation of direct evidence by defendant, with cross-examination, re-direct, and re-cross and then *defendant rests*; rebuttal evidence by plaintiff, and then by defendant; plaintiff's argument to jury; defendant's argument to jury; plaintiff's closing argument; instructions to jury by judge; and the jury verdict.

3. Nonjury Trial §1856

In a nonjury trial, the order is usually the same as above until the evidence has been presented, whereupon the parties may propose specific findings of facts and conclusions of law to the court.

E. PRESENTATION OF EVIDENCE

1. Control Over Presentation §1857

The presentation of evidence is usually the responsibility of the parties and their counsel, although most courts give a judge discretion to call his own witness.

2. Rules of Evidence §1858

Federal court proceedings are governed by the Federal Rules of Evidence. Many states' rules follow the Federal Rules. Some states have their own evidence codes, while others rely on common law rules.

plaintiff's opening statement (or at close of plaintiff's proof) if the statement of proof reveals that plaintiff's case is **legally insufficient**.

In a nonjury trial, after a party has been fully heard with respect to an issue, the court may enter a judgment against that party if it finds the party's proof is **unpersuasive**. The motion is analogous to the common law **demurrer** to the evidence. Today, some states call it a **motion to dismiss**, while in others it is a **motion for judgment**.

G.   ARGUMENT TO JURY

In federal practice and most state courts, counsels' arguments take place at the close of the evidence and **before** the jury receives the judge's instructions.

Counsel have an absolute right to argument in a jury trial. However, the trial judge has discretion to control the duration and manner of argument.

Counsels' comments must be **based on the evidence**, the argument must be within the limits of the **governing substantive law**, and counsel may **not appeal to the passions or prejudices** of the jurors.

H.   INSTRUCTIONS TO JURY

Before a jury deliberates, the judge instructs it on certain relevant matters.

A **judge** determines issues of **law** (e.g., interpretation of statute), while a **jury** decides disputed issues of **fact**. Questions of fact are specific and pertain to past events.

3.   **Burden of Persuasion**

The judge must explain to the jury which party has the burden of persuasion concerning each issue of fact the jury must decide.

In a civil case, the usual burden of persuasion is by **preponderance of the evidence**. However, issues of fraud, duress, or undue influence must be shown by **clear and convincing proof**.

Generally, a judge is allowed to comment to the jury on the quality of the evidence presented.

Although the responsibility for instructions rests with the judge, counsel has a duty to propose instructions that present the theory of the case. Proposed instructions must be *written* and served on opposing counsel. They must be filed by the close of evidence. Each party must be given the *opportunity to object* to an adversary's proposed instructions.

6. Appellate Review of Jury Instructions   §1920
Generally, errors in instructions are waived unless objections are timely made. Traditionally, courts have held that egregious ("*plain*") error may be reversible even without a timely objection, but some courts hold that there is no plain error exception.

I. JURY DELIBERATION AND VERDICT

1. Types of Verdicts

a. General verdict   §1922
The most common form of verdict, a general verdict is simply a decision in favor of one party or the other.

b. Special verdict   §1924
This consists of the jury's *answers to specific factual* questions that it is instructed to decide; it is not a direct decision as to which party should prevail on the law.

c. General verdict with special interrogatories   §1930
This verdict *combines the two forms* above. The jury makes a general decision as to which party should prevail on the law while simultaneously answering specific questions of fact. If there is an *inconsistency* between the *special finding and the general verdict*, a judge may ignore the verdict and enter judgment based on the special findings. However, inconsistency among *the special findings* usually requires a new trial.

2. Requirement of Unanimity   §1937
The general rule in federal and most state courts is that the jury must render a unanimous verdict unless the parties otherwise agree.

3. Jury Deliberation and Impeachment of Verdict

a. Standards of jury conduct   §1942
Only information presented at trial may be considered by the jury; any communication from the judge must be received in the *presence of counsel*. Each juror must make up his own mind; there can be no verdict of the average or by lots. *No coercion* by the judge is allowed.

b. Juror misconduct   §1948
At *common law*, juror misconduct had to be established by the testimony of a person *other than* a juror. The federal rule today is that a juror may testify to any "extraneous prejudicial information" or "outside influence." Some states allow jurors to testify to *any* improper influence, either inside or outside the jury room.

c. Impeachment of verdict   §1953
Impeachment can result from a juror's having concealed a ground for

disqualification on *voir dire* examination, as well as from misconduct during jury deliberations.

d. Announcement of verdict   §1956
The verdict must be announced in open court. At the request of either party, the jury may be *polled*. If the verdict is incomplete, the court may direct the jury to continue its deliberations.

J. MOTIONS AFTER VERDICT OR JUDGMENT

1. Renewed Motion for Judgment as a Matter of Law (Judgment N.O.V.)   §1960
A renewed motion for judgment as a matter of law is granted after a verdict when the trial judge concludes that there is *no substantial evidence* supporting the decision.

a. Procedural requirements   §1962
In federal practice, a renewed motion can be entered *only* on motion of a *party*; in some states it can be entered *by the court* sua sponte. The federal rule requires the motion to be made within 10 days after judgment was entered on the verdict; state requirements vary.

(1) Prior motion   §1966
In federal court, a renewed motion cannot be considered unless the moving party made a motion for judgment as a matter of law at the close of all the evidence.

2. Motion for New Trial   §1973
A trial judge has the power to order a new trial on all or some of the contested factual issues.

a. Grounds for motions—jury trial   §1974
A federal court may order a new trial in a jury case "for any of the reasons for which new trials have heretofore been granted in actions at law in the courts of the United States." Some state statutes are more explicit in specifying when a new trial is appropriate. Appropriate grounds include *prejudicial misconduct*, such as improper jury argument. Prejudicial error is *waived* if known and not raised prior to verdict. Some other grounds are surprise, newly discovered or improper evidence, verdict contrary to law, and a verdict contrary to the evidence.

b. Grounds for motion—nonjury trial   §1996
In a nonjury trial, such a motion may be granted on grounds of newly discovered evidence, erroneous findings of fact, and/or error in the conduct of the trial.

c. Procedural requirements   §1997
A federal court may order a new trial on its own motion; some states require a party to make the motion. In federal practice, the motion must be served not later than 10 days after the entry of judgment; state time limits vary.

d. Order   §2007
In nonjury cases, a court may order a full or partial new trial; in jury

cases, the court must grant or deny the motion but may do so in parts or on conditions. In federal court, a judge need not specify grounds on which the new trial is granted; in some states, grounds must be stated. Grounds include **excessive or inadequate damages and insufficiency of proof**.

(1) Conditional new trial §2014

A **remittitur** is an order for a new trial unless plaintiff consents to a **reduction** of the damage award. An **additur** (not allowed in federal court) orders a new trial unless defendant consents to an **increase** in the verdict amount.

3. Motion to Alter or Amend Judgment §2027

This is used to reopen judgments in both jury and nonjury cases and is used to correct **errors of law only**. Such a motion is subject to the same time limits as a motion for a new trial.

4. Motion for Relief from Judgment §2030

Such a motion may be used to correct a clerical error (no time limit); or on the grounds of mistake, inadvertence, or surprise; excusable neglect; newly discovered evidence; fraud; void judgment; change of circumstances; and under federal rules, for any other reason justifying relief. In federal court, the motion must be made within reasonable time; state rules vary.

a. Distinguish independent suit to set aside judgment §2045

This is an equitable proceeding usually based on **jurisdictional defects** or **fraud**. The independent suit may be addressed to a different court while a motion for relief from a judgment is made to the court that rendered the judgment. Grounds for an independent suit are more narrow and more strictly applied. Relief in federal court is authorized only **"to prevent a grave miscarriage of justice."**

5. Coram Nobis §2052

Abolished in federal courts, the common law writ of coram nobis is still available in some states. It is **cautiously applied** and is granted only where it is absolutely clear that a fact previously determined to be true is false and that the fact was crucial to the outcome of the case.

X. APPEAL

A. RIGHT TO APPEAL

1. Status as Right §2056

At **common law**, there was no right to appeal; a writ of error was discretionary with the court. Also, the Due Process Clause does not guarantee a right of appeal, at least in civil cases. However, the right to appeal is **statutorily created** in every state, and federal courts have a general right of appeal.

2. Waiver of Right §2061

The right of appeal may be lost through an express waiver, an untimely assertion, voluntary compliance with a judgment, or acceptance of benefits under the judgment.

B. APPELLATE PROCEDURE

1. Filing of Appeal
§2080

In the federal system, an appeal is commenced by filing a *notice of appeal* in the appellate or trial court within 30 days after entry of judgment (60 days if U.S. is a party). State rules vary. In any case, time limits are jurisdictional and usually *cannot be waived*.

2. Appeal Bonds
§2086

An appeal bond must generally be filed to secure the adversary's costs if the judgment is affirmed. Assurance that a judgment will be satisfied if affirmed may also have to be given by posting a *supersedeas bond*, which keeps the judgment from taking effect pending appeal.

3. Record on Appeal
§2090

Review on appeal is usually limited to the trial record.

4. Stay of Proceedings Below
§2093

While an appeal from a final judgment is pending, the trial court generally has *no power* to alter or vacate its judgment, and very limited power to make any other order affecting the rights of the parties with respect to the case on appeal.

C. RULINGS SUBJECT TO APPEAL

1. Final Decision Requirement

a. General rule
§2094

At *common law*, a writ of error could be taken only from a final judgment—*i.e.*, judgment that stated the outcome of the proceedings and manifested that the proceedings were complete. Now, the final decision rule is the basic rule, but it is subject to exceptions.

b. Jurisdictional character of rule
§2108

The final decision rule is jurisdictional in that it *cannot be waived*.

2. Exceptions to Final Decision Requirement

a. Partial final decisions
§2109

If multiple claims or parties are involved in an action, an order disposing of fewer than all claims is usually not a final judgment unless the trial court enters a partial final judgment (when that is authorized).

b. Review of equitable remedies
§2112

In early equity practice, the rule was not applied because personal orders (*e.g.*, injunctions), if erroneous, might result in irreversible consequences. Thus immediate appellate review was permitted. Modern practice preserves the right to interlocutory review from orders that might result in irreparable consequences, *e.g.*, grant or denial of injunction.

c. Discretionary review
§2114

Interlocutory appeals are also permitted in the federal system when the **trial court certifies** that determination of a controlling question of law would speed the ultimate resolution of the case, **and** the court of appeals **grants leave** to appeal. Appellate jurisdiction extends to any question included in the certified order and is not limited to the specific question formulated by the district judge.

<table>
<tr><td>d.</td><td>**Orders regarding class certification**</td><td>§2119</td></tr>
</table>

    d.   **Orders regarding class certification**   §2119

Such orders are immediately reviewable if application for review is made within 10 days. Whether to accept the application is completely within the appellate court's discretion and does not require district court certification.

    e.   **Collateral orders**   §2120

In federal court, an immediate appeal is permitted from orders as to collateral matters if (i) the issue the order concerns is an important one that is completely separate from the merits of the underlying case; (ii) deferred review would effectively destroy appellant's rights; and (iii) the trial court has made its final decision on the challenged issue. The collateral order exception is limited to a **small class of cases**.

    f.   **Practical construction of "finality"**   §2134

The U.S. Supreme Court has held that the final decision rule should be construed practically, not technically.

D. SCOPE OF APPELLATE REVIEW

    1.   **In General**   §2135

Appellate review does not extend to retrying facts or supplanting the trial judge's decision in discretionary matters.

    2.   **Findings of Fact Subject to Limited Review**

        a.   **Jury verdicts**   §2137

The role of the appellate court is to oversee the jury's adherence to the law. Verdicts must be supported by **substantial evidence**.

        b.   **Judicial findings in nonjury trials**   §2140

A judge's findings in a nonjury trial may be set aside if in **clear error**. Note that this is a less restrictive test, permitting reversal more often than the test for jury verdicts.

        c.   **"Fact" and "law" distinguished**   §2143

Only findings of fact are entitled to deference. **Errors of law** (e.g., improper jury instructions, erroneous conclusions of law by judge) are reviewed de novo and, if not harmless, result in reversal. The distinction between law and fact can be difficult, and there is no satisfactory test.

    3.   **Review of Discretionary Rulings**   §2152

A trial judge is entrusted by law with discretion as to certain matters, especially procedural questions. An appellate court will not reverse such decisions absent a clear **abuse of discretion**.

4. "Harmless Error" Standard   §2154

The general rule is that an appellate court will not reverse any judgment unless the trial court's error was *prejudicial* (*i.e.,* affected substantial rights of the parties) or the error was *egregious*.

5. Waiver of Objections in Lower Court

    a. General rule   §2159

    An appellate court will not reverse a judgment to correct any error that might have been avoided or corrected if the appellant had made a timely objection in the trial court.

    b. Exceptions   §2164

    An appellate court may review despite the lack of a timely objection if: (i) the trial court lacked *subject matter jurisdiction* or (ii) error is so clear and fundamental that it would be *unjust* to let the judgment stand.

6. Trial de Novo   §2167

Sometimes legislatively authorized, this is, in effect, a new trial in a court of general jurisdiction.

E. APPELLATE REVIEW BY EXTRAORDINARY WRIT

1. Prerogative Writs   §2168

The available writs, depending on the court system, are:

    (i)   *Mandamus*—order directing a judge to perform her legal duty; and

    (ii) *Prohibition*—an order enjoining a judge from conduct exceeding her lawful authority.

2. Source of Power to Issue Writs   §2169

State court writs are usually based on common law practice. Federal courts are statutorily empowered to issue prerogative writs.

3. Discretionary Character of Writ   §2171

The issuance of a prerogative writ is always discretionary with the appellate court. There is *no right* to a hearing.

4. Grounds for Issuance   §2172

A writ may issue for abuse of discretion, excess of jurisdiction, or refusal to exercise jurisdiction. There must be a *need for immediate review*, *i.e.,* when petitioner has no right to a present appeal and would suffer undue hardship or substantial prejudice if review was delayed until after a final judgment.

5. Common Uses of Writs   §2174

The courts of appeals use discretionary writs to correct erroneous denials of jury trial, to prevent the improper delegation of judicial power, and to prevent unlawful remand to state court.

6. Supervisory Mandamus   §2175

In rare circumstances, mandamus may be used to resolve *issues of first impression* that may be important in a significant number of cases.

estoppel may be limited in cases where the issue would not be conclusive between the parties to the original action or where unjust under the circumstances.

E. INTERJURISDICTIONAL PRECLUSIVE EFFECTS OF JUDGMENTS

1. Basic Rule §2265

If judgments are rendered in different court systems, generally the preclusion principles of the court system that rendered the judgment should be used to determine its preclusive effect.

a. State court judgments §2266

State court judgments are given effect in other states by the Full Faith and Credit Clause and also are given effect in other state courts, and in federal court, by federal statute.

b. Federal court judgments §2268

Federal court judgments are entitled to preclusive effect according to *federal common law,* but in diversity cases, the federal common law requires following the preclusive effect that the judgment would be given by the courts of the state in which the federal court sits.

2. Prohibition Against Broader Preclusion §2272

The Supreme Court has interpreted the Full Faith and Credit Clause as forbidding a federal court from giving more effect to a state court judgment than would the preclusion rules of that state.

Approach to Exams

Examination questions on civil procedure can concern a wide range of issues. The issues that you are most likely to encounter are discussed below and can be analyzed in the following sequence. (Note that these issues are discussed in greater detail in the chapter approach sections at the beginning of the appropriate chapters.)

1. **Jurisdiction**

    Does the court have *authority* to render judgment in the present action, consistent with constitutional requirements of due process?

    a. Does the court have jurisdiction *over the parties* (territorial jurisdiction of the state)?

    b. Does the court have jurisdiction *over the subject matter* (over the particular type of action)?

    c. Has *adequate notice* been given to all parties?

2. **Venue**

    Assuming the court does have jurisdiction, is it the *proper place* for trial of the action under the rules governing venue?

    a. If the action was originally filed in a court having proper venue, are there grounds for *transfer* or change of venue to another court?

3. **State and Federal Law**

    a. If the action is in federal court, does it concern a state law matter (usually this means it is a diversity case)? If so, the court will generally follow *state substantive law* and *federal procedural law.*

    b. Is there an *Erie* problem—*i.e.,* is there a *true conflict* between federal and state rules of law? (Only if there is a true conflict do you need to consider which rule, state or federal, applies.)

4. **Pleadings**

    a. Does the complaint contain a *valid substantive legal claim*?

    b. Does the complaint state the elements of a *prima facie case*?

    c. Is the complaint *sufficiently specific* so as to give fair notice of the basis of the claim(s) made?

d. Does the answer properly admit or deny the complaint's allegations? Does it properly raise any applicable defenses?

e. Is there a ground for allowing an *amendment*?

5. Parties

a. Are the named parties proper (*real party in interest* and *capacity to sue or be sued*)?

b. Are the named parties *properly joined*?

c. Are there *other parties* who should be joined under the necessary party rule or who may become parties by intervention or impleader?

d. Can the parties assert *claims against each other* in addition to those in the complaint—*i.e.*, counterclaims or cross-claims? Can the parties *implead* other parties?

e. Is a *class action* appropriate?

f. May additional parties *intervene*?

6. Discovery

Is there a controversy as to either party's right to obtain pretrial discovery from the other party or from some third person? If so, consider:

a. Have the parties satisfied the requirement of *disclosure*?

b. Is the information sought within the *permissible scope* of discovery (*i.e.*, is it relevant to the claim or defense of a party)?

c. Is the information protected by a *privilege* or as *work product*?

d. Is the *proper mechanism* used (*e.g.*, deposition, interrogatory, etc.)?

e. What limitations by *protective order* are needed to prevent abuse?

f. If a discovery order was violated, or if a disclosure obligation was not met, is a *sanction* appropriate?

7. Trial

a. Is there a *right to a jury trial*?

b. Are the issues before the court within the *scope* of the pleadings or pretrial order, or properly in issue because evidence on them was received without valid objection?

c. Who has the *burden of proof* as to a particular issue, and has the burden been met?

d. Were *instructions* properly given to the jury, and were they substantially correct?

e. Was there *improper conduct* by the judge, a counsel, party, witness, or juror?

f. Did plaintiff put on sufficient evidence to survive a *motion for judgment as a matter of law*?

8. Post-Trial

a. Is there relief that the *trial court* can give?

(1) Motion for a *new trial* (to overcome procedural error or if the verdict is against the weight of the evidence).

(2) *Renewed motion for judgment as a matter of law* (if the verdict is unsupported by sufficient evidence).

(3) *Extraordinary relief* (*e.g.*, if newly discovered evidence, fraud).

b. Can the *appellate court* provide relief?

(1) Is there a *final judgment* or other appealable order?

(2) Is *discretionary appeal* available?

(3) May review be obtained by *extraordinary writ*?

c. Does *res judicata* (claim preclusion) or *direct or collateral estoppel* (issue preclusion) bar relitigation of this matter in later trials?

Chapter One:
Territorial Jurisdiction and Related Matters

CONTENTS

Chapter Approach

Almost all civil procedure examinations will include a question regarding whether a court has the authority to hear a particular case. Such problems raise issues of personal jurisdiction (*i.e.*, a court's authority over the *parties* in the lawsuit), and related matters such as venue (*i.e.*, the geographic location where the case is heard). (Note that problems of subject matter jurisdiction—*e.g.*, whether a case can be brought in *federal* court are covered in Chapter II.) When faced with a question raising issues of territorial jurisdiction, ask yourself:

1. **Is there a statute or rule that gives the court a basis for the exercise of jurisdiction?** There must be some "enabling legislation" by which the court obtains authority to exercise jurisdiction in the case. Often you must analyze the specific wording of the statute or rule involved.

2. **Is this exercise of jurisdiction constitutional?** This analysis may look to one of a number of grounds for constitutional assertion of jurisdiction:

   a. Does the defendant have *minimum contacts* with the forum state (*i.e.*, the state where the court is located) to support the exercise of jurisdiction?

   b. Are the defendant's contacts with the forum state so substantial that she can be subjected to jurisdiction on claims not related to the lawsuit on a theory of *general jurisdiction*?

   c. Has *property* of the defendant been seized within the state? If so, is this a sufficient ground for the exercise of jurisdiction?

   d. Has the defendant *consented* to jurisdiction in the forum state?

   e. Was the defendant *personally served* within the forum state?

3. **Is venue proper?** If not, is it possible to *transfer* the case to a location that is a proper venue?

4. **Was proper notice given?** For a court to properly assert jurisdiction, the defendant also must have received *notice* of the lawsuit, and (in most cases) proper *service of process*, which is the summons to appear before the court and the complaint specifying what the lawsuit is about.

A. Introduction

1. **Types of Territorial Jurisdiction [§1]**

   Territorial jurisdiction (sometimes called personal jurisdiction) refers to a state's power to hear a case and enforce its judgment over the particular parties or property involved. This power is based on the state's connection to the parties or property. Territorial jurisdiction is divided into three categories:

   a. **In personam jurisdiction [§2]**

   In personam jurisdiction permits a court to enter a judgment that is *personally binding* on the defendant, either ordering her to do or refrain from doing a certain act (equitable or injunctive relief) or decreeing that the plaintiff may collect a certain amount of damages from the defendant (legal relief).

   b. **In rem jurisdiction [§3]**

   In rem jurisdiction permits a court *to adjudicate the rights of all possible claimants to a specific piece of property*, as in a condemnation proceeding. This authority originated from a state's power to determine controversies regarding real property within its borders: "The well-being of every community requires that the title to real estate therein shall be secure, and that there be convenient and certain methods of determining any unsettled questions respecting it." [**Arndt v. Griggs**, 134 U.S. 316 (1890)]

   c. **Quasi in rem jurisdiction [§4]**

   Quasi in rem jurisdiction formerly included cases of two types. The first category included cases involving *individual disputes related to property under the court's control* (such as actions for specific performance of a contract to purchase land). This type of quasi in rem jurisdiction continues to provide a constitutional basis for the exercise of jurisdiction. The second category of cases involved essentially *personal disputes where the court could not assert personal jurisdiction over the defendant*, but had jurisdiction over property belonging to the defendant. That property would be seized by the plaintiff and used to satisfy the claim if the plaintiff prevailed. The use of this second category of quasi in rem jurisdiction to provide a basis for exercise of jurisdiction over nonresident defendants has been severely limited on constitutional grounds. (*See infra*, §§60-78.)

2. ***Pennoyer v. Neff* and the Traditional Power Theory [§5]**

   In **Pennoyer v. Neff**, 95 U.S. 714 (1878), the Court found that for the state to exercise power over individuals or property there must be *valid service of process* on the individual (in in personam cases) *or attachment of property* in the state (in in rem actions). The methods by which jurisdiction may be obtained have broadened since *Pennoyer*.

a. **The *Pennoyer* decision [§6]**

In 1865, attorney Mitchell sued Neff in an Oregon state court, alleging that Neff owed him about $250 for legal work performed. Neff, a resident of California, was not personally served; instead, service was by publication based on Mitchell's assertion that Neff owned property in Oregon. When Neff did not appear in the action, Mitchell obtained a default judgment. A month later, Neff acquired title to a tract of land in Oregon, and Mitchell had the sheriff seize and sell the land to satisfy the judgment. Mitchell bought the land at the sheriff's sale and transferred title to Pennoyer shortly thereafter. Many years later, Neff sued Pennoyer in federal court, arguing that the sale was invalid because the Oregon court lacked jurisdiction to enter the judgment against him. The Supreme Court agreed, stating that there had been no in personam jurisdiction over Neff because he was never served with process, and there was no in rem jurisdiction because the court did not attach any Oregon property owned by Neff at the outset of the suit. Thus, the court had no jurisdiction over Neff or his property, and the judgment was invalid.

(1) Relation to due process

Because the Fourteenth Amendment did not become effective until 1868, after Mitchell had Neff's property sold, the Fourteenth Amendment Due Process Clause was not involved in the case. However, the Court made it clear in dictum that in the future, *due process would apply the same limitations on exercise of jurisdiction.*

b. **Territorial limits on process [§7]**

In keeping with its concept of a state's power being limited by its borders, the Court in *Pennoyer* determined that a state cannot serve an individual domiciled in another state with process and summon that person to respond to a lawsuit against him. This basic limitation on the power of state courts to exercise in personam jurisdiction over out-of-state defendants has been weakened by the modern shift to a minimum contacts analysis. (*See infra,* §§21-25.)

c. **Methods to obtain jurisdiction**

(1) Service within state sufficient [§8]

Pennoyer said that service of process on a defendant within the state was sufficient for jurisdiction. This conclusion is implicit in *Pennoyer's* reasoning, and is the basis for what has come to be known as ***transient jurisdiction***; *i.e.,* a court may obtain jurisdiction over a defendant by serving him when he is temporarily physically present in the state. It has been carried to great lengths.

Example—service in airplane: Passenger was on a nonstop scheduled commercial airline flight from Memphis, Tennessee, to Dallas, Texas. While the plane was over Pine Bluff, Arkansas, he was served with process. The service was held to be sufficient to establish jurisdiction in Arkansas. [**Grace v. MacArthur,** 170 F. Supp. 442 (E.D. Ark. 1959)]

(a) Limitation—fraudulent inducement into forum [§9]

However, courts decline transient jurisdiction where the defendant was fraudulently lured into the jurisdiction. [*See, e.g.,* **Wyman v. Newhouse,** 93 F.2d 313 (2d Cir. 1937)—service in Florida was invalid when defendant was enticed to Florida by a woman who falsely told him that she was leaving the country permanently and would like to see him one last time; *and see infra,* §112]

(b) Constitutional validity [§10]

A number of legal authorities questioned the constitutional validity of transient jurisdiction in the wake of **Shaffer v. Heitner,** 433 U.S. 186 (1997) (*see infra,* §111), but the Supreme Court has upheld the practice in **Burnham v. Superior Court,** 495 U.S. 604 (1990).

(2) Seizure of defendant's property [§11]

Pennoyer indicated in dictum that *prejudgment seizure* of a defendant's property was sufficient to permit a state to dispose of that property to satisfy *claims not related to the property*. Where such seizure was accomplished, the court had power to control disposition of the property, even absent service of process within the jurisdiction. This is an application of the second category of *quasi in rem jurisdiction* discussed above. (*See supra,* §4.)

(a) Need for prejudgment seizure [§12]

Quasi in rem jurisdiction was not available in *Pennoyer* itself because in the first action, the plaintiff, Mitchell, did not attach defendant Neff's property *before* entry of the judgment. The Court held that seizure after judgment was insufficient to support jurisdiction.

(b) Scope of "property"

1) Debt as property [§13]

In **Harris v. Balk,** 198 U.S. 215 (1905), the Court upheld assertion of quasi in rem jurisdiction over a debt owed to the defendant by a temporary visitor to the state. The Court reasoned that "[t]he obligation of the debtor to pay his debt clings to and accompanies him wherever he goes." Therefore, the debt was sufficiently "present" to permit its seizure to provide a basis for exercise of jurisdiction to the extent of the debt.

2) Insurance policies [§14]

Some states extended this idea to justify the seizure of an

insurer's obligation to defend and indemnify its insured. The obligation was said to be property of the insured, present wherever the insurer could be served, thereby justifying jurisdiction. [*See* **Seider v. Roth,** 17 N.Y.2d 111 (1966)] However, the Supreme Court *invalidated this practice* in **Rush v. Savchuk,** 444 U.S. 320 (1980) (*see infra,* §77).

d. Exceptions to in-state service or prejudgment seizure requirement [§15]

In *Pennoyer*, the Court recognized some exceptions to its rigorous rules:

(1) Status [§16]

Even absent service within the state, the *Pennoyer* Court acknowledged that a state court could determine the status of one of its citizens toward a nonresident. This exception bore principally on divorce cases and gave rise to the "Nevada divorce," in which one spouse would move to Nevada for the period required to establish residency and obtain a divorce there. Jurisprudentially, it led to the concept of the *divisible divorce*, under which the marital status was treated as a res that could be the subject of adjudication by the state in which either spouse resided, but alimony, child support, and other financial matters were viewed as in personam and beyond the authority of a state that had not obtained jurisdiction by personal service.

(2) Consent [§17]

Pennoyer suggested that states could require noncitizens to consent to suit as a condition for conducting activities in the state. As explained in *Pennoyer*, this depended on the state's right to forbid or exclude the activity. However, there were limitations on the power of a state to exclude noncitizens, and there gradually arose a doctrine of *implied consent*, which holds that a defendant's *in-state activities* are sufficient to justify service for suits *related to the activities*, despite doubts about the power to forbid them.

e.g. **Example—nonresident motorist statutes:** In **Hess v. Pawloski,** 274 U.S. 352 (1927), the Court upheld jurisdiction based on a statute that treated driving within the state as implied consent to suit in that state on claims arising from that driving.

e. Notice [§18]

Pennoyer had an ambivalent attitude toward the need for notice to the defendant of the pendency of the action.

(1) Notice not sufficient [§19]

The court proceeded from the notion that a state's power over individuals ends at its borders, so that process from a state's courts cannot run into another state and force persons domiciled there to appear in a legal proceeding. Therefore, notice to Neff in California of the suit filed by Mitchell in Oregon would not have any effect on the power of the Oregon court to enter a binding judgment.

(2) Notice not required [§20]

Pennoyer similarly did not indicate that notice was required for entry of a valid judgment. Instead, it indicated that prejudgment seizure of the defendant's property would be sufficient. *Rationale:* the law presumes that property is always in the possession of its owner, and therefore its seizure will inform the owner "that he must look to any proceedings authorized by law upon such seizure for its condemnation and sale." For examination of the current requirement that notice be given, *see infra,* §§225 *et seq.*

3. Shift to Minimum Contacts [§21]

In **International Shoe Co. v. Washington,** 326 U.S. 310 (1945), the Court shifted away from *Pennoyer's* insistence on service within the state to support in personam jurisdiction. Instead, it held that to subject a defendant to a judgment in personam, due process requires only that "he have certain minimum contacts with [the forum] such that the maintenance of the suit does not offend 'traditional notions of fair play and substantial justice.'"

a. Systematic and continuous activity [§22]

The Court has upheld in personam jurisdiction over a nonresident defendant based on *systematic and continuous contacts with the state.* In *International Shoe,* the defendant was a Delaware corporation headquartered in St. Louis, Missouri. It employed 11 to 13 salespeople in Washington, who were authorized only to solicit orders. The orders could be accepted or rejected only by the home office. Although it had no permanent office in Washington, the sales efforts there generated commissions of at least $31,000 per year. The state claimed that *International Shoe* was obligated to contribute to the state's unemployment compensation fund in amounts proportional to the activities there of its salespeople. The Court upheld Washington's jurisdiction, an easy decision given the volume and systematic and continuous nature of the contacts with the state, as well as the fact that the amount of the claim was directly related to the level of activities in the state.

b. Single contact [§23]

The Court has also upheld jurisdiction over a nonresident (Texas) defendant based on a *single contact with the forum* (California)—sending a contract for reinsurance to an insured in California. [**McGee v. International Life Insurance Co.,** 355 U.S. 220 (1957)] The Court emphasized that there was a trend toward expanding the permissible scope of state jurisdiction, based on a fundamental change in the national economy to a more nationalized form of commerce. This reduced the burden on a defendant of defending in any state in which it engages in economic activity. The Court indicated that it was sufficient that the contract sued on in *McGee* had "a substantial connection with the State." This conclusion was based in part on the presence in California of witnesses to the company's defense of suicide, and also on the existence of pervasive regulation of insurance companies in California. *McGee* is regarded by many as a high-water mark for extended state court jurisdiction.

c. **Purposeful availment limitation [§24]**

The Court cautioned, however, that "it is a mistake to assume that this trend heralds the eventual demise of all restrictions on the personal jurisdiction of state courts." [**Hanson v. Denckla**, 357 U.S. 235 (1958)] In *Hanson,* the Court said that there must be "some act by which the defendant *purposefully avails* itself of the privilege of conducting activities within the forum state, thus invoking the benefits and protections of its laws."

d. **Post-*International Shoe* trend [§25]**

For 30 years after *International Shoe* was decided, state courts and legislatures expanded state court jurisdiction. The usual impetus behind such expansions was to provide a forum for local plaintiffs claiming injury due to products or services provided by distant defendants. Given elastic limitations on jurisdiction, there were strong pressures to open the doors of the local courts to such plaintiffs.

B. Contemporary Constitutional Grounds for State Court Jurisdiction

1. **Contacts with Forum [§26]**

International Shoe's approach has generated a two-stage analysis for determining whether the exercise of jurisdiction over a nonresident defendant is proper. The first stage looks to the *purposeful availment* requirement introduced in *Hanson supra,* which is usually the harder requirement to satisfy. If that is satisfied, the analysis turns to questions of *reasonableness*.

a. **Purposeful availment—minimum contacts [§27]**

This criterion is the requirement on which the Supreme Court has usually relied in overturning overbroad extensions of jurisdiction by the lower courts. Usually the lower courts justified extensions of jurisdiction on grounds of reasonableness, lack of burden to the defendant, state interest in local adjudication, and convenience to the plaintiff. It is important to keep in mind that, unlike the reasonableness inquiry (*see infra,* §§46-52), the purposeful availment inquiry *focuses solely on the activities of the defendant* and not on the interests of the plaintiff.

Look **only at defendant's activities** to see if the defendant has **purposefully availed** himself of jurisdiction in the forum state, such as by:

- Having entered into a long term relationship with the forum state;
- Serving or seeking to serve the forum market;
- Delivering products into stream of commerce with the expectation that they will be purchased in the forum state (but additional conduct directed toward the forum might be required); or
- Targeting activities or intending effects in the forum (limited to wrongful or commercial activity).

NO

YES

No Jurisdiction

Look at defendant's activities **and** plaintiff's interests to see if it is **reasonable to assert jurisdiction** over defendant; consider factors such as:

- Interest of state in providing forum to plaintiff;
- Interest of state in regulating activity involved;
- Burden on defendant to defend in forum;
- Relative burden on plaintiff to prosecute elsewhere;
- Whether defendant's activity in forum is systematic and continuous;
- Extent to which claim is related to defendant's local activities; and
- Avoidance of multiplicity of suits and conflicting adjudications.

NO

YES

Minimum Contacts Exist

(1) Definition

Although far from absolutely clear, the purposeful availment inquiry looks to some *voluntary action by the defendant* establishing a *relationship with the forum*, usually one in which the defendant seeks to benefit from the relationship with the forum state.

(2) Rationale

This requirement gives defendants "fair warning that a particular activity may subject [them] to the jurisdiction of a foreign sovereign." [**Burger King Corp. v. Rudzewicz,** 471 U.S. 462 (1985)] It thereby "gives a degree of predictability to the legal system that allows potential defendants to structure their primary conduct with some minimum assurance as to where that conduct will and will not render them liable to suit." [**World-Wide Volkswagen Corp. v. Woodson,** 444 U.S. 286 (1980)]

(3) Foreseeability [§28]

Standing alone, the reasonable foreseeability that a suit might be filed in a forum is not sufficient. "[T]he foreseeability that is critical to due process analysis . . . is that the defendant's conduct and connection with the forum State are such that he should reasonably anticipate being haled into court there." [**World-Wide Volkswagen Corp. v. Woodson,** *supra*]

(a) Unilateral act of plaintiff—insufficient [§29]

It is said that the unilateral act of the plaintiff in bringing a product to the forum or relocating in the forum is insufficient to establish the requisite connection.

---

e.g. **Example—relocation to forum:** The settlor of a trust lived in Pennsylvania when she set up the trust. The trustee was a Delaware bank. Many years after creating the trust, the settlor moved to Florida. That unilateral act did not justify Florida's assertion of jurisdiction over the Delaware trustee even though the move was foreseeable. [**Hanson v. Denckla,** *supra,* §26]

---

e.g. **Example—taking product to forum:** Plaintiffs bought a car in New York and drove it to Oklahoma, where they were in an accident and suffered severe injuries allegedly caused by a defective design and placement of the car's gas tank. This action by plaintiffs (driving the car to Oklahoma) did not establish a contact between the New York retail seller and Oklahoma. [**World-Wide Volkswagen Corp. v. Woodson,** *supra*]

(b) Entering into a long-term relationship with a forum resident [§30]

Where the defendant has established a *long-term relationship* with a forum resident, that may suffice to establish minimum contacts.

> **e.g. Example—franchise agreement:** A Michigan defendant entered into a 20-year franchise agreement with a Florida fast-food corporation that required him to adhere to a detailed set of specifications in the operation of his franchised restaurant, to send payments to Florida, and to agree to the application of Florida law in construing the contract. The Court stated that Florida jurisdiction was proper because the defendant reached "out beyond Michigan and negotiated with a Florida corporation for the purchase of a long-term franchise and the manifold benefits that would derive from affiliation with a nationwide organization." [**Burger King Corp. v. Rudzewicz**, *supra*]

> **cf. Compare—acceptance of corporate directorship:** When defendants have accepted directorships in a corporation incorporated in the forum state, they may be subject to jurisdiction in that state. [*See* **Armstrong v. Pomerance**, 423 A.2d 174 (Del. 1980)] The rationale is that the defendants' status as directors and their power to act in that capacity arise exclusively under the forum state's laws. The Delaware court held that the directors accepted their directorships with explicit statutory notice that they could be haled into the forum state's courts "to answer for alleged breaches of the duties imposed on them by the very laws which empowered them to act in their corporate capacities."

(c) Seeking to serve [§31]

In *World-Wide Volkswagen, supra,* the Court indicated that Oklahoma contacts would have been sufficient to support jurisdiction if it were shown that the defendants "regularly sell cars at wholesale or retail to Oklahoma customers or residents or that they indirectly, through others, *serve or seek to serve* the Oklahoma market."

1) Single act [§32]

A single act seeking to serve the forum market has been held to suffice to support jurisdiction in an action asserting a claim growing out of the act. [*See* **McGee v. International Life Insurance Co.**, *supra*, §23]

(d) Stream of commerce [§33]

The Court has also said that a forum state may assert personal jurisdiction over a corporation that "delivers its products into the stream of commerce with the expectation that they will be purchased by consumers in the forum State." [**World-Wide Volkswagen Corp. v. Woodson**, *supra*]

1) Retail seller [§34]

In *World-Wide Volkswagen,* the Court held that the stream of commerce ends with the retail sale of the product, even if it is foreseeable that the purchaser will take the product to another state. (Note that a retail seller who regularly serves customers from a given state would be said to "seek to serve" that state's market even if located in another state.)

2) Manufacturer or component supplier [§35]

In *World-Wide Volkswagen,* the Court cited with seeming approval **Gray v. American Radiator & Standard Sanitary Corp.,** 176 N.E.2d 761 (Ill. 1961), which upheld jurisdiction over a component supplier whose product was sent into the forum state as part of a product manufactured by its customer. However, the Court more recently failed to resolve a similar issue involving a Japanese component manufacturer and a Taiwanese tire manufacturer whose product failed in California. [**Asahi Metal Industry Co. v. Superior Court,** 480 U.S. 102 (1987)] Justice O'Connor's opinion (not for a majority of the Court) indicated that placing a product in the stream of commerce is not sufficient, and that some "additional conduct" by which the defendant indicates "an intent or purpose to serve the forum state" is essential. The circumstances under which a manufacturer will be found subject to jurisdiction in a state because its product is sold there remain unclear.

(e) Targeting or intending effects in forum [§36]

The Court has indicated that, at least for *intentional torts,* jurisdiction can be obtained over a nonresident defendant in a forum if the defendant intended that his actions could have an effect in that forum. [**Calder v. Jones,** 465 U.S. 783 (1984)—Court indicated that the editor and author of an allegedly libelous story about a California plaintiff were subject to jurisdiction in California because "California is the focal point, both of the story and of the harm suffered"]

1) Limited to wrongful or commercial activity [§37]

The Court has stated that the effects test (above) "was intended to reach *wrongful activity* outside of the State causing injury within the State or *commercial activity* affecting State residents." [**Kulko v. Superior Court,** 436 U.S. 84 (1978)]

> **e.g.** **Example:** In *Kulko,* an ex-wife moved from New York to California and then sued her New Yorker ex-husband in California to modify child custody and child support arrangements (*see supra,* §16, regarding divisible divorce). The

Court held that the ex-husband's act of buying the couple's daughter a ticket to move to California, at her request, was not sufficient to support California jurisdiction, even though the ex-husband could have foreseen effects there. The Court reasoned that the ex-husband did not purposefully derive any benefits from activities related to California, and he had no other relevant contact with California. Thus, he could not reasonably anticipate being haled into court there.

2) Not applicable to all intentional torts [§38]

The test may not apply to all intentional torts. [*See* **IMO Industries, Inc. v. Kiekert AG,** 155 F.3d 254 (3d Cir. 1998)—for jurisdiction to be upheld, plaintiff must have felt brunt of harm of intentional tort in forum, and defendant must have expressly aimed its conduct at the forum]

(4) Relationship between contacts with forum and claim asserted [§39]

The Supreme Court has assumed that jurisdiction is proper for claims *related to the forum contacts* that satisfy the purposeful availment requirement. This involves what has been called *specific jurisdiction.* [*See* **Burger King Corp. v. Rudzewicz,** *supra,* §27] (For a discussion of the concept of general jurisdiction, *see infra,* §§79-92.) However, some cases present difficult problems that are often raised on examinations. Consider the following cases where the claim was not directly related to the forum contacts:

> **Example:** Recall that in **World-Wide Volkswagen Corp. v. Woodson,** *supra,* the plaintiffs purchased an Audi in New York, drove it to Oklahoma, were involved in an accident in Oklahoma, and alleged that they were injured because of design defects in the Audi. It seemed to be assumed that Oklahoma had specific jurisdiction for the plaintiffs' claim over Audi, the German manufacturer, and Volkswagen of America, the importer of Audi cars for the entire country, because both "seek to serve" the Oklahoma market. However, it is difficult to see how the plaintiffs' claim was related to Audi's and VW's contacts with Oklahoma (*i.e.,* their efforts to serve Oklahoma), since the Audi in question was sold in New York.

> **Example:** In **Buckeye Boiler Co. v. Superior Court,** 71 Cal. 2d 893 (1969), the plaintiff was injured in California by the explosion of a boiler manufactured by the defendant. The defendant regularly supplied boilers to a California purchaser, but these were of a different type from the one that injured the plaintiff, and nobody could explain how that boiler got to California. The California court upheld jurisdiction finding that the plaintiff's cause of action appeared to arise from the defendant's

economic activity in California: the totality of its sales of tanks to California customers or to other customers for foreseeable resale or use in California.

(a) Possible resolution

One resolution of this problem of similar claims not evidently connected with the forum contacts is to focus on the foreseeability elements mentioned above. (*See supra,* §§28-29.) If the claim actually asserted is of the type the defendant should have foreseen in the forum, it is not unfair to subject the defendant to jurisdiction even if this particular claim does not arise from the defendant's contacts. [*See* Twitchell, *The Myth of General Jurisdiction*, 101 Harv. L. Rev. 610, 661-62 (1988)] However, consider the "tricky problem of what constitutes adequate similarity. Must it be the identical product that is distributed? A similar make or model? . . . Would assertion of specific jurisdiction require that a similar product sent into the forum state have an identical defect?" [Brilmayer, *Related Contacts and Personal Jurisdiction*, 101 Harv. L. Rev. 1444 (1988)]

(5) Commercial vs. noncommercial [§40]

Purposeful availment may be found more easily with regard to a defendant's commercial activity than with regard to noncommercial activity. In assessing a defendant's contacts with the state, it is significant whether a defendant seeks "commercial benefit from solicitation of business" from a resident of the forum state.

Example—franchising agreement: In *Burger King, supra,* the defendant, a Michigan citizen, dealt face-to-face with the Michigan office of Burger King regarding opening a Burger King franchise in Michigan. However, he also negotiated via telephone with the Florida headquarters and agreed to send payments and notices there. Noting that the defendant was a *"commercial actor,"* the Court held that the Florida contacts constituted purposeful availment and thus upheld jurisdiction at Burger King's home in Florida.

Compare—suits against consumers: In *Burger King,* the Court indicated that suits against consumers to collect payments due on personal purchases would not be permitted at the distant sellers' locations as this was not commercial activity by the consumers.

Compare—family law: A court is less likely to find minimum contacts when the defendant has not sought any commercial benefits from contacts with the forum. Thus, the Court held that a divorced father who sent his daughter to live with his ex-wife did not thereby become subject to California jurisdiction in an action to modify support and child custody arrangements. The Court reasoned that "[a] father who agrees, in the interests of family harmony and his children's preferences, to allow them to spend more time in California than was required under a separation agreement can hardly be said to have 'purposefully availed himself' of the 'benefits and protections' of California's laws." [**Kulko v. Superior Court,** *supra,* §37]

(6) Choice of law distinguished [§41]

The Court has repeatedly emphasized that the fact that a given state's law may apply to a case under its conflict of laws rules is not relevant to the issue of whether the purposeful availment requirement is satisfied. [**Kulko v. Superior Court,** *supra*—fact that California may be "center of gravity" for choice-of-law purposes does not mean that California has personal jurisdiction over the defendant]

(a) Distinguish—choice of law clause [§42]

However, the parties' election that a certain state's law will govern their relations may support jurisdiction in that state. Thus, in *Burger King, supra,* the Court stated that the inclusion of a provision selecting Florida law in the parties' contract, although not sufficient of itself to support jurisdiction, "reinforced [defendant's] deliberate affiliation" with Florida.

(7) No relation to federalism [§43]

The Supreme Court has sometimes suggested that the limitations on personal jurisdiction are related to principles of interstate federalism, specifically to issues of a state's sovereignty vis-a-vis other states. [*See* **World-Wide Volkswagen Corp. v. Woodson,** *supra,* §39] However, the Court has since stated that the requirement of personal jurisdiction ultimately arises from the Due Process Clause and is unaffected by notions of federalism. If it were otherwise, it would not be possible for a defendant to waive the personal jurisdiction requirement, because this would interfere with state sovereignty. [*See* **Insurance Corp. of Ireland, Ltd. v. Compagnie des Bauxites de Guinee,** 456 U.S. 694 (1982)]

(8) Reasonableness insufficient to satisfy purposeful availment requirement [§44]

The Court has rejected the idea that other factors can outweigh the importance of the purposeful availment requirement: "Even if the defendant would suffer minimal or no inconvenience from being forced to litigate before the tribunals of another State; even if the forum State has a strong interest in applying its law to the controversy; even if the forum State is the most convenient location for litigation, the Due Process Clause . . . may sometimes act to divest the State of its power to render a valid judgment." [**World-Wide Volkswagen Corp. v. Woodson,** *supra*]

b.   Fair play and substantial justice—reasonableness [§45]

Besides focusing on the defendant's contacts with the forum, the jurisdictional inquiry takes account of a number of other factors that bear together on whether the *exercise of jurisdiction in the state is reasonable*. On this question, *consideration of the plaintiff's interests is proper*.

EXAM TIP	gilbert

Remember to distinguish between the *purposeful availment* and *reasonableness* portions of your due process discussion. Don't include discussion of plaintiff's convenience, etc., under purposeful availment, but focus on these concerns in relation to reasonableness. There are some circumstances supporting reasonableness in most exam questions.

(1)   Factors [§46]

A variety of factors can be considered:

(a)   The interest of the state in providing a forum to the plaintiff;

(b)   The interest of the state in regulating the activity involved;

(c)   The burden on the defendant of defense in the forum;

(d)   The relative burden on the plaintiff of prosecution elsewhere;

(e)   Whether the defendant's activity in the forum is systematic and continuous;

(f)   The extent to which the claim is related to the defendant's local activities; and

(g)   Avoidance of multiplicity of suits and conflicting adjudications.

(2)   Overlap [§47]

The same facts may be relevant to more than one of the above factors. For example, if the action arises out of an injury to the plaintiff in the forum, that may bear on the state's interest in opening its courts to the plaintiff, on the state's interest in regulating the allegedly injury-producing activity, and on the ease with which the plaintiff can sue elsewhere given the supposed presence in the forum of important witnesses to the event.

(3)   None critical [§48]

The fact that certain factors do not point toward forum jurisdiction is not fatal to jurisdiction. Thus, for example, the plaintiff need not be local for jurisdiction to be valid. [**Keeton v. Hustler Magazine, Inc.**, 465 U.S. 770 (1984)] Similarly, the fact that the defendant has conducted only one piece of business in the state does not by itself defeat jurisdiction over a claim arising out of that business. [**McGee v. International Life Insurance Co.**, *supra*, §32]

(4) Easy to satisfy [§49]

"[W]here a defendant who purposefully has directed his activities at forum residents seeks to defeat jurisdiction, he must present a compelling case that the presence of some other considerations would render jurisdiction unreasonable." [**Burger King v. Rudzewicz**, *supra*, §42]

Example: In **Keeton v. Hustler Magazine, Inc.**, *supra*, plaintiff sued in New Hampshire after her first suit in Ohio was dismissed. She had no prior contact with New Hampshire, but sued there only because the limitations period had expired in all other states. The Court found that the defendant's regular sale of 10,000 to 15,000 magazines in the state constituted purposeful availment and upheld jurisdiction as reasonable even though the plaintiff sought to recover damages for defamation worldwide under the "single publication rule." (*See* Torts Summary.)

---

(5) Greater concern with foreign defendants [§50]

The Court has indicated that it may be relevant that the defendant is a foreigner, recognizing the "unique burdens placed upon one who must defend oneself in a foreign legal system." [**Asahi Metal Industry v. Superior Court**, *supra*, §35]

Example: In *Asahi*, the Court held that it was unreasonable for California to exercise jurisdiction over a cross-complaint for indemnity by a Taiwanese manufacturer against a Japanese component manufacturer. In addition to the extra burdens placed on foreign defendants, the Court placed weight on the fact that the California plaintiff had settled his claim, leaving only the indemnification claim to be decided, and that it could be decided equally conveniently in Japan or Taiwan, where the dealings between the parties occurred.

(a) Caution

It is not clear whether *Asahi* indicates that as a general matter there is greater concern with the reasonableness of jurisdiction over foreign defendants. It may be that the Court would have viewed things differently had the California plaintiff been pursuing a claim against the Japanese component manufacturer who objected to jurisdiction.

(6) First Amendment concerns [§51]

Some lower courts felt that in certain defamation cases the risk of chilling the exercise of First Amendment rights warranted more demanding scrutiny of the reasonableness of jurisdiction. However, in **Calder v. Jones**, *supra*, §36, the Court rejected this reasoning: "[T]he potential chill on protected First Amendment activity stemming from libel and defamation actions is already taken into account in the constitutional limitations on the substantive law governing such suits. To reintroduce those concerns at the jurisdictional stage would be a form of double counting."

c. **Application—Internet activities [§52]**

The greatly increased use of the Internet in recent years has begun to produce rulings on the scope of personal jurisdiction in resulting litigation. Because this is a recent development, this is an *evolving area* and the *emerging rules remain unclear*. For purposes of illustration, however, some specifics can be provided.

(1) Same general analysis applied [§53]

The same minimum contacts analysis that is used for other litigation applies to suits arising from Internet activities as well (*see supra*, §21).

EXAM TIP   **gilbert**

Note that, like the regular minimum contacts analysis, the more important consideration in Internet cases (and usually the more difficult one to satisfy) is whether the *purposeful availment requirement* has been met.

(a) Contracts via Internet [§54]

As in *Burger King* (*supra*, §27), entering into an *ongoing contract* via Internet communications usually should suffice to support jurisdiction at the forum of either party for an action alleging breach of contract against the other. [*See* **CompuServe, Inc. v. Patterson**, 89 F.3d 1257 (6th Cir. 1996)—Ohio jurisdiction proper in suit based on software distribution agreement entered into on-line between Ohio plaintiff and Texas defendant]

(b) Causing effects in forum via Internet activities may suffice [§55]

Activities via the Internet have been reviewed under the "effects test" of *Calder* (*supra*, §36) to determine whether defendant should have realized that the effect in the forum would lead to suit there. [*See, e.g.*, **Blumenthal v. Drudge**, 992 F. Supp. 44 (D.D.C. 1998)—D.C. had jurisdiction over defamation suit against California-based electronic gossip columnist because numerous D.C. readers had defendant's column e-mailed to them, reader contributions from D.C. were solicited, stories in the column focused on D.C., and defendant visited D.C. to promote the column]

(c) Relation to state long arm statute requirements [§56]

Courts apply their usual long arm analysis when determining personal jurisdiction in Internet cases. A state has long arm jurisdiction when the defendant commits an act enumerated in the long arm statute and thereby submits to the state's personal jurisdiction for any cause of action arising out of that act. (*See infra*, §119.) [*See, e.g.*, **Bensusan Restaurant Corp. v. King**, 126 F.3d 25 (2d Cir. 1997)—alleged trademark infringement on passive Web page set up in Missouri did not constitute tortious act committed in New York under its long arm statute; *compare* **Blumenthal v. Drudge**, *supra*—defendant's interactive Web page satisfied long arm statute in defamation case due to the impact of the story in D.C., and to defendant's "persistent course of conduct" consisting of contacts with forum residents in connection with subjects addressed on the Web page, as well as solicitation of information from D.C. residents for use in the on-line column]

(2) Specific issues relating to Internet

(a) Ability of forum residents to access Internet site usually not sufficient [§57]

Most courts hold that the ability of forum residents to access a Web page does not, standing alone, support forum jurisdiction. [*See* **GTE New Media Services, Inc. v. BellSouth Corp.**, 199 F.3d 1343 (D.C. Cir. 2000)—fact that forum residents could access defendant's Web page was not sufficient to uphold jurisdiction; *compare* **Inset Systems, Inc. v. Instruction Set, Inc.**, 937 F. Supp. 161 (D. Conn. 1996)—foreign corporation's advertising via Internet was solicitation of sufficient repetitive nature to satisfy solicitation of business provision of long arm statute]

(b) Level of interaction and nature of Web page relevant [§58]

Courts often look to the level of interaction of a Web page to determine whether or not the purposeful availment requirement has been met. If the Web page is *passive* (*e.g.*, merely provides information), jurisdiction will not be found. [*See* **Bensusan Restaurant Corp. v. King,** *supra*—local Missouri club with Web page could not be subject to trademark suit under New York long arm statute by New York club with same name] Even a Web page that permits interaction may not support jurisdiction if it is essentially "local" in nature. [*See* **Millennium Enterprises, Inc. v. Millennium Music, L.P.**, 33 F. Supp. 2d 907 (D. Or. 1999)—defendant's interactive Web page about its retail outlets in North Carolina insufficient to support jurisdiction in Oregon because content was essentially local, and when it became aware of plaintiff's trademark concerns, defendant posted notice saying it would not fill orders from Oregon]

(3) Possible relaxation of reasonableness requirements [§59]

Because communication via the Internet is easier than by other means, the advent of this new mode of communication may cause courts to relax the reasonableness requirements. [*See* **McGee v. International Life Insurance Co.,** *supra,* §23—in upholding jurisdiction, Court emphasized the "fundamental transformation of our national economy" and the fact that "modern transportation and communication have made it much less burdensome for a party sued to defend himself in a State where he engages in economic activity"]

2. Presence of Defendant's Property in Forum [§60]

Quasi in rem and in rem jurisdiction have been curtailed since **Harris v. Balk,** *supra,* §13. Nevertheless, the presence of the defendant's property in the jurisdiction often may suffice to make jurisdiction constitutional, but ordinarily only because it establishes a relevant contact between the defendant and the forum.

a. Location of property

(1) Tangible property [§61]

Tangible property (*e.g.,* real estate, chattels) is located in a state if it is physically present therein.

(2) Intangible property [§62]

Generally, states may declare that intangible property is located within their jurisdiction if some transaction related to the property occurred within the state. When intangible property is embodied in an instrument (*e.g.,* negotiable paper), however, it is usually said to be located in the state where the instrument is located.

Examples: A *debt* (such as a bank account) may be deemed located where the debtor (the bank) is located, but generally shares of stock are said to be located where the certificate is located.

(a) Absence of constitutional limitations [§63]

The Court has placed no constitutional limitations on the power of a state to declare intangible property present within its borders. It has upheld multiple death taxation of property by different states that all claim the property is within their jurisdiction [**Blackstone v. Miller,** 188 U.S. 189 (1903)], but has held that when a debt may be located in more than one state, due process forbids a state from declaring the property escheated unless it can guarantee that no other state would make a conflicting and duplicative claim [**Western Union Telegraph Co. v. Pennsylvania,** 368 U.S. 71 (1961)].

Example—corporate stock: In **Shaffer v. Heitner,** *supra,* §10, Delaware, unique among the 50 states, declared that shares of stock in corporations it chartered were located in that state rather than where the certificate was located. The Court did not question this.

---

e.g. **Example—insurer's duty to defend and indemnify:** In **Rush v. Savchuk,** *supra,* §14, the Court did not question the state's conclusion that the insurer's obligation to defend and indemnify the insured constituted property in the state, while holding that contact insufficient to support jurisdiction.

---

b. Contacts test [§64]

Shaffer held that the minimum contacts analysis of *International Shoe* should be applied to jurisdiction over property. *Rationale:* Jurisdiction over a thing is an "elliptical way of referring to jurisdiction over the interests of *persons* in a thing" and should therefore be viewed as analogous to personal jurisdiction in terms of protection of those interests.

(1) Caution

In **Burnham v. Superior Court,** *supra,* §10, Justice Scalia indicated doubts about the continuing validity of the reasoning in *Shaffer,* stating that, "while our holding today does not contradict *Shaffer,* our basic approach to the due process issue is different." Although Justice Scalia's opinion announced the Court's judgment, it was not joined by a majority. Nevertheless, it has been suggested that this view may lead to curtailing *Shaffer.* [*See* Weintraub, *An Objective Basis for Rejecting Transient Jurisdiction,* 20 Rutgers L.J. 611, 621-23 (1991)]

c. Presence of property supports jurisdiction [§65]

In *Shaffer,* the Court recognized that "the presence of property in a State may bear on the existence of jurisdiction by providing contacts among the forum State, the defendant, and the litigation."

(1) True in rem cases [§66]

The Court appeared to leave untouched the state's power to exercise true in rem jurisdiction, which "affects the interests of all persons in designated property." Therefore, the *state would have jurisdiction* based on the presence of the property in true in rem cases (*e.g.,* condemnation).

(2) Preexisting claim to property [§67]

Actions for specific performance or otherwise to perfect a claim to the property (*e.g.,* actions to remove a cloud on title) *should also still be permissible* in the state where the property is located.

(a) But note

This reasoning would not necessarily apply to an action by the owner of local property to force a nonresident to perform an alleged contract to purchase the property, as the presence of the property may not imply any connection between the defendant and the state.

(b) Must be claim to specific property [§68]

Note that the legal right asserted must be to recover the specific property located in the forum state, such as in a replevin action. Property attached as security for an eventual money judgment would not suffice.

(3) Claim related to rights and duties arising from ownership [§69]

The Court also noted that jurisdiction could be sustained on the basis of presence of the property where the *claim relates to the duties of the owner.*

---

e.g. **Example:** In **Dubin v. Philadelphia,** 32 Pa. D. & C. 61 (1938), jurisdiction was upheld in a suit against an absentee owner of property for injuries sustained on the property. The court reasoned that "[i]t is just as important that nonresident owners of Philadelphia real estate should keep their property in such shape as not to injure our citizens as it is that nonresident owners of cars should drive about our streets with equal care. It is only a short step beyond this to assert that defendants in both classes of cases should be answerable in this forum."

(a) Movable property [§70]

Note that injuries may be inflicted by movable property, such as construction equipment or an airplane. If that produces a claim against the owner, seizure of the property may support jurisdiction even if the owner did not cause the property to be in the forum (*e.g.,* because the property was leased).

(b) Distinguish—property unrelated to claim [§71]

In **Rush v. Savchuk,** *supra,* the Court held that the presence of "property" (the insurer's obligation to defend and indemnify the insured) was jurisdictionally insignificant since "[t]he insurance policy is not the subject matter of the case, . . . nor is it related to the operative facts of the negligence action."

(4) Real property [§72]

Justices Powell and Stevens argued in concurring opinions that *Shaffer* should not invalidate jurisdiction in actions against nonresident owners of real property in the state.

(5) Absence of other forum [§73]

In a footnote in *Shaffer,* the Court noted that "[t]his case does not raise, and we therefore do not consider, the question whether the presence of a defendant's property in a State is a sufficient basis for jurisdiction when no other forum is available to the plaintiff." This may sanction *jurisdiction by necessity.*

---

e.g. Example: In **Mullane v. Central Hanover Bank & Trust Co.,** 339 U.S. 306 (1950), the Court upheld New York jurisdiction to determine the interests of all beneficiaries (including claims of mismanagement by the trustee) in trusts established in New York without examining the beneficiaries' personal affiliation with New York. Eschewing an attempt to categorize this jurisdiction as in rem or in personam, the Court reasoned that "the interest of each state in providing means to close trusts that exist by the grace of its laws and are administered under the supervision of its courts is so insistent and rooted in custom as to establish beyond doubt the right of its courts to determine the interests of all claimants, resident or nonresident, provided its procedure affords full opportunity to appear and be heard." The *scope* of this "jurisdiction by necessity" is *unclear.*

---

(6) Securing judgment in another forum [§74]

In *Shaffer,* the Court rejected the argument that quasi in rem jurisdiction is necessary to prevent a defendant from moving his assets to a state in which he is not subject to suit. The Court suggested that in such a situation it might be proper for the plaintiff to attach the property as security for a judgment being pursued in a state that has in personam jurisdiction over the defendant. (For an example upholding jurisdiction to attach defendant's assets pending judgment in a jurisdiction that has personal jurisdiction over defendant, *see* **Carolina Power & Light Co. v. Uranex,** 451 F. Supp. 1044 (N.D. Cal. 1977).)

(7) Enforcing valid judgment [§75]

Similarly, the Court noted that once a judgment is entered by a court with in personam jurisdiction, it is proper for another state to enforce the judgment, even if it did not have jurisdiction to decide the case as an original matter. [*See* **Shaffer v. Heitner,** *supra*]

d. Presence of unrelated property insufficient for jurisdiction [§76]

Shaffer holds that when property is "*completely unrelated to the plaintiff's cause of action*" its presence alone will not suffice to support jurisdiction. This *overrules* **Harris v. Balk,** *supra,* §13.

e. Insurance obligations [§77]

States cannot obtain jurisdiction over nonresident defendants in automobile tort actions by treating the defendant's insurer's obligation to defend and indemnify as property in the state and garnishing the insurer. [**Rush v. Savchuk,** *supra,* §71]

f. In personam alternative [§78]

Whenever the defendant may be subject to in rem jurisdiction, it is important to consider in personam jurisdiction as well.

Example: In *Shaffer,* Justice Brennan, while agreeing that *International Shoe* should be applied to quasi in rem jurisdiction, argued that the defendants' acceptance of positions as officers or directors in Delaware corporations should support jurisdiction over them in Delaware. After the decision in *Shaffer,* the Delaware legislature promptly enacted a statute so providing, and such exercise of in personam jurisdiction was upheld. [**Armstrong v. Pomerance,** *supra,* §30]

---

3. General Jurisdiction

a. Introduction [§79]

The Supreme Court distinguishes between *specific* and *general* personal jurisdiction. If general jurisdiction is justified, the defendant is subject to suit on *any claim* in the forum. Specific jurisdiction, on the other hand, gives rise to jurisdiction only for *claims related to the jurisdictional contact* with the state. [*See* **Burger King Corp. v. Rudzewicz,** *supra,* §27]

(1) Relation to claim [§80]

The general jurisdiction analysis usually becomes important when the relation between the defendant's contacts with the jurisdiction and the claim sued upon is not sufficient for specific jurisdiction. (*See supra,* §39, for purposeful availment focus on relation between contacts and claim.) Where there is not a sufficient relation between the contacts and the claim, one may look for a basis to exercise general jurisdiction.

Example: In **Helicopteros Nacionales de Colombia v. Hall,** 466 U.S. 408 (1984), plaintiffs sued in Texas to recover for the deaths of workers killed in a helicopter crash in Peru. The helicopter was operated by defendant, a Colombian company. The parties conceded that the claims did not arise out of defendant's contacts with Texas, and so there was no basis for specific jurisdiction. Neither did the Court find a basis for general jurisdiction. (Justice Brennan dissented, arguing that the claims were sufficiently related to defendant's Texas contacts to permit specific jurisdiction because defendant negotiated the contract it was performing in Texas, bought in Texas the helicopter that crashed, and sent its pilots to Texas for training, but the majority did not agree.)

---

(2) Rationale

Since *International Shoe* forbids jurisdiction only where it would violate fair play and substantial justice for the state to exercise jurisdiction, one might well question the need for general jurisdiction in other cases. The general idea is to provide a *"safe harbor"* where the plaintiff may bring suit without the worry that a court might later question the existence of sufficient contacts under *International Shoe.*

(a) Comment—possible narrowing of general jurisdiction

Although the threshold for general jurisdiction is relatively low, particularly for corporate defendants, the expansion of specific jurisdiction may call for a more cautious use of general jurisdiction. [*See* **Nichols v. G.D. Searle & Co.,** 991 F.2d 1195 (4th Cir. 1993)— because specific jurisdiction has "expanded tremendously," general jurisdiction, "which functioned primarily to ensure that a forum was available for plaintiffs to bring their claims [has] been rendered largely unnecessary. Thus, broad constructions of general jurisdiction should generally be disfavored."]

b. Natural persons [§81]

General jurisdiction is available in the state of a person's *domicile*. [**Milliken v. Meyer,** 311 U.S. 457 (1940)] One acquires a domicile by *being present* in a state *with the intent* to make it one's home for an indefinite period.

(1) Distinguish—diversity of citizenship subject matter jurisdiction

Domicile is also important for determining diversity of citizenship in connection with the subject matter jurisdiction of federal courts. (*See infra,* §314.) Be sure to keep the concepts of personal jurisdiction and subject matter jurisdiction separate.

c. Corporations

(1) State of incorporation [§82]

A corporation is subject to general jurisdiction in its state of incorporation.

(2) Headquarters [§83]

A corporation is also subject to general jurisdiction in the state in which its headquarters are located, if different from its state of incorporation. This may produce problems if the executive offices are in one state and the manufacturing headquarters are in another. (*See infra,* §§317 *et seq.*, regarding citizenship of corporation for diversity purposes.)

(3) Substantial contacts [§84]

Corporations have been held subject to suits on unrelated claims in states in which they conduct *"substantial activity."* The level of activity that is sufficient for this purpose is ambiguous. Although one could argue that only a very large volume of activity should suffice, some courts have seemingly lowered the threshold. A number of examples provide touchstones:

(a) Temporary headquarters in forum [§85]

In **Perkins v. Benguet Consolidated Mining Co.**, 342 U.S. 437 (1952), a Philippine corporation was unable to operate due to the Japanese occupation of the Philippines during World War II. Its president and general manager maintained an office in Ohio that seems to have been a substitute head office. The Court stated that defendant had been "carrying on in Ohio a *continuous and systematic*, but limited, part of its general business." Jurisdiction in Ohio was upheld.

(b) Ongoing operations in forum [§86]

In older cases, even a relatively small office of a defendant corporation would suffice to uphold general jurisdiction, but courts may be tightening those requirements.

1) Office in forum—sufficient [§87]

In **Bryant v. Finnish National Airline**, 15 N.Y.2d 426 (1965), the New York Court of Appeals upheld jurisdiction over a claim for injuries sustained in Europe based on defendant's operation of a one-and-a-half room office in New York, staffed by three full-time and four part-time employees, and maintenance of a bank account in New York, even though defendant had no flights to or from American airports.

2) Distinguish—sales in forum not sufficient [§88]

In **Nichols v. G.D. Searle & Co.**, *supra*, §80, 116 plaintiffs from other states sued Searle in Maryland, basing jurisdiction on the fact that although Searle had no office in the state, it did have 17 to 21 employees regularly working there to market its products, resulting in annual sales of $9-13 million in the state, but the court found these activities insufficient to justify general jurisdiction.

3) Problem—nationwide business activities [§89]

In *Rush*, *supra*, §77, the Supreme Court stated that State Farm Insurance Co. was subject to garnishment in Minnesota because "State Farm is 'found,' in the sense of doing business, in all 50 states." The propriety of basing general jurisdiction over companies with nationwide business activities is unclear.

(c) Distinguish—purchase of equipment and execution of contract in forum [§90]

In **Helicopteros Nacionales de Colombia v. Hall**, *supra*, §80, defendant, a Colombian corporation, had contracted to provide transportation services in Peru, in connection with a project being built there by a Texas-based joint venture, and had been paid over $5 million for its services under the contract. Defendant had also purchased most of its helicopter fleet from a Texas manufacturer and sent its pilots to Texas for training. The Court held the defendant's contacts with Texas to be *insufficient* as a basis for general jurisdiction over the defendant.

(d) Regular purchases in forum [§91]

Similarly, in **Rosenburg Bros. & Co. v. Curtis Brown Co.,** 260 U.S. 516 (1923), an Oklahoma retailer's purchase of a large portion of its merchandise in New York was held *not to be sufficient* for jurisdiction, even when coupled with regular visits to New York in connection with the purchases. The Supreme Court cited this case with approval in *Helicopteros*.

(e) Possible reasonableness limitation [§92]

In **Metropolitan Life Insurance Co. v. Robertson-Ceco Corp.,** 84 F.3d 560 (2d Cir.), *cert. denied,* 519 U.S. 1006 (1996), the Court found that the defendant manufacturer had systematic and continuous contacts with the state so as to satisfy general jurisdiction, but it declined jurisdiction, finding that the exercise of jurisdiction over the manufacturer was unreasonable because there was no cognizable interest in the forum on the part of the plaintiff or the state. *Criticism:* Because the common law doctrine of forum non conveniens, *infra*, §208, is available to support dismissals for inconvenience, holding jurisdiction unconstitutional on reasonableness grounds even when suit is brought at corporate headquarters seems unwarranted.

4. Consent [§93]

A defendant may consent to jurisdiction in the forum. This consent may be *express, implied,* or due to the making of a *general appearance* in the minority of states that do not follow federal practice.

a. Express consent [§94]

Express consent can be made either before or after suit is filed, and suffices to support jurisdiction without reference to other contacts with the forum.

EXAM TIP **gilbert**

Although in your class you have probably had the need for minimum contacts with the forum drummed into your head, remember that for the traditional bases of jurisdiction—consent, domicile, and service within the state—the minimum contacts analysis is irrelevant! Therefore if the defendant has **consented** to jurisdiction, was **served with process within the state**, or was **domiciled** in the state, you do not even need to discuss minimum contacts in your answer. If, however, there would be some reason that the consent or service was not valid (*e.g.,* if it was fraudulently obtained), then you would have to look for other bases for jurisdiction such as minimum contacts.

---

e.g. **Example:** In **National Equipment Rental, Ltd. v. Szukhent,** 375 U.S. 311 (1964), defendant Michigan farmers signed the plaintiff's form lease for farm equipment providing that one Florence Weinberg of Long Island would be their agent for service of process in New York. Defendants did not know Weinberg, who was the wife of an officer of the plaintiff, but the Court upheld the effectiveness of service on her to establish jurisdiction in New York.

(1) Registration by corporation [§95]

In many states, foreign corporations that engage in business in the state are required to register and appoint an agent for service of process in the state, thereby consenting to suit there.

(a) Commerce Clause limitations [§96]

The power of a state to insist on consent to general jurisdiction may be questionable to the extent that it unreasonably burdens interstate commerce. [*Compare* **Pennsylvania Fire Insurance Co. v. Gold Issue Mining & Milling Co.,** 243 U.S. 93 (1917)—state could require corporations wishing to do business to consent to jurisdiction on unrelated claims—*with* **Bendix Autolite Corp. v. Midwesco Enterprises, Inc.,** 486 U.S. 888 (1988)—state may not deny protection of statute of limitations to foreign corporation that refuses to consent to jurisdiction on unrelated suits]

(b) Implied consent contrasted [§97]

As an adjunct to the registration requirements, states often treat conduct of business in the state to be impliedly appointing a state official, often the secretary of state, as agent for service of process. This is not based on a true consent theory, but on the constitutionality of exercise of state jurisdiction over claims arising from the corporation's activities in the state.

(2) Limitation—local actions [§98]

In cases involving title to land, courts will proceed only if the land is located in the jurisdiction. (*See infra,* §175.) In such cases *consent of the parties is insufficient.*

b. Implied consent [§99]

By filing suit, the plaintiff is deemed to have consented to the jurisdiction of the forum for the purpose of a counterclaim by the defendant. [**Adam v. Saenger,** 303 U.S. 59 (1938)] However, this implied consent does not extend to a counterclaim unrelated to the subject matter of plaintiff's claim against the defendant.

(1) Consent in class actions [§100]

In class actions, the failure of unnamed *plaintiff* class members to opt out of the class action constitutes consent to adjudication of their claims in the forum. [**Phillips Petroleum Co. v. Shutts,** 472 U.S. 797 (1985)] The Supreme Court has not resolved the question of whether the same reasoning would apply to a defendant class.

c. Appearance [§101]

A party's voluntary appearance in an action is sufficient by itself to support jurisdiction.

(1) What constitutes an appearance? [§102]

In general, an appearance occurs when the defendant defends litigation on the merits. Depending on the prevailing rules in the jurisdiction, the issue turns on the extent to which the defendant raises issues other than jurisdiction.

(a) State courts [§103]

In many states, a defendant who wishes to preserve objections to personal jurisdiction must make a *special appearance* raising *only jurisdictional issues*. Raising any other matter subjects the defendant to the risk of having made a general appearance and thereby consenting to jurisdiction.

(b) Federal courts [§104]

In federal courts and in most state courts, a defendant need not make a special appearance; all grounds of defense, including lack of personal jurisdiction, can be asserted in a motion or answer. [*See* Fed. R. Civ. P. 12(b)]

1) Waiver [§105]

However, if the defendant fails to raise personal jurisdiction in her initial motion or answer, that objection is waived. [Fed. R. Civ. P. 12(h)(1)]

2) Consent to jurisdiction to decide jurisdiction [§106]

By moving to dismiss for lack of personal jurisdiction, the defendant consents to the power of the court to decide that question, *including the power to order discovery pertinent to the jurisdictional question.* [**Insurance Corp. of Ireland, Ltd. v. Compagnie des Bauxites de Guinee,** *supra,* §43]

a) Binding effect [§107]

A defendant who appears and litigates jurisdiction may not later raise jurisdiction as a bar to full faith and credit. (*See infra,* §141.) To preserve the jurisdictional objection, defendant must default. (*See infra,* §109.)

(c) Extent of jurisdiction conferred [§108]

A general appearance may be limited to the claims made or issues raised in the action at the time of the appearance.

(d) Alternative of default [§109]

A defendant who believes that jurisdiction in the forum is improper may disregard the suit and permit a default judgment to be taken against him. When the plaintiff later attempts to enforce the default judgment in another jurisdiction under the Full Faith and Credit Clause, the defendant can then challenge on the ground that the rendering court lacked jurisdiction. If the enforcing court finds jurisdiction was proper, however, there will be no further opportunity to defend on the merits. (*See infra*, §138.)

5. Service Within the Jurisdiction [§110]

Under *Pennoyer, supra*, §5, service of process within the jurisdiction was *presumptively sufficient* to support jurisdiction.

a. Possible minimum contacts requirement [§111]

In *Shaffer, supra*, §64, the Court stated that "all assertions of state court jurisdiction must be evaluated according to the standards set forth in *International Shoe*." However, in **Burnham v. Superior Court,** 495 U.S. 604 (1990), the Supreme Court, without a majority opinion but with no dissents, *upheld* the constitutionality of "*transient jurisdiction,*" obtained by service on a nonresident temporarily within the state, even though the suit was unrelated to the defendant's activities in the state. *Caution:* This ground for jurisdiction may not suffice, according to some Justices' opinions, if the defendant's presence in the state was not intentional or voluntary.

b. Fraudulent inducement [§112]

Where the defendant is personally served in the forum state, the court will *not* exercise jurisdiction on that ground if the defendant was lured into the jurisdiction by the plaintiff's *false statements*. [*See* **Wyman v. Newhouse,** *supra,* §9]

(1) Distinguish—trickery to effect service [§113]

Although fraudulently inducing a defendant into the jurisdiction is generally a defense to service, using trickery *to effect service* on a defendant already in the jurisdiction generally *does not interfere with the effectiveness of service.*

(2) In rem cases [§114]

When the plaintiff relies on seizure of the defendant's movable property to establish jurisdiction, the seizure should be disregarded if the *property is moved* to the forum as the result of some *trickery by the plaintiff.* [*See* **Commercial Air Charters v. Sundorph,** *57* F.R.D. 84 (D. Conn. 1972)—

jurisdiction refused because plaintiff's friend "rented" defendant's airplane, misrepresenting his intentions, and took it into forum so that plaintiff could levy attachment]

CHECKLIST OF BASES FOR JURISDICTION — gilbert

A COURT WILL HAVE JURISDICTION OVER A DEFENDANT IF:

- ☑ Defendant has sufficient *minimum contacts* with the forum so that the forum's exercise of jurisdiction over defendant is reasonable

- ☑ Defendant's *property has been seized within the forum* and there is an appropriate relationship between the property and the claim

- ☑ Defendant's contacts with the forum are *so substantial* that jurisdiction on *unrelated claims* can be exercised (general jurisdiction)

- ☑ Defendant expressly, impliedly, or by appearance *consented* to forum's exercise of jurisdiction

- ☑ Defendant was *personally served within the forum*

6. Territorial Jurisdiction of Federal Courts [§115]

In most cases, federal courts *do not exercise nationwide jurisdiction*. Except in the few situations where such powers are conferred by rule or statute, the territorial jurisdiction of a federal court is usually no broader than that of the state in which the federal court is located. (*See infra*, §§127 *et seq.*)

a. Constitutional limitations on nationwide service [§116]

It appears that Congress *could* constitutionally create nationwide personal jurisdiction for the federal courts. [*See* **United States v. Union Pacific Railroad**, 98 U.S. 569 (1878)—asserting that Congress could have created a single federal district court with nationwide jurisdiction] There may, however, be *limitations under the Due Process Clause* of the Fifth Amendment on extremely inconvenient exercises of jurisdiction. [*Compare* **Republic of Panama v. BCCI Holdings**, 119 F.3d 935 (11th Cir. 1997)—finding nationwide exercise of jurisdiction subject to Fifth Amendment due process limitations—*with* **FTC v. Jim Walter Corp.**, 651 F.2d 251 (5th Cir. 1981)—rejecting Fifth Amendment limitation on federal court jurisdiction]

b. National contacts [§117]

Some have argued that in actions against aliens, contacts with the United States should be aggregated in order to determine whether together they would support jurisdiction in this country, even though no state has sufficient contacts to justify jurisdiction. The Supreme Court has not passed on this argument. [*See* **Omni Capital International v. Rudolf Wolff & Co., Ltd.**, 484 U.S. 97 (1988)]

C. Statutory Authorization for Jurisdiction

1. Introduction [§118]

For a court to assert jurisdiction over an out-of-state defendant, there must be a statute or rule that gives the court the authority to exercise jurisdiction. In state court, such authority is usually in the form of a *long arm statute*, which operates as *enabling legislation*. Thus, the *first step* in a jurisdictional analysis (*i.e.,* before any analysis of minimum contacts or other jurisdictional basis) is to examine this legislation and determine whether it covers the case presented. This often involves a problem of *statutory interpretation*—deciding what the legislators or rule-makers meant by the words selected for the statute or rule.

2. Long Arm Statutes [§119]

In the wake of *International Shoe*, legislatures began to enact statutes extending the reach of their courts' jurisdiction ("the long arm of the law").

a. Full power statutes [§120]

Long arm statutes in a few states explicitly authorize exercise of jurisdiction *whenever it would not violate the Constitution*. [*See, e.g.,* Cal. Civ. Proc. Code §410.10] In such states, the only question that need be considered is the constitutionality of jurisdiction. Note that some courts have interpreted statutes that do not expressly provide this broad jurisdiction to nevertheless have this effect. (*See infra,* §126.)

b. Specific acts [§121]

Most long arm statutes *designate specific acts* as warranting the exercise of jurisdiction. Common examples include:

(i) The *transaction of any business* within the state;

(ii) The *commission of a tortious act* within the state;

(iii) Ownership, use, or possession of *real property* within the state;

(iv) *Contracting to insure* any person, property, or risk located in the state at the time of contracting; and

(v) The maintenance of a *marital domicile* in the state in an action for divorce.

With such a statute, one must consider (i) whether the defendant's activities fall within the terms of the statute and (ii), if so, whether the exercise of jurisdiction in this case is constitutional.

(1) Common sense reading [§122]

In general, courts say that they will give the words of the rule or statute their ordinary meaning. In some instances, however, they seem to over-extend that reading. Thus, in **Gray v. American Radiator & Standard Sanitary Corp.**, *supra*, §35, the court read the Illinois statute's provision of jurisdiction for "the commission of a tortious act within this State" to cover the manufacture in Ohio of an allegedly defective valve that was shipped to a manufacturer in Pennsylvania and incorporated into a boiler made there. [*Compare* **Feathers v. McLucas**, 15 N.Y.2d 443 (1965)—language "tortious act within the state" too clear to include tortious act outside the state that causes an injury within the state]

(2) Different legal theory [§123]

If the defendant's specific act is within the statute, claims based on the same act but a different legal theory usually can also be asserted in the action. [**Mack Trucks, Inc. v. Arrow Aluminum Castings Co.**, 510 F.2d 1029 (5th Cir. 1975)—products liability suit based on "tortious act" long arm provision can assert both negligence and breach of contract theories]

(3) "Arising out of" requirement [§124]

Usually, long arm statutes that designate specific acts require that claims arise out of that act. This presents a problem similar to that in determining whether there is a relationship between the claim and the contacts on a minimum contacts analysis (*supra*, §39) and whether specific or general jurisdiction is being invoked (*supra*, §79). However, in this instance, the analysis made is of the relationship between the contacts and the claim as a matter of state law, rather than as a matter of federal constitutional law.

(4) "Tortious act" [§125]

The tortious act requirement is generally held to be satisfied whenever the plaintiff *alleges* that the defendant's act was tortious. [**Nelson v. Miller**, 11 Ill. 2d 378 (1975)] If an actual tortious act were required and the defendant won the case on the ground that the act was not tortious, that could mean that there was no jurisdiction.

(5) Full power through interpretation [§126]

Some long arm statutes specifically extend jurisdiction to the constitutional limit. (*See supra*, §120.) In those states that have specific act statutes, some courts have interpreted the statutes to extend jurisdiction to the constitutional limit. [*See* **World-Wide Volkswagen Corp. v. Woodson**, *supra*, §44—Oklahoma statute interpreted as conferring jurisdiction to the limits permitted by constitution; **Nelson v. Miller**, *supra*—same with regard to Illinois statute]

(a) Rationale

Often the reasoning behind such extensions is that the legislature had no reason to deny residents access to the courts in cases in which jurisdiction would be constitutional.

(b) Caution

States that have taken this approach sometimes balk at pursuing it as far as possible. Thus, after *Nelson, supra,* the Illinois Supreme Court cautioned that "[a] statute worded in the way ours is should have a fixed meaning without regard to changing concepts of due process." [**Green v. Advance Ross Electronics Corp.,** 427 N.E.2d 1203 (Ill. 1981)] *But note:* Illinois later amended its long arm statute to extend to the constitutional limit. [*See* Ill. Code Civ. P. §2-209(c)]

3. Federal Court Jurisdiction [§127]

In general, federal courts exercise jurisdiction no broader than that authorized by state long arm statutes.

a. In personam jurisdiction

(1) Subject to jurisdiction of state court [§128]

Process from a federal court will confer jurisdiction over a defendant if the defendant would be subject to jurisdiction of a court of general jurisdiction in the state in which the federal court is located. [Fed. R. Civ. P. 4(k)(1)(A)] In other words, if the defendant could be served in a suit in the state where the federal court is located, the defendant can also be served in a federal court suit.

(a) Constitutionality

Where this is the ground for exercise of personal jurisdiction, the constitutionality of that exercise is the same as if the case were in state court.

(2) Rule 14 or Rule 19 joinder [§129]

Even if local law does not permit service, a party who is served within a judicial district and within 100 miles of the place from which the summons was issued is subject to jurisdiction if joined under Rule 14 (impleader, *see infra,* §§1071 *et seq.*) or Rule 19 (necessary parties, *see infra,* §§1042 *et seq.*). [Fed. R. Civ. P. 4(k)(1)(B)] This is commonly known as *"bulge jurisdiction."*

(3) Interpleader or other federal statutory basis [§130]

Sometimes a federal statute authorizes **nationwide jurisdiction**. If so, federal courts can exercise jurisdiction even though state courts could not. Examples include interpleader [28 U.S.C. §2361] and securities fraud actions [15 U.S.C. §78aa]. [Fed. R. Civ. P. 4(k)(1)(C), (D)]

(4) Minimum contacts with United States [§131]

For *claims arising under federal law*, federal courts can exercise jurisdiction even though the defendant is *not subject* to the jurisdiction of the courts of general jurisdiction *in any state*, if this would be consistent with the Constitution. [Fed. R. Civ. P. 4(k)(2)] This situation usually involves a foreign defendant.

(a) National vs. state contacts [§132]

This provision could apply if defendant's national contacts permit exercise of jurisdiction although no state has sufficient contacts to support it. [*See, e.g.,* **Go-Video, Inc. v. Akai Electric Co.,** 885 F.2d 1406 (9th Cir. 1989)]

(b) Narrow long arm statute [§133]

Alternatively, this provision could apply if the state in which the court is located has a narrow long arm statute that does not apply to the circumstances presented in the case although there are constitutionally sufficient grounds for exercise of jurisdiction.

(c) Showing defendant not subject to jurisdiction in any district [§134]

A plaintiff who invokes this ground of jurisdiction must certify that, based on available information, the defendant cannot be sued in any district. To avoid jurisdiction on this basis, the burden is then on the defendant to show that it is subject to suit in some district. [*See* **United States v. Swiss American Bank,** 191 F.3d 30 (1st Cir. 1999)]

b. In rem jurisdiction [§135]

The federal court may assert jurisdiction by seizing a defendant's assets found within the district only if *defendant cannot be served by an otherwise authorized means*, and then only in the *manner provided by the law of the state* in which the district court is located. [Fed. R. Civ. P. 4(n)(2)] *But note:* It may still be possible to challenge the seizure under **Shaffer v. Heitner.** (*See supra,* §§63 *et seq.*)

c. No court-created authority [§136]

In **Omni Capital International v. Rudolf Wolff & Co.,** *supra,* §117, the Court rejected arguments that it should authorize nationwide service of summons in connection with a federal claim for which Congress had not provided for such service. The Court found it "likely that Congress has been acting on the assumption that federal courts cannot add to the scope of service of summons Congress has authorized." The addition of Rule 4(k)(2), (*supra,* §131) provided the authority the Court had found lacking.

D. Litigating Jurisdiction

1. Introduction [§137]

Implicit in the idea of consent (*supra*, §§93-109) is the need for the defendant to raise personal jurisdiction objections in a timely fashion. In reality, the defendant faces a variety of options.

2. Default [§138]

A party served with summons who believes that the court lacks personal jurisdiction or authority to serve process on her may disregard the process and allow her default to be taken. If an effort is later made to enforce the resulting default judgment, she can argue that full faith and credit should not be given to the judgment because it was entered by a court without jurisdiction. However, if this argument is rejected, the defendant may not then defend on the merits.

3. Appearance to Litigate Jurisdiction [§139]

The defendant can appear in the action and litigate jurisdiction in the court in which the suit was filed. In federal court and in most state courts, the jurisdictional objection can be raised along with other defenses (*see supra*, §104), but in a few states, the defendant would have to enter a special appearance (*see supra*, §103), which raises only the jurisdictional issue.

4. Discovery [§140]

Where factual issues (*e.g.*, defendant's level of contacts with the forum) are pertinent to resolution of a personal jurisdiction objection, the court may order discovery regarding those issues. By making a *personal jurisdiction objection*, the defendant *consents to the court's jurisdiction with respect to such discovery*. [**Insurance Corp. of Ireland, Ltd. v. Compagnie des Bauxites de Guinee**, *supra*, §106]

5. Binding Effect [§141]

Once the defendant has appeared and litigated jurisdiction, she may not re-raise the issue collaterally to resist full faith and credit; she is estopped from re-litigating the issue. [**Baldwin v. Iowa State Traveling Men's Association**, 283 U.S. 522 (1931)]

a. Appellate review [§142]

A defendant whose jurisdictional objections are rejected can appeal that decision. However, in the federal courts and many state systems, appellate review is available only after a final decision is rendered, usually only after a trial. (*See infra*, §§2094 *et seq.*) In some state systems, earlier review is possible. [*See* Cal. Civ. Proc. Code §418.10(e)—defendant whose motion to quash service is denied must petition for writ of mandate within 10 days or enter general appearance and waive jurisdictional objection]

E. Venue

1. Introduction [§143]

Venue is a statutory limitation on where a suit may be brought. It may prevent a plaintiff from bringing suit in a particular court even though the court has jurisdiction. The venue rules are designed to prevent the plaintiff from suing where it would be burdensome for the defendant to appear and defend. Venue usually is considered after it is determined that there is statutory authorization for the exercise of jurisdiction and that the exercise of jurisdiction is constitutional.

a. Federal system [§144]

Venue statutes in the federal system limit the *federal districts* in which suit may be brought.

b. State courts [§145]

Venue statutes in state court systems usually limit the *counties* in which suit may be brought.

EXAM TIP   **gilbert**

Don't confuse venue with jurisdiction. Jurisdiction involves the *power* of the court to decide a case (subject matter jurisdiction) and to exercise its power over a particular defendant or piece of property (territorial or personal jurisdiction). Venue involves the *proper place* to bring the action. Remember that you need not even consider whether venue is proper until you have already determined that the court has jurisdiction. If so, then you look at the particular venue statute to see if venue is proper.

---

2. Federal Venue Limitations [§146]

Most suits in federal courts are considered *transitory actions* (*i.e.*, they may be brought wherever the defendant can be served). Transitory actions are subject to the following venue rules. Cases involving land may be considered *local actions* (*i.e.*, they may be brought only where the land that is the subject of the suit is located). Local actions are subject to special venue rules (*see infra*, §175). Generally, for most federal question and diversity cases, venue is proper as follows:

a. Defendant's residence [§147]

Venue is proper in a judicial district where any defendant resides, if all defendants reside in the same state, whether federal subject matter jurisdiction is based on diversity of citizenship or a federal question. [28 U.S.C. §1391(a)(1), (b)(1)]

(1) Residence of natural person [§148]

Ordinarily, residence of a natural person refers to domicile—the place she resides with intent to remain indefinitely. In this sense, it is analogous to citizenship for purposes of jurisdiction. (*See supra*, §81.) But some cases have interpreted residence to refer also to a district in which a person has a second home. [**Arley v. United Pacific Insurance Co.,** 379 F.2d 183 (9th Cir. 1967)]

(2) Residence of corporation [§149]

A corporation is deemed a resident of any judicial district in which it is *subject to personal jurisdiction* at the time the action is commenced. [28 U.S.C. §1391(c)]

(3) Unincorporated associations [§150]

Large unincorporated associations (*e.g.*, labor unions) normally have the capacity to sue or be sued as an entity. Venue is proper in districts in which they are *doing business.* [**Denver & Rio Grande Western Railroad v. Brotherhood of Railroad Trainmen,** 387 U.S. 556 (1967)]

(4) Partnerships [§151]

It has been held that partnerships should be treated like unincorporated associations [**Penrod Drilling Co. v. Johnson,** 414 F.2d 1217 (5th Cir. 1969)], although some older cases have used the residence of the partners to determine venue.

b. Location of substantial part of events or omissions or of property [§152]

Venue is proper in "a judicial district in which a substantial part of the events or omissions giving rise to the claim occurred, or a substantial part of property that is the subject of the action is situated," whether federal subject matter jurisdiction is based on diversity of citizenship or a federal question. [28 U.S.C. §1391(a)(2), (b)(2)]

(1) Rationale

These provisions are intended to cope with the problem of *venue gaps,* which could arise when there are multiple defendants and there is no state that is the residence of all of them.

(2) Distinguish—where claim arose [§153]

Until 1990, venue was proper "where the claim arose." This term had generated substantial litigation to determine which of several districts was the *single one* "where the claim arose" in cases involving multiforum transactions, and the term received a narrow interpretation by the Supreme Court. [**Leroy v. Great Western United Corp.,** 443 U.S. 173 (1979)] Unlike this narrow interpretation, the amended venue statute contemplates that in a number of cases venue may be proper on this ground in *more than one district.*

(3) Application [§154]

Problem areas in the application of the new statutory provision include the following:

(a) "Giving rise" [§155]

It is not clear whether Congress intended that the pertinent events be only those on which liability is predicated under the relevant substantive law. For example, in a products liability action against a manufacturer, it is likely that the retail sale of the product would not be an element of the claim (*see infra,* §649, regarding privity), but the place of retail sale may nevertheless be a proper venue even if the injury occurred in another district.

(b) "Substantial part" [§156]

Although the amended statute contemplates that more than one district may qualify, it is not clear how many events (or omissions) suffice as a "substantial part."

Example: Where a creditor's demand letter was forwarded to a district by the Postal Service from plaintiff's old address, receipt of the letter in the district was held to satisfy the venue requirements for an action under the Fair Debt Collection Practices Act [15 U.S.C. §§1692 *et seq.*]. The harm Congress sought to protect against occurred when the letter was received. [**Bates v. C & S Adjusters, Inc.,** 980 F.2d 865 (2d Cir. 1992)]

Example: A government enforcement action against a defendant that had mailed 15 million postcards nationwide could be brought in Iowa, where 200,000 postcards were directed. [**United States v. Hartbrodt,** 773 F. Supp. 1240 (S.D. Iowa 1991)]

(4) "Property present" [§157]

The problem of location of property is similar to the question of location of property for purposes of personal jurisdiction (*see supra,* §§61-63), but turns in this instance on the intent of Congress, which may be to have the federal courts develop federal rules regarding the location of property for venue purposes.

(a) Property subject of the action

The property must be the subject of the action for this venue provision to apply.

(b) Distinguish—local actions

In some actions, the local action rule (*see infra,* §§175-178) may apply instead of the provisions of section 1391.

c. Fallback venue—used when other venue requirements cannot be satisfied in any district [§158]

In multidefendant cases, "if there is *no other district in which the action may otherwise be brought,*" there are fallback provisions for venue. [28 U.S.C. §1391(a)(3), (b)(3)] The fallback provisions apply only if the other two venue rules (*supra,* §§147, 152) do not apply, and they differ depending on whether the case is based solely on diversity jurisdiction.

(1) Diversity cases—venue proper where defendant is subject to personal jurisdiction [§159]

In *diversity of citizenship* cases, venue is proper in any district in which a defendant is *"subject to personal jurisdiction at the time the action is commenced."* [28 U.S.C. §1391(a)(3)]

(a) Service within jurisdiction not sufficient [§160]

Personal service within the jurisdiction would *not* suffice to establish venue under section 1391(a)(3) because it would not be a ground for personal jurisdiction that exists *"at the time the action is commenced."* Federal civil actions are "commenced by filing a complaint with the court" [Fed. R. Civ. P. 3], and the summons issues only upon "the filing of the complaint." [Fed. R. Civ. P. 4(a)] Thus, service of the summons does not establish that the defendant was subject to personal jurisdiction at the time the action was commenced.

EXAM TIP   **gilbert**

Note that venue is proper in any district in which *one* defendant is subject to personal jurisdiction. Thus, in a multidefendant case, the absence of personal jurisdiction over the other defendants will not preclude on *venue* grounds suit against the defendant for which there is personal jurisdiction.

---

(2) Federal question cases—venue proper where a defendant is "found" [§161]

In cases in which federal subject matter jurisdiction is *not based solely on diversity of citizenship*, venue is proper in a district in which a defendant can be "found." [28 U.S.C. §1391(b)(3)] It appears that "found" means a district in which she *can be served with process.*

EXAM TIP   **gilbert**

Remember that in venue questions you must analyze venue under the first two bases for venue—defendant's residence and location of a substantial part of the events or omissions or of the property—*before* considering the fallback provisions. *Only if the first two bases do not apply* do you consider what type of case it is (diversity or federal question) and then use the appropriate fallback provision.

---

(3) Application—as a fallback only [§162]

A plaintiff who wishes to rely on the fallback provisions must show that venue cannot be established in any other district.

(a) Defendant's residence [§163]

The fallback provision may not be used if all defendants are residents of a single state, since sections 1391(a)(1) and (b)(1) would apply. In single-defendant cases, this means that venue is not proper in a district in which personal jurisdiction can be obtained if the defendant is a resident of another state. [**Samuelson v. Honeywell,** 863 F. Supp. 1503 (E.D. Okla. 1994)—in malpractice action, defendant who had established citizenship in Louisiana after providing treatment in Oklahoma was not subject to venue in Oklahoma although personal jurisdiction requirements were satisfied]

(b) Substantial portion of acts giving rise to the claim [§164]

The fallback provision cannot apply if there is any district in which a substantial portion of the acts or omissions giving rise to the liability occurred, because that would suffice for venue under section 1391(a)(2) or (b)(2). Thus, the fallback provision can only apply if no substantial portion of the acts or omissions giving rise to liability happened in this country.

SUMMARY OF FEDERAL VENUE RULES		**gilbert**
BASIS FOR VENUE	**TYPE OF SUBJECT MATTER JURISDICTION**	
	DIVERSITY	**FEDERAL QUESTION**
Residence of *any* defendant *if all reside in same state*	Yes	Yes
Location of *substantial part of events or omissions giving rise to the claim*, or of the *property* that is the subject of the action	Yes	Yes
Fallback venue: Where a defendant is *subject to personal jurisdiction* at the time the action is commenced	Yes	No
Where a defendant *may be found* (served with process)	No	Yes

d. Special venue statutes [§165]

Congress has altered the general rules of venue in connection with certain types of cases:

(1) Additional venue options [§166]

In some types of cases, venue may be proper in certain locations in addition to the districts allowed under the general rules.

(a) Patent infringement actions [§167]

In *addition* to the districts specified by the general venue statutes, venue in a patent infringement action is also proper in the district where the defendant committed acts of infringement if the defendant has a "regular and established place of business in that district." [28 U.S.C. §1400(b)]

(b) Copyright suits [§168]

Similarly, in addition to the districts specified by the general venue statutes, venue in copyright suits is proper in any district in which the defendant or her agent may be found. [28 U.S.C. §1400(a)]

(2) Substitute venue [§169]

In a few types of cases, venue is proper *only* in the districts specified by the special statute.

(a) Federal tort claims actions [§170]

Venue for federal tort claims actions is proper only in the district where the plaintiff resides or where the act complained of occurred. [28 U.S.C. §1402(b)]

(b) Statutory interpleader [§171]

In statutory interpleader actions, venue is proper only in a district where a claimant to the fund resides. [28 U.S.C. §1397]

e. Aliens [§172]

In a suit against an alien, venue is proper in *any district*. [28 U.S.C. §1391(d)]

(1) Distinguish—citizenship for determination of diversity of citizenship [§173]

Where the residence of an alien must be considered to determine whether there is *subject matter jurisdiction* due to complete diversity of citizenship, an alien admitted to the United States for permanent residence is deemed a citizen of the state in which the alien is domiciled. (*See infra*, §297.)

f. Removed cases [§174]

Where a case is removed from state court to federal court, it is assigned to the district encompassing the state court in which the action was pending, regardless of the residence of the parties. [28 U.S.C. §1441(a)] In a sense, removal creates its own venue.

g. Local actions [§175]

Certain types of cases involving title to property are considered "local," and venue is regarded as proper only in the district where the property is located. In effect, this is an *unwritten limitation* on the federal venue statutes, treating them as applicable to "transitory" actions only.

---

e.g. **Example:** In **Livingston v. Jefferson,** 15 Fed. Cas. 660 (C.C.D.Va. 1811), plaintiff charged former President Jefferson with trespass to plaintiff's land in Louisiana. The Court refused to proceed with the case because it was a "local action" that could be brought only in Louisiana (where personal jurisdiction could not be obtained over Jefferson).

---

(1) In rem analogy [§176]
One court has explained that the difference between local and transitory actions is the same as that between in personam and in rem jurisdiction, and that an action is a local action only if the court needs to have jurisdiction over the real property in order to grant relief. [**Raphael J. Musicus, Inc. v. Safeway Stores, Inc.,** 743 F.2d 503 (7th Cir. 1984)]

(2) Property in multiple districts [§177]
Where the property is located in more than one district in the same state, the action may be brought in any of those districts. [28 U.S.C. §1392(b)]

(3) Treated as a matter of subject matter jurisdiction [§178]
Some courts treat the local action rule as a limitation on subject matter jurisdiction. (*See infra,* §371.)

3. State Venue Limitations [§179]
State venue provisions involve similar considerations to federal venue rules.

a. Defendant's residence [§180]
Traditionally, in personam actions can be brought in the county where the defendant resides; and where multiple defendants are sued, the action may be proper in any county where one of them resides. [*See* Cal. Civ. Proc. Code §395]

b. Where claim arose [§181]
In some jurisdictions, most or some types of claims (*e.g.,* tort claims) can be brought where the claim arose. [*See* Cal. Civ. Proc. Code §395(a)—in action for personal injury, venue is proper in county where injury occurs]

c. Actions affecting real property [§182]
Where the action affects title to real property, venue is usually in the county where the property is located. [*See* Cal. Civ. Proc. Code §392(1)]

d. Nonresident defendant [§183]
In general, nonresidents are regarded as having no venue rights, and the

plaintiff may often sue them in any county. [*See* Cal. Civ. Proc. Code §395(a)]

(1) Equal protection challenge rejected [§184]

A state may allow an out-of-state corporation to be sued in *any* county without violating the Equal Protection Clause, even when it limits suits against an in-state corporation to the county of its principal place of business. It is rational to weigh differently (i) the inconvenience of a domestic corporation in defending a suit in a forum distant from its principal place of business and (ii) the burden on an out-of-state corporation that must defend away from home in any event. [**Burlington Northern Railroad v. Ford,** 504 U.S. 648 (1992)]

4. Litigating Venue [§185]

As with personal jurisdiction, improper venue may be *waived* unless raised in the proper way. In federal court, for example, it is waived unless it is raised in the first Rule 12 motion or in the answer if there is no Rule 12 motion. [*See* Fed. R. Civ. P. 12(h)(1)]

a. Effect of timely venue objection [§186]

Where the defendant timely objects to venue, the court *cannot proceed* with the case. It may dismiss, but in most jurisdictions it can also transfer the case to a court that is a proper venue. (*See infra.*)

5. Federal Transfer Provisions [§187]

A federal case may be transferred to another federal court in the following circumstances:

a. Venue or jurisdiction improper in original court [§188]

Where venue or jurisdiction is improper in the court selected by the plaintiff and the defendant properly objects, the court *may transfer the case to a proper court* rather than dismiss it. [28 U.S.C. §1406(a)]

(1) Transfer where jurisdiction also improper [§189]

Although the statute only talks of transfer where venue is improper, the Supreme Court has held that it authorizes transfer where both jurisdiction and venue are improper. [**Goldlawr, Inc. v. Heiman,** 369 U.S. 463 (1962)]

(2) Transfer where venue proper but jurisdiction lacking [§190]

Lower courts have upheld transfer where venue is proper but there is no personal jurisdiction. [**Aguacate Consolidated Mines v. Deeprock,** 566 F.2d 523 (5th Cir. 1978)]

(3) Court may dismiss, not transfer [§191]

Although the district court may choose to relieve the plaintiff of some adverse consequences of filing suit in a district in which venue or jurisdiction is improper by transferring to a proper venue, it may dismiss instead of transferring. [*See* **Nichols v. G.D. Searle & Co.,** *supra,* §88—district court within its discretion when dismissed rather than transferred where plaintiff's attorney committed "obvious error" in filing suit in the wrong court, and thereby imposed substantial unnecessary costs on defendant and the legal system]

b. Transfer for convenience [§192]

Where venue and jurisdiction are proper in the court selected by the plaintiff, the court can transfer the action "for the convenience of the parties and witnesses in the interests of justice." [28 U.S.C. §1404(a)]

(1) Distinguish—forum non conveniens [§193]

This transfer provision considers many factors that bear on the question of whether to dismiss on forum non conveniens grounds (*see infra,* §214), but it permits transfer on a *lesser showing of inconvenience.* [**Norwood v. Kirkpatrick,** 349 U.S. 29 (1955)]

(2) Proper transferee court [§194]

The statute authorizes transfer only to a district in which the action "*might have been brought.*" This means that the transferee district must be a *proper venue* and have *valid personal jurisdiction.* The moving party's willingness to waive objections to venue or personal jurisdiction does not satisfy this requirement. [**Hoffman v. Blaski,** 363 U.S. 335 (1960)]

(3) Procedure

(a) Proper moving parties [§195]

Either the plaintiff or the defendant can move to transfer under this section. [**Ferens v. John Deere Co.,** 494 U.S. 516 (1990)—plaintiffs moved to transfer, arguing that they had sued in an inconvenient district] A defendant who has removed a case from a state court can still move to transfer after removal. [**Chicago Rock Island & Pacific Railway v. Igoe,** 212 F.2d 378 (7th Cir. 1954)]

(b) Showing required [§196]

In general, it is said that the *plaintiff's initial choice of forum should be respected,* and that transfer is proper only when the balance of conveniences *strongly favors transfer.* This showing should look to the identity and location of witnesses, access to items of real evidence, and any other factor that would make trial in the transferee forum more convenient.

(4) Forum selection clause [§197]

Where the parties have entered into a contract containing a forum selection clause concerning the dispute in question, the Supreme Court has stated that the presence of the clause should be "a significant factor" in determining whether to transfer the case to the forum designated. [**Stewart Organization, Inc. v. Ricoh Corp.,** 487 U.S. 22 (1988)]

c. Multidistrict litigation [§198]

When cases pending in different districts raise a common question of law or fact, they can be transferred to one district. [28 U.S.C. §1407]

(1) Showing required [§199]

All that need be shown is that the actions share a common question of fact or law; unlike transfers for convenience under section 1404(a) (*supra,* §196), there is no preference for plaintiff's choice of forum.

(2) For pretrial purposes only [§200]

This transfer is for pretrial purposes only; the cases should be remanded to the original court for trial. [28 U.S.C. §1407(a)] The transferee court has full power to pass on any pretrial matters, however.

(3) Follow-up transfer for trial not authorized [§201]

Despite widespread support for the practice among lower courts, the Supreme Court has held that section 1407(a) does not authorize the judge who receives a multidistrict transfer to use section 1404(a) to transfer cases to her court for trial. [**Lexecon, Inc. v. Milberg Weiss Bershad Hynes & Lerach,** 523 U.S. 26 (1998)]

(4) Procedure [§202]

Motions for transfer are directed to the *Judicial Panel on Multidistrict Litigation,* which holds hearings and has the authority to transfer to any district *without reference to venue or jurisdiction.*

d. Effect on choice of law [§203]

In cases in federal court on grounds of diversity of citizenship, the transfer could affect choice of law because in such cases the federal court is required to look to the choice of law rules of the state in which it sits to determine choice of law issues. [**Klaxon Co. v. Stentor Electric Manufacturing Co.,** 313 U.S. 487 (1941)]

(1) Venue and jurisdiction proper in original court [§204]

In cases where the plaintiff sues in a court that has proper venue and jurisdiction, a transfer for the convenience of the parties *does not affect choice of law* because the transferee court is to apply the same choice of law rules that the transferor court would have applied. [**Van Dusen v. Barrack,** 376 U.S. 612 (1964)] The *Van Dusen* rule applies even when the transfer is on motion of the plaintiff who chose the inconvenient forum in the first place and thus could shop for more favorable law. [**Ferens v. John Deere & Co.,** *supra,* §195]

(2) Venue or jurisdiction improper in original court [§205]

If the plaintiff could not have overcome the defendant's venue or jurisdiction objections in the original court, the *choice of law rules of the transferee state should usually be applied.* [**Wisland v. Admiral Beverage Corp.**, 119 F.3d 733 (8th Cir. 1997)]

(3) Federal claims [§206]

Because the federal circuits sometimes disagree on issues of federal law, it is possible for similar choice of law problems to arise where a claim is transferred from one circuit to another. Ordinarily, the interpretation of the transferee circuit is applied in this circumstance. [*In re* **TMJ Implants Products Liability Litigation**, 97 F.3d 1050 (8th Cir. 1996); *In re* **Korean Air Lines Disaster of Sept. 1, 1983**, 829 F.2d 1171 (D.C. Cir. 1987), *aff'd on other grounds, sub nom.* **Chan v. Korean Air Lines**, 490 U.S. 122 (1989)]

6. Transfer in State Court [§207]

State courts often have transfer provisions analogous to the federal provisions. [*See, e.g.,* Cal. Civ. Proc. Code §§396—transfer where jurisdiction lacking, 397(c)—transfer for convenience of witnesses; Cal. Rules of Court §§1501 *et seq.*—coordination of actions involving common questions of fact or law]

F. Forum Non Conveniens

1. Background [§208]

Even when jurisdiction and venue are proper, courts may decline to exercise jurisdiction on the ground that the location the plaintiff selected for the case is *grossly inconvenient.* This ancient common law doctrine was endorsed by the Supreme Court as a matter of federal common law in **Gulf Oil Corp. v. Gilbert,** 330 U.S. 501 (1947), and is recognized in almost all state courts.

2. Present Use

a. Federal courts [§209]

When the inconvenience problem can be solved by transfer to *another federal district,* the court may not dismiss; but if the proper forum is in another country, the federal court can dismiss. [**Piper Aircraft Co. v. Reyno,** 454 U.S. 235 (1981); *In re* **Union Carbide Corp. Gas Plant Disaster at Bhopal, India,** 809 F.2d 195 (2d Cir.), *cert. denied,* 484 U.S. 871 (1987)]

b. State courts [§210]

When the more convenient court is not within the state and transfer is therefore not possible (*see supra,* §207, regarding in-state transfer) forum non conveniens remains an important device.

(1) Uniform Act [§211]

The National Conference of Commissioners on Uniform State Laws has recommended a Uniform Transfer of Litigation Act that would permit transfers similar to those between federal courts pursuant to 28 U.S.C. section 1404(a) if adopted by both the transferor and transferee states, but the uniform act has not been widely adopted.

3. Rationale

Courts are not required to make their jurisdiction available to parties who engage in unfair forum shopping and thereby impose substantial inconvenience on other parties and expense and burden on the courts of the forum selected by the plaintiff.

4. Procedure [§212]

The defendant must make a motion to dismiss on grounds of inconvenience.

a. Showing required [§213]

The defendant must show that the plaintiff has selected a *grossly inconvenient* location for the suit.

(1) Distinguish—transfer

In federal court, the showing necessary to justify transfer is not as compelling as the showing needed to justify dismissal on forum non conveniens grounds.

b. Factors [§214]

The court is to consider a number of private and public factors in making a decision whether to dismiss on forum non conveniens grounds. (*See* chart, *infra*.)

c. Weight given plaintiff's choice [§215]

Usually *substantial weight* is given to the plaintiff's choice to sue in a forum where venue and jurisdiction requirements are satisfied. When the plaintiff is foreign, however, that deference is not warranted. [**Piper Aircraft Co. v. Reyno**, *supra*, §209]

d. Change in substantive law [§216]

The fact that the law in the more convenient forum is less favorable to plaintiffs usually has no significant weight. [**Piper Aircraft Co. v. Reyno**, *supra*]

e. Alternative forum available [§217]

The court *cannot dismiss* unless the alternative forum is available, but problems of jurisdiction in the alternative forum can be solved by stipulation by the moving party to submit to jurisdiction there.

f. Conditions on dismissal [§218]

The court can condition the dismissal to protect against unfairness to the plaintiff. A common example is insistence on a stipulation by the defendant that the statute of limitations will be deemed tolled as of the time suit was filed in the inconvenient forum, so that plaintiff does not risk a limitations defense based on the delay between the filing of the original case and the filing of suit in the preferred forum.

FACTORS FOR FORUM NON CONVENIENS DISMISSAL

PRIVATE FACTORS

☑ **Relative ease of access to sources of proof**—*i.e.,* will access to needed proof be significantly easier in another forum?

☑ **Availability of compulsory process**—*i.e.,* as to **unwilling witnesses** whose testimony is important, will there be compulsory process to compel them to attend trial in another forum that is not available in the forum chosen by the plaintiff?

☑ **Cost of obtaining attendance of willing witnesses.**

☑ **Need to view premises**—*i.e.,* will having the jury view the premises involved in the litigation be important at trial? If so, this weighs in favor of having the trial near the premises.

PUBLIC FACTORS

☑ **Local interest** in having localized controversies decided at home;

☑ **Interest in having trial in forum familiar with the law** to be applied;

☑ **Avoiding unnecessary problems with conflict of laws**; and

☑ **Unfairness of burdening citizens** of an unrelated forum with jury duty.

5. Effect on Choice of Law [§219]

Because forum non conveniens results in a dismissal, the plaintiff must file a new suit, and the choice of law rules that apply are determined by the forum for the new suit.

6. Contractual Limitations on Forum [§220]

Dismissal in favor of litigation in another forum can also occur where the dispute arises out of a contract in which the parties have agreed to litigate in a specific forum, but transfer to that forum is not possible.

a. Federal law—generally enforceable [§221]

The Supreme Court has declared that, as a matter of federal common law, such clauses are generally enforceable even where they result in dismissal because the forum chosen is in another country. [*See* **The Bremen v. Zapata Off-Shore Co.**, 407 U.S. 1 (1972)—clause should be enforced absent showing that doing so "would be unreasonable and unjust, or that the clause was invalid for such reasons as fraud or overreaching"] Moreover, the Supreme Court has held that a forum selection clause on a *printed passenger ticket* is enforceable even though not the subject of bargaining, unless enforcing it would violate fundamental fairness. [**Carnival Cruise Lines, Inc. v. Shute**, 499 U.S. 585 (1991)] *Note:* Congress invalidated such clauses in ship passenger tickets [46 U.S.C. App. §183c], but later re-amended the statute to restore the original language, although apparently intending still to change the result in *Carnival Cruise Lines*. Such clauses may be valid in other consumer situations, however.

b. State law—enforcement limited [§222]

In many states, the enforcement of such clauses is limited, on the theory that the parties cannot by agreement "oust" a court with jurisdiction to decide the dispute. [*See, e.g.,* **Stewart Organization, Inc. v. Ricoh Corp.**, *supra*, §197—"Alabama looks unfavorably upon contractual forum-selection clauses"]

c. Choice between state and federal rules in federal court [§223]

Where state law claims are presented in federal court, there may be a serious problem determining whether to apply state or federal common law. The Supreme Court has not decided this question. [*See* **Stewart Organization, Inc. v. Ricoh Corp.**, *supra*] It has, however, decided that where transfer to the selected forum is possible under 28 U.S.C. section 1404(a), the existence of such a clause is a significant factor in deciding whether to transfer.

G. Notice

1. Introduction [§224]

In addition to personal jurisdiction and venue, problems of notice should be considered. Notice is not a substitute for these other factors, but is essential to a valid judgment.

2. Constitutional Requirements [§225]

Due process requires that *reasonable efforts to provide notice* be made with regard to persons whose interests are to be determined. [**Mullane v. Central Hanover Bank & Trust Co.,** *supra,* §73]

a. In rem cases [§226]

The notice requirement applies even to pure in rem actions. [**Walker v. City of Hutchinson,** 352 U.S. 112 (1956)]

b. Method [§227]

The method of giving notice must have a *reasonable prospect of giving actual notice*: "The means employed must be such as one desirous of actually informing the absentee might reasonably adopt to accomplish it." [**Mullane v. Central Hanover Bank & Trust Co.,** *supra*]

(1) Personal delivery [§228]

Personal delivery of the notice (ordinarily the summons and complaint) is the traditional method of giving notice.

(2) First class mail [§229]

In *Mullane, supra,* the Court required mailed notice to those whose addresses were known, reasoning that "the mails today are recognized as an efficient and inexpensive means of communication."

(a) Class actions [§230]

In class actions brought under Federal Rule 23(b)(3) (common question suits), there must be mailed notice to all identifiable class members. [**Eisen v. Carlisle & Jacquelin,** 417 U.S. 156 (1974)]

(3) Posted notice [§231]

Notice by posting on the defendant's residence may *not* be sufficient. [**Greene v. Lindsey,** 456 U.S. 444 (1982)—state procedure for giving notice of eviction proceedings by posting on the front door of apartment invalid in view of testimony that notices were often torn off doors; notice by mail required]

c. Effort to identify [§232]

Reasonable efforts to identify and locate affected persons are required. As to named defendants, the identification issue should not be a problem, but in other instances, such as in rem actions, it can prove more difficult.

Example—mortgagee: Where property was sold for nonpayment of taxes, the mortgagee with a mortgage on file with the county recorder was held entitled to notice of the sale. [**Mennonite Board of Missions v. Adams,** 462 U.S. 791 (1983)]

Example—creditor of decedent: Application of a state requirement that claims against a decedent be presented to his executor within two months of publication of notice of the commencement of probate proceedings was held to violate due process where it cut off rights of creditors whose identity was reasonably ascertainable to a decedent's executor and who were not given notice. [**Tulsa Professional Collection Services, Inc. v. Pope**, 485 U.S. 478 (1988)]

---

(1) Class actions [§233]

In class actions, the Court has accepted failure to identify significant numbers of class members. [*See* **Eisen v. Carlisle & Jacquelin**, *supra*—inability to locate more than half of six million class members] *Rationale:* In **Mullanne v. Central Hanover Bank & Trust Co.**, *supra*, the Court explained that "notice reasonably certain to reach most of those interested in objecting is likely to safeguard the interests of all, since any objection sustained would inure to the benefit of all."

(a) Distinguish—future claims class action

In a class action involving "future" claims by class members who had not yet manifested illness due to exposure to asbestos, the Supreme Court cautioned that providing adequate notice to such individuals might be impossible due to problems of identification and to the uncertainty caused for those who may not even know of the asbestos exposure at the time of any notice that is given. [**Amchem Products, Inc. v. Windsor**, 521 U.S. 591 (1997)]

d. Contents [§234]

The notice must intelligibly advise the defendant of the *nature and place* of the proceeding.

e. Constructive notice [§235]

In some instances where a person cannot be located *after reasonable efforts*, published or other constructive notice will suffice. [*See, e.g.*, Cal. Civ. Proc. Code §415.50—service by publication where party cannot by reasonable diligence be served another way]

f. Effect of failure to receive [§236]

If a constitutionally valid procedure is used, the *judgment is binding* even if some interested parties do not actually receive notice.

3. Service of Process [§237]

The usual method for giving notice is service of a *summons* and complaint on the defendant directing that the defendant file an answer to the complaint or suffer a default.

a. **Jurisdiction distinguished [§238]**

Although service of process implies an exercise of jurisdiction, the questions of jurisdiction and method of service should be kept separate. Even where the method of service is proper, the defendant can still challenge the exercise of personal jurisdiction; although some forms of service may by themselves suffice to establish personal jurisdiction. [**Burnham v. Superior Court**, *supra*, §10—personal service in state sufficient to establish jurisdiction]

b. **Methods of service [§239]**

Service of process can be accomplished by the following methods:

(1) **Personal delivery [§240]**

Process may be served on the person. In the case of a corporation, partnership, or unincorporated association, service may be made on an officer or managing agent, or on an agent authorized by law.

(2) **Substituted service [§241]**

Other means of service may be authorized by statute or court rule.

(a) **Federal Rules**

1) **At defendant's home [§242]**

A copy of the summons and complaint can be left at the "usual place of abode" of the person to be served with a "person of suitable age and discretion" residing therein. [Fed. R. Civ. P. 4(e)(2)]

EXAM TIP gilbert

To be proper, service of process must be by the book; *i.e.*, you have to check the facts carefully to see that the rules were followed. Keep in mind that *personal service is best*—the defendant cannot claim that she did not receive notice—but it is not always possible. In that case, *substituted service* may be allowed, but be sure that the facts show that it was proper. Things to consider include *where* the service is made—is it the defendant's "usual abode" and not a vacation home, her mother's house, etc.? Check on *how* service was made—tacking a copy of the summons and complaint to the door of the home is not sufficient under most statutes; the papers must be left with a person at the home. And consider the person *who accepts* the papers; he must be of "suitable age and discretion," which means that leaving the papers with defendant's spouse would most likely be fine but leaving them with her four-year-old son would not. The technical rules must be followed or the service is improper and the notice requirement not met.

---

2) **In accordance with state law [§243]**

Service also may be made pursuant to the law of the *state in which the district court is located*, or pursuant to the law of the *state in which service is effected*. [Fed. R. Civ. P. 4(e)(1)]

3) Waiver of service [§244]

A plaintiff may ask a defendant to waive formal service. This is done by sending a request for waiver of service to the defendant by first class mail. Because a defendant has a duty to avoid unnecessary costs of service, a defendant located within the United States who fails to waive service without good cause can be liable for the costs of formal service. A defendant who waives service receives additional time to answer the complaint compared to one who is served in the usual manner. [Fed. R. Civ. P. 4(d)]

4) On defendant in foreign country [§245]

A defendant served in another country may be served by an internationally agreed means or, if there is not an agreed means, as directed by the law of the place of service, including, unless forbidden by the law of that country, personal delivery or any form of mail requiring a signed receipt, or as directed by the court. [Fed. R. Civ. P. 4(f)]

(b) State law [§246]

State law on substituted service varies. In California, for example, such service may be accomplished in the following ways:

1) At defendant's office or home [§247]

A copy of the summons and complaint can be left at the person's office or abode *plus* mailing a copy to that place. [Cal. Civ. Proc. Code §415.20]

2) By mail within state [§248]

A copy of the summons and complaint can also be mailed to a person within the state, if the person executes and returns an acknowledgment of service. [Cal. Civ. Proc. Code §415.30]

3) By mail outside state [§249]

A copy of the summons and complaint can be served on a person outside the state by using return-receipt mail, without the need for execution of an acknowledgement by the defendant. [Cal. Civ. Proc. Code §415.40]

(3) Service in diversity cases [§250]

In diversity cases, the service procedures of Federal Rule 4 are to be applied (*supra*, §§242-245). [**Hanna v. Plumer**, 380 U.S. 460 (1965)]

c. Immunity from service [§251]

In some jurisdictions, there are rules that forbid service of process on a person who is in the state only to participate in a legal proceeding. *Rationale:* This immunity is designed to protect against the risk of people being unwilling to attend trials for fear of being served with process. These rules have been severely limited in recent times.

4. Timing of Notice—Prejudgment Seizures

a. Introduction [§252]

At common law, a plaintiff could have a defendant's property seized as a method of coercing the defendant to appear for trial. Over time, this seizure—variously called replevin, attachment, garnishment, sequestration—came to be used to provide *security for any judgment* the plaintiff might obtain in the action. Very often, such prejudgment remedies were available before defendant was given notice of the action.

b. State law requirements [§253]

Partly in response to constitutional decisions (*see infra,* §§255 *et seq.*), states placed *limits on such prejudgment remedies.* Thus, before considering possible constitutional objections to state procedures, first consider whether the prejudgment seizure sought by the plaintiff is authorized by state law.

e.g. **Example—California:** In California, attachment is available only in contract actions for more than $500 for a fixed or readily ascertainable amount. In an action against a natural person, attachment is available only if the claim arises out of the defendant's conduct of a trade, business, or profession. [Cal. Civ. Proc. Code §483.010]

e.g. **Example—New York:** Prejudgment attachment is allowed in New York only where there is a showing that the defendant has, or "is about to," assign, dispose of, or secrete property, or that the defendant is a nondomiciliary, or a resident who cannot be served in the state. [New York Civ. Prac. Law §6201]

(1) Federal courts [§254]

Federal courts *must apply state law* concerning the availability of prejudgment remedies, unless a federal statute provides a prejudgment remedy. [Fed. R. Civ. P. 64]

c. Procedural due process requirements for prejudgment seizure [§255]

In a series of cases, the Supreme Court has considered the constitutional requirements for procedures attending issuance of prejudgment remedies. Because these cases are difficult to reconcile, it is worthwhile to consider them one by one.

(1) *Sniadach*—garnishment of wages [§256]

In **Sniadach v. Family Finance Corp.**, 395 U.S. 337 (1969), the Court held that the state violated a defendant's due process rights by allowing prejudgment garnishment of wages. The opinion contained suggestions that wages might be viewed as a *special type of property* because they are essential to everyday life.

(2) *Fuentes*—seizure of chattels [§257]

In **Fuentes v. Shevin**, 407 U.S. 67 (1972), by a 4-3 decision, the Court invalidated Florida and Pennsylvania procedures for writs of replevin that authorized the seizure of property, because there was no provision for *notice and a preseizure hearing*.

(a) Purpose of hearing [§258]

The Court emphasized that the notice and hearing requirement ensured a "fair process of decisionmaking," but it was not clear on whether this was limited to reducing the risk of erroneous issuance of writs of replevin.

(b) Alternative safeguards against error [§259]

The plurality viewed alternative safeguards against error as significant factors in determining the type of hearing afforded, but the safeguards were "far from enough by themselves to obviate the right to a prior hearing of some kind." One dissenter argued that the bond requirement, coupled with the creditor's desire to have the transaction completed, should provide sufficient protection.

(c) Unimportance of cost of hearing [§260]

The Court placed little importance on the possible cost of more elaborate hearing procedures, noting that "[t]he Constitution recognizes higher values than speed and efficiency."

(d) Exception for "extraordinary situations" [§261]

The plurality recognized in dictum that the right to preseizure notice and hearing could be overcome in "extraordinary situations." It specified three factors that appeared to be necessary:

1) Such seizures should be *directly necessary* to secure an *important governmental or general public interest*, *e.g.*, *public health* or *the war effort*.

2) Such seizures without notice may occur only where *delay would be inimical to the public interest*; and

3) Such seizures should be limited to circumstances in which the *state controlled the initiation of proceedings*.

(3) *Mitchell* **[§262]**

In **Mitchell v. W.T. Grant Co.,** 416 U.S. 600 (1974), the Court *upheld* Louisiana's procedure allowing the seller of several household appliances to obtain a writ for their seizure when the defendant missed payments.

(a) *Fuentes* **overruled? [§263]**

One could argue that *Mitchell* overruled *Fuentes* since the situation was difficult to fit within the "extraordinary situations" analysis of *Fuentes*. (In dissent, the author of the *Fuentes* opinion asserted that the case had been overruled.)

(b) *Mitchell's* **requirements—***Fuentes* **distinguished [§264]**

However, the majority in *Mitchell* said that it was applying *Fuentes*, and that the Louisiana procedures were different in ways that made them constitutional because:

1) They *required more than the conclusory claims of ownership* called by the state procedures at issue in *Fuentes*;

2) Where this case arose, the practice was that a *judge* (rather than a clerk) *would pass on the application* for the writ;

3) *"Narrowly confined" issues* were presented by the application for the writ in Louisiana in contrast to the broad "fault" standard applicable in the statutes at issue in *Fuentes*; and

4) The defendant in Louisiana had a *right to an immediate hearing* on whether the plaintiff was entitled to the writ, and the burden remained on the plaintiff to justify the issuance of the writ.

(c) **Explanation for shift [§265]**

The easiest explanation for the shift from *Fuentes* to *Mitchell* is that two new Justices—Powell and Rehnquist—were added to the Court in the interim.

(4) *Di-Chem* **[§266]**

In **North Georgia Finishing, Inc. v. Di-Chem, Inc.,** 419 U.S. 601 (1975), the Court struck down Georgia garnishment procedures. Its description of the distinguishing factors that made the case different from *Mitchell* provide a guide to important constitutional criteria.

(a) **Property not subject of suit [§267]**

Unlike *Fuentes* and *Mitchell*, the property in *Di-Chem* (a bank account) had no intrinsic relation to the claim.

(b) Purpose of due process requirements [§268]

The majority opinion found that the procedure in *Fuentes* was unconstitutional because the seizures there were "carried out without notice and without opportunity for a hearing *or other safeguard against mistaken repossession*." This seemed to revise the thrust of the *Fuentes* opinion, which treated the presence of safeguards as bearing on the type of hearing required, not the need for preseizure notice at all.

(5) *Doehr* [§269]

In **Connecticut v. Doehr,** 501 U.S. 1 (1991), the Court struck down Connecticut's provision for attachment of real property without prior notice and an opportunity for a hearing "as applied in this case." The Court followed a three-step analysis based on **Mathews v. Eldridge,** 424 U.S. 319 (1976):

(a) Private interest [§270]

The Court held that the interests of a homeowner were *significantly affected* by attachment even though it did not interfere with possession of the property because attachment can cloud title, impede sale, and interfere with borrowing on the property.

(b) Risk of erroneous deprivation [§271]

The Court found that there was a *substantial risk of an erroneous deprivation* because the state practice allowed decisions based on a conclusory affidavit without prior notice and adversary hearing, and the underlying issue in the case (an alleged assault) did not lend itself to documentary proof.

(c) Governmental interest [§272]

Connecticut had *no significant interest* in allowing a private plaintiff to attach defendant's property without notice or a showing of exigent circumstances, in view of the fact that other states have more exacting requirements for seizure without notice.

(d) Application to drug forfeiture seizure [§273]

In **United States v. James Daniel Good Real Property,** 510 U.S. 43 (1993), the Court held that seizure of defendant's home after his conviction for drug trafficking there violated due process because he did not receive preseizure notice and an opportunity to be heard. The seizure deprived him of use of the property, created an unacceptable risk of error because owners are entitled to an affirmative defense of innocent ownership, and was unnecessary to protect the government's interest because real property cannot abscond.

(e) Cognovit notes [§274]

Related issues arise in connection with cognovit notes, in which the debtor agrees that in the event of a default in payments, the creditor may immediately and without notice obtain a judgment against the debtor. The Supreme Court has held that if such arrangements are the result of arm's length negotiation between sophisticated commercial entities, they are enforceable over procedural due process objections. [**D.H. Overmyer Co. v. Frick Co.,** 405 U.S. 174 (1972)]

(6) Effect of *Doehr* [§275]

Doehr, supra, appears to have the following effects besides prescribing the three-part analysis of *Mathews, supra*:

(a) Exigent circumstances [§276]

The Court's opinion suggests that proof of exigent circumstances may be constitutionally necessary to permit seizure without notice. (*Compare supra,* §261, regarding "extraordinary situations" under *Fuentes.*)

(b) Effect of preexisting interest in property [§277]

The Court distinguished its summary affirmance in another case involving a mechanic's lien, suggesting that less rigorous standards might apply when the plaintiff is asserting an interest in the property that *antedates the suit*.

(c) Type of claim [§278]

The Court's emphasis on the difficulty of evaluating the assault claim before it on the basis of filings by plaintiff suggests that only claims that can be reliably evaluated on documentary proof may be the basis for seizure without notice.

(d) Due process limitations if hearing held before seizure [§279]

Even if a hearing is held before seizure, procedural due process may limit seizure unless the above criteria are satisfied.

Chapter Two: Subject Matter Jurisdiction of the Federal Courts

CONTENTS

Chapter Approach

Subject matter jurisdiction questions are an examination staple. When presented with litigation in federal court, remember that there must be a basis for the exercise of jurisdiction and keep in mind the following possibilities:

1. **Diversity Jurisdiction**

   a. **Complete diversity**

   Are any defendants of the same citizenship as any plaintiffs? If so, complete diversity is missing.

   b. **Jurisdictional amount**

   Does the plaintiff's claim in good faith put *more than $75,000* in controversy in the suit?

2. **Federal Question Jurisdiction**

   a. **Federal claim**

   Is the plaintiff seeking relief on the basis of a federal claim?

   b. **Federal issue in state law claim**

   If not, does the plaintiff's nonfederal claim turn on a substantial issue of federal law that is included in the *well-pleaded complaint*?

3. **Removal Jurisdiction**

   a. Was a *timely notice* of removal filed by *all* defendants?

   b. Would the case have been within the *original jurisdiction* of the federal court?

   c. If not, is the removing defendant the subject of a *separate and independent claim arising under federal law*?

   d. If the case was properly removed, should it be *remanded* because all federal claims have been dismissed, or because plaintiff in a diversity case has been allowed to amend to add nondiverse defendants?

4. **Supplemental Jurisdiction**

   If there is a claim properly within federal jurisdiction, does the court have jurisdiction over other claims against existing parties or claims against additional parties as well?

   a. Would the exercise of such jurisdiction be *constitutional* because the added claim forms part of *the same constitutional case* as the claim within federal jurisdiction?

b. If the case is in federal court *solely on grounds of diversity*, is the exercise of supplemental jurisdiction over claims by a plaintiff against a person made a party through *third party practice, joinder of necessary parties, permissive joinder, or intervention*, or over claims by a person seeking to be joined as a necessary party or seeking to intervene? If so, if exercising supplemental jurisdiction would destroy diversity jurisdiction, the court may *not* exercise supplemental jurisdiction.

c. If supplemental jurisdiction is properly invoked, should the court exercise its *discretion* to dismiss the supplemental claims due to *complexity of state law*, because the *state law claim substantially predominates*, or because the court has *dismissed* the claim over which it had original jurisdiction?

A. Introduction

---

1. Nature of Subject Matter Jurisdiction [§280]

Historically—sometimes by mere accident—many courts obtained authority to decide only certain types of actions; *i.e.*, they had jurisdiction over only particular subject matters (*e.g.*, only cases involving claims in excess of $75,000, or only claims involving land). Thus, whether a court has authority to hear a particular case can depend on the subject matter involved. The most significant limitations on subject matter jurisdiction today, for purposes of this Summary, involve the subject matter limitations on the federal courts. These limitations often reflect notions of the "proper" relation between federal and state power.

2. Territorial Jurisdiction Distinguished [§281]

Subject matter jurisdiction differs from territorial jurisdiction. Territorial jurisdiction limits the power of courts over persons based on geographic location. Subject matter jurisdiction limits the power of courts based on *case type*. Subject matter jurisdiction allocates authority between courts systems (*e.g.*, only courts in the federal system have subject matter jurisdiction over admiralty cases), or among courts of a given system (*e.g.*, some states provide that only state "family law courts" have subject matter jurisdiction over divorces). The two concepts of jurisdiction should not be confused. It is incorrect, for example, to say that the court "has diversity jurisdiction over the defendant" because diversity jurisdiction refers to jurisdiction over the type of case, not over the defendant. To proceed with a case, the court must possess *both personal jurisdiction* over the defendant and *subject matter jurisdiction* over the claim.

3. Defects Not Waivable [§282]

Lack of subject matter jurisdiction is not waivable so it may be raised as a basis for dismissing a case at any time. It can lie in the background as a sort of "time bomb" in the plaintiff's lawsuit.

a. **Plaintiff must allege grounds for subject matter jurisdiction [§283]**
Ordinarily, the plaintiff must include in the complaint allegations stating the subject matter jurisdiction of the court. [*See* Fed. R. Civ. P. 8(a)(1)]

b. **Defendant may raise objection at any time [§284]**
The defendant may raise lack of subject matter jurisdiction *at any time* during the pendency of the case, even after final judgment has been entered and the case has been appealed on other grounds. [Fed. R. Civ. P. 12(h)(3)] Indeed, the defendant may even remove the case to federal court, lose there, and then raise lack of subject matter jurisdiction as a ground for invalidating the judgment for the plaintiff. [*See* **American Fire & Casualty Co. v. Finn**, 341 U.S. 6 (1951)] Subject matter jurisdiction defects sometimes can even be raised on "collateral" attack, after all appeals have been exhausted or waived and the judgment has become completely final.

(1) **Distinguish—personal jurisdiction [§285]**
The defendant's failure to raise *personal jurisdiction* at the earliest time waives objections to personal jurisdiction. (*See supra*, §87.)

EXAM TIP	gilbert

Be sure to remember the important distinction regarding waiver. Defects in *personal jurisdiction* can easily be waived—a defendant's mere failure to raise the issue in an initial motion or answer constitutes a waiver. Defects in *subject matter jurisdiction* are *not* waivable; the defendant can even raise it for the first time on appeal.

c. **Court to raise sua sponte [§286]**
Even if the parties do not raise the issue, the court is to raise subject matter jurisdiction on its own motion. [*See, e.g.,* **Louisville & Nashville Railroad v. Mottley**, 211 U.S. 149 (1908)—Court dismissed appeal for lack of subject matter jurisdiction even though neither party raised issue]

d. **Jurisdiction must be resolved before court addresses merits of suit [§287]**
The question of whether a court has jurisdiction must be resolved *before* the court may decide the merits of the case. [**Steel Co. v. Citizens for Better Environment**, 523 U.S. 83 (1998)—rejecting "doctrine of hypothetical jurisdiction," followed by some appellate court circuits, under which a court would assume it had jurisdiction to decide the case on its merits where the merits question is more readily resolved than the jurisdiction question and the party that would prevail on the merits is the same party that would prevail if jurisdiction were denied]

(1) Personal jurisdiction challenge may be resolved before subject matter jurisdiction challenge [§288]

Although a federal court must resolve challenges to its jurisdiction before deciding the merits of a case, there is no unyielding jurisdictional hierarchy requiring a federal court to resolve challenges to its subject matter jurisdiction before resolving challenges to its personal jurisdiction. **[Ruhrgas AG v. Marathon Oil Co.,** 526 U.S. 574 (1999)—district court properly dismissed action removed from state court to federal court for lack of personal jurisdiction even though there were challenges to the court's removal jurisdiction]

4. State Courts [§289]

This chapter focuses on the subject matter jurisdiction of federal courts. Except for claims within the exclusive jurisdiction of the federal courts (*infra*, §§294-297), state court systems usually exercise "general jurisdiction"; *i.e.*, a state court is available for every type of claim. Within the state court system, however, there may be subject matter jurisdiction limitations that should be kept in mind:

a. Specialized courts [§290]

In many states, there are specialized courts that deal with certain types of cases. For example, probate proceedings or matrimonial disputes may have to be raised before a specialized court, or a specialized division of the court.

b. Monetary limitations [§291]

In some states, there are courts that have jurisdiction over claims below a certain dollar amount. Many states have *small claims courts* with authority to decide cases involving small sums [*see, e.g.,* Cal. Civ. Proc. Code §116.220(a)—less than $5,000], using very informal procedures that may even forbid the participation of lawyers. In addition, there may be more formal courts with jurisdiction limited to claims under a certain amount.

c. General jurisdiction [§292]

Each state has some court of "general jurisdiction." This means that *any type of claim* can be brought in this court, except those claims within the exclusive jurisdiction of the federal courts. (*See infra*, §294, regarding exclusive jurisdiction.)

d. Concurrent jurisdiction of federal claims [§293]

Generally, state courts have jurisdiction concurrent with the federal courts to hear federal claims. If there is concurrent jurisdiction, a plaintiff may choose to file her case in either federal or state court. Indeed, under the Supremacy Clause of the Constitution [U.S. Const. art. VI, §2], state courts may not refuse to enforce federal claims unless federal law provides otherwise. Thus, even if for some reason the plaintiff may not file her entire case in federal court, she can still file it in state court.

(1) Exception—exclusive jurisdiction [§294]

Federal law grants the federal courts *exclusive* jurisdiction over some types of cases, and state courts therefore cannot adjudicate such claims. Examples of such exclusive jurisdiction include the following:

(a) Patents, copyrights, and trademarks [§295]

Federal courts have exclusive jurisdiction when the plaintiff's patent, copyright, or trademark claim arises under a federal statute. [28 U.S.C. §1338] State courts have concurrent jurisdiction, however, to decide claims arising under the common law (*e.g.*, for unfair competition) and to decide claims for breach of contract concerning the license, sale, or other disposition of patents, even if the validity of the patent is challenged. [**Lear, Inc. v. Adkins**, 395 U.S. 653 (1969)]

(b) Federal antitrust regulations [§296]

Claims for violation of the federal antitrust laws have been held to be within the exclusive jurisdiction of the federal courts. [*See* **Freeman v. Bee Machine Co.,** 319 U.S. 448 (1943)] States may, however, have parallel state law antitrust provisions within the jurisdiction of the state courts.

(c) Federal securities acts [§297]

Federal jurisdiction is exclusive in actions brought under the Securities Exchange Act of 1934, including actions under *rule 10b-5* for "manipulative or deceptive conduct" in connection with the purchase or sale of securities. [15 U.S.C. §78a] States may, however, entertain claims for common law fraud arising out of the same events.

(d) Distinguish—federal defense [§298]

When an issue of federal law arises *as a defense* to a state law claim, the fact that a claim for affirmative relief on the federal ground would be subject to exclusive federal jurisdiction does not prevent the state court from considering the defense. Indeed, under the Supremacy Clause, the state court cannot refuse to entertain the defense.

5. Federal Courts' Jurisdiction

a. Limited jurisdiction [§299]

Unlike state courts, federal courts are courts of limited jurisdiction.

(1) Constitutional grant [§300]

Article III, section 1 of the United States Constitution establishes the Supreme Court and gives Congress the power to create inferior federal courts. Section 2 of Article III sets out the scope of the federal judicial power. It provides that, among others, the federal courts may hear cases: arising under the Constitution or federal law, affecting ambassadors, or between citizens of different states. To be constitutional, an exercise of jurisdiction by a federal court must be within the scope of power granted by Article III, section 2.

(2) Statutory grant [§301]

It is not enough that an exercise of federal jurisdiction is merely permissible under the Constitution. There must also be some statutory grant by Congress vesting the federal courts with jurisdiction. Unless Congress has vested a federal court with jurisdiction, the fact that it might do so without violating the Constitution is irrelevant.

(a) Historical background

It was uncertain at the outset whether Congress would create lower federal courts. Thus, it was also unclear whether any of the Article III jurisdiction would be used. In fact, until 1875, the primary grant of jurisdiction to the lower federal courts was authority to decide diversity cases (*i.e.*, cases in which the opposing parties were from different states).

SUMMARY OF BASIC STATUTES ON FEDERAL SUBJECT MATTER JURISDICTION	**gilbert**
DIVERSITY JURISDICTION	Under 28 U.S.C. §1332, federal courts may hear cases where (i) no defendant is a citizen of the same state as any plaintiff in the case, **and** (ii) more than $75,000 is in controversy.
FEDERAL QUESTION JURISDICTION	Under 28 U.S.C. §1331, federal courts may hear cases involving a federal question. There is no amount in controversy requirement, but the federal question must appear in the plaintiff's well-pleaded complaint; allegations in the complaint anticipating a defense are not sufficient.
SUPPLEMENTAL JURISDICTION	Under 28 U.S.C. §1367, once a federal court has jurisdiction over a claim under §1331 or §1332, it may hear all claims that are related to the claims over which it has "original" jurisdiction.
REMOVAL JURISDICTION	Under 28 U.S.C. §1441, a defendant may usually "remove" a case filed by plaintiff in state court if plaintiff could originally have filed the suit in federal court, provided defendant does so at the outset of the case.

b. Tactical considerations [§302]

Litigants with a choice between state and federal court often prefer federal court for a variety of tactical reasons.

(1) Location [§303]

Federal courts are usually located in metropolitan areas, while many state courts are in less populated areas.

(2) Broad discovery [§304]

Federal courts may afford broader opportunities for discovery (*i.e.,* pre-trial devices to obtain information about a case—generally from the other party), although the breadth of federal discovery has been curtailed, *see infra,* §§1421-1428.

(3) Speedy trial [§305]

In some locations, state court dockets are backlogged and federal courts are able to offer parties shorter delays to trial. By the same token, where the delay is greater in federal court, a party desiring delay might want to litigate in federal court for that reason.

(4) Single assignment system [§306]

In most federal courts, cases are assigned to a single judge from the outset. Some litigants believe that this arrangement is more efficient and effective than having the case assigned on a "master calendar" basis that assigns different aspects to different judges. Most states use the master calendar approach, although some are shifting to a single assignment system.

(5) Source of jurors [§307]

Federal juries are drawn from the entire federal district, while state court juries are usually drawn from a more limited area, such as a county or part of a county.

B. Diversity Jurisdiction

1. Introduction [§308]

Most cases brought in federal courts are brought under one of two subject matter jurisdiction statutes: the diversity statute [28 U.S.C. §1332] or the federal question statute [28 U.S.C. §1331]. This section of the Summary will discuss diversity jurisdiction; federal question jurisdiction will be discussed *infra.*

2. Constitutional Authorization [§309]

Article III, Section 2 of the Constitution provides that the judicial power of the United States may extend to controversies between two or more states, between a state and a citizen of another state, *between citizens of different states*, or between a state (or the citizens thereof) and foreign states, citizens, or subjects.

a. Rationale

The usual justification for creating diversity jurisdiction is to afford an alternative forum to out-of-state litigants who might be victims of local prejudice against outsiders.

b. What constitutes diversity [§310]

The plaintiff and defendant have diverse citizenship if one is a citizen of one state and the other is a citizen of another state or an alien or foreign national. There is no diversity jurisdiction, however, in a suit between two aliens, even if from different countries (*e.g.*, a citizen of India and a Canadian).

c. "Minimal" diversity constitutionally required [§311]

The Constitution requires only that one plaintiff be of different citizenship from one defendant, even if there are co-parties who are not of diverse citizenship. [**State Farm Fire & Casualty Co. v. Tashire**, 386 U.S. 523 (1967)] Absent minimal diversity, the federal courts are forbidden to entertain a case unless it involves a federal question (discussed *infra*, §§375 *et seq.*).

3. Diversity Statute [§312]

The First Congress not only created lower federal courts, but also vested them with diversity jurisdiction by passing the predecessor to 28 U.S.C. section 1332. That statute closely tracked the constitutional language. There are two main prerequisites to diversity jurisdiction under the statute: diversity of citizenship and a minimum amount in controversy.

a. Diversity of citizenship

(1) Complete diversity requirement [§313]

In 1806, the Supreme Court interpreted the diversity statute to *require complete diversity*, i.e., that there be *no defendant* having the same citizenship as any plaintiff. [**Strawbridge v. Curtiss**, 7 U.S. 267 (1806)] Although it has made some changes to the statute since then, Congress has not tried to change this interpretation. The supplemental jurisdiction statute (granting federal courts jurisdiction to hear "supplemental" claims related to the claim over which they have "original" jurisdiction; *see infra*, §§424 *et seq.*) appears to embrace the complete diversity requirement, but could be interpreted to weaken it; *see infra*, §§425 *et seq.*

(2) How citizenship determined

(a) Natural persons [§314]

For United States nationals, "citizenship," in substance, has the same meaning as *domicile*. A new citizenship may be established by physical presence in the new state and an intention to remain there—*i.e.*, no present intent to go elsewhere.

EXAM TIP	gilbert

Although a person's domicile is important in determining both personal jurisdiction and diversity jurisdiction, be sure to keep these concepts separate. Personal jurisdiction gives a court *power over the defendant*, while diversity jurisdiction, a type of subject matter jurisdiction, gives the court the authority to hear the *type of case*.

---

1) **United States national living abroad [§315]**

An American citizen permanently living abroad has no domicile within the United States and is *not a citizen of any state*. Such a person cannot sue or be sued in federal court on grounds of diversity of citizenship.

2) **Citizens of District of Columbia, Puerto Rico, and U.S. territories [§316]**

Although citizens of the District of Columbia, Puerto Rico, and U.S. territories might have suffered a similar fate to that of the expatriates, Congress instead provided that they should be *treated as citizens of states* for purposes of diversity jurisdiction, and the Supreme Court upheld this as constitutional. [28 U.S.C. §1332(d); **National Mutual Insurance Co. v. Tidewater Transfer Co.,** 337 U.S. 582 (1949)] Thus, a citizen of Puerto Rico can sue a citizen of Illinois in federal court under diversity jurisdiction.

(b) **Corporations [§317]**

For diversity purposes, a corporation is deemed to be a citizen of *every state* in which it is *incorporated and* of the state in which it has its *principal place of business*. [28 U.S.C. §1332(c)]

1) **"Principal place of business" [§318]**

Where the corporation's executive office and its other activities are in the same state, the concept causes no trouble. However, where the executive offices are in one state and its principal production facilities are in another state, the courts may have more trouble determining the principal place of business. Some courts consider the executive office as the *nerve center* of the corporation (and thus the principal place of business), while other courts hold that the *main physical plant* is the principal place of business.

2) **Distinguish—venue [§319]**

For venue purposes, a corporate defendant is usually treated as a resident of every state in which it is *subject to personal jurisdiction*, not merely its principal place of business. (*See supra*, §149.)

EXAM TIP　　　　　　　　　　　　　　**gilbert**

Remember that subject matter jurisdiction and venue are two distinct concepts, and thus the rules regarding corporate citizenship are different. For purposes of *diversity jurisdiction*, the corporation is a citizen of its state(s) of *incorporation and* of the state of its *principal place of business*. For *venue* purposes, the corporation is deemed to reside in any state in which it is *subject to personal jurisdiction*, which allows venue in the state of incorporation, where its principal place of business is, and also in every other state where it *has substantial contacts*.

(c) Artificial entities [§320]

For purposes of diversity, unincorporated associations and other noncorporate artificial entities created by state law are viewed as citizens of *each state in which any member is a citizen*. As a result, complete diversity is often destroyed and diversity jurisdiction is unavailable.

1) Partnerships [§321]

A business partnership is viewed as an association for diversity purposes. Therefore, the citizenship of each partner must be considered. [**Cresswell v. Sullivan & Cromwell**, 922 F.2d 60 (2d Civ. 1990)—American law firm partnership could not be sued in federal court on diversity grounds because it included partners who were United States nationals but were domiciled abroad, *see supra*, §315]

a) Limited partnerships [§322]

In a general partnership, the partners have full individual liability for the partnership's debts. In a limited partnership, the liability of the "limited" partners is restricted to the amount of their investment and they have negligible power to control the partnership. Nonetheless, the Supreme Court has held that the citizenships of *all limited partners* must be taken into account for purposes of determining complete diversity. [**Carden v. Arkoma Associates**, 494 U.S. 185 (1990)]

b) Distinguish—professional corporation [§323]

Some enterprises (such as law firms) that formerly operated as partnerships now operate as "professional corporations" (mainly for tax reasons). Because the "shareholder" attorneys in such corporations remain individually liable for legal malpractice, arguably their citizenship should be considered for purposes of determining complete diversity. Lower federal courts have held, though, that only the citizenship *of the professional corporation* should be considered. [*See, e.g.,* **Coté v. Wadel**, 796 F.2d 981 (7th Cir. 1986)]

2) Labor unions [§324]

The Supreme Court has held that unions are unincorporated associations for purposes of diversity jurisdiction, and thus the citizenship of all union members is considered. [**United Steel Workers v. R.H. Bouligny, Inc.**, 382 U.S. 145 (1965)]

3) Underwriting syndicate [§325]

Lloyd's of London, the underwriting syndicate, has been held to have the citizenship, for purposes of diversity, of every "name" (*i.e.*, investor). [**Indiana Gas Co. v. Home Insurance Co.,** 141 F.3d 314 (7th Cir.), *cert. denied*, 525 U.S. 931 (1998); *but see* **Certain Interested Underwriters at Lloyd's of London v. Layne,** 26 F.3d 39 (6th Cir. 1994)—as real party in interest, only Lloyd's itself need be considered in determining whether there is diversity]

4) Business trusts [§326]

A business trust involves investments by "shareholders" who entrust their investments to trustees who control the activities of the trust. State law may give the trustees power to sue and be sued as individuals in their capacity as trustees in connection with trust affairs. When state law does so, and the trustees sue or are sued in their own right, their citizenship and *not that of nonparty shareholders* is to be considered in determining the existence of diversity in an action involving the trust. [**Navarro Savings Association v. Lee,** 446 U.S. 458 (1980)]

(d) Permanent resident aliens [§327]

Aliens admitted to the United States for *permanent residence* are deemed citizens of the states in which they are domiciled for purposes of determining diversity. [28 U.S.C. §1332(a)]

1) Caution—possible constitutional challenge [§328]

Although the constitution requires only minimal diversity (*see supra*, §311), minimal diversity does not exist between two aliens. Therefore section 1332(a) might authorize jurisdiction beyond the constitutional grant of federal judicial power.

---

e.g. **Example:** In a suit by a citizen of India, domiciled in Virginia, against a German manufacturer and its American distributor, which was a citizen of Delaware, the court upheld jurisdiction because there was citizen-vs.-alien diversity, given the presence of the Delaware citizen, but noted possible constitutional problems had that defendant not been sued. [**Singh v. Daimler-Benz AG,** 9 F.3d 303 (3d Cir. 1993)]

---

cf. **Compare—statute held not to authorize:** Another court held that section 1332(a) was intended to narrow federal court jurisdiction, and that it therefore should not be interpreted to authorize a suit between aliens even if one were domiciled in an American state. In part, the court so interpreted the statute to avoid constitutional difficulties. [**Saadeh v. Farouki,** 107 F.3d 52 (D.C. Cir. 1997)]

---

2) Distinguish—aliens generally [§329]

Otherwise, the only persons who can become citizens of a state are United States nationals. Thus, an alien in this country for an extended stay would still be an alien for purposes of diversity jurisdiction.

(e) Class actions [§330]

In a class action (*i.e.,* an action brought by representatives on behalf of a class consisting of a large number of persons), only the citizenship of the *named representatives* is considered in determining diversity. [**Supreme Tribe of Ben Hur v. Cauble,** 244 U.S. 356 (1921)]

EXAM TIP   **gilbert**

Note that because only the citizenship of the *named representatives* is considered in determining diversity in a class action, it is irrelevant that some members of the class are citizens of the defendant's state; diversity still exists. Don't be fooled by a fact pattern where the defendant is a large company, like Firestone, and members of the plaintiff class live in every state. Diversity may be preserved by carefully selecting the class representatives.

(f) Executors, guardians, and trustees [§331]

The legal representative of an estate or of an infant or incompetent is deemed to have the citizenship of the decedent, infant, or incompetent. [28 U.S.C. §1332(c)(2)]

(g) Fictitious defendants [§332]

When the plaintiff in a civil case is unable to ascertain the name of a potential defendant, some states allow the plaintiff to sue the unknown defendant under a fictitious name (*e.g.,* "John Doe"). A number of federal courts have held that such cases could not be heard under diversity jurisdiction because of the uncertainty of the citizenship of the unnamed defendant. [*See, e.g.,* **Othman v. Globe Indemnity Co.,** 759 F.2d 1458 (9th Cir. 1985)] In 1988, a federal statute [28 U.S.C. §1441; *see infra,* §465] providing for removal of cases from state court to federal court was amended. The amendment provides that for purposes of removal, the citizenship of defendants sued under fictitious names is to be disregarded. The diversity jurisdiction statute [28 U.S.C. §1332] was *not* similarly amended. Nevertheless, after the 1988 amendment, at least one court has held that inclusion of a fictitious defendant neither destroys diversity jurisdiction nor requires that the fictitious defendant be named or dropped from the case. [*See* **Macheras v. Center Art Galleries,** 776 F. Supp. 1436 (D. Haw. 1991); *but see* **Howell v.**

Tribune Entertainment Co., 106 F.3d 215 (7th Cir. 1997)—fictitious defendants are not permitted in federal diversity suits] The Supreme Court has not resolved the issue.

(3) Time for determination [§333]

Diversity need only exist at the *commencement* of the action.

(a) Change before filing [§334]

It is immaterial that the parties had the same citizenship when the claim arose, and a party may even move to another state to create diversity, as long as there is a genuine change of citizenship.

(b) Change after filing [§335]

Similarly, a change in either party's citizenship after the filing of the suit does not deprive the court of jurisdiction.

(c) Substituted party [§336]

Sometimes after a case is filed, a plaintiff will transfer his interest in the case and the transferee will be substituted for the plaintiff. The general rule is still followed: Because diversity "is assessed at the time the action is filed," diversity is not destroyed even if the substituted plaintiff is a citizen of the same state as one of the defendants. **[Freeport-McMoRan, Inc. v. KN Energy, Inc.,** 498 U.S. 426 (1991)]

(d) Partial exception—removal [§337]

Where an action is removed to federal court from state court on grounds of diversity, diversity must exist at the time of *filing of the suit and* on the date of *filing of the notice of removal.*

(4) Realigning parties [§338]

In determining diversity, the court will look to the *real interests* of the parties and may realign them (as plaintiffs or defendants) according to their real interests. In general, the court will look to the *ultimate interests* of the parties in realigning them.

(a) Shareholders' derivative actions

In a shareholder derivative action (in which a shareholder brings a suit to enforce a right of the corporation because the officers of the corporation refuse to bring the suit directly), the corporation, even though nominally joined as a plaintiff, is likely to be realigned as a defendant for diversity purposes if (as is usually the case) it is controlled by persons antagonistic to the shareholder-plaintiff. [**Smith v. Sperling,** 354 U.S. 91 (1957)]

(5) Efforts to create diversity [§339]

28 U.S.C. section 1359 provides that there shall be no jurisdiction when a

person has collusively or improperly been made a party or joined in order to invoke federal jurisdiction.

(a) Assignment of claim [§340]

When a claim is assigned to establish diversity, or assigned without significant consideration, the assignment will not create diversity if diversity would not exist had the action been brought in the name of the assignor. [**Kramer v. Caribbean Mills, Inc.,** 394 U.S. 823 (1969)] However, if substantial consideration is given for the assignment, jurisdiction exists even though there would be no diversity between the assignor and the defendant.

(b) Appointment of executor [§341]

Appointment of an out-of-state executor will not create diversity, because the executor is deemed to be a citizen of the decedent's state. (*See supra,* §331.)

(c) Distinguish—change of citizenship [§342]

A genuine change of citizenship can create diversity. (*See supra,* §334.)

(6) Efforts to defeat diversity [§343]

There is no similar statute forbidding efforts to defeat diversity, and plaintiffs have some latitude in doing so.

(a) Joinder of nondiverse defendants [§344]

Under federal practice, a plaintiff can bring a single action against a number of defendants, as long as the claims against the defendants arise out of the same series of occurrences or transactions and there is a question of law or fact common to all the parties. (*See infra,* §§1033, 1037.) Often the plaintiff may add claims against nondiverse defendants and thereby defeat diversity.

1) Limitation—valid claims [§345]

The plaintiff must have a valid claim against the nondiverse defendant or the presence of this defendant will be disregarded in making the diversity determination.

2) Limitation—alternative grounds for federal jurisdiction [§346]

Removal may be possible if nondiverse defendants are sued if federal jurisdiction can be justified on some other basis, such as federal question jurisdiction (*i.e.,* a case arising under federal law; *see infra,* §379).

(b) Appointment of nondiverse representative [§347]

The appointment of a nondiverse executor or administrator cannot defeat diversity because the citizenship of such persons is deemed to be the same as that of the decedent. (*See supra*, §331.)

(7) Effect of lack of diversity

(a) Dismissal of nondiverse party [§348]
The plaintiff often can solve the lack of diversity problem by dismissing the nondiverse party. [**Newman-Green, Inc. v. Alfonzo-Larrain**, 490 U.S. 826 (1989)]

(b) Necessary party [§349]
Where the nondiverse party is a necessary party (*i.e.*, a party needed for just adjudication, *see infra*, §1044), the plaintiff may be unable to proceed in federal court. (*See infra*, §1048—discussing decision whether to proceed with action in absence of necessary party.)

(c) Other grounds for federal jurisdiction [§350]
Remember to consider other grounds for federal jurisdiction if diversity is absent. For example, if a federal question is presented, the case may proceed in federal court even though there is no diversity.

b. Jurisdictional amount [§351]
From the outset, the diversity statute limited federal jurisdiction to cases in which more than a certain ***minimum amount*** was ***"in controversy."*** Currently, diversity jurisdiction is limited to cases involving ***more than $75,000***. *Rationale:* The monetary limitation seeks to ensure that only "substantial" cases will be brought in federal court.

(1) Time for computing [§352]
The amount is computed as of the ***date of commencement*** of the action. Subsequent events (*e.g.*, part payment) do not defeat jurisdiction.

(2) Legal certainty test [§353]
The jurisdictional amount requirement is satisfied unless the plaintiff's complaint shows to a "legal certainty" that she could not recover *more* than the minimum amount. [**St. Paul Mercury Indemnity Co. v. Red Cab Co.**, 303 U.S. 283 (1938)]

(a) No need to itemize damages in complaint [§354]
The plaintiff ordinarily need not indicate in the complaint how she arrived at the amount of damages claimed.

1) But note—disclosure
Early in most cases the Federal Rules require that certain disclosures be made, including a computation of any damages claimed. (*See infra*, §1299.)

(b) Good faith limitation [§355]

The claim for damages set forth in the complaint is determinative of the amount in controversy if the claim was made in good faith; there need only be some *legal possibility* of recovering the minimum amount.

1) Removed cases [§356]

Determination of the amount in controversy may be less strict in actions removed from state court to federal court under the removal statute, since the plaintiff would presumably have no incentive to inflate her claim to satisfy federal jurisdictional requirements when filing in state court.

(c) Effect of judgment for lesser amount [§357]

The fact that the actual recovery does not exceed the jurisdictional amount does not affect the jurisdiction of the court, as long as the claim was made in good faith. The court may, however, deny the plaintiff costs of suit or impose them on the plaintiff. [28 U.S.C. §1332(b)] However, this power is rarely used.

(d) Valuing claims for nonmonetary relief [§358]

Where the remedy sought is not money (*e.g.*, where the plaintiff seeks an injunction ordering the defendant to refrain from doing some act) the courts are split on whether the relief should be valued from the *plaintiff's perspective* (value to plaintiff) or the *defendant's perspective* (cost to defendant) in the minority of cases in which the values would differ.

> **e.g.** **Example—plaintiff's perspective:** Plaintiff sued to restrain defendant from erecting poles and wires in a way that would injure plaintiff's poles and wires. Although the cost to defendant of changing its operation would be less than the jurisdictional amount, the Supreme Court upheld jurisdiction because the value to plaintiff would exceed that amount. [**Glenwood Light & Water Co. v. Mutual Light, Heat & Power Co.**, 239 U.S. 121 (1915)]

> **e.g.** **Example—defendant's perspective:** Plaintiffs sued a railroad to quiet title to water rights that were worth far less than the jurisdictional amount to plaintiffs, but a good deal more to defendant, and the court upheld jurisdiction. [**Ronzio v. Denver & Rio Grande Railroad**, 116 F.2d 604 (10th Cir. 1940)]

(e) Valuing claims for declaratory relief [§359]

In declaratory relief actions where the plaintiff seeks a determination that he is not liable to the defendant, the amount in controversy is the amount of the claim that would be asserted by the declaratory relief defendant against the declaratory relief plaintiff. With other sorts of declaratory claims (*e.g.,* that plaintiff may continue a course of conduct defendant claims is illegal), the analysis should resemble that for nonmonetary relief.

(f) Interest and costs [§360]

Interest and costs are *excluded.* However, attorneys' fees that are recoverable by contract or by statute are considered part of the matter in controversy, rather than as costs, and are included.

(3) Aggregation of claims to satisfy requirement [§361]

Whether separate claims for less than the jurisdictional amount can be aggregated to satisfy the jurisdictional requirement depends on a number of factors.

(a) Claims of single plaintiff against single defendant [§362]

All claims of the plaintiff against the defendant, whether or not related, *can be aggregated* to meet the minimum.

---

e.g. **Example:** Plaintiff sues defendant for $50,000 in damages arising from a car accident and for $30,000 arising from an unrelated breach of contract. These amounts may be aggregated to reach the jurisdictional amount.

(b) Claims of single plaintiff against several defendants [§363]

Only claims for which all defendants are *jointly liable* to the plaintiff may be combined. "Joint liability" is defined narrowly for this purpose; claims arising from closely related conduct do not satisfy the test. "Joint" liability would arise in a few situations such as where the defendants are co-owners of property; it would not arise where the defendants are *joint tortfeasors.*

1) Note

When the plaintiff alleges that the defendants inflicted separate harms on her as part of a conspiracy, *allegations of conspiracy* may make defendants jointly liable and therefore *permit aggregation* of amounts.

(c) Claims of several plaintiffs against single defendant [§364]

The claims of multiple plaintiffs can be aggregated only if they have a *common undivided ownership interest* in the claims.

---

e.g. **Example:** A and B are tenants in common in a parcel of land (*i.e.,* each owns an "undivided" 50% interest). They sue D for trespass, alleging $120,000 in total damages to the property. Each plaintiff has suffered only $60,000 damage to her own interest, but the plaintiffs' undivided interest in the property has been injured. Under these circumstances, the plaintiffs may aggregate their claims to meet the $75,000 requirement.

(d) Counterclaims [§365]

In general, the amount sought on a counterclaim cannot be aggregated with a plaintiff's small claim to satisfy the jurisdictional minimum.

1) Note

A 1961 Supreme Court case [**Horton v. Liberty Mutual Insurance Co.,** 367 U.S. 348 (1961)] appears to look to the counterclaim as the basis for jurisdiction in a case involving Texas workers' compensation. It is regarded by many as limited to its quite unusual facts.

2) Distinguish—jurisdiction over counterclaim where plaintiff has satisfied minimum [§366]

When the defendant's counterclaim arises out of the same transaction and is therefore *compulsory* (*see infra*, §883), it need *not* satisfy the jurisdictional minimum requirement because it is clearly within the supplemental jurisdiction of the court (*see infra*, §§426-429). With a *permissive* counterclaim (*see infra*, §882), however, there must be an *independent jurisdictional basis* and the jurisdictional minimum requirement must therefore be satisfied.

3) Distinguish—compulsory counterclaim sometimes considered when defendant does not move to dismiss [§367]

A few lower federal courts will allow the amount of defendant's compulsory counterclaim to be used to establish jurisdiction if: (i) the case was *originally filed* in federal court; (ii) the amount of the counterclaim satisfies the jurisdictional minimum of $75,000; and (iii) defendant does not move to dismiss for lack of subject matter jurisdiction. [*See, e.g.,* **Spectacor Management Group v. Brown,** 131 F.3d 120 (3d Cir. 1997), *cert. denied,* 523 U.S. 1120 (1998)] But this approach does not justify using a counterclaim to satisfy the jurisdictional amount for *removal* because that would permit the defendant to override plaintiff's choice to sue in state court. [*See, e.g.,* **Independent Machine Co. v. International Tray Pads & Packaging, Inc.,** 991 F. Supp. 687 (D.N.J. 1998)—emphasizing narrow construction required for removal jurisdiction]

c. **Exceptions to exercise of diversity jurisdiction [§368]**

Although the diversity statute does not limit the subject matter of cases brought in federal court, the courts decline to exercise jurisdiction in some types of cases.

(1) Domestic relations [§369]

As a matter of long-standing statutory construction, there is an exception to diversity jurisdiction that prohibits issuance by a federal court of divorce, alimony, or child custody decrees. However, the exception does not permit a federal district court to refuse to exercise diversity jurisdiction over a tort action for damages, even when the claims are brought by one divorced parent on behalf of children allegedly abused by the other parent. [**Ankenbrandt v. Richards,** 504 U.S. 689 (1992)]

(2) Probate proceedings [§370]

Federal courts will not take jurisdiction over proceedings maintainable in probate courts (*e.g.,* cases challenging the validity of a will), but will take jurisdiction over actions by and against fiduciaries maintainable in state courts of general jurisdiction.

(3) Local actions [§371]

Some federal courts treat the rule that actions regarding title to real property should be litigated at the location of the property (*supra,* §175) as limiting the subject matter jurisdiction of courts to entertain such actions elsewhere. [*See, e.g.,* **Hayes v. Gulf Oil Corp.,** 821 F.2d 285 (5th Cir. 1987)—"federal and state courts lack jurisdiction over the subject matter of claims to land located outside the state in which the court sits"]

d. **Proposals to repeal diversity statute [§372]**

For some time, there have been calls for the repeal of the diversity statute. Proponents of this move argue that any residue of prejudice against outsiders is insufficient to justify imposing the burden of deciding diversity cases on the federal courts. Those who favor retaining diversity jurisdiction urge that prejudice does persist, and that it is important to preserve options for litigants. It is impossible to forecast the future of this debate.

(1) Complex litigation [§373]

Whatever the future of diversity jurisdiction generally, there is also sentiment favoring expanding it to cope with the demands of repeated litigation of related matters.

(2) Increase in jurisdictional minimum [§374]

As a partial compromise in the ongoing debate over the continued existence of diversity jurisdiction, Congress raised the jurisdictional amount from $10,000 to $50,000 in 1988 and then to $75,000 in 1996, thus cutting down the number of cases that come within diversity jurisdiction.

C. Federal Question Jurisdiction

1. Constitutional Grant

a. Constitutional provisions [§375]
Article III, Section 2 of the Constitution provides that federal judicial power shall extend to:

(1) Cases in law and equity *arising under the Constitution, the laws of the United States, and treaties* (this is the major area of federal question jurisdiction);

(2) Cases affecting *ambassadors, consuls,* etc.;

(3) Cases involving *admiralty* and maritime jurisdiction; and

(4) Cases to which the *United States is a party.*

b. Broad view of federal question power [§376]
In 1824 the Supreme Court upheld a statute that it read to grant federal courts jurisdiction over any case to which the Bank of the United States (a private bank created by Congress) was a party. It found this acceptable because, even if the suit were about a state law debt, the bank was a federal creation, and in every case there would be a question about whether it could legally sue—a federal question. The fact that this question would not be important after it was resolved did not bother the Court: "The question forms an original ingredient in every cause. Whether it be in fact relied on or not, in the defense, it is still a part of the cause, and may be relied upon [to uphold federal question jurisdiction]." [**Osborn v. Bank of the United States,** 22 U.S. 738 (1824)]

(1) Criticism
Some have criticized this broad view of federal question power as including too many cases in which the background federal question would not really be a viable issue in the case at all. Thus, it is suggested that under the broad view of *Osborn,* all land disputes in western states could be heard in federal court on the ground that the land was originally the subject of a federal land grant even though that fact had nothing to do with the dispute between the parties. Nevertheless, the *Osborn* holding stands and permits Congress to define federal question jurisdiction extremely broadly. However, the courts have concluded that Congress has

not defined federal question jurisdiction this broadly under the **general** federal question statute. [28 U.S.C. §1331]

(2) Special federal question statutes [§377]

The Supreme Court has, however, found such broad definition in some *special* "federal question" jurisdiction statutes, such as the Foreign Sovereign Immunities Act, 28 U.S.C. section 1330 [**Verlinden B.V. v. Central Bank of Nigeria,** 461 U.S. 480 (1983)—congressional regulation of foreign sovereigns' immunity permits federal jurisdiction over alien's suit against foreign government entity even without any federal cause of action], and the federal statute chartering the American National Red Cross, 36 U.S.C. section 2 [**American National Red Cross v. S.G.,** 505 U.S. 247 (1992)—chartering statute's language confers original jurisdiction over suits involving the Red Cross, a private but federally chartered corporation, even in cases involving state law claims].

c. Claim based on federal substantive law [§378]

It may be that (except where a federal creation such as the Bank of the United States is involved, *see supra*) Congress can assign to the federal courts jurisdiction over claims it creates only by promulgating or providing for a body of federal substantive law to govern the claims or delegating authority to create such substantive law to the courts.

---

e.g. **Example—Labor Management Relations Act:** In the Labor Management Relations Act, Congress granted the federal courts jurisdiction over suits to enforce collective bargaining agreements between employers and unions. The Court found this grant of jurisdiction valid despite lack of diversity, stressing the need for national uniformity in enforcement of such agreements and concluding that "the legislation does more than confer jurisdiction in the federal courts" because "the substantive law to apply in suits under [the Act] is federal law, which the courts must fashion from the policy of our national labor laws." [**Textile Workers Union v. Lincoln Mills,** 353 U.S. 448 (1957)]

---

2. Federal Question Statute

a. Introduction [§379]

Except for a brief period, Congress did not grant lower federal courts general jurisdiction to hear cases based on federal law (*i.e.,* "general federal question jurisdiction") until 1875, when it passed the predecessor to 28 U.S.C. section 1331. The statute used language very similar to that in the Constitution, granting the federal courts jurisdiction to hear "all civil actions arising under the Constitution, laws, or treaties of the United States."

(1) Statute interpreted more narrowly than Constitution [§380]

Despite the similarity between the language of the statute and the Constitution, the Supreme Court has interpreted the statute more narrowly;

the remainder of this section, therefore, examines the ways in which the Court has limited the reach of the statute.

(2) State court jurisdiction over cases raising federal questions [§381]

Until 1875, the only courts in which federal question cases could usually be litigated, absent diversity of citizenship, were state courts. Note that as to most federal question issues, jurisdiction in such cases is now *concurrent* between the state and federal courts. (*See supra*, §§293-298.)

(3) Supreme Court jurisdiction to review state court decisions of federal questions [§382]

Often, when the lower federal courts do not have jurisdiction under the federal question statute, the Supreme Court has jurisdiction to review decisions of state courts involving federal law issues. [*See* 28 U.S.C. §1257]

b. Standards for determining whether a federal question is raised [§383]

The Supreme Court's decisions under the federal question statute are sometimes difficult to reconcile, but look to two basic possibilities:

(1) Federal law creates claim [§384]

If federal law creates the claim sued upon, there generally is no problem in finding that the federal courts have subject matter jurisdiction. As Justice Holmes put it, "a suit arises under the law that creates the cause of action." [**American Well Works Co. v. Layne & Bower Co.**, 241 U.S. 257 (1916)]

(a) Test underinclusive [§385]

The Court has since recognized that this description is "more useful for describing the vast majority of cases that come within the district courts' original jurisdiction" than for distinguishing among cases in which jurisdiction is doubtful. [**Franchise Tax Board v. Construction Laborers' Vacation Trust**, 463 U.S. 1 (1983)]

(b) Implied claims [§386]

Note that federal claims include claims implied by the courts in addition to private rights of action explicitly created by Congress. [*See, e.g.,* **J.I. Case Co. v. Borak**, 377 U.S. 426 (1964)—implied private right of action for violation of Federal Securities Exchange Act of 1934] However, the Supreme Court has recently taken a cautious attitude toward implying causes of action. (For details on implied claims, *see* Federal Courts Summary.)

(2) Nonfederal claim that turns on construction of federal law [§387]

If the claim being sued upon is not one created by federal law but resolution of the suit turns on construction of federal law, application of the federal question statute is more difficult. The Supreme Court has confirmed that federal question jurisdiction can be proper "where the vindication of a right under state law necessarily turned on some construction of federal law." [**Merrell Dow Pharmaceuticals, Inc. v. Thompson,** 478 U.S. 804 (1986)]

---

e.g. **Example:** A landowner challenged building restrictions resulting from landmark designation based on state administrative review law. The landowner's challenge to the administrative action was based on federal constitutional objections, and the right to relief under state law therefore required resolution of a substantial question of federal law. [**City of Chicago v. International College of Surgeons,** 522 U.S. 156 (1997)]

---

e.g. **Example:** A shareholder sued to enjoin a corporation in which he held stock from purchasing bonds issued by federal land banks. The shareholder asserted that under state law the corporation was forbidden to invest in bonds that were not legally issued. The only issue in the case was whether the bonds were validly issued under federal law, and the Supreme Court held that there was federal question jurisdiction. [**Smith v. Kansas City Title & Trust Co.,** 255 U.S. 180 (1921)]

---

cf. **Compare:** A railroad employee sued his employer for injuries sustained on the job, which he alleged were caused by a defective uncoupling lever that did not comply with federal standards for safety equipment. The Supreme Court held that the fact the alleged violation of the federal standard was an element of the state law tort claim did not fundamentally change the state law nature of the action and that jurisdiction was absent. [**Moore v. Chesapeake & Ohio Railway,** 291 U.S. 205 (1934)]

(a) **Absence of implied federal claim [§388]**

In *Merrell Dow, supra,* the Court held that there was no federal question jurisdiction over a state tort claim for negligent manufacture of a drug, although the claim relied on the defendant's alleged violation of the Federal Food, Drug, and Cosmetic Act ("FDCA"). The parties agreed that there was no implied federal cause of action, and the Court reasoned that in that circumstance it would "flout" the will of Congress to allow federal jurisdiction over a state law claim turning on a violation of the FDCA.

(b) **Substantial bearing on outcome [§389]**

Where federal law is an element of a state law claim, it suffices to support federal question jurisdiction only where it is important to the outcome of the case: "The right or immunity must be such that it will be supported if the Constitution or laws of the United States are given one construction or effect, and defeated if they receive another." [**Gully v. First National Bank,** 299 U.S. 109 (1936)]

1) But note—constitutional power

Under **Osborn v. Bank of the United States,** *supra,* §376, the unimportance of the question to the dispute before the court may not matter.

(c) Nature of federal interest [§390]

In *Merrell Dow, supra,* the Court suggested that it would be helpful to focus on the nature of the federal issues at stake and that this approach could reconcile the results in the *Moore* and *Smith* cases, *supra.* In *Smith,* jurisdiction was proper because the validity of an act of Congress was directly drawn into question, and there was a substantial federal interest in this question. On the other hand, in *Moore* the federal issue related to the employer's compliance at one place and time with one federal safety standard, and there was little federal interest in this isolated incident.

1) Split over interpretation of Merrell Dow

There is debate in the lower federal courts over whether an implied federal right of action is *necessary* for federal question jurisdiction over a state claim under *Merrell Dow,* or whether the federal interest could in other ways have the nature and importance seemingly required by the opinion. [*Compare* **Jairath v. Dyer,** 154 F.3d 1280 (11th Cir. 1998)—absence of private cause of action not fatal to federal question jurisdiction over state law claim that incorporates federal duty, *with* **Seinfeld v. Austen,** 39 F.2d 761 (7th Cir. 1994)—implied right of action necessary]

c. Well-pleaded complaint rule [§391]

Generally, a federal court will not have federal question subject matter jurisdiction unless the federal question appears in the plaintiff's "well-pleaded complaint." Federal questions raised by an *answer* to a complaint are *not* sufficient. The well-pleaded complaint rule serves as a quick and reliable sorting device for allocating subject matter jurisdiction between the state and federal courts.

(1) Federal element of nonfederal claim properly included under pleading rules [§392]

Sometimes a plaintiff who has a state-law claim will want to sue in federal court but cannot bring a diversity action. Such a plaintiff might try to get the case into federal court by injecting a federal law issue into the complaint even though it is not required to be included by the rules governing pleading (*infra,* §§595-634). This does not suffice to support federal question jurisdiction. The federal issue must be an *element of the state-law claim* that is *required to be included in the complaint to state a claim* under the applicable rules of pleading, for that is what makes these allegations "well pleaded."

(2) Anticipation of defense insufficient [§393]

Similarly a plaintiff who wants to sue in federal court might try to raise a federal question to invoke jurisdiction by including in his complaint allegations relating to a federal-law defense that the defendant might raise. Such an allegation—in anticipation of a defense—is not a sufficient basis for federal question jurisdiction. Under the well-pleaded complaint rule, allegations going to an anticipated defense are not required to be in a complaint.

---

e.g. **Example:** Plaintiffs sued defendant railroad in federal court alleging that the railroad had breached a contract to provide plaintiffs with free lifetime passes to ride the railroad. Breach of contract is a state law claim. The railroad had granted plaintiffs the passes to settle the plaintiffs' personal injury claims against it. Diversity jurisdiction was not available. In an attempt to invoke federal question jurisdiction, plaintiffs, in their complaint, alleged that D would defend the breach of contract action by claiming that a newly enacted federal statute prohibited such lifetime passes. They further alleged that the statute should not apply to them or that the statute unconstitutionally deprived them of their property without due process of law. The Supreme Court held that the federal courts did not have federal question jurisdiction over the case because the allegations relating to the federal statute were not essential to Plaintiffs' action for breach of contract; they merely anticipated a defense that the railroad would have to plead and prove. [**Louisville & Nashville Railroad v. Mottley,** *supra,* §286]

---

(3) Removed cases [§394]

As discussed earlier, usually state courts have concurrent jurisdiction to hear federal question cases, and sometimes a plaintiff will choose to file a federal-law based action in state court. As will be discussed later (*infra,* §455), in some circumstances a *defendant* has a right to remove such cases from the state court to the federal courts. In removal cases, the general rule discussed above applies: A case cannot be removed on the basis of federal question jurisdiction unless the federal question appears on the face of the *plaintiff's* well-pleaded complaint. The fact that the defendant has raised a federal defense is irrelevant.

(a) Criticism

One of the reasons for the well-pleaded complaint rule that courts are not to consider federal claims raised in anticipation of a federal defense is that there is no way to be certain what defenses will be raised in a defendant's answer. Thus, there is no way to predict whether a federal question will actually be involved. But this argument loses its bite in removed cases, since removal must be on the defendant's motion, and the defendant can definitively establish whether he will raise a federal defense in his answer.

(b) Plaintiff's election not to assert federal claim [§395]

To prevent the defendant from removing the case to federal court, a plaintiff might "artfully plead" her case to avoid a federal question. Generally, this is permissible on the rationale that the plaintiff is the master of her complaint and cannot be compelled to assert a claim that she chooses not to assert.

1) Partial exception—federal displacement of state law [§396]

The Supreme Court of the United States Constitution (making federal law the supreme law of the land) makes it possible for a state cause of action to be preempted by federal law. Ordinarily, preemption is a defense, and the possibility that federal law preempts a state law claim does not provide a basis for federal question jurisdiction. However, Congress may so completely preempt a particular area that any claim in that area is necessarily federal in character. This is *rare*; Congress has displaced state law in only a few statutory schemes. [*See, e.g.,* **Metropolitan Life Insurance Co. v. Taylor,** 481 U.S. 58 (1987)—state law "displaced" by Employee Retirement Security Act; *and see* **Avco Corp. v. Machinists,** 390 U.S. 557 (1968)—state law disputes between employers and employees displaced by §301 of Labor Management Relations Act] When Congress has so displaced state law in the area, a plaintiff may not—through artful pleading—elude federal jurisdiction by electing not to plead the federal claim because there is no other claim in the area. *The case may be removed on federal question grounds because the only possible claim in the area is federal.*

2) Distinguish—federal claim preclusion [§397]

If a federal court enters a final judgment on a federal claim, under the doctrine of claim preclusion (or res judicata—*see infra,* §§2183-2224) any related claim is barred. But this effect does not "displace" state law in the same manner as Congress has done in the statutory schemes mentioned above, and claim preclusion is an affirmative defense. Hence, if a plaintiff later files a state court suit asserting only a state-law claim based on the same events, that would usually be subject to res judicata, but that fact would not be a ground for removal. [**Rivet v. Regions Bank,** 522 U.S. 470 (1998)]

(4) Declaratory judgment cases [§398]

Congress has adopted the Declaratory Judgment Act [28 U.S.C. §2201] which allows parties to seek a declaration of rights rather than a specific remedy. The Supreme Court has held that when actions are filed under the act, jurisdiction does not depend on whether a federal question appears in the complaint seeking the declaratory judgment. Instead, the federal court should essentially pretend that the action is for a coercive remedy (*e.g.,* an injunction, specific performance, damages) and determine whether a hypothetical, well-pleaded complaint for the coercive remedy would have presented a federal question. [**Skelly Oil Co. v. Phillips Petroleum Co.,** 339 U.S. 667 (1950)] The rationale is that the Declaratory Judgment Act was not intended to expand federal court jurisdiction, and a well-pleaded complaint in a declaratory judgment action might contain a federal question, but that federal question would only be a defense in a coercive action.

Example: If in *Louisville & Nashville Railroad, supra,* the railroad had sued the Mottleys for declaratory relief, its complaint might have alleged that the Mottleys claimed a contract right to continue receiving free passes, but that an Act of Congress had invalidated such passes. Had this hypothetical suit been filed in federal court, the court should determine whether it had subject matter jurisdiction by asking whether it would have jurisdiction over a breach of contract action brought by the Mottleys. As we have already seen, the impact of the federal legislation would only be a defense in such a suit, and it therefore would not provide a basis for jurisdiction over the railroad's hypothetical declaratory relief action.

EXAM TIP **gilbert**

When answering an exam question, be sure to remember that in almost every case the plaintiff's *complaint is the only pleading that is considered* when determining whether federal question jurisdiction is present. If the federal question arises in the plaintiff's well-pleaded complaint, there is federal question jurisdiction. On the other hand, if the plaintiff artfully pleads a claim under state law so that no federal question appears in the complaint, there generally is no federal question jurisdiction; a defendant may not remove the action to federal court alleging a federal defense. The only *exception* to the general rule arises where the plaintiff has artfully pleaded a state law claim to avoid a federal question, and the defendant can show that federal law has completely displaced the state law claim.

(5) Supreme Court jurisdiction [§399]

The well-pleaded complaint rule does not apply to cases appealed from state courts to the United States Supreme Court. Thus, even though a lower federal court does not have subject matter jurisdiction to hear a case because the federal claim arises only as a defense, the Supreme Court may hear an appeal from a state court judgment entered in essentially the same case. [28 U.S.C. §1257; *and see* **Louisville & Nashville Railroad v. Mottley**, 219 U.S. 467 1911—Court reaches the Mottleys' federal arguments—that federal statute did not apply to them and that if it applied it unconstitutionally deprived them of property—on merits on appeal from state court judgment; *compare supra*, §393]

d. Plausible assertion of federal right sufficient [§400]

A federal claim or question is sufficient to vest the court with jurisdiction unless it "clearly appears to be immaterial or made solely for the purpose of obtaining jurisdiction, or where the claim is wholly insubstantial and frivolous." The litigant need not show that he will prevail on the merits of the claim; the federal claim need only be arguable. [**Bell v. Hood**, 327 U.S. 678 (1946)] *Rationale:* A court is not to delve too deeply into the merits of the federal claim at this point because the court is required to determine whether it has subject matter jurisdiction *before* it considers the merits. [**Steel Co. v. Citizens for Better Government**, *supra*, §287]

---

e.g. **Example:** In *Merrell Dow, supra*, §387, the Supreme Court accepted the parties' concession that the FDCA did not give rise to an implied federal claim and, therefore, provided no basis for exercise of federal question jurisdiction. Yet when other plaintiffs sued, contending that the FDCA gave rise to implied claims, those were held sufficient to support federal question jurisdiction: "Until this court or the Supreme Court holds that there is no implied private right of action under the FDCA, the opposite position cannot be deemed either frivolous or insubstantial." [*In re* **Bendectin Litigation**, 857 F.2d 290 (6th Cir. 1988)]

---

(1) Effect of dismissal on pleadings [§401]

Once the court has decided that a federal question is present, it has subject matter jurisdiction over the case. If the court later dismisses the case for failure to state a federal claim, the decision is on the merits. There are differences between the effect of a dismissal for lack of subject matter jurisdiction and dismissal for failure to state a claim.

(a) Res judicata [§402]

If the court dismisses for failure to state a federal claim, that decision on the merits acts as res judicata. (*See infra*, §2208 for discussion of res judicata.) A dismissal for lack of subject matter jurisdiction has no res judicata effect.

(b) Supplemental jurisdiction [§403]

If a court dismisses for lack of jurisdiction, it cannot hear any part of the case. However, if the court decides it has jurisdiction and then dismisses for failure to state a federal claim, it may exercise supplemental jurisdiction (*see* below) over related state law claims and retain the case. But, because state law claims should usually be dismissed as a matter of discretion if the federal claims are dismissed early in the action (*see infra*, §446), this possibility is rarely important.

e. No jurisdictional amount [§404]

Where the court's federal question jurisdiction is properly invoked, there is *no minimum amount in controversy requirement* (except in a few minor categories of cases).

D. Supplemental Jurisdiction

1. Introduction

a. Historical basis [§405]

From an early date, the Supreme Court recognized that federal question jurisdiction could not be limited to a decision of federal issues presented in a case. In 1824, the Court confirmed that a lower court exercising federal question jurisdiction could decide all issues in a case, not just the federal questions. [**Osborn v. Bank of the United States**, *supra*, §376] *Rationale:* The basis for this reasoning was that the federal courts had jurisdiction over "*a whole case*, as expressed by the constitution." As joinder of claims and parties relaxed, the concept of the scope of the "constitutional case" expanded to encompass claims based on state law and claims against additional parties.

b. Goal [§406]

The goal of supplemental jurisdiction is to *promote judicial economy and consistency of decision* by removing obstacles to having all related controversies decided in one proceeding. As the Supreme Court put it, "Under the [Federal] Rules [of Civil Procedure], the impulse is toward entertaining the broadest possible scope of action consistent with fairness to the parties." [**United Mine Workers v. Gibbs**, 383 U.S. 715 (1966)]

c. Effect—decision may be based on state law alone [§407]

Federal courts exercising federal question jurisdiction can rest a decision entirely on issues of state law, without reaching issues of federal law. Where federal constitutional issues are raised, this is often the preferable approach, because it is said that courts should try to avoid unnecessary decision of matters of constitutional law. [**Siler v. Louisville & Nashville Railroad**, 213 U.S. 175 (1909)]

2. Background of Supplemental Jurisdiction—Pendent and Ancillary Jurisdiction [§408]

Supplemental jurisdiction, provided by statute in 1990, must be understood against the background of the preexisting doctrines of pendent and ancillary jurisdiction, which had developed in court decisions over several decades. (*Note:* Instructors have different preferences concerning the attention to be devoted to these topics. Your instructor might not emphasize these preexisting doctrines. In that case, you may find it best to skip from this point to §424, where discussion of the supplemental jurisdiction statute begins.)

a. Ancillary jurisdiction [§409]

The doctrine of ancillary jurisdiction originated in cases where the federal court controlled property that was claimed by a litigant who was properly before the court. In such cases, ancillary jurisdiction allowed the court to entertain claims of others to the property even though the court had no independent basis for jurisdiction over those claims. [**Freeman v. Howe,** 65 U.S. 450 (1860)] Thereafter, the doctrine was expanded. Generally, ancillary jurisdiction involved assertion of a claim by a *party other than the plaintiff* that was related to the claim made by the plaintiff. The operation of ancillary jurisdiction is best understood from an examination of the various contexts in which it arose:

(1) Counterclaims [§410]

When a plaintiff brings a suit against a defendant, the defendant may file a counterclaim against the plaintiff. A counterclaim arising from the same transaction as the plaintiff's claim fell within the ancillary jurisdiction of the court. Note that under Federal Rule 13(a), such a counterclaim is compulsory, meaning that it would be barred by res judicata unless asserted. *Compare:* If a counterclaim did not arise from the same transaction as the plaintiff's claim (a "permissive counterclaim" under Fed. R. Civ. P. 13(b)), it was not within the court's ancillary jurisdiction and there had to be an independent basis for federal jurisdiction.

(2) Third-party practice—impleader [§411]

Federal Rule 14 permits the *defendant* to assert a claim against another person not originally a party (called a third-party defendant) to the action, seeking indemnity in whole or in part for the claim the plaintiff has asserted against the defendant. There was ancillary jurisdiction over the third-party claim.

(a) Distinguish—claim by plaintiff against third-party defendant [§412]

If the *plaintiff* asserted a claim against the third-party defendant in a diversity case, however, there had to be an *independent basis for federal jurisdiction over that claim.*

 Example: Plaintiff sued a power district for causing the death of her husband when a crane hit a high tension wire. The power district impleaded the operator of the crane and later obtained summary judgment against plaintiff's claim. Plaintiff amended her complaint to assert a claim against the operator of the crane, but there was no diversity between plaintiff and the third-party defendant. The Supreme Court held that there was no jurisdiction over plaintiff's claim against the third-party defendant. [**Owen Equipment & Erection Co. v. Kroger**, 437 U.S. 365 (1978)] *Rationale:* If ancillary jurisdiction were permitted in such cases, plaintiff could circumvent the requirement of complete diversity by suing only diverse potential defendants and waiting for them to implead other nondiverse, potentially responsible, parties.

(b) Contrast—claim by third-party defendant against plaintiff [§413]

A number of cases held that there is ancillary jurisdiction over a claim by the third-party defendant against the plaintiff. [*See, e.g.,* **Revere Copper & Brass, Inc. v. Aetna Casualty & Surety Co.**, 426 F.2d 709 (5th Cir. 1970)]

1) Compulsory counterclaim by plaintiff [§414]

If the third-party defendant filed a claim against the plaintiff, and the plaintiff had a counterclaim arising out of the same events from which the defendant's claim arose, the counterclaim would have been within the court's ancillary jurisdiction because it would be compulsory. (*See supra,* §410.)

(3) Cross-claims [§415]

Federal Rule 13(g) allows one defendant to assert a cross-claim against another defendant if it arises out of the transaction sued upon by the plaintiff. Because of the relation to the original claim filed by the plaintiff, there was ancillary jurisdiction over the cross-claim. [**LASA per L'Industria v. Alexander**, 414 F.2d 143 (6th Cir. 1969)]

(4) Intervention [§416]

Federal Rule 24 allows persons who claim an interest in the litigation to intervene and become either plaintiffs or defendants in the suit. When they could intervene *of right*—because the litigation would inevitably affect their rights or because the present parties would otherwise be subjected to the risk of inconsistent judgments (*see infra,* §§1090 *et seq.*)—it was ordinarily held that *ancillary jurisdiction* covered their participation.

(a) But note

When intervention was merely *permissive,* an independent jurisdictional basis was required.

(5) Necessary parties [§417]

Under Federal Rule 19, certain nonparties are considered "necessary parties" because their rights are implicated in the action or because the present parties run the risk of inconsistent or multiple liabilities if they are not joined. (*See infra,* §§1090 *et seq.*) As to such parties, an ***independent basis*** for jurisdiction was required. If there was no independent basis for jurisdiction, the court might have had to dismiss the case. [*See* Fed. R. Civ. P. 19(b)—enumerating factors that affect decision whether to dismiss when necessary party cannot be joined; *see infra,* §1048]

b. **Pendent jurisdiction [§418]**

Pendent jurisdiction developed in cases where the plaintiff had both federal and nonfederal claims against a nondiverse defendant arising from the same event. The court was said to have jurisdiction over the state law claims, which are "appended" to the federal claim. Thus, it referred to the assertion of ***nonfederal claims by the plaintiff*** that are related to the plaintiff's federal claim.

ANCILLARY AND PENDENT JURISDICTION COMPARED	gilbert
ANCILLARY JURISDICTION	**PENDENT JURISDICTION**
A party (usually the defendant) could assert a related claim against ***another*** defendant, the plaintiff, or a third party, even though the second claim was not itself within the court's jurisdiction.	A plaintiff with a jurisdictionally sufficient claim (usually a federal question) could join a related claim against the ***same*** defendant even though the second claim was not itself within the court's subject matter jurisdiction.

 Example: Plaintiff copyrighted a play, revised it, and submitted both versions to defendant for possible production. When defendant did not produce the play, plaintiff sued, claiming that defendant had stolen parts of both the copyrighted and uncopyrighted versions for use in a play produced by defendant. Plaintiff asserted a federal copyright claim and two state law claims of unfair competition, one for use of the copyrighted version and the other for use of the uncopyrighted version. The Supreme Court held that there was pendent jurisdiction over the unfair competition claim relating to the copyrighted version because it "results from the same acts which constitute the infringement and is inseparable therefrom." But in a narrow ruling the Court later rejected as "unnecessarily grudging," it also held that there was no jurisdiction over the unfair competition claim related to the uncopyrighted version because that claim was "independent of the claim of copyright infringement." [**Hurn v. Oursler,** 289 U.S. 238 (1933)]

 Example: Plaintiff claimed that defendant union violated federal labor laws and committed the state law tort of interference with contract by pressuring customers of plaintiff not to employ his services. Both federal and state claims arose from the same series of actions by defendant's agents. The federal court could grant plaintiff judgment on the state law claims even if it decided after trial that plaintiff had not established a violation of federal law. [**United Mine Workers v. Gibbs,** *supra,* §406]

---

(1) Pendent party jurisdiction [§419]

If plaintiff has a claim within original federal jurisdiction against D1 and a claim not within original federal jurisdiction arising out of the same event against D2, plaintiff might seek to "append" the claim against D2 to the claim against D1. Noting that "the addition of a completely new party would run counter to the well-established principle that federal courts, as opposed to state trial courts of general jurisdiction, are courts of limited jurisdiction" [**Aldinger v. Howard,** 427 U.S. 1 (1976)], the Supreme Court took a limited approach to pendent party jurisdiction.

(a) Diversity claim [§420]

The Supreme Court refused to allow a plaintiff to assert a claim against a nondiverse, third-party defendant because allowing this maneuver would enable plaintiffs to circumvent the complete-diversity requirement. [**Owen Equipment & Erection Co. v. Kroger,** *supra,* §412]

(b) Federal question claim [§421]

Even where there was exclusive federal jurisdiction over a federal claim against one defendant, the Supreme Court held that there could be no jurisdiction over a related, nonfederal claim against a nondiverse party because "a grant of jurisdiction over claims involving particular parties does not itself confer jurisdiction over additional claims by or against different parties." [**Finley v. United States,** 490 U.S. 545 (1989)]

(2) Class actions [§422]

Pendent jurisdiction over class actions was complicated. While the issue of diversity was determined only by looking to the named class representative (*see supra,* §330), the Supreme Court held that where a class action was brought under diversity jurisdiction, *each class member had to have a sufficient claim,* unless the claims were legally "joint." [**Zahn v. International Paper Co.,** 414 U.S. 291 (1973)]

(a) Distinguish—federal question class action

In a federal question class action, ordinarily there was no jurisdiction problem since the amount in controversy requirement would not apply and each class member would have a claim within the subject matter jurisdiction of the federal court.

c. Lack of statutory basis [§423]

In a 1989 decision regarding pendent party jurisdiction, the Supreme Court stressed that pendent and ancillary jurisdiction appeared to contravene the principle that:

> [a]s regards all courts of the United States inferior to this tribunal, two things are necessary to create jurisdiction, whether original or appellate. The Constitution must have given to the court the capacity to take it, and an act of Congress must have supplied it . . . . To the extent that such action is not taken, the power lies dormant.

[**Finley v. United States,** *supra*] Although *Finley* left existing pendent *claim* precedents undisturbed, it cast doubt on all extensions of ancillary jurisdiction to claims against added *parties* without express congressional authorization.

3. Supplemental Jurisdiction Statute [§424]

In 1990, largely to restore the law to its pre-*Finley* state, Congress enacted the supplemental jurisdiction statute. [28 U.S.C. §1367]

a. Jurisdictional power to limit of Constitution [§425]

The statute grants federal courts that have original jurisdiction over a claim supplemental jurisdiction over all other claims that form part of the same case or controversy under Article III of the Constitution. [28 U.S.C. §1367(a)] The focus of the constitutional inquiry is whether the claims sought to be added to those within federal jurisdiction are part of *one constitutional case.* [**United Mine Workers v. Gibbs,** *supra*, §418; *see also* §405]

(1) Standard for supplemental jurisdiction in federal question cases [§426]

In *United Mine Workers v. Gibbs, supra,* the Supreme Court articulated the following three-part test to determine whether a federal court has the power to entertain pendent claims:

(a) Substantial federal claim [§427]

The federal claim must be sufficiently substantial to support federal question jurisdiction. (*See supra,* §§400 *et seq.*)

(b) Common nucleus of operative fact [§428]

The federal and nonfederal claims must derive from a common nucleus of operative fact.

(c) One judicial proceeding [§429]

The federal and nonfederal claims must be such that the plaintiff "would ordinarily be expected to try them in one judicial proceeding."

(2) Diversity cases [§430]

The Supreme Court has suggested that the same test may apply to determine the outer constitutional limits of diversity jurisdiction. [**Owen Equipment & Erection Co. v. Kroger,** *supra,* §420]

(a) Note

Because only minimal diversity is required by the Constitution (*see supra,* §311), as long as one defendant is diverse from one plaintiff, there is no constitutional difficulty with exercise of jurisdiction over the whole case, including nondiverse parties.

(3) Pendent party jurisdiction [§431]

Section (a) of the supplemental jurisdiction statute explicitly grants supplemental jurisdiction over "claims that involve the joinder or intervention of additional parties."

(4) Time of decision [§432]

"The question of [constitutional] power will ordinarily be resolved on the pleadings." [**United Mine Workers v. Gibbs,** *supra*]

(5) Contrast to original jurisdiction statutes [§433]

Unlike the statutes granting federal question and diversity jurisdiction, which have been interpreted not to go to the constitutional limit (*see supra,* §§313, 380), subsection (a) of the supplemental jurisdiction statute *does go* to the maximum extent allowed by the Constitution.

(6) Mandatory exercise [§434]

It has been held that federal courts should exercise supplementary jurisdiction granted by 28 U.S.C. section 1367(a) unless a ground for declining jurisdiction exists under 28 U.S.C. section 1367(c) (*see infra,* §§443-447). [**Executive Software North America, Inc. v. District Court,** 24 F.3d 1545 (9th Cir. 1994)]

b. Exception for diversity cases [§435]

When federal subject matter jurisdiction is founded *solely on diversity of citizenship,* supplemental jurisdiction is limited. [28 U.S.C. §1367(b)] The legislative history indicates that this was done to implement the rationale of *Owen Equipment, supra.* This represents Congress's explicit adoption of the complete diversity requirement long ago adopted by the Supreme Court (*see supra,* §313).

(1) Claims by plaintiffs [§436]

In diversity-only cases, there is no supplemental jurisdiction over claims by *plaintiffs* against persons made parties under Rule 14 (impleader), Rule 19 (necessary party joinder), Rule 20 (permissive party joinder), or Rule 24 (intervention).

(2) Claims by parties joined as plaintiffs under Rule 19 or 24 [§437]

There is no supplemental jurisdiction over claims by persons *proposed to be joined* pursuant to Rule 19 or 24. *Note:* This effects a change. Formerly there was thought to be jurisdiction over claims by plaintiff intervenors of right (*see supra,* §416).

(a) Distinguish—Rule 20 joinder of plaintiffs [§438]

The supplemental jurisdiction statute makes no reference to claims by parties to be joined permissively pursuant to Rule 20, so such additional parties may be joined under the court's supplemental jurisdiction. [**Stromberg Metal Works, Inc. v. Press Mechanical, Inc.,** 77 F.3d 928 (7th Cir. 1996)—claim of co-plaintiff joined under Rule 20 came within supplemental jurisdiction, even though it did not satisfy jurisdictional amount, because lead plaintiff's claim satisfied jurisdictional minimum]

1) Criticism

Such a reading of the statute goes far toward abolishing the complete-diversity rule, and is contrary to the intent of *Owen Equipment, supra,* to preclude devices by which plaintiffs could evade the jurisdictional requirements of the diversity statute.

(b) Distinguish—class actions [§439]

The legislative history states that the statute is not intended to affect the requirement in most state law class actions that each class member satisfy the amount in controversy requirement. (*See supra,* §422.) However, since section 1367(b) nowhere limits the use of supplemental jurisdiction under Rule 23 (class actions), and such claims could constitutionally be appended to the jurisdictionally sufficient claims of other members, the statute might not preserve this rule. Lower courts are in disagreement, and the Supreme Court has failed to resolve this conflict. [*Compare* **Meritcare, Inc. v. St. Paul Mercury Insurance Co.,** 166 F.3d 214 (3d Cir. 1999)—section 1367 did not alter the requirement that each class member satisfy the amount in controversy requirement, *with* **Free v. Abbott Laboratories,** 51 F.3d 524 (5th Cir. 1995), *aff'd by an equally divided Court,* 529 U.S. 333 (2000)—section 1367(b) places no limitation on use of supplemental jurisdiction in class actions, so that class members need not satisfy amount in controversy requirement]

(c) Distinguish—compulsory counterclaims by plaintiff [§440]

Under prior law (*see supra,* §385), there would be ancillary jurisdiction over a compulsory counterclaim by plaintiff against a third-party defendant in a diversity case. [**Evra Corp. v. Swiss Bank Corp.,** 673 F.2d 951 (7th Cir.), *cert. denied,* 459 U.S. 1017 (1982)]

It is *unclear* whether this rule survives the supplemental jurisdiction statute's prohibition of jurisdiction over "claims by plaintiffs" against such parties, although the legislative history's expression of intent to preserve most prior case law suggests that this form of supplemental jurisdiction may survive.

(3) Inconsistent with jurisdictional requirements of section 1332 [§441]

The above limitations on supplemental jurisdiction apply only insofar as exercising jurisdiction "would be inconsistent with the jurisdictional requirements of section 1332." This may allow an argument that in some instances claims by plaintiffs against parties joined under Rules 14, 19, 20, or 24, and joinder of parties as plaintiffs under Rules 19 or 24 could be entertained.

e.g. Possible example: Pre-*Finley* case law allowing ancillary jurisdiction over plaintiff's compulsory counterclaim against a third-party defendant in a diversity case (*see supra*, §414) could support an argument that despite section 1367(b)'s apparent ban on supplemental jurisdiction over some types of claims by diversity plaintiffs, such jurisdiction over the counterclaim would be permissible because exercising it would not be "inconsistent with the jurisdictional requirements of section 1332."

c. Discretionary decline of jurisdiction [§442]

The statute explicitly authorizes district courts to decline jurisdiction in *certain circumstances* that largely implement discretionary factors identified in **United Mine Workers v. Gibbs**, *supra*, §§426-429). [28 U.S.C. §1367(c)]

(1) Grounds to decline [§443]

A federal court may decline to exercise supplemental jurisdiction, but only on the basis of one of the following four grounds. [**Executive Software North America, Inc. v. District Court**, *supra*, §434]

(a) Novel or complex issue of state law [§444]

If the law to be applied to the nonfederal claim is uncertain, the district court may decline to entertain that claim so that the parties can get a "surer-footed reading of applicable law" from a state court. [§1367(c)(1); **United Mine Workers v. Gibbs**, *supra*]

(b) Nonfederal claim substantially predominates [§445]

The federal court may conclude that the nonfederal claim is the real body of the case. [28 U.S.C. §1367(c)(2)] The court should not "tolerate a litigant's effort to impose upon it what is in effect only a state law case." [**United Mine Workers v. Gibbs**, *supra*]

(c) All original jurisdiction claims dismissed [§446]

If all claims over which the federal court had original jurisdiction are dismissed, the court may dismiss the nonfederal claims. [28 U.S.C. §1367(c)(3)] In deciding whether to do so, the court should consider the *amount of time invested in the case by the court.*

(d) Extraordinary circumstances [§447]

The federal court may also decline to exercise supplementary jurisdiction in extraordinary circumstances if there are *"other compelling reasons for declining jurisdiction."* [28 U.S.C. §1367(c)(4)]

1) Complication of case [§448]

In *United Mine Workers,* the Supreme Court said that complication of the case in federal court would justify refusal to entertain the nonfederal claims. It has been held that this ground for decline of jurisdiction was limited by the statute to instances in which the district court finds that "exceptional circumstances" exist in the case and that these provide "compelling reasons" for decline of jurisdiction. [**Executive Software North America, Inc. v. District Court**, *supra*]

(2) Distinguish—state law tied to questions of federal policy [§449]

When the state claim is closely tied to a question of federal policy, this link argues in favor of exercise of supplemental jurisdiction.

---

e.g. **Example:** When the allowable scope of the state law claim implicates the federal doctrine of preemption, it is desirable for the federal court to employ supplemental jurisdiction. [**United Mine Workers v. Gibbs**, *supra*]

---

cf. **Compare—preemption defense:** Preemption is usually an affirmative defense and therefore not a ground for exercise of original federal question jurisdiction under the well-pleaded complaint rule. (*See supra*, §396.)

---

(3) Timing of decision [§450]

The question whether to decline to exercise supplemental jurisdiction remains open throughout the case. However the longer the court waits, the more effort it puts into the case, and the effort invested by the court may be a reason to retain jurisdiction. Nevertheless, the court may decide, even after trial, not to entertain nonfederal claims.

d. Tolling of limitations [§451]

The limitations period for any claim asserted under supplemental jurisdiction, or any other claim in the same action voluntarily dismissed at the same time or later, is tolled while the claim is pending in federal court and for 30 days after the federal court dismisses it. [28 U.S.C. §1367(d)]

(1) Rationale

The rationale for the tolling is that a plaintiff should not be subjected to the risk that her claim will be barred by limitations if the federal court declines to exercise supplemental jurisdiction, or if the plaintiff is mistaken about whether the claim actually falls within supplemental jurisdiction.

(2) Voluntary dismissal of claim within original jurisdiction [§452]

If a claim asserted under supplemental jurisdiction is dismissed, the tolling provision will also apply to any claim that was properly within federal jurisdiction that plaintiff dismisses along with the supplemental claim. *Rationale:* If plaintiff prefers to combine all the claims in state court, limitations should not be an obstacle.

E. Removal

1. Introduction [§453]

Removal allows a defendant to shift a case from state court to federal court when the plaintiff has chosen to sue in state court. Although there is no mention of removal jurisdiction in the Constitution, some form of removal jurisdiction has existed since the federal court system was created by the first Congress in 1789.

2. Grounds for Removal [§454]

In general, if the plaintiff files an action in state court but *could originally have filed in federal court*, the defendant can remove the action to the federal court. [28 U.S.C. §1441(a)] Note that there are exceptions to this rule (*e.g.*, a defendant who is a citizen of the state in which the federal court is located cannot remove to state court).

a. Federal question [§455]

If the plaintiff's state court complaint raises a federal question, the defendant may remove.

(1) Federal defenses not considered [§456]

The *well-pleaded complaint rule* applies in the removal situation. Thus, the fact that the defendant has raised a federal defense to the plaintiff's state law claim is not sufficient to support removal. [**Oklahoma Tax Commission v. Graham**, 489 U.S. 838 (1989)]

(2) Federal counterclaim not considered [§457]

The fact that the defendant has interposed a counterclaim asserting a federal claim does not provide a basis for removal on federal question grounds.

(3) Plaintiff omits federal claim [§458]

If the plaintiff chooses not to assert a possible federal claim, the defendant may not remove the case by citing the unasserted claim.

(a) Amendment to assert federal claim [§459]

If after filing in state court, the plaintiff amends his complaint to assert a federal claim, the defendant *can then remove the case*. Note that if the plaintiff does not amend his complaint, res judicata may bar assertion of the federal claim in a later action.

(b) Exception—complete preemption [§460]

If federal law completely preempts state law on the matter and converts the plaintiff's claim into one of federal law, that satisfies the well-pleaded complaint requirement and makes the case removable. [**Metropolitan Life Insurance Co. v. Taylor,** *supra*, §396]

(4) Effect of supplemental jurisdiction statute [§461]

The Supreme Court has stated that the supplemental jurisdiction statute [28 U.S.C. §1367] "applies with equal force to cases removed to federal court as to cases initially filed there." [**City of Chicago v. International College of Surgeons,** *supra*, §387] Under the supplemental jurisdiction statute, any case in which a federal claim is asserted in state court should be removable even though it includes defendants against whom only state law claims are asserted, as long as the claims against these defendants form part of the same federal constitutional "case."

(5) Effect of Eleventh Amendment immunity [§462]

If a state is a defendant and joins in removing a federal question case that includes claims barred by the Eleventh Amendment (which limits federal court jurisdiction over many private claims against state governments—*see* Federal Courts Summary), the federal court may not hear the barred claims, but it still has jurisdiction over the remaining claims against the nonstate parties. [**Wisconsin Department of Corrections v. Schacht,** 524 U.S. 381 (1998)]

b. Diversity of citizenship [§463]

If the plaintiff could have filed the action in federal court using diversity of citizenship jurisdiction, the defendant may remove the case to federal court. Note that the *complete diversity* requirement applies in this situation.

(1) Local defendant [§464]

However, such removal is not permitted if any defendant is a citizen of the state in which the action is brought. [28 U.S.C. §1441(b)] *Rationale:*

Since diversity jurisdiction is designed to protect against local prejudice, there is no reason to invoke it on behalf of a local party. *Compare:* A local plaintiff can file an action in federal court invoking diversity jurisdiction.

(2) Fictitious defendants [§465]

If the plaintiff has named fictitious "John Doe" defendants in the complaint, they are disregarded for purposes of determining whether there is complete diversity in cases that are removed from state to federal court. [28 U.S.C. §1441(a)] Note that the effect of naming a "John Doe" defendant in a case originally filed in federal court is uncertain. (*See supra,* §332.)

(3) Fraudulent joinder [§466]

To prevent the defendant from removing the case to federal court, a plaintiff might join a defendant who is a resident of the state the plaintiff lives in or who otherwise would destroy diversity jurisdiction. If the plaintiff joins such a defendant and there really is no basis for the claim against that nondiverse party, the presence of that defendant will not defeat removal.

(4) Jurisdictional amount [§467]

The jurisdictional amount requirement applies to cases removed on grounds of diversity. (*See supra,* §§351 *et seq.*) It has been held that the plaintiff can prevent removal by suing in state court for less than the jurisdictional amount, even though the claim could be for a larger sum. [**Hick v. Universal Housing,** 792 F. Supp. 482 (S.D. W. Va. 1992)]

c. Separate and independent federal claim [§468]

A defendant sued on a "separate and independent claim or cause of action" within *federal question jurisdiction* may remove, even if the plaintiff has joined nonremovable claims. [28 U.S.C. §1441(c)] For example, a defendant sued for breach of contract and an unrelated violation of federal antidiscrimination laws can remove the case to federal court. *Rationale:* Such removal protects the defendant's right of removal of a federal claim so that the plaintiff cannot prevent removal by joining a wholly unrelated claim.

(1) Entire action removed [§469]

Where the separate and independent claim requirement is satisfied, the court may retain jurisdiction over otherwise nonremovable claims or remand them to state court.

(a) Criticism

The retention of claims not otherwise within federal jurisdiction is anomalous. The court should retain jurisdiction over state claims only if the interests of efficiency dictate (*i.e.,* where the claims are part of one constitutional case). Here, the case qualifies for removal precisely because the federal claim and state law claim are unrelated, "separate and independent" claims.

(2) Limitation to federal question claims [§470]

Prior to 1990, section 1441(c) allowed removal of separate and independent claims in diversity cases as well as in federal question cases. But the Supreme Court narrowly construed the power to remove such diversity cases. [*See, e.g.,* **American Fire & Casualty Co. v. Finn**, *supra*, §284] Most cases removed on diversity grounds involved state law claims against some diverse and some nondiverse defendants. But few claims qualified for removal because state procedural rules typically allowed joinder of parties only if there was some relationship between the claims asserted, thus making the presence of a separate and independent claim unlikely. In 1990, Congress amended section 1441(c) to limit removal of cases with separate and independent claims to those involving a federal question.

(a) Possible constitutional problems [§471]

Recall that the federal courts are courts of limited jurisdiction. Because they have jurisdiction over "cases" (and not merely "issues"), they can hear claims related to a case that otherwise would be outside the court's jurisdiction, but they may not hear unrelated claims absent a jurisdictional ground. (*See supra,* §405.) Recall also that the supplemental jurisdiction statute [28 U.S.C. §1367] gives the federal courts power to hear all claims that form part of the same case or controversy. (*See supra,* §§425-429.) Such claims would seemingly be removable under sections (a) and (b) of the removal statute. Thus, section (c) either has no useful function or it purports to expand federal court jurisdiction beyond what is constitutionally permissible.

(b) Power to remand matters as to which state law predominates [§472]

The district court has discretion to remand all "matters in which state law predominates." Whether this gives the district court power to remand the federal claim as well is unsettled. [*Compare* **Eastus v. Bell Creameries, L.P.**, 97 F.3d 100 (4th Cir. 1996)—asserting that courts have "overwhelmingly" held that remand of the entire action is allowed, *with* **In re City of Mobile**, 75 F.3d 605 (11th Cir. 1996)—there is no authority to remand a properly removed federal claim, *and* **Borough of West Mifflin v. Lancaster**, 45 F.3d 780 (3d Cir. 1995)—discretion to remand under §1441(c) applies only to claims based on state law]

d. Special removal statutes [§473]

In certain cases, special removal statutes apply. For example, when a state court defendant in a civil or criminal case cannot adequately protect her *federal civil rights regarding racial equality* in state court, she may remove to federal court. [28 U.S.C. §1443] Also, suits against *federal officers* sued for *acts performed under color of office* are removable. [28 U.S.C. §1442]

e. Removal forbidden in employment injury cases [§474]

Suits brought in state court against a railroad under the *Federal Employers' Liability Act* ("FELA") or under state *workers' compensation laws* are not removable. [28 U.S.C. §1445] The rationale for this limitation is to allow injured workers to pick the court in which they wish to have their claims decided.

3. Procedure for Removal [§475]

A defendant seeking removal must file a notice setting forth the facts supporting removal in the federal district court and division within which the action is pending. A copy of the notice should be sent to the other parties and to the state court.

a. Only defendant can remove [§476]

Only the defendant has the power to seek removal. Even if the defendant asserts a federal claim as a counterclaim, the plaintiff may not remove. [**Shamrock Oil Co. v. Sheets,** 313 U.S. 100 (1941)]

b. All defendants must join [§477]

All defendants who have been served with process must join in the notice of removal. [**Chicago, Rock Island & Pacific Railway v. Martin,** 178 U.S. 245 (1900)] However, when the ground for removal is a *separate and independent claim*, only the defendant against whom this claim is asserted need seek the removal.

c. Timing [§478]

The notice of removal must be filed within 30 days after the time the case becomes removable. If the action is removable as filed, the 30 days begin running from the time process is served on the defendant. If the action becomes removable only due to some later development (*e.g.,* amendment to add a federal claim to the complaint, or dismissal of nondiverse defendants), the 30 days begin running from that point. However, removal on grounds of diversity is not allowed more than one year after the commencement of the action. [28 U.S.C. §1446(b)]

(1) Service of process required to trigger running of time limit for removal [§479]

Section 1446(b) says that the time to remove starts when defendant receives a copy of the complaint "through service *or otherwise.*" However, the Supreme Court has held that the 30 days do not begin to run until the defendant is *formally* served. [**Murphy Brothers, Inc. v. Michetti Pipe Stringing, Inc.,** 526 U.S. 344 (1999)]

(2) Grounds for removal obscured on complaint [§480]

In some situations, the lower courts have found that the time for removal does not start running until defendant learns more about the claim so as to be able to determine that it is removable. [*See* **Lovern v. General Motors Corp.,** 121 F.3d 160 (4th Cir. 1997)—citizenship of plaintiff not known until discovery obtained; *and see* **Huffman v. Saul Holdings, Ltd.,** 194 F.3d 1072 (10th Cir. 1999)—time to remove did not start running until deposition testimony showed that claim exceeded jurisdictional minimum]

d. Effect of removal [§481]

The case is considered to be removed as soon as the notice of removal is filed and served. After that, the state court may take no further action on the case. The remedy for improper removal is to seek a *remand* to state court. (*See infra,* §§483-489.)

e. State court lack of subject matter jurisdiction [§482]

The federal court has jurisdiction over an otherwise properly removed action even if the state court lacked jurisdiction over the claim. [28 U.S.C. §1441(e)]

Example: Plaintiff sues defendant in state court for violation of federal antitrust laws, a claim over which there is exclusive federal jurisdiction. Defendant may remove to federal court.

SUMMARY OF REMOVAL ISSUES — gilbert

THE KEY REMOVAL ISSUES ARE:

☑ A federal court *must have jurisdiction* over the case; jurisdiction need not have been proper in the state court.

☑ Removal is to the federal district court whose *territory encompasses the state court*.

☑ *Only defendants* can remove; *all* defendants must join in the removal.

☑ A case may *not be removed on diversity grounds* if any defendant is a citizen of the forum state.

☑ *Notice of removal* must be filed within 30 days of the date defendant receives a copy of the initial pleading unless the case becomes removable later (as by dismissal of a nondiverse defendant), in which case the case may be removed within 30 days of the date it becomes removable, but a case removable on diversity grounds may be removed only within one year after it was brought in state court.

☑ If the case contains a *separate and independent claim based on a federal question*, defendant may remove the whole case.

4. Remand

a. Improper removal [§483]

If the case was improperly removed, the federal court should remand it to state court. [28 U.S.C. §1447(c)] Remand is required whenever the court determines that removal was improper, unless final judgment has been entered.

(1) Jurisdictional defect cured before final judgment entered [§484]

If there was a jurisdictional defect at the time of removal, so that the case should have been remanded but was not, and the defect is cured before final judgment is entered, interests of finality, efficiency, and economy justify disregarding that defect on appellate review even if the plaintiff timely moved to remand and the district court erroneously denied that motion. [**Caterpillar, Inc. v. Lewis**, 519 U.S. 61 (1996)—nondiverse defendant dismissed after motion to remand was denied but before trial]

(2) Time limit for motion to remand on ground other than lack of subject matter jurisdiction [§485]

If the ground for the motion to remand is something other than lack of subject matter jurisdiction (*e.g.*, a defect in removal procedure), the motion must be made *within 30 days* after the notice of removal is filed. [28 U.S.C. §1447(c)]

b. Supplemental claims after dismissal of federal claims [§486]

When a court would otherwise dismiss the supplemental claims after disposing of the federal claims (*see supra*, §446), it may instead remand them to state court. [**Carnegie-Mellon University v. Cohill**, 484 U.S. 343 (1988)]

c. Other grounds for remand [§487]

The Supreme Court has indicated that remand is *usually not allowed where a case was properly removed*. [**Thermtron Products, Inc. v. Hermansdorfer**, 423 U.S. 336 (1976)—remand improper when based on expectation that there would be greater delay in obtaining a trial date in federal court than in state court]

(1) Distinguish—addition of nondiverse defendants [§488]

In 1988, Congress added 28 U.S.C. section 1447(e), providing that if the plaintiff seeks to *add additional defendants* whose addition would destroy subject matter jurisdiction, the court may *permit joinder and remand*.

d. Appellate review [§489]

An order remanding a case to state court *on grounds of lack of subject matter jurisdiction or a defect in removal procedure* is "not reviewable on appeal or otherwise." [28 U.S.C. §1447(d)] [**Things Remembered, Inc. v. Petrarca**, 516

U.S. 124 (1996)] However, this prohibition is not as unqualified as it seems. The Supreme Court has upheld *review via mandamus* (a writ procedure seeking an order from a superior court to an inferior court to perform some act) when a district court openly remanded on a ground not authorized by the statute. [**Thermtron Products, Inc. v. Hermansdorfer,** *supra*] In addition, the Supreme Court has upheld review of a remand order based on "abstention" principles under the *collateral order doctrine*. [**Quackenbush v. Allstate Insurance Co.,** 517 U.S. 706 (1996); *see infra*, §§2020-2133; for a discussion of abstention, *see* Federal Courts Summary]

(1) Distinguish—remand motion erroneously denied

If a motion to remand is erroneously denied, the plaintiff need not attempt to obtain interlocutory review to preserve the error for review after final judgment, although denial of the motion to remand will not justify reversal if the jurisdictional defect is cured before entry of final judgment. [**Caterpillar, Inc. v. Lewis,** *supra*, §484]

5. No "Reverse" Removal [§490]

There is presently no method by which a defendant can remove a case originally filed in federal court to state court.

a. Distinguish—abstention [§491]

Federal courts may, however, decline to proceed in certain situations where "abstention" is proper. This may be due to the presence of an uncertain issue of state law pertinent to a federal constitutional claim, or due to deference to litigation already pending in state court. (For details on abstention, *see* Federal Courts Summary.)

Chapter Three:
Relation Between State and Federal Law

CONTENTS

Chapter Approach

Chapter Approach

1. ### *Erie* Doctrine

    In a number of situations and for certain issues, the federal courts are required to apply state rather than federal law. Determining whether to apply state or federal law is known as an *Erie* problem.

    "Erie" problems are a favorite source of examination questions. They usually arise in diversity cases, but can arise in others (*e.g.*, supplemental state claims in federal question cases are analyzed similarly). In very general terms, in state law matters in the federal courts, **state substantive** and **federal procedural law** are followed. However, determining which law to apply is often more complex; the role and definition of the concepts of "substance" and "procedure" vary in different contexts. When either state or federal law might apply, it can help to approach the problem in two stages.

    a. **First,** ask whether there is a *"true conflict"*—are there both federal and state rules of law that purport to apply and cannot be harmonized? There is no true conflict if a federal rule or practice does not exist and state law is of a substantive nature, or the federal and state rules—while related—do not speak to exactly the same point, or the two rules agree. In such cases, no choice of one or the other is necessary.

    b. **Second,** if—but only if—there is a "true conflict," look to the **source** of the potentially applicable **federal** rule of law; the test for the federal rule's validity and governing force varies depending on whether it derives from the Constitution, a statute enacted by Congress, a court rule promulgated under the Rules Enabling Act, or purely from decisional law (as opposed to interpretation of the Constitution, an Act of Congress, or a Federal Rule).

        (1) Is the federal rule of law grounded in the **Constitution** itself (*e.g.*, the Seventh Amendment guarantee of jury trial in actions at law in the federal courts)? If so, the **federal rule governs**, period, without regard to the source, importance, or substantive nature of any contrary state rule.

        (2) Is the federal rule of law found in an Act of Congress (*e.g.*, a federal statute providing for nationwide service of process)? If so, **it governs** as long as it is constitutional—*i.e.*, (i) it falls within the broad powers of Congress (which include regulation of procedure and "arguably procedural" matters in the federal courts) and (ii) it does not violate any independent federal constitutional right.

        (3) Is the federal rule of law a **Federal Rule of Civil Procedure** (or Evidence or Appellate Procedure)? If so, the Rules Enabling Act [28 U.S.C. §2072]

provides the principal test for its validity: It must be "arguably procedural," dealing with practice, procedure, or evidence, **and** must not "abridge, enlarge or modify any substantive right." If it passes these tests (and is constitutional, which is practically certain if it satisfies the standards of section 2072), the *federal rule governs*.

(4) Is the federal rule of law *judge-made* (*e.g.*, the equitable doctrine of laches)? If so, it *should not govern* in federal court if it fails the "twin-aims" test of *Erie*, as stated in *Hanna v. Plumer*:

> *If* the federal courts do *not* follow the state rule, will it encourage forum shopping between state and federal courts and inequitable administration of the laws by providing different, and possibly outcome-affecting, regimes of applicable law?

Certain "judge-made law" cases involve an "essential characteristic" of the federal court system, such as relations among the jury, trial judge, and appellate court. In such cases, it might be necessary to balance state interests against those served by a decisional federal rule, or to see whether the state and federal interests both can be accommodated.

2. Federal Common Law

Some civil procedure courses will also include coverage of "federal common law." Although in *Erie* the Supreme Court stated that "there is no federal *general* common law" (emphasis added), in several areas of special federal authority or interest, the federal courts may develop federal common law by borrowing or even preempting state law. You may need to ask whether a case involves: (i) a need to borrow state law (such as a statute of limitations for a federal claim when Congress has enacted none); (ii) an express or implied authorization from Congress for the federal courts to develop federal common law; or (iii) a federal interest significant enough to call for uniform federal decisional law.

A. State Law in the Federal Courts

1. Rules of Decision Act [§492]

The starting point for the applicability of state law in the federal courts is the Rules of Decision Act [28 U.S.C. §1652], originally adopted in 1789. In its present form the Act provides, "The laws of the several states, except where the Constitution or treaties of the United States or Acts of Congress otherwise require or provide, shall be regarded as rules of decision in civil actions in the courts of the United States, in cases where they apply."

2. Former Rule—*Swift v. Tyson* [§493]

For almost a century, the prevailing interpretation of the reference to state "laws" in the Rules of Decision Act was that it did not include state common law of a general, as opposed to local, nature. Thus, the federal courts could and did follow their own view of what the "general" common law was or should be. [**Swift v. Tyson,** 41 U.S. (16 Pet.) 1 (1842)] The federal courts' decisions on this "general" common law, however, were not binding precedent on the courts of the states; consequently, different rules of law could apply to the same transaction, depending on whether litigation took place in state or federal court.

a. Note

Even under *Swift*, federal courts *were* bound by applicable state *statutes* (as long as they were constitutional) and *"local" common law* (*e.g.,* state common law regarding rights in real property within the states).

3. Difficulties of *Swift* Regime [§494]

The approach taken in *Swift* became vulnerable for several reasons.

a. Changing attitudes toward law [§495]

Swift appeared to rest in part on a view that a "true" common law existed and could be "found" by the courts. However, many legal authorities moved away from this view and accepted the idea that each state could have its own internally authoritative common law, and that variations among states on the same point did not mean that some had to be "wrong."

b. Failure to achieve uniformity [§496]

Swift also became vulnerable because it failed to help develop a uniform common law, due to the disagreement of many state courts with the "general" common law established by the federal courts. Thus, *Swift* came to be seen as allowing the federal courts to add one more regime of common law rather than taking part in the development of one "true" set of common law doctrines.

c. Practical difficulties and unfairness [§497]

Swift led to forum shopping. Because the federal courts often applied common law rules different from the law of the states in which they sat, litigants could manipulate federal jurisdiction to gain favorable substantive law. That is unfair since parties who are similarly situated except for litigating in different court systems within the same state can be governed by different substantive rules. This undermines the ends of state common law rules and complicates private planning, because parties cannot be sure what law will govern their affairs.

---

e.g. **Example—*Black & White Taxicab Co.*:** The height of such manipulation came in **Black & White Taxicab Co. v. Brown & Yellow Taxicab Co.,** 276

U.S. 518 (1928), in which the plaintiff avoided a state common law anti-monopoly rule by reincorporating in another state and then bringing a diversity action in federal court, which followed a different rule under which the challenged exclusive-dealing agreement was lawful.

d. Doubts about *Swift* interpretation [§498]

Swift also came into doubt because historical research on the adoption of the original Rules of Decision Act questioned whether the drafters had intended to exclude "general" common law from the term "laws of the several states" (*see supra,* §§492-493). [Warren, *New Light on the History of the Federal Judiciary Act of 1789,* 37 Harv. L. Rev. 49 (1923)]

e. Views on the constitutional scope of federal power [§499]

Finally, there seemed to be no constitutional basis for the federal courts' law-making authority that existed under *Swift*. The decision appeared to presume a *general* law-making power in the federal courts of a sort that the Constitution does not grant to Congress, and which Congress had not attempted to confer on the federal courts. (*See infra,* §508.)

4. Overruling of *Swift* by *Erie* [§500]

The combination of the above problems contributed to the overruling of *Swift* in **Erie Railroad v. Tompkins,** 304 U.S. 64 (1938). *Erie* held that in the absence of an Act of Congress providing governing law, a federal court should follow applicable state common law principles rather than developing and applying its own "general" common law. At issue was the liability of a railroad for injury to a person who was struck by an object protruding from a passing train. Today the issue of what substantive law governs in cases like *Erie* itself is often simple, but the decision made broad changes whose ramifications are still being worked out in the federal courts today.

a. Reasoning of *Erie* [§501]

Erie clearly identified three distinct rationales for the decision.

(1) Statutory interpretation [§502]

The Court accepted the argument that the language of the Rules of Decision Act was not intended to exclude all state "general" common law. (*See supra,* §498.) Instead, the term "laws of the several states" includes state common law, general and local, as well as "positive" law like state constitutions, statutes, regulations, and ordinances.

(2) Lack of uniformity and resulting discrimination [§503]

The *Erie* majority also noted the persistence of differing views on common law questions between the state and federal courts, and the possibility this created for discrimination among litigants depending on the forum in which the case was tried.

(a) Note—"equal protection" red herring [§504]

In this *nonconstitutional* portion of its opinion, the Court stated that the *Swift* doctrine had rendered impossible the "equal protection of the law." This misleading phrasing often makes students think that *Erie* rests on the Equal Protection Clause of the Fourteenth Amendment. This cannot be true because *Swift* was a *federal* law ruling; the Equal Protection Clause speaks to the *states*, and had not yet been held applicable to the federal government at the time *Erie* was decided. Instead, the term "equal protection" here must refer to the serious, but nonconstitutional, problems of nonuniformity in administration of state law and unfairly disparate treatment of litigants depending on whether a case is in state or federal court.

(b) "Discrimination by noncitizens against citizens" [§505]

In this second part of the opinion, the *Erie* majority also said that *Swift* had "introduced grave discrimination by noncitizens against citizens," a concept repeated in some later opinions in the *Erie* line of cases. The reference is to the ability that an out-of-state party often has to control the choice of forum—federal or state—in diversity litigation (*e.g.,* out-of-state plaintiff may decide to sue in defendant's home state court, in which case defendant cannot remove to federal court [28 U.S.C. §1441(b); *see supra,* §464]; out-of-state defendant often—but not always—can effect removal to federal court if sued in state court; *see supra,* §§453 *et seq.*). Regardless of who controls the forum choice, discrimination among litigants depending on the forum and what law it may apply remains a concern.

(3) Unconstitutionality of *Swift* interpretation [§506]

Whatever the persuasiveness of the above two points (erroneous statutory interpretation and resulting discrimination), the Court in *Erie* stated that it would not have been prepared to abandon the long-established *Swift* doctrine were it not convinced of *Swift's* unconstitutionality.

(a) Holding, not dictum [§507]

Because the Court explicitly said that the constitutional ground was essential to the result in *Erie*, the constitutional portion of the opinion—despite some questioning—qualifies as *holding* rather than dictum.

(b) Basis of unconstitutionality [§508]

The Court did not clearly explain why the *Swift* interpretation of the Rules of Decision Act was unconstitutional. It did not find that *Swift* violated any specific clause, but rather noted the *absence* of any clause in the Constitution purporting to confer upon either Congress or the federal courts a general "power to declare substantive rules of common law applicable in a state." The Court explained that the Constitution preserves the autonomy of the states, and supplanting their law with federal law is permissible only pursuant to powers specifically granted to the federal government by the Constitution.

1) Note—Tenth Amendment alone not basis of *Erie* [§509]

The Tenth Amendment's reservation of undelegated powers to the states or the people reinforces this argument, but by itself does not establish the unconstitutionality of *Swift*. The *Swift* interpretation probably would be unconstitutional under modern views even if there were no Tenth Amendment, because the interpretation presumes a *general* law-making power that has not been granted to the federal government.

2) Commerce power a possible basis? [§510]

Because the accident giving rise to the *Erie* litigation involved an interstate railroad, students sometimes wonder whether *Erie* did not overlook a possible basis for federal law in the commerce power. The Constitution does grant Congress pervasive power over interstate commerce. Pursuant to this power, Congress *could have* provided for substantive tort law to govern accidents involving interstate commerce or, perhaps, it could have authorized the federal courts to develop applicable common law in the area. However, Congress *had not done so* (and still has not). Thus, the Court had to examine whether the federal courts had the power to create a "general" federal common law. It concluded that they did not, leaving state law the only law that could govern without congressional legislation.

b. *Erie* as part of a revolution in federal court practice [§511]

Erie coincided with the adoption of the Federal Rules of Civil Procedure, before which federal courts had largely followed the procedural rules of the state courts in which they sat. Thus in the same year, the federal courts moved sharply in opposite directions: (i) under *Erie* toward *more application of state substantive law* rather than "general" common law and (ii) under the Federal Rules toward *uniform federal procedural law* in place of diverse local practice. The approach to deciding when to apply federal "procedural" law in diversity cases, however, remained problematic for some time.

c. Principal cases developing *Erie* [§512]

Erie solved many old problems but opened up new ones, especially in cases in which the competing federal and state rules that might apply were in the borderland between substance and procedure. The Supreme Court has repeatedly said that in matters in the federal courts arising under state law, the *general guideline* is that *state substantive law* and *federal procedural law* govern. However, the distinction between substance and procedure is not always clear, unvarying, or mechanical; the role and definition of these concepts vary depending on the context. Major cases in the first decades after *Erie* dealt in differing ways with these problems; two of them—*York* and *Byrd, infra*—often receive great emphasis in teaching, but are of limited practical significance today.

(1) *Guaranty Trust Co. v. York* [§513]

Guaranty Trust Co. v. York, 326 U.S. 99 (1945), on somewhat complicated facts, presented the question whether a state statute of limitations or the more flexible federal decisional rule of "laches"—which asks whether delay has been excessive and caused the other side prejudice—should determine the timeliness of an equitable state law claim filed in federal court.

(a) Specific holding [§514]

The Court ruled that the New York statute of limitations governed, rather than the federal laches doctrine. This makes sense because statutes of limitations, although partly reflecting procedural concerns about courts' ability to deal with "stale" claims, also have strong substantive overtones in that they provide for "repose"—when the time to sue has passed, people can stop worrying about being sued, close their books on past transactions, make plans unaffected by the possibility of litigation, and get on with their lives and businesses.

1) Note

Regardless of the fluctuations in the *Erie* doctrine since *York*, this holding—treating state statutes of limitations as "substantive" for *Erie* purposes—still stands.

(b) "Outcome determination" test [§515]

In explaining the *York* ruling, the Court articulated what came to be a major test for whether state law should be regarded as substantive for *Erie* purposes: Will application of federal law instead of the state law significantly affect the outcome of the litigation?

1) Difficulties of the test [§516]

It is hard to know where to stop in applying the *York* test. If applied broadly, almost any procedural rule could qualify as substantive because (especially if disobeyed) it could affect the outcome of a case. In fact, some cases applying the test appeared to raise doubts about whether many Federal Rules of Civil Procedure could govern when state law differed, but the Supreme Court has subsequently drawn back from the most far-reaching readings of *York*.

2) Possible overreading of test [§517]

It seems doubtful that the "outcome determination" test should have been read with such a vengeance, for it was contrasted with whether a state rule "concerns merely the manner or means" by which a right to recover is enforced (*i.e.*, even under *York*, if a state rule concerned only the manner or means of enforcement, federal law could govern). The opinion also pointed out that the concern was to avoid providing litigants with a second, conflicting body of law. This "dual-regime" concern remains valid and is often a useful tool for discerning whether a serious *Erie* problem exists.

(2) *Byrd* and the "interest balancing" approach [§518]

In **Byrd v. Blue Ridge Electric Cooperative, Inc.,** 356 U.S. 525 (1958), the Court appeared to signal another departure by at least demoting the "outcome determination" factor to one among several—to be balanced along with federal and state interests in the rules that could be applied. This came to be known as an "interest balancing" approach to *Erie* problems.

(a) Specific holding [§519]

Byrd was a federal diversity case. The issue was whether federal or state law should govern the manner of determining an ancillary state law issue (the status of an outside contractor's employee under a workers' compensation law). Under state practice, the judge determined status; in federal court, such issues went to the jury. The Court held in favor of the federal rule.

1) Note

A federal court would probably reach the same result today (if *Byrd* arose as a case of first impression) by application of the Seventh Amendment jury trial right as it is now interpreted. At the time, though, the Court did not treat the result as required by the Seventh Amendment.

(b) "Balancing" approach [§520]

Byrd discusses three main types of factors that could bear on the choice between the state and federal rules.

1) **Relation between state rule in question and underlying state right [§521]**

   The Court first asked whether the state practice was "bound up with" the underlying state law rights and obligations being enforced, and concluded that it was not. The aim of this inquiry seems to have been to determine whether the *state procedural practice was an integral part of the state substantive right*, or if the state system followed it for some independent reason that might relate more to state court internal housekeeping and, therefore, have less call to be followed in federal court.

---

   cf. Compare—malpractice screening panels: Several federal courts have followed state law requirements for screening panels in medical malpractice suits, on the theory that the procedural mechanism was adopted for purposes related to the legislature's views on the enforcement of the underlying tort claims themselves. [*See, e.g.,* **DiAntonio v. Northampton-Accomack General Hospital,** 628 F.2d 287 (4th Cir. 1980)]

---

2) **Countervailing interests of the federal judicial system [§522]**

   The *Byrd* Court also looked to the strength of the federal policy involved—*i.e.,* the relationship between judge and jury in federal court—and the danger that following the state rule would disrupt that policy. The federal interests relevant to this inquiry fall into a narrow range; they do not pertain to the substance of the law, but rather involve the federal courts' interest in their own smooth functioning and in the uniformity and coherence of the decisional principles they have evolved to govern their procedures.

3) **Likelihood of effect on outcome [§523]**

   Finally, the Court looked to the *York* "outcome determination" test and decided that following the federal practice would not likely have an effect on the outcome of the suit.

(c) **Views on "balancing" approach [§524]**

   Byrd drew praise for recognizing the relevance of federal as well as state concerns, for bringing to the surface factors bearing on choices between state and federal law in a complex system, and for reducing the threat that the Federal Rules of Civil Procedure would so often have to yield to state rules as to produce a patchwork and undermine the uniformity sought and achieved by adoption of the Rules. However, *Byrd* suffers from the common difficulties of multifactor balancing approaches: It has the apples-and-oranges problem, for it is hard to find a scale on which to balance state and federal interests of different types, and inconsistency in application can often result.

(d) Status of *Byrd* test [§525]

For many years, starting with *Hanna v. Plumer* (discussed below), the Supreme Court virtually ignored *Byrd* and emphasized other approaches set out in *Hanna* and applied in later cases. However, the Court never disavowed or overruled *Byrd*, thus leaving doubt as to whether that case remained good law in any respect. In 1996, the Court revived *Byrd* to a limited extent, invoking it when the possibly applicable federal rule of law was purely decisional *and* might involve an "essential characteristic" of the federal court system (*e.g.*, some aspects of the relationship among the jury, trial judge, and appellate court). [**Gasperini v. Center for Humanities, Inc.,** 518 U.S. 415 (1996)] In *Gasperini*, a diversity defendant appealed a jury award, claiming that it was excessive. Had the case been in state court, appellate review would have been de novo and the court would apply the state standard for excessiveness, which looked to whether the verdict departs materially from what would be reasonable compensation. Federal appellate courts, by contrast, apply the deferential abuse-of-discretion standard when reviewing federal trial courts' rulings on such matters. The Supreme Court held that the state interest in application of its substantive standard, and the federal interest in the relationship between federal trial and appellate courts, could be accommodated by having the federal trial court apply the state's "departs materially" standard, with federal appellate review of the district court's resulting ruling being for abuse of discretion only.

5. Approach Under *Hanna v. Plumer* [§526]

Until 1965, the Supreme Court treated many federal vs. state law problems as subject to a general *Erie* approach, as developed through *York* and *Byrd*. However, when Federal Rules of Civil Procedure arguably conflicted with the law that would apply in state courts, a parallel but mostly independent line of cases developed. The Court sorted out the different law choice situations and refined the approaches applicable to each in **Hanna v. Plumer,** 380 U.S. 460 (1965). It is now clear that one should not think of any *single* test or approach—substance vs. procedure, outcome determination, interest balancing—as applicable to all *Erie* situations.

a. Specific holding [§527]

In *Hanna* the Supreme Court held that Federal Rule of Civil Procedure 4(d)(1), allowing "substituted" service of process on a defendant's spouse at their home, rather than the personal service required by Massachusetts law, was valid and controlling, even though the "substituted" service would not have sufficed had the same action been brought in Massachusetts state court.

(1) Note

The situation incidentally illustrates the possible overextension of the "outcome determination" test, for if the state rule applied in federal court, the suit would have been dismissed because state requirements had not been met.

b. Two parts of *Hanna* opinion [§528]

It is perhaps not frequently enough noticed that the majority opinion in *Hanna* has two parts: the first, technically dictum, about the *Erie* rule and the second, being the Court's holding, about the tests for the validity of a rule adopted pursuant to the Rules Enabling Act [28 U.S.C. §2072].

(1) *Erie* "dictum" in *Hanna* [§529]

The first part of the opinion confirms the scaling back of the *York* "outcome determination" test. It suggests—and later opinions appear to confirm—that while the test survives, it is to be applied in modified form in light of "the policies underlying the *Erie* rule." The Court identified these policies as the *"twin aims"* of "discouragement of forum shopping and avoidance of inequitable administration of the laws."

(a) Application

Although the Court decided that *Hanna* was not the type of case to which the modified *York* test applied (*see infra*), the Court implied that if it *did* apply, the Federal Rule would govern because the different rules in federal and state court regarding service of process would neither encourage forum shopping nor cause unfair discrimination among litigants.

(b) Comment on forum shopping

Forum shopping is not always an evil; the very existence of diversity jurisdiction, concurrent with state courts' general jurisdiction, reflects an intent to let some litigants choose between forums. By itself, forum shopping seems at most a minor irritant, involving some procedural shuffling. The main difficulty appears to be with what litigants may get when they forum shop—an unfairly different rule of law from what would have governed in state court. Consequently, although Supreme Court opinions regularly mention the forum shopping concern, it should not be treated in isolation, but rather should be considered in tandem with the aim of discouraging inequitable administration of the laws.

(2) Holding with respect to validity of Federal Rules [§530]

In the holding portion of *Hanna*, the Court found that the modified

York approach (developed in the dictum portion of *Hanna, supra*) applied to the "typical, relatively unguided *Erie* choice," but did not apply here because Congress had provided a different standard in the Rules Enabling Act, under which the Federal Rules are promulgated. That Act gives the Supreme Court the power to adopt Federal Rules regarding practice, procedure, and evidence in the federal courts, as long as the Rules do not "abridge, enlarge or modify any substantive right." Under the Enabling Act, the *Hanna* Court ruled that the Federal Rules are to be applied in federal courts unless they violate the Constitution or the terms of the Enabling Act itself.

(a) Constitutional restrictions [§531]

Recall that the power of the federal courts to create "general" common law was held unconstitutional because it did not rest on a power granted to the federal government by the Constitution. (*See supra*, §508.) The power to regulate *procedure* in the federal courts, however, has been granted to Congress under the constitutional provision creating lower federal courts [Art. III, §1] as augmented by the Necessary and Proper Clause [Art. I, §17] (*see* Constitutional Law Summary), and Congress has delegated part of this power to the Supreme Court through the Rules Enabling Act. The only *constitutional* restriction on this power is that the rules be "arguably procedural": the power to make procedural rules is broad enough to include "matters which, though falling within the uncertain area between substance and procedure, are rationally capable of classification as either." [**Hanna v. Plumer,** *supra*]

(b) Enabling Act limitations

1) "Practice and procedure" requirement [§532]

In *Hanna*, the Court reiterated that a rule passes muster under the "practice and procedure" portion of the Enabling Act if it *"really regulates procedure*—the judicial process for enforcing rights and duties recognized by substantive law and for justly administering remedy and redress for disregard or infraction of them." It is highly unlikely that any Federal Rule the Court might plausibly promulgate could fail this test.

2) "Substantive rights" limitation [§533]

The second sentence of the Rules Enabling Act requires that the Rules not "abridge, enlarge or modify any substantive right," and to be valid a rule technically must not transgress this proscription. However, in *Hanna* the Court pointed out that this limitation is not addressed to merely "incidental effects" on the rights of litigants.

(c) Strong presumption of validity [§534]

The *Hanna* Court made it clear that when there is a conflict between a federal rule and state law, there is a very strong presumption in favor of the validity of the Federal Rule. It stated that the Rule is to be applied unless it appears that the Rules Advisory Committee, the Supreme Court, and Congress erred in their initial judgment that the Rule did not transgress the Enabling Act or the Constitution. Indeed, the Supreme Court has never held a Federal Rule invalid.

SUBSTANCE VS. PROCEDURE—HISTORICAL CASES	gilbert
***YORK* OUTCOME DETERMINATION TEST**	Will application of federal instead of state law *significantly affect the outcome of litigation*?
***BYRD* INTEREST BALANCING APPROACH**	(1) Is the state practice rule *bound up with the underlying state law rights* being enforced? (2) Would following the state practice rule *interfere with the relationship between the judge and jury* in federal court? (3) Would following the state practice rule *affect the outcome of the lawsuit*?
***HANNA* MODIFICATIONS**	Distinguish between situations in which the possibly applicable federal rule has been *promulgated under the Rules Enabling Act* and those in which it is *purely decisional*. If the rule has been promulgated under the Rules Enabling Act (*e.g.,* a Federal Rule of Civil Procedure), it is to be applied in federal court unless it violates the Constitution or the Rules Enabling Act, including its ban on affecting substance (which is *very unlikely*). If the federal rule is purely decisional, in most instances you should analyze the case in light of the twin aims of (i) *discouragement of forum shopping* and (ii) *avoidance of inequitable administration of the laws*.

c. Justice Harlan's concurrence [§535]

Justice Harlan concurred in the *Hanna* judgment, but criticized the majority as going too far in the direction of favoring the Federal Rules. He characterized the Court's approach as: "arguably procedural, ergo constitutional." As to the Federal Rules, this characterization may understate *Hanna's* requirements, at least if the Court were to give some effect to the Enabling Act's substantive rights limitation. On the other hand, Harlan's characterization seems accurate when Congress itself has enacted legislation regulating procedure in the federal courts (*e.g.,* venue rules, *see supra,* §§143 *et seq.*). However, such a relaxed standard for validity is not objectionable in the context of a procedural rule for federal courts enacted by Congress. *Rationale:* Congress has broad power over procedure in the federal courts and is not bound by the Enabling Act's restriction against affecting substantive rights.

(1) "Primary private activity" [§536]

Justice Harlan also argued for an approach to federal vs. state rule choice that would have emphasized state power over "primary private activity" (*i.e.*, state rule would apply if it would affect the primary, out-of-court stages of activity from which a case arises; federal rule would apply if it affected in-court behavior following the "primary" stages). Although thoughtfully advocated, this view has not prevailed; and if turned into a single approach, it would overlook the multiple nature of modern *Erie-Hanna* analyses.

6. Modern Approach Under *Erie* and *Hanna* [§537]

The *Hanna* opinion suggests an approach to analysis of many federal-state law choice issues, amplified in an important article. [Ely, *The Irrepressible Myth of Erie*, 87 Harv. L. Rev. 693 (1974)] First, it is necessary to see whether any choice is needed; there may be no conflict to resolve between federal and state rules. Second, if conflict exists, one should determine the *source* of the arguably applicable federal rule of law—the Constitution; an Act of Congress; a Federal Rule of Civil or Appellate Procedure or Evidence; or a decisional rule developed by the federal courts and not resting on interpretation of one of the foregoing sources. The *source* of the federal rule determines the *test* for its validity and governing force.

a. Conflict-determination stage [§538]

For several reasons, federal and state rules of law that might apply in a situation may not conflict; *e.g.*, only one system may purport to have an applicable rule at all; or the two rules may address somewhat different, even if closely related, points and may both be applied; or the rules may agree and thus call for the same result, whichever is applied. If so, no *Erie-Hanna* choice analysis is necessary.

(1) Illustration—no federal rule [§539]

After *Erie*, in the absence of action by Congress, there is no federal law that purports to govern in many common tort situations. The only substantive law that can govern is state law.

(2) Illustration—no direct conflict [§540]

Federal Rule 3, which states that a "civil action is commenced by filing a complaint with the court," need not be read as speaking to when a state statute of limitations is tolled on a state cause of action. Thus, if state law provides that the action is not tolled until *process is served*—the service requirement being an integral part of the state limitations statute—

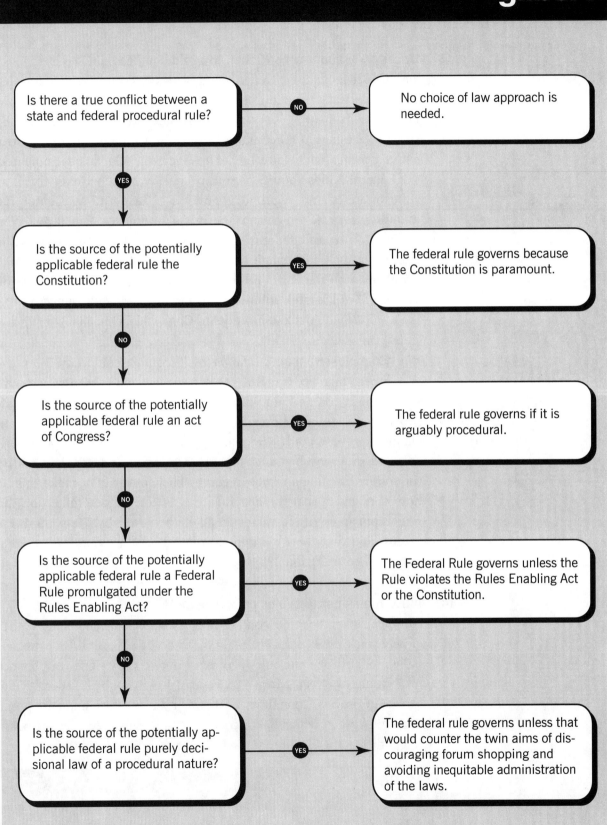

Is there a true conflict between a state and federal procedural rule?

NO → No choice of law approach is needed.

YES ↓

Is the source of the potentially applicable federal rule the Constitution?

YES → The federal rule governs because the Constitution is paramount.

NO ↓

Is the source of the potentially applicable federal rule an act of Congress?

YES → The federal rule governs if it is arguably procedural.

NO ↓

Is the source of the potentially applicable federal rule a Federal Rule promulgated under the Rules Enabling Act?

YES → The Federal Rule governs unless the Rule violates the Rules Enabling Act or the Constitution.

NO ↓

Is the source of the potentially applicable federal rule purely decisional law of a procedural nature?

YES → The federal rule governs unless that would counter the twin aims of discouraging forum shopping and avoiding inequitable administration of the laws.

the state rule applies in state law actions in federal court, without any conflict requiring the *Hanna* analysis. [**Walker v. Armco Steel Corp.**, 446 U.S. 740 (1980); **Ragan v. Merchants Transfer & Warehouse Co.**, 337 U.S. 530 (1949)]

(3) Uncertainty about construction to avoid conflict [§541]

The Court has stated that Federal Rules "should be given their plain meaning"; if that reading leads to a direct collision with state law, the *Hanna* analysis applies. [**Walker v. Armco Steel Corp.**, *supra*] This position suggests that a Federal Rule should not be narrowly construed to avoid conflict with state law. However, the Court has indicated that the Federal Rules should be interpreted "with sensitivity to important state interests and regulatory policies" [**Gasperini v. Center for Humanities,** *supra*], which may permit a finding of "no direct conflict" between state and federal laws. The Court has also been willing to adopt limiting constructions of Federal Rules to minimize or avoid problems with the Rules Enabling Act's substantive-right limitation (*see supra*, §533) [**Semtek International Inc. v. Lockheed Martin Corp.**, 531 U.S. 497 (2001); **Ortiz v. Fibreboard Corp.**, 527 U.S. 815 (1999)]

---

e.g. **Example—*Hanna*:** In *Hanna* itself, conflict could have been avoided by reading Federal Rule 4(d)(1) to deal only with service to commence the action and not with tolling the statute of limitations. State law provided for tolling *either* by personal service *or* by filing a notice of claim in probate court; the plaintiff might thus have followed both federal and state law by using substituted service under Rule 4 and tolling the statute by filing a notice of claim. The Court did not take this course, however, saying that the Federal Rule reflected a determination that the notice purposes of state law could be achieved by "less cumbersome" means, and that the Rule implied that in-hand service was not required in federal court actions.

---

(4) Illustration—parallel rules or borrowing [§542]

Another reason why no conflict may exist is that many state court rules closely track the Federal Rules (and some of the Federal Rules were originally modeled on state rules), so that the two provisions may be identical in phrasing or effect. Moreover, Federal Rules, such as Federal Rule 4 on service of process, sometimes borrow certain types of state law provisions from the state in which the district court sits. This precludes the possibility of conflict to the extent that the federal rule is borrowed state law.

EXAM TIP	gilbert

Be alert to ways in which the federal and state rules can be *reconciled or applied in a side-by-side manner* (e.g., no direct conflict, narrow construction to avoid conflict, parallel rules or borrowing). Don't assume that there is a conflict.

b. Conflict-resolution stage [§543]

If the federal and state rules conflict, it is necessary to proceed to the *Hanna* analysis. In applying that analysis, it is essential first to determine the **source** of the potentially applicable federal rule of law. The answer to that inquiry provides the approach for determining whether the federal rule is valid; if so, under the Supremacy Clause [U.S. Const. art. VI, §2] it prevails over contrary state law.

(1) Federal Constitution [§544]

Some procedural rules that govern in federal court derive from the text and judicial interpretations of the United States Constitution, such as the Seventh Amendment guarantee of the right to trial by jury in suits at common law (which does not apply to state courts). Because the Constitution is our paramount law, if it speaks to a situation before a court, **it governs,** without regard to any contrary state law or practice. This situation provides a possibly oversimplified example of why one should not invariably think in the *Erie* context in terms of "substance" vs. "procedure"; such labels, about either state or federal law, are totally beside the point if the source of a rule of federal law is the Constitution itself.

(2) Acts of Congress [§545]

Because of Congress's broad constitutional power over federal courts (*see supra*, §531), if Congress passes a statute governing federal court procedure, that statute is valid and prevails over any contrary state law **if** it is "arguably procedural." Thus, one should look **only** to the "procedural" nature of the *federal* statute in determining whether it is valid and governing; the substantive nature of any contrary state rule would be irrelevant, and there is no place for *Byrd's* balancing of state and federal interests, because Congress has already done the balancing.

(a) Illustration—federal transfer of venue statute [§546]

Although Alabama law that would govern in an action conducted in Alabama state court disfavored contractual forum-selection clauses, 28 U.S.C. section 1404(a) on transfer of venue between federal courts (*see supra*, §§192 *et seq.*) was sufficiently broad to cover, and governed in a state law case in Alabama federal court. Thus, the federal court could consider the effect of the parties' forum-selection clause on possible transfer to federal court in New York. [**Stewart Organization v. Ricoh Corp.,** *supra*, §223]

(3) Federal Rules [§547]

A Federal Rule promulgated pursuant to the Rules Enabling Act is judged by the standards of the Act, as reflected in the holding portion of **Hanna v. Plumer,** *supra*. The Rule (including court interpretations of the Rule) is to be applied instead of contrary state law unless it appears that the relevant Advisory Committee (Advisory Committees on Civil Rules, Appellate Rules, Rules of Evidence, etc., draft proposed rules for the Judicial Conference of the United States, which recommends them for promulgation by the Supreme Court), the Supreme Court, and Congress erred in their initial judgment that the Rule did not transgress the Enabling Act or the Constitution. (Congress does not usually vote on proposed Rules, but they must be submitted to Congress at least seven months before they are to take effect. [28 U.S.C. §2074] If Congress does not act, the rules go into effect.)

EXAM TIP   **gilbert**

On your law school exam, if a question involves a lawsuit in federal court under diversity jurisdiction and there is both a federal law and a state law on a particular issue, be sure to mention the basic rule: Under *Erie*, a federal court sitting in diversity jurisdiction will **apply state substantive law and federal procedural law**. If there is a conflict between the requirements of a Federal Rule of Civil Procedure and a state procedural rule, you should note that under the modern approach, the federal courts will apply a Federal Rule of Civil Procedure unless the court determines that the rule violates the Rules Enabling Act or the federal Constitution. Think carefully before blazing new trails on this point and arguing that the rule involved is invalid. In most cases, you can probably finish off your answer by stating that it is highly unlikely that the drafters of the rule, the Supreme Court, and Congress erred in their initial judgment that the rule did not violate the Rules Enabling Act and the Constitution.

Example: Federal Rule of Appellate Procedure 38, which allows *discretionary* penalties for frivolous appeals, prevailed in federal court over an Alabama statute *requiring* penalties for unsuccessful appeals in state court. [**Burlington Northern Railroad v. Woods**, 480 U.S. 1 (1987)]

Compare—possible counterexample: The leading case in a court of appeals declining to apply an applicable Federal Rule, because of conflict with a state rule it regarded as substantive, involved a liberal Massachusetts rule on relation back for party changes in pleading amendments. The First Circuit held that then-applicable Federal Rule 15(c)'s restrictive approach to relation back (since relaxed by amendment of the Rule, *see infra*, §935) would "defeat rights arising from state substantive law" and followed the state rule. [**Marshall v. Mulrenin**, 508 F.2d 39 (1st Cir. 1974)] It seems doubtful that the Supreme Court would approve the approach in *Mulrenin* if a similar case were to come before it today, because of its strong emphasis on the presumptive validity of a Federal Rule that qualifies as "procedural" and its willingness to tolerate "incidental" effects of the Rules on the enforcement of state law rights.

(a) Rules Enabling Act's "substantive right" limitation [§548]

Whether the Court would ever strike down a Federal Rule for violating the Enabling Act seems to depend primarily on whether it would be willing to give significant independent force to the portion of the Enabling Act that requires that the Rules "not abridge, enlarge or modify any substantive right." Most often, procedural rules will not have anything like the forbidden effect, so the problem will rarely arise.

1) "Incidental" effects [§549]

The Court has disregarded "incidental" effects that leave untouched the content of state substantive law, while providing a somewhat different "manner or means" to enforce it.

---

e.g. **Example:** The Court has held that any effect on substantive rights resulting from the imposition of Rule 11 (regarding improper assertion of claims or defenses, *see infra*, §§768 *et seq.*) sanctions is incidental, and that the Rule governs in diversity cases. [**Business Guides, Inc. v. Chromatic Communications Enterprises, Inc.**, 498 U.S. 533 (1991)]

---

2) Possibility of conflict with substantive right [§550]

The Court has not, thus far, entertained the possibility that a generally valid Federal Rule might, in particular contexts, impermissibly conflict with a substantive right, as the First Circuit concluded had happened in *Marshall, supra*. The Court has, however, been willing to adopt limiting constructions of Federal Rules of Civil Procedure to minimize or avoid problems with the Rules Enabling Act's substantive-right limitation (*see supra*, §533). [**Semtek International Inc. v. Lockheed Martin Corp.**, *supra*, §541; **Ortiz v. Fibreboard Corp.**, *supra*, §541]

(4) Judge-made federal procedural rules [§551]

If a potentially applicable federal rule is purely *decisional—i.e., not* the result of an interpretation of positive law found in the Constitution, an Act of Congress, or a Federal Rule—the "twin aims" *Erie* test articulated in the dictum portion of the *Hanna* opinion governs: If applying the federal judge-made rule would counter the aims of discouraging forum shopping and avoiding inequitable administration of the laws, the federal court should follow state law. The "twin aims" approach might also apply, and cut against the applicability of state law in federal court, if state courts have a rule governing purely internal housekeeping matters—such as judicial attire or length of paper for court filings—and federal courts have nothing that amounts to a rule but do have a practice differing from that followed in state court.

(a) Caution

The Court has also shown a willingness to consider possible outcome variation and forum-choice influence in interpreting a Federal Rule of Civil Procedure, thus possibly making the twin-aims approach relevant in at least some cases besides those involving purely decisional federal procedural rules or non-rule practices. [*See* **Semtek International Inc. v. Lockheed Martin Corp.**, *supra*, §541—declining to give Rule 41(b)'s provision that most dismissals operate "as an adjudication on the merits" full claim-preclusive effect in a case where the district court dismissed based on the statute of limitations and courts of state in which district court sat would not treat such a dismissal as extinguishing the substantive right; the Court noted that otherwise defendants would have an incentive to remove diversity cases to federal court to obtain a broader preclusive effect]

Example: *Guaranty Trust, supra*, §513, remains a prime illustration of such a situation, although the Court's analysis when it decided *York* was somewhat different from the modern approach under *Hanna*. Today, federal courts would apply the state law rule in a case like *York* because following the federal rule would fail the "twin aims" test: a party who would be barred by a statute of limitations in state court, but might be able to argue around a more flexible federal judge-made "laches" rule, would be tempted to file in federal court; and entertaining the action in federal court, when it would be barred by limitations in state court, would also deprive the defendant of the benefits of repose meant to be conferred by the state statute.

(b) Illustration—sufficiency of evidence [§552]

In state law cases in the federal courts, the lower federal courts are divided on whether to apply state or judge-made federal standards to the issue of whether the evidence is sufficient for a case to go to the jury. The trend in the cases, however, appears to be toward the federal standard because the question goes to whether judge or jury should evaluate the sufficiency of the evidence, not to the elements of the claim or the definition of the persuasion burden. [**Mayer v. Gary Partners & Co.**, 29 F.3d 330 (7th Cir. 1994)]

1) But note—standard for reviewing jury awards [§553]

When a federal trial judge considers a new trial motion based on alleged excessiveness of a jury's award in a state-law case, state, rather than federal, law supplies the governing standard because it reflects state policy on how much of a check to place on excessive damages. [**Gasperini v. Center for Humanities, Inc.**, *supra*, §525]

(c) Relative infrequency of problems of this sort [§554]

Because federal statutes and the Federal Rules cover federal procedural issues fairly broadly, and because federal decisional rules often will not conflict with potentially applicable state rules, judge-made federal law infrequently comes into play in state vs. federal law conflicts. Nevertheless, later cases discussing *Hanna* explicitly endorsed the "twin aims" analysis for this type of situation. [*See, e.g.,* **Stewart Organization v. Ricoh Corp.,** *supra,* §546]

1) *NASCO* case

In 1991, for the first time since before *Hanna*, the Supreme Court faced a case involving what it viewed as a conflict between state law and judge-made federal procedural law. [**Chambers v. NASCO, Inc.,** 501 U.S. 32 (1991)] *NASCO* involved the inherent power of federal courts to impose sanctions for bad faith conduct in litigation before the courts, even in state law cases where the state courts would not have a similar sanctioning power. The majority opinion routinely invoked the "twin aims" approach, found no forum shopping incentives or inequity, and upheld the federal rule.

2) Cautionary note

Because the two prominent intermediate cases of *York* and *Byrd* involved what the Court treated as a conflict between state law and judge-made federal law, students often mistakenly regard them as dominating the field of *Erie* problems. The Court has, however, made it clear that other tests for the validity and governing force of a federal rule apply when the rule is grounded in the Constitution itself, enacted by Congress, or promulgated pursuant to the Enabling Act.

(d) Limited survival of *Byrd* approach [§555]

The survival of *Byrd's* balancing or accommodation of state and federal interests appears to be limited to a subpart of this category of cases involving judge-made federal procedural law—when an as of yet not clearly defined "essential characteristic of the federal court system," likely implicating relations among jury, trial judge, and appellate court, is involved. [*See* **Gasperini v. Center for Humanities, Inc.,** *supra*] Such balancing or accommodation appears uncalled for in cases involving positive federal law, because other authoritative lawmakers—the Constitution drafters, Congress, or the Federal Rules makers—have already done the balancing or accommodating. Even with purely decisional federal rules, the Court's decisions since *Hanna* indicate that the purposive "twin aims" modified version of the *York* test, rather than *Byrd* interest analysis, is the approach to be followed, unless an "essential characteristic" of the federal-court system is involved.

Example—*Hanna:* In *Hanna* itself, the Court said that the "importance" of a state rule is relevant in the *Erie* context only for purposes of determining whether failing to follow the state rule in federal court would disserve the "twin aims" of discouraging forum shopping and avoiding inequitable administration of the laws.

Example—*NASCO:* In *NASCO* (*supra*), in upholding the federal courts' decisionally established inherent authority to impose sanctions for bad-faith conduct in state-law litigation before them despite contrary state law, the Court relied on *Erie*, *York*, and *Hanna* but ignored *Byrd*.

Example—*Gasperini:* In *Gasperini* (*see supra*, §525), the Court relied on *Byrd*, but only concerning the scope of federal appellate review of trial court denials of motions seeking remittitur, which involves relations among federal juries, trial judges, and appellate courts. In choosing state law over the federal standard for trial judges' review of jury verdicts for excessiveness in state law cases, however, the Court in *Gasperini* again used the "twin aims" test and relied on *Erie*, *York*, and *Hanna* while ignoring *Byrd*.

7. Which State's Law Applies? [§556]

Because diversity cases—and most of the state law cases in the federal courts are diversity cases—by definition involve parties from different states, federal courts must often decide *which* state's law is to govern.

a. General rule [§557]

In diversity cases, as to matters for which the federal court is required to follow state law, it will apply the ***law of the state in which it sits***. This includes the state's choice of law rules, *i.e.*, the rules the state courts use to determine what law to apply to cases such as involving a nonresident party or events that occurred out of state. Thus, if the state's choice of law rules require application of another state's law, the federal court is to do the same. [**Klaxon Co. v. Stentor Manufacturing Co.**, 313 U.S. 487 (1941)]

EXAM TIP   **gilbert**

Exam questions involving diversity jurisdiction sometimes are based on a cause of action involving people or events in several states and include provisions of substantive law from each state. You will have to decide what law the federal district court should apply. Remember to state the basic rule: A federal district court will apply the *law of the state in which it is sitting*, including its conflict of laws rules. Thus, if P, a resident of State Green, is hit by D, a resident of State Yellow, while driving through State Red, and P brings a diversity action against D in State Yellow, the federal district court should apply State Yellow law. However, if the facts tell you that under State Yellow conflict of laws rules, a State Yellow court would apply the law of the state where the accident occurred, the federal district court should apply State Red law, because in diversity jurisdiction cases, the federal court applies the *choice of law rules of the state in which it sits*, as well as that state's substantive law.

b. **Questionable extension of *Klaxon* to statutory interpleader [§558]**

In a companion case decided the same day as *Klaxon* [**Griffin v. McCoach**, 313 U.S. 498 (1941)], the Supreme Court applied the *Klaxon* rule to a case arising within federal statutory interpleader jurisdiction. (For discussion of interpleader, *see infra*, §§1117 *et seq*.) Although *Griffin* apparently remains the law for federal statutory interpleader actions, no one has defended its application of the conflicts rules of the state in which the federal court sits, since federal statutory interpleader jurisdiction was created precisely because it might not be possible to bring scattered claimants before the same state court.

c. **Modern reaffirmance of *Klaxon* [§559]**

Despite some academic criticism of the *Klaxon* rule, the Supreme Court strongly and summarily reaffirmed it in an extreme case in which the Texas courts would have followed Cambodian law. [**Day & Zimmermann, Inc. v. Challoner**, 423 U.S. 3 (1975)] By contrast, the heavily criticized extension of the *Klaxon* rule to statutory interpleader in *Griffin*, *supra*, has not been relitigated at the Supreme Court level.

d. **Exceptions [§560]**

In some instances, federal legislation may provide a *federal* choice of law rule. [**Richards v. United States**, 369 U.S. 1 (1962)] For example, the Federal Tort Claims Act requires courts to apply the law—including choice of law rules— "of the place where the [allegedly tortious] act or omission occurred." [28 U.S.C. §1346(b)]

8. **Determining Applicable State Law [§561]**

Erie referred to the law of a state as declared by the state's "highest court." Often, of course, because a state statute or supreme court decision is on point, the state substantive law to be followed by a federal court will be clear. However, in other cases, the state court system may never have faced a question, or only lower state courts may have ruled, or it may seem likely that the state supreme court would overrule an old precedent if given the opportunity.

a. **General guideline—"proper regard" to state court rulings [§562]**

Although the Supreme Court has not recently spoken directly on how federal courts should approach the problem of determining unclear state law, it has stated that "proper regard" must be given to state court precedents. In some cases, a *federal court will not be bound* by the ruling of a state intermediate appellate court on a point of state law, and *a fortiori* not by a state trial court decision. Such courts' opinions are, however, relevant data for ascertaining state law. [**Commissioner v. Estate of Bosch**, 387 U.S. 456 (1967)]

b. **Implementation in light of *Erie* aims [§563]**

The determination of unclear state law seems best approached with the *Erie* "twin aims" of avoiding forum shopping and inequitable administration of the laws in mind. Adoption of simplistic or rigid tests (*e.g.,* being bound by a recent holding of a state's intermediate appellate court—even if the ruling seems contrary to what the state supreme court would probably do) could encourage forum shopping by making available in the federal system law that would not, ultimately, govern in the state system. Therefore, many lower federal courts look to *all* relevant sources, giving due regard to the varying weights of different authorities within the state system, in an attempt to discern how the state supreme court would decide the issue. [*See, e.g.,* **McKenna v. Ortho Pharmaceutical Corp.,** 622 F.2d 567 (3d Cir. 1980)] In any event, a federal court is supposed to *apply* state law and *not* attempt to change it to what the court thinks might be a better rule.

EXAM TIP   **gilbert**

If an exam question involves diversity jurisdiction and you are told that the state supreme court has never ruled on the substantive issue involved or that it has ruled on it but it did so a very long time ago, you should explain that the federal court should give proper regard for state court rulings. However, this does not mean that the court must blindly follow state appellate court precedent. The court should consider the twin aims of *avoiding forum shopping and inequitable administration of the laws*. It should apply the law it thinks the state supreme court would apply; not the law it thinks is the best rule.

---

c. **No deference to local federal judges [§564]**

The Supreme Court has ruled that federal appellate courts are not to defer to the interpretation of state law by federal trial judges, but must review district courts' state law determinations de novo. [**Salve Regina College v. Russell,** 499 U.S. 225 (1991)]

d. **State certification laws [§565]**

Many states authorize their highest courts to answer questions of state law certified by federal courts before which cases are pending. Where this procedure is available, a federal court may seek an authoritative answer to uncertain questions about state law rather than speculating on them. [*See* **Lehman Bros. v. Schein,** 416 U.S. 386 (1974)]

B. Federal Common Law

1. **No "Federal General Common Law" [§566]**

Erie's repudiation of *Swift* (*see supra,* §§506 *et seq.*) included the flat statement, "[t]here is no federal general common law." However, the very day *Erie* was decided, the Court held that federal common law governed on the specific issue of apportionment of waters in an interstate stream. [**Hinderlider v. La Plata River Co.,** 304 U.S. 92 (1938)] The resolution to this apparent contradiction lies in the fact that the federal courts do have authority to create common law in *particular* areas of federal authority or interest, subject to overruling by Congress.

2. Examples of Federal Common Law Areas [§567]

The range of federal interests and grants of authority that could support federal common law is fairly broad, and the subject receives more extended treatment elsewhere. (*See* Federal Courts Summary.)

a. Borrowed state law [§568]

In some cases, federal statutes may be silent as to particular issues arising under them (*e.g.*, statutes of limitations for federal claims and definitions of family status for purposes of some federal law entitlements). In such cases, the federal courts often fill the interstices in federal law by borrowing the law of the relevant state, as long as that law does not undermine the purposes of the underlying federal law.

(1) Illustration—derivative action demand requirement [§569]

A derivative action is a lawsuit brought by corporation's shareholder(s) to vindicate corporate rights where the corporation's board of directors has not filed an action. In most states, before filing a derivative action, shareholders must make a demand on the board before they bring the action. However, a number of states have an exception allowing shareholders to bring an action without making a pre-complaint demand if the demand would be futile (*e.g.*, because the suit would be against members of the board). The federal Investment Company Act allows shareholders to bring certain derivative actions after making demand on the board. The Supreme Court has held that under the act, the scope of the "futility" exception to the pre-complaint demand requirement should be borrowed from state law. [**Kamen v. Kemper Financial Services, Inc.**, 500 U.S. 90 (1991)]

b. Authorization by Congress [§570]

In some areas (*e.g.*, portions of the law of labor relations), the Supreme Court has interpreted congressional legislation as intending that the federal courts develop substantive law to further national uniformity. [*See* **Textile Workers Union v. Lincoln Mills**, 353 U.S. 448 (1957)]

c. Sufficient federal interest [§571]

The Court sometimes regards the federal government as having a strong enough interest in a transaction that it should be governed by uniform federal common law to further that interest, even in the absence of congressional authorization and despite contrary state law. [*See, e.g.*, **Clearfield Trust Co. v. United States**, 318 U.S. 363 (1943)—federal common law governed on issue of delay in notice of forgery of federal government check] There must, however, be a significant federal interest. [*See, e.g.*, **Bank of America v. Parnell**, 352 U.S. 29 (1956)—state law governed in suit between private parties on issue of good faith of holder of previously stolen government bonds; that federal government issued the paper involved in the suit does not by itself suffice to require the creation of uniform federal common law]

d. **Interstate disputes [§572]**

In interstate disputes involving governments of, or in, different states (*e.g.*, disputes over interstate pollution), it may be inappropriate for the law of one of the interested states to govern. The federal courts consequently may develop federal common law when no congressional legislation deals with the area. [**Illinois v. City of Milwaukee,** 406 U.S. 91 (1972)]

e. **United States foreign relations [§573]**

When questions of American foreign relations are involved, the need for uniform federal common law may be especially clear. [*See, e.g.,* **Banco Nacional de Cuba v. Sabbatino,** 376 U.S. 398 (1964)]

EXAM TIP   **gilbert**

For some reason almost everyone who has been to law school seems to remember *Erie's* admonition that "there is no federal general common law." This often results in a knee-jerk response whenever they hear the suggestion that a federal court is to apply federal common law. They respond that there is no such thing. This, of course, is incorrect. Federal common law exists in a significant range of cases, including those where Congress has appeared to authorize federal common law development (*e.g.*, labor relations), where there is a strong federal interest in developing a uniform federal common law (*e.g.*, requirements for notice of forgery on government checks), where interstate disputes are involved (*e.g.*, pollution issues), and where American foreign relations are involved. So don't be fooled on an exam question. Remember, federal common law exists in some areas.

Chapter Four:
Pleading

CONTENTS

Chapter Approach

Chapter Approach

Questions on pleadings generally concern one or more of the following issues:

1. **Complaint**

   a. Does the plaintiff's complaint *state a claim upon which relief can be granted?* To do so, it must allege the *elements* required by substantive law to constitute a cause of action. If it is deficient, the complaint may be challenged by *demurrer* (in code pleading states) or by *motion to dismiss* (in Federal Rules systems.)

   b. Does the complaint make its allegations with the *specificity* required under applicable pleading rules? In code pleading systems, the complaint must include "*facts* constituting the cause of action." In the federal courts and in most state systems that are based on the Federal Rules of Civil Procedure, "*notice pleading*" suffices: In addition to any required statement of jurisdiction and a prayer for relief, the complaint need contain only a "short and plain statement of the claim showing that the pleader is entitled to relief." However, the plaintiff still needs to set forth factual matter to support each element of the claim.

2. **Answer**

   a. Does the defendant's answer *deny* the material allegations of the complaint? To the extent it does not, the allegations may be taken as *admitted.*

   b. Does the answer raise *affirmative defenses* to the complaint?

   c. Does the answer set forth *counterclaims*?

   — A counterclaim arising out of the transaction or occurrence that is the subject matter of the opposing party's claim is a *compulsory counterclaim* and should be included in the answer.

   — Any other counterclaim is *permissive* and may be included at the option of the pleader. In federal court, there generally is *no supplemental jurisdiction* over permissive counterclaims; there must be an *independent basis of federal jurisdiction.*

3. **Investigation of Claims and Defenses**
   Federal Rule 11 and similar state rules require investigation of the claims and defenses made in pleadings. Be sure to consider the following:

a.   Was *reasonable inquiry* made concerning the legal and factual bases of the claim or defense?

b.   Does the claim or defense have *evidentiary support*?

c.   Is the claim or defense *warranted by existing law* or a good faith argument for extension of the law?

d.   Was the claim or defense interposed for an *improper purpose*, such as to harass the opposing party?

e.   If the claim or defense was improperly asserted, what *sanctions,* if any, are appropriate?

Besides these topics, be sure to review briefly the rules discussed in this chapter on amended and supplemental pleadings, default, judgment on the pleadings, and voluntary dismissal by the plaintiff.

A. Introduction

1.   In General [§574]

The plaintiff begins a civil action by filing in a court of appropriate jurisdiction a *complaint* seeking some sort of judicial relief against specified defendants. The court thereupon issues its process (*e.g.,* summons) directing the named defendants to appear. A defendant "appears" by filing some sort of response (*e.g.,* answer, motion, demurrer), after which other pleadings and motions may be filed until the case is "at issue."

2.   Objectives [§575]

The basic purpose of pleadings is to give notice of the general character of the controversy between the parties. Under code pleading (*see infra,* §581; used in such states as California, Illinois, and New York), the pleadings are also intended to narrow and formulate the issues involved in the case. The pleading process thus helps to determine the scope of the action for the trial and the scope of any judgment in the action.

3.   Background [§576]

At common law, the courts relied exclusively on the pleadings to define the issues. The result was that the pleading process was all-important and pleading rules were extremely technical. Mistakes in the pleading process often proved fatal to the pleader's case, and prevented a hearing on the merits of the case. However, under modern practice, the pleadings are merely one stage of the issue-defining process. Discovery devices and the pretrial conference (*infra,* Chapters VI and VIII) are also available. Consequently, there has been a strong trend toward liberalizing the rules of pleading and streamlining the pleading process.

B. History of Pleading

1. Common Law Pleadings [§577]

The original common law courts could grant relief only in accordance with certain recognized *forms of action,* each representing a particular theory of substantive law (*e.g.,* trespass, case, trover, assumpsit, etc.) and pleadings had to be drawn in terms of one of these recognized forms. Thus, the plaintiff was forced to fit the out-of-court transaction of which he was complaining into the mold of one of the forms. Amendments to change the form of action were not allowed, so once a plaintiff chose a particular form, he could recover—if at all—only under the substantive theory of law represented by the form; *e.g.,* if the plaintiff chose trespass, but the facts established trover, the plaintiff could not recover.

a. Objective [§578]

The basic objective of pleading at common law was to narrow the issues as finely as possible (preferably to a single issue), so that the case could be determined by deciding that issue.

b. Numerous pleadings [§579]

For this purpose, distinct pleadings and counterpleadings were employed; *e.g.,* declaration, answer, replication, rejoinder, surrejoinder, etc. Each party was required to either demur (challenge sufficiency of the pleading responded to; *see infra,* §697) or counterplead to each pleading by his adversary. The submission of numerous pleadings was time-consuming, and a defendant could often use the pleading rules for purposes of delay.

c. Compare—equity pleading [§580]

The courts of equity were distinct from common law courts and were governed by different procedures. Relief was available from the equity courts only where there was no right to recover under any of the forms of action recognized in the law courts (*i.e.,* where the remedy at law was inadequate). Therefore, pleaders in equity had to go outside the forms of action to state their claims; the plaintiff recited *facts* showing that he had a grievance that ought to be remedied. This concept of *fact pleading* was the basis of code pleading (below).

2. Code Pleading [§581]

The New York Code of 1848 (known as the Field Code) originated code pleading to relax some of the rigidities of common law pleading. This code, or adaptations thereof, was subsequently adopted in most states, and is still retained in several today. It incorporates several important departures from common law pleading rules.

a. **Single form of action [§582]**

Unlike the rigid common law forms, the fundamental requirement of code pleading is that the plaintiff's complaint be in the form of a *statement of facts showing a right to a remedy.* This has been described as abolishing the forms of action and providing for *one form of action.* [Fed. R. Civ. P. 2; Cal. Civ. Proc. Code §307]

(1) Effect

Under code pleading, the plaintiff no longer has to select and set forth in the pleadings the particular legal theory of his case. He is entitled to recover under *any* legal theory applicable to the *facts* pleaded and proved.

Example: P's complaint alleged that D published statements that were injurious to P's reputation (that P committed a hijacking) and that unnecessarily specified P as the person involved. The complaint failed to state a cause of action for libel because the published statements were admittedly true; but it was held sufficient to state a claim for invasion of privacy. If *any* legal theory will sustain recovery on the facts pleaded, the complaint is sufficient. [**Briscoe v. Reader's Digest,** 4 Cal. 3d 529 (1971)]

Example: A federal statute prohibits states from violating a person's constitutional rights. P filed a complaint alleging that the manager of D's store had an arrangement with the local police under which the police would assist the store in refusing service to African Americans at its lunch counter. The complaint was held sufficient to state a claim for violation of P's civil rights under federal statutes, since even if the store itself was not governed by the statute, the police were so governed and the complaint alleged concerted action between D (through its manager) and the police. [**Adickes v. S.H. Kress & Co.,** 398 U.S. 144 (1970)]

---

b. **Merger of law and equity [§583]**

Another major aspect of code pleading is the elimination of separate courts of law and equity, and of the separate procedures in each court. This change has persisted under modern practice, where the same court is vested with jurisdiction to grant both equitable and legal relief. [Fed. R. Civ. P. 1]

(1) Remedies—distinct [§584]

Note that while the distinctions between legal and equitable *procedure* have been abolished, the distinctions between legal and equitable *remedies* remain intact. The nature of the relief available depends upon the circumstances shown (*e.g.,* whether damage has actually resulted).

Example: Equitable relief is generally said to be available only where the legal remedy (damages) is shown to be *inadequate.* This is called the "irreparable injury" rule. *But note:* The irreparable injury rule is said to have been replaced by a rule that legal damages are inadequate unless they can be used to replace the specific thing that the plaintiff lost. [Laycock, The Death of the Irreparable Injury Rule, 103 Harv. L. Rev. 688 (1990)] Equitable relief will be more widely available under this narrow definition of "inadequate."

Example: Similarly, various defenses are recognized where an equitable remedy is sought (laches, hardship, unclean hands, etc.), but are not recognized in actions at law.

(a) Jury trial [§585]

Also note that the distinction between legal and equitable remedies is relevant to whether a jury trial is available. While a jury trial is usually available in an action at law, equitable actions are normally tried by the court alone (although the court may impanel a jury for an advisory verdict on disputed questions of fact). (*See* further discussion *infra,* §§1777 *et seq.*)

c. Limited number of pleadings [§586]

Far fewer pleadings are allowed under code pleading than in the old common law system, since there is no objective to reduce the case to a single issue through a pleading "dialogue."

(1) Types of pleadings [§587]

The basic pleadings allowed under existing codes are shown in the chart on the next page. Note that in contrast to the practices in some other code states, California and New York do not permit a reply to matters of affirmative defense in the defendant's answer. Such matter is "deemed controverted" without the necessity of a response by the plaintiff. [Cal. Civ. Proc. Code §431.20(b)]

d. Fact pleading [§588]

A pleading under the codes must set forth "the facts constituting *the cause of action* in ordinary and concise language." [Cal. Civ. Proc. Code §425.10(a)] This is interpreted as requiring an allegation of the *"ultimate facts"* of the cause of action (or defense) involved.

(1) "Ultimate facts" [§589]

Ultimate facts are those facts that describe *in adequate detail but without legal argument* the circumstances that the plaintiff believes entitle him to a remedy. If the allegations are too general, they are deemed "conclusions"; and if too much detail is given, it is an impermissible pleading of "evidence."

EXAMPLES OF BASIC PLEADINGS

gilbert

PLAINTIFF'S PLEADINGS	DEFENDANT'S PLEADINGS
California Civ. Proc. Code §§422.10, 430.30	
Complaint	Demurrer to complaint; Answer
Demurrer to answer	
Demurrer to cross-complaint	Cross-complaint
Answer to cross-complaint	Demurrer to answer to cross-complaint
New York Civ. Prac. Law §§3011, 3019, 3211	
Complaint	Motion to dismiss; Answer
Motion to dismiss counterclaim	Counterclaim
Reply to counterclaim	
Illinois Code Civ. Proc. §§2-602, 2-608, 2-614, 2-615	
Complaint	Motion to dismiss; Answer
Reply to affirmative matter in answer	
Motion to dismiss counterclaim	Counterclaim
Answer to counterclaim	

> **e.g.** **Example:** Suppose the plaintiff's complaint makes the following allegations in a negligence action:
>
> (i) "D operated her automobile in violation of Vehicle Code section 23101, and injured P."
>
> (ii) "D consumed one gallon of wine at the Green Frog Cafe, less than two hours before the accident in which P was injured."
>
> (iii) "D drove her car while intoxicated and on the wrong side of the highway, causing it to strike the car in which P was riding."
>
> Allegation (i) could be attacked as a conclusion of law. Allegation (ii) might be found to contain only "evidentiary" matter. Allegation (iii) is a sufficient statement of ultimate fact.

(2) Consequences of improper pleading of facts [§590]

Failure to allege ultimate facts constituting every essential element of the cause of action (or defense) involved makes the pleading insufficient and subject to a *general demurrer* or, under some codes, a motion to dismiss (which is the equivalent of a general demurrer). (*See* discussion, *infra*, §§697 *et seq.*)

(a) *If sufficient ultimate facts are alleged,* evidentiary allegations and conclusions of law can be treated as surplusage (but are subject to a motion to strike; *see infra*, §712).

(b) *If the allegations are too vague* (*i.e.,* mere conclusions), the complaint is also subject to a special demurrer (*see infra*, §§708-709).

(3) Criticism

Under the code pleading system, there is considerable difficulty in determining what constitute the requisite "ultimate facts" (as opposed to "evidentiary matter" or "legal conclusions") in various situations. As a result, pleaders tend to use stereotyped allegations and form complaints that have previously been held sufficient.

3. Pleading Under the Federal Rules [§591]

The Federal Rules have *further liberalized* pleading standards and have eliminated many of the technical requirements under the Field Code. Today, most states have also adopted the Federal Rules.

a. Pleadings permitted [§592]

The Federal Rules authorize even fewer pleadings than the code pleading states (above). The basic pleadings allowed by Federal Rule 7(a) are shown in the chart below.

FEDERAL PLEADINGS	**gilbert**
PLAINTIFF'S PLEADINGS	**DEFENDANT'S PLEADINGS**
Complaint Reply to counterclaim	Answer, which may contain a counterclaim against plaintiff

(1) Note

The *demurrer has been eliminated* in federal courts. In its place, the *motion to dismiss for failure to state a claim* is used. [Fed. R. Civ. P. 12(b)(6)]

b. Notice pleading [§593]

The Federal Rules eliminate the code requirement of pleading "facts constituting a cause of action." Instead, the Rules simply require a *"short and plain statement of the claim showing the pleader is entitled to relief."* [Fed. R. Civ. P. 8(a)(2)] This has been called "notice pleading."

(1) Rationale

The purpose of pleading under the Federal Rules is simply to *identify* the transaction out of which the plaintiff's claim arises, so that the defendant has *notice* of the claim. Discovery and other pretrial procedures are relied on for full development of the facts. [**Conley v. Gibson**, 355 U.S. 41 (1957)] Under the Federal Rules, the distinctions among "ultimate facts," "evidentiary facts," and "conclusions of law" (above) are therefore unimportant. Any claim may be stated in general terms, and stylized precision in identifying the cause of action is not required. However, generality can be taken too far. A pleading must "show that the pleader is entitled to relief," and courts may insist that pleadings include sufficient support for the claims included.

EXAM TIP	**gilbert**

If you are asked to write a complaint on your exam under a notice pleading system, remember that while pleading is more relaxed than under a code pleading system, mere conclusions are not enough. You must set forth *factual assertions* sufficient to support each claim.

C. Complaint

1. In General [§594]

In most jurisdictions, a civil action is commenced by the filing of the plaintiff's complaint. [Fed. R. Civ. P. 3; Cal. Civ. Proc. Code §411.10] (In New York, an action is commenced by service of process; and the complaint can be filed thereafter.)

2. Form [§595]

The essential parts of the complaint are: the caption, jurisdictional allegations, body, prayer for relief, and subscription.

a. Caption [§596]

The complaint must set forth:

(i) The name of the court;

(ii) The number assigned to the action (stamped by the clerk when the action is filed);

(iii) A designation of the pleading (*e.g.*, "Complaint for Damages"); and

(iv) The names of the parties.

[Fed. R. Civ. P. 10; Cal. Civ. Proc. Code §§422.30; 422.40]

(1) Note

Suing *"John Doe" defendants* is permitted in some states if the plaintiff does not know the true names of all the defendants. [Cal. Civ. Proc. Code §474]

(a) Caution—"Doe" defendants questionable in federal court [§597]

Due to subject matter jurisdiction concerns, use of Doe defendants may not be allowed in cases based on diversity jurisdiction. (*See supra,* §332)

(2) Effect of errors [§598]

Under modern rules, pleadings are "so construed as to do substantial justice." [Fed. R. Civ. P. 8(f)] Accordingly, the courts will disregard errors in the form or caption of the complaint that do not mislead the other party.

(a) Name of party wrong or incomplete [§599]

An error or incompleteness in designating a party in the *complaint* is generally harmless error. However, if there is also error in the *summons* and as a result the intended defendant is not adequately warned that he is being sued, the action may be subject to dismissal for insufficient process.

b. Jurisdictional allegations [§600]

In *federal* court, the complaint must contain allegations showing the ground (or grounds) upon which the subject matter jurisdiction of the federal court is invoked. [Fed. R. Civ. P. 8(a)(1)] Since federal courts are courts of *limited* jurisdiction, a complaint that fails to set forth the jurisdictional grounds must be dismissed unless the ground can be supplied by amendment. (*See infra,* §§912 *et seq.*)

Example: If jurisdiction is founded on diversity of citizenship, a sufficient statement might be: "Plaintiff is a citizen of New York and defendant is a citizen of California. The matter in controversy exceeds, exclusive of interest and costs, the sum of $75,000."

(1) Contrast—state practice [§601]

Jurisdictional allegations generally are *not* required in state court practice, because state courts usually have general jurisdiction.

c. Body [§602]

The complaint must also contain a statement of the facts upon which recovery is sought. In code pleading states, this requires a "statement of the (ultimate) facts constituting the cause of action" (*supra,* §588), while under the Federal Rules there must be a "short and plain statement of the claim showing that the pleader is entitled to relief" (*supra,* §593).

(1) Separate causes of action [§603]

Each claim or cause of action should be set forth in a separate group of serially numbered paragraphs; and each paragraph should be limited to a statement of a single set of circumstances. [Fed. R. Civ. P. 10(b)]

(a) *Under code pleading practice,* this was an essential requirement. A complaint that lumped together several causes of action was subject to demurrer.

(b) *Under modern law,* however, failure to state separate claims separately (*e.g.,* "First Cause of Action," "Second Cause of Action") is simply a formal defect—and is not even a basis of objection in some states (*e.g.,* California).

(c) *Under certain circumstances,* it may be important for the defendant to know exactly the grounds on which the plaintiff is proceeding (*e.g.,* where several different claims have been lumped together and the statute of limitations is different on each claim). In such cases, the defendant's remedy is to file a demurrer for uncertainty under code pleading practice (*infra,* §699) or a motion for more definite statement under federal practice (*infra,* §739).

(2) Direct allegations [§604]

The allegations in the complaint should be "simple, concise and direct." [Fed. R. Civ. P. 8(e)]

(a) Recitals [§605]

It is improper to allege essential facts only by way of recitals (*e.g.,* an allegation that "A, *while acting as D's agent,* executed a contract with P"). The proper form is "At all times herein, A was the agent of D. On or about _____, A made an agreement with P."

(b) Exhibits [§606]

Essential allegations may appear in an exhibit attached to the complaint if *incorporated by reference* into the complaint. [Fed. R. Civ. P. 10(c)]

> **e.g. Example:** Where the essential allegation is that P gave D notice to quit the premises by a certain date, P can attach a copy of the written notice as an exhibit to the complaint and incorporate it by reference therein. The date can then be ascertained from the exhibit.

(c) Consequences of defect [§607]

Noncompliance with these rules of form is at most the basis for a *demurrer* or *motion* objecting to the defect. In modern practice, such defects are usually disregarded.

(3) Allegations on "information and belief" [§608]

Ordinarily, the plaintiff's allegations should be based on personal knowledge. However, if the plaintiff lacks personal knowledge of some element of his claim (*e.g.,* is relying on hearsay or conjecture), in *code pleading states* the plaintiff may still make the allegation on "information and belief." "Information and belief" may be insufficient under the Federal Rules, however. In federal courts, allegations can be made only after reasonable inquiry and with a belief that the pleading is likely to have evidentiary support. [Fed. R. Civ. P. 11; *see infra,* §§768 *et seq.*]

(a) Denials [§609]

Similarly, in code pleading states, a defendant may *deny* allegations based on "lack of information and belief." [Cal. Civ. Proc. Code §431.30] And under the Federal Rules, a statement that the defendant is "without knowledge or information sufficient to form a belief as to the truth of an averment" has the effect of a denial. [Fed. R. Civ. P. 8(b)]

(b) Importance [§610]

The use of allegations on information and belief is important where a pleading is to be *verified* by a party (where the pleading party includes an affidavit that the pleading is true to the best of the pleader's knowledge; *see infra,* §630), since the plaintiff should not swear facts to be true when she has no personal knowledge thereof.

(c) Limitation [§611]

Allegations on information and belief are improper as to matters which the pleader obviously knows or has *reason to know* (*e.g.,* events that she witnessed), or matters as to which she has *constructive knowledge* (*e.g.,* matters of *public record*). In such cases, pleadings on information and belief will be disregarded, leaving the complaint subject to a demurrer or motion to dismiss.

> ### EXAM TIP gilbert
>
> Exam questions will sometimes ask you to draft a complaint but tell you that your client has no personal knowledge of a certain allegation. Generally this should not be a stumbling block. A complaint generally can include allegations based on *"information and belief"* (or in federal court, with a belief that the pleading is likely to have evidentiary support). Similarly, an allegation can be denied in a code pleading state based on *"lack of information or belief,"* or under the Federal Rules, on the basis defendant is *"without knowledge or information sufficient* to form a belief as to the truth of the averment." *But remember:* If the pleader should have personal knowledge of the matter (*e.g.,* it concerns an event the pleader witnessed), the above allegations may not properly be used.

(4) Alternative and inconsistent allegations

(a) Inconsistent legal theories [§612]

A plaintiff *may* properly allege facts based on inconsistent legal theories. Note that Federal Rule 11 may limit this latitude. (*See infra,* §§768 *et seq.*)

Example: P claims damages as the result of surgery performed on him by Dr. D. P may plead in one count that the surgery was performed without his informed consent (hence a battery) and alternatively, in a separate count, that the surgery was negligently performed. P is entitled to go to trial on *both* theories, so that if the facts do not sustain one theory, they may sustain the other.

Example: P claims that D fraudulently induced him to execute a contract. P may plead one count for damages based on the fraud and alternatively, in another count, seek rescission of the contract based on the fraud.

1) Limitation—election of remedies [§613]

However, while a plaintiff may go to trial on both theories and have a verdict on each, he will have to elect one theory *prior to judgment* because he cannot have two remedies (*e.g.,* duplicate damages) for the same injury. [**Savage v. Van Marle,** 39 Cal. App. 3d 241 (1974)]

a) Time of election [§614]

The plaintiff is not required to make this election until *after* a jury verdict (or fact findings by the court) and before judgment. Otherwise, the plaintiff would have to guess which version of the facts will be sustained and thereby lose the benefit of alternative pleading. [**McCormick v. Kopmann,** 161 N.E.2d 720 (Ill. 1959)]

(b) Inconsistent facts [§615]

A pleader is also permitted to plead inconsistent versions of the facts. [Fed. R. Civ. P. 8(e)] However, some jurisdictions require that the facts alleged indicate some reason why the plaintiff could not know which version was true (*e.g.*, plaintiff was unconscious at the time of the injury, or injury-causing events occurred outside the pleader's observation).

(c) Alternative defendants [§616]

The plaintiff can also plead one version of the facts against one defendant and another version against another defendant. Again, some jurisdictions require a reason why the plaintiff could not know which version is true.

---

e.g. **Example:** After P's husband left a tavern operated by D-2, he was killed in a head-on collision with a truck driven by D-1. In her wrongful death action, P alleged that the accident was caused by the driving of D-1, whom she alleged had crossed the center line. To recover from D-1, P had to prove that her husband was free of contributory negligence. But P also asserted a claim against D-2, alleging that the accident was caused by her husband's intoxication, which resulted from the drinking her husband did at D-2's tavern. Under this version, P's husband would have been guilty of contributory negligence in connection with the crash. [**McCormick v. Kopmann,** *supra*]

EXAM TIP	gilbert

If you are asked to draft a pleading on an exam question, remember that it may include *alternative and inconsistent allegations*. For example, suppose your client in the question tells you facts regarding a contract dispute, and you think the facts support an argument that your client was fraudulently induced into making the contract, and they also support an argument that the other party did not fully perform. The fraud argument essentially seeks to negate the validity of the contract, while the performance argument admits there is a contract, but raises a defense to your client's failure to perform. Even though these theories are inconsistent, they may be pleaded in the alternative. Similarly pleadings can allege inconsistent facts in different claims if there is some reason why your client might not know which version is true.

(5) Defenses need not be anticipated [§617]

Ordinarily the plaintiff is not required in the complaint to anticipate any defense that the defendant may raise.

(a) Well-pleaded complaint rule [§618]

The rule regarding anticipating defenses corresponds to the well-pleaded complaint rule for federal question subject matter jurisdiction (*supra*, §391), which provides that the existence of a federal defense is not considered in deciding whether plaintiff's claim arises under federal law.

(b) Reply to affirmative defense [§619]

Although it is not automatically required, a court may order a plaintiff to reply to an affirmative defense asserted in an answer. (An affirmative defense is a defense relying on "new matter" that the defendant must prove to avoid the plaintiff's claim.) [Fed. R. Civ. P. 7(a)] The Supreme Court has observed that such a reply may be appropriate when a defendant asserts a defense of qualified immunity [**Crawford-El v. Britton,** 523 U.S. 574 (1998)], and some courts now require a reply in that situation [*See* **Reyes v. Sazan,** 168 F.3d 158 (5th Cir. 1999)—district court abused its discretion in failing to require plaintiffs to file reply to defendant's answer containing defense of qualified immunity].

d. Prayer for relief [§620]

A complaint must also contain a prayer for relief, *i.e.,* a statement of the relief sought.

(1) In default cases [§621]

If the defendant defaults by failing to defend, the relief granted cannot exceed what is prayed for in the complaint or differ from it in kind (*e.g.,* an injunction when the prayer was only for damages). *Rationale:* By failing to appear and contest the action, the defendant has, in effect, acquiesced in the entry of judgment against her; but the judgment entered must conform to the "consent" given. [Fed. R. Civ. P. 54(c); Cal. Civ. Proc. Code §580; *infra,* §§958 *et seq.*]

(2) In contested cases [§622]

In a contested case, the plaintiff is *not* limited to the relief prayed for in the complaint. The court may award *any relief to which a party is entitled* under the pleadings and proof—even if different from or greater than that prayed for in the complaint. [Fed. R. Civ. P. 54(c); Cal. Civ. Proc. Code §580]

EXAM TIP	gilbert

The distinction between damages available in a default case versus a contested case is sometimes tested on law school exams. Remember that in federal court and in most states, in a default case, damages **cannot exceed those asked for in the complaint** because that is what the defendant consented to by defaulting. It would be unfair to let a party default in an action where the plaintiff was seeking $1,000 damages and then allow the plaintiff to recover $10,000, for if the defendant knew $10,000 was at stake, she might have defended the action. On the other hand, if the defendant defends and the plaintiff proves damages in excess of those asked for in the complaint, the defendant can't complain, for she had an opportunity to be heard.

(a) Limitations [§623]

In a few states, a plaintiff is not permitted to state the amount of his demand in *personal injury or wrongful death actions*. [Cal. Civ. Proc. Code §425.10(b)] *Rationale:* This rule is intended to prevent sensational publicity for large demands. (However, the plaintiff must provide a statement of the damages claimed if the defendant demands one; in any event, such a statement must be made before trial.)

(b) Caution [§624]

Some decisions hold that where the complaint alleges *specific amounts* of damages, the allegations may be treated as *binding admissions* with respect to the amount of damage sustained. Hence, it may be error to award a greater sum; and such a judgment may be reduced accordingly. [**Brown v. North Ventura Road Co.,** 216 Cal. App. 2d 227 (1963)]

1) Trial tactic [§625]

Where evidence at trial indicates that the verdict may exceed the damages pleaded, the plaintiff should seek leave of court to *amend* the damage allegations and prayer upward. This may prevent the problem noted above. (Note that pleadings may be amended even after trial; *see infra,* §952.)

(3) Other functions of prayer [§626]

The prayer is ordinarily determinative of the *amount in controversy* for jurisdictional purposes. (*See supra,* §§351 *et seq.*) In state courts, it may also determine the nature of the action (legal or equitable), on which the *right to jury trial* depends.

e. Subscription [§627]

The complaint must be signed by the attorney (or by the party himself, where he is acting as his own counsel). [Fed. R. Civ. P. 11; Cal. Civ. Proc. Code §446]

(1) Effect of signature—federal practice [§628]

In federal practice, the signature on a pleading by a party or his attorney constitutes a certification by him that to the best of his knowledge, information, and belief, formed after reasonable inquiry, the evidentiary contentions have evidentiary support or are likely to have such support after discovery. The signature also certifies that the claims or defenses are warranted by existing law or a good faith argument for change in existing law, and that the claim or defense is not interposed primarily for any improper purpose such as harassment, delay, or increasing costs. [Fed. R. Civ. P. 11; *see infra,* §§768 *et seq.*]

EXAM TIP   **gilbert**

It is important to remember the effect of a signature on a pleading in federal court. Under Rule 11, the signature certifies that:

- To the best of the pleader's knowledge, formed after *reasonable inquiry*, the allegations have evidentiary support or are likely to after further investigation or discovery;

- The claims or *defenses* are *warranted by existing law* or a good faith argument for change in existing law; and

- The claims or defenses are *not interposed primarily for an improper purpose*.

As will be discussed later, the court may impose sanctions if a party or attorney improperly certifies a pleading.

(a) State practice [§629]

In state practice, subscription sometimes remains a mere formality. [**Hancock v. Bowman,** 49 Cal. 413 (1874)]

(2) Verification [§630]

A verification is an affidavit at the end of a pleading which avers that the pleading is true to the best of affiant's knowledge, information, or belief. The affidavit is made by the party, or by his attorney or other person on her behalf if the pleader cannot do so (*e.g.*, because she is incapacitated), or if another person with better knowledge of the facts is willing to make the verification for the party.

(a) Federal practice [§631]

In view of the importance attached to an attorney's subscription in federal practice (above), verification by a party is the exception rather than the rule in federal courts. Federal Rule 11 expressly provides that pleadings need *not* be verified except where specifically required by rule or statute.

 Example: The Federal Rules specifically require verification in shareholders' derivative suits. [Fed. R. Civ. P. 23.1]

(b) State practice [§632]

Some code pleading rules provide that any pleading *may* be verified; and verification is frequently required by statute as to certain kinds of proceedings (*e.g.*, quiet title actions, unlawful detainer proceedings, divorce suits).

1) Effect of verification [§633]

If a pleading is verified, the responsive pleading must also be verified (*e.g.,* if P files a verified complaint, D's answer *must* be verified by D). Moreover, a defendant cannot use a mere general denial (*infra,* §817) in answering a verified complaint. [Cal. Civ. Proc. Code §431.30(d)]

2) How to attack lack of verification [§634]

If a pleading that requires verification is not verified, the pleading is subject to a *motion to strike* (*infra,* §712).

PARTS OF A COMPLAINT   **gilbert**

A COMPLAINT GENERALLY MUST INCLUDE THE FOLLOWING:

☑ *Caption* (name of court, number assigned to action, designation of pleading, names of parties)

☑ Allegations of *subject matter jurisdiction*

☑ Allegations of *facts upon which recovery is sought*

☑ *Prayer for relief*

☑ *Signature* of attorney or unrepresented party

---

3. Pleading Specific Claims [§635]

As noted previously, the body of the complaint must contain allegations showing that the plaintiff has a right to recover.

a. In general [§636]

The elements of any particular cause of action involve both a *substantive* and a *procedural* aspect.

(1) Substance [§637]

Substantive law determines whether a specific incident or transaction *results in liability* to the plaintiff. For example, calling someone a "subversive" results in liability for defamation only if the substantive law so provides.

(2) Procedure [§638]

The procedural aspect is one of *allocation:* The plaintiff must allege enough particulars about the incident to constitute a *prima facie case.* Other particulars may be relevant, but will be considered only if they are injected into the case by the *defendant,* ordinarily in an affirmative defense.

> **e.g.** **Example:** When P alleges that D called him a subversive, does P also have to allege that the statement is *false* in order to state a claim for libel? Or must defendant raise the issue by pleading truth as an *affirmative defense*? The rule varies from state to state. [*See* **Brewster v. Boston Herald-Traveler,** 188 F. Supp. 565 (D. Mass. 1960)]

(a) State pleading [§639]

The following discussion of pleading requirements in particular causes of action is primarily important for *code pleading* states, where the general rule is that every essential element of the cause of action sued upon must be pleaded by allegations of "ultimate fact." (*See supra*, §589.)

(b) Federal pleading [§640]

This is not to imply that the elements of a cause of action may be disregarded in *notice pleading* jurisdictions: Federal Rule 8(a) requires that the complaint show that the plaintiff has a "right to relief"; and Federal Rule 12(b) authorizes a motion to dismiss for "failure to state a claim upon which relief can be granted" (*see infra*, §718). However, under the Federal Rules:

1) *Less detail and specificity* are required;

2) *Omission of allegations is never fatal* (*i.e.*, they can be supplied by amendment); and

3) *Only where the allegations indicate that the plaintiff cannot recover* as a matter of law is the action subject to dismissal for failure to state a claim. [**Conley v. Gibson,** *supra*, §593]

b. Trespass to land—elements [§641]

The essential elements in a trespass action are as follows:

(1) *Plaintiff's possession or right to possession* of the described property (as owner or otherwise) at the time of defendant's wrongful act. In most code pleading states, an allegation of "ownership" is sufficient to establish at least constructive possession, as long as there is nothing in the complaint to indicate that anyone else was in actual possession.

(2) *Defendant's wrongful intrusion* on the described property.

(3) *Damage* proximately caused by defendant's intrusion.

c. Recovery of possession (ejectment)—elements [§642]

In an action for ejectment, the plaintiff must allege:

(1) *Ownership* by plaintiff of some interest in the real property, adequately described. Ownership may be generally alleged; *i.e.,* "P was owner and in possession of Blackacre." This is a legal conclusion, but it is the best practical form of allegation, and hence is treated as an ultimate fact rather than a conclusion of law.

(2) *Defendant's possession and withholding.*

(3) *Damage* to plaintiff.

d. Negligence

(1) Elements [§643]
A complaint asserting negligence must contain allegations of: duty, breach of duty, damages, and causation.

(a) Duty [§644]
The plaintiff must allege the *specific facts from which the defendant's duty arose* (or from which it is inferred), *e.g.,* plaintiff was "driving on public highway"; "customer in defendant's store"; "patient under defendant's care"; etc.

Example: An allegation that "the defendant owed the plaintiff a duty of care" is a conclusion of law, and the complaint would be subject to a general demurrer. But an allegation that "the defendant was operating her automobile on Main Street near the intersection of Benton Way, and plaintiff was standing in a bus loading zone in the middle of that intersection" is a sufficient allegation of ultimate facts. From these facts, it can be inferred that the defendant, as a reasonable person, owed a duty of due care to the plaintiff in the operation of her automobile.

Compare: If the duty to be inferred rests upon unusual or special circumstances, they must be specifically alleged in the complaint—*e.g.,* a landlord ordinarily owes a duty to his tenant only with respect to known, latent defects (*see* Torts Summary), so that the landlord's knowledge and the latency of the defects must be alleged.

(b) Negligent action or omission (breach of duty) [§645]
In most code pleading states, the plaintiff can allege the defendant's breach of duty *generally—i.e.,* merely alleging that whatever the defendant did was "negligently" done, or that the defendant "negligently" failed to do something.

1) Allegation of "negligence"

An allegation of negligence is admittedly a conclusion of law; but in most instances it is still the best way to describe how the act was done. Thus, in most jurisdictions an allegation of negligence is treated as a sufficient allegation of the ultimate fact of breach of duty—as *a rule of convenience and fairness.* [**Rannard v. Lockheed Aircraft Corp.,** 26 Cal. 2d 149 (1945)]

EXAM TIP   **gilbert**

In code pleading states it is important to remember the distinction between *ultimate facts* and *conclusions of law*. Ultimate facts are facts, generally without legal argument or conclusion, that establish that the plaintiff is entitled to relief. However, in most code pleading states, in certain circumstances what is essentially a conclusion of law may be treated as an ultimate fact where the conclusion is the *best practical form of an allegation*. For example, rather than force a plaintiff to plead facts explaining how he came to possess the land upon which the defendant trespassed, the plaintiff may simply plead "at all times herein plaintiff owned the property at 123 Main Street."

---

2) Allegation of negligent acts

Alternatively, a general allegation of negligence may be replaced or supplemented by allegations of negligent acts showing that the defendant breached a duty of care (*e.g.,* "failed to keep a lookout"; "failed to maintain control of her car").

a) But note

Ordinarily, a general allegation by itself is preferable, because it does not tie the plaintiff down to any particular set of facts he must prove on trial.

b) And note—res ipsa loquitur

If the plaintiff intends to invoke the presumption of res ipsa loquitur at trial (a presumption that the defendant was negligent based on the harm that occurred to the plaintiff without proof of the defendant's exact conduct; *see* Torts Summary), some authorities hold that he must plead facts showing that he does not know the specific details of the defendant's negligence. In most states, however, res ipsa loquitur is no longer a matter of pleading, but one of proper instructions to the jury, to be given when the evidence of negligence is circumstantial. [**Newing v. Cheatham,** 15 Cal. 3d 351 (1975)]

(c) Damages [§646]

No cause of action in negligence will lie unless injury has been sustained. (For rules on pleading damages, *see infra,* §§663-672.)

(d) Allegation of causation [§647]

The courts are fairly liberal with respect to pleading causation and will allow allegations in *general terms*—*e.g.*, that plaintiff's injuries were "proximately caused" by the defendant's wrongful act. However, the courts insist that the *causal chain* between each step of the transaction be clearly alleged. Causation will not be inferred if there is an apparent gap between the defendant's wrongful act and the injuries to the plaintiff.

---

e.g. **Example:** P simply alleges that she suffered emotional distress "as a result" of defendant's conduct. This general statement of causation is insufficient, since P must allege facts showing the causal chain between D's conduct and P's distress—*i.e.*, the time, manner, and manifestations of the distress. [**Deboe v. Horn,** 16 Cal. App. 3d 221 (1971)]

---

(2) Defenses need not be anticipated [§648]

Ordinarily, the plaintiff is *not* required in the complaint to anticipate any defense that the defendant may raise (*e.g.*, assumption of risk, contributory negligence) and allege freedom from fault thereunder. The plaintiff can introduce such facts for the first time at trial, if the defendant has raised contributory negligence as a defense in her answer. In short, affirmative defenses in the answer are "deemed controverted." [**Mahoney v. Coralejo,** 36 Cal. App. 3d 966 (1974)]

EXAM TIP **gilbert**

Note that the pleading rule that the plaintiff need not anticipate defenses corresponds to the "well-pleaded complaint" rule that a federal defense to a state law claim does not provide a basis for federal question jurisdiction.

---

e. Products liability

(1) Elements [§649]

The essential elements of a cause of action for strict liability against the manufacturer or seller of a defective product are that:

(i) *Defendant was in the business* of making or selling the product in question;

(ii) *Defendant made or sold* the product in question;

(iii) *The product was in defective condition* (unreasonably dangerous for its foreseeable use) when it left defendant's control and when plaintiff used it; *and*

(iv) *Use of the product proximately caused injury* to plaintiff.

[**Read v. Safeway Stores,** 264 Cal. App. 2d 404 (1968)]

(2) Note

Under modern cases, it is generally *not* necessary to allege or prove: (i) privity of contract between the parties (as required in a warranty action); (ii) the plaintiff's reliance as a user or consumer on the reputation, skill, or judgment of the seller; (iii) any representation or undertaking on the part of the seller; or (iv) compliance with the provisions of the Uniform Commercial Code applicable to warranty actions. (*See* Torts Summary.)

f. Fraud

(1) Action at law [§650]

If the action for fraud is one at *law,* the necessary elements are:

(a) *Representation;*

(b) *Falsity;*

(c) *Knowledge* of falsity (*scienter*);

(d) *Intent to deceive* plaintiff;

(e) *Justifiable reliance* by plaintiff; and

(f) *Damages.*

(2) Suit in equity [§651]

If the suit is in *equity* (*e.g.,* to rescind a contract because of a fraudulent misrepresentation), the necessary elements are the same, except that scienter and damages need *not* be shown. (*See* Remedies Summary.)

(3) Special pleading requirement [§652]

In any event, the *ultimate facts* in a fraud action must always be pleaded *with particularity;* general allegations are not sufficient. [*See* Fed. R. Civ. P. 9(b); **Searle & Co. v. Superior Court,** 49 Cal. App. 3d 22 (1975)]

(a) Pleading securities fraud

For federal securities fraud claims, the Private Securities Litigation Reform Act of 1995 requires that the complaint "state with particularity facts giving rise to a strong inference that the defendant acted with the requisite state of mind" in cases where scienter is an element of the claim. [15 U.S.C. §78u-4(b)(2)] Although the courts have differed some in interpreting this Act, it has been held to require *very detailed allegations.* [*In re* **Silicon Graphics, Inc., Securities Litigation,** 183 F.3d 970 (9th Cir. 1999)—plaintiff must "plead, in great detail, facts that constitute strong circumstantial evidence of deliberately reckless or conscious misconduct"]

g. Defamation [§653]

The elements of a defamation claim are as follows:

(1) *Publication by defendant* to third persons of specified false matter which is "of or concerning" plaintiff.

(2) *Defamatory nature* of statement.

    (a) *If the statement is defamatory per se* (*e.g.,* an assertion that plaintiff committed a felonious crime), alleging the statement is sufficient. [**Megarry v. Norton,** 137 Cal. App. 2d 581 (1955)]

    (b) *If the statement on its face does not appear to be defamatory,* it must be alleged that:

        (i) *Extrinsic facts* make the statement defamatory ("inducement"); and

        (ii) The statement was *understood as defaming plaintiff* ("innuendo").

    [**Yorty v. Chandler,** 13 Cal. App. 3d 467 (1970)]

(3) *Causation* (*i.e.,* the publication of the defamatory statement caused harm to the plaintiff's reputation).

(4) *Special damages,* where the matter:

    (i) Is not defamatory on its *face* (some jurisdictions);

    (ii) Is *oral* (slander) rather than written (libel) and does not fall into one of the slander per se categories; *or*

    (iii) Appeared in a *newspaper* or *magazine* and no timely *demand for retraction* had been made (some jurisdictions).

    [**Briscoe v. Reader's Digest,** 4 Cal. 3d 529 (1971)] (*See* Torts Summary.)

h. Contract actions [§654]

A contract action should allege the following:

(1) Terms [§655]

The making of the contract must be alleged as well as its *terms,* by:

    (i) Stating the specific terms of the contract;

(ii) Attaching and incorporating by reference a copy of the contract, if it is in writing; *or*

(iii) Giving a general description of the terms of the agreement.

Note: In a few states, the plaintiff must also indicate whether the contract was *oral* or *in writing*. [Cal. Civ. Proc. Code §430.10(g)]

(a) Consideration [§656]

Whether consideration is required to make a promise enforceable is a matter of substantive law, determined by the particular promise. If consideration is required, merely alleging that there was consideration is neither necessary nor proper.

1) Enforceable promise [§657]

If the consideration is specifically alleged or other allegations show the promise is enforceable (*e.g.,* because under seal), such allegations indicate consideration. Hence, a general allegation that there was consideration is a mere conclusion.

2) Written contract [§658]

In some states, an allegation that the agreement is *in writing* will satisfy any requirement of pleading consideration, since a written contract is *presumed* to have been executed for sufficient consideration. [Cal. Civ. Code §1614]

3) Adequacy of consideration [§659]

Adequacy of consideration may have to be alleged in suits to enforce contracts in equity (*e.g.,* specific performance), because the equitable remedy is available only if the contract is fully fair and just.

(2) Performance by plaintiff [§660]

If the contract required the plaintiff to perform in whole or part before the defendant was obliged to perform, the plaintiff must allege performance on his part *or* show facts excusing his performance.

(a) Note

In some states, the plaintiff may allege this generally (*e.g.,* "plaintiff has performed all conditions on his part"). [Cal. Civ. Proc. Code §457]

(3) Conditions precedent [§661]

If some external condition must occur before the defendant's obligation arises, the plaintiff must allege that the condition occurred *or* allege facts constituting an *excuse* (*e.g.,* impossibility).

(a) Note

The occurrence of conditions precedent can be alleged generally. [Fed. R. Civ. P. 9(c); Cal. Civ. Proc. Code §457] If *excuse* is relied on, however, it must be specifically alleged. [**Gruenberg v. Aetna Insurance Co.,** 9 Cal. 3d 566 (1973)]

(b) Distinguish—conditions subsequent

The plaintiff need not concern himself with alleging nonoccurrence of a condition subsequent. Occurrence of a condition subsequent is "new matter" to be raised by the defendant in the answer. (*See infra*, §842.)

(4) Breach [§662]

The complaint must allege that the defendant *failed to perform* her obligation; *e.g.*, "Defendant failed to construct the structure in a proper and professional manner"; "Defendant failed to pay the sum agreed to be paid or any part thereof."

(5) Damages

See below.

i. Damages [§663]

The requisite allegations concerning damages depend on whether the action is in contract or in tort and—if in tort—what kind of injury is involved.

(1) Contract actions

(a) Promise to pay money [§664]

The measure of damages for breach of a promise to pay money is the amount of money unpaid, plus interest. An allegation that no part of the sum has been paid (or "no part except $_____") states the damages due.

(b) Promise to do an act or sell a thing [§665]

The measure of damages in this situation ordinarily is the difference between the agreed price and the price at which the plaintiff could obtain equivalent goods or services with reasonable effort at the time of breach. This difference is recoverable on a general allegation of damage in a specified amount—*i.e.*, it is *not* necessary to allege specifically the contract price "computation." [**Myers v. Stephens,** 233 Cal. App. 2d 104 (1965)]

(c) "Consequential" or "special" damages [§666]

The defendant is not liable for other damages in a contract action unless she was apprised in advance of facts indicating that they would result if she breached the contract. When such damages are sought, facts must be pleaded to show that the defendant was made aware that such losses could result. [Fed. Rule Civ. P. 9(g); **Shook v. Pearson,** 99 Cal. App. 2d 348 (1950)]

(2) Tort

(a) Negligence and products liability [§667]

From the fact of injury, *pain and suffering* may be inferred; and no special allegations are required for these elements of damage. However, other losses—wages, hospital expenses, etc.—must be alleged.

(b) Defamation [§668]

Earlier rules distinguished between damages recoverable for slander (oral defamation) and libel (written defamation). Today, allegations showing a defamatory statement are sufficient in most states to permit recovery of damages for indignation and injury to personal reputation, but *loss of income or damages to business* or profession must be specifically alleged. [**Smith v. Los Angeles Bookbinders Union,** 133 Cal. App. 2d 486 (1955)]

(c) Other torts [§669]

At common law, there were complicated distinctions between general and specific damages. In modern procedure, it is proper to describe the nature of the injuries sustained—loss of profits, shock and humiliation, etc.—and allege their monetary value.

1) *Whether a particular type of loss* (*e.g.,* loss of profit, humiliation) is *recoverable* is a matter of substantive law.

2) *Whether a particular type of loss* must be *pleaded* is a matter of *fair notice.* If the loss in question is not one that obviously would result from the conduct complained of, the facts showing the loss must be pleaded. [**Continental Nut Co. v. Robert L. Berner Co.,** 345 F.2d 395 (7th Cir. 1965); **Triodyne, Inc. v. Superior Court,** 240 Cal. App. 2d 536 (1966)]

(d) Punitive damages [§670]

Punitive damages are allowed only in some types of intentional torts—those involving fraud or willfully inflicted injury. Even when allowed, a claim for them must be made in either the statement of the cause of action or the prayer for relief, so that the defendant is on notice that they are being sought.

(e) Prohibition on pleading amount of personal injury or punitive damages [§671]

In some states, plaintiffs are not allowed to state in their complaints the amount of personal injury or punitive damages that they seek. [*See, e.g.,* Cal. Civ. Proc. Code §425.010(b)] *Rationale:* There is too great a likelihood that the amounts sought in these categories may be overly inflated and misleading.

(3) Distinguish—initial disclosure of computation of damages [§672]
Ordinarily the plaintiff need not plead in detail the computation of damages sought. In federal court, however, initial disclosure rules direct each party seeking to recover damages to provide "a computation of any category of damages" and make pertinent documents available for copying early in the litigation. [Fed. R. Civ. P. 26(a)(1)(C); *see infra,* §1299]

j. Pleading the "common counts"

(1) Definition [§673]
A "common count" is a simple pleading form seeking contractual or quasi-contractual relief—*e.g.,* to recover the value of goods or services rendered to another, money due on a loan, a balance owing on an account, etc. [*See* Fed. R. Civ. P. Forms 4-8]

---

e.g. **Example:** "D is indebted to P in the sum of $_____ for goods sold and delivered by P to D at D's request" is an example of the common count form. The common counts are conclusions of law, but are sufficient to state a cause of action under code pleading.

---

(2) Limitation [§674]
Pleading by means of a common count cannot overcome a substantive deficiency in the plaintiff's claim—as where the plaintiff supplied goods to the defendant in circumstances *not* reasonably implying a duty on the defendant's part to pay for them (*e.g.,* plaintiff voluntarily sent goods to defendant through the mail and then demanded payment for them).

(a) Consequences [§675]

1) *If the plaintiff pleads a common count in this situation,* the *pleading* is sufficient; but the substantive sufficiency of the plaintiff's claim may be attacked in a motion for summary judgment (*see* Chapter VIII.). [**Berk v. Alperin,** 206 Cal. App. 2d 240 (1962)]

2) *If the plaintiff pleads the common count along with an alternative count* that pleads the facts, the alternative count will be looked to in order to determine whether the underlying claim is substantively valid. [**White Lighting Co. v. Wolfson,** 68 Cal. 2d 336 (1968)]

3) *In any event, if the common count leaves the defendant uncertain* as to what is being complained of, various *discovery devices* are available by which she may ascertain the facts underlying the complaint. (*See* Chapter VI.)

k. Form complaints [§676]

In many jurisdictions, complaint forms are published for the types of claims that are commonly made. These complaints are usually *presumptively sufficient*. For example, the forms appended to the Federal Rules of Civil Procedure are explicitly declared to be "sufficient under the rules." [Fed. R. Civ. P. 84]

4. Splitting of Claims [§677]

A pleader cannot split a single claim or cause of action into several different parts and file separate suits on each one. If the plaintiff sues on only part of the cause of action he has against the defendant, he is barred from suing later on the balance. This results from the doctrine of *res judicata, i.e.*, that a judgment on any portion of a single cause of action merges the cause of action into the judgment, so that there is nothing left to sue on (*see* Chapter XI.). Where judgment has not been entered, and two cases are pending, attacks on the pleadings are possible.

a. Obvious splitting [§678]

If the plaintiff is proceeding in two separate actions and the splitting appears *on the face* of either complaint (unlikely), some states permit a special demurrer on the ground that "there is another action pending between the same parties for the same cause." [Cal. Civ. Proc. Code §430.10(c)]

b. Splitting not obvious [§679]

More frequently, the splitting will not appear on the face of either complaint, in which case the objection must be raised by the defendant in her answer (again, on the ground that another action is pending between the same parties for the same cause).

5. Joinder of Claims

a. No compulsory joinder of claims [§680]

While res judicata may force the plaintiff to bring suit upon her entire claim or cause of action (above), there is *no* requirement that she join in a single action what are separate and independent claims. Even where the claims are factually related, the plaintiff has the option of instituting a separate suit on each separate claim although, as a practical matter, plaintiffs usually join related claims because of the danger of *collateral estoppel*. (*See infra,* §§2226 *et seq.*)

b. Permissive joinder of claims

(1) Early common law rules [§681]

At common law, the joinder of separate claims was permitted only if all claims were in the same *form* of action and there was *identity* of parties to each claim.

---

e.g. **Example:** Slander could be joined with nuisance or negligent infliction of bodily injury because both claims had the same form of action (*i.e.*, trespass on the case). Moreover, joinder was permitted regardless of whether there was any factual relationship between these claims.

---

cf. **Compare:** A claim for slander (trespass on the case) could not be joined with one for assault and battery (trespass)—even where both claims arose out of the same event—because the two claims involved different forms of action.

---

(2) Equity rules [§682]

In equity suits, it was generally sufficient if the claim arose out of the same transaction or transactions and involved a common question of law or fact—*i.e.*, a requirement of subject matter relationship.

(3) Code pleading rules [§683]

Under the original Field Code, a plaintiff was restricted as to the causes of action that could be joined in a single complaint. All causes joined had to be the *same type* of claim (*e.g.*, all for injury to person, for injury to property, or all contract claims, etc.), or at least arise out of the same transaction; all such causes had to affect all parties to the action; and no cause could require a venue different from the others.

(a) Criticism

These rules frequently prevented a plaintiff from settling all claims against a defendant in a single action, and drastically narrowed the rules on permissive joinder of parties (because *all* causes joined had to affect *all* parties). In effect, the rules fostered a multiplicity of suits.

(b) Note

To remedy this situation, many states have now adopted rules similar to the more liberal Federal Rule on joinder, below. [*See* Cal. Civ. Proc. Code §427.10]

(4) Federal Rules [§684]

The modern viewpoint on joinder of claims is represented by Federal Rule 18(a), which *abolishes all restrictions* on the joinder of claims and provides that a party asserting a claim for relief may join as many claims as she has against an opposing party, regardless of subject matter.

EXAM TIP	gilbert

On your exam, remember that a party may assert as many claims as she has against an opposing party. This may be especially important if the plaintiff sues in federal court relying on diversity jurisdiction, for it means that if plaintiff has a $60,000 contract claim against a particular person and a $50,000 tort claim **against the same person** arising from a separate transaction, he can join the actions to meet the jurisdictional amount requirements.

(a) Limitation in multi-party cases [§685]

While there are no restrictions on the number or nature of claims that may be joined where a *single* plaintiff is suing a *single* defendant, the rules on joinder of parties impose limitations where there are several co-plaintiffs or co-defendants. When there are multiple parties, *at least one* of the claims by or against each party must arise out of "the same transaction or series of transactions" *and* must involve a "common question of law or fact" affecting each of the parties joined. [Fed. R. Civ. P. 20(a)]

1) Effect

The joinder of parties rules thus limit the joinder of claims in multi-party cases to those among which there is a *subject matter relationship*.

Example: P may sue D1 and D2 for personal injuries sustained in a three-car collision, asserting claims against both D1 and D2 because the same transaction is involved. P may also join a separate claim she has against D2 for nonpayment of a promissory note, even though this does not affect D1 in any way, because there are common questions of law affecting D1 and D2 in the personal injury claim.

(b) Separate trials [§686]

In its discretion, the trial court may remedy any possible inconvenience or prejudice caused by the joinder of claims by ordering separate trials. [Fed. R. Civ. P. 20(b), 42(b)]

Compare: If the claims are brought in *separate suits,* but have related subject matter, the defendant may move to have the trials *consolidated.* [Fed. R. Civ. P. 42(a), below]

(c) Distinguish—subject matter jurisdiction [§687]

In federal court, subject matter jurisdiction requirements must also be satisfied. For claims that arise out of the same transaction, there would ordinarily be *supplemental jurisdiction* (*see supra,* §§424-452) as long as one claim is a federal claim, but otherwise there must be an independent basis for subject matter jurisdiction (such as diversity of citizenship) with regard to permissively joined claims.

6. Consolidation of Separate Actions [§688]

The trial judge has the power to order separate lawsuits tried together or have them consolidated into a single action, if they involve a "common question of law or fact." [Fed. R. Civ. P. 42(b); Cal. Civ. Proc. Code §1048]

a. Actions pending in different courts [§689]

If separate actions involving related facts are pending in different courts, many jurisdictions permit one or more of the actions to be *transferred* so they can be consolidated or joined for trial in the same court. The cases may be transferred in whole or in part.

(1) State procedure [§690]

Transfer in state courts may be ordered where it will "promote the just and efficient control" of the various cases involved, and may involve transfer of the whole action or only certain issues (*e.g.,* liability). [Cal. Civ. Proc. Code §404]

(2) Federal practice [§691]

Federal "multi-district" litigation may be consolidated in one district for all *pretrial* purposes (development of issues, discovery, pretrial conference). [28 U.S.C. §1407] However, the parties have a right to *trial* in the district where the action was filed unless the action was transferred to another district where it "might have been brought." [28 U.S.C. §1404(a); *see supra,* §§187 *et seq.*]

D. Challenges to Complaint

1. In General [§692]

Before responding to the factual allegations in the plaintiff's complaint (by admitting or denying them, or setting forth some defense or offset thereto), a defendant may challenge the legal sufficiency of the complaint.

2. Common Law [§693]

At common law, defects in the pleadings could be raised by a demurrer. There were two kinds of demurrer:

a. General demurrer [§694]

A general demurrer *challenged the substantive sufficiency* of the cause or causes in the complaint. It did not specifically state the reason for demurring, but asked the court to pause (demur) and look at the complaint to see if it stated a valid case. Otherwise, why prolong the proceeding? This is still the basic idea of a general demurrer.

b. Special demurrer [§695]

This common law demurrer *specially stated* a matter to be scrutinized in the complaint—*e.g.,* incapacity of plaintiff, allegations that were too vague, etc. Hence, the special demurrer challenged *matters of form.*

3. State Practice [§696]

The Field Code, as adopted in states such as California, preserved the demurrer. In other states, such as New York, a motion to dismiss or (when the objection is that the pleading is vague) a motion to make more definite and certain is used instead. (*See infra,* §739.) However, the functions of these challenges are similar.

a. Demurrer [§697]

A demurrer is a pleading filed by one party for the purpose of challenging the *legal sufficiency* of the other party's pleading.

(1) Pleadings subject to demurrer [§698]

The most frequent use of the demurrer is to challenge the plaintiff's complaint. However, the plaintiff may demur to an affirmative defense, counterclaim, or cross-complaint filed by the defendant.

(2) Grounds for demurrer [§699]

The grounds for demurrer usually include the following [Cal. Civ. Proc. Code §430.10]:

(a) *Lack of jurisdiction over the subject* of the action (note that lack of *personal* jurisdiction usually must be challenged by a motion to quash because a demurrer constitutes a "general appearance," which would have the effect of waiving the personal jurisdiction challenge);

(b) *Plaintiff lacks legal capacity* to sue;

(c) *Another action is pending* between the same parties for the same cause;

(d) *Defect or misjoinder* of parties;

(e) *Failure to state facts sufficient to constitute a cause of action*—the "general demurrer" (below);

(f) *Complaint is uncertain* (ambiguous, unintelligible); *and*

(g) In an action upon a contract, *inability to ascertain whether the contract is oral or written.*

(3) "General" vs. "special" demurrer [§700]

A demurrer for failure to plead facts sufficient to constitute a cause of action is considered a "general" demurrer. A demurrer on any other ground is a "special" demurrer.

(a) Issue

In ruling on a general demurrer, the court must accept all facts pleaded as though they were true. The issue is whether—assuming that the well-pleaded facts are true—*the facts would entitle the plaintiff to some form of judicial relief.*

(b) Standard

If the complaint alleges facts sufficient to constitute *some* valid cause of action, the general demurrer will be overruled. The test is whether the complaint sets forth *any* good cause of action.

(4) Defect appearing on face of complaint [§701]

The demurrer challenges only defects that appear on the face of the pleading or matters of which the court can take *judicial notice* (well-known facts or facts that can readily and reliably be confirmed by resort to, *e.g.,* an almanac; *see* Evidence Summary). A demurrer *cannot* be used to introduce facts to controvert what is alleged in the pleading; *i.e.,* "speaking demurrers" are not allowed.

(a) Note

For this reason, certain grounds of demurrer—*e.g.,* plaintiff's lack of legal capacity or nonjoinder of parties—are rarely sustained. Such defects rarely appear on the face of the plaintiff's complaint and thus must be raised by motion (*see* below) or by affirmative defense in the answer.

(b) But note

Where the plaintiff's own allegations disclose some *complete defense* (*e.g.,* running of statute of limitations) *on the face of the complaint,* a general demurrer will lie unless the plaintiff has somehow "pleaded around" the defense.

(5) Procedure [§702]

A demurrer normally must be filed within the time permitted to answer the complaint. (*See infra,* §863.) The defendant may choose to demur and answer at the same time—as where the demurrer goes to only one portion of the complaint.

(a) Demurrer must specify defect [§703]

The defendant's demurrer must be in writing and must specify the ground for objection. Unless it does so, it may be disregarded. [Cal. Civ. Proc. Code §430.60]

> **Example:** "P's complaint fails to state a cause of action in that it does not allege what consideration, if any, was given for D's promise" is a sufficient demurrer.

(6) Ruling on demurrer—effects

(a) Ruling limited to grounds raised [§704]
Normally, the court has no power to raise grounds for demurrer on its own; its ruling must be based on the grounds raised by the demurring party.

1) Exception
However, the court may always raise lack of subject matter jurisdiction and the question of whether the pleading alleges facts sufficient to constitute a cause of action.

(b) Where demurrer is overruled [§705]
If the demurrer is overruled, the defendant will be ordered to answer the complaint within a period of time designated by the court. The defendant will then have to make a decision either to: (i) file an answer; or (ii) refuse to do so, allow the plaintiff to obtain a *default* judgment, and appeal the default judgment.

1) *If the defendant files an answer,* she *waives* any error in the overruling of a *special* demurrer. However, the defendant retains the right to object that the complaint does not state a cause of action.

2) *If the defendant does not file an answer* and appeals the resulting default judgment, she takes a big risk: An appellate court will not reverse unless the judgment was so plainly erroneous as to constitute an "abuse of discretion." [**Bristol Convalescent Hospital v. Sone,** 258 Cal. App. 2d 848 (1968)]

(c) Where demurrer is sustained

1) Specify grounds [§706]
In some states, the court must specify the particular ground or grounds upon which the demurrer is sustained. [Cal. Civ. Proc. Code §472d]

2) Leave to amend [§707]
Having sustained the demurrer, the court normally grants the plaintiff *leave to amend* the complaint.

a) *If the court is convinced that the defect cannot be cured* by amendment (especially where the plaintiff has already tried unsuccessfully to amend), it may sustain the demurrer *without* leave to amend. In that event, a *judgment of dismissal* is entered (from which the plaintiff can appeal).

b) *If the plaintiff is granted leave to amend and amends* the complaint within the time permitted, the defendant again has the choice of answering or demurring to the amended complaint.

c) *If the plaintiff chooses not to amend* (or fails to amend within the time permitted), a judgment of dismissal will be entered. The plaintiff can then obtain appellate review; but the appellate court will affirm the dismissal if:

1/ The complaint was *defective in substance,* even though the trial judge was incorrect as to the ground on which it was defective [*see, e.g.,* **Friendly Village Community Association v. Silva & Hill Construction Co.,** 31 Cal. App. 3d 220 (1973)]; *or*

2/ The complaint was *defective in form and the party failed to use an opportunity* given him in the trial court *to clarify* his pleading [*see, e.g.,* **Cooper v. Leslie Salt Co.,** 70 Cal. 2d 627 (1969)]. *Note:* Appellate courts do sometimes give plaintiffs a second chance to amend in this situation. [*See e.g.,* **Gillispie v. Goodyear Service Stores,** 128 S.E.2d 487 (N.C. 1963)—remand to allow plaintiff to replead]

(7) Effect of failure to raise ground for demurrer [§708]

Grounds for demurrer are *waived* unless raised in the defendant's *initial pleading*—demurrer *or answer.* (Where the defect does not appear on the face of the complaint—*e.g.,* plaintiff's lack of capacity to sue—it will, of course, have to be raised in the answer.) [Cal. Civ. Proc. Code §430.80]

(a) Exceptions [§709]

Failure to state facts sufficient to constitute a cause of action and the court's *lack of subject matter jurisdiction* are never waived. These objections can be raised at any time. [Cal. Civ. Proc. Code §430.80]

(b) Waiver of personal jurisdiction and process [§710]

Since a general demurrer constitutes an appearance in the action, it results in a waiver of objections to *personal* jurisdiction and to sufficiency of process.

(8) Criticism of demurrers [§711]

Modern writers generally condemn the demurrer as encouraging dilatory tactics by the defendant. Although a general demurrer undoubtedly serves a valuable function in weeding out claims without any legal basis, demurrers that merely attack the form of the complaint can be used for the sole purpose of delay, and thus perpetuate technical objections and technical rules of pleading.

b. Motion to strike [§712]

The only other challenge usually permitted against the form or contents of a pleading is a motion to strike, which normally lies to reach defects not subject to demurrer. Filing a motion to strike *extends the time within which to answer* the complaint. This enables the defendant to obtain a court order striking improper allegations from the complaint before being obliged to answer them. [Cal. Civ. Proc. Code §435(c)]

(1) Formal defects [§713]

The usual grounds for a motion to strike are that the pleading attacked contains *irrelevant or redundant matter* (*e.g.,* evidentiary matters or conclusions of law) or has some *defect in form* which is not a ground for demurrer (*e.g.,* lack of verification or subscription, late filing).

(2) Substantive defects [§714]

A motion to strike can also be used to eliminate *part* of a claim that is otherwise valid (*e.g.,* punitive damages sought in a suit for breach of contract). [**Goldman v. City Specialty Stores, Inc.,** 285 App. Div. 880 (1955)]

4. Federal Practice [§715]

The Federal Rules have deemphasized pleadings (*see supra,* §591), and accordingly limit the form and manner in which pleadings can be attacked.

a. Motion to dismiss [§716]

Under the Federal Rules, the motion to dismiss is the basic challenge to the legal sufficiency of adversary pleadings. [Fed. R. Civ. P. 12(b)] Making such a motion is *always optional* with the defendant, since he can raise the same objections in his answer (below).

(1) Permissible grounds [§717]

The motion to dismiss can be made *only* on the following grounds (with any other defenses or objections raised in the answer):

(a) *Lack of jurisdiction over the subject matter;*

(b) *Lack of jurisdiction over the person;*

(c) *Improper venue;*

(d) *Insufficiency of process;*

(e) *Insufficiency of service* of process;

(f) *Failure to state a claim* upon which relief can be granted; and

(g) *Failure to join a party whose joinder is required by Rule 19* (necessary or indispensable parties).

GROUNDS FOR DEMURRER VS. FEDERAL RULE 12(b) **gilbert**	
TYPICAL GROUNDS FOR DEMURRER	**GROUNDS TO DISMISS UNDER FEDERAL RULE 12(b)**
Lack of subject matter jurisdiction	Lack of subject matter jurisdiction
Plaintiff lacks capacity to sue	Lack of jurisdiction over the person
Another action is pending	Improper venue
Defect or misjoinder of parties	Insufficiency of process
Failure to state sufficient facts	Insufficiency of service
Complaint uncertain	Failure to state a claim upon which relief can be granted
Inability to ascertain whether contract was oral or written	Failure to join a party whose joinder is required

(2) Failure to state a claim [§718]

When the motion is made under Federal Rule 12(b)(6) (failure to state a claim), its function is basically that of a general demurrer (*supra,* §700): Assuming the facts pleaded are true, do they constitute a legal claim upon which the plaintiff is entitled to judicial relief?

(a) Test for sufficiency of complaint [§719]

In testing the sufficiency of the complaint in connection with a Rule 12(b)(6) motion, the following principles are generally applied.

1) "Facts" not explicitly required [§720]

The complaint generally need not contain the ultimate facts; Federal Rule 8(a)(2) requires only a "short and plain statement of the claim showing that the pleader is entitled to relief."

2) Liberal standard for sufficiency [§721]

The Supreme Court has stated that the complaint should not be dismissed unless the court is certain that the plaintiff cannot prove a set of facts in support of his claim that would entitle him to relief. [**Conley v. Gibson**, *supra*, §640]

(e.g.) **Example:** A complaint charging "slanderous utterances" by defendant was held sufficient notwithstanding its failure to state, in so many words, that there had been a *publication* of the alleged defamations, because that could fairly be inferred from the allegations made. [**Garcia v. Hilton Hotels**, 97 F. Supp. 5 (D.P.R. 1951)]

---

b) **Liberal standard questioned [§722]**

Despite the Supreme Court's grand pronouncement in *Conley*, the lower courts have continued to pay attention to whether the plaintiff indicates in the complaint that there is a factual basis for the claim. As one court put it, "although the exceedingly forgiving attitude toward pleading deficiencies that was expressed by Justice Black for the Supreme Court in *Conley* . . . continues to be quoted with approval, it has never been taken literally." [**Sutliff, Inc. v. Donovan Companies**, 727 F.2d 648 (7th Cir. 1984)]

c) **Code pleading standard compared [§723]**

Nevertheless, the federal standard is more lenient than the requirements imposed by many state courts under code pleading. For example, Form 9 of the Federal Rules states that the following is sufficient to allege negligence: "Defendant negligently drove a motor vehicle against plaintiff." This relaxes the requirement in some code states that the plaintiff specify the underlying failure of the defendant upon which the claim of negligence is based. (*See supra*, §645.)

3) **Continuing need to set out factual matter [§724]**

Despite the absence of a specific requirement for allegations of fact in the rules, the federal courts require the plaintiff to "set out sufficient factual matter to outline the elements of his cause of action or claim, proof of which is essential to his recovery." [**Daves v. Hawaiian Dredging Co.**, 114 F. Supp. 643 (D. Haw. 1953)]

EXAM TIP	gilbert

It is important to remember the function of a Rule 12(b)(6) motion to dismiss for failure to state a claim. The court will look at the complaint, *assume the facts are true* (provided the complaint sets out sufficient facts to outline the cause of action), and assess whether, even if all the facts are true, the complaint fails to set out a legal claim that would entitle the plaintiff to relief. If a sufficient claim is not set out, the court will grant the motion.

4) Fraud or mistake [§725]

When claims are based on fraud or mistake, the Federal Rules require the plaintiff to plead *"with particularity."* [Fed. R. Civ. P. 9(b)]

a) Claims affected [§726]

This requirement of added specificity applies only to claims where the substantive right to relief depends on proof of fraud or mistake. Examples include common law fraud, securities fraud, and actions to rescind or modify a contract for mutual mistake. (Recall that for federal securities fraud claims, the Private Securities Litigation Reform Act requires *very detailed allegations*; *see supra*, §652.)

b) Rationale

Courts explain that the added specificity is important to provide added notice and that it protects defendants against unfounded claims that damage their reputations.

c) Criticism

It is difficult to understand why the claims covered give rise to especially troubling problems compared with other claims not covered by the rule.

d) Application

Courts usually look to whether the plaintiff has provided specifics concerning the date and content of representations on which a fraud claim is based. In cases involving multiple defendants, it may be necessary for the plaintiff to specify the involvement of each one that allegedly gives rise to liability, sometimes requiring very great detail. However, some courts say that to satisfy Rule 9(b), the plaintiff need provide only "slightly more" than that which is required by Rule 8(a)(2). [*See, e.g.,* **Tomera v. Galt,** 511 F.2d 594 (7th Cir. 1975)]

e) State of mind [§727]

Rule 9(b) also provides that "[m]alice, intent, knowledge, and other condition of mind" can be *averred generally*. This exempts all allegations on these subjects from the particularity requirement of the rule. Nevertheless, some courts apply the particularity requirement to allegations relating to state of mind. [*See, e.g.,* **Ross v. A.H. Robins Co.,** 607 F.2d 545 (2d Cir.), *cert. denied*, 446 U.S. 946 (1980)—in securities fraud action, plaintiffs required to plead facts giving rise to a "strong inference" that defendants knew falsity of their statements]

5) Heightened specificity for other types of claims [§728]

With regard to certain other types of claims, some federal courts have developed pleading requirements that seem to go beyond the liberality of *Conley*.

a) Civil rights claims [§729]

The most prominent examples are *civil rights claims.* In such claims courts often insist that plaintiffs allege with specificity the basis for their belief that the defendants acted with forbidden animus. [*See, e.g.,* **Fisher v. Flynn,** 598 F.2d 663 (1st Cir. 1979)—requiring employment discrimination plaintiff to plead basis for believing that firing was in retaliation for her rejection of supervisor's sexual overtures; **Albany Welfare Rights Organization Day Care Center, Inc. v. Schreck,** 463 F.2d 620 (2d Cir. 1972)—plaintiff required to plead basis for believing that defendant officials refused to deal with plaintiff in retaliation for plaintiff's political activities]

b) Other claims "analogous" to fraud [§730]

Lower courts have also found that more stringent pleading requirements are appropriate in cases that involve contentions or litigation problems "analogous" to fraud. [*See, e.g.,* **Chiron Corp. v. Abbott Laboratories,** 156 F.R.D. 219 (N.D. Cal. 1994)—particularized pleading required for defense of inequitable conduct by plaintiff in obtaining patent in suit; **Cash Energy, Inc. v. Weiner,** 768 F. Supp. 892 (D. Mass. 1991)—more specific pleading required for claims made personally against corporate officers in environmental cleanup suit]

c) Qualified immunity [§731]

Another area in which lower courts have required that plaintiffs plead with more specificity are cases in which local officials claim qualified immunity against suit. [**Elliott v. Perez,** 751 F.2d 1472 (5th Cir. 1985)—in cases against government officials involving the likely defense of immunity, trial judges must demand that the plaintiff's complaint state with factual detail and particularity the basis for the claim, including why the defendant-official cannot successfully maintain the defense of immunity]

d) Stimulus for heightened pleading requirements [§732]

The motivation for this intensification of pleadings scrutiny is *concern about the settlement value of frivolous or groundless claims.* [*See, e.g.,* **Blue Chip Stamps v. Manor Drug Stores,** 421 U.S. 723 (1975)—Court stated that the liberal discovery provisions can give complaints with little chance of success on the merits a disproportionately high settlement value to plaintiff, as long as he can prevent suit from being resolved against him by dismissal]

e) Court disapproved heightened specificity [§733]
In **Leatherman v. Tarrant County Narcotics Intelligence and Coordination Unit,** 507 U.S. 163 (1993), the Supreme Court has disapproved of heightened specificity requirements regarding qualified immunity in civil rights cases, which are not governed by Rule 9(b). However, it does not appear that courts need accept mere conclusions in such cases, and some lower courts have held that special pleading requirements still apply to civil rights suits against local officials entitled to claim immunity. [*See, e.g.,* **Jordan v. Jackson,** 15 F.3d 333 (4th Cir. 1994)— even after *Leatherman,* district courts should not tolerate plaintiffs seeking "unlimited discovery from municipal defendants in the mere hope of obtaining tidbits of information from which they can cobble together support for what were conclusory allegations of an impermissible municipal policy"] The long-term impact of *Leatherman* is *unclear.*

f) Alternative of requiring reply or entertaining motion for more definite statement [§734]
The Supreme Court has stated that in suits involving official immunity, a district court "must exercise its discretion so that officials are not subjected to unnecessary and burdensome discovery or trial proceedings." If the plaintiff can overcome a public official's defense of immunity only with proof of a wrongful motive, the court may insist that the plaintiff "put forward *specific, nonconclusory factual allegations*" that establish the motive. A court has "two primary options" for accomplishing this: (i) "the court may order a reply to the defendant's or a third party's answer under Federal Rule of Civil Procedure 7(a)," or (ii) the court may "grant the defendant's motion for a more definite statement under Rule 12(e)." [**Crawford-El v. Britton,** *supra,* §619]

1/ Reply required [§735]
One lower court has ruled that it is an abuse of

discretion for a district court to fail to require a plaintiff to file a reply after defendants have raised qualified immunity unless plaintiff's complaint was pleaded with particularity. [**Reyes v. Sazan,** *supra,* §619]

2/ Rule 8(a) not applicable to a reply [§736]

The same lower court has concluded that because Rule 8(a) (which requires a "short and plain" statement of the grounds for jurisdiction and of the facts showing a right to relief in a complaint) does not list Rule 7 replies, Rule 8(a)'s "short and plain" standard does not govern Rule 7 replies. [**Schultea v. Wood,** 47 F.3d 1427 (5th Cir. 1995)]

(3) Amendment by plaintiff if motion to dismiss is granted [§737]

Granting or denying leave to amend rests in the discretion of the court, but leave must be liberally granted. [**Foman v. Davis,** 371 U.S. 178 (1962)]

(a) *If the plaintiff amends,* he waives any error in the ruling on the original complaint, unless he can show that the outcome of the action was prejudiced by the erroneous dismissal of the original complaint.

(b) *If the plaintiff chooses not to amend* (or if leave to amend is denied), the court will enter a judgment of dismissal. The ruling on the motion is not an appealable order, but the judgment can be appealed.

   1) *If the plaintiff appeals and wins,* the complaint is reinstated, and the defendant must answer.

   2) *If the plaintiff loses on appeal* or fails to appeal, this generally bars any further proceedings in the action. However, the appellate court has discretion to remand in order to permit an amended complaint to be filed.

(4) Answer by defendant if motion is denied [§738]

If the defendant's Rule 12(b) motion is denied, she must answer and proceed with the litigation—*i.e.,* the appellate court will not reexamine the denial of the defendant's motion as such. However, the defendant can raise the same issues on appeal from the final judgment and by subsequent motions (motions for judgment as a matter of law, for directed verdict, for judgment notwithstanding the verdict, etc.), which can also be reviewed on appeal from the final judgment.

b. Motion for more definite statement [§739]

Rule 12(e) permits a very limited attack on the *form* of the pleadings (and to this extent serves somewhat the same function as the special demurrer for uncertainty in code pleading practice). However, the motion will be granted only where the pleading under attack is *so vague and ambiguous* that it would be *unreasonable* to require the moving party to reply to it. [Fed. R. Civ. P. 12(e)]

EXAM TIP	gilbert

On your exam, if you are asked to judge the sufficiency of a motion for a more definite statement, be sure to remember that such motions are rarely granted. If the pleading is sufficiently definite that a reply *can* reasonably be made, the motion will be denied; and any vagueness or uncertainty must be addressed through discovery (see Chapter VI.).

(1) When available [§740]

A motion for a more definite statement is appropriate only if the pleading being attacked requires a response. If no response is permitted to the pleading under attack (*e.g.,* defendant's answer), the motion is *never* proper.

(2) As predicate for Rule 12(b)(6) motion [§741]

Numerous cases have found that the motion for a more definite statement should not be used as a predicate for a Rule 12(b)(6) motion to dismiss for failure to state a claim. [*See, e.g.,* **United States v. Board of Harbor Commissioners,** 73 F.R.D. 460 (D. Del. 1977)] But the Supreme Court has recognized that in some circumstances it is an important way of making plaintiffs "put forward specific, nonconclusory factual allegations." [**Crawford-El v. Britton,** *supra,* §734] Thus, although there may be a bias against using a Rule 12(e) motion as a precursor to a Rule 12(b)(6) motion, it appears to be proper to do so if there actually is a substantial threshold question that may be dispositive (*e.g.,* whether facts are sufficient to overcome official immunity).

(3) Motion available even if complaint states claim [§742]

If a complaint is unduly wordy or otherwise in improper form, a court may require a more definite statement even though the complaint states a claim. Moreover, if the plaintiff fails to comply, the complaint may be dismissed even if it is not wholly without merit. [**McHenry v. Renne,** 84 F.3d 1172 (9th Cir. 1996)]

c. Motion to strike [§743]

Either party may move to strike an insufficient defense or any "redundant, immaterial, impertinent or scandalous" matter in the other's pleadings. [Fed. R. Civ. P. 12(f)]

(1) Limited use [§744]

The motion to strike is said to be "disfavored" and generally will be denied unless the allegations attacked have absolutely *no* possible relation to the controversy (*e.g.*, allegations that a tribunal was a "kangaroo court"). [**Skolnick v. Hallett,** 350 F.2d 861 (7th Cir. 1965)] If the alleged matter is merely of doubtful relevancy or doubtful legal value, the motion will be denied. *Rationale:* Pleadings are not read to the jury in federal court (except in unusual circumstances where they have special relevance—*e.g.*, when they contain an admission). Consequently, it serves little purpose to strike allegations in the pleadings.

(2) Strike portions of complaint [§745]

A motion to strike may also be used to attack separate portions of the complaint which are insufficient as a matter of *law*—*e.g.*, where plaintiff seeks punitive damages in a breach of contract action even though, as a matter of law, such damages are not available on such a claim, or where defendant asserts an affirmative defense that is not applicable to plaintiff's claim.

d. Procedure on motions under Rule 12 [§746]

A motion under Rule 12 must be in writing and must specify the ground (or grounds) upon which it is based. [Fed. R. Civ. P. 7(b)(1)]

(1) Facts [§747]

If the motion is based on asserted facts, these must be established by accompanying affidavits, depositions, or other evidence. (The opposing party may, of course, submit controverting evidence.) *Note:* On a Rule 12(b)(6) motion, scrutiny is ordinarily limited to the face of the complaint. (*See infra*, §§756-758.)

(2) Time [§748]

The motion must be served within the time permitted the defendant to serve the answer (normally 20 days after service of a summons and complaint; *infra*, §860). The filing of the motion operates to extend the time within which the answer is due until the court rules on the motion.

e. Waiver of defenses [§749]

The defendant is never compelled to file a motion under Rule 12; but if she does, she must include therein *all defenses and objections that she could then raise by motion.* If she omits an available defense or objection, she may not make a further motion on the omitted ground. [Fed. R. Civ. P. 12(g)] She will, however, be able to raise the ground in her answer, unless it is a ground that is waived by failure to raise in the first responsive pleading or motion.

(1) Waiver [§750]

The following defenses are *waived* unless raised in the first responsive pleading [Fed. R. Civ. P. 12(h)(1)]:

(i) *Objections to the form* of the complaint;

(ii) *Objections to venue, personal jurisdiction,* or to *sufficiency of process.*

(a) Rationale

A party who invites the court to pass upon a "threshold" defense should bring forth *all* such defenses, in order to prevent waste of time by piecemeal presentation of defects.

(b) Defenses not included in answer

Most other defenses must be raised in the answer to be asserted later in the case. If defendant fails to raise a given defense in the answer, it is sometimes said that it is "waived," but actually it can later be raised if defendant obtains leave to amend the answer to add the omitted defense.

(2) Defenses that need not be raised in answer [§751]

The following basic defenses need not be raised in the answer to be raised later by motion [Fed. R. Civ. P. 12(h)(2), (3)]:

(a) *Lack of subject matter jurisdiction;*

(b) *Failure to join an indispensable party;*

(c) *Failure to state a claim* upon which relief can be granted.

DEFENSES WAIVED BY FAILURE TO ASSERT	**gilbert**
DEFENSES WAIVED IF NOT FILED IN FIRST RESPONSIVE PLEADING	**DEFENSES THAT NEED NOT BE RAISED IN RESPONSIVE PLEADING AND WHICH MAY BE RAISED LATER**
Objections to *form of the complaint* Objections to *venue* Objections to *personal* jurisdiction Objections to *sufficiency of process*	Objections based on *subject matter jurisdiction* Objections based on *failure to join an indispensable party* Objections claiming *failure to state a claim* upon which relief can be granted

(3) Limitation [§752]

Keep in mind that the waiver pertains only to the defenses that *could* be raised by a Rule 12 motion. Thus, there is no waiver of substantive defenses (*e.g.,* release, novation, payment, etc.), which can be raised in *only* the answer.

(4) Distinguish—forfeiture of defense due to delay in asserting [§753]

Under some circumstances, even where a defendant complies with Rule 12(h) and includes a preliminary defense in her answer, her failure to assert that defense by motion in a timely fashion may be found to forfeit the defense. [*See, e.g.,* **Hamilton v. Atlas Turner, Inc.,** 197 F.3d 58 (2d Cir. 1999)—defendant's failure to move to dismiss for lack of personal jurisdiction for over four years, while there was substantial pretrial activity in the case, constituted a forfeiture of its objection to personal jurisdiction]

5. Other Procedures [§754]

While the demurrer (state practice) and Rule 12 motion (federal practice) are the procedures most commonly used to attack the sufficiency of a pleading, other procedures are likewise available—the most important of which is the *motion for judgment on the pleadings* (discussed *infra,* §§967-972).

6. Additional Rules of Pleading [§755]

In both state and federal practice, the following additional principles apply:

a. Materials considered

(1) Pleading on its face [§756]

In general, challenges to the sufficiency of the pleadings are limited to the allegations of the pleadings alone, and consideration of evidentiary materials, no matter how persuasive, is not allowed.

(a) Distinguish—summary judgment [§757]

Evidentiary materials are the basis for decision on a motion for summary judgment. (*See* Chapter VII.)

(b) Conversion to summary judgment [§758]

In federal court, if materials outside the complaint are submitted with a motion to dismiss for failure to state a claim and are not excluded by the court, the motion is to be considered a motion for summary judgment. [*See* Fed. R. Civ. P. 12(b); *and see* **Vesely v. Sager,** 5 Cal. 3d 153 (1971)—motion to strike complaint based on materials outside the complaint treated as motion for summary judgment]

(2) "Speaking" demurrers [§759]

In some code pleading jurisdictions, there was once a practice of allowing "speaking" demurrers, which went beyond the face of the complaint and called other materials to the attention of the court. This practice has generally been disapproved.

(3) Exhibits [§760]

When a document is an exhibit to the complaint, it is "a part thereof for all purposes." [Fed. R. Civ. P. 10(c)] Therefore, it can be considered in connection with a motion to dismiss.

(a) Caution

The fact that the court may consider the exhibit in connection with the motion to dismiss does not mean that all assertions in the exhibit are taken as true for purposes of the motion. For example, in a defamation action based on assertions in a letter, the plaintiff might attach the letter as an exhibit to the complaint without admitting that the assertions in the letter are true.

(4) Superseded pleadings [§761]

Reference to earlier pleadings filed by the same party present several kinds of problems:

(a) Inconsistent allegations [§762]

Because parties may ordinarily make inconsistent allegations within a given pleading (*see supra,* §615), the fact that the plaintiff made an inconsistent allegation in a previous complaint does not render the current complaint inadequate.

(b) Omission of fatal details [§763]

Where, however, a party has attempted to "cure" a defect simply by omitting an allegation, the court may look to the previous complaint to determine the sufficiency of the current complaint. [**Lee v. Hensley,** 103 Cal. App. 2d 697 (1951)—where original complaint showed that claim was barred by limitations, amendment to delete these allegations was ineffective to avoid dismissal]

(5) Matters judicially noticed [§764]

Finally, a pleading is construed in light of facts that may be *judicially noticed:* historical facts, geography, etc. [Cal. Civ. Proc. Code §430.30(a)]

(6) Materials referred to in complaint but not attached [§765]

In some instances, the lower courts have considered materials not attached to the complaint in deciding a Rule 12(b)(6) motion (failure to state a claim upon which relief may be granted). In general, the courts explained that these materials were *"central"* to the complaint [*In re* **Burlington Coat Factory Securities Litigation,** 114 F.3d 1410 (3d Cir. 1997)], that they were *referred to in the plaintiff's complaint* [**GFF Corp. v. Associated Wholesale Grocers, Inc.,** 130 F.3d 1381 (10th Cir. 1997), and that there was *no dispute about their authenticity* [**Watterson v. Page,** 987 F.2d 1 (1st Cir. 1993)].

b. Anticipatory defenses [§766]

A complaint need *not* anticipate affirmative defenses that the defendant might raise.

Example: P is injured, but executes a release of her claim. Later, P sues for her injuries on the premise that the release was given by mistake. P should not anticipate the defense of release, but should simply allege her claim for injury, await the defense of release, and then *avoid* it by proof at trial.

Compare: If P *does* anticipate a defense in her complaint, the complaint must also plead facts to avoid it. For example, if P in the previous example alleges the release, she must also allege facts showing a mistake that would make the release ineffective. **[Powell v. Lampton,** 30 Cal. App. 2d 43 (1938); **Hoshman v. Esso Standard Oil Co.,** 263 F.2d 499 (5th Cir. 1959)]

(1) Duty to investigate [§767]

Before filing a complaint, the plaintiff's attorney should investigate defenses. (*See* below.)

E. Attorney's Duty to Investigate Claims and Defenses

CHECKLIST OF MATTERS CERTIFIED UNDER RULE 11   **gilbert**

THE FOLLOWING MATTERS ARE CERTIFIED UNDER RULE 11 BY THE PERSON SIGNING THE PLEADING:

☑ The signer has made a *reasonable inquiry into the factual and legal grounds* for the pleading

☑ The *factual allegations have evidentiary support* or will likely have evidentiary support after the signer has a reasonable opportunity to further investigate and use discovery

☑ The position taken in the pleading is *warranted by existing law* or a nonfrivolous argument for a change in existing law or the establishment of new law

☑ The *paper was not filed for an improper purpose*

1. Introduction [§768]

Verification and signature requirements for pleadings have long existed. (*See supra*, §§627-634.) From 1938 through 1983, however, the original *Rule 11* of the Federal Rules of Civil Procedure used a *subjective standard* for the obligations of a lawyer signing a pleading. The Rule looked to actual bad faith of the lawyer in signing the pleading. In 1983, the Rule was amended to fortify its requirements and became a major consideration in assessing the obligations of lawyers filing suits and answers (as well as other papers). In 1993, substantial further revisions were made.

a. Rationale
The rationale for enhanced scrutiny of lawyer behavior was to *promote self-policing* by lawyers and *deter groundless and frivolous claims.*

b. Conflicting interpretations
Under the 1983 version, courts gave the Rule conflicting interpretations on a number of key issues.

c. Policy concerns
Many courts (and law professors) expressed concern that the 1983 version of the rule *unduly constricted creative advocacy.*

d. Distinguish—state court provisions
A number of state courts retain *subjective* standards. [*See, e.g.,* Cal. Civ. Proc. Code §128.5—authorizing sanctions for "bad faith actions or tactics that are frivolous or solely intended to cause unnecessary delay"]

2. Certification Requirement

a. Signature on paper [§769]
Rule 11 focuses on the signature on a paper filed in court, although it may also apply to later oral argument advocating a position in a paper (*see infra,* §797).

b. Applicable to all filings except discovery [§770]
The rule applies to every filing in court, but may be most important with regard to complaints and answers.

(1) Discovery [§771]
With regard to discovery filings, Federal Rule 26(g) imposes similar certification requirements, and Rule 11 does not apply.

(2) Applicable to nonattorneys [§772]
The rule applies to nonattorneys (*e.g.,* parties appearing pro se and, with regard to certain matters, parties represented by attorneys), as well as to attorneys.

3. Matter Certified by Signature [§773]
By signing a paper filed in court, a person certifies the following:

a. Reasonable inquiry [§774]
With regard to the factual and legal grounds for the position taken in the paper, the person signing the paper certifies that she has made an "inquiry reasonable under the circumstances" to support that position.

(1) Attorney pre-filing investigation [§775]

Ordinarily, it is expected that a lawyer will investigate factual and legal assertions before making them in a filing. This can include factual investigation of allegations and legal research regarding legal assertions.

b. Allegations or factual contentions have evidentiary support [§776]

Rule 11 provides that signing a paper filed in court certifies that factual assertions "have evidentiary support." [Fed. R. Civ. P. 11(b)(3)]

(1) Prior law [§777]

Under the 1983 version of Rule 11, the similar certification was that allegations were "well grounded in fact," and there was no explicit reference to evidentiary support.

(2) Option for party lacking evidentiary support [§778]

The rule provides that a party may make allegations without evidentiary support for them if the allegations, are *"likely to have evidentiary support after a reasonable opportunity for further investigation or discovery."* This option is available, however, only as to allegations *"specifically so identified."*

(3) Applicable to denials [§779]

These certification requirements apply fully to denials of factual contentions. Denials may, however, be *based on lack of information or belief*, but only if *specifically so identified.* [Fed. R. Civ. P. 11(b)(4)]

(4) Reliance on client [§780]

Reliance on the client for the factual assertions may be dangerous, although prospective testimony of a client who has personal knowledge of the circumstances would seem to meet the rule's standard. [*See, e.g.*, **Finance Investment Co. v. Geberit AG,** 165 F.3d 526 (7th Cir. 1998)—attorney not justified in accepting client's word that it had a right to pursue the claim asserted; **Southern Leasing Partners, Ltd. v. McMullan,** 801 F.2d 783 (5th Cir. 1986)—"blind reliance on the client is seldom a sufficient inquiry"]

(a) Possible shift under 1993 amendment [§781]

Some courts read the 1993 amendments to Rule 11 as indicating that attorneys need only do "an inquiry reasonable under the circumstances," and that so long as the client provides prospective evidentiary support for allegations, the attorney has acted properly. [**Hadges v. Yonkers Racing Corp.,** 48 F.3d 1320 (2d Cir. 1995)—under the Rule 11 amendments it is clear that an attorney is entitled to rely on the "objectively reasonable representations of the client"]

(b) Distinguish—sanction on client where attorney reasonably relies on client [§782]

Where the lawyer properly relies on the client, the client can be sanctioned for signing documents filed in court in violation of Rule 11, even if the lawyer committed no violation of the rule. [**Business Guides, Inc. v. Chromatic Communications Enterprises,** 498 U.S. 533 (1991)]

(5) Waivable affirmative defense [§783]

It is *unclear* whether a lawyer violates the rule by filing a complaint where the investigation shows that there is a valid affirmative defense that could be waived.

(a) Effect or burden of pleading [§784]

If Rule 11 forbids filing a complaint in such circumstances, it in essence has converted the affirmative defense into a part of the plaintiff's pleading burden, because the plaintiff would not be allowed to proceed despite being able to plead all the affirmative elements of his claim.

c. Supported by law [§785]

The signature also certifies that the claim, defense, or other legal position taken in the paper is "warranted by existing law or by a nonfrivolous argument for the extension, modification, or reversal of existing law or the establishment of new law." [Fed. R. Civ. P. 11(b)(2)]

(1) Need to research [§786]

The lawyer is expected to do research to determine whether there is a legal basis for claims or defenses that are asserted.

(2) Objective standard [§787]

The rule is intended to create an objective standard. As explained under the 1983 version, it calls for sanctions "where it is patently clear that the claim has absolutely no chance of success under the existing precedents, and where no reasonable argument can be advanced to extend, modify or reverse the law as it stands." [**Eastway Construction Corp. v. City of New York,** 762 F.2d 243 (2d Cir. 1985)]

(a) Conflict among district courts [§788]

The Supreme Court has said that when there is a conflict on an issue among district courts, it is not frivolous to rely on the issue even if the position is contrary to controlling circuit precedent, where the question had not yet been decided by the Supreme Court. [**McKnight v. General Motors Corp.,** 511 U.S. 659 (1994)]

(b) Attorney's unfamiliarity with area of law no excuse [§789]

The fact that the attorney is new to the area of law is no excuse for making a claim or defense that is unwarranted by law. [**Zuk v. Eastern Pennsylvania Psychiatric Institute,** 103 F.3d 294 (3d Cir. 1996)—

although this was attorney's first copyright case, that did not excuse his failure to ascertain that the claim was groundless under copyright law]

(3) Specifying that existing law unfavorable [§790]

The courts disagreed under the 1983 version of the rule on whether lawyers were required to state that they were arguing for an extension of existing law. [*Compare* **Golden Eagle Distributing Corp. v. Burroughs Corp.,** 801 F.2d 1531 (9th Cir. 1986)—no need to explain that argument is for an extension of law; *with* **Thornton v. Wahl,** 787 F.2d 1151 (7th Cir. 1986)—failure to clarify that argument was not based on existing law can be sanctioned] The 1993 amendment does not require identification, but the Advisory Committee Notes observe that a contention so identified "should be viewed with greater tolerance under the rule." [146 F.R.D. at 587]

(4) Concern about chilling lawyer creativity [§791]

In scrutinizing new arguments, courts are concerned that they might "stifle the enthusiasm or chill the creativity that is the very lifeblood of the law." [**Eastway Construction Corp. v. City of New York,** *supra*]

(5) Monetary sanction not allowed against represented party [§792]

A monetary sanction may not be awarded against a represented party for violation of the Rule 11 requirement that claims and defenses be supported by law. [Fed. R. Civ. P. 11(c)(2)(A)]

d. Improper purpose [§793]

The signature also certifies that the paper was not filed "for an improper purpose, such as to harass or to cause unnecessary delay or needless increase in the cost of litigation."

(1) Collateral purpose [§794]

Some courts have focused on whether a given litigation action seemed to have a collateral purpose (*i.e.*, some objective other than relief in court), finding this to indicate improper purpose. [*See, e.g.,* **Szabo Food Service, Inc. v. Canteen Corp.,** 823 F.2d 1073 (7th Cir. 1987)—objectively reasonable pleading may be sanctioned based on bad intent; **Appeal of Licht & Semonoff,** 796 F.2d 564 (1st Cir. 1986)—litigation used as method for obtaining information to be used in proxy battle between parties]

(2) Purpose irrelevant if complaint not frivolous [§795]

Other courts have decided that the improper purpose standard is satisfied as long as the complaint is not frivolous. [*See, e.g.,* **Sussman v. Bank of Israel,** 56 F.3d 450 (2d Cir. 1995)—suit designed to generate adverse publicity about defendant cannot be sanctioned unless frivolous; **National Association of Government Employees, Inc. v. National Federation**

of Federal Employees, 844 F.2d 216 (5th Cir. 1988)—"if an initial complaint passes the test of nonfrivolousness, its filing does not constitute harassment for the purposes of Rule 11"]

4. Objective Standard [§796]

The Rule 11 standard with regard to the factual and legal basis for the claim is objective, and the actual state of mind of the lawyer is not important. "An empty head but a pure heart is no defense." [**Thornton v. Wahl,** *supra*]

5. Duty to Reevaluate [§797]

Although Rule 11 focuses on assertions in written filings with the court, it can be violated by *"later advocating"* a position previously taken in such a paper.

a. Rationale

Oral statements made to the court about matters arising for the first time in court may be made under circumstances where there is insufficient opportunity to investigate, but litigants' obligations with respect to assertions contained in papers should not be measured solely with regard to what they know at that time, and later advocacy of those positions should be based on all information reasonably available.

b. No requirement of formal withdrawal

To comply with Rule 11, a party need not formally withdraw an earlier filing; the proscription applies only to later advocacy of the assertion found to be groundless after the paper was filed.

6. Sanctions

a. Discretionary [§798]

On finding a violation of the certification requirements, a court *may* impose sanctions. [Fed. R. Civ. P. 11(c)]

(1) Distinguish—former law [§799]

The 1983 version of Rule 11 provided that a court "shall" impose sanctions for a violation. This was read to make sanctions *mandatory*.

b. Nature and measure of sanction [§800]

The court has substantial latitude in selecting the sanction, which may include directives of a monetary or nonmonetary nature. [Fed. R. Civ. P. 11(c)(2)]

(1) Limited to deterrence [§801]

The sanction is to be limited to that which is *"sufficient to deter repetition of such conduct or comparable conduct by others similarly situated."*

(2) Ordinarily paid into court [§802]

If the sanction is to pay money, that money ordinarily is to be paid into court and not to the opposing party. Thus, Rule 11 sanctions are ***not a fee shifting device*** to make the violator pay the victim's attorneys' fees or other legal costs.

(a) Costs of motion [§803]
The court may, however, award the moving party the costs of making the Rule 11 motion. [Fed. R. Civ. P. 11(c)(1)(A)]

(b) Payment to movant warranted for deterrence [§804]
If it is *"warranted for effective deterrence,"* however, the court may direct a payment to the moving party of some or all of its attorneys' fees and other expenses incurred as a direct result of the violation.

(c) Only nonmonetary sanctions against represented party regarding legal basis [§805]
Monetary sanctions cannot be imposed on a represented party for violation of the requirement that contentions made be warranted by law. [Fed. R. Civ. P. 11(c)(2)(A)]

(d) Sanctions on law firm [§806]
Ordinarily, a law firm should be held ***jointly responsible*** with its partners, associates, or employees for violations of Rule 11. [Fed. R. Civ. P. 11(c)(1)(A)]

7. Procedure

a. Separate motion [§807]
A motion for sanctions must be made "separately from other motions." Accordingly, parties cannot simply append a request for sanctions to other papers they file. [Fed. R. Civ. P. 11(c)(1)]

b. Twenty-one day "safe harbor" [§808]
The motion is not to be filed with the court until 21 days after it is served on the opposing party, and then only if the challenged paper is not withdrawn or corrected. This provides a safe harbor for parties to reassess their filings without suffering sanctions for realizing that an earlier paper was not supported. [Fed. R. Civ. P. 11(c)(1)]

(1) Must not be too late to withdraw challenged paper [§809]
A party may not move for sanctions at a time when it is too late for the opposing party to withdraw the challenged paper. [**Barber v. Miller,** 146 F.3d 707 (9th Cir. 1998)—defendant could not move for Rule 11 sanctions after its motion to dismiss was granted; **Ridder v. City of Springfield,** 109 F.3d 288 (6th Cir. 1997)—defendant could not satisfy safe harbor requirement by serving motion for sanctions after its summary judgment motion had been granted]

EXAM TIP   **gilbert**

If an exam question includes facts indicating that a party has violated Rule 11, remember to mention that the court has *discretion* to impose sanctions. The sanction should be limited to what is needed to *deter future similar violations* of the rule, and generally if the sanction is to pay money, the money will be paid into court. However, if appropriate, the court may order the violator to pay the other party's costs or other expenses related to the violation, including attorneys' fees. Finally, remember that a motion for sanctions must be made separately from other motions, and it must be served upon the party against whom sanctions are sought at least 21 days before filing with the court.

---

  c. Sanctions on court's initiative [§810]

The court may, on its own initiative, enter an order directing an attorney or party to show that it has not violated Rule 11 (a so-called show cause order). [Fed. R. Civ. P. 11(c)(1)(B)] But monetary sanctions cannot be imposed under these circumstances unless the court issues the order before voluntary dismissal or settlement of the case. [Fed. R. Civ. P. 11(c)(2)(B)]

  d. Sanctions order [§811]

If the court imposes sanctions, it should describe the conduct determined to constitute a violation of the rule and explain the basis for the sanction imposed. [Fed. R. Civ. P. 11(c)(3)]

  e. Appellate review [§812]

Rule 11 orders should be reviewed under an *abuse of discretion* standard. [**Cooter & Gell v. Hartmarx Corp.,** 496 U.S. 384 (1990)]

8. Sanctions for "Multiplying Proceedings" [§813]

A federal statute authorizes courts to impose sanctions on a person who "multiplies the proceedings in any case unreasonably and vexatiously." [28 U.S.C. §1927] This section looks to *delaying tactics* or *excessive litigation activity*. Ordinarily such sanctions depend on a finding of *willful bad faith* by the offending person. [**Zuk v. Eastern Pennsylvania Psychiatric Institute,** *supra*, §789]

9. Inherent Power to Sanction [§814]

Federal courts have inherent power to impose substantial sanctions on a party guilty of bad faith conduct not involving signing of filings even when Rule 11 does not apply. [**Chambers v. NASCO, Inc.,** 501 U.S. 32 (1991)—repeated acts of deception of court led to imposition of almost $1 million in sanctions]

F. Answer

1. In General [§815]

The function of the answer is to put at issue the factual allegations in the complaint. The answer accomplishes this by *denying* the allegations of the claim and/

or by setting forth some affirmative defense ("new matter") that *avoids* the effect of the plaintiff's allegations.

2. Denials [§816]

To put at issue the allegations of the complaint, the defendant's answer must contain *effective* denials. Allegations not denied are *deemed admitted* (below).

a. Form

(1) General denials [§817]

A single "general" denial will controvert all of the allegations in the complaint (*e.g.*, "D denies each and all of the allegations in P's complaint"). In most jurisdictions, this is no longer good practice.

(a) Federal pleading [§818]

In federal practice, the basic requirement of *good faith* based upon reasonable inquiry in pleading [Fed. R. Civ. P. 11] means that a general denial is rarely proper because there is usually *something* in the plaintiff's complaint (*e.g.*, allegations about plaintiff's personal identity and jurisdictional allegations) which the defendant in good faith *should* admit.

(b) State pleading [§819]

In some states a general denial is not allowed in response to a *verified* complaint. In such a case, the answer must also be verified and *specific denials* are required. [Cal. Civ. Proc. Code §431.30(d); *and see supra*, §632]

1) Exception [§820]

Verified general denials to a verified complaint may be allowed where the amount in controversy is small.

(2) Specific denials [§821]

Anything less than a general denial can be considered a "specific" or "qualified" denial. Several different types of allegations may be used in this regard:

(a) Specific denial by parts [§822]

The defendant can go through the complaint, paragraph by paragraph or sentence by sentence, admitting or denying each part as appropriate. Where only part of a paragraph or allegation therein is true, the defendant should admit that which is true and deny the balance. [Fed. R. Civ. P. 8(b); **Zielinski v. Philadelphia Piers, Inc.**, 139 F. Supp. 408 (E.D. Pa. 1956)]

 Example: "Answering paragraph 12 of plaintiff's complaint, defendant admits providing medical treatment to plaintiff on or about May 15, 1999, and, except as expressly so admitted, denies each and every allegation of paragraph 12."

(b) Negativing plaintiff's allegations [§823]

A denial may be effected merely by repeating the allegation but prefacing it with a word of denial.

1) Caution—denials in the conjunctive ("negative pregnant" rule) [§824]

This type of denial, if carelessly employed, may be deemed "pregnant" with an admission of that which the defendant is attempting to deny.

e.g. Example: P's complaint alleges that D "struck and kicked P." D's answer that "D did not strike and kick P" is pregnant with an admission that he may have struck *or* kicked P.

a) How to avoid

To avoid the negative pregnant problem, the defendant should make the denial in the *disjunctive*—e.g., "D did not strike or kick P."

2) Denials of times, dates, or places [§825]

Similarly, if the complaint alleges that an event occurred at a certain time, date, or place *not* material to the statement of the plaintiff's cause of action, a specific denial thereof may be held pregnant with an admission that the event occurred at some *other* time, date, or place.

e.g. Example: P's complaint alleges "P fully and completely performed the contract *on June 1*." D's answer stating that D "denies that P fully and completely performed the contract on June 1" may be held to admit performance on another date.

a) How to avoid

It is generally a good idea to add "or at any other time," "at any other place," etc., to avoid this negative pregnant problem.

3) Ease of avoiding [§826]

These problems can be easily avoided by denying "each and every allegation of plaintiff" except as expressly admitted, as indicated in §822, *supra*. As a result, the negative pregnant problem has virtually vanished from the scene under liberalized pleading rules.

(3) Denial on lack of information [§827]

If the defendant is without sufficient knowledge or information to enable her to form a belief as to the truth of allegations in the complaint, she may so state in her answer. Such a statement operates as an effective denial. [Fed. R. Civ. P. 8(b); Cal. Civ. Proc. Code §431.30]

(a) Information that is peculiarly within defendant's control [§828]

If the information of which the defendant claims ignorance is peculiarly within the defendant's control, use of the denial on information and belief may be forbidden.

Example: Where defendant bought out the assets of the company that manufactured a product that injured plaintiff, information about the extent to which defendant assumed the tort liabilities of the manufacturer was peculiarly within defendant's control, and defendant could not claim to be ignorant of it. [**David v. Crompton & Knowles Corp.,** 58 F.R.D. 444 (E.D. Pa. 1973)]

(b) Public record [§829]

If matters are of public record, the defendant may not deny for lack of information and belief. [**Porto Transportation Co. v. Consolidated Diesel Electric Corp.,** 20 F.R.D. 1 (1956)] *Compare:* In assessing the adequacy of the complaint, the court may refer to matters of which it can take judicial notice. (*See supra,* §752.)

b. Effect of failure to deny [§830]

Failure to make an effective denial of allegations to which a responsive pleading is required constitutes an *admission* of the allegations.

(1) Exception—damages [§831]

Under federal practice, allegations of *damages* are deemed at issue, even if not effectively denied. [Fed. R. Civ. P. 8(d)] State practice is generally contra—*i.e.,* allegations of damages, like any other material allegation, must be denied.

(2) Material vs. immaterial allegations [§832]

Note that only *material* allegations are deemed admitted. "Material" allegations are those essential to the claim and which could not be stricken from the pleading without leaving it insufficient. [*See* Cal. Civ. Proc. Code §431.10]

---

cf. **Compare:** Failure to deny *immaterial* allegations does *not* constitute an admission thereof, the immaterial allegations being treated merely as "surplusage."

(a) But note

In practice, few pleaders feel confident enough to decide what is "material" and "immaterial" and hence deny *all* allegations. Alternatively, the defendant can *move to strike* from the complaint whatever she considers to be "immaterial" allegations before filing her answer (*see supra,* §712), so she will not have to admit or deny them.

3. Affirmative Defenses [§833]

In addition to or in lieu of a denial, the defendant in her answer must plead any defenses or objections that constitute "new matter" or an affirmative defense. Such matter is *not in issue* (and hence may not be introduced in evidence at trial) *under a simple denial.*

a. Definition [§834]

Basically, "new matter" is anything that the defendant must prove in order to *avoid* the plaintiff's claim—*i.e.,* even assuming plaintiff's allegations were true, an independent reason why plaintiff cannot recover. The test usually is whether the defendant would bear the *burden of proof* on the issue at trial; if so, it is "new matter."

b. Federal practice [§835]

Although burden of proof is generally deemed to be a "substantive" question for *Erie* purposes (and hence controlled by appropriate state law), pleading rules are clearly "procedural." Hence, if an affirmative defense falls within Federal Rule 8(c), below, it must *always* be specially pleaded; and this is true whether or not the defendant would have the burden of proof on this issue under state law. [**Palmer v. Hoffman,** 318 U.S. 109 (1943)]

(1) Rule 8(c) [§836]

Federal Rule 8(c) lists various defenses that must be affirmatively alleged, but this list is not all-inclusive. The Rule provides that *"any other matter constituting an avoidance or affirmative defense"* must also be specially pleaded.

c. Application [§837]

The following are the most common types of "new matter" in state and federal practice:

(1) Tort cases [§838]

In tort cases:

(a) *Self-defense, consent, justification, or other privilege,* as defenses to intentional torts, are new matter and must be specially pleaded in the answer.

(b) *Contributory negligence and assumption of the risk,* as defenses to negligence, are new matter in most jurisdictions.

(c) *Privilege or license (as a defense to trespass); consent (as a defense to conversion)* are other examples of new matter.

(d) *But lack of causation is not new matter.* Causation is one of the ultimate facts in any tort complaint, and thus *lack* of proximate cause need not be specially pleaded. It is in issue under a general denial of an allegation that the defendant's acts "caused" plaintiff's injuries.

(2) Contract cases [§839]

In a contract action, new matter that must be specially pleaded (*i.e.,* not in issue under a denial) includes *fraud, mistake, duress, incapacity, release, waiver, and estoppel.*

(a) Illegality [§840]

Illegality is of course a "defense" to a contract action, but evidence of the illegality can come in even if not pleaded.

1) Rationale

Public policy to nullify illegal contracts is so strong that it should not require specific pleading. Indeed, the court can raise the issue on its own motion. [**Santoro v. Carbone,** 22 Cal. App. 3d 721 (1972)]

(b) Lack of consideration [§841]

Wherever the plaintiff has alleged consideration, lack of consideration will be in issue under a simple denial. However, consideration need not always be alleged (*see supra,* §656); and where it need not be alleged, lack of consideration is new matter which must be specially pleaded.

(c) Failure of conditions

1) Condition subsequent [§842]

Occurrence of a condition subsequent that the defendant claims *discharged* his duty to perform is an affirmative defense, and hence must be specially pleaded as new matter. [**Pierce v. Wright,** 117 Cal. App. 2d 718 (1953)]

2) Conditions precedent or concurrent [§843]

However, because the plaintiff must allege the occurrence or performance of all conditions precedent or concurrent (in order to show that the defendant was under an absolute, unconditional duty to perform), a denial by the defendant sufficiently controverts the plaintiff's allegations concerning such conditions. [*See* Cal. Civ. Proc. Code §457]

a) But note

Federal Rule 9(c) requires that the defendant's denial pinpoint the particular failure or condition on which she wishes to rely—in effect requiring an affirmative allegation. [**Ginsburg v. Insurance Co. of North America,** 427 F.2d 1318 (6th Cir. 1970)]

(d) Payment [§844]

If the plaintiff sues on an obligation for payment of money, she bears the burden of pleading and proving *nonpayment* as part of her case. However, if the defendant intends to rely on payment as a defense in the action, most jurisdictions require that she *affirmatively plead* it in her answer. [Fed. R. Civ. P. 8(c); **Pastene v. Pardini,** 135 Cal. 431 (1902)]

(e) Mitigation of damages [§845]

Although the defendant bears the burden of proof as to mitigation of damages, it does *not* always require special pleading.

e.g. Example: Defendant may prove that plaintiff's damages have been *offset or reduced* by other income (as where a wrongfully discharged employee obtains another job) without special pleading. Such proof goes to the computation of plaintiff's damages, and is thus in issue under defendant's denial of the sum complained of. [**Erler v. Five Points Motors,** 249 Cal. App. 2d 560 (1967)]

cf. Compare: If defendant claims that plaintiff has *failed* to mitigate damages (*e.g.,* failing to seek comparable employment), this is treated as new matter in order to alert the plaintiff. [**Erler v. Five Points Motors,** *supra*]

(f) Statute of Frauds [§846]

The federal rule (also followed in most states) is that the Statute of Frauds is new matter and must be specially pleaded. [Fed. R. Civ. P. 8(c)]

1) Minority view [§847]

Some code pleading states take the position that the Statute of

Frauds is in issue under a simple denial of the contract. This position was originally based on the theory that noncompliance with the Statute of Frauds rendered a contract void, rather than merely voidable; although this theory is no longer recognized (*see* Contracts Summary), the pleading rule has remained. [**Aero Bolt & Screw Co. v. Iaia,** 180 Cal. App. 2d 728 (1960)]

(3) Statute of limitations [§848]

Running of the statute of limitations is new matter and must be specially pleaded.

(a) But note

If it appears from the dates alleged *on the face of the complaint* that the plaintiff's action is barred, *some* courts allow the defendant to raise this defense (*e.g.,* by a motion to dismiss) even though not pleaded in the answer (*see supra,* §766).

(b) Title obtained by adverse possession [§849]

If the running of the statute of limitations establishes title in an adverse possessor and the former owner then sues for ejectment, the adverse possessor's title is in issue under a simple denial of the owner's allegations in the ejectment action—since one of the necessary allegations is a claim of title. [**Denham v. Cuddeback,** 311 P.2d 1014 (Or. 1957)]

(4) Pleas in abatement (dilatory pleas) [§850]

Pleas in abatement are *not* defenses on the merits, but assert some reason why the present action should be put off or should not be heard. Matters of abatement often appear on the face of the complaint, and when they do, the complaint is subject to demurrer or similar motion. However, where the matter of abatement does not appear on the face of the complaint—which is the usual case—it must be raised in the answer or, in federal practice, by answer or motion; and it must be *specially pleaded* as new matter.

(a) Grounds [§851]

The principal pleas in abatement are:

1) *Plaintiff lacks capacity* to sue;

2) *Nonjoinder* of parties;

3) *Another action pending* between the parties on the *same issues*;

4) *An action brought prematurely;* and

5) Lack of *personal jurisdiction* (including improper service of process) and *improper venue:*

    a) ***In federal practice,*** these issues may be raised by motion or answer, as long as it is in the defendant's first appearance [Fed. R. Civ. P. 12(b)];

    b) ***In state practice,*** lack of personal service must be raised by a motion to quash, while improper venue must be raised by motion at or before the time defendant files a demurrer or answer [Cal. Civ. Proc. Code §418.10].

AFFIRMATIVE DEFENSES—EXAMPLES		**gilbert**
TORT	**CONTRACT**	**OTHER**
Self-defense	Illegality	Statute of limitations
Consent	Lack of consideration	Pleas in abatement (*e.g.*, plaintiff lacks capacity, non-joinder of parties, another action on the same issue is pending between the parties, the action is premature, lack of personal jurisdiction, improper venue)
Justification	Failure of conditions	
Privilege	Payment	
Contributory negligence	Statute of Frauds	
	Failure to mitigate damages	

(b) Special hearing available [§852]

Statutes or rules often require that on motion of either party (or the court itself), matters of abatement be heard first—since they would dispense with the litigation if proved. [*See, e.g.,* Fed. R. Civ. P. 12(d)]

(c) Pleas disfavored [§853]

A plea of abatement is a disfavored defense because it is generally an attempt to "put off" or "hold in abeyance" rather than to defend squarely on the merits. Accordingly, the courts require that such matters be raised ***promptly*** or the objection will be deemed ***waived.*** Thus, for example, such defenses generally cannot be raised for the first time in an amended answer. [**Collins v. Rocha,** 7 Cal. 3d 232 (1972)]

d. Effect of failure to plead new matter [§854]

If not pleaded in the answer, new matter is not in issue and the ***defendant may not offer evidence*** of such defenses at the time of trial—unless the plaintiff fails to object to the introduction of such evidence or the court allows leave to *amend* (*see infra,* §937). [**Jetty v. Craco,** 123 Cal. App. 2d 876 (1954)]

(1) Personal jurisdiction, improper service, and improper venue [§855]

In federal practice, objections to personal jurisdiction, venue, or manner of service are *permanently waived* unless asserted at the earliest time, so a later motion to amend cannot revive these waived defenses. [Fed. R. Civ. P. 12(h)(1)]

4. Procedure in Answering Complaint

a. Form [§856]

The requirements for allegations in a complaint (*supra,* §§594 *et seq.*) also apply to the allegations of an answer.

b. Signing [§857]

In federal practice, the same standards apply to the answer as apply to the complaint. [Fed. R. Civ. P. 11(b)(4); *see supra,* §§629, 768 *et seq.*]

(1) Lack of sufficient information [§858]

Rule 11(b)(4) permits defendant to deny if the denial is "reasonably based on a lack of information or belief." The Advisory Committee Note accompanying the 1993 amendment explained that a denial would be permissible if "after an appropriate investigation, a party has no information concerning the matter or, indeed, has a reasonable basis for doubting the credibility of the only evidence relevant to the matter. A party should not deny an allegation it knows to be true; but it is not required, simply because it lacks contradictory evidence, to admit an allegation that it believes is not true."

(2) Verification [§859]

Under state practice, an answer must be verified if the complaint is verified (otherwise, it may be stricken by the court). [Cal. Civ. Proc. Code §431.30]

c. Time limitations [§860]

Under federal practice, the defendant must file her answer within 20 days after being served with process, except that if she chooses during that time to file a motion under Rule 12(b), this extends the time for filing her answer until 10 days after the Rule 12(b) motion is denied. [Fed. R. Civ. P. 12(a)(1)(A)]

(1) Service waived [§861]

If defendant waives service of process (*supra,* §244), the answer is not due until 60 days after the request for waiver was sent, if addressed to a defendant within the United States, or 90 days if defendant is outside the country. [Fed. R. Civ. P. 12(a)(l)(B)]

(2) Service on United States [§862]

The United States, an agency of the United States, or an officer or employee of the United States sued for actions occurring in connection with the performance of official duties, is allowed 60 days to file an answer. [Fed. R. Civ. P. 12(a)(3)]

(3) State practice [§863]

State practice is similar. For example, in California, the defendant must answer or demur within 30 days after service of process (although the 30-day period is measured from different dates, depending on whether defendant was served personally, by mail, or by publication). [Cal. Civ. Proc. Code §412.20(3)]

(4) Effect of failure to file timely answer [§864]

See discussion of default procedure *infra*, §§958-966.

5. Allegations of Answer Deemed Controverted [§865]

Except where the answer contains a counterclaim (below), no reply to an answer is permitted in federal practice unless the court so directs. [Fed. R. Civ. P. 7(a)] Allegations of new matter in the answer are *"deemed controverted"*—meaning that the plaintiff has the right, without further pleading, to introduce evidence to defeat or avoid the allegations. [Fed. R. Civ. P. 8(d); Cal. Civ. Proc. Code §431.20(b)]

---

e.g. **Example:** P's complaint charges negligence. D's answer sets up the defense of contributory negligence by P. This is "deemed controverted," and P can introduce evidence to overcome the contributory negligence defense (*see* Torts Summary) even though he has never formally denied D's allegations of P's negligence.

---

a. Reply required [§866]

The Supreme Court has observed that a reply may be appropriate when a defendant asserts a defense of qualified immunity [**Crawford-El v. Britton**, *supra*, §734], and some courts now require a reply in that situation [*see* **Reyes v. Sazan**, *supra*, §735].

6. Challenges to Answer [§867]

A plaintiff who desires to challenge the legal sufficiency of an affirmative defense may file a *demurrer* (state practice) or a *motion to strike* "any insufficient defense" under Federal Rule 12(f).

a. And note

In addition, the plaintiff may employ a motion for judgment on the pleadings or motion for summary judgment to challenge the new matter. (*See infra*, §967.)

G. Counterclaims and Cross-Claims

1. Federal Practice

a. Counterclaims [§868]

As part of her answer, the defendant may set forth by way of counterclaim any claims that she has *against the plaintiff.* Such claims *need not be related* to the claims set forth in the complaint. [Fed. R. Civ. P. 13(b)]

(1) Subject matter jurisdiction

(a) Compulsory counterclaim [§869]

If the counterclaim is compulsory (*i.e.,* based on the same transaction or occurrence as the plaintiff's claim; *see* below), it is deemed "*ancillary*" to the plaintiff's claim, and therefore within supplemental jurisdiction (*see supra,* §§424 *et seq.*).

(b) Permissive counterclaim [§870]

However if the counterclaim is merely permissive (below), subject matter jurisdiction requirements must ordinarily be satisfied on some *independent ground* of federal jurisdiction (*e.g.,* if plaintiff's claim is based on a federal question, defendant's counterclaim would have to be based on some federal question or on diversity).

(2) Venue [§871]

Counterclaims have no effect on venue. The venue statutes regulate where the "*action* may be brought"; and this refers solely to where the plaintiff files his complaint.

(3) Pleading [§872]

The sufficiency of a counterclaim is tested by the same rules of pleading applicable to a complaint (*see supra,* §§715 *et seq.*).

(a) Form [§873]

The counterclaim should be set forth as *part of the defendant's answer,* rather than as a separate pleading. [Fed. R. Civ. P. 13(a)]

(b) Caption [§874]

A counterclaim should always be labeled as such, since a reply to a counterclaim by the plaintiff is mandatory only if it is so denominated. [Fed. R. Civ. P. 7(a)] However, failure to label a counterclaim as such has no other effect: The court may still treat it as a counterclaim and award whatever relief is appropriate. [Fed. R. Civ. P. 8(c)]

(c) Plaintiff's reply [§875]

A responsive pleading by the plaintiff is required to a counterclaim labeled as such. The reply may contain denials, affirmative defenses, or even a counterclaim to the counterclaim. [**Great Lakes Rubber Corp. v. Herbert Cooper Co.,** 286 F.2d 631 (3d Cir. 1960)]

1) Note
All matters in the reply are deemed "denied or avoided" under Federal Rule 8(d).

2) But note
The defendant can attack the reply by a motion for judgment on the pleadings or a motion to strike under Federal Rule 12.

(4) Joinder of other parties to counterclaim [§876]
Although a counterclaim is against the plaintiff, it can be an occasion for the joinder of additional parties.

(a) Permissive joinder [§877]
When making a counterclaim, the defendant may join other persons in accordance with the provisions of Rule 20. [Fed. R. Civ. P. 13(h); *see infra,* §§1031-1041]

1) Caution—subject matter jurisdiction [§878]
Note, however, that when a counterclaim is *permissive*, there must be some independent basis for federal subject matter jurisdiction (*see supra*, Chapter II).

(b) Joinder by order of court [§879]
If the defendant does not join a party that should be joined under Rule 19(a) (*see infra,* §§1042-1047), the court may order that party joined on motion of the plaintiff or, if the party is not joined, proceed to determine whether the case should be dismissed pursuant to Rule 19(b) (*see infra,* §1048) if it is not possible to join the additional party.

1) Subject matter jurisdiction [§880]
If the defendant has asserted a *compulsory counterclaim*, ordinarily supplemental jurisdiction would permit the addition of claims against parties who should be joined under Rule 19(a).

(5) Voluntary dismissal by plaintiff [§881]
To protect the defendant's right to relief on the counterclaim, Federal Rule 41(a)(2) provides that once a counterclaim is asserted, the *plaintiff cannot dismiss the action without the defendant's consent* (unless the counterclaim remains pending for independent adjudication; *see infra,* §981).

(6) Permissive vs. compulsory counterclaims

(a) Permissive counterclaims [§882]
If the defendant's claims against the plaintiff are **unrelated** to the

claims set forth in the complaint, it is optional (or permissive) for the defendant to assert them by way of counterclaim; *i.e.*, the defendant may, if she chooses, assert the claims in an independent action.

(b) Compulsory counterclaims [§883]

However, if the defendant's claim against the plaintiff arises out of the *same transaction* as the claim set forth in the complaint, the counterclaim is *compulsory*—meaning that it must be asserted in the action or it will be barred. (This bar is implicit in Rule 13(a).)

1) When counterclaim is "compulsory" [§884]

A counterclaim is compulsory if it:

a) *Arises out of the transaction or occurrence* that is the subject matter of the plaintiff's claim; *and*

b) *Does not require the presence of third parties* over whom the court has no jurisdiction. This provision invokes the requirements of Rule 19 (*see infra,* §§1042-1047).

2) Scope of "transaction or occurrence" [§885]

In determining whether a counterclaim is compulsory, the phrase "transaction or occurrence" appears to be construed differently depending on the context:

a) **Broad view—jurisdiction in first action [§886]**

When the question is whether the counterclaim is *within the court's supplemental jurisdiction,* a *broad* definition of "transaction" is used—the object being to permit the counterclaim and thereby to avoid multiplicity of suits. [**Albright v. Gates,** 362 F.2d 928 (9th Cir. 1966); *see* 28 U.S.C. §1367(a)]

b) **Narrower view: scope of preclusion in later action [§887]**

On the other hand, if the question is whether a defendant who *failed* to interpose a counterclaim is barred from later suing on it, a *narrower* definition may be used if it would be inequitable to bar the later suit. [**LaFollette v. Herron,** 211 F. Supp. 919 (E.D. Tenn. 1962)]

(7) Statute of limitations problem [§888]

An important issue is whether a counterclaim is barred by the statute of limitations if it is filed *after* the statute has run, but the action (plaintiff's complaint) was filed before the statute ran. The question is considered "substantive" for *Erie* doctrine purposes, and hence is resolved by appropriate state law. [**Keckley v. Payton,** 157 F. Supp. 820 (N.D. W. Va. 1958)]

(a) Majority view [§889]

The general view is that if the counterclaim arises out of the *"same transaction"* as the plaintiff's claim, it will not be barred if the plaintiff's complaint was filed before the running of the statute. *Rationale:* The plaintiff's filing of the complaint places before the court all rights and obligations of the parties to the transaction in question. [**Liberty Mutual Insurance Co. v. Fales,** 8 Cal. 3d 712 (1973)] In addition, in terms of the policies of the statute of limitations, a plaintiff who files suit is clearly on notice of the transaction and has an incentive to preserve evidence about it.

EXAM TIP   **gilbert**

If an exam question sets out grounds for a counterclaim, the statute of limitations for the counterclaim has a shorter limitation period than the plaintiff's claim, and the shorter period has already run, remember to address the issue of whether the counterclaim is barred. In most states, the counterclaim will **not be barred if it arises out of the same transaction or occurrence** as the plaintiff's claim. For example, if the plaintiff files a malpractice action three years after the defendant provides medical services, the defendant can file a counterclaim that plaintiff never paid for the services, even if the limitations period for such contracts claims is two years and has already expired. However, if the counterclaim is unrelated to the plaintiff's claim, it will be barred.

(b) Minority view [§890]

A minority view goes further and allows *any* counterclaim (same transaction or not) to be used *defensively*—*i.e.*, as an offset to the plaintiff's claim—even though the statute has run. [**Hawkeye Security Insurance Co. v. Apodaca,** 524 P.2d 874 (Wyo. 1974)]

1) "Cross-demands deemed compensated" [§891]

Other states reach the same result via statutes that provide that where *cross-demands for money* have existed between the parties at any point in time, they are "deemed compensated"—*i.e.*, plaintiff's claim is *deemed paid* to the extent of defendant's off-setting claim. If plaintiff later sues defendant, defendant can set up her cross-demand to show payment (an affirmative defense), even though an independent action on defendant's claim would then be barred by the statute of limitations. [Cal. Civ. Proc. Code §431.70]

2) Limitation [§892]

Such statutes apply only if the cross-demands are *for money*. Thus, if the plaintiff is suing for recovery of property, the statute of limitations will continue to run on any cross-demand which the defendant has against the plaintiff.

b. Cross-claims [§893]

In federal court actions, the defendant may set forth in the answer any claims that she has against a *co-defendant* that relate to the *"transaction or occurrence"* or to any property that is the subject of the plaintiff's complaint. Such cross-claims are *never compulsory,* however. [Fed. R. Civ. P. 13(g)]

---

e.g. Example: P sues D1 and D2, claiming they were jointly negligent in causing his injuries. Either defendant may cross-claim against the other on any claim arising out of the same accident, but is not required to do so. [**Scott v. Fancher,** 369 F.2d 842 (5th Cir. 1966)] Alternatively, either defendant may file a cross-claim for *contribution* against the other, asserting that both are *jointly* liable to the plaintiff and requesting that any judgment be fashioned accordingly. (If one defendant is only secondarily liable, he may cross-claim *for indemnification* against the other who is primarily liable.) [**Lumbermen's Mutual Insurance Co. v. Massachusetts Bonding and Insurance Co.,** 310 F.2d 627 (4th Cir. 1962)]

---

(1) Jurisdiction [§894]

Since the cross-claim must relate to the transaction in the existing action, the better view is that it is within the supplemental jurisdiction of the court, and no independent ground for federal jurisdiction is required. [**LASA per L'Industria del Marmo Societa per Azioni v. Alexander,** 414 F.2d 143 (6th Cir. 1969)]

(2) Pleading

(a) Form [§895]

Like a counterclaim, the cross-claim should be set forth as *part of the defendant's answer* rather than as an independent pleading.

(b) Responsive pleading [§896]

The co-defendant against whom the claim is asserted must file an *answer to cross-claim.* [Fed. R. Civ. P. 7(a)]

(3) Parties [§897]

The basic cross-claim must be against a co-defendant. As with counterclaims, however, the cross-claimant may add new parties against whom it has claims growing out of the same transaction. [Fed. R. Civ. P. 13(h)]

(a) Note

A cross-claim is also proper in a case where there are several plaintiffs (P1 and P2) and defendant has counterclaimed against only one of them (P1). In such a case, P1 could cross-claim against his co-party (P2) for contribution or indemnification as to the claim asserted in D's counterclaim.

(4) Other procedures compared

(a) Counterclaims and cross-claims [§898]

Counterclaims lie only against the *opposing* party (plaintiff), whereas a cross-claim lies against a *co-party* (D2).

1) And note

A counterclaim is sometimes compulsory, whereas a cross-claim is always permissive. [**Augustin v. Mughal,** 521 F.2d 1215 (8th Cir. 1975)]

(b) Impleaders and cross-claims [§899]

Impleaders are claims against a *third person* who is a stranger to the action, whereas a cross-claim lies against a *co-party* (D2). Moreover, an impleader claim is limited to a claim for indemnification or contribution, whereas a cross-claim can be asserted for *any* claim D1 has against D2 arising out of the transaction that is the basis for the plaintiff's action.

2. State Practice—Cross-Complaint [§900]

Most state rules governing pleading of claims by a defendant against the plaintiff or third parties follow the Federal Rules (above). However, some states (*e.g.,* California) do not recognize the counterclaim or cross-claim, but provide that a defendant's claims against *any* party (plaintiff, co-defendant, or a third person not yet a party to the action) may be asserted in a *cross-complaint.*

a. Form [§901]

The cross-complaint is a *separate pleading* (*i.e.,* not a part of the answer). [Cal. Civ. Proc. Code §428.40]

(1) Procedure [§902]

If the cross-complaint is filed *at the same time as the answer,* it may be filed as a matter of right. Otherwise, leave of court must first be obtained for a cross-complaint against current parties to the case. Cross-complaints against new parties can be filed without leave of court until a trial date has been set. [Cal. Civ. Proc. Code §428.50]

(2) Service [§903]

The cross-complaint must be served on *every* party to the action. [Cal. Civ. Proc. Code §428.60]

b. Joinder of parties [§904]

As noted above, a cross-complaint may be filed against the plaintiff, a co-defendant, *or* a third person not yet a party to the action. In the latter case, a separate summons is issued on the cross-complaint.

(1) Note

The usual rules with respect to necessary and indispensable parties (*see infra,* §§1042 *et seq.*) apply here as well.

c. Joinder of claims

(1) Against plaintiff—unlimited scope [§905]

The defendant may assert any and all claims she has against the plaintiff. There is *no* requirement of any subject matter relationship to the plaintiff's complaint. [Cal. Civ. Proc. Code §428.10(a)]

(a) Compulsory cross-complaints [§906]

However, if the defendant's cause of action *is* related to the subject of the plaintiff's complaint, failure to assert it constitutes a waiver thereof. [Cal. Civ. Proc. Code §426.30] Basically, the same rules apply as for federal "compulsory counterclaims." (*See supra,* §883.)

(2) Against other parties—subject matter relationship [§907]

A defendant can assert a cross-complaint against a co-defendant or third party only if the cause of action sued upon is *related to the plaintiff's complaint—i.e.,* arises out of same transaction or series of transactions, or involves the same property or controversy. [Cal. Civ. Proc. Code §428.10(b)]

(a) Effect

As long as there is *one* such cause of action, the defendant can join with it *any other* causes of action she has against any of the cross-defendants. [Cal. Civ. Proc. Code §428.30] Defendant may join additional cross-defendants although they were not formerly parties. [Cal. Civ. Proc. Code §428.20]

---

e.g. **Example:** P, while operating a car, collides with T, who is operating a car owned by O. P sues O for personal injuries. O may file a cross-complaint against P for the damages to O's car; and against T as a third-party defendant, seeking indemnity for any liability that O may be subjected to in favor of P, and also for the damages to O's car.

(b) Note

The California cross-complaint can thus be used to assert the claims asserted under the Federal Rules by compulsory counterclaim (same transaction), permissive counterclaim (different transaction), cross-claim (against co-party), or impleader (bringing stranger in as third-party defendant).

d. Responsive pleading required [§908]

Each cross-defendant must file an answer (or demurrer) to the cross-complaint. [Cal. Civ. Proc. Code §432.10] If no such response is filed, a default judgment may be entered on the cross-complaint.

(1) Grounds for demurrer [§909]

The grounds for demurrer to a cross-complaint are the same as for a demurrer to the original complaint.

(2) Additional cross-complaints [§910]

A cross-defendant, in turn, is permitted to file a cross-complaint against any other party or against any stranger to the action (just as if the cross-complaint filed against him had been the original complaint). [Cal. Civ. Proc. Code §428] *Note:* This means that the cross-defendant is subject to the **compulsory** cross-complaint provisions (above).

(3) Note—indemnification [§911]

A special statute in California allows broader defenses where the cross-complaint is for indemnification (*e.g.*, P sues D; D cross-complains against T, alleging that T is liable to indemnify D against P's claim, so that if P wins against D, T is liable to D). In such cases, the cross-defendant (T) is permitted to assert any defenses to the underlying cause of action (P vs. D) that could be asserted by the person seeking indemnification from him (D). [Cal. Civ. Proc. Code §428.70(b)]

(a) Rationale

The purpose of this rule is to protect against collusion on the underlying cause of action (*i.e.*, D admitting or defaulting to P's claim, in order to saddle T with the liability).

H. Amended and Supplemental Pleadings

1. In General [§912]

Since it is the basic function of pleadings to define the issues in controversy (and thus limit the proof at trial), the rules allowing amendments and supplements to pleadings are of vital importance. The problem is the extent to which a party, by amending or supplementing pleadings, can alter or expand his case from that originally set forth in the complaint or answer. As will be seen, this depends to a significant degree on the **stage of the proceedings** at which an amendment is sought.

2. Amendments Prior to Trial

a. Amendments as a matter of right [§913]

Either party may amend his pleading **once** as a matter of right, either (i) before a responsive pleading (as opposed to a mere motion) is served by the other party or (ii) if the pleading is one to which no responsive pleading is permitted (*e.g.,* defendant's answer) and the action has not been placed on the trial calendar, at any time within 20 days after the pleading is served. [Fed. R. Civ. P. 15(a)]

(1) Note

Even though there is a right to amend, the alteration must be within the *permissible scope* of amendment (*see infra,* §§918 *et seq.*) or it is subject to being stricken.

b. Amendment by permission of court [§914]

In any other situation, a party may amend his pleading only by leave of court; however, such permission is usually granted liberally prior to trial.

(1) Rationale

Modern courts stress that the primary function of the pleadings is to give *notice* of the pleader's claim (or defense). As long as the original pleading gave such notice, the claim may be expanded or changed in the course of litigation.

(2) Effect

Leave to amend will usually be granted unless some *actual prejudice* to the other party appears or the *trial schedule* will be disrupted. In the absence of such prejudice or disruption, refusal to permit an amendment may be an *abuse* of the court's discretion. [**Foman v. Davis,** *supra,* §737; **Greenberg v. Equitable Life Assurance Society,** 34 Cal. App. 3d 994 (1973)]

(3) Stipulation

Ordinarily, leave of court is not required when the opposing party stipulates to the amendment.

c. Procedure

(1) Motion for leave to amend [§915]

Unless the amendment is a matter of right or the parties consent, the party seeking leave to amend must file a formal motion with the court, attaching a copy of the proposed amended pleading, and an appropriate showing (usually by affidavit) of the grounds upon which the amendment is sought.

(2) Service [§916]

If leave to amend is granted, the amended pleading must then be filed and served in the same manner as the original pleading.

(3) Response to amended pleading [§917]

If a response to the original pleading was required (*e.g.,* complaint or counterclaim), then a response to the amended pleading is required as well. The response to the pleading—be it an answer, reply, or motion—must be served within 10 days after service of the amended pleading. [Fed. R. Civ. P.15(a)]

d. Permissible scope of amendment

(1) State practice [§918]

Under the early codes, an amendment would not be permitted if it changed the basic cause of action or defense asserted in the original pleadings. The plaintiff was not allowed to amend his complaint to set up a "wholly new and different cause of action"; neither was the defendant allowed to amend her answer to set up a "wholly new and different" defense.

(a) Modern rule [§919]

Even under code pleading, however, the test now employed is simply whether the proposed amended pleading is based on the *same general set of facts* as the original pleading. [**Austin v. Massachusetts Bonding Co.,** 56 Cal. 2d 596 (1961)]

(2) Federal practice [§920]

Under the Federal Rules, the basic question is whether (and to what extent) the amendment results in *prejudice* to the opposing party.

(a) Effect

Under federal practice, therefore, it is immaterial that the proposed amendment changes the theory of the case, states a claim arising out of a transaction different from that originally sued on, or causes a change in parties. [**Sherman v. Hallbauer,** 455 F.2d 1236 (5th Cir. 1972)]

(b) Amended answer [§921]

The same liberal rules apply to the defendant's answer, *except that* defenses that are waived if not asserted in the defendant's first pleading (answer or motion)—*e.g.,* improper venue, defective service of process—cannot be revived by amendment.

(c) Effect of trial date and Rule 16 limitations on time to file motions [§922]

Another factor that increasingly bears on whether a party is granted leave to amend is the court's schedule for completion of pretrial activities and trial of the case (*see infra,* §§1689 *et seq.*). If the motion is made after the cutoff for making motions under a Rule 16 scheduling order, or if the scheduled date for trial might be disrupted, the court may deny leave to amend.

e. **"Relation back doctrine"—statute of limitations problems [§923]**

If the plaintiff seeks to amend the complaint after the statute of limitations would otherwise have run on the claim, there is a question of whether the amended claim "relates back" to the date of filing of the original complaint.

Example: P sues D for breach of contract. Then, after the statute of limitations on an independent fraud action has run, P amends his complaint to seek damages for fraud in connection with the same contract. Should the amended claim be deemed filed at the time the original claim was filed?

---

(1) **"Relation back" usually permitted [§924]**

In most jurisdictions, the amended claim "relates back"—*i.e.*, is deemed filed as of the date of the original complaint—as long as the claim asserted in the amended pleading arose out of the *same conduct, transaction, or occurrence* set forth in the original pleadings. [Fed. R. Civ. P. 15(c)(2); **Parrish & Sons v. County Sanitation District,** 174 Cal. App. 2d 406 (1959)]

EXAM TIP	gilbert

The relation back doctrine often arises in law school exam questions. Be sure to mention the basic rule: A plaintiff usually can amend her complaint after the statute of limitations period otherwise would have run on the claim as long as the claim asserted in the amended pleading arose out of the *same conduct, transaction, or occurrence* set forth in the original pleadings.

(a) **Effect**

As long as the same basic transaction is involved, the plaintiff may therefore amend his complaint to establish new theories of recovery, or even to show new facts entitling him to recover, after the statute of limitations would otherwise have run.

(b) **Rationale**

The defendant is not prejudiced because she had notice, within the limitations period, that the plaintiff was asserting *some* claim against her on the basis of the transaction involved. Consequently, a change in the nature or theory of the plaintiff's claim does not prejudice the defendant. [**Tiller v. Atlantic Coast Line,** 323 U.S. 574 (1945)]

(c) **Rule regarding new parties [§925]**

An amendment of the complaint cannot avoid the statute of limitations with respect to a totally new party (as plaintiff or defendant). *Rationale:* The fact that the plaintiff has filed an action against one defendant does not toll the statute of limitations on such claims as he may have against other defendants. [**Anderson v. Papillion,** 445 F.2d 841 (5th Cir. 1971)]

(d) Federal rule for relation back [§926]

In federal court, relation back is permitted if an amendment "changes the party or the naming of the party against whom a claim is asserted." [Fed. R. Civ. P. 15(c)(3)] This relation back is permitted only in cases in which the new claim arises from the *same transaction* as that asserted in the original complaint [Fed. R. Civ. P. 15(c)(2); *see supra* §924], and the new party had *notice of the suit*.

1) Liberal interpretation superseded [§927]

Some earlier cases interpreted the rule liberally to permit the addition of defendants involved in the events subject to suit so long as they were on notice of the filing of the suit. [**Swartz v. Gold Dust Casino, Inc.,** 91 F.R.D. 543 (D. Nev. 1981)] Later cases have taken a stricter view of relation back in such circumstances. (*See infra.*) Courts may continue to use the more liberal approach in situations in which: (i) the added defendant is an entity related to the original defendant, (ii) plaintiff has a strong interest in obtaining relief against the added defendant, and (iii) the entity will suffer no prejudice due to the delay in naming it.

2) Misnamed defendant [§928]

The relation back provision was clearly directed to the situation in which the plaintiff simply uses the wrong name for the defendant. [*See e.g.,* **Schiavone v. Fortune, Inc.,** 477 U.S. 21 (1986)—in libel action, plaintiff named defendant as "Fortune," a division of Time, Inc., which should have been named as defendant] Restrictive recent cases have said that this is the only situation in which relation back is allowed. [**Barrow v. Wethersfield Police Department,** 66 F.3d 466 (7th Cir. 1995)—"the rule is meant to allow an amendment changing the name of a party to relate back to the original complaint only if the change is the result of an error, such as misnomer or misidentification"]

3) Unnamed defendants [§929]

If plaintiff knew the identities of some but not all defendants, earlier cases might permit relation back to add those additional defendants when their identities became known. More recent cases have disapproved relation back in such circumstances. [**Worthington v. Wilson,** 8 F.3d 1253 (7th Cir. 1993)—plaintiff not allowed to amend to add claims against "unknown police officers" identified in original complaint]

RELATION BACK DOCTRINE—A SUMMARY OF POSSIBLE DEFENDANTS	**gilbert**

ADDITIONAL DEFENDANT	Recent cases do *not* allow a plaintiff to add a new defendant after the statute of limitations has run *unless* the new defendant is an entity related to the original defendant, plaintiff has a strong interest in obtaining relief, and the added defendant will not suffer prejudice
MISNAMED DEFENDANT	If the plaintiff technically *misnamed* the defendant, the plaintiff should be allowed to fix the error and have the claim relate back to the original filing
UNNAMED DEFENDANTS	If a plaintiff knew the identities of some defendants but not others, recent cases do *not* allow the plaintiff to add the unnamed defendant after the statute of limitations has run

4) **Time and nature of notice [§930]**

For relation back to apply with regard to a claim against a defendant different from the one originally sued, that defendant must have been on notice *within the time allowed by Rule 4(m)* for service of the complaint—120 days after the filing of the complaint. The notice need not be by service of the complaint, but may come from any source. However, the notice must alert the new defendant that, but for a mistake concerning the identity of the proper party, plaintiff would have brought the action against this defendant. This may sometimes be found lacking if the theory of the claim against the new defendant is different from that against the original defendant. [**Lundy v. Adamar of New Jersey, Inc.**, 34 F.3d 1173 (3d Cir. 1994)—suit against casino for premises liability in connection with care provided by nurse did not notify doctor who employed nurse, because he had no reason to know he was not sued due to a mistake concerning identity]

5) **Added plaintiffs [§931]**

Rule 15(c)(3) speaks only of adding defendants, not plaintiffs, so ordinarily relation back is not allowed for claims of new plaintiffs. However, relation back has been allowed in situations in which the new plaintiff is the real party in interest [**Tidewater Marine Towing, Inc. v. Dow Chemical Co.**, 689 F.2d 1251 (5th Cir. 1982)], or to permit the original plaintiff to assert a claim in another capacity [**Williams v. United States**, 405 F.2d 234 (5th Cir. 1968)—mother who sued as next friend of her minor son permitted to add claims asserted in her own right for loss of her son's services after limitations period expired].

a)　Distinguish—class actions [§932]

The filing of the class action tolls the running of the statute of limitations for all members of the class. Class members may therefore be included in the suit after a class is certified, or benefit from this tolling of the limitations period if a class is not certified, or if they opt out of a class that is certified. (*See infra*, §§1216-1221.)

(e)　Distinguish—"Jane Doe" defendants named (state practice) [§933]

Some states permit the filing of a complaint against fictitious defendants ("Jane Does") where the true name of the defendant is not known when the action is filed. In such states, the complaint can be amended to name the defendant when her identity is discovered—even if the statute of limitations has then run! [Cal. Civ. Proc. Code §474; **Contract Engineers, Inc. v. California-Dorian Co.,** 258 Cal. App. 2d 546 (1968)]

(2)　Amendments in federal diversity cases [§934]

The Federal Rule permitting "relation back" [Fed. R. Civ. P. 15(c), *supra*] is applied by federal courts in diversity cases even if there is no similar local rule. Thus, a plaintiff may be able to assert a claim in an amended pleading that would be barred by the state court under the same circumstances. [**Skidmore v. Syntex Laboratories, Inc.,** 529 F.2d 1244 (5th Cir. 1976)]

(a)　State rule may be more liberal [§935]

Where the state rule regarding relation back is more liberal (*e.g.,* by dispensing with the requirement of notice to the new defendant within the limitations period), the state rule should be applied if state law provides the applicable statute of limitations. [Fed. R. Civ. P. 15(a)(1)]

f.　Amendment supersedes original pleading [§936]

An amended pleading *supersedes* the original, and the original has no further effect as a pleading. The pleader cannot "resurrect" the original pleading by attempting to dismiss or strike the amended pleading; but she can seek leave to re-amend if she wants to return to the claim originally pleaded.

(1)　Note

While superseded as a pleading, the original pleading can still be used *in evidence* against the pleader where appropriate—*e.g,* as an admission or prior inconsistent statement. (*See* Evidence Summary.)

(2)　And note

In many code pleading states, if the amended pleading contains *contradictory allegations on material matters without explaining the inconsistency* from the original pleading, the adverse party may move to strike the amended pleading as a sham. This applies to both verified and unverified pleadings. [**Hills Transportation Co. v. Southwest Forest Industries,** 266 Cal. App. 2d 702 (1968)]

3. Amendments at Trial [§937]

Because a basic purpose of pleading is to define the scope of the issues at trial, problems arise when a party seeks to amend the pleadings—and thus change the triable issues—during the course of the trial.

a. Common law background—doctrine of "variance" [§938]

At common law, a party could prevail (if at all) only on the claim stated in the pleadings. Issues outside the pleadings could not be tried; and any "variance" between the facts pleaded and those proved was often fatal to recovery. It made no difference that the other side failed to object or even *consented* to the variance.

b. Modern code practice [§939]

The common law rules have been relaxed in most code pleading states today. Where the evidence offered at trial is only a *partial* variance from the pleadings, the court may grant leave to amend the pleadings at trial to conform to the proof. If the variance is prejudicial, however, no such amendment can be permitted.

(1) Nonprejudicial variance [§940]

A nonprejudicial variance exists where the evidence at trial differs from the pleadings but concerns the *same transaction* as that originally alleged *and* the difference was *not prejudicial* to the opposing party (*i.e.,* did not mislead her in preparing her defense). [**General Credit Corp. v. Pichel,** 44 Cal. App. 3d 844 (1975)]

(2) Prejudicial variance [§941]

A prejudicial variance exists where the facts proved at trial show an entirely "new and different" cause of action or theory of recovery, or otherwise differ so materially from the pleadings as to be prejudicial.

> **Example:** P's complaint for malpractice alleged liability of defendant hospital by reason of the negligence of doctors who performed an operation. At trial, plaintiff sought to prove negligence on the part of members of the hospital's own staff. This was held to be a prejudicial variance, and amendment of the pleadings to assert the new theory was not permitted. [**Rainer v. Community Memorial Hospital,** 18 Cal. App. 3d 240 (1971)]

(3) Determinative factors [§942]

Whether a variance will be deemed prejudicial depends on several factors:

(a) *Surprise* to the opponent—*i.e.,* whether the opponent was put on notice of the new claim or defense, through discovery or pretrial disclosures;

(b) *Whether a continuance* would enable the opponent to meet the new evidence;

(c) *Any elements of inconvenience or unfairness* in granting a continuance (prejudice from delay, extra expense in trial, etc.); and

(d) *Policy favoring amendment*—to obtain complete and final disposition on the merits.

c. Federal practice [§943]

The pleadings are considerably less important in federal than in code pleading practice, and amendments are therefore allowed more liberally—even during trial. The doctrine of variance is effectively *abolished* in federal practice.

(1) Evidence received without objection [§944]

First, any variance between the pleadings and the proof at trial is *waived* unless a specific, timely, and proper objection to the evidence is made when offered. [Fed. R. Civ. P. 15(b)—"all issues tried with the *express or implied consent* of the parties shall be treated in all respects as if they had been raised in the pleading"]

(a) Aider by verdict [§945]

This embodies the doctrine of "aider by verdict"; *i.e.,* that evidence received at trial without objection by the adverse party supplies the missing allegations in the pleadings, so that the defective pleadings are "aided" by the verdict.

(b) Tactic—amend to conform to proof [§946]

It is still sound practice to seek leave to amend to conform to proof (which can be granted even after trial and judgment)—so there will be a correlation between the judgment and pleadings. However, failure to amend to conform to proof does *not* affect the result of the trial or the validity of the judgment as entered. [Fed. R. Civ. P. 15(b)]

(c) Problem of relevance [§947]

The usual objection that could be made would be relevance—that the proffered evidence is not relevant to the issues made out in the pleading. In many instances, however, this may not be clear, and one can argue that evidence was relevant even without an amendment. If that is true, failure to object would not necessarily be a waiver of objections to an amendment.

(2) Amendments over objection [§948]

If evidence *is* objected to on the ground that it is outside the issues framed by the pleadings, the proponent of the evidence must seek leave to amend his pleadings. Federal Rule 15(b) provides that the court may allow the pleadings to be amended (during trial) and *"shall do so freely"* if it appears that the amendment will aid in the presentation of the case and will not prejudice the objecting party in the presentation of her action or defense.

(a) Effect [§949]

It is up to the objecting party to show *prejudice* on the merits, or the requested amendment must be granted. Refusing leave to amend without such showing constitutes an abuse of judicial discretion and will be reversed on appeal. [**Hodgson v. Colonnades, Inc.**, 472 F.2d 42 (5th Cir. 1973)]

(b) Tactic—continuance [§950]

The proper remedy for surprise resulting from a change of theory at trial is a continuance. And in granting a continuance, the court can assess *costs* against the party at fault. [**Watson v. Cannon Shoe Co.**, 165 F.2d 311 (5th Cir. 1948)]

(3) Distinguish—modification of final pretrial order [§951]

Due to managerial judging, it often happens that the pleadings are superseded by a final pretrial order that specifies the claims and defenses to be tried. (*See infra*, §§1710-1718.) If so, the final pretrial order is to be modified only *"to prevent manifest injustice."* [Fed. R. Civ. P. 16(e)]

4. Amendments After Trial [§952]

In federal practice, the pleadings can be amended to conform to proof at any time, even after trial and entry of judgment (*see* above). [Fed. R. Civ. P. l5(b)] Such a motion for amendment can be made for the first time *on appeal*. However, this is subject to the general rule of appellate practice that a reviewing court will not consider grounds for appeal (other than jurisdictional) that were not reasonably raised in the trial court. (*See infra*, §§2159-2166.)

EXAM TIP	gilbert
Remember that while the federal rules allow a party to amend a pleading only once *as a matter of right*, in federal courts, pleadings may be amended *by leave of court*, and such leave is liberally granted. Indeed, a party may be given leave to amend even after trial.	

5. Supplemental Pleadings [§953]

The function of supplemental pleadings is to call the court's attention to material facts that have occurred *subsequent* to the filing of the original complaint.

Example: In an action for personal injuries, a supplemental pleading might allege aggravation of injuries or increments of damage sustained after filing of the original complaint.

---

a. **Discretion of court [§954]**

There is *no right* to file a supplemental pleading. The filing of such pleadings is permissive, within the sound discretion of the court. [Fed. R. Civ. P. 15(d)]

(1) But note

The same policy factors favoring liberality in amendment of pleadings (above) likewise support supplemental pleadings. Indeed, there is even less chance of prejudice to the other party in this situation, since the supplemental pleading does not alter the claim or defense originally asserted.

b. **Procedure [§955]**

The party seeking leave to supplement a pleading must file a written motion with a copy of the proposed supplemental pleading attached.

(1) Response [§956]

Whether a response to a supplemental pleading may be filed is also discretionary with the court. If the court orders a response, it will likewise set the time within which such a response must be served and filed. [Fed. R. Civ. P. 15(d)]

c. **Effect on original pleading [§957]**

The function of a supplemental pleading is merely to *add to,* not modify, the original pleadings. If permitted, it does not replace the original pleading (as would an amended pleading), but it is a supplement to the original.

(1) *Under state practice,* a supplemental complaint is not permitted to change the basic nature of the case by alleging what amounts to a totally different cause of action. [**Flood v. Simpson,** 45 Cal. App. 3d 644 (1975)]

(2) *Federal practice* is more liberal. Federal Rule 15(d) gives the court discretion to allow supplemental pleadings despite the fact that the original pleading is defective, or that the supplement would change the nature of the relief sought.

I.   Default Procedure

1. **In General [§958]**

As discussed (*supra,* §860), if a defendant fails to answer or otherwise plead within the time permitted, the clerk of the court is required to enter a default. [Fed. R. Civ. P. 55(a)]

2. Effect of Default Entry [§959]

The defendant's failure to plead is regarded as an *admission* of the claim against her. So long as the default stands, any attempt by defendant to "answer" or file any other pleading in the case will be disregarded.

3. Obtaining Judgment [§960]

After an entry of default, the plaintiff must proceed to obtain a default judgment. If he is suing on a promissory note or other sum certain, the judgment may be entered directly by the clerk of the court. In all other cases, the plaintiff must present his evidence to the court in order to obtain judgment. [Fed. R. Civ. P. 55(b)]

a. Relief limited to prayer [§961]

In default cases, the judgment cannot exceed the *amount or type of relief requested in the prayer of the complaint*. (*See supra*, §621.)

b. Defendant not entitled to appear [§962]

Unless she made an earlier appearance in the action, the defendant is *not* entitled to any notice of the plaintiff's application for default judgment; nor is she entitled to appear or submit evidence in opposition.

4. Setting Aside Default [§963]

If the defendant's default has been entered, her remedy is to move the court to set aside the default (and any judgment entered pursuant thereto).

a. Time limits [§964]

In federal practice, a motion to set aside the default can be made at any time until judgment is entered. [Fed. R. Civ. P. 55(c)] Thereafter, a motion to set aside the judgment can be made at any time within *one year* after the judgment or order is entered. [Fed. R. Civ. P. 60(b)]

b. Grounds [§965]

Ordinarily, the defendant must show:

(1) *That she has a valid excuse* for her default (*e.g.,* excusable neglect, fraud, inadvertence);

(2) *That she has a meritorious defense* to the action; *and*

(3) *That plaintiff will not be prejudiced.*

c. Appellate review [§966]

Review of a trial court's decision on a motion to set aside default is limited. Appellate courts will not overturn the trial court decision unless both of the above factors (time limit and grounds) are so clearly satisfied or not satisfied that the trial court ruling was an *abuse of discretion.*

J. Judgment on the Pleadings

1. Purpose [§967]

A motion for judgment on the pleadings is closely analogous to a demurrer or motion to dismiss under Federal Rule 12(b)(6), and is used at common law for the same purpose—*i.e.,* to challenge the adversary's pleadings on the ground that they are *insufficient to establish any valid claim or defense.*

2. Making of Motion [§968]

A motion for judgment on the pleadings may be made by either party at any time after the pleadings have joined issue, but within such time as will not delay the trial. [Fed. R. Civ. P. 12(c)]

3. Issues Raised

a. Legal sufficiency of pleading [§969]

A motion for judgment on the pleadings challenges only the sufficiency of the adversary's pleading in posing a legally meritorious contention.

b. Matters beyond the pleading [§970]

Under common law and code practice, a motion for judgment on the pleadings could not raise defects that did not appear on the face of the pleadings. However, modern practice permits the moving party to present matters beyond the pleadings; and where this is done, the motion is treated as a motion for summary judgment. [Fed. R. Civ. P. 12(c)]

4. Hearing on Motion [§971]

As with other pretrial matters, a motion for judgment on the pleadings is generally heard before commencement of the trial (although the court may order the motion deferred until the time of trial). [Fed. R. Civ. P. 12(d)]

5. Adversary's Right to Amend Pleadings [§972]

Once a responsive pleading has been filed, a pleader no longer has an absolute right to amend the pleading; any amendment must be by leave of court or by written consent of the adverse party. [Fed. R. Civ. P. 15(a)] For this purpose, a motion for judgment on the pleadings is *not* a "responsive pleading" and hence does not cut off an adversary's right to amend without leave of court if no answer has been filed. [**Breier v. Northern California Bowling Proprietors' Association**, 316 F.2d 787 (9th Cir. 1963)]

K. Voluntary Dismissal by Plaintiff

1. **Common Law [§973]**

   At common law, a plaintiff had the right to dismiss his own action at any time before verdict. While a dismissal ordinarily would result in an award of costs against the plaintiff, the dismissal was without prejudice to a later suit on the same claim.

2. **Code Practice [§974]**

   The common law procedure was subject to some abuse by plaintiffs taking dismissals to prevent decisions on the merits favoring their adversaries. As a result, code pleading states limited the right of plaintiffs to dismiss their actions without prejudice: Such a dismissal had to occur *before* the commencement of trial; otherwise it was deemed to be with prejudice (*i.e.,* a bar to relitigation). This is still the rule in some states. [*See, e.g.,* Cal. Civ. Proc. Code §581(b)(1)]

   a. **Note**

      The filing of a counterclaim or cross-demand for affirmative relief may also prevent a voluntary dismissal without prejudice. [Cal. Civ. Proc. Code §581(i)]

3. **Federal Practice—Notice of Dismissal (Voluntary)**

   a. **Filing of notice [§975]**

      Under federal practice, a plaintiff retains the right to dismiss his own action by filing a notice of dismissal. [Fed. R. Civ. P. 41(a)(1)(i)] But the right to do so is even more narrowly limited than in code pleading states.

   b. **Time for filing [§976]**

      An effective notice of dismissal must be filed before the filing of the adversary's *answer or motion for summary judgment.* Thereafter, the plaintiff cannot dismiss without the defendant's consent or court order. [Fed. R. Civ. P. 41(a)(2)]

      ---

      cf. Compare: It has been held that a *motion to dismiss for failure to state a claim* is not tantamount to a motion for summary judgment, and does not terminate the plaintiff's right to file a voluntary dismissal. [**Kilpatrick v. Texas & Pacific Railway,** 166 F.2d 788 (2d Cir. 1948); *but see* **Tele-Views News Co. v. S.R.B. TV Publishing Co.,** 28 F.R.D. 303 (E.D. Pa. 1961)]

      ---

   c. **Number of dismissals [§977]**

      The plaintiff is limited to one (voluntary) dismissal by notice. Thereafter, any dismissal operates as a dismissal *with prejudice.* [Fed. R. Civ. P. 41(a)]

   d. **Trial court cannot set aside proper dismissal [§978]**

      An order striking a timely notice of dismissal is reversible error, and any judgment subsequently entered against the plaintiff will be reversed on appeal after trial. [**Plains Growers, Inc. v. Ickes-Braun Glasshouses, Inc.,** 474 F.2d 250 (5th Cir. 1973)]

e. Effect on power to sanction [§979]

Unless the court has already issued an order to show cause why sanctions should not be imposed at the time of the voluntary dismissal, it may not impose monetary sanctions on its own initiative. [Fed. R. Civ. P. 11(c)(2)(B)]

4. Federal Practice—Dismissal by Leave of Court

a. Time for motion [§980]

The court may grant the plaintiff's motion for leave to dismiss without prejudice at any time *prior to judgment*—*i.e.,* even after the trial has commenced. [Fed. R. Civ. P. 41(a)(2)]

b. Discretion to refuse limited [§981]

The discretion of the court to refuse a dismissal without prejudice is limited.

Example: A plaintiff making a good faith request based on newly discovered evidence has been held entitled to a dismissal without prejudice (to allow refiling of the action and a new trial) unless a substantial right of the defendant would be jeopardized thereby. [**Durham v. Florida East Coast Railroad,** 385 F.2d 366 (5th Cir. 1971)]

Compare: The court should not order a dismissal without prejudice merely to accommodate the plaintiff's desire to get another 10-day period within which to demand a jury trial. [**Noonan v. Cunard Steamship Co.,** 375 F.2d 69 (2d Cir. 1967)]

(1) Counterclaims preserved

The court may not dismiss over the objection of a defendant who has filed a counterclaim unless the counterclaim can remain pending for independent adjudication. [Fed. R. Civ. P. 41(a)(2); *see* Chapter II. regarding subject matter jurisdiction]

c. Number of dismissals [§982]

The court is not limited as to the number of times it may grant motions to dismiss the same action without prejudice—provided, of course, that there is a legitimate reason for the repeated requests. [**American Cyanimid Co. v. McGhee,** 317 F.2d 295 (5th Cir. 1963)]

d. Conditions of dismissal [§983]

A plaintiff seeking dismissal *without* prejudice may be required to bear the full cost of the litigation to date, including the adversary's attorneys' fees. [Fed. R. Civ. P. 41(a)(2)] But such conditions may not be imposed on a plaintiff seeking to dismiss his claim *with* prejudice. [**Smoot v. Fox,** 353 F.2d 830 (6th Cir. 1965)] *Note:* Under Rule 11, sanctions may not be imposed on a plaintiff who voluntarily dismisses a groundless suit in response to service of a motion for sanctions. (*See supra,* §§768 *et seq.*)

e. Continuing jurisdiction—stipulated dismissal [§984]

When dismissal by stipulation pursuant to Rule 41(a)(2) provides that the court shall retain jurisdiction to enforce a settlement agreement, the court has continuing jurisdiction, but otherwise dismissal terminates the court's jurisdiction. [**Kokkonen v. Guardian Life Insurance Co.,** 511 U.S. 375 (1994)—court without jurisdiction to enforce provision of parties' settlement agreement after dismissal pursuant to that agreement because the parties' obligation to comply was not made part of the order of dismissal]

Chapter Five:
Parties

CONTENTS

Chapter Approach

Chapter Approach

Modern procedural rules make available several devices for joinder of parties beyond the "single plaintiff vs. single defendant" paradigm of a lawsuit. The standards for joinder vary with the functions served by the various procedural devices. When you face a problem involving more than just one plaintiff vs. one defendant, consider the following:

1. Before you even get to joinder issues, you may need to think about the requirements of *real party in interest* and *capacity to sue or be sued:*

   a. Is the action brought in the name of the *real party in interest, i.e.,* the party who under governing substantive law has the right to enforce the claim?

   b. Do the parties have legal competence to be parties to a lawsuit; do they have *capacity to sue or be sued?* Partnerships (as opposed to partners) and infants and incompetent persons, for example, may lack legal capacity.

2. If the situation in your question calls for joinder of someone not a party to the suit, is joinder *compulsory?*

   a. Is the absentee one whose nonjoinder would prevent the granting of *complete relief,* or *prejudice* his or the present parties' interests? Such a person should be joined if joinder is feasible. If it is not feasible (as when joinder would destroy complete diversity in a diversity case in federal court), the court must decide whether it can proceed with only the present parties before it.

   — If the court can proceed, the absentee is characterized as merely a *"necessary"* party, and the action can proceed in his absence.

   — If the court cannot proceed, the absentee is regarded as an *"indispensable"* party, and the action must be dismissed.

3. To determine whether *permissive* joinder is appropriate:

   a. Is the relief sought *jointly, severally, or in the alternative;*

   b. Does the claim *arise out of the same transaction* or series of transactions; and

   c. Is there a *common question of law or fact?*

4. Sometimes someone not already a party to the suit seeks to *intervene.* In that case consider:

   a. Is the case one for *intervention of right,* in which disposition in his absence could impair or impede his ability to protect an interest he claims in the property or transaction sued on, and the existing parties do not adequately represent his interest; or

b. Is the case one in which the court may allow *permissive intervention*, with the prospective intervenor's claim or defense having a question of law or fact in common with the main action?

5. When you see facts that have two (or more) persons asserting a claim to money or property in the hands of a third party (the "stakeholder"), think of *interpleader*. The stakeholder may deposit the property with the court and seek a ruling as to which of the adverse claimants is entitled to the property.

6. A defendant in your question may seek *impleader* of a third-party defendant. If so, is the third party one (*e.g.*, an insurer) who is or may be liable to the defendant for all or part of the plaintiff's claim against the defendant?

7. In federal court when an effort is made at joinder adding a party, if there is no independent basis of federal jurisdiction, think about whether there is *supplemental jurisdiction* over the added claim.

8. If the situation seems to call for a *class action*

a. Ask:

(1) Are the class members so *numerous* that joinder of all is impracticable;

(2) Are there *common questions* of law or fact;

(3) Are the representative's *claims or defenses typical* of those of the class; and

(4) Will the representative *adequately represent* the interests of the class?

b. And in addition, ask:

(1) Might there be *prejudice from separate actions*;

(2) Has the class's opponent acted or refused to act on grounds generally applicable to the class, making *class injunctive or declaratory relief* appropriate; *or*

(3) Do *common questions predominate* over individual ones, and is a class action *superior* to other methods?

If you find that the case may be conducted as a class action, has required *notice* been given?

A. Real Party in Interest Rule

1. Background [§985]

At common law, only the legal "owner" of a right could bring an action for infringement of that right. Since the common law did not recognize equitable interests (*e.g.*, rights of subrogees, beneficiaries of various kinds of trusts, etc.), the holder of such an interest could not sue at law for its enforcement, but instead had to rely on the legal owner to bring suit. This burdensome practice has been abolished, and today, suit can be brought only in the name of the real party in interest. [Fed. R. Civ. P. 17]

2. Definition [§986]

The real party in interest rule has two parts; the person who is suing must: (i) use her *own name* as plaintiff, *and* (ii) have a *legal right* to enforce the claim in question under the applicable substantive law.

a. Exception—permission to sue using fictitious name [§987]

In limited circumstances, a court may permit a plaintiff to proceed under a fictitious name, such as Jane Doe, to protect against serious harm that would result from revealing the party's name. However, this is allowed only if the plaintiff shows a compelling need to proceed anonymously. [*See, e.g.*, **Southern Methodist University Association of Women Law Students v. Wynne & Jaffe**, 599 F.2d 707 (5th Cir. 1979)—female lawyers asserting that law firm discriminated against women could not proceed anonymously]

b. Burden of proof [§988]

The plaintiff has the burden of proving that she is a real party in interest; *i.e.*, that she should be allowed to sue to protect the interest involved.

c. Under Federal Rules and state rules [§989]

The following parties have a right to sue as representative parties even though they may have no beneficial interest in the claims at issue [Fed. R. Civ. P. 17(a)]:

(1) *The executor, administrator, guardian, or trustee* of an estate;

(2) *A party to a contract made for the benefit of another party* (*e.g.*, an agent contracting on behalf of the principal or the promisee of a third-party beneficiary contract); and

(3) *A private claimant suing in the name of the United States Government* if such a claim is expressly authorized by statute.

d. In all other cases [§990]

In all other cases, a determination of the real party in interest is made according to applicable substantive law. In a federal diversity action, the applicable state law is applied.

3. Determination of Real Party in Interest [§991]

The following situations illustrate the types of problems encountered in determining the real party in interest.

a. Assignments [§992]

Whether an assignee is the real party in interest depends primarily on the nature of the assignment.

(1) Complete assignment [§993]

If the assignor's *entire interest* has been transferred to the assignee, the assignee has become the real party in interest. The assignee may then prosecute any action to enforce the assigned right in her own name without joining the assignor.

(a) Gratuitous assignment [§994]

In state and federal practice, the assignee can sue even if she paid nothing for the claim and is merely an *assignee for collection*. However, in federal court, the citizenship of the *assignor* determines whether diversity exists. (*See supra*, §340.)

(b) Assignment after commencement of suit [§995]

If the assignment takes place after suit has been filed, the assignee may either continue the action in the name of the assignor or be substituted as the plaintiff. [*See* Fed. R. Civ. P. 25(c)]

(c) Effect of judgment [§996]

A judgment in the assignee's action will bar any subsequent suit on the same claim by the assignor, because of the *privity* between the assignee and assignor. [**Nemeth v. Hair,** 146 Cal. App. 2d 405 (1956); *and see* discussion on res judicata, *infra*, §§2184 *et seq.*]

(2) Partial assignments [§997]

At common law, the assignee of part of a claim could not enforce the claim at all. However, partial assignees could enforce their claims in *equity* if the assignor and all other partial assignees joined as parties in the same suit.

(a) Modern rule [§998]

Today, the assignor and all partial assignees are considered *"necessary parties"* in any suit to enforce the claim, and on appropriate motion, the court will order their joinder. [**United States v. Aetna Casualty & Surety Co.,** 338 U.S. 366 (1949)]

(3) Assignment may create diversity [§999]

When an assignee seeks to base federal court subject matter jurisdiction on diversity of citizenship, and there was no diversity between the assignor and the defendant, jurisdiction exists only if substantial consideration was given for the assignment. (*See supra*, §340.)

b. Subrogation [§1000]

Subrogation is an equitable principle through which an assignment occurs by operation of law. Under the doctrine of subrogation, the person who *pays* another for a loss or injury caused by the act of some third person is entitled to enforce whatever claim the injured person had against the third person. Most jurisdictions allow the person who paid (subrogee) to sue in his own name without joining the injured party (subrogor). [**United States v. Aetna Casualty & Surety Co.,** *supra*]

Example: X Insurance Co. insures P's house and pays P for damages to the house caused by D's wrongful act. X becomes subrogated to P's claim against D and is entitled to sue D in its own name. [**Auto Insurance Co. v. Union Oil Co.,** 85 Cal. App. 2d 302 (1948)]

---

(1) Tactical problem [§1001]

An insurance company will usually prefer to sue in the name of its *insured*, rather than in its own name, to avoid any jury prejudice against insurers. Consequently, most insurance settlements contain provisions expressly authorizing the insurer to sue the wrongdoer "in the name of the insured."

(a) Note

The traditional view did not permit such suits because the insured, having been fully paid and having assigned the claim to the company, had no further interest in the matter. [*See* **Sosnow v. Storatti Corp.,** 295 N.Y. 675 (1946)] However, most states now permit suits in the name of the insured. [*See* **Anheuser-Busch, Inc. v. Starley,** 28 Cal. 2d 347 (1946)]

(b) And note

Even states that do not permit suit in the name of the insured may recognize the "loan receipt" device. Here, the insurer—instead of paying off the insured—makes him a "loan" repayable only out of proceeds from the insured's recovery against the third person. The insured gets his money but still "owns" the claim. The insurance company then brings suit in the name of the insured, and the insurer keeps the proceeds if it wins.

c. Trusts

(1) Trustee [§1002]

The trustee of a trust holds legal title to the trust estate and is therefore the real party in interest for redress of any *wrong to the trust estate.* [Fed. R. Civ. P. 17] Suit is maintained in the trustee's name as trustee (*e.g.,* "John Smith, as trustee of the Mary Doe Trust"). [See **Powers v. Ashton,** 45 Cal. App. 3d 783 (1975)]

(2) Beneficiary [§1003]

The beneficiary of a trust may sue the trustee to protect her rights as beneficiary—*e.g.,* for an accounting, for distributions of assets, etc. [**DeOlazabel v. Mix,** 24 Cal. App. 2d 258 (1937)]

(a) But note

A beneficiary cannot sue third persons for wrongs to the trust estate unless the trustee refuses to bring suit for such injuries. In the latter situation, the beneficiary can sue the third party by joining the trustee and alleging his failure to act. [**Triplett v. Williams,** 269 Cal. App. 2d 135 (1969)]

d. Executors and administrators [§1004]

Executors and administrators are the proper parties to sue on behalf of decedents' estates at law or in equity.

(1) Note

Problems do arise about the capacity of a representative appointed in one state to sue in another, but such problems do not result from the real party in interest provision. They concern primarily the policy of the forum state of protecting local creditors. This has led to the general rule that an executor or administrator has capacity to sue only in the state of her appointment, unless she obtains ancillary appointment in another state.

(2) Beneficiary of an estate pursuing claims [§1005]

Ordinarily the legatee or distributee of an estate may not bring suit to pursue claims of the estate, although exceptions have been recognized in situations parallel to the exceptions for beneficiaries of a trust.

(3) Survival statutes and wrongful death acts [§1006]

Claims under survival statutes are generally part of the decedent's estate and are to be pursued by his executor or administrator just as any other asset of the estate would be. Wrongful death acts generally specify the proper party to an action under them. Some of them name one or more of the beneficiaries, and in such a case, the party named is, of course, the real party in interest. Many of them require suit to be brought by the personal representative of the deceased—*i.e.,* the executor or administrator. However, when suing under such a statute, the executor or administrator is not

PARTY	EXAMPLE
ASSIGNEE	Becomes the real party in interest if assignor assigns entire interest; if less than entire interest is assigned, assignor and assignee both are "necessary parties" and on appropriate motion court will order that both be joined.
SUBROGEE	Most jurisdictions allow a subrogee (*i.e.,* a person who has paid another's obligation to a third party—the subrogor) to sue in his own name without joining the subrogor.
TRUSTEE	The trustee is the real party in interest for redress of any wrong to the trust estate.
BENEFICIARY OF A TRUST	The beneficiary of a trust may sue the trustee to protect her rights as a beneficiary, but may not bring suit on behalf of the trust.
EXECUTORS AND ADMINISTRATORS	Executors and administrators are the real parties in interest to sue on behalf of decedents' estates.
PRINCIPAL	If an obligation on a contract made by an agent on behalf of a principal is owed to the principal alone, the principal is the only real party in interest.
AGENT	If an agent enters into a contract on behalf of a principal and the obligation is owed to both the principal and the agent, the agent is a real party in interest in addition to the principal.
THIRD-PARTY BENEFICIARY	If a third-party beneficiary has enforceable rights under a contract, she is a real party in interest and may sue in her own name.

acting as a representative of the estate, but rather as a person designated by statute. Consequently the judgment or recovery under the statute will not be an asset of the estate at all, but instead will belong to the statutory beneficiaries, who may or may not be the same persons who would take as legatees or distributees of the estate.

e. Principal and agent [§1007]
If a contract has been executed by an agent acting for a principal, the following rules apply:

(1) *If the obligation is owed to the principal alone,* the principal is the only proper plaintiff.

(2) *If the obligation is owed to both the agent and the principal,* either party may sue (*e.g.,* if there was a promise to both the agent and the principal). [**Warren Insurance Agency v. Surpur Timber Co.,** 250 Cal. App. 2d 99 (1967)—suit by agent; **Ford v. Williams,** 62 U.S. 287 (1858)—suit by undisclosed principal]

f. Third-party beneficiary [§1008]
If a third-party beneficiary has enforceable rights under a contract, he is the real party in interest and is entitled to sue in his own name to enforce his rights. [**Orcutt v. Ferranini,** 237 Cal. App. 2d 216 (1965)]

(1) Note
The *promisee* under a contract may also be entitled to sue to enforce the promise given for the benefit of a third party. In such case, *both* the promisee and the third-party beneficiary would have enforceable rights and would be deemed real parties in interest.

4. Attacking Violation of Real Party in Interest Rule

a. If defect apparent

(1) Federal practice [§1009]
If a violation of the real party in interest rule is apparent on the face of a complaint in federal court, the defendant should make a *motion to dismiss* for failure to state a claim upon which relief may be granted (since the plaintiff has no right to recovery). [Fed. R. Civ. P. 12(b)(6)]

(2) Code practice (some states) [§1010]
Under code pleading practice, a *general demurrer* is appropriate to attack defects on the face of the complaint. (*See supra,* §700.)

b. Where defect not apparent [§1011]
If the defect is not apparent on the face of the complaint, the defendant may

move for summary judgment (supported by appropriate affidavits to establish the defect) or may raise the matter as an affirmative defense in her answer.

5. Nonjoinder of Necessary Party [§1012]

If the named plaintiff has some kind of interest in the claim (assignor or assignee, principal or agent, trustee or beneficiary), and the objection is that someone else should also be the named plaintiff (another partial assignee, principal, etc.), this is an objection to nonjoinder of a *necessary party*.

a. When objection can be raised [§1013]

The objection as to the named plaintiff can be raised by motion before trial or at the trial itself [Fed. R. Civ. P. 12(h)(2)], but delay may result in estoppel against raising it. If the objection is first made on appeal, it is too late unless serious injustice would inevitably result from the nonjoinder. [**Provident Bank & Trust Co. v. Patterson**, 390 U.S. 102 (1968)]

b. No cause of action [§1014]

If the named plaintiff has *no* substantive interest in the claim being enforced, he has no cause of action. This objection is therefore proper at any time prior to judgment. Note, however, that under the usual rules governing appeal, a claim that the plaintiff has no cause of action cannot be raised on appeal for the first time, and the objection *cannot* be made in collateral attack on the judgment.

B. Capacity of Party to Sue or Be Sued

1. Definition [§1015]

"Capacity" refers to legal competence to be a party to a lawsuit. The plaintiff must have the capacity to sue, and the defendant must have the capacity to be sued.

2. Individuals [§1016]

The capacity of an individual to sue or be sued is determined by the law of her domicile. [Fed. R. Civ. P. 17(b)] If the plaintiff lacks capacity (as in the case of a minor or an incompetent), suit must be maintained by a duly authorized or appointed guardian. If there is none, the court must appoint one for the particular action (a "*guardian ad litem*"). [Fed. R. Civ. P. 17(c)]

a. Pleadings by guardian [§1017]

If a guardian or conservator appears in the action, the pleadings are usually drawn in the name of the guardian "for and on behalf of" the incompetent or minor. [Fed. R. Civ. P. 17(c)] Note that state practice on such pleadings varies. For example, in California, the pleadings are drawn in the name of the minor or incompetent "by a guardian or conservator. . . ." [Cal. Civ. Proc. Code §372]

b. Incompetent's right to disaffirm judgment [§1018]

If a minor (or incompetent) is a party to the action but is not represented by a guardian, any judgment rendered is *voidable by him* within a reasonable time after attaining majority (or being restored to competency) *if* it appears that his legal interests were inadequately protected in the action. [**Withers v. Tucker,** 145 N.W.2d 665 (Wis. 1966)—minor represented by attorney]

3. Corporations [§1019]

The capacity of a corporation to sue (or be sued) is determined by the law of the state in which it was organized.

Example: Statutes in some states provide for suspension of powers of a corporation that is delinquent in paying its state taxes. [*See, e.g.,* Cal. Rev. & Tax Code §23301] In such a case, the corporation would have no power to sue, defend itself, or appeal from a judgment as long as it is under the suspension. [**Mather Construction Co. v. United States,** 475 F.2d 1152 (Ct. Cl. 1973)]

a. Limitation

A state cannot impose a disability on a corporation if doing so would violate federal law.

Example: An attempt to deny an out-of-state corporation the right to sue in local courts to enforce a contract made in interstate commerce would violate federal law. [**Allenberg Cotton Co. v. Pittman,** 419 U.S. 20 (1974)]

4. Partnerships [§1020]

Two issues arise with respect to the capacity of partnerships: (i) whether the partnership can (or must) sue as an entity, distinct from its members; and (ii) if the suit is by one or more of the members of the partnership, whether they should be named individually or should sue in the name of the partnership.

a. Federal practice—entity vs. aggregate [§1021]

In federal courts, a partnership can always *sue or be sued as an entity if the litigation involves a federal question.* However, in other cases—including a diversity action—the partnership's capacity to sue or be sued is determined by the law of the state in which the federal court is located. [Fed. R. Civ. P. 17(b)]

b. State law varies [§1022]

About half the states permit a partnership to be sued, but not to sue, as an entity (in its common name). In those states, actions on a partnership claim must be brought in the names of the individual partners (*e.g.,* "A, B, and C, as co-partners doing business as Acme Partnership"). Other states allow the partnership to both sue and be sued as an entity. [*See* Cal. Civ. Proc. Code §369.5]

5. Unincorporated Associations [§1023]

At common law, unincorporated associations lacked capacity to sue or be sued as entities. [**Ostrom v. Greene,** 161 N.Y. 353 (1900)]

a. State practice [§1024]

Many states now treat unincorporated associations like corporations. [*See* Cal. Civ. Proc. Code §369.5; **Wright v. Arkansas Activities Association,** 501 F.2d 25 (8th Cir. 1974)]

b. Federal practice [§1025]

In federal courts, an association has capacity to sue or be sued when a *federal right* is being enforced by or against the association. But when a *state* law right is being enforced, as in a *diversity* action, the capacity of an unincorporated association is determined by the law of the state in which the federal action is brought. [Fed. R. Civ. P. 17(b)]

(1) Existence of diversity [§1026]

For purposes of determining the existence of diversity of citizenship, the association is considered a citizen of each state of which any one of its members is a citizen. (*See supra,* §320.)

c. Real party in interest rule [§1027]

Even where an unincorporated association has the capacity to sue, it must assert a claim that belongs to it rather than to its members individually.

___

Example: An unincorporated association of businesses has standing to seek an injunction against conduct constituting unfair competition to its members, but not to seek damages for past injury to the members, as such rights do not belong to the association. [**Travel Agents Malpractice Action Corps v. Regal Cultural Society,** 287 A.2d 4 (N.J. 1972)]

___

6. Attacking Lack of Capacity

a. Lack of capacity on face of complaint [§1028]

If lack of capacity appears on the face of the complaint, the complaint is subject to a *motion to dismiss* (or demurrer, in some states). Usually, however, it does not appear on the face and must be raised by motion for summary judgment or in the *answer.*

b. Lack of capacity not raised by time of answer [§1029]

If lack of capacity is not raised by the time of the answer, the defect is waived. The judgment entered will determine the rights of the party despite his lack of capacity, unless the party can show that she was inadequately represented (*see supra,* §1018).

C. Joinder of Parties

1. In General [§1030]

Determining which parties are to be joined as plaintiffs or defendants requires consideration of the rules of compulsory and permissive joinder. Compulsory joinder rules cover parties who *must* be joined ("indispensable parties") and those who *should* be joined if possible ("conditionally necessary parties"). The rules of permissive joinder apply to parties who *may* be joined ("proper parties").

2. Permissive Joinder [§1031]

At common law and under the early codes, a plaintiff's joinder options were limited. Under the Federal Rules and modern codes, however, a plaintiff may join anyone involved in the *transaction* that is the subject matter of the suit.

a. Early approach [§1032]

Under the original codes, parties could be joined only if they each had "an interest" in both the subject of the action and the relief sought. The rules governing joinder of causes of action required that causes joined "affect" *all* parties joined. These rules prevented joinder in many cases where the need was obvious.

Example: Wife, injured by D's negligence, sues for her injuries. Husband attempts to join his claim for loss of her services. Joinder was not proper under the early approach because Husband had no "interest" in the relief sought by Wife, and vice versa. [**Ryder v. Jefferson Hotel Co.**, 113 S.E. 474 (S.C. 1922)]

b. Modern approach [§1033]

Today, parties may join or be joined in one action if:

(i) A right to relief is asserted by (or against) them *jointly, severally, or in the alternative;*

(ii) The right to relief *arises out of the same transaction or series of transactions;* and

(iii) There is *at least one question of law or fact common to all parties* sought to be joined.

[Fed. R. Civ. P. 20(a)]

(1) Relief sought

(a) Separate or joint [§1034]

Each plaintiff is not required to have an interest in every cause of action in all the relief prayed for. If there are several plaintiffs, they have the option to seek separate relief or joint relief. Likewise, if several defendants are joined, the relief sought may be against each separately or against them jointly.

(b) "In the alternative"—plaintiff "in doubt" [§1035]

Sometimes, a plaintiff may be in doubt as to which of several defendants is liable for his injuries (*e.g.,* P is injured by a bullet fired by either D-1 or D-2). In such a case, it is proper for the plaintiff to set forth a claim against each defendant in the alternative, so that their respective liabilities can be determined.

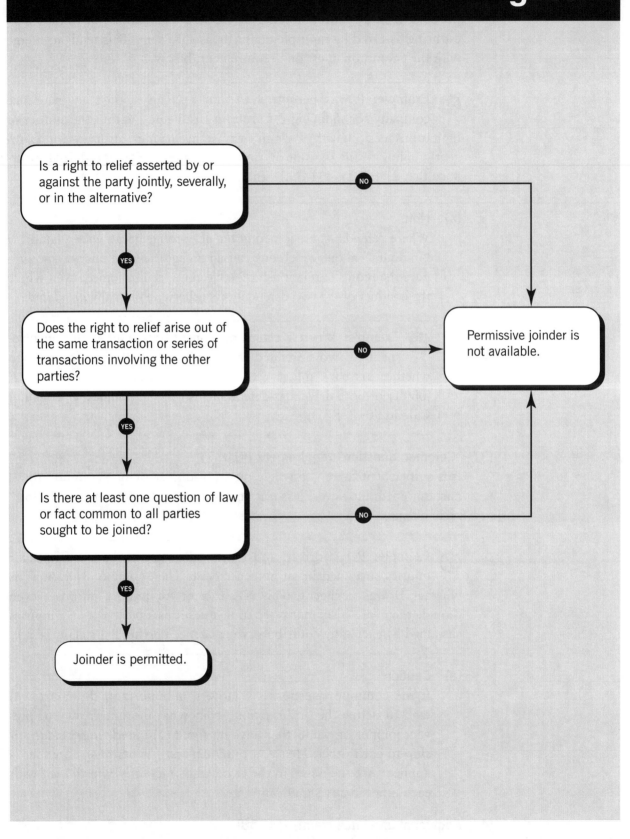

Is a right to relief asserted by or against the party jointly, severally, or in the alternative?

NO → Permissive joinder is not available.

YES ↓

Does the right to relief arise out of the same transaction or series of transactions involving the other parties?

NO → Permissive joinder is not available.

YES ↓

Is there at least one question of law or fact common to all parties sought to be joined?

NO → Permissive joinder is not available.

YES ↓

Joinder is permitted.

(2) "Same transaction" requirement [§1036]

The requirement that the right to relief arise from the "same transaction or series of transactions" is construed very broadly. *Some causal relationship or interrelation* among the defendants' conduct, or in the interest being asserted by multiple plaintiffs, is sufficient. This tends to merge with the "common question" requirement, below.

Example: P was permitted to join a claim against an insurance company for inducing P to refrain from suing within the statute of limitations period with a claim against his former attorney for negligently failing to file the suit on time. [**Rekeweg v. Federal Mutual Insurance Co.**, 27 F.R.D. 431 (N.D. Ind. 1961)]

(a) Note

Where defendants are joined *in the alternative* because the plaintiff is "in doubt" about which one caused his injuries, the injury issue supplies the requisite relationship between the claims joined, even where the conduct of the two defendants is otherwise factually *unrelated.*

Example: Where P claims permanent back injuries after involvement in two unrelated traffic accidents, alleging doubt as to whether his back injury was caused by accident 1 or accident 2, joinder of both drivers as defendants is proper. [**Landau v. Salam**, 4 Cal. 3d 901 (1971)]

(3) "Common question" requirement [§1037]

It is sufficient if there is a *single* question of law or fact common to all parties joined. However, it is *not* necessary that the "common question" be in dispute.

Example: P-1, a driver, and P-2, a passenger in the car, sue D for injuries sustained in an auto accident. The "common question" is whether D was negligent. This is sufficient for joinder purposes even though there are also many separate questions involved (*e.g.*, injuries sustained by each, any contributory negligence barring P-1's claim, etc.).

(a) Caution

If the common question is relatively unimportant, the court will tend to define the "transaction" somewhat more narrowly to prevent joinder of claims that have no significant *evidentiary relationship* to each other. Hence, a *practical test* for permissive joinder is applied: Are the issues in the two claims *factually intertwined* with each other in any significant way?

(4) Additional unrelated claims [§1038]

As long as the requirements for joinder of parties (above) are met, each of the parties joined may assert as many *claims* as she has against any opposing party. [Fed. R. Civ. P. 18] The policy of the law is to allow *unlimited* joinder of claims as long as there is a transactional connection among all of the parties.

> **Example:** P joins D-1 against whom he claims injuries while a passenger in D-2's vehicle, and D-2 against whom he claims for the same injuries in the accident, and also for failure to pay a promissory note that D-2 executed in favor of P. This joinder is proper.

(5) Power of court to order separate trials [§1039]

To curb expense or delay, or to avoid prejudice that might result from the joinder of numerous parties asserting numerous separate claims against one another, the court may order separate trials for various claims joined, or otherwise regulate the proceedings to minimize the difficulties involved. [Fed. R. Civ. P. 20(b)]

(6) Attacking improper joinder [§1040]

Under the Federal Rules, a misjoined claim may be dismissed on motion of the party against whom it is asserted; and the whole action may be dismissed as to that party if no claim for relief remains against him. [Fed. R. Civ. P. 21] Under code pleading practice, a demurrer will lie for misjoinder of claims. [Cal. Civ. Proc. Code §430.10(d)]

c. Subject matter jurisdiction [§1041]

In addition to the requirements of personal jurisdiction over defendants, federal subject matter jurisdiction requirements must be satisfied as to all parties (whether plaintiffs or defendants) permissively joined. Supplemental jurisdiction does not extend to permissive joinder when the permissively joined matter is not part of the same case or controversy with the claim over which the federal court has original jurisdiction, or in diversity cases where banned by 28 U.S.C. section 1367(b). (*See supra,* §§424-441.)

EXAM TIP | **gilbert**

Be sure to remember subject matter jurisdiction limitations when you encounter an exam question involving permissive joinder in federal courts. *Federal subject matter jurisdiction requirements* must be met *for all parties*, and supplemental jurisdiction will not help when joinder is of a matter that is not part of the same case or controversy as the claim over which the federal court has original jurisdiction. For example, suppose P has a state-law claim against D1, who is diverse, for breach of P's lease of an apartment from D1. Although P may also have a claim against D2, the leasing agent, that arises from the same transaction, there would not be supplemental jurisdiction to add D2 if she were not diverse. On the other hand, if there were also a claim of violation of federal anti-discrimination statutes against D2, the state-law breach of lease claim could be in federal court as supplemental to the federal claim. Even then, however, P's claim that D2 also failed to deliver a $300 table to P in breach of a contract unrelated to the lease could not be asserted in federal court, because that claim would not be within supplemental jurisdiction, although allowed by claim joinder rules.

3. Compulsory Joinder [§1042]

Joinder is required for *any person who has a material interest in the case and whose absence would result in substantial prejudice* to the absentee or to other parties before the court. [Fed. R. Civ. P. 19]

a. Traditional approach—"necessary" vs. "indispensable" parties [§1043]

Historically, the statutes and cases drew a distinction between "necessary" and "indispensable" parties.

(1) "Necessary parties" [§1044]

Necessary parties were those who *ought* to be joined *if possible.* However, if their interests were *"severable"* and if one or more were not joined (*e.g.,* could not be located), the court could still determine the rights and liabilities of the parties before the court.

(2) "Indispensable parties" [§1045]

Indispensable parties, on the other hand, were those whose interests were so unavoidably involved (nonseverable) that the court could not proceed without them. Failure to join such parties meant that the action had to be dismissed. [**Shields v. Barrow**, 58 U.S. 130 (1855)]

(3) Criticism

A party's interest could always be "severed" somehow, simply by leaving his interests out of the judgment and allowing them to be adjudicated later. Hence, the issue in distinguishing necessary and indispensable parties was not whether the absentee's interests were in fact severable (they always were), but whether they should be adjudicated along with those already present in the action.

b. Modern approach—practical considerations [§1046]

Modern rules recognize that the labels "necessary" and "indispensable" merely reflect conclusions arrived at for other reasons. Hence, these rules focus on the *practical consequences* if a party with an interest in the action is not before the court. [**Provident Bank & Trust Co. v. Patterson**, *supra*, §1013]

(1) Persons to be joined if feasible [§1047]

Federal Rule 19(a) provides that any person with an interest in the subject matter of a pending action shall be joined as a party if:

(i) In his absence, *complete relief* cannot be accorded those already parties [Fed. R. Civ. P. 19(a)(1)]; *or*

(ii) His interest is such that to proceed without him would be *substantially prejudicial* as a practical matter because it would:

    i. Impair his ability to protect his interest in later proceedings [Fed. R. Civ. P. 19(a)(2)(i)]; or

ii. Expose the *parties already before the court* to the risk of double liability or inconsistent obligations [Fed. R. Civ. P. 19(a)(2)(ii)].

(For examples, *see infra*, §§1049-1060.)

(a) Caveat

Although the modern pragmatic approach has been adopted in the federal courts and in many states, some decisions still assert that *certain types of parties* (*e.g.,* partial assignees, *infra*, §1054) always must be joined—*i.e.,* that these parties are indispensable. A review of the case law, therefore, reveals two conflicting rules: (i) that compulsory joinder is a pragmatic problem, and (ii) that it is "jurisdictional" in that an action cannot proceed without an indispensable party.

(2) Effect of nonjoinder—possible dismissal [§1048]

If a person to be joined cannot be made a party (*e.g.,* because he is not subject to the court's jurisdiction), the court must determine whether *"in equity and in good conscience"* the action can proceed without him or whether the action should be dismissed. The court's determination is based on the following practical considerations [Fed. R. Civ. P. 19(b)]:

(a) The extent to which any judgment rendered in the action would be *prejudicial* to the interest of the absent party, or the interests of those already before the court;

(b) The extent to which such prejudice could be *lessened or avoided* by appropriate court action;

(c) Whether relief rendered without the absent party would be *adequate;* and

(d) Whether the plaintiff has any *other adequate remedy* if the action is dismissed for nonjoinder of the absent party.

(3) Application [§1049]

Situations in which compulsory joinder issues commonly arise involve:

(a) Joint obligors

1) Parties to contract [§1050]

Joint promisors under a *contract* (and other joint debtors) should be joined as defendants wherever possible. However, if one cannot be joined, the court can still proceed against those before the court. [**Jett v. Phillips & Associates**, 439 F.2d 987 (10th Cir. 1971)]

a) Rationale

There is no "substantial prejudice" to the parties before the court that would justify dismissal, since an obligor held responsible on the joint debt has a *right of contribution* against the other joint obligors.

2) Tortfeasors [§1051]

Although the plaintiff may join in one action all defendants potentially liable to her as a result of a given transaction or occurrence (*see supra*, §1033), ordinarily she is not required to do so, and a joint tortfeasor is *not considered a necessary party.* [**Temple v. Synthes Corp.**, 498 U.S. 5 (1990)—"It has long been the rule that it is not necessary for all joint tortfeasors to be named as defendants in a single lawsuit"]

a) Rationale

The plaintiff is the "master of her lawsuit" and can choose to sue as many or as few potential defendants as she desires.

b) Distinguish—impleader [§1052]

Often there is a right of contribution among joint tortfeasors. Where this is so, those defendants who are sued can file third-party complaints or cross-complaints (depending on the jurisdiction) against the other tortfeasors for *indemnity* (*see infra*, §1071). [**American Motorcycle Association v. Superior Court**, 20 Cal. 3d 578 (1978)] *Note:* This maneuver does not make the new party a defendant on the plaintiff's complaint unless the plaintiff amends to assert a claim against the new defendant. The only claim asserted against the new defendant is to indemnify the original defendant.

(b) Joint obligees [§1053]

Where persons are jointly owed a duty under a contract, the courts have usually held that they are not only necessary, but also *indispensable* parties, and have dismissed for nonjoinder. [**Jenkins v. Reneau**, 697 F.2d 160 (6th Cir. 1983)]

1) Rationale

A promise made to the obligees jointly should be enforced jointly since otherwise there is a risk that the right of the absent obligee to enforce the promise may be prejudiced, that the defendant might be subjected to inconsistent obligations in an action brought by the absent obligee, and that the court would be unable to afford complete relief because it could not provide in its decree for the defendant's obligations to the nonparty while enforcing the same promise for the plaintiff.

(c) **Partial assignees or subrogees [§1054]**

In an action by a partial assignee or subrogee to enforce its share of a debt, all other partial owners are necessary parties who should be joined if feasible. [**National American Corp. v. Federal Republic of Nigeria,** 420 F. Supp. 954 (S.D.N.Y. 1976); **Peerless Insurance Co. v. Superior Court,** 6 Cal. App. 3d 358 (1970)—insured with claims over policy limit was necessary but not indispensable party in suit by insurer-subrogee who had paid up to policy limit]

(d) **Co-owners of property [§1055]**

Co-owners of property are necessary parties in situations where the interests of all should be decided on a consistent basis (*e.g.,* rescission granted to one should be granted to all). [**Worthington v. Kaiser Health Plan,** 8 Cal. App. 3d 435 (1970)]

1) **Conflicting claims [§1056]**

If the action seeks to determine conflicting claims between persons claiming co-ownership of property, *all co-owners* are necessary parties (*e.g.,* action for partition by one of several tenants in common, suit to fix shares of beneficiaries in a trust, suit by one of several partners to dissolve the partnership).

2) **Suits to establish adverse interest [§1057]**

Similarly, in suits by a *third person* to establish or enforce an interest in the property, all co-owners must be joined if possible (*e.g.,* suits to foreclose a mortgage, remove an easement, and the like).

(e) **Third-party beneficiary suits**

1) **Original parties to contract need not be joined [§1058]**

If a third-party beneficiary sues on a contract, the federal courts have uniformly rejected the argument that the original parties to the contract must be joined. [**Sandobal v. Armour & Co.,** 429 F.2d 249 (8th Cir. 1970)]

2) **Third-party beneficiary need not be joined [§1059]**

If an original party to a contract sues, a third-party beneficiary is not an indispensable party. [**Prudential Oil & Minerals Co. v. Hamlin,** 277 F.2d 384 (10th Cir. 1960)]

(f) **Shareholder's derivative suit [§1060]**

In a derivative suit by a shareholder (*i.e.,* suing on a cause of action belonging to the corporation because the corporation refuses to sue), the *corporation* is an *indispensable* party. Its rights are so inextricably involved that no complete judgment can be rendered unless it is subject to the court's jurisdiction.

PERSONS TO BE JOINED IF FEASIBLE—EXAMPLES	**gilbert**
NECESSARY PARTIES	**NONNECESSARY PARTIES**
• Joint obligors • Joint obligees • Partial assignees and subrogees • Co-owners of property (if case involves interest of all) • Corporation in a shareholder's derivative action	• Joint tortfeasors • Original parties to a contract when third-party beneficiary sues • Third-party beneficiary when original party to a contract sues

c. Procedure for compelling joinder

(1) Must name all necessary parties [§1061]
In the complaint, the plaintiff should set forth the names of all necessary persons who have not been joined, and the reasons for their nonjoinder. [Fed. R. Civ. P. 19(c)]

(a) Criticism
This provision is not effective because plaintiffs rarely concede that nonparties are necessary parties.

(2) Failure to name all necessary parties [§1062]
If the plaintiff fails to allege the existence of such parties, the defendant can raise the matter in a motion to dismiss under Federal Rule 12 or in the answer. Failure to object may constitute *waiver*. (*See infra*, §1068.)

(3) Joinder of necessary parties ordered if feasible [§1063]
If the plaintiff has failed to join necessary parties, the court will order that they be joined unless it is impossible to do so because their joinder would destroy subject matter jurisdiction or because the court lacks personal jurisdiction over them.

(a) Involuntary plaintiff [§1064]
If the absentee should be aligned as a plaintiff, he may be joined as an involuntary plaintiff. [Fed. R. Civ. P. 19(a)]

(b) Necessary parties too numerous [§1065]
If the necessary parties are too numerous to be joined, it is possible that the case might be handled as a *class action*. (*See infra*, §§1139 *et seq*.)

(c) Venue [§1066]

If addition of the necessary party would make venue improper, the added party must be dismissed if she objects to venue. Then the court must decide whether to dismiss.

(4) Dismissal if joinder not feasible [§1067]

If the court cannot order the necessary parties joined because of lack of personal jurisdiction or because their presence would destroy diversity of citizenship, it must decide whether to dismiss the action. (*See supra*, §1048 for criteria used to decide whether to dismiss.)

d. Waiver of right to compel joinder [§1068]

Nonjoinder of an absentee should be raised at the earliest possible opportunity by the parties to the action; otherwise, delay may constitute waiver of the right to compel joinder.

(1) If absentee is indispensable [§1069]

If the absentee is determined to be indispensable, his nonjoinder can be raised at any time by pleading or motion, even at the trial of the action. [Fed. R. Civ. P. 12(h)(2)] However, delay in raising the objection is one of the factors the court will consider in exercising its *discretion* as to whether to dismiss the action (*i.e.*, in deciding whether the absentee *is* indispensable). [**Provident Bank & Trust Co. v. Patterson**, *supra*, §1046]

(2) No waiver by absentee [§1070]

The failure of the parties to raise the defect of nonjoinder in no way constitutes a "waiver" by the absentee. Since she is not a party to the action, the judgment is not legally binding on her. [**Martin v. Wilks**, 490 U.S. 755 (1989)]

4. Impleader [§1071]

Impleader is a procedure that permits the defendant to bring into the lawsuit a third person who is or may be liable for all or part of the plaintiff's claim against the defendant. [Fed. R. Civ. P. 14] In some states, the same remedy may be secured by a cross-complaint bringing in the third person. Two features of impleader guard against prejudice to the third party: (i) the third party may plead any defenses that the defendant might have against the plaintiff's claim and may participate fully in defending against the claim; and (ii) the court may grant a separate trial on any separate issues of the third-party claim if needed to prevent undue confusion or prejudice.

a. Limited to claims for indemnification [§1072]

Impleader under the Federal Rules is confined to those situations in which the defending party has a *right to indemnity*, in whole or in part, against the impleaded third party—*i.e.*, where the defendant asserts that if he is held liable to the plaintiff, he would be entitled to collect all or some part of the judgment from the third party. This includes a claim to contribution in states where a defendant is allowed to claim contribution from a person that the plaintiff did not originally join as a defendant.

(1) How right is determined [§1073]

Whether the defendant has any such right to indemnification, etc., is a question of substantive law, and under the *Erie* doctrine, the federal court must therefore refer to the appropriate state statutes and case law.

(a) No right to indemnification under state law [§1074]

If the appropriate state law does not recognize such a right, the fact that the impleader procedure is available in federal court does not create one for the defendant.

(b) Liability under state law may be "accelerated" [§1075]

However, federal impleader may "accelerate" liability created by state law. For example, if, under state law, the defendant can seek indemnity from a third person only after paying a judgment to the plaintiff, the defendant in federal court may implead the third person and *assert his claim conditionally.* If the plaintiff recovers, the defendant should get judgment—thereby closing the time gap between liability to the plaintiff and receipt of an indemnity judgment against the third party. [**Glen Falls Indemnity Co. v. United States,** 229 F.2d 370 (9th Cir. 1955)]

(c) Contribution among tortfeasors [§1076]

Most states allow contribution among tortfeasors only when *judgment* is rendered against *all* of them. For federal impleader purposes, this means that the defendant in a personal injury action *cannot* implead other tortfeasors to seek contribution, because their liability arises only after the plaintiff obtains judgment against all of them. [**McPherson v. Hoffman,** 275 F.2d 466 (6th Cir. 1960)]

1) But note

If state law allows contribution where judgment is obtained against only one tortfeasor, the situation is essentially one of partial indemnity, and the tortfeasor who is sued can implead the other to recover it. [*See* **American Motorcycle v. Superior Court,** *supra,* §1052]

(2) Potential liability sufficient [§1077]

Rule 14 authorizes impleader of any person who is or *may be* liable for any part of the plaintiff's claim. Thus, impleader is proper before any loss actually has been paid by the defendant.

(a) No direct action by plaintiff against defendant's liability insurer [§1078]

In a liability suit, a plaintiff usually would be delighted to join the defendant's insurance carrier as a co-defendant—to let the jury know that the defendant is insured. However, most states do *not* permit this, on the ground that the plaintiff has no right to relief against the defendant's insurance carrier until she has first obtained a judgment against the defendant (after which, the plaintiff would have an enforceable claim as third-party beneficiary of the insurance company's promise to indemnify the defendant).

1) Minority rule contra [§1079]

A few states are contra, with "direct action statutes" that permit joinder of the defendant's insurance carrier in the original action. [*See* **Watson v. Employers Liability Assurance Corp.,** 348 U.S. 66 (1954)—direct action statute may constitutionally apply despite provision in insurance contract conditioning duty to indemnify on entry of judgment against insured]

EXAM TIP   **gilbert**

Insurance companies are sometimes lurking in the background of civil procedure questions. Remember that while Rule 14 authorizes impleader of any person who may be liable for any part of a plaintiff's claim, most courts do *not allow* a plaintiff to implead a defendant's insurance company until after the plaintiff has obtained a judgment against the defendant.

(b) Defendant's right to implead insurer [§1080]

It may be that the defendant himself will seek to bring his liability insurer into the action—*e.g.,* when the insurer has failed or refused to defend the action. Where this is the case, impleader may be permitted to obtain a prompt determination of the defendant's insurance coverage and avoid multiplicity of suits. [**Government Employees Insurance Co. v. United States,** 400 F.2d 172 (10th Cir. 1968)]

(3) Distinguish—alternative liability to plaintiff [§1081]

It is not sufficient for impleader that the third-party defendant may be liable to *the plaintiff* for the plaintiff's injuries; only when the law gives the present *defendant a right to relief in the form of indemnity from the third-party defendant* is impleader permitted.

Example: Plaintiff contracted trichinosis and sued D1, which manufactured a cooker Plaintiff claimed had failed properly to cook pork she ate on July 9. D1 sought to implead the college that plaintiff attended, claiming that her trichinosis had actually resulted from eating pork in the college cafeteria on July 8. The court dismissed the third-party complaint because "[c]ontribution will not arise from distinct causes of action, regardless of how similar the events may have been or how close in time they may have occurred." [**Klotz v. Superior Electric Products Corp.,** 498 F. Supp. 1099 (E.D. Pa. 1980)]

(4) Supplemental jurisdiction over related claims [§1082]

In federal court litigation, the court has supplemental jurisdiction to adjudicate a claim by the original defendant (third-party plaintiff in the impleader) for his *own* injuries when joined with a claim for indemnity.

(a) But note

At least in diversity actions, there is *no* supplemental jurisdiction over a claim by the original plaintiff against the third-party plaintiff even if it arises out of the transaction originally sued on.

Example: P sues D, who impleads T, a citizen of the same state as P. P may not assert a separate claim against T, because there is no diversity between them and ancillary jurisdiction will not be permitted. [**Owen Equipment & Erection Co. v. Kroger,** 437 U.S. 365 (1978); 28 U.S.C. §1367(b)]

b. Pleadings and procedure [§1083]

Leave of court is not required for impleader if the defendant (third-party plaintiff) files a third-party complaint of impleader within 10 days after he serves his original answer. Thereafter, leave of court is required, and grant of the motion is at the *discretion* of the court. [Fed. R. Civ. P. 14]

(1) Answer [§1084]

The impleaded party must file an answer to the third-party complaint, and the answer may raise whatever defenses could be asserted to the *original* cause of action (P vs. D). *Rationale:* The purpose is to prevent collusion between the original parties—D admitting or defaulting to P's claim, in order to affix liability on the impleaded party.

(2) Counterclaim or cross-claim [§1085]

The impleaded party may also file a *counterclaim or cross-claim* against existing parties, or may implead any person who may be liable to him, subject to the jurisdictional limits noted below. [Fed. R. Civ. P. 14(a)]

c. Possibility of separate trials [§1086]

The trial court has discretion to order a separate trial of the impleaded claim to avoid undue trial confusion or prejudice. [Fed. R. Civ. P. 42(b)]

d. Effect on jurisdiction and venue [§1087]

An impleader claim is usually deemed ancillary to the main claim and has *no* effect on jurisdictional and venue requirements. Thus, an independent ground of federal jurisdiction need not be established, and the impleaded defendant cannot object to venue. [**Dery v. Wyer**, 265 F.2d 804 (2d Cir. 1959); 28 U.S.C. §1367]

e. Distinguish—cross-claim [§1088]

Impleader is somewhat similar to the cross-claim procedure discussed *supra*, §§893 *et seq.* However, there are significant differences:

(1) *An impleader can be asserted only against a person not yet a party*, whereas a cross-claim is filed by one party against another party to the action.

(2) *Impleader must be based on a claim for indemnification* or contribution, while there is no such limitation on cross-claims.

5. Intervention [§1089]

Intervention is a procedure whereby a *nonparty*, upon timely application, may become a party in a lawsuit in order to protect her interests in that action. Whether intervention is allowed depends on a balancing of two conflicting policies: (i) that the plaintiff should be allowed to be "master of his action," in the sense of joining such parties with him or against him as he wishes; and (ii) that other interested parties and the court have an interest in avoiding multiplicity of litigation or inconsistency of result, which may require overriding the plaintiff's choice of parties.

a. Types of intervention in federal cases [§1090]

There are several types of intervention under Federal Rule 24:

(1) Intervention of right—federal statute [§1091]

Intervention is granted as a matter of right where a federal statute confers an unconditional right to intervene (*e.g.*, 28 U.S.C. section 2403—intervention by United States is a matter of right in any suit in which the constitutionality of an Act of Congress is in question). [Fed. R. Civ. P. 24(a)(1)]

(2) Intervention of right—to protect intervenor's interest [§1092]

Intervention of right is also granted when the applicant claims an interest relating to the property or transaction that is the subject of the action and is so situated that the disposition of the action may, as a practical matter, impair or impede the applicant's ability to protect that interest. [Fed. R. Civ. P. 24(a)(2)]

(a) Nature of interest [§1093]

The Supreme Court has stated that only a "significantly protectable interest" suffices to support intervention of right. [**Donaldson v. United States**, 400 U.S. 517 (1971)] Some lower courts emphasize a direct, substantial, and legally protectable interest to satisfy this standard, while others take a more relaxed attitude.

e.g. Example: Opponents of abortion could intervene in an action challenging a city's moratorium on abortion clinics in an area on ground that they owned houses in the area and were defending their property values, but not on ground that they were opposed to abortion. "Interests in property are the most elementary type of right that Rule 24(a) is designed to protect." [**Planned Parenthood v. Citizens for Community Action,** 558 F.2d 861 (8th Cir. 1977)]

e.g. Example: Rate-payers of a utility could not intervene in a contract action between the utility and a supplier concerning the amounts the utility would have to pay for boiler fuel. Although the outcome of the litigation could affect the rates intervenors would have to pay, they had no legally protectable interest in the contract dispute. [**New Orleans Public Service, Inc. v. United Gas Pipe Line Co.,** 732 F.2d 452 (5th Cir. 1984)]

1) Standing [§1094]
The Supreme Court has not decided whether an intervenor must have standing to intervene [*see, e.g.,* **Diamond v. Charles,** 476 U.S. 54 (1986)], and the lower courts are divided on whether standing is required [*compare* **Ruiz v. Estelle,** 161 F.3d 814 (5th Cir. 1998)—intervenors need not satisfy standing requirements, *with* **Mova Pharmaceutical Corp. v. Shalala,** 140 F.3d 1060 (D.C. Cir. 1998)—party that seeks to intervene as of right must satisfy standing requirements].

(b) Outcome of litigation may impair intervenor's interests [§1095]
The intervenor must also show that the resolution of the litigation would impair her interest. This is not limited to legally binding effects, such as res judicata, but looks to the practical impact of resolution of the litigation on the intervenor's interest.

e.g. Example: Plaintiff brought suit against a federal agency, claiming that the agency was improperly allowing the state to issue licenses to run uranium mills without first requiring preparation of environmental impact statements. Companies with license applications pending were allowed to intervene. *Rationale:* As a practical matter, such applicants would be affected by the outcome of the litigation if it caused the state agency to alter its mode of operation and require more of applicants for licenses. [**Natural Resources Defense Council v. United States Nuclear Regulatory Commission,** 578 F.2d 1341 (10th Cir. 1978)]

cf. Compare: Where a commercial tenant of a shopping center sought to enjoin a lease to another prospective commercial tenant on the ground that plaintiff's lease limited the number of jewelry stores in the shopping center, interests of the prospective tenant might be affected if it could not compel performance of defendant's commitment to lease space to it, but the court nevertheless held that the prospective tenant was not a necessary party. [**Helzberg's Diamond Shops, Inc. v. Valley West Des Moines Shopping Center, Inc.**, 564 F.2d 816 (8th Cir. 1977)]

1) Stare decisis effect [§1096]

It is sometimes argued that the stare decisis effect alone is sufficient to justify intervention of right. When a unique issue of law is involved, and there is little likelihood that it will be reconsidered after it is decided in the current litigation, that may be sufficient. [*See* **Atlantis Development Corp. v. United States**, 379 F.2d 818 (5th Cir. 1967)—issue of application of the Outer Continental Shelf Lands Act to specific islands that intervenor sought to develop] More generally, however, the fact that resolution of a question of law might affect cases to which the intervenor is, or may in the future be, a party would more properly be considered a ground for amicus curiae (briefs from "friends of the court") than for intervenor status.

(c) Intervenor not adequately represented by present parties [§1097]

If the intervenor claims the right kind of interest and shows a threat of practical impairment, intervention could be denied on the ground that the intervenor's interest is adequately represented by the present parties.

1) "Minimal" burden [§1098]

The Supreme Court has said that the burden of demonstrating inadequacy of representation is "minimal." [**Trbovich v. United Mine Workers**, 404 U.S. 518 (1972)]

2) Factors [§1099]

A variety of factors can be considered in evaluating the adequacy of representation, including the amount at stake for the intervenor and the present parties, the ability and resources of the present parties to litigate effectively, and the existence of any conflicts of interest between the present party and the intervenors.

3) Concern with complication of action [§1100]

Although it is said that the burden of showing inadequacy is minimal, in order to avoid complication of the action due to the addition of too many new parties, courts will resist multiple intervention applications by parties in similar situations.

(d) Distinguish—compulsory joinder [§1101]

The grounds for intervention of right are analogous to the grounds for finding nonparties to be necessary parties under Rule 19(a)(2)(i). (*See supra*, §1047.) As a result, if there is a question on an examination raising issues under one of these rules, the effect of the other should be considered:

1) **Intervention more flexible [§1102]**

Even though the language of the rules for intervention and necessary parties is similar, courts seem more willing to find a nonparty's interests are of the protected type and are threatened, and therefore protected, when intervention is sought. This is because the nonparty intervenor has indicated a desire to participate in the litigation and the conclusion that intervention of right is proper does not mean that the litigation should not proceed unless all similarly situated nonparties are joined. Under Rule 19, the finding that a person with a certain interest should be joined means that all others with that interest should also be joined.

2) **Adequacy of representation requirement [§1103]**

This difference in treatment is confirmed by the adequacy of representation requirement for intervention. Under Rule 19, the adequacy of the present parties to protect the interests of the nonparty ordinarily does not relieve the court of the duty to add the necessary party. When Rule 19 is invoked but representation seems adequate, treatment as a class action may be in order. (*See infra*, §§1139 *et seq.*)

(e) **Conditions on intervention [§1104]**

Although this form of intervention is designated "of right," the court may nevertheless impose conditions, such as limiting the intervenor to claims already raised by other parties, or requiring that the intervenor obtain permission from one of the original parties to make motions and take discovery. This authority derives from the court's general power to control the litigation before it. [**Stringfellow v. Concerned Neighbors in Action**, 480 U.S. 370 (1987)]

(3) **Permissive intervention [§1105]**

The court has discretion to permit a nonparty to intervene if:

(i) *A federal statute* confers a conditional right to intervene; *or*

(ii) *A question of law or fact in common* with the main action is part of the applicant's claim or defense.

[Fed. R. Civ. P. 24(b)]

(a) **"Common question"**

Example: In a suit to set aside a zoning ordinance, adjoining property owners may intervene if their claims present common questions of law or fact. [**Wolpe v. Poretsky**, 144 F.2d 505 (D.C. Cir. 1944)]

---

1) Distinguish—permissive joinder rules [§1106]

Permissive intervention is the counterpart of permissive joinder under Federal Rule 20(a). The standard for permissive intervention corresponds to that for permissive joinder—*i.e.*, a common question, interpreted as claims arising from the same or a related transaction.

(b) Broad discretion in court [§1107]

The trial court has very broad discretion under Federal Rule 24(b) in granting or denying permissive joinder; and a reversal on appeal is almost impossible to obtain.

(c) Conditions imposed by court [§1108]

The court will often condition intervention in a lawsuit by limiting the intervenor's claims to those directly involved in the pending action.

INTERVENTION OF RIGHT VS. PERMISSIVE INTERVENTION	**gilbert**
INTERVENTION OF RIGHT	**PERMISSIVE INTERVENTION**
Federal statute grants a right to intervene *or* Intervenor claims an interest in the litigation that may be impaired by the litigation and is not adequately represented by the present parties	Federal statute grants a *conditional* right to intervene *or* A question of law or fact in common with the main action is part of the applicant's claim or defense

(4) Timeliness of intervention [§1109]

Whether the intervention sought is of right or permissive, the motion for leave to intervene must be made in a timely fashion. However, since a potential intervenor of right may be seriously harmed if excluded from the action, intervention motions rarely should be denied as being untimely.

b. Effect of intervention in federal cases

(1) Subject matter jurisdiction [§1110]

If the action is in federal court solely on grounds of diversity, there is no supplemental jurisdiction over claims by intervenors or claims by the plaintiff against persons who intervene. [28 U.S.C. §1367(b); *see supra*, §§424-441] In those circumstances there must be an independent basis for federal court jurisdiction to permit assertion of the claim. If federal jurisdiction does not depend solely on diversity of citizenship, there would usually be supplemental jurisdiction over claims by or against intervenors of right. [28 U.S.C. §1367(a)]

(2) Venue [§1111]

The intervenor cannot question the propriety of venue in the original action, since her act of intervening is a submission to the court in question. [**Trans World Airlines, Inc. v. Civil Aeronautics Board**, 339 F.2d 56 (2d Cir. 1964)] Venue objections, however, may be raised by someone who is already a party to the action.

(3) Judgment [§1112]

Any judgment rendered subsequent to intervention is binding on the intervening party as if she had originally been a party, and she has a similar right of appeal. [**Spangler v. United States**, 415 F.2d 1242 (9th Cir. 1969)]

c. State practice [§1113]

Most states have intervention provisions patterned on the Federal Rules. In other states, statutes on intervention provide that a person having an "interest in the matter in litigation *may* intervene" in an action between other parties. [*See* Cal. Civ. Proc. Code §387]

(1) Broad discretion in court [§1114]

The term "interest" in such statutes is very vague, but usually has been limited to a "legal" interest. The term "may" indicates that intervention is never of right. Thus, intervention in state court actions largely depends on the discretion of the trial court. Often, permission is denied on the ground that the plaintiff has the right to choose the parties to his action.

(2) Modern trend to permit intervention [§1115]

However, under the influence of federal intervention rules (*supra*), state courts are becoming more liberal in permitting intervention.

6. Consolidation of Separate Actions [§1116]

Even when joinder rules do not permit the addition of new parties to an action, almost the same result can be achieved by consolidating separate suits pending in the same court. The court has broad discretion, on its own motion or on the motion of a party, to consolidate actions involving *common issues* (*e.g.*, liability of common carrier in mass accident litigation). Consolidation can be complete so that the separate suits effectively become one, although they are technically not merged; or it may be partial—*e.g.*, consolidation for purposes of determining liability, with separate trials on the issue of damages. [*See* Fed. R. Civ. P. 42]

7. Interpleader [§1117]

Interpleader is a device that enables a party against whom conflicting claims with respect to the same debt or property are asserted (the "stakeholder") to join all the adverse claimants in the same action and require them to litigate among themselves to determine which, if any, has a valid claim to the debt or property involved. Once the stakeholder's right to interplead is established and he has deposited the funds or property in court, he can be released or "discharged" from the litigation; it is up to the adverse claimants to litigate their claims to the property. (If the stakeholder denies any liability at all, or if he has a claim to the fund, he remains a party.)

---

e.g. **Examples:** An escrow holder may interplead funds deposited with him, as to which parties are making adverse claims. Or a life insurance company, upon the death of the insured, may interplead the policy proceeds if they are claimed by both the named beneficiary and some third person.

---

a. Background [§1118]

Interpleader originated in the equity courts as a way to protect a stakeholder from possible legally inconsistent liability, and to avoid multiplicity of actions and the risk of inconsistent results. Historically, the plaintiff had to admit liability on the obligation in question, and the conflicting claims had to be mutually exclusive, but these limitations are not recognized under modern law. [*See* 28 U.S.C. §1335; Fed. R. Civ. P. 22]

b. Procedure [§1119]

The party against whom claims are being made may institute the interpleader action himself (naming all claimants as defendants); or he may interplead in any action pending between the adverse claimants. If he is named as a defendant in such an action, he may interplead by filing a *counterclaim* (*see infra*, §1134).

(1) Deposit "stake" with court [§1120]

To invoke *statutory* interpleader (*see infra*, §1125), the plaintiff must deposit (or give security for) the entire amount in his possession that is claimed by the claimants, and may not hold back amounts that he claims. [**Miller & Miller Auctioneers, Inc. v. G.W. Murphy Industries, Inc.,** 472 F.2d 893 (10th Cir. 1973)]

(a) No deposit required for rule interpleader [§1121]

Where Rule 22 interpleader is properly invoked (*see infra*, §§1127 *et seq.*), there is no requirement that the stake be deposited in court.

(2) Plaintiff may claim interest [§1122]

As indicated above, interpleader is permitted even if the plaintiff denies *any* liability or claims some offset or defense. Such cases are often referred to as *"actions in the nature of interpleader,"* following old English practice. The difference is that classic interpleader involves a "disinterested" stakeholder, making no claim to the property, while an "action in the nature of interpleader" is brought by an "interested" stakeholder, such as an insurance company denying liability. [*See, e.g.,* **State Farm Fire & Casualty Co. v. Tashire,** 386 U.S. 523 (1967)]

(3) Defendants may cross-file claims [§1123]

Where the stakeholder initiates interpleader, the adverse claimants can—and usually do—file cross-claims (*see infra,* §1134) against each other to obtain a judicial determination of their respective rights in the fund or property interpleaded.

c. Types of federal interpleader actions [§1124]

In federal practice, there are two distinct interpleader remedies:

(1) Statutory interpleader [§1125]

Interpleader is permitted by 28 U.S.C. section 1335, which contains special provisions as to jurisdiction, venue, and service of process, if:

(a) *Two or more claimants of diverse citizenship* are making adverse claims to the same debt, instrument, or property owed or held by the plaintiff; *and*

(b) *The debt, instrument, or property has a value of at least $500.*

(2) Rule 22 interpleader [§1126]

Federal Rule 22 permits interpleader in any action that meets the normal jurisdictional requirements in federal court—*i.e.,* a sufficient amount in controversy (if applicable) and proper diversity or federal question.

d. Differences between statutory and Rule 22 interpleader [§1127]

The existence of two forms of federal interpleader can be confusing. Rule interpleader is needed for cases that do not meet the specialized requirements of statutory interpleader. Statutory interpleader is framed to focus on situations involving scattered claimants (below). The basic differences between interpleader under section 1335 and under Rule 22 are as follows:

(1) Requirements for diversity jurisdiction [§1128]

Depending on the type of federal interpleader action, either minimal or complete diversity is required.

(a) Statutory interpleader [§1129]

In statutory interpleader, it is sufficient that diversity of citizenship exists between *any two adverse claimants*, but at least two claimants must be diverse. As long as such *minimal diversity* exists, the citizenship of the plaintiff-stakeholder and any other claimants is immaterial. [**State Farm Fire & Casualty Co. v. Tashire,** *supra*]

---

e.g. **Example:** I, an Illinois insurance company, is confronted by claims to insurance proceeds by A, a citizen of Illinois, B, another citizen of Illinois, and C, a citizen of Wisconsin. There is sufficient diversity for statutory interpleader even though I (as plaintiff in the action) and A and B (as defendants) are co-citizens, and A and B (as competing claimants) are co-citizens; the required minimal diversity is present because one of the claimants, C, is not a co-citizen of the other claimants.

(b) Rule 22 interpleader [§1130]

In an interpleader action under Rule 22, there must be *complete* diversity between the plaintiff-stakeholder and *all* of the adverse claimants, or a federal question must be involved.

(c) Distinguish—all claimants citizens of one state [§1131]

Where all the claimants are citizens of one state and the stakeholder is a citizen of another, the suit can be brought only under Rule 22, since statutory interpleader requires some diversity among the *claimants* (*see supra*).

(2) Jurisdictional amount [§1132]

Statutory interpleader requires only that the debt or property involved be valued at *$500* or more. Under Rule 22, if the case relies on diversity jurisdiction, the jurisdictional amount is the same as in any other civil action ($75,000).

(3) Limits of process [§1133]

In *statutory* interpleader, the reach of process is nationwide. [28 U.S.C. §2361] Under *Rule 22*, service of process is the same as in any other civil action—*i.e.*, within the territorial limits of the state in which the district court is located, except as extended by any applicable long arm statute.

(4) Cross-claims and counterclaims [§1134]

The interpleaded claimants may (and usually do) cross-claim against each other, counterclaim against the plaintiff, and implead third parties, unless jurisdictional problems prevent their doing so.

(a) Subject matter jurisdiction [§1135]

Such additional claims must have an independent basis of jurisdiction unless they relate to the original impleaded claim (and thus fall within supplemental jurisdiction).

(b) Service of process [§1136]

When a defendant is before the court only because of nationwide process under *statutory* interpleader, he is subject to additional claims through cross-claim, etc., only if they are part of "cleaning up" the original interpleader claim.

e.g. **Example:** A, a driver insured by I for $20,000, injures B and C, each of whom claims more than $20,000 in damages. I interpleads A, B, and C, contending that there is no liability on A's part, but that if there is, the claims of B and C to the insurance coverage should be interpleaded. A seeks to cross-claim against C for A's own injuries. This would be disallowed if C was before the court only through nationwide process, because it does not relate to I's interpleader claim. [*See* **Allstate Insurance Co. v. McNeill,** 382 F.2d 84 (4th Cir. 1967)]

(5) Venue [§1137]

In *statutory* interpleader, venue is proper in the district in which *any* claimant resides. [28 U.S.C. §1397] With interpleader under *Rule 22,* venue is the same as in any other civil action—*i.e.*, in the district in which a defendant resides, if all reside in the same state, or a district in which a substantial part of the events or omissions giving rise to the claim occurred. [28 U.S.C. §1391(a)(1)-(2); *see supra,* §§146-157] Alternatively, venue is proper in a district "in which a substantial part of the property that is the subject of the action is located." [28 U.S.C. §1391(a)(2)] The location of the property may be a convenient venue in many interpleader cases.

EXAM TIP | **gilbert**

If an exam question raises the possibility of interpleader, it is, of course, important to keep the two types of interpleader straight. The following mnemonic device may be helpful: *R*ule 22 interpleader must follow the *R*egular *R*ules; *S*tatutory interpleader has *S*pecial, *S*impler *S*tandards.

RULE INTERPLEADER VS. STATUTORY INTERPLEADER — gilbert

	RULE INTERPLEADER	STATUTORY INTERPLEADER
DIVERSITY REQUIREMENTS	Complete diversity between plaintiff stakeholder and all adverse plaintiffs	Only two claimants need be of diverse citizenship
JURISDICTIONAL AMOUNT	More than $75,000	At least $500
PROCESS	Process is limited to the territorial boundaries of the state in which the district court sits	Process is nationwide
VENUE	In the district where a defendant resides, if all reside in the same state, or where a substantial part of the claim occurred or in which a substantial part of the property involved is located	Where any claimant resides

e. **_Erie_ doctrine [§1138]**

The question of whether the interpleader remedy is available is a procedural matter and is decided pursuant to federal interpleader standards. To determine the law to be applied to the merits of the case, the federal court will look to appropriate state law.

D. Class Actions

1. In General [§1139]

One or more members of a class of persons similarly situated may *sue or be sued* on behalf of all members of that class. Such lawsuits are permitted where considerations of *necessity or convenience* justify an action on behalf of the group rather than multiple actions by (or against) the class members individually.

2. Background

a. Original development in equity [§1140]

Class actions originally were permitted only in equity, and then only if it was shown (i) that joinder of all parties having similar interests was *impractical* because the parties were too numerous, were presently unascertainable, or were not yet in being (*e.g.,* unborn heirs); and (ii) a few members could fairly represent all in the litigation. In such cases, the chancellors in equity permitted suit to be maintained by or against representatives of the class and, in some instances, held that the decree rendered in such an action was binding on *all* members of the class.

(1) Comment

Unless the joinder of all necessary parties was not practical (usually because they were too numerous), the class action device was not needed, since adequate relief could be obtained in an ordinary action.

b. Class actions under code pleading [§1141]

The grounds for maintenance of class suits in equity were carried over in the Field Code, which authorized such suits wherever there were "questions of common or general interest of many persons," or when the parties were "numerous" and it would be "impracticable" to bring them all before the court. [*See* Cal. Civ. Proc. Code §382]

(1) But note

The courts usually limited class actions to those asserting what formerly had been equitable (as distinct from common law) claims—*e.g.,* stockholder derivative suits, creditors' bills to reach the assets of debtors, and injunction suits.

(2) And note

The decisions were split as to whether the judgment in a class suit was binding on the absent members of the class.

c. Class actions under the Federal Rules

(1) Former Federal Rule 23 [§1142]

As originally adopted in 1938, Federal Rule 23 provided for three different kinds of class actions.

(a) "True class" action [§1143]

A "true class" action was one where the rights of all members of the class were "joint" or "common." A judgment rendered in such an action bound *all* members of the class, including absentees. For example, stockholders' suits and suits by or against the members of labor unions or other unincorporated associations were "true class" actions.

(b) "Hybrid class" action [§1144]

A "hybrid class" action was one in which the subject of the action was a specific fund or property, and the members of the class had "separate" rights therein (*e.g.*, suit on behalf of numerous co-owners of an oil well against a drilling company to enforce a royalty contract). A judgment in such an action was conclusive upon the rights of all members in the specific fund or property involved, but did not otherwise affect or bind class members not before the court. [**Dickinson v. Burnham**, 197 F.2d 973 (2d Cir. 1952)]

(c) "Spurious class" action [§1145]

A "spurious class" action was one in which there was simply a "common question of law or fact" affecting all members of the class, and the claims of each member were separate. A judgment in such an action bound *only* those members of the class actually before the court. Accordingly, this was not really a class action, but rather a permissive joinder device.

(2) Present Federal Rule 23 [§1146]

In 1966, Rule 23 was completely revised, eliminating the distinctions above and providing that members of a class can sue or be sued *with binding effect on the class as a whole.*

(3) State courts [§1147]

Most states have adopted the present Rule 23, sometimes with modifications. In California, the Rule has been effectively adopted by judicial decisions. [**Vasquez v. Superior Court**, 4 Cal. 3d 800 (1971)]

3. Prerequisites to Class Action [§1148]

Under Federal Rule 23(a), *all four* of the following conditions must be established in any type of class suit. All class actions must also fit into one of the categories of Rule 23(b) (*infra*, §§1173-1196).

(i) *Numerous parties*—the class must be so numerous that joinder of all members individually is impractical [Rule 23(a)(1)];

First determine whether all four conditions are present:

☑ Class members are so *numerous* that joinder of all is impracticable.

☑ There are *common questions* of law or fact.

☑ The *representative's claims or defenses are typical* of those in the class.

☑ The *representative will adequately represent* the interests of the class.

If all four conditions are present, a class action may be based on *any one* of the following grounds:

☑ Prosecution of separate actions would create a significant risk of (i) requiring *inconsistent conduct* by the defendant or (ii) *substantially impairing the interests* of other members of the class.

☑ *Declaratory or injunctive relief* would be appropriate for the class as a whole.

☑ *Questions of law or fact common to the class predominate* over questions affecting only individual members and a class action is superior.

(ii) *Common question*—the action must involve questions of law or fact common to the class [Rule 23(a)(2)];

(iii) *Representative's claims typical*—the claims (or defenses) of the persons maintaining the action on behalf of the class must be typical of those of the class generally [Rule 23(a)(3)]; *and*

(iv) *Adequacy of representation*—the persons representing the class must be able fairly and adequately to protect the interests of all members of the class [Rule 23(a)(4)].

a. Numerous parties requirement [§1149]

As indicated by the treatment of the real party in interest problem (*see supra*, §§985-1014), ordinarily litigation is to be conducted by the persons whose rights are involved as named parties. Only where they are too numerous to be joined is class treatment considered necessary.

(1) No fixed minimum [§1150]

There is no fixed minimum number required to make a class "too numerous" for joinder of all members individually. Some cases have held 25 enough, while others have held that 39 is not enough. If the number is *50 or less,* whether a class will be permitted usually turns on the following factors, and note that the trial court has considerable discretion in this matter [**De Marco v. Edens,** 390 F.2d 836 (2d Cir. 1968)]:

(i) The *size of each member's claim* (the smaller the claim, the more likely a class suit will be allowed);

(ii) The *practical likelihood that individual suits will be brought* (the lower the likelihood, the more likely a class suit be allowed);

(iii) The *public importance of the right* being enforced (the greater the public importance, the more likely a class action will be permitted); and

(iv) The *geographic location of class members* (the more difficult the geographic location makes it for class members to intervene, the more likely a class suit will be allowed).

Example: In a case involving a price fixing conspiracy, the district court found a proposed class of 350 members not numerous enough to justify a class action. The claims involved were large and, based on the district judge's prior experience with decision of such claims, he found that the claims could best be handled by intervention and individual participation. [**American Pipe & Construction Co. v. Utah,** 414 U.S. 538 (1974)]

EXAM TIP	gilbert

If an exam question involves a small number of plaintiffs (*e.g.,* 35) and you must determine whether the court would likely allow a class action, a good ***rule of thumb*** is that the less likely it is that individuals would bring their own suits or intervene (*e.g.,* because damages are small or the individuals are spread out geographically) the more likely the court will allow a class action.

(2) No fixed maximum [§1151]

Similarly, there is no fixed maximum size for a class action. In **Eisen v. Carlisle & Jacquelin,** *supra,* §230, for example, the Court dealt with a class of six million members, and while it put severe limitations on the class action, discussed below, it did not disqualify it as a class action because of its size. More recently, a lower court described a class action against tobacco companies on behalf of all "nicotine-dependent" smokers as "the largest class action ever attempted in federal court." [**Castano v. The American Tobacco Co.,** 84 F.3d 734 (5th Cir. 1996)]

(a) Limitation—class must be manageable [§1152]

In actions brought under Rule 23(b)(3) (*i.e.,* cases where questions of law or fact common to the class predominate; *see infra,* §§1180-1186), "difficulties likely to be encountered in management of the class" is one of the factors that the court must consider in deciding whether to permit the case to proceed as a class action: The larger the class, the greater the problems of manageability are likely to be.

(b) Limitation—notice requirements [§1153]

In some class suits, all identifiable members of the class must be given individual notice of the action, and the larger the class, the more cumbersome and expensive this becomes.

(3) Need for ascertainable class [§1154]

The class must be defined with sufficient clarity that its members can be identified. *Rationale:* If the class action is successful, it is necessary to know who is entitled to relief under the court's decree, and if the class action is not successful, it is necessary to know who is bound by the class's loss. This concern may be ***less important*** in actions for ***injunctive relief*** under Rule 23(b)(2) (*see infra,* §§1178-1179), because injunctive relief can be fashioned without knowing the identities of all class members. [**Yaffe v. Powers,** 454 F.2d 1362 (1st Cir. 1972)]

b. Common question requirement [§1155]

There must be "questions of law or fact common to the class." [Fed. R. Civ. P. 23(a)(2)] *Rationale:* Unless there is some common question, there would be no efficiencies to be achieved by adjudicating the rights of the class members in a single proceeding.

Example: In a securities fraud action where defendant made separate representations to various groups of investors, the common question requirement was satisfied because defendant engaged in a "common and consistent course of conduct." [**Green v. Wolf Corp.**, 406 F.2d 291 (2d Cir. 1968)]

(1) Predominance of common questions [§1156]

In actions brought under Rule 23(b)(3) (*i.e.,* cases where questions of law or fact common to the class predominate; *see infra*, §§1180-1186), there must not only be a common question, but also common questions must predominate. Under Rule 23(a)(2), on the other hand, predominance is not required.

(2) Fact question needed [§1157]

As a practical matter, it is usually essential that the common question have factual content that would make common litigation desirable.

(3) Distinguish—permissive joinder [§1158]

Ordinarily, a closer factual connection is required to satisfy the class action common question requirement than the common question requirement for permissive joinder. (*See supra*, §1037.)

(4) Problem of individual damages [§1159]

If class members have suffered individual damages, that presents individual (as opposed to class) questions. However the need to assess individual damages will not always prevent a class action because there may also be common questions regarding liability.

(5) Problem of variation in state law [§1160]

If the claims asserted in a class action are based on state law, and class members live in a number of states with varying laws, common questions might not be present because the factual questions to be resolved turn on different legal principles. [*See* **Castano v. The American Tobacco Co.**, *supra*] The court may not "homogenize" the law of various states to overcome this problem. [*In re* **Rhone-Poulenc Rorer, Inc.**, 51 F.3d 1293 (7th Cir. 1995)] In some cases, however, the laws of the various states will fit into a few patterns so that recurrent common questions are presented. [*In re* **School Asbestos Litigation**, 789 F.2d 996 (3d Cir. 1986)—state laws fit into four basic categories, and the jury could return verdicts based on the four legal standards]

c. Typical claim requirement [§1161]

The claims of the representative suing on behalf of the class must be typical of the class generally. *Rationale:* Because the class representative acts on behalf of others, the court wishes to be assured that she will have the same objectives as the class members and sufficient motivation to protect their interests. This should flow from the fact that her claim makes her typical of the class members. [*See* **Gonzales v. Cassidy,** 474 F.2d 67 (5th Cir. 1973)]

---

e.g **Example:** A Mexican-American employee who challenged the denial of a promotion was not typical of a class of Mexican-American job applicants who had not been hired, even though he alleged that the job applicants had, like him, allegedly been discriminated against on grounds of national origin. His claim of denial of a promotion in a specific instance was not typical of the claims of job applicants who were not hired. [**General Telephone Co. of the Southwest v. Falcon,** 457 U.S. 147 (1982)]

---

(1) Size of claim relevant [§1162]

The size of the representative plaintiff's personal claim is relevant to the issue of whether she is properly motivated to protect the interests of the class generally. [**Jenkins v. General Motors Corp.,** 354 F. Supp. 1040 (D. Del. 1973)]

(2) Distinguish—common question requirement [§1163]

The Supreme Court has observed that "[t]he commonality and typicality requirements of Rule 23(a) tend to merge. Both serve as guideposts for determining whether under the particular circumstances maintenance of a class action is economical and whether the named plaintiff's claim and the class claims are so interrelated that the interests of the class members will be fairly and adequately protected in their absence." [**General Telephone Co. of the Southwest v. Falcon,** *supra*]

(3) Effect of mootness of representative's claim [§1164]

When the class representative's claim becomes moot, it may be necessary to locate a new class representative who has a live claim. [*See* **United States Parole Commission v. Geraghty,** 445 U.S. 388 (1980)—named plaintiff whose claim expires before certification may be unable to continue as class representative; **Sosna v. Iowa,** 419 U.S. 393 (1975)—class representative whose claim expired allowed to continue representing class]

d. Adequate representation requirement [§1165]

This requirement is similar to the typical claim requirement, but also focuses on whether there is any *actual or potential conflict of interest* between the representative and the class she seeks to represent and whether the representative can prosecute or defend the suit with adequate vigor and resources.

(1) Constitutional requirement [§1166]

Due process requires that the class representative not have interests adverse to members of the class.

> **Example:** Whites seeking to enforce a racially restrictive covenant forbidding sale of houses in area to Blacks could not represent Black who desired to buy house in area. [**Hansberry v. Lee,** 311 U.S. 32 (1940)]

(2) "Future" vs. present personal injury tort claimants [§1167]

At least in the tort claimants context, the Supreme Court has implied that those who presently have claims for current injuries are not adequate representatives of those who may in the future fall ill because those with current claims would want to maximize payouts presently, while those who may fall ill in the future would want to preserve resources for later compensation. [**Amchem Products, Inc. v. Windsor,** 521 U.S. 591 (1997)]

(3) Present vs. past employees [§1168]

A union representing airline stewardesses in challenging the airlines' policy of discharging pregnant stewardesses could not "adequately represent" former stewardesses who had been discharged on this ground and were seeking reinstatement because their reinstatement might harm those currently employed, thus creating a potential conflict of interest. [**Air Line Stewards Association v. American Air Lines,** 490 F.2d 636 (7th Cir. 1973)]

(4) Failure to object does not bar later objection [§1169]

If the representative does not meet the adequate representation requirement but no one objects and the action proceeds to judgment, the judgment can be attacked by an absent member of the class on the ground that his interests were not adequately represented. [**Hansberry v. Lee,** *supra*] And this is true even if the court hearing the class suit expressly found the representative to be "adequate."

(5) Time when adequate representation measured [§1170]

The adequacy of representation can be measured at two different times: (i) Prior to certifying the action as a class action, the judge must believe that the named plaintiff will furnish an adequate representation of the class members. (ii) After a class action ends, if an unnamed class member sues the party that was the defendant in the class action and the defendant argues that the plaintiff should be bound by the result of the class action, the court will evaluate whether the representation in the class action was in fact adequate. If not, the unnamed plaintiff will not be bound. [**Gonzales v. Cassidy,** *supra*, §1161]

(6) Decertification [§1171]

Another possibility is that the court will determine, after deciding that the case is a proper class action, that the class representative is not adequate. In that situation the court can "decertify" the class and change the case back into an individual action.

(7) Subclasses [§1172]

If an action is otherwise properly brought as a class action, but there is a significant divergence of interest among segments of the overall class, the court may divide the class into *subclasses,* appoint a representative for each subclass, and allow the suit to proceed in that manner. [**Amchem Products, Inc. v. Windsor,** *supra*]

4. Three Grounds for Class Actions [§1173]

If the foregoing conditions are all present, the class action may be based on *any one* of the following grounds. [Fed. R. Civ. P. 23(b)]

EXAM TIP   **gilbert**

Be sure to remember that while *all four conditions* (numerosity, commonality, typicality, and adequacy) must be satisfied, *only one of the three grounds* (prejudice, declaratory or injunctive relief sought, or questions of law or fact common to the class predominate) need be shown.

---

a. Prejudice from separate actions [§1174]

Under Federal Rule 23(b)(1), a class action is permitted if the prosecution of separate actions would create either of the following risks:

(1) Establishing incompatible standards of conduct for defendant through inconsistent adjudications [§1175]

To justify a class action on this ground, the court must find that a number of individual actions are otherwise likely to be filed, and that the *conduct* required of the defendant under various judgments might be inconsistent. [Fed. R. Civ. P. 23(b)(1)(A); **Larionoff v. United States,** 533 F.2d 1167 (D.C. Cir. 1976)]

Examples: Paradigm examples of proper actions under this part of the rule are actions by taxpayers to invalidate municipal action or by stockholders to compel the declaration of a dividend. In such situations, there is a risk that other similarly situated plaintiffs might sue to compel defendants to take a different course of action (*e.g.,* to proceed with the intended municipal action or to withhold a dividend).

(a) Note

There is no such risk of inconsistency where injured parties are simply seeking *damages* for separate tort claims arising out of a single occurrence. The fact that the defendant might be held liable in one case and not liable in another is not enough to justify a class action on this basis. [**McDonnell Douglas Corp. v. District Court,** 523 F.2d 1083 (9th Cir. 1975)]

(2) Substantially impairing the interests of other members of the class [§1176]
To permit a class action under this subsection, the court must find that separate actions would interfere with the interests of other absent persons having similar claims. [Fed. R. Civ. P. 23(b)(1)(B)]

---

e.g. Examples: (i) One of several beneficiaries of a trust sues the trustee for an accounting and distribution which would affect the interests of all the beneficiaries. [**Redmond v. Commerce Trust Co.**, 144 F.2d 140 (8th Cir. 1944)] (ii) One of numerous claimants to a fund that is not sufficient to pay all claims seeks recovery (since satisfaction of any single claim in full would impair others). [**Bradford Trust Co. v. Wright**, 70 F.R.D. 323 (E.D.N.Y. 1976)]

(a) "Limited fund" mass tort situation
An increasingly important occasion for invoking this part of the rule is the situation in which it is claimed that a large number of tort plaintiffs have claims exceeding the assets and insurance of the manufacturer of goods or services that injured them. In this situation, the concern is that if the first successful plaintiffs recover full damages, there will not be sufficient assets left to pay compensation to later plaintiffs. The courts have resisted allowing class actions in this situation. [*See, e.g.,* **In re Northern District of California "Dalkon Shield" IUD Products Liability Litigation**, 693 F.2d 847 (9th Cir. 1982), *cert. denied*, 459 U.S. 1171 (1983)] The Supreme Court has held that a "limited fund" class action is not permitted when the limitation on the fund is the result of the parties' settlement agreement, as opposed to being limited by the funds actually available, but it has not ruled definitively on whether other limited fund class actions might be allowed. [**Ortiz v. Fibreboard Corp.**, 527 U.S. 815 (1999)—"fund" created by settlement among plaintiff class, counsel, defendant, and its insurers not acceptable even though agreement provides that claims must be asserted against this fund]

b. Equitable relief sought as to rights held in common [§1177]
Under Federal Rule 23(b)(2), a class action is also warranted if the basis on which the opposing party has acted is generally applicable to the class and *declaratory or injunctive relief* would benefit the class as a whole.

---

e.g. Example: P sues on equal protection grounds to invalidate a statutory provision that divorce actions can be maintained only by persons who have resided in the state for at least a year. The effects on particular members of the class in question (persons who have resided in the state less than a year) may vary; but a class action is proper because the determination will benefit the class as a whole. [**Sosna v. Iowa**, *supra*, §1164]

---

(1) Problem of monetary relief [§1178]

In some cases, monetary relief may be sought as well as injunctive relief. When the amounts due to class members can be calculated by a formula or on principles uniformly and easily applicable to the class, courts sometimes allow certification of *"hybrid (b)(2) classes."* When individualized determination of money damages is involved, however, this route is held improper. [**Rice v. City of Philadelphia**, 66 F.R.D. 17 (E.D. Pa. 1974)]

(2) Caution—Title VII employment discrimination class actions [§1179]

Because back pay awards in Title VII cases involving employment discrimination were considered "equitable," courts considered them suitable for certification under Rule 23(b)(2) even though they involved monetary claims. But in 1991, Congress amended Title VII to permit recovery of compensatory and punitive damages, and it has been held that certification under Rule 23(b)(2) is not proper as a result. [**Allison v. Citgo Petroleum Corp.**, 151 F.3d 402 (5th Cir. 1998)]

c. Common predominant question [§1180]

The third—and most common—basis for a class suit is under Federal Rule 23(b)(3)—the situation in which questions of law or fact common to the class *predominate* over questions affecting only individual members, *and, on balance, a class action is superior to other available methods* for adjudicating the controversy. The Supreme Court has called this provision "the most adventuresome" innovation in the 1966 amendments to Rule 23. [**Amchem Products, Inc. v. Windsor**, *supra*, §1167]

(1) Relevant factors [§1181]

In deciding whether common issues "predominate" and whether a class action is "superior" to individual litigation, the court will consider:

(i) *The interest of individual members* in personally controlling their cases;

(ii) *The nature and extent of any litigation* in progress involving the same controversy;

(iii) *The desirability of consolidating* all claims in a single action before a single court; and

(iv) *Any probable difficulties* managing a class action.

[Fed. R. Civ. P. 23(b)(3)]

(2) Predominance of common questions [§1182]

To find that common questions predominate, the court must *compare the relative importance* of the common questions and the individual questions presented by the case. It cannot merely compare the number of common and individual questions. Damages, for example, may present individual questions as to each class member, but may not defeat a finding that common questions predominate. Instead, the court is to determine whether the common questions are so important to the resolution of the lawsuit, and whether they will occupy sufficient time and effort in the resolution of the case, that it may fairly be said that they predominate over individual questions.

(a) Existence of common issue [§1183]

It is important to focus carefully on whether there really is a common factual issue. For example, in many products liability cases, it may be that the common issue regarding liability can be stated only in the most general terms, because so much depends on the individual circumstances of each plaintiff. In such cases, one may conclude that there really is no common factual issue. [*See, e.g.,* **Mertens v. Abbott Laboratories**, 99 F.R.D. 38 (D.N.H. 1983)—in action against manufacturer of DES, allegedly common issue of defendant's knowledge of risks of DES not important, since "there is nothing to show that knowledge at a given point in time essentially settles anything with respect to liability of a particular claimant"]

(b) Single issue certification [§1184]

The existence of numerous and important individual issues can be partly solved by certifying the class action as to certain issues only. [Fed. R. Civ. P. 23(c)(4)(A)] However, it is unlikely that this device may properly be used to circumvent the requirement of predominance of common questions, and in most instances the court should hesitate to sidestep the problem of predominance by limiting the class action aspects to common issues.

EXAM TIP **gilbert**

On exam questions involving class actions, pay particular attention to the *nature of the damages* sought. If individual amounts of damages will have to be proved, that might undercut class certification under Rule 23(b)(3) (for cases where common questions predominate). But, of course, class certification might still be proper under Rule 23(b)(3) *if other common questions* predominate (*e.g.,* as to liability).

(c) "Maturity" factor in tort class actions [§1185]

In mass tort class actions, courts have resisted finding that there is a predominant common issue where the claim is of a new and untested sort. [**Castano v. The American Tobacco Co.**, *supra*, §1151—claim that tobacco companies were liable for addicting smokers new and untested; *In re* **Rhone-Poulenc Rorer, Inc.**, *supra*, §1160—

claims by HIV positive hemophiliacs against producers of blood solids on theory that heat treatment of blood solids designed to remove risk of hepatitis would also eliminate HIV risk] However, in situations where the court is well familiar with the claims, this problem is not present. [**Jenkins v. Raymark Industry, Inc.,** 782 F.2d 316 (5th Cir. 1986)—"state of the art" issue in asbestos litigation very familiar to court due to number of trials that had already addressed it]

(d) Variation in state law [§1186]

In Rule 23(b)(3) class actions, the problems of variation in applicable state laws (*see supra*, §1181) are compounded because the common questions must predominate.

(3) Manageability and superiority [§1187]

Assuming common issues predominate, the court must also ask whether a class action would be manageable, and whether it would be superior to other methods of adjudicating the case.

(a) Comparative analysis [§1188]

It is important to understand that manageability is only one *factor in evaluating superiority*. Accordingly, the fact that the case will be difficult to manage as a class action does not necessarily preclude a finding that handling the case as a class action is superior to other methods of adjudicating the dispute. Only in the most extreme instances would problems of manageability alone be decisive in evaluating superiority.

(b) Illustration—class action superior [§1189]

In litigation brought on behalf of thousands of military personnel exposed to the defoliant Agent Orange in Southeast Asia, the court recognized that it confronted massive problems of manageability. Nevertheless, it compared the difficulties presented by handling the case as a class action with the enormous problems of handling the litigation as individual cases, and concluded that class action treatment had advantages over the other methods. [*In re* **Agent Orange Product Liability Litigation,** 506 F. Supp. 762 (E.D.N.Y. 1980)]

(c) Illustration—class action not manageable [§1190]

A suit on behalf of all residents of Los Angeles County (over seven million persons) to enjoin 293 large industrial companies from further pollution of the atmosphere was dismissed as unmanageable, because of the number of parties, the diversity of their interests, and the multiplicity of issues involved. [**Diamond v. General Motors Corp.,** 20 Cal. App. 3d 374 (1971)]

(d) Effect of settlement [§1191]

A settlement that makes a trial unnecessary may remove manageability obstacles that were present when the case was proceeding as a litigation class action. [**Amchem Product., Inc. v. Windsor,** *supra* §1172; *and see* below]

(4) Mass tort class actions under Rule 23(b)(3) [§1192]

In 1966, the Advisory Committee included a note cautioning against use of class actions in mass accident cases on the ground that individual issues would predominate, and the cases would "degenerate in practice into multiple lawsuits separately tried." [Fed. R. Civ. P. Adv. Comm. Note] Nevertheless, since the 1970s, courts have certified such cases despite the note, and the Supreme Court has recognized this trend with seeming acceptance. [**Amchem Products, Inc. v. Windsor,** *supra*—"The text of the Rule does not categorically exclude mass tort cases from class certification, and district courts, since the late 1970s, have been certifying such cases in increasing number"]

d. Certification for settlement only [§1193]

A court need not conclude that it would certify a class for all purposes, including full trial, in order to approve class certification for the purpose of effectuating a proposed class settlement. The prospect of settlement has on occasion prompted courts to certify cases for settlement discussions only.

(1) Criticism [§1194]

A lawyer representing a class only with regard to a possible settlement is without significant leverage because she is unable to threaten to proceed to full litigation if settlement demands are not met. Moreover, the defendant may be tempted to "shop" among prospective class counsel to locate one willing to accept a settlement along the lines defendant wants to embody in a court decree. This risk is sometimes described as a *reverse auction*.

(a) Counter to criticism

The Supreme Court has recognized that settlement classes are sometimes permissible. [*See* **Amchem Products, Inc. v. Windsor,** *supra*] *Rationale:* The court has at least some role in selecting counsel who will negotiate on behalf of the class if it certifies for purposes of settlement only, even if the case cannot proceed to trial.

(2) Requirements for certification for settlement [§1195]

When certifying a class for settlement only, the court may overlook the likely difficulties of managing a trial. But the judge must still find that all of the Rule 23(a) prerequisites (*see supra*, §§1148-1172) have been satisfied, and that the case falls within one of the Rule 23(b) categories. Subclassing may be necessary to assure adequate representation under

Rule 23(a)(4) in the case of a large and disparate class, and in classes certified under Rule 23(b)(3), the fact of settlement does not supersede the rule's requirement that common issues predominate. [*See* **Ortiz v. Fibreboard Corp.**, *supra*, §1176; **Amchem Products, Inc. v. Windsor**, *supra*]

e. Application of different grounds to same case [§1196]

In a given case, the plaintiff may try to satisfy different parts of Rule 23(b) in the alternative, and the case may be certified as to certain matters on one ground while certification is denied as to other parts.

Example: Plaintiffs charged that the Philadelphia police illegally detained persons accused of crimes for as long as 20 hours without food or medical care, and sought declaratory, injunctive, and compensatory relief on behalf of a class. The court certified a class with respect to declaratory and injunctive relief under Rule 23(b)(2), but held that the action could not be certified under Rule 23(b)(3) with respect to damages. [**Rice v. City of Philadelphia**, *supra*, §1178]

5. Jurisdictional Requirements in Class Suits

a. Subject matter jurisdiction [§1197]

In class actions in federal court not involving federal claims, subject matter jurisdiction issues may arise.

(1) Diversity of citizenship [§1198]

For purposes of federal diversity jurisdiction, only the citizenship of the *representative* is considered. This facilitates maintenance of a class suit in federal court. Note also that the named representatives must also meet the requirements of venue. [**Supreme Tribe of Ben-Hur v. Cauble**, *supra*, §330]

(2) Jurisdictional amount [§1199]

However, in any class action in which the individual class members would be entitled to *separate* recoveries (rather than a recovery in common), where the amount in controversy requirement is applicable, *each* member of the class must have a claim in excess of $75,000—*i.e.*, no aggregation of claims is permitted. [**Zahn v. International Paper Co.**, *supra*, §422—refusal to permit class action where claims of representatives exceeded jurisdictional amount, but claims of unnamed members of class did not]

(a) Effect [§1200]

The effect of this requirement has been to exclude most *diversity* consumer class actions from federal courts, because the claims of each member in such cases usually do not exceed $75,000.

(b) State courts [§1201]

There is usually a state court of general jurisdiction, so state law class actions can be filed in that court. Where the state court of general jurisdiction has a jurisdictional minimum (*see supra*, §291), it is usually possible to aggregate claims to meet that minimum.

1) Possible impact of supplemental jurisdiction statute [§1202]

The supplemental jurisdiction statute [28 U.S.C. §1367(b)] does not explicitly preclude supplemental jurisdiction over the claims of class members that do not exceed $75,000, but the legislative history says the statute should not affect the rule in *Zahn, supra*. The courts are divided on whether the statute nullified *Zahn*. (*See supra*, §439.)

EXAM TIP   **gilbert**

Be sure to remember that diversity jurisdiction is a bit quirky when it comes to class actions. For *purposes of diversity* of citizenship, *only the class representative* is considered, but for *purposes of the jurisdictional amount*, each and *every class member* is considered and must surpass the $75,000 threshold individually. Thus, most consumer class actions must be brought in state, rather than federal, court because most will not meet the jurisdictional amount requirement for diversity jurisdiction in federal court.

---

b. Personal jurisdiction [§1203]

It has been held that in an action involving a nationwide class, a state court could assert personal jurisdiction over absent members of the plaintiff class if they were afforded an opportunity to opt out and chose not to do so. [**Phillips Petroleum Co. v. Shutts,** 472 U.S. 797 (1985)]

(1) Requirement of right to opt out [§1204]

It is *unclear* whether the right to opt out is required to justify personal jurisdiction in all cases, such as actions brought under Rule 23(b)(1) or 23(b)(2). The Supreme Court reserved ruling on this point in *Shutts, supra*, and has since declined to decide whether a right to opt-out is required. [*See* **Adams v. Robertson,** 520 U.S. 83 (1997)—certiorari dismissed in case raising issue]

(2) Defendant classes [§1205]

It is also *unclear* whether the same analysis would apply to a defendant class when the right to opt out was afforded the unnamed members of the class.

6. Procedure in Conducting Class Suits

a. Certification hearing [§1206]

As soon as practicable after commencement of an alleged class suit, a hearing should be held to decide whether the action should proceed as a class suit. If the court finds that the class action requirements (above) are met, it decides that the case can proceed as a class action. [Fed. R. Civ. P. 23(c)(1)] This is commonly called "class certification." If the court finds that no class action is possible, the suit may be continued as an individual action.

(1) Based on evidence [§1207]

In determining whether the suit can proceed as a class action, the court can take evidence on any of the issues raised (*i.e.,* it is **not** restricted to the pleadings).

(a) Discovery on class certification [§1208]

Because the class certification decision is to be based on evidentiary materials, it is said to be necessary to allow precertification discovery relevant to whether the case should be certified as a class action. [**Stewart v. Winter,** 669 F.2d 328 (5th Cir. 1982)] Some courts try to limit this to "class action" issues, as distinguished from "merits" issues (going to the merits of the case), but this may prove difficult since commonality and typicality are class certification issues that depend in large measure on merits information.

(2) Consideration of merits [§1209]

The Supreme Court has stated that the court may not make a preliminary inquiry into the merits of the suit to decide whether it can be maintained as a class action. [**Eisen v. Carlisle & Jacquelin,** *supra,* §1151]

(a) Distinguish—determining whether claim satisfies Rule 23 [§1210]

The court may, however, determine whether the claim is of a type that would satisfy Rule 23, and to do so it must examine the grounds for the action to identify common issues and decide whether the plaintiff has a typical claim. One court said that the court should look "between the pleading and the fruits of discovery. . . . [E]nough must be laid bare to let the judge survey the factual scene on a kind of sketchy relief map, leaving for later view the myriad of details that cover the terrain." [**Sirota v. Solitron Devices, Inc.,** 673 F.2d 566 (2d Cir.), *cert. denied,* 459 U.S. 838 (1982)]

(3) Precertification decision of merits [§1211]

The premise of the 1966 amendments to Rule 23 was that the class action would be binding on all class members, whether or not it was successful. Otherwise, class members could benefit from *"one-way intervention,"* finding out how the merits were decided before they elected to remain in the action or to opt out. As a result, it was widely assumed that the court could not decide the merits until it ruled on the certification issue, but the courts have modified this view (*see* below).

(a) Criticism

Where the certification process was likely to be protracted and expensive, it might give a plaintiff who added class action allegations to his groundless complaint undue settlement leverage to prevent defendants from attacking the merits of the case until certification was decided.

(b) Motions to dismiss [§1212]

To counteract the risk that plaintiffs will add class action allegations to groundless complaints, courts generally will entertain motions to dismiss under Rule 12(b)(6) (*see supra*, §718) before certification is decided.

(c) Summary judgment motions [§1213]

Many courts will also allow defendants to move for summary judgment. The theory to support this is that defendants can waive the rule's protection against one-way intervention by filing motions for summary judgment if they choose to. [**Cowen v. Bank United of Texas,** 70 F.3d 937 (7th Cir. 1995)]

(4) Certification order may be modified [§1214]

The certification order is only tentative. At any time before trial, the court may revise class certification if it decides changes are necessary, by decertifying or altering the class configuration. Indeed, it may expand class size even after judgment if this would not unfairly subject the defendant to liability. [**Payne v. Travenol Laboratories, Inc.,** 673 F.2d 798 (5th Cir.), *cert. denied,* 459 U.S. 1038 (1982)]

(5) Immediate appellate review of certification decisions [§1215]

Rule 23 provides for interlocutory appellate review of orders granting or denying class status. [Fed. R. Civ. P. 23(f)] The court of appeals has discretion to entertain such an immediate appeal if a party applies for review within 10 days after entry of the order.

b. Statute of limitations [§1216]

The *filing* of a suit as a class action *suspends the running of the statute of limitations* for all putative members of the class until class certification is decided. [**American Pipe & Construction Co. v. Utah,** *supra*, §1150] *Rationale:* Unless they could rely on the pendency of the class action to protect their rights, unnamed members of the class would have to file their own suits to guard against the running of the limitations period. This would defeat the purpose of Rule 23 to achieve the efficient combined resolution of cases suitable for class action treatment.

(1) Effect [§1217]

From the date the class action is filed until class certification is decided, the running of limitations is suspended. If class certification is denied, the limitations period begins to run again, and class members have the remainder of the period to file their own actions or intervene. [**Nelson v. County of Allegheny,** 60 F.3d 1010 (3d Cir. 1995)—tolling ceased when district court denied class certification] If class certification is granted, class members who remain in the class action are protected against a limitations defense, provided the class action was filed in time.

(2) Opt-outs [§1218]

If class certification is granted and some class members opt out, the limitations period begins to run again and they must file individual actions to protect themselves against the running of limitations.

(3) Tolling not dependent on grounds for denial [§1219]

The suspension of the running of the limitations period applies even if the class certification motion is denied for lack of commonality or typicality. [**Crown, Cork & Seal Co. v. Parker,** 462 U.S. 345 (1983)] *Criticism:* This means that the defendant is really not on notice of the claims that are protected from the running of limitations by the filing of the defective class action.

(4) Defendant class actions [§1220]

The suspension of limitations has been held to apply to a defendant class action in which the unnamed member of the defendant class did not even have notice of the filing of the suit within the limitations period. [**Appleton Electric Co. v. Graves Truck Line, Inc.,** 635 F.2d 603 (7th Cir. 1980), *cert. denied,* 451 U.S. 976 (1981)]

(5) Successive class actions [§1221]

The suspension of limitations has been held not to be available in a second class action that is timely only because a deficient class action earlier suspended the running of limitations. [**Basch v. Ground Round, Inc.,** 139 F.3d 6 (1st Cir. 1998)]

c. Notice requirements

(1) When notice to individual class members is discretionary [§1222]

If the basis for a class action is to avoid the risk of inconsistent adjudications [Fed. R. Civ. P. 23(b)(1), *supra,* §1174], or the claim is for injunctive or declaratory relief for the class as a whole [Fed. R. Civ. P. 23(b)(2)], the appropriate form of notice to class members is left to the discretion of the court. [Fed. R. Civ. P. 23(d)(2)] Individual notice to class members is not required by due process if the class representation is adequate. [**Wetzel v. Liberty Mutual Insurance Co.,** 508 F.2d 239 (3d Cir. 1975)]

(2) When individual notice is mandatory

(a) Damages class action [§1223]

In a damages class action based on a predominant question common to the class [Fed. R. Civ. P. 23(b)(3), *supra*, §1181], members of the class must be given "the best notice practicable under the circumstances, *including individual notice to all members who can be identified through reasonable effort.*" [**Eisen v. Carlisle & Jacquelin**, *supra* §1151—requiring individual notice to 2,250,000 class members; Fed. R. Civ. P. 23(c)(2)]

(b) Settlement or dismissal [§1224]

Once a suit has been certified as a class suit, some type of notice to the class is required before *any* type of class action may be settled or dismissed. [Fed. R. Civ. P. 23(e)]

(c) State rules may be more flexible [§1225]

State courts usually require individual notice only where members of the class have *"substantial" claims*, because in such cases it is essential for them to decide whether to remain in (and be bound by res judicata) or opt out and pursue their independent remedies. Where the membership of the class is large and damages to each member small, individual notice might not be required and notice by publication may be sufficient. [**Cooper v. American Savings & Loan Association**, 55 Cal. App. 3d 274 (1976)]

(3) Form and content of notice [§1226]

Federal Rule 23 does not establish any specific form or manner of giving notice.

(a) Form [§1227]

Clearly, the notice itself need *not* be in the form of a complaint or summons. Letters, bulletins, or circulars mailed to members of the class are commonly used. However, when notice to each member is mandatory, it must be given at least the formality of mail. [**Eisen v. Carlisle & Jacquelin**, *supra*] In other instances, the court has discretion as to form. [**Greenfield v. Villager Industries, Inc.**, 483 F.2d 824 (3d Cir. 1973)]

(b) Contents [§1228]

The notice must advise the class member of the existence of the suit, the nature of the claim and relief requested, provisions for costs of maintaining the suit, and the identity of the person or persons suing on behalf of the class. When based on Rule 23(b)(3)—the predominant question ground—it must also advise each member that he will be bound by the judgment unless he opts out. [Fed. R. Civ. P. 23(c)(2)]

(c) Effect of notice [§1229]

In the ordinary civil action, notice has the effect of making the notified person a *party* to the action who will be bound by any judgment in the action (including a default judgment if he does not appear). In a class suit, however, the notified person is already provisionally bound through representation by the class representative. Hence, notice has the following effects:

1) *If accompanied by an "opt out" directive* in a Rule 23(b)(3) suit, the notice allows the notified person to terminate his involvement in the action (*see infra*, §1232.)

2) *In other types of class suits,* the notice:

   a) Gives absent members of the class the opportunity to intervene and protect themselves; *and*

   b) Gives the opposing party more assurance that the eventual judgment cannot subsequently be attacked by an absentee claiming that the representation was inadequate (*see supra*, §1169).

(4) Plaintiff must pay costs of notice [§1230]

Under Rule 23(c), the plaintiff initially must pay the costs of notifying all members of the class. [**Eisen v. Carlisle & Jacquelin**, *supra*] If the plaintiff *wins* the action, she can ultimately recover such expenses from the defendant as necessary court costs.

(a) Cost of identifying class members [§1231]

The plaintiff must also pay the cost of identifying class members. [**Oppenheimer Fund, Inc. v. Sanders**, 437 U.S. 340 (1978)—$16,000 in computer costs to identify certain class members properly charged to plaintiff]

(b) Effect

The cost of notice has inhibited large class actions in federal court, because the larger the class, the less likely it is that any single plaintiff can afford to bear the costs of notice (and thus "fairly and adequately" represent the class).

EXAM TIP   **gilbert**

Notice issues may be important in an exam question involving a class action. Recall that if the class is certified under Rule 23(b)(3) (*i.e.,* common questions predominate), class members must be given "the best notice practicable under the circumstances," which includes *individual notice to class members who can be readily identified*. If the class is large, notice may stifle the suit because the plaintiff must bear the costs of notice (although such costs are ultimately recoverable if the plaintiff wins). Also remember: The form of the notice must usually be approved by the court; it should advise class members of the existence and nature of the suit and relief sought, the provisions for costs, and the identity of the class representative. Finally, the notice must indicate that members may opt out of the class action.

d. Opting out by class members [§1232]

In class actions under Rule 23(b)(3), unnamed members of the class may opt out, thereby excluding themselves from the binding effects of the class action.

(1) Timing [§1233]

Usually the decision to opt out must be made before the court decides the merits, to avoid the risk of one-way intervention. (*See supra*, §1211.)

(2) Effect on statute of limitations [§1234]

Once a class member opts out, she loses the class action's effect of suspending the limitations period and must file her own suit within the remainder of the limitations period to protect her rights. (*See supra*, §1216.)

(3) Rule 23(b)(1) and 23(b)(2) class actions [§1235]

There is no mandatory opt-out right in the rule for actions under Rule 23(b)(1) or 23(b)(2). In some cases, the court may, in its discretion, permit opting out, but that could undermine the purpose of certifying a case of this type in the first place. When class members have monetary claims, however, it may be an abuse of discretion to deny the right to opt out. [**Holmes v. Continental Can Co.,** 706 F.2d 1144 (11th Cir. 1983)]

(4) Constitutional right argument [§1236]

It may be argued that the Supreme Court's decision that the right to opt out permits exercise of personal jurisdiction over the claims of unnamed class members (*see supra*, §1203) means that there must always be a right to opt out where unnamed class members are not subject to the personal jurisdiction of the court.

(5) Right to claim collateral estoppel [§1237]

It has been held that where class members opt out and the class action is successful, the *opt-outs may not claim collateral estoppel* (*i.e.,* claim that the issues decided against the defendant in the class action control here as well). That would be tantamount to one-way intervention. [**Becherer v. Merrill Lynch, Pierce, Fenner & Smith, Inc.,** 193 F.3d 415 (6th Cir. 1999); **Amati v. City of Woodstock,** 176 F.3d 952 (7th Cir. 1998)]

e. Intervention by class members [§1238]

Intervention by class members in the class action is allowed on the same terms that govern intervention otherwise. (*See supra*, §§1089-1115.)

(1) Adequacy of representation [§1239]

A problem arises from this rule because intervention is not allowed where the intervenor is adequately represented by the present litigant (*see supra*, §1097), and the court must find the class representative (*i.e.,* the present litigant) adequate to certify the class (*see supra*, §1165). Some courts solve the problem by saying that the finding of adequacy under Rule 23(a) for class certification does not require a finding of adequacy under Rule 24(a) (dealing with intervention). [**Woolen v. Surtran Taxicabs, Inc.,** 684 F.2d 324 (5th Cir. 1982)]

(2) Role of intervenor [§1240]

Rule 23 makes no provision for participation by a party who is not the class representative. Some courts suggest that when intervention is proper, the certification decision should be reconsidered or the intervenor should be designated a new class representative. [**Lelsz v. Kavanagh,** 710 F.2d 1040 (5th Cir. 1983)]

(3) Entering an appearance [§1241]

In Rule 23(b)(3) actions, a class member may "enter an appearance through counsel." This does not entitle the class member to take an active role in the litigation, but rather only entitles the class member to receive copies of pleadings and other filings. It is, thus, a way to monitor the progress of the case.

f. Discovery [§1242]

Class members are treated as "quasi-parties" for discovery purposes. The opposing party is not given the full rights (*e.g.*, to depose each class member) that he ordinarily has against opposing litigants. However, he can obtain fair discovery of the "typicality" of claims, the factual basis for determining inclusion in the class, individual damages, and the like. Interrogatories for these purposes are proper, as are depositions when necessary. [**Brennan v. Midwestern United Life Insurance Co.,** 450 F.2d 999 (7th Cir. 1971)]

g. Communications with class members [§1243]

Courts are concerned about the risk that unnamed members of the class may be victimized by misleading or overreaching on the part of the litigants or their lawyers, and may therefore sometimes limit contacts with class members.

(1) Showing of need [§1244]

The Supreme Court has held that limitations on communications with class members by class counsel may be imposed only where there is some showing of need. [**Gulf Oil Corp. v. Bernard,** 452 U.S. 89 (1981)] The showing should indicate a *likelihood of misleading or overreaching class members.*

(2) Effect of certification [§1245]

After the class is certified, class counsel is for some purposes the attorney for the class members, and the court's power to interfere with her communications is limited.

(3) Communications by class opponent [§1246]

After the class is certified, the court has broader authority to regulate communications by the class opponent, particularly when there is a risk that the class opponent will try to subvert the class action by pressuring class members to opt out.

---

e.g. **Example:** In a class action against a bank alleging that it defrauded its borrowers by inflating the prime rate it charged them, the court properly punished the bank for embarking on a campaign to have loan officers call class members and pressure them to opt out of the action. [**Kleiner v. First National Bank of Atlanta,** 751 F.2d 1193 (11th Cir. 1985)]

(a) Attorney contacts [§1247]

After certification, class members should be considered "represented by counsel," and the attorney for the class opponent is therefore forbidden by ethical rules to communicate with the class members. [**Resnick v. American Dental Association,** 95 F.R.D. 372 (N.D. Ill. 1982)]

(4) Remedies for violations [§1248]

When a valid rule against communication with class members is violated, the court may hold the person who violated the rule in *contempt.* In addition, when the communication resulted in opt-outs, the court can *invalidate the opt-outs* tainted by the communication.

h. Dismissal and compromise

(1) Court approval required [§1249]

Because of the fiduciary nature of a class action, it may not be dismissed or settled by the class representative without court approval. [Fed. R. Civ. P. 23(e)]

(a) Fairness inquiry does not substitute for satisfaction of Rule 23(a) requirements [§1250]

In a class action that is settled, the Rule 23(a) prerequisites to a class action apply even if the court finds that the proposed settlement is fair and adequate. [**Amchem Products, Inc. v. Windsor,** *supra,* §1167] Indeed, the fact that class counsel and defendants have reached a settlement without formal certification of a litigation class action may mean that the court should be more exacting with regard to questions of adequacy of representation and typicality.

(2) Notice required [§1251]

Notice of the proposed dismissal or compromise must be given to all members of the class before the court can give its approval. [Fed. R. Civ. P. 23(e)]

(3) Settlement before certification [§1252]

If a class action is settled before certification, the notice and hearing requirements depend on the nature of the settlement.

(a) Settlement of class claims [§1253]

If the settlement purports to resolve class claims by releasing the defendant from further liability to class members, notice and a hearing are required. [**Philadelphia Electric Co. v. Anaconda American Brass Co.,** 42 F.R.D. 324 (E.D. Pa. 1967)]

(b) Settlement of individual claims [§1254]

If the settlement purports only to settle the individual claims of the proposed class representatives, the court usually will determine whether there is any *indication of abuse* of the class action device or *prejudice to absent class members.* If there is, it should order notice and a hearing. [**Shelton v. Pargo, Inc.,** 582 F.2d 1298 (4th Cir. 1978)]

i. Distribution of proceeds of action

(1) Class members file individual claims [§1255]

Ordinarily, any fund obtained by settlement or judgment in a class action will be held intact, and members of the class will be notified to file individual claims to establish their shares.

(2) Rebate approach [§1256]

However, when the class is numerous and the claims are small, this approach may be impractical. In this situation, some courts have adopted what amounts to a rebate approach: Where the identity of the class members at the time of the wrong cannot be determined or the amounts of their respective claims are very small, the recovery will be distributed to those persons who are *now* members of the class.

Example: Taxi fare overcharges to former customers may be refunded by reducing fares to *future customers.* [*See* **Daar v. Yellow Cab Co.,** 67 Cal. 2d 695 (1967)]

(a) Criticism

This approach may distort market structure, resulting in temporary underpricing, overuse, and competitive advantage for the wrongdoer.

j. Award of attorneys' fees [§1257]

Although there is no authority under the Federal Rules for awarding fees to counsel in a successful class suit, federal and state courts generally award fees out of the proceeds recovered by the class. This is based on the court's inherent equity powers under the "common fund doctrine"—*i.e.*, the plaintiff who hired the attorney should not be required to pay the entire legal fees incurred in obtaining a "common fund" benefiting all class members. [**Mills v. Electric Auto Lite Co.,** 396 U.S. 375 (1970)] However, the fee award is carefully considered by the court on behalf of the class. [**Lindy Brothers Builders, Inc. v. American Radiator Corp.,** 540 F.2d 102 (3d Cir. 1976)]

7. Effect of Judgment in Class Action [§1258]

A central issue in class actions is whether the judgment binds members of the class who were not actually before the court.

a. State rules [§1259]

Some states retain the distinctions between true, hybrid, and spurious class actions (the former Federal Rule), under which the "nature" of the action determines whether the judgment is binding on absentees. (*See supra*, §§1142-1145.)

b. Federal Rule [§1260]

Under Federal Rule 23, however, these distinctions are eliminated. A valid judgment in any class action (whether or not favorable to the class) *binds all members of the class who do not affirmatively request exclusion (opt out).* A person who excludes herself from the action will not be bound by an adverse judgment. Conversely, however, she may be unable to assert collateral estoppel in her own action if the judgment turns out to be favorable to the class. (*See supra*, §1237.)

8. Defendant Class Actions [§1261]

Rule 23 states that suits may be brought against a defendant class. For such actions, the Rule does not provide any procedures different from those for actions on behalf of a plaintiff class. Nevertheless, the *courts tend to approach defendant class actions differently* in ways that should be noted.

a. Adequacy of representation [§1262]

There is a risk that a plaintiff will select a weak representative for a defendant class. Adequacy of representation may therefore be *examined more closely.*

(1) Incentive problem [§1263]

The defendant class representative may have less incentive to litigate vigorously, and the lawyer for the class lacks the entrepreneurial incentive of a plaintiff class lawyer, who looks forward to a large fee award if the case is successful.

(2) Courts' attitude [§1264]

Despite these problems, many courts realize that defendants will try to escape service as class representative. The courts resist such efforts: "[C]ourts must not readily accede to the wishes of named defendants in this area, for to permit them to abdicate so easily would utterly vitiate the effectiveness of the defendant class action." [**Marcera v. Chinlund,** 595 F.2d 1231 (2d Cir.), *vacated on other grounds,* 442 U.S. 915 (1979)] Hence, when the representatives will adequately protect the class by protecting their own interests, courts will find them adequate.

b. **Qualitative differences between plaintiff and defendant postures [§1265]**
Many courts view defendants' stakes as qualitatively different. The distinction is that the unnamed plaintiff stands to gain while the unnamed defendant stands to lose. [**Thillens, Inc. v. Community Currency Exchange Association,** 97 F.R.D. 668 (N.D. Ill. 1983)]

   (1) Criticism
   This represents a skewed view of litigation, because both defendants and plaintiffs stand to lose and gain. The absent plaintiff class member who has a valid claim stands to lose if the class action is decided adversely, and the absent defendant class member stands to gain res judicata protection against future suits if the defendant class is successful.

c. **Rule 23(b)(2) class actions [§1266]**
Rule 23(b)(2) authorizes actions for injunctive or declaratory relief against "the party opposing the class," seemingly precluding a defendant class action. Nevertheless, there is a division in the courts on whether it is permissible to have a class action seeking an injunction against a defendant class. [*See* **Marcera v. Chinlund,** *supra*—defendant class allowed; **Henson v. East Lincoln Township,** 814 F.2d 410 (7th Cir. 1987)—defendant class not allowed]

d. **Personal jurisdiction [§1267]**
In upholding the authority of a state court to exercise personal jurisdiction over absent plaintiff class members (*see supra*, §1203), the Supreme Court distinguished the situation of defendants, for "an out-of-state defendant summoned by a plaintiff is faced with the full powers of the forum state *against* it." [**Phillips Petroleum Co. v. Shutts,** *supra*, §1203] It is uncertain whether this mandates granting unnamed defendant class members more than the right simply to opt out to overcome their personal jurisdiction objections.

e. **Bilateral class action [§1268]**
Some of the most troubling class action problems involve "bilateral" class actions, *i.e.*, involving a plaintiff class suing a defendant class. One reaction of courts has been to hold that *each plaintiff class member must have a claim against each defendant class member* in such actions. [**La Mar v. H & B Novelty & Loan Co.,** 489 F.2d 461 (9th Cir. 1973)] There are two principal ways to satisfy this requirement.

   (1) Conspiracy [§1269]
   When it is alleged that the defendant class members conspired with each other, that provides a basis for holding each conspirator liable to each plaintiff and solves the problem.

(2) Juridical link [§1270]

The courts have also allowed bilateral class actions where there is a "juridical link" among the defendants. Usually this means that defendants are officers of the same governmental unit, such as the state. [*See, e.g.,* **Marcera v. Chinlund,** *supra*—action against sheriffs of state for denying contact visits to pretrial detainees]

Chapter Six: Discovery

CONTENTS

Chapter Approach

Chapter Approach

Procedural rules make available several modes of discovery:

(i) *Initial disclosure;*

(ii) *Depositions;*

(iii) *Interrogatories;*

(iv) Requests for *admissions;*

(v) Requests for *production and inspection;* and

(vi) *Physical or mental examination.*

Through the use of these devices, by the time a case gets to trial, each side should know as much as possible about its own case and that of the adversary.

For examination purposes, questions most commonly center on the following issues related to discovery:

1. **Scope of discovery**

   Is the matter *relevant* to the claims or defenses in the action and *not privileged*? If so, it is within the scope of discovery, although discovery may be limited or denied as to *work product* (trial preparation material) or *expert analysis.*

2. **Protective orders**

   Is there good cause for a protective order *limiting, conditioning,* or *delaying* the discovery?

3. **Sanctions**

   Has a party's resistance to discovery or *noncompliance* with discovery rules and orders been sufficient to warrant judicial imposition of sanctions?

4. **Use at trial**

   Is the deposition that of a *party* or an *unavailable or distant witness*? If so, it may be introduced for *any* purpose. If it is the deposition of a witness appearing at trial, it may be used to *impeach* the witness's testimony.

A. Introduction

1. History of Discovery

a. Common law [§1271]

Under common law procedure, the pleadings were to disclose factual contentions and information to the adversary parties. Neither party could compel the other to disclose additional information that might support his case, even such crucial information as the identity of an eyewitness. A party was not compelled to reveal in advance the evidence he would present at trial; neither were third parties required to make disclosures except pursuant to a subpoena requiring their attendance at trial.

b. Equity [§1272]

In early equity practice, a bill in equity could be used to compel the adversary to disclose information, and such bills frequently were accompanied by interrogatories which the defendant was required to answer under oath. In addition, parties or witnesses could be required to appear for depositions where interrogation through written questions could be conducted. Since answers to interrogatories and depositions were a part of the record on which the decision was made, they were really part of the trial and not merely preparatory discovery. Live testimony was usually not allowed at the hearing, so cases were decided on the basis of the material developed through discovery.

c. Equity in aid of law [§1273]

A litigant in a law court could sometimes take advantage of the equitable procedures by bringing a bill in equity to compel discovery of information needed to present a claim or defense at law. Such a bill could issue if the evidence sought would be admissible in the specific legal proceeding (*i.e.,* if the moving party was not embarked on a "fishing expedition") and would be helpful to the moving party in meeting a burden of proof imposed on him.

d. Code procedure [§1274]

Nineteenth-century reforms merged the bill of discovery into legal proceedings, but did not significantly enlarge its availability. Thus, heavy reliance on the pleadings continued.

e. Federal Rules [§1275]

Ultimately, the Federal Rules made pretrial discovery an integral part of the process of defining the issues for trial. Similar discovery procedures have now been adopted in almost every state. However, increasing concern about excessive discovery has led to repeated revision of discovery rules.

2. Purpose and Effect of Discovery Procedures

a. Obtaining factual information [§1276]

A party who has made effective use of discovery can go to trial with the best evidence available to prove his contentions and with a good knowledge of the presentation that his adversary will make. Surprise and delay are thus largely avoided, and the chance that the judgment will rest on accurate findings of fact is enhanced.

b. Narrowing the issues [§1277]

Discovery can help to eliminate fictitious issues, claims, or defenses by revealing overwhelming evidence on one side, thereby paving the way for stipulations, settlements, and summary disposition. *Caution:* Many lawyers say that broad discovery has not in fact narrowed cases, although it may have facilitated summary judgment (*see infra*, §§1616 *et seq.*).

c. Promoting settlements [§1278]

It was hoped that discovery would facilitate more and earlier settlements by providing each side fuller knowledge of the strengths and weaknesses of its case.

d. Simplification of pleading [§1279]

The availability of discovery makes it unnecessary to rely heavily upon the pleadings for exchanging information, narrowing issues, or disposing of untenable claims or defenses. Accordingly, where discovery is available, pleading is simplified and technical challenges to pleadings are disfavored.

e. Costs to litigants [§1280]

To the extent that discovery produces settlements and stipulations, it can substantially cut down costs to one or both parties. At the same time, the discovery process itself can be very costly in terms of time spent by lawyers, parties, witnesses, and court reporters.

f. Substantive consequences [§1281]

The foregoing effects of discovery can have substantive implications as well. Claims and defenses otherwise difficult to establish may be made effective by the availability of discovery. Antitrust claims, for example, are often proved with evidence discovered in the possession of the defense. And the availability of discovery may enable a tenacious and resourceful litigant to wear down one who is weaker or less energetic.

3. Problems in Discovery

a. Collateral purpose problem [§1282]

An ongoing concern with discovery is the risk that litigants may seek to obtain discovery for some *purpose other than preparation for trial*.

(1) Harassment [§1283]

Because of its cost, discovery can be used to harass an opponent or club an opponent into settlement. The court has power to limit discovery having these tendencies [Fed. R. Civ. P. 26(b)(2)] and to sanction the person who so uses it [Fed. R. Civ. P. 26(g)].

(2) Nonlitigation use of information [§1284]

Alternatively, a litigant may seek information that is pertinent to the litigation to use it for some nonlitigation purpose.

> **Example:** In litigation between business competitors, one litigant may seek to force its opponent to reveal information that can be used to obtain competitive advantages in the marketplace.

> **Example:** In an action between Jacqueline Kennedy Onassis and a professional photographer who specialized in unauthorized candid photos of the Kennedy family, there was concern that the photographer would use Ms. Onassis's deposition as an occasion for photographing her. [**Galella v. Onassis,** 487 F.2d 986 (2d Cir. 1974)—upholding protective order excluding plaintiff from defendant's deposition]

b. "Stonewalling" and failure to respond properly [§1285]

Another prominent discovery concern is that some litigants do not comply with their obligations to respond to discovery in a timely or thorough manner. Some reportedly withhold materials that should be turned over, while others may use "dump truck" tactics—turning over vast amounts of irrelevant material that the opponent must sift through rather than only the items requested.

B. Basic Discovery Devices

1. Prediscovery Disclosure [§1286]

Federal Rule 26(a) provides for disclosure of certain information *before commencement of formal discovery*. *Rationale:* Formal discovery is too time-consuming and expensive as to certain *core information* that will undoubtedly be revealed during the formal discovery process.

a. Early conference of counsel [§1287]

To accomplish the objectives of the disclosure provisions, counsel are to meet and confer "as soon as practicable" after the suit is filed. The purpose of this conference is to allow the parties to "discuss the *nature and basis* of their claims and defenses" and to "*develop a proposed discovery plan*," as well as to specify the materials that should be included in the prediscovery disclosures. [Fed. R. Civ. P. 26(f)]

(1) Presented to court [§1288]

The discovery plan is to be presented to the court in writing within 14 days, or orally at the court's scheduling conference pursuant to Rule 16 (*see infra,* §§1691-1696).

b. No formal discovery until meeting of counsel [§1289]

Formal discovery may not be undertaken, except on stipulation or court order, until the Rule 26(f) conference has been completed. [Fed. R. Civ. P. 26(d)]

(1) Exception for witnesses leaving country [§1290]

A party may take a deposition earlier if the witness is expected to leave the country and be unavailable for deposition in this country unless examined before the meeting of counsel. [Fed. R. Civ. P. 30(a)(3)(C)]

c. Disclosure of materials disclosing party may use [§1291]

As amended in 2000, prediscovery disclosure regarding witnesses and documents that the disclosing party *"may use to support its claims or defenses."*

(1) Particularity no longer important to disclosure [§1292]

Before the 2000 amendments, disclosure was limited to information relevant to facts alleged with particularity in the pleadings. The 2000 disclosure requirement applies whether or not matters are pled with particularity. *Rationale*: If a party is required to disclose only materials it may use to support its case, the party's need for more complete allegations about the claim is minimized.

(2) Impeachment materials excluded [§1293]

Materials that a party would use solely for impeachment are not subject to the disclosure requirement. *Caution*: Very few materials fall within this category; if they are relevant for some purpose other than impeachment, a court may hold this exemption inapplicable.

(3) Categories of cases exempted [§1294]

A limited number of categories of cases in which substantial discovery is unlikely are exempted from the disclosure requirement, and the accompanying attorney conference and discovery moratorium provisions. [Fed. R. Civ. P. 26(a)(1)(E)] Examples include habeas corpus petitions, actions to enforce an administrative subpoena, and actions on guaranteed student loans.

(4) Objection suspends duty to disclose [§1295]

If a party objects during the Rule 26(f) attorney conference that disclosure is "not appropriate in the circumstances of the action" and states that objection in the Rule 26(f) report to the court (*see supra,* §1288), the obligation to disclose is suspended until the court rules on the objection.

(5) Disclosure by later added parties [§1296]

A party first served or otherwise joined after the Rule 26(f) conference must make its disclosures within 30 days.

d. Material to be disclosed

(1) Identity of witnesses [§1297]

Each party is to disclose the name and, if known, the address and telephone number of each person whom it may use to support its claims or defenses. [Fed. R. Civ. P. 26(a)(1)(A)]

(2) Documents that may be used [§1298]

Each party is to disclose a copy or description by category of all documents in its possession that it may use to support its claims or defenses. [Fed. R. Civ. P. 26(a)(1)(B)]

(a) Broad concept of "use"

The expected use of a document or witness that mandates disclosure is not limited to use at trial. The expectation that a document or witness will be used in connection with any motion or a pretrial conference is sufficient. Sufficient use even includes certain discovery events, such as questioning a witness by using a document. However, the concept of use here does not extend to the mere use of a document or witness's name to respond to another party's discovery inquiry.

EXAM TIP   **gilbert**

Whenever a party attempts to make any use of a document or witness (whether at a hearing or through an affidavit) that has **not been previously disclosed**, consider whether the party may have failed to satisfy its initial disclosure obligations. As noted *infra* (§1305), failure to do so may result in an "automatic" refusal by the court to permit the use of the material. Keep in mind that the rule calls for disclosure as long as the party "*may*" use the document; its use need not be certain.

---

(3) Damages computation [§1299]

Each party claiming damages should disclose a computation of those damages and *produce the documents* on which the computation is based. [Fed. R. Civ. P. 26(a)(1)(C)]

(4) Insurance agreements [§1300]

Each party against whom a claim has been asserted should produce for inspection and copying each insurance agreement that might cover the claim. [Fed. R. Civ. P. 26(a)(1)(D)]

UNDER THE FEDERAL RULES, THE FOLLOWING MUST BE DISCLOSED BEFORE FORMAL DISCOVERY BEGINS:

- ☑ Name, address and (if known) phone number of any person the disclosing party may use to support its case.

- ☑ Copies or description of all documents in the party's possession that it may use to support its position in the case.

- ☑ Computation of damages and documents on which computation is based.

- ☑ Insurance agreements that might cover the claim.

e. Timing of disclosures [§1301]

Under the 2000 amendments, these disclosures should be made at, or within 14 days after, the meeting of counsel pursuant to Rule 26(f) (*supra*, §1287) unless otherwise agreed by the parties or ordered by the court. *Note:* A different period applies to later-added parties. (*See supra*, §1296.)

f. Form of disclosures [§1302]

Every disclosure is to be *signed* by at least one attorney of record for the disclosing party. The signature represents that to the best of the lawyer's knowledge, *formed after a reasonable inquiry*, the disclosure is complete and correct as of the time it is made. [Fed. R. Civ. P. 26(g)(1)]

g. Duty to supplement [§1303]

If a party learns that its disclosures were *incorrect*, or if *additional or corrective information* comes to its attention, the party is to supplement the disclosure with the added information. [Fed. R. Civ. P. 26(e)(1)]

h. Sanctions for failure to disclose [§1304]

A party failing to disclose as required by Rule 26(a)(1) or to supplement as required by Rule 26(e)(1) is subject to sanctions. [Fed. R. Civ. P. 37(c)(1)]

(1) Exclusion of evidence [§1305]

Unless the failure to disclose was harmless, the party will not be permitted to use the material in evidence. This sanction is said to be *automatic*, and it applies not only at trial but also at motion hearings, as on a motion for summary judgment.

(2) Additional sanctions [§1306]

In addition, the court may impose the sanctions authorized by Rule 37(b), which usually require an order compelling discovery as a prerequisite (*see infra*, §§1567-1572), and can *inform the jury* of the failure to make disclosure.

i. Stipulation to limit disclosure obligation [§1307]

The parties may stipulate to limit or alter the initial disclosure obligation.

j. District court opt-out of disclosure regime not allowed [§1308]

When the prediscovery disclosure rule was first introduced in 1993, it was controversial and district courts were allowed to "opt out" by adopting local rules changing disclosure practice or invalidating the requirement altogether. Many districts did so, and individual judges also developed standing orders. As a result, disclosure existed only in a patchwork condition in the federal court system. Some districts required more disclosure than the national rule, and some required less or none. Under the 2000 amendments, disclosure has become *nationally uniform*.

EXAM TIP   **gilbert**

If a test question focuses on discovery, you will likely need to know not only what constitutes a violation of the rules of discovery, but also **what sanctions** can be imposed and under what conditions. The sanctions and their prerequisites vary from one discovery device to the next, but it is important to remember that if a party fails to make or supplement a prediscovery disclosure as required by Rule 26 and the failure was harmful, the party who failed to disclose will be prohibited from using the undisclosed evidence. Other sanctions may be imposed (*e.g.,* a contempt charge) if the court first orders disclosure and the party still does not disclose.

---

2. Depositions [§1309]

A deposition is an examination of a witness under oath in the presence of a court reporter. All parties have a right to be represented by counsel at a deposition; and counsel may examine and cross-examine the witness. The examination may be held in the presence of a judge if the witness is recalcitrant.

a. When timely

(1) Before suit filed [§1310]

A deposition may be taken *before* an action is filed or while an appeal is pending from a final judgment, but only by leave of court granted for the purpose of perpetuating testimony based on a showing that the party seeking to perpetuate testimony is unable to cause the action to be brought. [Fed. R. Civ. P. 37(a)]

(2) Moratorium after commencement of suit [§1311]

Federal Rule 26(d) provides that formal discovery (except depositions of witnesses about to leave the country; *see supra,* §1290) must be deferred until after the parties meet and confer on a discovery plan pursuant to Rule 26(f).

(a) Defendant's head start

Where the moratorium does not apply, as in state court, defendants usually are protected against initiation of formal discovery by the plaintiff until a certain time after service of the complaint [*e.g.,* Cal. Code Civ. Proc. §2025(b)(2)—20-day period for noticing depositions]

(3) Simultaneous proceedings [§1312]

All parties may take depositions simultaneously unless the court otherwise directs. [Fed. R. Civ. P. 26(d)] Hence, neither side is entitled to discovery "priority" before the other side can commence discovery.

b. Optional to parties [§1313]

Depositions are optional. Each party has the right to take the deposition of *any* witness—without a showing of good cause—but is not required to do so. A party is also entitled to interview any willing nonparty witness without court supervision. [**Corley v. Rosewood Care Center, Inc.,** 142 F.3d 1041 (7th Cir. 1998)]

c. Numerical cap on depositions [§1314]

To curb abuse, Rule 30 imposes a *10-deposition limit.* [Fed. R. Civ. P. 30(a)(2)(A)]

(1) Limit per "side" [§1315]

The 10-deposition limit is not per party, but rather is calculated cumulatively for plaintiffs, defendants, and third-party defendants.

(2) One deposition per witness [§1316]

In addition, the rules provide that a given witness's deposition may be taken only once. [Fed. R. Civ. P. 30(a)(2)(B)]

(3) Change by stipulation or order [§1317]

The parties may stipulate in writing to vary the deposition limitation, and the court may so order.

d. Durational limit on depositions [§1318]

The 2000 amendments added a durational limitation on depositions in response to concerns that some depositions were too long. Depositions are limited to one, seven-hour day. [Fed. R. Civ. P. 30(d)(2)]

e. Compulsory appearance of witness

(1) Issuance of subpoena [§1319]

At the request of a party, the court clerk will issue a subpoena commanding the named witness to appear and give testimony at the designated time and place. An attorney admitted to practice before the court may also issue a subpoena. [Fed. R. Civ. P. 45(a)]

(2) Service of subpoena [§1320]

A subpoena is served on the witness personally and must be accompanied by a tender of the fee for one day's attendance, plus reimbursement for mileage. [Fed. R. Civ. P. 45(b)(1)]

(3) Place of deposition [§1321]

A witness may be required to appear at a deposition at any place within 100 miles of the place where he resides, is employed, or transacts business. [Fed. R. Civ. P. 45(c)(3)(A)(ii); *compare* Cal. Civ. Proc. Code §2025(e)(1)—75 miles]

(4) Subpoena not necessary for party-witness [§1322]

It is not necessary to serve a subpoena on an *adverse party*, or an officer or managing agent of a party, in order to compel attendance. [Fed. R. Civ. P. 37(d); Cal. Civ. Proc. Code §2025(h)(1)] A deposition of a party-witness may be scheduled at any reasonable place.

(5) Deposition of corporation or organization [§1323]

Where a corporation (or an association or governmental body) is to be deposed, the party taking the deposition need not identify the individual who is compelled to give the deposition. She need state only the *matters* on which she proposes to examine the organization, and the organization must then designate the appropriate witness. [Fed. R. Civ. P. 30(b)(6)] The adversary need not guess which employee is in possession of the required information; and the organization itself is bound by its deponent's answers.

(a) Scope of inquiry [§1324]

Problems can arise where the party doing discovery inquires into matters relevant to the suit but beyond the expertise of the witness. If the witness has some knowledge of the matters, she may have to answer and the organization may be bound by her testimony.

> **Example:** Where defendant manufacturer designated a doctor as its witness in a products liability action, the doctor could be required to answer questions about company policy as well as technical matters on which he had expertise. [**Lapenna v. Upjohn Co.,** 110 F.R.D. 15 (E.D. Pa. 1986)]

f. Notice to parties

(1) Form of notice [§1325]

A party wishing to depose a witness must give written notice to every other *party*, identifying the deponent and the time and place of the deposition. [Fed. R. Civ. P. 30(b); Cal. Civ. Proc. Code §2025(c), (d)]

(2) Time for notice [§1326]

In federal proceedings, notice must be given a "reasonable" length of time in advance of the scheduled date for the deposition. [Fed. R. Civ. P. 30(b)] Some state codes are more explicit in regard to the time period. [*See, e.g.*, Cal. Civ. Proc. Code §2025(f)—10 days]

g. Production of documents [§1327]

The subpoena (when necessary) or the notice may direct the witness to bring along and produce at the deposition any documents that could properly be sought by a request for production of documents (*see infra*, §§1384-1402). [Fed. R. Civ. P. 30(b)(5); Cal. Civ. Proc. Code §2025(d)(4)]

(1) Effect on timing [§1328]

Where the witness is to produce documents at the deposition, more notice is required. [Fed. R. Civ. P. 30(b)(5)—time required for Rule 34 document production: 30 days; Cal. Civ. Proc. Code §2025(f)—20 days]

h. Questioning of deponent

(1) Oral [§1329]

Ordinarily, the examination of deponents is conducted orally, with the examining party questioning first, and the others in turn.

(a) Examination by witness's attorney [§1330]

Usually the attorney for the witness will not question the witness except to clear up important matters left uncertain by other interrogation. *Rationale:* The witness's lawyer does not wish to assist the other parties by making the content of the witness's testimony at trial more evident to them than their own questions have made it.

(2) Depositions in writing [§1331]

The examining party may choose to conduct the examination in writing. If so, the questions are submitted in writing; the adversary may review the questions in advance and submit cross-questions to be answered at the same time; and the cross-questions may be followed by re-direct and re-cross-questions. Even though the questions are written, the answers of the deponent are given orally. [Fed. R. Civ. P. 31; Cal. Civ. Proc. Code §2028]

(a) Practicality [§1332]

This form of deposition may be more economical because it does not require the attendance of lawyers at the place of the deposition. On the other hand, it does not give the examiner an opportunity to follow up answers effectively, and hence is not used where the witness may be evasive or where the subject under examination is complex.

(3) Depositions by telephone [§1333]

In federal practice, the deposition may be taken by telephone upon leave of court or if both parties so stipulate in writing. [Fed. R. Civ. P. 30(b)(7)]

(4) Objections to questions [§1334]

The lawyer for the witness may object to a question and instruct the witness not to answer.

(a) Limitation on instructions [§1335]

In federal court, a witness may be instructed not to answer a question only to *preserve a privilege* (*see infra,* §§1443-1478), to *enforce a limitation on evidence imposed by the court* in the case, or to *present a motion for a protective order.* [Fed. R. Civ. P. 30(d)(1)] Furthermore, some federal courts have imposed stricter restraints on the behavior of the lawyer for the witness. [*See, e.g.,* **Hall v. Clifton Precision**, 150 F.R.D. 525 (E.D. Pa. 1993)—deponent's attorney forbidden to talk to deponent between commencement and completion of deposition, except to decide whether to assert a privilege]

(b) Motion to compel [§1336]

When a witness is instructed not to answer, the examining party may move for an order of the court *compelling* an answer. [Fed. R. Civ. P. 37(a); Cal. Civ. Proc. Code §2025(o)]

(c) Failure to obey order [§1337]

If the witness disobeys an order to answer, the witness may be held in *contempt*; and a party-witness may be subject to other sanctions as well. [Fed. R. Civ. P. 37(b); Cal. Civ. Proc. Code §2025(o)]

(d) Protective order for witness [§1338]

On the other hand, if questioning is conducted in an unreasonably oppressive manner, the witness may move for a protective order *limiting or terminating* the examination. [Fed. R. Civ. P. 30(d)(3)]

(e) No waiver [§1339]

Failure of the witness to object to a question on deposition does *not* constitute a waiver of her right to object to the same question or answer at trial. [Fed. R. Civ. P. 32(b)]

1) Exception—matters of form [§1340]

Errors in the taking of a deposition that *might be cured if promptly presented* but which were not, *may not be raised as grounds for exclusion* of the deposition evidence at trial. This includes objections to the form of questions or answers or in the manner of taking of the deposition. [Fed. R. Civ. P. 32(d)(3)]

DEPOSITIONS — **gilbert**

A SUMMARY UNDER THE FEDERAL RULES:

WHO	A party may depose *any witness* once, but each side is *limited to 10* depositions; parties must attend on reasonable notice while nonparties must be subpoenaed to compel their attendance.
WHAT	Usually a deposition involves *oral* questioning of the witness, but a deposition may be in writing or, upon the parties' stipulation or leave of court, by phone. The notice or subpoena may also direct the witness to produce documents.
WHERE	The deposition must be within 100 miles of where the witness resides, is employed, or transacts business.
PENALTIES	If a party refuses to answer, the examining party may make a motion to compel. Further refusal can result in contempt or other sanctions.

---

i. Transcription of deposition

(1) Review of transcript [§1341]

If requested before completion of the deposition, a deponent is entitled to review the transcript of her testimony and make corrections in it, subject to the right of the examining party to comment on the changes if the deposition is used at trial. [Fed. R. Civ. P. 30(e)]

(2) Videotape [§1342]

In federal practice, a deposition may be recorded by "other than stenographic means" if the party noticing the deposition so chooses. [Fed. R. Civ. P. 30(b)(2)] Some states also permit a videotape deposition. [Cal. Civ. Proc. Code §2025(p)]

j. Use of deposition testimony at trial

(1) Generally inadmissible [§1343]

Statements in depositions are *hearsay* and thus are generally inadmissible at trial to prove the truth of matters asserted by deponents.

(2) Exceptions [§1344]

In the following circumstances, however, statements made in depositions may be admissible:

(a) Party admissions [§1345]

Deposition statements by party-witnesses are admissible against those parties. [Fed. R. Civ. P. 32(a)(2); Cal. Civ. Proc. Code §2025(u)(2)]

(b) Impeachment [§1346]

A deposition by a nonparty witness that contradicts testimony given at trial may be admitted for the purpose of impeaching the witness who has changed her story. [Fed. R. Civ. P. 32(a)(1); Cal. Civ. Proc. Code §2025(u)(1)]

(c) Unavailability of deponent [§1347]

If the deponent is dead, infirm, or beyond the reach of subpoena process at the time of trial, the deposition may be used in lieu of her live testimony. [Fed. R. Civ. P. 32(a)(3); Cal. Civ. Proc. Code §2025(u)(3)(B)]

1) Note

This rule also applies to the deposition of a party seeking to use his own deposition instead of testifying at trial, *unless* that party is responsible for his own absence. [**Richmond v. Brooks,** 227 F.2d 490 (2d Cir. 1955)]

(3) Objectionable evidence in deposition [§1348]

A party may object to the admission of deposition testimony on any ground that would be available if the witness were testifying in person. This is true even if the objection was not raised at the time the deposition was taken, except as to matters of form. [Fed. R. Civ. P. 32(b), (d)]

3. Interrogatories [§1349]

Interrogatories are written questions from one party to another party requiring written responses. [Fed. R. Civ. P. 33(a); Cal. Civ. Proc. Code §2030]

a. Distinguish—depositions [§1350]

Be sure to distinguish interrogatories from depositions.

(1) *Depositions* can be taken from a party *or* nonparty witness, while interrogatories may be addressed *only to a party* to the action.

(2) *Deposition* questions may be oral or written, but the answers are ***always*** given ***orally*** before a court reporter or similar official who transcribes what is said. In contrast, answers to written interrogatories are prepared in ***writing***, usually by counsel for the answering party.

(3) *A deponent* may limit her answers to matters of which she has ***personal knowledge.*** Interrogatories require the party to answer not only of her own knowledge, but ***also*** on the basis of information to which she has reasonable access.

b. Who must answer

(1) Any other party [§1351]
A nonparty witness is not subject to interrogatories.

(2) Co-parties [§1352]
Co-parties generally are obliged to respond to interrogatories (although a few states adhere to an older rule that interrogatories may be served only upon an "adverse" party).

(3) Corporate parties [§1353]
Interrogatories served on a corporation may be answered by any officer or agent designated by the corporation. [Fed. R. Civ. P. 33(a)]

c. When served

(1) Federal practice [§1354]
In federal practice, interrogatories, like other formal discovery, may be served only after the Rule 26(f) conference on a discovery plan. [Fed. R. Civ. P. 26(d)]

(2) State practice [§1355]
Some state rules require the plaintiff to delay service of interrogatories for a fixed period following service of the complaint. [*See, e.g.,* Cal. Civ. Proc. Code §2030(b)—10 days]

d. Numerical limit [§1356]
In federal practice parties are limited to 25 interrogatories, including subparts. [Fed. R. Civ. P. 33(a)] This limitation applies to each *party*, so that co-parties (such as co-plaintiffs) may *each* use 25 interrogatories even though represented by the same lawyer. The limit may be varied by stipulation or court order. Some states have similar numerical limitations. [*See, e.g.,* Cal. Civ. Proc. Code §2030(c)—35 interrogatories]

e. Duty to respond

(1) Time for response [§1357]

A party must answer or object to interrogatories within 30 days after their date of service. [Fed. R. Civ. P. 33(b)(3); Cal. Civ. Proc. Code §2030(h)]

(2) Duty to investigate [§1358]

A party to whom interrogatories are propounded must give all information responsive to the questions that is under her control. This generally includes all information that might be discovered in her own files or by further questioning of her agents or employees.

(3) Option where extensive search required [§1359]

If an answer can be supplied only by extensive search of the responding party's records and the burden of ascertaining the information is substantially the same for the inquiring and responding parties, the responding party may specify the pertinent records and allow the inquiring party to examine and copy them. [Fed. R. Civ. P. 33(d); *and see* Cal. Civ. Proc. Code §2030(f)(2)]

f. Failure to make adequate response to interrogatories

(1) Motion to compel response [§1360]

If an answer to interrogatories is incomplete or evasive, on motion the court will order the responding party to answer fully. [Fed. R. Civ. P. 37(a); Cal. Civ. Proc. Code §2030(l)] If the responding party defies the order, she is subject to sanctions. [Fed. R. Civ. P. 37(b)(2)]

(2) Time for motion [§1361]

In federal proceedings, a motion to compel an answer may be made at any time. Under state rules, the motion may have to be made promptly after receipt of the unsatisfactory answer or the matter will be deemed waived. [*See, e.g.,* Cal. Civ. Proc. Code §2030(l)—45 days after response served]

(3) Objections to interrogatories [§1362]

A motion to compel an answer to an interrogatory will be denied if the question propounded is subject to a valid and timely objection.

(4) Costs of proceedings [§1363]

A party moving to compel an answer without substantial justification therefor, or a party making an objection that lacks substantiality, is subject to an award to the adversary of costs, including attorneys' fees incurred in the discovery dispute. [Fed. R. Civ. P. 37(a)(2)]

INTERROGATORIES **gilbert**

A SUMMARY UNDER THE FEDERAL RULES:

WHO	Interrogatories may be served *only* on other *parties*; each party may be served with up to 25 interrogatories from each other party.
WHAT	Interrogatories are *written* questions from one party to another requiring written responses.
WHEN	Interrogatories may be served only after the Rule 26(f) meeting of counsel; responses are due within 30 days after the interrogatories are served.
PENALTIES	If a party refuses to answer an interrogatory or gives an incomplete or evasive answer, on motion the court may order the party to respond; further refusal can result in contempt or other sanctions.

4.   Requests for Admission

a.   Device to eliminate issues [§1364]

A request for an admission imposes a duty on the party served to acknowledge the existence of facts that are not in doubt and that should not be necessary to prove at trial. [Fed. R. Civ. P. 36(a); Cal. Civ. Proc. Code §2033]

b.   On whom served [§1365]

A request for admission may be served by any party on any other *party*, whether or not adverse. [Fed. R. Civ. P. 36(a)]

c.   Subject of request

(1)   Facts or application of law to fact [§1366]

A request may ask the party served to admit the *genuineness* of a document, the truth of factual allegations, or the applicability of legal concepts to specified facts in issue.

(2)   Conclusions of law [§1367]

A party may request another party to make an admission about the circumstances underlying the case that includes a legal conclusion, *e.g.*, that a person was acting as an agent, or that the speed limit at a point of impact was 50 miles per hour.

(a)   But note

It is *not* proper to request an admission to an abstract statement of law (*e.g.*, that speeding constitutes negligence). [Fed. R. Civ. P. 36(a)]

(3) Ultimate issues [§1368]

Under the Federal Rules, a party may be requested to admit an ultimate fact—*i.e.,* one that controls the outcome of the controversy (such as causation). [Fed. R. Civ. P. 36(a)] Not all states adhere to this rule, however.

(4) Opinions [§1369]

A party may also request another party to make an admission regarding a matter of opinion (such as the value of property or the extent of damages). A request is not improper merely because the matter to be admitted is in controversy or in doubt.

(5) Matters unknown to responding party [§1370]

A party may also be requested to admit a fact that is outside his knowledge.

d. Time limits

(1) For serving requests [§1371]

Under the Federal Rules, a request to admit may be served at any time after the Rule 26(f) conference. [Fed. R. Civ. P. 26(d), 36(a)] In some states, leave of court is required if the plaintiff wishes to serve requests within 10 days after service of process. [Cal. Civ. Proc. Code §2033(b)]

(2) For responses [§1372]

The party upon whom a request is served must file a response within 30 days. [Fed. R. Civ. P. 36(a); Cal. Civ. Proc. Code §2033(h)]

e. Appropriate responses

(1) Admit [§1373]

The responding party may choose to make the requested admission; and if he does so, he will not be permitted to controvert the admission at trial. But the admission is binding only in the present action; it may not be used against the party in any other proceeding. [Fed. R. Civ. P. 36(b)]

(2) Deny [§1374]

If the responding party chooses to deny the matter that he is asked to admit, and the matter is subsequently proved, the party may be liable for the full costs of proving that matter, unless the court finds that there were "good reasons" for the denial or that the admissions sought were of "no substantial importance." [Fed. R. Civ. P. 37(c)(2); Cal. Civ. Proc. Code §2033(o)]

(a) Impact [§1375]

The matter of an award of costs is generally within the court's *discretion*. The court's power to impose sanctions is *not* affected by which party ultimately wins the lawsuit. Even the winner may end up having to pay sanctions to the loser if the winner was guilty of a "bad faith" refusal to admit (necessitating extra expenses of proof by the loser). [**Smith v. Circle P Ranch Co.**, 87 Cal. App. 3d 267 (1978)]

(b) Equivocal denial [§1376]

An equivocal denial (*e.g.*, "defendant is not presently certain . . ." or "plaintiff reserves the right to contest this assertion") may be treated as an admission or, on motion, the court may order a proper response. Alternatively, the court might treat an equivocal denial as a "false denial" (above) and award the full costs of proof to the requesting party.

(3) Reasons for not admitting or denying [§1377]

If the responding party has good reasons for objecting to the request, she may decline to admit or deny, and instead must state her refusal and the grounds therefor. However, there are few valid objections to be made.

(a) Nature of matter sought to be admitted [§1378]

That the matter is one of opinion, or an ultimate issue, or a conclusion of law is *not* an adequate reason for refusing to admit or deny.

(b) Ignorance of matter sought to be admitted [§1379]

However, it is sufficient for a refusal to admit that the responding party is ignorant of the matter in question, *provided she has made reasonable inquiry* and still found the information unavailable.

EXAM TIP — **gilbert**

There are a few quirks to requests for admissions that could be tested on an exam. Be sure to remember that an admission establishes the fact *only for the current litigation*; it cannot be used in other proceedings. Also remember that a party can be *assessed costs* if the other party proves the denied matter, even if the proving party loses the case. Finally, remember that *for good cause* (*e.g.*, ignorance of the matter, to protect the right against self-incrimination, etc.) a party can decline to admit or deny.

(c) Self-incrimination [§1380]

A party can refuse to answer on the ground that her response may tend to incriminate herself.

(d) Consequences of giving insufficient reasons [§1381]

The party seeking the admission may move to determine the sufficiency of any objections to his request. If the reasons are insufficient, the court may order a proper response and may impose other sanctions on the party making the inadequate response. Even if no such motion is made, the party making the request may prove the matter, in which event the court can order the objecting party to pay the full costs of proof.

(4) Failure to respond [§1382]
If there is no timely response to a request, the matter is deemed *admitted*. [Fed. R. Civ. P. 36; Cal. Civ. Proc. Code §2033]

f. Withdrawal of admissions [§1383]
If presentation of the merits will be served, the court may allow a party to amend or withdraw an admission previously made. [Fed. R. Civ. P. 36(b); Cal. Civ. Proc. Code §2033(m)]

REQUESTS FOR ADMISSIONS	gilbert
A SUMMARY UNDER THE FEDERAL RULES:	
WHO	A request for admission may be served by a party on *any other party*.
WHAT	A request for admission asks the party to acknowledge the existence of facts that are not in dispute; the request may even go to an "ultimate fact" (*i.e.,* a fact controlling the outcome of the litigation) or a party's opinion about the application of law to fact.
WHEN	A request for admission may be served any time after the Rule 26(f) meeting of counsel; responses must be made within 30 days.
PENALTIES	If a party fails to respond to a request for admission, the matter will be *deemed admitted*. If the party denies the matter and the matter is subsequently proved, the court may order the denying party to pay the proving party's costs unless there was good reason for the denial or the admissions were of no substantial importance.

5. Requests for Inspection of Documents and Other Things

a. Materials discoverable [§1384]
A party is entitled to inspect and copy a variety of items in the possession of any other party, including documents, photographs, maps, records (however kept), and correspondence.

(1) Computerized information [§1385]
Included among the things that are properly subject to inspection is information stored on computers. [Fed. R. Civ. P. 34(a)—"data compilations from which information can be obtained"] To assist in this, discovery about the computer system of a party is usually permitted

[**Fautek v. Mongomery Ward & Co.**, 96 F.R.D. 141 (N.D. Ill. 1982)], and a party may be required to supply data in computer-readable form [**National Union Electric Corp. v. Matsushita Electric Industrial Co.**, 494 F. Supp. 1257 (E.D. Pa. 1980)].

EXAM TIP	gilbert

Discovery of e-mail and other computerized information has assumed great importance in litigation recently and might show up on exam questions. Searching for all e-mail messages on a given subject can impose an *immense burden* and also raise *confidentiality concerns* about the expectations of privacy that attend the use of e-mail. Requests for discovery of all interim drafts of documents created on word processing systems can also raise burden and confidentiality issues. Thus, if you encounter a question seeking discovery of computerized information, be prepared to look for facts relating to those issues.

---

b. Scope of examination [§1386]

Examination may include testing and sampling of materials, and may involve an entry onto the property of a party. With computerized material, this may sometimes involve access to an opposing party's computer system.

c. Making request for inspection

(1) No court action required [§1387]

The party seeking discovery may serve a request for inspection without prior court order or a showing of good cause.

(a) Inspection of premises [§1388]

When *inspection of premises* is sought, a general showing of "relevancy" may not be enough. Since entry upon one's premises may entail greater burdens and risks than mere production of documents or other physical evidence, some degree of *necessity* is generally required for such inspection. [**Belcher v. Bassett Furniture**, 588 F.2d 904 (4th Cir. 1978)]

(2) Timing [§1389]

Under the Federal Rules, a request for inspection may be served at any time after the Rule 26(f) conference. [Fed. R. Civ. P. 26(d), 34] Some state rules require leave of court if the request is served concurrently with the initial pleadings. [*See, e.g.,* Cal. Civ. Proc. Code §2031(b)—leave of court required if request served by plaintiff within 10 days after service of summons]

d. Designation of items [§1390]

The moving party must describe the items to be produced with sufficient certainty to enable a person of ordinary intelligence to know which items are sought. Other forms of discovery are sometimes needed to identify the real evidence to be inspected.

(1) Designation by category [§1391]

Often a party will request all materials that fall within a category (*e.g.,* "all documents that relate or refer to the meeting on January 1, 2000") rather than specifying individual items. This is done because the party requesting production cannot know for certain what materials the responding party possesses and wishes to avoid omitting valuable information.

(2) Relation to initial disclosures [§1392]

The initial disclosures pursuant to Rule 26(a)(1)(B) (*see supra,* §1298) may enable the requesting party to be more specific in the document request.

e. Timing of inspection [§1393]

The request for inspection must specify the proposed time, place, and manner of making the inspection. [Fed. R. Civ. P. 34(b); Cal. Civ. Proc. Code §2031(c)(2)]

f. Objection to requests

(1) Timing [§1394]

In federal actions, the party receiving a request for inspection may file written objections within 30 days following service of the request. [Fed. R. Civ. P. 34(b); *compare* Cal. Civ. Proc. Code §2031(h)—20 days]

(2) Motion with respect to objections [§1395]

If objections are made, the requesting party may move for an order compelling the requested inspection; and the merits of the objections will then be determined by the court.

g. Items in responding party's control [§1396]

The responding party is to produce all requested items (unless objections are interposed) that are within its possession, custody, or control. Some courts hold that the "control" idea requires the responding party to make efforts to obtain documents from others if it has "influence" over the possessor. [*See, e.g.,* **Cooper Industries, Inc. v. British Aerospace, Inc.,** 102 F.R.D. 918 (S.D.N.Y. 1984)]

h. Organization of produced materials [§1397]

In federal court and in some state courts, the responding party is required to produce the requested materials either as they are kept in the ordinary course of business or organized and labeled to correspond to the requests. [Fed. R. Civ. P. 34(b); Cal. Civ. Proc. Code §2031(f)(1)]

(1) Stimulus for requirement [§1398]

This requirement was included to prevent responding parties from "hiding" embarrassing materials among mounds of uninteresting materials (*e.g.*, placing an inculpatory memorandum among thousands of invoices instead of leaving it in the memorandum file where it is normally kept).

(a) Ethical requirements

"Hiding" relevant material as described above is probably a violation of a lawyer's ethical responsibilities, even if it were permitted by the discovery rules. (*See* Legal Ethics Summary.)

(2) Course of business format usually employed [§1399]

Most responding parties will produce records in the way they are kept in the normal course of business. They do this because it is usually difficult to determine exactly which request is the pertinent one for given materials, and several requests may apply to a given item. Therefore, not only would reorganizing the files be a great deal of difficult work, it would often assist the opposing party.

i. Failure to respond [§1400]

Failure to respond to a request for inspection exposes the nonresponding party to sanctions, including the striking of portions of pleadings and a determination of facts on the assumption that inspection would have provided the requesting party with persuasive evidence.

j. Materials in possession of nonparties

(1) Subpoena for inspection [§1401]

Under federal practice, a subpoena can order a nonparty to permit inspection and copying of documents in its control, or to permit inspection of premises. [Fed. R. Civ. P. 45(a)(1)(C)] Some states have similar provisions. [*See, e.g.,* N.Y. Civ. Prac. Law §3120]

(a) But note

Other states require a ***showing of good cause*** in an affidavit (usually a showing of ***relevance*** to the claims or defenses raised in the action) as a condition to issuance of a subpoena. [Cal. Civ. Proc. Code §1985(b)]

(2) Independent action [§1402]

Alternatively, real evidence not otherwise discoverable may be examined through an adequate suit in equity for discovery in aid of the original action.

REQUESTS FOR DOCUMENT INSPECTION   gilbert

A SUMMARY UNDER THE FEDERAL RULES:

WHO	A party may request that another *party* allow him to inspect documents and other things in control of the other party. The request may designate the material sought by category rather than by individual item. Similar inspection may be sought from *nonparties* through subpoena.
WHAT	Inspection can be of documents, photographs, maps, records, correspondence. To facilitate inspection of computer files, a responding party may be required to provide data in a computer readable format or to disclose details about its computer system. A party may also seek inspection of another party's, or (with subpoena) a nonparty's, premises.
WHEN	A request for inspection can be made any time after the Rule 26(f) meeting of counsel.
HOW	The responding party is required to produce the requested materials: (i) as they are kept in the ordinary course of business, or (ii) organized and labeled to correspond to the requests.
PENALTIES	If a party fails to allow inspection, he is subject to sanctions, including striking portions of his pleadings relating to the items for which inspection was prohibited.

---

6. Medical Examinations

a. Court action required [§1403]

If the physical or mental condition of a party is in issue, in *federal court* a motion is necessary to require a party to submit to examination by experts in the service of other parties.

(1) Distinguish—state practice

In some states, prior court action is not required for the defendant to obtain a physical examination of the plaintiff in a personal injury suit. [Cal. Civ. Proc. Code §2032(c)]

b. Condition must be in issue [§1404]

The condition that is the subject of the examination must be raised directly by the pleadings or by the factual contentions of the parties through discovery; and the court-ordered examination must be limited to such conditions. [**Schlagenhauf v. Holder,** 379 U.S. 104 (1964)]

c. Good cause [§1405]

If court action is required, an examination will not be ordered except upon a showing of good cause. [Fed. R. Civ. P. 35; Cal. Civ. Proc. §2032(d)] In this context, "good cause" means that the examination sought must be shown to be reasonably likely to produce information about the condition in issue.

d. Only parties subject to examination [§1406]

Court rules generally provide for the examination only of parties or persons in the custody or control of parties. [Fed. R. Civ. P. 35(a)] Some states also provide for the examination of agents of parties. [*See, e.g.,* Cal. Civ. Proc. Code §2032(a)(2)]

e. Qualifications of examiner [§1407]

Historically, court-ordered examinations were done only by medical doctors. In federal court, however, examinations may be ordered by any "*suitably licensed or certified examiner.*" [Fed. R. Civ. P. 35(a); *and see* Cal. Civ. Proc. Code §2032(b)—"licensed physician or other appropriate licensed health care professional"]

(1) Selected by party [§1408]

Ordinarily the courts will order examination by the examiner selected by the party wanting the examination, but if reasonable objection is made to the moving party's selection, the court has the power to appoint an "impartial examiner" of its own choosing.

f. Place of examination [§1409]

The examination ordinarily will be ordered at the place selected by the examining party; but the court can have the examination conducted elsewhere to diminish the burden on the examinee.

g. Types of procedure [§1410]

If the information sought to be obtained is important, the court may permit an examination procedure that is novel or even uncomfortable, as long as it is reasonably safe.

h. Presence of council or other observer [§1411]

Federal and state courts follow widely different approaches when it comes to allowing the presence of counsel or an observer at a physical or mental examination. A majority of federal courts do not permit the presence of the examinee's counsel, a third party, or an unattended videotape machine at a physical or mental examination, absent some compelling circumstance. [*See, e.g.,* **Holland v. United States,** 182 F.R.D. 493 (D.S.C. 1998)] Other courts, however, have found a right to the presence of an observer, and still others decide on a case-by-case basis. [*See* **Galieti v. State Farm Mutual Automobile Insurance Co.,** 154 F.R.D. 262 (D. Colo. 1994)]

i. Copies of reports

(1) Examinee's right to receive copy [§1412]

Upon request, the examinee has the right to receive a copy of the examiner's report. [Fed. R. Civ. P. 35(b); Cal. Civ. Proc. Code §2032(h)]

(2) Waiver of privilege [§1413]

However, an examinee who requests a copy of the report *waives* the doctor-patient privilege with respect to any previous examinations of the same condition by his own physician [Fed. R. Civ. P. 35(b); Cal. Civ. Proc. Code §2032(i)]; any reports of such other examinations must be provided on request to the examining party. Note that even absent such a request, a plaintiff in a personal injury case waives the privilege in regard to medical examinations of the injury for which recovery is sought.

MEDICAL EXAMINATIONS   **gilbert**

A SUMMARY UNDER THE FEDERAL RULES:

WHO	A party may seek a medical examination only of another *party* and *only if:* (i) the condition that is the subject of the examination is in issue, and (ii) the court determines that there is good cause for the exam.
WHAT	The examination can be of physical or mental condition, and can be done by any suitably licensed or certified examiner selected by the party requesting the exam and approved by the court.
WHERE	The examination is usually held at the place selected by the examining party.
HOW	The court may authorize an examination that is novel or even uncomfortable as long as it is reasonably safe.
PENALTIES	A party who refuses an examination may *not* be held in contempt, but facts that could be proved by the examination can be deemed established by the refusal.

---

7. Duty to Supplement Responses

a. Federal practice—broad duty to supplement [§1414]

Rule 26(e) requires supplementation of prior responses if *in some material respect* Rule 26(a) disclosures or discovery responses are *incomplete or incorrect* or if there is *additional or corrective information* that has been acquired since the response was made.

(1) Inapplicable if information otherwise made known [§1415]

The obligation to supplement is satisfied if the additional or corrective information has otherwise been made known during the discovery process or if it is supplied in writing.

(2) Application to deposition testimony [§1416]

The supplementation requirement ordinarily *does not apply to deposition answers*, but it *is* applicable to *testimony of an expert witness*.

b. State practice compared [§1417]

Some states have supplementation requirements similar to those in the Federal Rules, but many do not; in such states, cautious practitioners must attempt to obtain the same information by sending out *supplemental interrogatories* before the trial. Still other states use different procedures for the same purpose.

(1) Pretrial conference orders [§1418]

If a pretrial conference is held, the court (on a showing of good cause) may require either side to update its responses to earlier interrogatories, particularly in connection with disclosing expert witnesses who will be called to testify at trial. A party failing to disclose an expert at this point may be barred from using that person as a witness at trial, except on such terms as the court finds appropriate. [**Sanders v. Superior Court,** 34 Cal. App. 3d 270 (1973); **Crumpton v. Dickstein,** 82 Cal. App. 3d 166 (1978)]

(2) Demand to exchange lists of expert witnesses [§1419]

California has a separate procedure whereby, at the time a case is set for trial, either side may serve the other with a demand to exchange information on the identity, qualifications, and expected testimony of expert witnesses. Failure to disclose the information demanded bars the use of such experts at trial, except for purposes of impeachment or on terms as the court may order. [Cal. Civ. Proc. Code §2034]

C. Scope of Discovery

1. Relation of Discovery to Proof [§1420]

Generally, discovery may inquire into all information not otherwise privileged that is *relevant* to the claim or defense of a party, whether or not the material would be admissible as proof. It is sufficient if the information sought appears reasonably calculated to lead to the discovery of admissible evidence. [Fed. R. Civ. P. 26(b)(1); Cal. Civ. Proc. Code §2017(a)] However, a few jurisdictions retain the old equity practice, under which discovery is limited to *admissible* evidence needed by the discovering party to bear his burden of proof. Moreover, the federal courts have become increasingly uneasy with broad discovery and have moved to limit it.

a. Scope of discovery in federal court [§1421]

In 2000, the Supreme Court promulgated an amendment to Rule 26(b)(1), defining the scope of discovery. Under the amendment, party-controlled discovery is available only with regard to matter *"relevant to the claim or defense of any party."*

(1) Uncertain dividing line [§1422]

Before the 2000 amendment, Rule 26(b)(1) allowed discovery of material relevant to the subject matter of the litigation. The Committee Note accompanying the amendment recognizes that the dividing line between material relevant to the subject matter of the litigation and that relevant to the claims or defenses "cannot be defined with precision." But the Note explains that the change is intended to signify to parties that they are not entitled to use discovery to "develop new claims or defenses that are not already identified in the pleadings." [Fed. R. Civ. P. 26(b)(1) Committee Note]

(2) Court may expand [§1423]

Note that under the amended rule, the court is authorized to expand discovery to any information relevant to the subject matter of the action if good cause is shown.

(3) Case-by-case determination [§1424]

A determination of whether information is "relevant to the claim or defense of any party," depends on the facts of each case, and types of information that are not directly pertinent to the incident in suit could be relevant to the claims or defenses.

Example: Other incidents of the same type, or involving the same product, could be properly discoverable under the revised standard. [Fed. R. Civ. P. 26(b)(1) Committee Note]

Example: Information about organizational arrangements or filing systems of a party could be discoverable if likely to yield or lead to the discovery of admissible information. [Fed. R. Civ. P. 26(b)(1) Committee Note]

Example: Information that could be used to impeach a likely witness, although not otherwise relevant to the claims or defenses, might be properly discoverable. [Fed. R. Civ. P. 26(b)(1) Committee Note]

EXAM TIP   **gilbert**

Keep in mind that the standard for discovery changed in 2000, so older cases in your casebook might not use the current standard. Formerly, material was discoverable if it was relevant to the subject matter of the action. The new standard is subtly narrower: To be discoverable, the matter must be *relevant to a claim or defense*.

---

b. Judicial limitation of disproportionate discovery [§1425]

In federal court, the court *must* limit discovery if it finds one of the following circumstances to exist [Fed. R. Civ. P. 26(b)(2)]:

(1) Discovery unreasonably cumulative [§1426]

If the discovery is unreasonably cumulative or duplicative, or if it is obtainable from some other source that is more convenient, less burdensome, or less expensive, the court may limit or forbid the discovery.

(2) Party has already had opportunity for discovery [§1427]

If the party seeking discovery has already had ample opportunity in the action to obtain discovery of the information sought, the court may limit or forbid the discovery.

(3) Discovery unduly burdensome [§1428]

If the discovery is unduly burdensome or expensive in view of the needs of the case, the amount in controversy, the limitations on the parties' resources, and the importance of the issues at stake in litigation, the court may limit or forbid the discovery. *Criticism:* This authority appears to permit the judge to truncate discovery in cases she does not think are "important." This is probably not what the drafters of the rule's changes had in mind.

2. Scope of Relevant Material

a. Meaning of relevance [§1429]

Information will be deemed relevant (and therefore may be discoverable) if the information tends to prove or disprove a given proposition. In federal court, "relevant evidence means evidence having any tendency to make the existence of any fact that is of consequence to the determination of the action more probable or less probable than it would be without the evidence." [Fed. R. Evid. 401; for more detail, *see* Evidence Summary]

(1) Fact of consequence [§1430]

The concept of a "fact of consequence" includes all matters that are pertinent to the decision of the case. This would include all issues raised by the pleadings.

(2) Low threshold for relevance [§1431]

The federal standard creates a very low threshold for relevance.

(3) Common sense determination [§1432]

The determination of whether evidence is relevant depends on a common sense examination of the probative impact of the information in question on the issue it is said to bear upon.

(4) Distinguish—substantial evidence [§1433]

A party with the burden of proof on an issue has the obligation on that issue to produce substantial evidence to justify submitting the issue to the trier of fact. (*See infra*, §1862, regarding burden to produce evidence.) The fact that such a party has some relevant evidence on the issue does not mean that she has satisfied the burden of production. Put differently, evidence may be relevant, but by itself insufficient to support a jury verdict on a given issue.

b. Relation to claims and defenses [§1434]

Although the 2000 amendments have narrowed the scope of discovery, it is clear that discovery may relate to the claims or defenses of either party and is not limited to information that the discovering party needs to satisfy his own burden of proof.

(1) Comment

This enables each party to evaluate his adversary's case as well as his own. This in turn may lead to earlier and more realistic settlement efforts—which is one of the main purposes of discovery.

c. Matters not in dispute [§1435]

Information may be subject to discovery even though it bears on issues that are not in dispute. Again, the test is relevancy to the claims and defenses rather than admissibility at trial. [Fed. R. Civ. P. 26(b)]

d. Information about witnesses [§1436]

The identity and location of witnesses are discoverable facts. Likewise, information bearing on the *credibility* of witnesses (*e.g.*, possible grounds for impeachment) may be discovered.

e. Insurance coverage [§1437]

Although not admissible as evidence, the existence and scope of insurance coverage is discoverable in most jurisdictions. [Fed. R. Civ. P. 26(a)(1)(D); **Laddon v. Superior Court**, 167 Cal. App. 2d 391 (1959)] *Rationale:* Settlement negotiations are an essential part of the action, and insurance coverage is relevant at least to this aspect of the claims.

f. Financial status [§1438]

Financial condition generally is not relevant even though the information might affect settlement negotiations.

(1) Defendant's financial status [§1439]

A general inquiry into the financial ability of the defendant to satisfy a judgment usually is not permitted. However, the defendant's financial condition may be pertinent in some cases, as where punitive damages are sought. In such cases, the defendant may be required to disclose her financial condition.

(2) Plaintiff's financial status [§1440]

If the plaintiff's loss of earnings is in question, he may be compelled to produce copies of his financial records, including federal income tax returns.

(3) Bank records [§1441]

If pertinent, bank records may be subject to subpoena, although the bank may be under a duty to notify its customer before complying, in order to give the customer an opportunity to resist disclosure. [**Valley Bank v. Superior Court,** 15 Cal. 3d 652 (1975)]

g. Contentions [§1442]

A party may be asked to particularize his contentions as to the facts (or the application of law to facts) for the purpose of narrowing the issues at trial. However, answers to such questions may be delayed by court order until pretrial, when the party can be expected to know with some precision what his contentions are.

3. Privilege [§1443]

Privileged material is universally excluded from obligatory disclosure through discovery. Most civil procedure courses do not examine any privilege in detail, except the *attorney-client privilege*, which will be the main focus here. It is the oldest and most frequently invoked privilege.

a. Reasons for the privilege [§1444]

The traditional rationale for the attorney-client privilege has been labeled the "*utilitarian rationale.*" It justifies the privilege on the ground that it is necessary to *promote full and frank disclosure* to the lawyer by the client. Unfortunately, there is little evidence that the existence of the privilege is necessary, or perhaps even important, to achieve that objective. Accordingly, some authorities have argued that the privilege is necessary to protect the *personal autonomy* of persons faced with legal proceedings, because it ensures that there is at least one knowledgeable person from whom they can seek help with the assurance that this person will not become a witness for the other side. (*See* Evidence Summary.)

b. Requirements [§1445]

The widely cited definition of the requirements for application of the attorney-client privilege comes from Dean John Wigmore [8 Wigmore on Evidence §2292]:

(1) Legal advice sought [§1446]

The privilege applies only to communications in which legal advice is sought. Thus, where the client is seeking *business advice*, no protection exists.

(2) From lawyer [§1447]

The privilege applies only to communications seeking legal advice from a professional legal adviser acting in that capacity. In most jurisdictions, it applies whenever the client reasonably believes that the person from whom he seeks advice is a lawyer, even if the belief turns out to be wrong.

(3) Communications relating to legal advice [§1448]

The privilege applies only to communications relating to obtaining legal advice; communications on entirely different subjects are not protected.

(4) Made in confidence [§1449]

The privilege applies only to communications made in confidence. In general, this means that the parties must behave as though they intend the communication to be confidential.

(a) Presence of other people [§1450]

The presence of other people during the communication may indicate that the communication is *not confidential*, unless the presence of these people is *necessary* to the communication. Thus, the lawyer's secretary might be present to assist the lawyer. Similarly, a friend or close relative might properly be present if the client is unusually young or old or otherwise in need of moral support or guidance.

(b) Eavesdroppers [§1451]

If the communication is overheard by an eavesdropper, the privilege usually is held not to preclude testimony by that eavesdropper, even if reasonable precautions were taken to protect confidentiality. However, if electronic surveillance was used by the eavesdropper, most courts will forbid use of the fruits of the eavesdropping.

(5) By client [§1452]

The traditional formulation of the privilege was that the privilege protected only information communicated to the lawyer by the client. There was no need to protect the information communicated to the client by the lawyer, it was thought, except to the extent that it revealed the content of communications to the lawyer by the client.

(a) Criticism

It was often difficult to distinguish communications by the lawyer that revealed client communications from others, and this limitation threatened to intrude into the relationship between the lawyer and the client.

(b) Modern view

The modern view is increasingly that *communications by the lawyer to the client* are protected also. [*See, e.g.,* **Upjohn Co. v. United States,** 449 U.S. 383 (1981)—privilege exists to protect "the giving of professional advice"]

(c) Corporate client

See infra, §§1463-1469, for discussion of the problem of the corporate client.

(d) Distinguish—communication by lawyer with others [§1453]

When the lawyer communicates with persons other than the client, such as witnesses, the privilege does not apply. [**Hickman v. Taylor,** 329 U.S. 495 (1947)—interviews with witnesses]

ATTORNEY-CLIENT PRIVILEGE CHECKLIST

THE ATTORNEY-CLIENT PRIVILEGE WILL APPLY ONLY IF THE FOLLOWING CONDITIONS ARE MET:

☑ The client must be *seeking legal advice*.

☑ The advice must be sought *from one whom the claimant reasonably believes is an attorney*.

☑ The communication for which privilege is being asserted must *relate to the legal advice sought*.

☑ The communication must have been *made in confidence*.

---

c. Permanently protected at client's request

(1) Need to invoke [§1454]

The privilege is not self-executing and applies only when invoked. Usually, however, the *lawyer is under a duty to invoke the privilege* on behalf of the client.

(2) Absolute protection [§1455]

The protection is absolute, in the sense that it cannot be outweighed by other considerations, such as the social interest in full disclosure of relevant evidence in the case.

(3) Applies to disclosure by client or lawyer [§1456]

Once invoked, the privilege precludes disclosure by the lawyer and the client (including employees of the client covered by the privilege; *see infra*, §1465, regarding corporate clients). Thus the privilege can preclude disclosure by a person who is willing to reveal privileged information.

d. Waiver [§1457]

Just as the client must invoke the privilege, so can the client waive it.

(1) Breadth of waiver [§1458]

In general, waiver of the privilege applies to *all communications* with counsel on the subject matter regarding which the waiver has occurred. *Rationale:* If the waiver did not apply to all related communications, the client could "pick and choose" the favorable pieces of information for revelation while keeping secret unfavorable pieces of information that are necessary to make the picture whole.

(2) No need for intentional waiver [§1459]

The act that constitutes a waiver need not be intentional, and in litigation unintentional disclosure of privileged material often works a waiver of the privilege.

(3) Application in other litigation [§1460]

Once the privilege is waived, it cannot be revived for other litigation.

e. Federal vs. state law

(1) Federal claim or defense [§1461]

In *federal court* the privileges available are to be determined by "principles of common law as they may be interpreted by the courts of the United States." [Fed. R. Evid. 501] Thus, the federal courts may alter the rules governing federal privilege law.

(2) State law claim or defense [§1462]

In *federal court*, when state law supplies the rule of decision with respect to an element of a claim or defense, however, privilege issues are to be determined in accordance with state law. [Fed. R. Evid. 501]

f. Corporate clients

(1) Privilege applicable [§1463]

The Supreme Court early held that the attorney-client privilege applied to corporate clients. This did not answer the question, however, of who was the client.

(2) Control group test [§1464]

Many courts limited the privilege to communications between the lawyer and those persons who could be considered the "control group" of the corporation, *i.e.,* the persons who controlled the corporation and who could act on the lawyer's advice. But this was imperfect because often the members of the control group did not have the information the lawyer needed to evaluate the corporation's legal problems, and the lawyer would then be subjected to a "Hobson's choice" about whether to inquire of other employees of the corporation.

(3) *Upjohn* test [§1465]

In **Upjohn Co. v. United States** (*supra,* §1452), the Supreme Court rejected the control group test as a matter of federal common law of evidence. (*See supra,* §1461.) Instead, the Court adopted a test that can extend the privilege to *any employee.* Although the contours of the test are unclear, it turns basically on the following factors:

(a) Matters within scope of employment [§1466]

The protection extends only to communication about matters within the scope of the employee's job with the corporation.

(b) Information not available from higher management [§1467]

The protection is justified for "non-control group" employees when higher management cannot itself supply the information.

(c) Other requirements satisfied [§1468]

In the course of its opinion, the Court emphasized the importance of other requirements of the privilege. Thus, the employee must know that the communication is designed to *obtain legal advice for the corporation* and that it is to be *held in confidence.*

(d) Criticism

This new formulation appears to overextend the privilege in that it provides no safeguards for the employee who makes full disclosure to the corporation's lawyer. The *corporation can waive the privilege and disclose* the employee's confidences without the permission of the employee.

(4) State law [§1469]

At least some states have refused to follow the Supreme Court's expansion of privilege protection for corporate clients. Illinois, for example, has continued to adhere to the control group test. [*See* **Consolidation Coal Co. v. Bucyrus-Erie Co.,** 432 N.E.2d 250 (Ill. 1982)]

g. Other communicational privileges [§1470]

Other privileges protect other communications from disclosure. For more information on these, *see* the Evidence Summary.

(1) Spousal communications [§1471]

Confidential communications between husband and wife during the marriage are privileged at the request of either spouse. [Cal. Evid. Code §980]

(a) Distinguish—testimony against spouse [§1472]

A husband or wife also has the privilege not to testify against the other spouse on any subject. [Cal. Evid. Code §§970-972; **Trammel v. United States**, 445 U.S. 40 (1980)] Note that no similar privilege is extended to other relatives, such as parents and children of a litigant.

(2) Doctor-patient [§1473]

A patient usually has a limited right to prevent disclosure of information she disclosed to her doctor in connection with medical treatment. [Cal. Evid. Code §§990-1007]

(a) Easily waived [§1474]

This privilege is easily waived, and is usually held waived by a plaintiff who sues for personal injuries and thereby puts her medical condition "in issue." [Cal. Evid. Code §996]

(3) Psychotherapist-patient [§1475]

The Supreme Court has held that there is a psychotherapist/patient privilege for confidential communications even if the psychotherapist is not a doctor. [**Jaffee v. Redmond**, 518 U.S. 1 (1996)—psychotherapy sessions by licensed social worker privileged]

(4) Priest-penitent [§1476]

A priest is privileged to refuse to disclose information revealed by a penitent. [Cal. Evid. Code §§1030-1034]

(5) Distinguish—tenure review materials [§1477]

The Supreme Court has held that universities have no privilege against disclosure of confidential tenure review materials. [**University of Pennsylvania v. EEOC**, 493 U.S. 182 (1990)]

h. Specificity of privilege claim [§1478]

If a party withholds information—particularly documents—from discovery on grounds of privilege, it should describe the materials withheld with sufficient specificity *to enable other parties to assess the applicability of the privilege.* [Fed. R. Civ. P. 26(b)(5)]

4. Trial Preparation Materials

a. "Work product"—*Hickman v. Taylor* rule

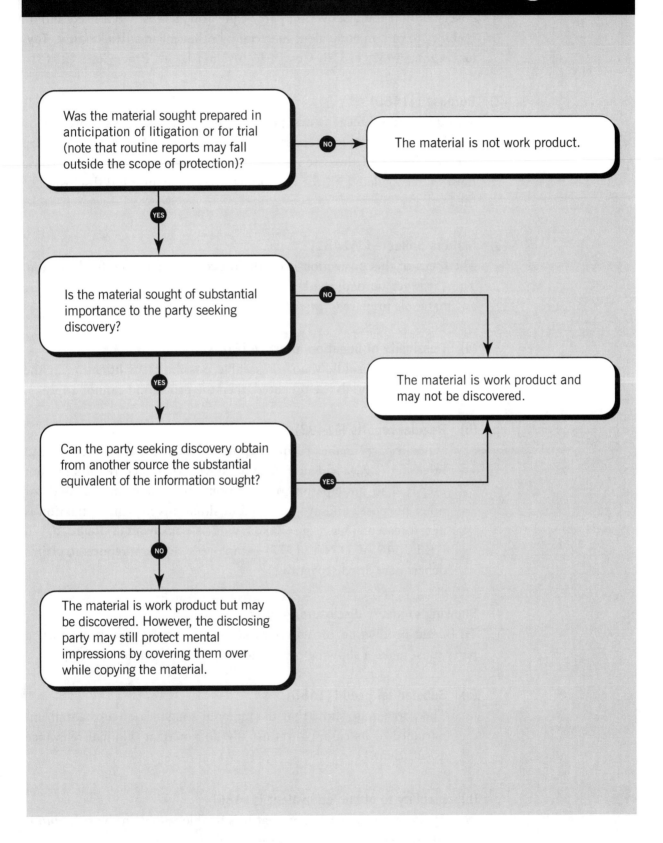

Was the material sought prepared in anticipation of litigation or for trial (note that routine reports may fall outside the scope of protection)?

NO → The material is not work product.

YES

Is the material sought of substantial importance to the party seeking discovery?

NO →

The material is work product and may not be discovered.

YES

Can the party seeking discovery obtain from another source the substantial equivalent of the information sought?

YES →

NO

The material is work product but may be discovered. However, the disclosing party may still protect mental impressions by covering them over while copying the material.

(1) Qualified privilege [§1479]

Materials prepared and information developed by or under the direction of a party or her attorney in anticipation of litigation are subject to discovery *only if* the discovering party can show a substantial need and an inability to obtain equivalent material by other means. [**Hickman v. Taylor**, *supra*, §1453; Fed. R. Civ. P. 26(b)(3); Cal. Civ. Proc. Code §2018]

(2) Purpose [§1480]

This qualified privilege is designed to maintain the adversary process by enabling each party to prepare her own case, with free rein to develop her own theory of the case and her own trial strategy; but this purpose must be reconciled with the overriding need to require full disclosure of the facts.

(3) Matters protected [§1481]

The focus of this protection is on the process of preparing for litigation. Thus, it is very broad; the Federal Rule [Fed. R. Civ. P. 26(b)(3)] covers any materials prepared *"in anticipation of litigation or for trial."*

(a) Possibility of litigation foreseen [§1482]

If there is absolutely no foreseeable possibility of litigation at the time the materials are prepared, then the protection cannot apply.

(b) Regular reports [§1483]

When a party makes regular reports of incidents that often lead to litigation (*e.g.*, accidents), it may be held that such reports are not prepared in anticipation of litigation, since they can be used for other purposes and are prepared in situations in which litigation is not foreseen. [*See, e.g.*, **Rakus v. Erie-Lackawanna Railroad**, 76 F.R.D. 145 (W.D.N.Y. 1977)—employees' accident reports to claims department are discoverable]

(4) Showing to justify disclosure [§1484]

To obtain production of material that is protected as work product, a party must make a showing of substantial need and undue hardship.

(a) Substantial need [§1485]

The party must show that the material sought is of substantial importance to its case; courts usually do not treat minimal relevance as sufficient.

(b) Inability to obtain equivalent [§1486]

The party must also show that it is unable to obtain the *substantial equivalent* without *undue hardship*.

(5) Special protection for mental impressions of attorney [§1487]

If a showing has been made to justify disclosure, materials containing the mental impressions of an attorney are given special protection.

---

e.g. **Example:** A memorandum prepared by an attorney may include her observations at the scene of the accident, which would be ordinary work product. The memo could also include the attorney's theories about possible grounds of liability and promising avenues of investigation, as well as her assessments of the persuasiveness of various possible witnesses. All this material, except her observations at the scene, would be considered *opinion work product* and would receive special protection.

(a) Protection under Federal Rules [§1488]

Federal Rule 26(b)(3) states that in ordering discovery of work product, the court "shall" protect against disclosure of the mental impressions and legal theories of an attorney. This has been held to provide absolute protection to such items. [**Duplan Corp. v. Moulinage et Retorderie de Chavanoz**, 509 F.2d 730 (4th Cir. 1974), *cert. denied*, 420 U.S. 997 (1975)] The Supreme Court, however, has declined to take this step: "we are not prepared at this juncture to say that such material is always protected by the work-product rule." [**Upjohn Co. v. United States**, *supra*, §1452] And several lower courts have denied absolute protection. [*See, e.g.,* **Holmgren v. State Farm Mutual Automobile Insurance Co.**, 976 F.2d 573 (9th Cir. 1992)—lawyer's mental impressions a pivotal issue and need for their disclosure compelling]

(b) State law [§1489]

Under the law of some states, protection for such materials is absolute. [*See, e.g.,* Cal. Civ. Proc. Code §2018(c)—"Any writing that reflects an attorney's impressions, conclusions, opinions, or legal research or theories shall not be discoverable under any circumstances"]

(c) Method—redaction [§1490]

If materials containing opinion work product are ordered produced, the portions containing the opinion work product may be "redacted" by covering them over in the copying process so they cannot be read.

(6) Rule 26(b)(3) and *Hickman* contrasted [§1491]

In federal court, the protections of Rule 26(b)(3) and *Hickman* both continue to apply, although usually they overlap. There are significant differences, however:

(a) Trial preparation by nonlawyers [§1492]

Hickman protects only the work of lawyers. It applies to their assistants, and perhaps to experts hired by them or others acting at their direction. Rule 26(b)(3) is broader; it also includes trial preparation by the party's "consultant, surety, indemnitor, insurer, or agent."

(b) Tangible materials [§1493]

Rule 26(b)(3) is more limited than *Hickman,* however, in protecting only "documents and tangible things." It therefore has no application, for example, to a deposition of the attorney inquiring into her trial strategies, etc. *Hickman* would apply in such a situation, however, since it is not limited to tangible items.

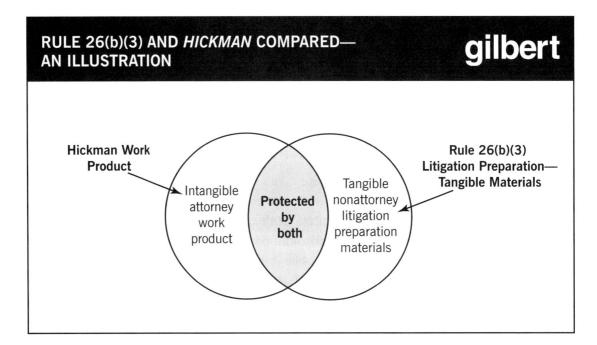

RULE 26(b)(3) AND *HICKMAN* COMPARED— AN ILLUSTRATION　　**gilbert**

Hickman Work Product

Intangible attorney work product

Protected by both

Tangible nonattorney litigation preparation materials

Rule 26(b)(3) Litigation Preparation— Tangible Materials

(7) Protection after litigation terminated [§1494]

It is not entirely clear whether work product protection endures after termination of the litigation for which the material was prepared. The Supreme Court has held in a case involving the Freedom of Information Act that the protection continues. [**FTC v. Grolier, Inc.,** 462 U.S. 19 (1983)] It has also been held that the protection can apply in a case that was not anticipated at the time the material was prepared, as long as it was prepared in anticipation of some litigation. [**Duplan Corp. v. Moulinage et Retorderie de Chavanoz,** *supra,* §1488]

(8) Distinguish—attorney-client privilege [§1495]

The qualified work product rule must be distinguished from the absolute privilege afforded confidential communications from client to counsel.

(9) Witness statements [§1496]

Because witness statements illustrate the application of work product and the attorney-client privilege, it is worthwhile to examine them in detail. Some statements of witnesses to lawyers may be subject to the attorney-client privilege, while other communications made to lawyers or investigators may be treated as work product and thus be subject to disclosure only on a showing of substantial need.

(a) Statements made by party to own attorney [§1497]

If the statements were made in confidence regarding past events, the communications are privileged under the attorney-client privilege.

1) Attorney's employees [§1498]

The privilege may also apply to statements made to an investigator *employed* by the party's counsel. [**Brakhage v. Graff**, 206 N.W.2d 45 (Neb. 1973)]

2) Caveat [§1499]

Note, however, that a party cannot put documents beyond the reach of discovery by turning them over to counsel. Nor can a party relieve himself of the obligation to disclose by making disclosure to his own lawyer. All that is protected is the content of the communication from client to lawyer.

(b) Statements by employees of corporation [§1500]

The attorney-client privilege applies to communications made in confidence by employees of a corporation, including nonsupervisory employees in many jurisdictions. (*See supra,* §1465-1468.)

1) Confidential reports [§1501]

The attorney-client privilege may also apply to routine reports that are intended to be *confidential* records of the corporation, prepared for the corporation's attorney; *e.g.,* accident reports prepared by a truck driver according to company policy that such reports be submitted immediately following any accident for confidential use of the corporation's lawyers. [**D.I. Chadbourne, Inc. v. Superior Court**, 60 Cal. 2d 723 (1964)]

2) Other reports [§1502]

Other reports of employees to corporate counsel are not covered by the attorney-client privilege, but may be subject to the qualified work product privilege *if* they were made or prepared in anticipation of litigation. [**Xerox v. IBM**, 64 F.R.D. 367 (S.D.N.Y. 1974)] However, remember that regular reports may be found to not meet the "in anticipation" requirement. (*See supra,* §1483.)

(c) Statements of nonparty witnesses [§1503]

Statements obtained from nonparty witnesses are usually held to be work product of the attorney, so they are not subject to discovery by an adversary unless he is not reasonably able to obtain a similar statement from the witness by his own effort.

1) Note

Under federal practice, the witness himself is entitled to a copy of his statement *as a matter of right*. [Fed. R. Civ. P. 26(b)(3)]

2) Not covered by attorney-client privilege

Witness interviews are not covered by the attorney-client privilege. [**Hickman v. Taylor,** *supra,* §1453]

(d) Statements made by party to adversary counsel [§1504]

Usually, no privilege (absolute or qualified) protects statements of a party made to adversary counsel. Such statements are subject to discovery without a showing of need—*i.e.,* a party-witness is entitled to a copy of statements given to adversary counsel as a matter of right. [Fed. R. Civ. P. 26(b)(3)]

b. Expert reports [§1505]

Lawyers are increasingly dependent on retained experts to help them prepare for trials and to testify at trials. Often the subject matter of a litigation is unfamiliar to the lawyer, and the lawyer therefore needs the assistance of a person schooled in the field to prepare adequately for trial. At trial, the technical subject matter of the litigation may make it essential that an expert testify to support the party's case. (For more detail on the rules governing the presentation of expert testimony at trial, *see* the Evidence Summary.)

(1) Nontestifying experts

(a) Role [§1506]

Where the lawyer needs the help of an expert to prepare for trial, he will often retain one to advise him on trial strategy and help develop legal and factual theories for the case. The expert can also help the lawyer prepare to cross-examine the opponent's expert.

(b) Discoverability of facts known and opinions held [§1507]

Under Federal Rule 26(b)(4)(B), facts known to and opinions held by nontestifying experts are discoverable only in exceptional circumstances, *e.g.,* when one party has monopolized the qualified experts. *Rationale:* Allowing discovery would give the party seeking it a *free ride* where it could hire its own expert.

1) Reimbursement for fees [§1508]

Where discovery is ordered, the court is to require the discovering party to reimburse the party who retained the expert for a fair portion of the fees and expenses paid for the facts and opinions developed by the expert. [Fed. R. Civ. P. 26(b)(4)(C)]

(c) Nontestifying expert as witness for opponent [§1509]

Experts can differ in their opinions, and when a lawyer hires an expert she will not always know the expert's opinion of her client's case. What happens if the expert develops an opinion unfavorable to the client? The opposing side will likely want to hire the expert because the circumstances tend to make her opinion very believable. At least one court has held that the opposing party may not do so in the absence of extraordinary circumstances; *i.e.,* Rule 26(b)(4)(B) (*supra*, §1507) must be satisfied [**Durflinger v. Artiles,** 727 F.2d 888 (10th Cir. 1984)], but other courts might not adopt this rule. The rationale is that if such use of the nontestifying expert's opinions were allowed, lawyers might be deterred from consulting experts whose opinions are unknown.

EXAM TIP   **gilbert**

An important guiding principle of litigation is that an attorney should never call a witness unless she already knows how the witness will testify. But how will the attorney know? In the case of expert witnesses, she will ask the expert before trial. What happens if, in an exam question, an attorney does this, the expert's opinion is unfavorable, and the attorney's opponent has found out about the expert and can't wait to make the expert his own witness at trial? At least one court has prohibited such unsporting conduct, holding that the opponent cannot call the expert absent extraordinary need. Your answer should note this, but should also note the fact that this issue is unresolved.

(d) Discovery of identity of nontestifying expert [§1510]

The courts are split on whether the identity of the nontestifying expert can be discovered. [*Compare* **Ager v. Jane C. Stormmont Hospital,** 622 F.2d 496 (10th Cir. 1980)—discovery not permitted because it subverts protective purposes of the rule—*with* **Baki v. B.F. Diamond Construction Co.,** 71 F.R.D. 179 (D. Md. 1976)—discovery allowed because it does not involve disclosure of facts known or opinions held by expert]

(e) Informally consulted experts [§1511]

The protections of Rule 26(b)(4)(B) apply only to experts who are "retained or specially employed" by a party. The courts have held that discovery regarding experts who were only informally consulted is not available. [**Procter & Gamble Co. v. Haugen,** 184 F.R.D. 410 (D. Utah 1999)]

(2) Testifying experts [§1512]

The Federal Rules allow broad discovery regarding testifying experts and impose a requirement to provide a written report that applies to most such experts.

(a) Required disclosure [§1513]

Without a formal discovery request, each party must identify each person that party will call to offer expert testimony at trial. [Fed. R. Civ. P. 26(a)(2)(A)]

(b) Timing of disclosure [§1514]

In the absence of other direction from the court, this disclosure must be made at least *90 days before trial.* [Fed. R. Civ. P. 26(a)(2)(C)] However, courts may stagger the disclosures and the party with the burden of proof may be required to disclose first.

1) Rebuttal [§1515]

Within 30 days after the disclosure by an opposing party, a party may add another expert intended to offer testimony solely to rebut or contradict expert evidence identified by the opposing party.

(c) Required report by expert witness [§1516]

In addition to identifying its expert witnesses, a party must ordinarily provide a detailed report from the expert. [Fed. R. Civ. P. 26(a)(2)(B)]

1) Experts covered [§1517]

A report must be prepared for any specially retained expert and for any employee of a party whose duties regularly include giving expert testimony. This ordinarily does *not* include a party's *treating doctor* if the doctor will offer opinions only on the basis of observations during treatment. [**Riddick v. Washington Hospital Center,** 183 F.R.D. 327 (D.D.C. 1998)]

2) Signed by expert [§1518]

The report is to be signed by the witness, although it is contemplated that counsel will assist in drafting the report.

3) Statement of expert's opinions [§1519]

The report is to include a *complete statement* of all opinions the expert will express in testimony, along with the *basis* therefor and the *data or other information* on which they are based. This makes all materials provided the expert, including privileged materials, subject to mandatory disclosure.

4) Exhibits [§1520]

Disclosure should also include all exhibits that will be used in connection with the testimony.

5) Expert's qualifications [§1521]

The report must include the witness's qualifications, including *all publications during the preceding 10 years* and a list of *all cases in which the expert testified during the preceding four years.*

6) Expert's compensation [§1522]

The report should include the compensation the expert will be paid.

7) Supplementation [§1523]

The report should be supplemented with new information that is developed after it is submitted. [Fed. R. Civ. P. 26(e)(1)]

REQUIRED DISCLOSURES CONCERNING TESTIFYING EXPERTS

AT LEAST 90 DAYS BEFORE TRIAL, A PARTY ORDINARILY IS REQUIRED TO DISCLOSE:

☑ The *identity* of all experts expected to be called at trial.

☑ A statement of all *opinions* the expert will express in testimony, along with the basis for the opinions.

☑ All *exhibits* that will be used in connection with the expert's testimony.

☑ The expert's *qualifications*, including a list of anything the expert has published in the last 10 years and cases in which the expert has testified in the last four years.

☑ The expert's *compensation*.

(d) Deposition of right [§1524]

Any party has a right to take the deposition of a testifying expert. [Fed. R. Civ. P. 26(b)(4)(A)] Where a report is required, however, this deposition may not take place until *after the report is provided.*

1) Supplementation of expert's testimony [§1525]

Although supplementation is not required with other deposition testimony, a party has a duty to supplement the deposition testimony of its expert witness. [Fed. R. Civ. P. 26(e)(1)]

2) Compensation of expert for responding to discovery [§1526]

The party taking the deposition must compensate the expert for the time spent on the deposition. *Compare:* There is no requirement to compensate the expert for the time spent on the report.

(e) State practice compared [§1527]

States often have similar statutory procedures for pretrial identification of expert witnesses, including provisions for pretrial depositions. [*See, e.g.,* Cal. Civ. Proc. Code §§2034(f), 2034(i)]

(3) Unaffiliated experts [§1528]

Rule 26(b)(4) makes no provision for a person who has expertise that may be pertinent to a lawsuit, but who has not consented to assist any party in connection with the case. On occasion, litigants subpoena such persons to compel them to testify. It has been held that they may sometimes be compelled to give such testimony, albeit perhaps only on being paid a fee for it. [*See, e.g.,* **Wright v. Jeep Corp.**, 547 F.2d 871 (E.D. Mich. 1982)—professor who prepared report on Jeep rollover problems compelled to testify]

(a) Rationale

Experts should be treated like other witnesses who have information that is pertinent to the resolution of a lawsuit.

(b) Criticism

Society pays a price if such experts are required to spend substantial time attending depositions or trials, and they may not be adequately compensated for being required to reveal their expertise.

(c) Protection against subpoenas [§1529]

Rule 45 provides that if a subpoena "requires disclosure of an unretained expert's opinion or information not describing specific events or occurrences in dispute and resulting from the expert's study made not at the request of any party," the court may quash or modify the subpoena. Alternatively, "if the party in whose behalf the subpoena is issued shows a substantial need for the testimony or material that cannot be otherwise met without undue hardship and assures that the person to whom the subpoena is addressed will be reasonably compensated, the court may order appearance or production only upon specified conditions." [Fed. R. Civ. P. 45(c)(3)(B)]

(d) Distinguish—expert as fact witness [§1530]

Whether or not experts should be protected against being compelled to testify regarding matters within their expertise, they are not immune to the civic duty to testify regarding the facts of the case. Thus, if a Nobel Prize winner witnesses an accident, she must testify about what she saw just like any other witness.

D. Protective Orders

1. Introduction [§1531]

Protective orders are designed to *prevent undue burdens* that might otherwise be imposed by discovery. The availability of protective orders recognizes both that discovery can be extremely intrusive and that parties may seek to abuse it. Both concerns can be ameliorated through protective provisions.

2. Requirement of Good Cause [§1532]

A protective order should be granted only on a showing of good cause by the party seeking protection. [Fed. R. Civ. P. 26(c)] Appropriate grounds include the following.

a. Confidential information [§1533]

A protective order may be entered to protect "trade secret or other confidential research, development, or commercial information." [Fed. R. Civ. P. 26(c)(7)]

(1) Showing required

(a) Confidentiality [§1534]

Such protection is available only for information that is in fact confidential. To justify an order, the party must show that the information has been held in confidence.

(b) Specific harm from disclosure [§1535]

There must also be a showing that a specific harm is likely to flow from disclosure of the information.

(c) Not limited to technical information [§1536]

The protection is not limited to technical trade secret information, but rather may extend to wide varieties of commercial data whose disclosure could give commercial advantage to competitors. It has therefore been applied to *customer lists* [**Chesa International, Ltd. v. Fashion Associates, Inc.**, 425 F. Supp. 234 (S.D.N.Y. 1977)], *profit and gross income data* [**Corbett v. Free Press Association**, 50 F.R.D. 179 (D. Vt. 1970)], and *terms of a contract* [**Essex Wire Corp. v. Eastern Electric Sales Co.**, 48 F.R.D. 308 (E.D. Pa. 1969)].

It is not uncommon in real life for a person to seek discovery of information for improper purposes, and this could be reflected in an exam question. For example, the Coca-Cola Company might file an unfair competition action against the bottlers of Dr. Pepper just so it can force the bottlers to disclose Dr. Pepper's secret flavor ingredient during litigation (some say it's cherry; others say it's prune—the debate continues). If this occurs on your exam, remember that the court can grant a protective order limiting the disclosure and use of the information if:

- The information is confidential; and

- Disclosure will likely cause a specific harm.

(d) Privacy interests [§1537]

Related arguments can be made to justify the protection of privacy interests of litigants because Rule 26(c)(7) allows protection against annoyance or embarrassment. [*See, e.g.,* **Galella v. Onassis,** *supra,* §1284—Jacqueline Onassis protected against being photographed by plaintiff during her deposition]

(2) Stipulated orders [§1538]

Despite the showing requirement, confidentiality orders are often entered into on stipulation. In such situations, there are *no findings* regarding either confidentiality or the risk of harm to any person. *Caution:* Some courts question the propriety of such orders.

(3) Format—"umbrella" orders [§1539]

Protective orders to protect confidentiality can take a number of forms. One would be to forbid discovery altogether. More often, however, the information is validly sought for trial preparation and the court places *limitations on use and dissemination* of the confidential information. Because these orders often are self-executing and apply throughout the discovery process, they are referred to as "umbrella" orders.

(a) Designation of confidential information [§1540]

Usually, any person producing information is allowed to designate it as confidential and, therefore, subject to the protection of the order. Often this is done by stamping documents "Confidential."

1) No judicial scrutiny [§1541]

Note that there is no judicial involvement in the designation process, which is left entirely to the parties.

(b) Effect of designation [§1542]

Usually, all designated documents are to be *held in confidence* by the other parties, *used only for trial preparation*, and *disclosed only to specified persons*, usually including the client and witnesses.

(c) Challenges to designation [§1543]
Any party may move the court to set aside a confidentiality designation on the ground that the material is not in fact confidential.

1) Burden on producing party [§1544]
At this point, the burden is on the producing party to establish that the material is indeed entitled to protection under Rule 26(c).

2) Exception—blanket challenges [§1545]
In some cases where large volumes of material have been designated confidential, however, the court may impose on the challenging party the duty to specify which confidentiality designations are challenged and why. [*See, e.g.,* **Zenith Radio Corp. v. Matsushita Electric Industrial Co.,** 529 F. Supp. 866 (E.D. Pa. 1981)—through discovery plaintiff sought to unseal hundreds of thousands of documents designated confidential]

(4) Public access [§1546]
The public may have an interest in materials covered by confidentiality orders. Were the material to be offered in evidence at trial, there would be a constitutional and common law right of *public access to court trial* that would enable the public to have access to the information. Before trial, there are two possible arguments:

(a) Discovery presumptively public [§1547]
Some courts say that discovery is presumptively public unless closed, and that orders limiting access to the public need special justification. This argument appears not to apply to material covered by proper protective orders, and the Supreme Court has stated that *there is no tradition of public access to discovery.* [**Seattle Times Co. v. Rhinehart,** 467 U.S. 20 (1984)]

1) Filing of discovery discontinued [§1548]
Formerly, discovery materials were automatically filed with the court. However, pursuant to a 2000 amendment, filing is no longer automatic. This amendment may further weaken arguments that there should be some presumptive public access to discovery materials because there is no reason to expect them to be in a public file.

(b) Material involved in pretrial rulings [§1549]
Where materials covered by a confidentiality order are involved in

pretrial rulings by the court, the public access argument is stronger because the constitutional and common law rights are designed to allow the public meaningful access to observe judicial decision-making. The application of this concept is not always easy:

1) **Access allowed—decision on merits of case [§1550]**
   If pretrial rulings resolve the merits, access to discovery materials relied on should be granted. [*See, e.g.,* **Cianci v. New Times Publishing Co.,** 88 F.R.D. 562 (S.D.N.Y. 1980)—summary judgment granted]

2) **Access denied—decision that privileged materials should not be produced [§1551]**
   If a discovery motion presents the question of whether materials sought are privileged, and, based on an in camera review of the materials, the court decides that they should not be produced, public access should not be allowed because it would undermine the privilege.

3) **Intermediate situations [§1552]**
   A problem arises in cases: (i) not involving resolution of the merits, or (ii) involving non-merits decisions that would be undermined by disclosure. Courts tend to deem *all materials considered in connection with a motion* to be subject to *presumptive public access*. [*See, e.g.,* **Zenith Radio Corp. v. Matsushita Electric Industrial Co.,** *supra*—public right of access to all materials offered in good faith in connection with summary judgment motion]

EXAM TIP	gilbert

If an exam question involves materials covered by a confidentiality order and a member of the press or public seeks access to the material during discovery, you must assess the procedural context. Generally, the press and public have *no right to access* material that was disclosed to a party during discovery and is subject to a confidentiality order. However, the United States Constitution provides for *open trials*, so if a pretrial ruling is based on confidential discovery material the courts will generally:

- Allow public access if the pretrial rulings resolve the merits of the case;

- Prohibit public access if access would undermine the court's ruling, such as a ruling that the materials are privileged; and

- Start with a presumption of public access in all other cases.

---

(5) Sharing with other litigants [§1553]

An issue of growing importance is the possibility that materials covered by a confidentiality order could be shared with other litigants in similar cases. This would tend to *reduce discovery expense* for other litigants, which would be a legitimate objective. [**United States v. Hooker Chemical Co.**, 90 F.R.D. 421 (W.D.N.Y. 1981)] Courts often allow such sharing.

(6) First Amendment limitations on protective orders [§1554]

Protective orders can limit expression by forbidding litigants to disclose information gained through discovery.

(a) Prior restraint analysis [§1555]

Some courts held that such orders could be justified under the First Amendment only where a prior restraint would be warranted, a very demanding standard. [*See, e.g., In re* **Halkin**, 598 F.2d 176 (D.C. Cir. 1979)] (For more on the prior restraint doctrine, *see* Constitutional Law Summary.)

(b) Supreme Court ruling [§1556]

The Supreme Court *rejected the prior restraint analysis* and held that a protective order supported by good cause is valid under the First Amendment. [**Seattle Times Co. v. Rhinehart**, *supra*, §1547]

(c) Continuing concern about First Amendment [§1557]

There is disagreement in the lower courts about whether courts should continue to consider First Amendment values in deciding whether to issue or modify protective orders. [*Compare* **Cipollone v. Liggett Group, Inc.**, 785 F.2d 1108 (3d Cir. 1986)—First Amendment irrelevant—*with* **Anderson v. Cryovac, Inc.**, 805 F.2d 1 (1st Cir. 1986)—First Amendment still a "presence" in protective order decisions]

b. Inconvenient place of examination [§1558]

If a deposition has been scheduled at a place that is unnecessarily inconvenient for the deponent or adversary, a protective order may issue.

(1) Federal practice [§1559]

Under the Federal Rules, protective orders are the only method available for controlling the place at which the deposition of a *party* can be scheduled, since the adverse party can notice his deposition to be taken anywhere. (*Compare:* A *nonparty* witness cannot be required to appear except by subpoena, and the range of a subpoena is limited; *see supra*, §1321.)

(a) Nonresident defendants [§1560]

On applications for protective orders as to the place of deposition, courts are inclined to hold that a nonresident defendant should be deposed at his residence rather than at the place where the suit is pending.

1) But note

A contrary result may be reached if the plaintiff is willing to pay the defendant's expenses to travel to the forum, or if it is shown that the defendant will be in the forum anyway.

(b) Nonresident plaintiff [§1561]

The courts appear more inclined to require a nonresident plaintiff to appear locally for his deposition, since he chose to file his action in the local forum.

(2) State practice compared [§1562]

Instead of requiring a nonresident deponent to obtain a protective order, state rules frequently put the burden on the party seeking the deposition to obtain a prior court order if he wishes to compel the other party to give her deposition beyond the range of a subpoena. [Cal. Civ. Proc. Code §2025(e)]

c. Unreasonable conduct of deposition [§1563]

If a deposition is conducted in a manner that is unduly annoying, embarrassing, or oppressive to a witness or party, a protective order may issue. When the court terminates a deposition for this reason, it may not be resumed or rescheduled except by court order. [Fed. R. Civ. P. 30(d)(3); Cal. Civ. Proc. Code §2025(n)]

d. Unduly burdensome discovery [§1564]

When discovery is unduly expensive, unnecessarily burdensome, or otherwise clearly excessive in relation to the importance of the case, a protective order may be sought to limit discovery. (*See supra*, §§1425-1428, regarding judicial limitation of discovery.)

3. Relation Between Protective Orders and Other Discovery Orders

a. Effect of prior orders [§1565]

Protective orders are rarely appropriate in regard to discovery conducted pursuant to a prior court order. The circumstances and limitations to be imposed on a medical examination, for example, are generally determined at the time the examination is ordered. Consequently, absent some new information or a change of circumstances, there is no occasion to reconsider the initial order.

b. No waiver [§1566]

A party or witness who does not seek a protective order in advance of a deposition or before the response date for interrogatories, does not thereby waive her right to make objections. She remains free to object to questioning at deposition and she may refuse answers to interrogatories, thereby forcing the discovering party to invoke the power of the court to compel answers to those questions which the court deems proper. [Fed. R. Civ. P. 37(a)]

E. Failure to Disclose or to Comply with Discovery

1. Order Compelling Response—Necessary Prerequisite [§1567]

Before discovery sanctions can be imposed, a party seeking discovery must usually obtain an order compelling discovery. [Fed. R. Civ. P. 37(a)]

a. Evasive or incomplete answer [§1568]

If a motion to compel discovery is made, an evasive or incomplete answer is treated as a failure to answer. [Fed. R. Civ. P. 37(a)(3)] This means that the responding party can be ordered to provide a proper answer.

b. Exception—complete failure to respond [§1569]

If a party completely fails to file a response to a discovery request or to attend his properly noticed deposition, discovery sanctions can be sought immediately, without the need for a prior order compelling discovery. [Fed. R. Civ. P. 37(d)]

c. Exception—failure to make required disclosures or supplementation [§1570]

If a party fails to make disclosures required by Rule 26(a), or to supplement disclosures as required by Rule 26(e)(1), the court should usually *exclude undisclosed materials from evidence*, and it may also *impose Rule 37(b) sanctions*, which are usually reserved for failures to comply with discovery orders. *Note:* The 2000 amendments add failure to supplement discovery responses—such as interrogatories or requests to produce—as required by Rule 26(e)(2), as a ground for this "automatic" sanction. [Fed. R. Civ. P. 37(c)(1)]

(1) Grounds for declining to sanction nondisclosure [§1571]

The court should not impose sanctions on a party who has *substantial justification* for its failure to disclose, or when the failure to disclose was *harmless*.

d. Need to meet and confer before motion [§1572]

Before filing a motion to compel discovery, a party must attempt to meet and confer with the opposing party in an effort to secure compliance without court action. [Fed. R. Civ. P. 37(a)(2)(A), (d)]

2. Sanctions for Failure to Comply with Order [§1573]

If sanctions are authorized because of disobedience of an order compelling discovery, the court has a variety of options available. [Fed. R. Civ. P. 37(b)(2)] Many of them affect the merits of the case and may therefore be called *merits sanctions.*

a. Order establishing facts [§1574]
The court may order that matters pertinent to the discovery be taken as established in the favor of the party seeking discovery. [Fed. R. Civ. P. 37(b)(2)(A)]

b. Order disallowing claims or defenses [§1575]
The court may deny the offending party the right to present claims or defenses raised by the pleadings, or exclude certain matters from evidence.

Example: When plaintiff failed to provide adequate answers to interrogatories regarding damages, the court precluded plaintiff from introducing evidence of damages, leaving it with only a claim for injunctive relief. [**Cine Forty-Second Street Theatre Corp. v. Allied Artists,** 602 F.2d 1062 (2d Cir. 1979)]

---

c. Dismissal or default [§1576]
The court can use the "*litigation death penalty*" and dismiss or default the offending party, rendering judgment in favor of the party seeking discovery.

d. Contempt [§1577]
The court may also impose contempt sanctions on the offending party. (*See infra*, §§1591-1594, regarding contempt.)

CHECKLIST OF DISCOVERY SANCTIONS

IF A PARTY DISOBEYS A COURT'S DISCOVERY ORDER OR IF SANCTIONS ARE OTHERWISE APPROPRIATE, THE COURT MAY:

☑ Order that *facts pertinent to the undisclosed material be established* in favor of the party seeking discovery.

☑ *Deny* the nondisclosing party the *right to present claims or defenses* related to the material sought.

☑ *Dismiss or default* the nondisclosing party.

☑ Hold the nondisclosing party *in contempt*.

---

e. Discretion to select proper sanction [§1578]
The trial court has substantial discretion to select the proper sanction. However, there are some guidelines in the area:

(1) Least severe sanction [§1579]
Some courts of appeals direct district judges to use the least severe sanction, but others do not. [*Compare* **Gonzalez v. Trinity Marine Group,**

Inc., 117 F.3d 894 (5th Cir. 1997)—district court abused its discretion by dismissing because that was not the least onerous sanction that would redress plaintiff's conduct, *with* **Angulo-Alvarez v. Aponte de la Torre**, 170 F.3d 246 (1st Cir. 1999)—district court did not abuse its discretion by dismissing without first considering less severe sanctions] In any case, the district court clearly has discretion to use less severe sanctions if it concludes that would serve the interests of justice.

(2) General deterrence [§1580]

The Supreme Court, however, has stated that *general deterrence* can justify sanctions more severe than would be necessary to deter the offending party from future discovery misconduct (*i.e.*, the courts can impose a harsh sanction against this recalcitrant litigant in order to deter future litigants from similar misconduct). [**National Hockey League v. Metropolitan Hockey Club, Inc.**, 427 U.S. 639 (1976); *and see* **Brockton Savings Bank v. Peat, Marwick, Mitchell & Co.**, 771 F.2d 5 (1st Cir. 1985)—no requirement that lesser sanction first be considered]

3. Culpability Necessary for Sanctions

a. Due process requirements [§1581]

There are due process limitations on the power of a court to impose sanctions that affect the merits.

(1) No merits sanctions for misconduct unrelated to merits [§1582]

A party has a constitutional right to have her case decided on the merits, whether or not she obeys every directive of the court. Hence, it is a violation of due process for the court to enter judgment against a party merely for disobeying an order. [**Hovey v. Elliott**, 167 U.S. 409 (1897)] However, if a party's misconduct taints the merits, that is sufficient to justify a sanction order that redresses the effects of the misconduct. Thus, the failure to comply with discovery usually will support an inference that the violator's case lacks merit and justify a merits sanction. [**Hammond Packing Co. v. Arkansas**, 212 U.S. 322 (1909)]

(2) Ability to comply [§1583]

Even if the failure to comply relates to the merits of the case, it would violate due process to enter judgment against a party for failing to do something that he was unable to do. [**Societe Internationale v. Rogers**, 357 U.S. 197 (1958)]

b. Willfulness, bad faith, or other fault [§1584]

The ordinary formulation looks to whether the party to be sanctioned was guilty of willfulness, bad faith, or other fault in connection with the failure to comply with the court's order. The broadest ground is "other fault," and it is unclear whether it would extend to simple negligence. [*See* **Cine Forty-Second Street Theatre Corp. v. Allied Artists,** *supra,* §1575—gross negligence sanctionable]

c. Punishing client for lawyer's misconduct [§1585]

Often it will not be clear that the client (who is directly affected by merits sanctions) was responsible for misconduct by the lawyer.

(1) Lawyer as agent of client [§1586]

The Supreme Court has said that the lawyer is the agent of the client, and that the client is therefore responsible for the conduct of the lawyer. [**Link v. Wabash Railroad,** 370 U.S. 626 (1962)]

(2) Need to show client involvement [§1587]

Most lower courts, however, insist on some showing of client involvement before imposing harsh sanctions on the client. [*See, e.g.,* **Cine Forty-Second Street Theatre Corp. v. Allied Artists,** *supra*—plaintiff's principal officer "intimately involved" in litigation; **Shea v. Donohoe Construction Co.,** 529 F.2d 1071 (3d Cir. 1986)—trial court to provide direct warning about risk of dismissal to parties before imposing ultimate sanction]

4. Taxation of Costs of Discovery Proceedings

a. Motion to compel discovery [§1588]

Unless the court finds that the losing party on a discovery motion was substantially justified in taking the position it did, the court will require the losing party to pay the other side the cost of making or defending against the motion to compel. [Fed. R. Civ. P. 37(a)(4)]

b. Failure to obey order compelling discovery [§1589]

The party who fails to comply with a discovery order may, in addition to other sanctions, be required to pay the moving party the cost of seeking sanctions. [Fed. R. Civ. P. 37(b)]

c. For failure to attend deposition [§1590]

Federal Rule 30(g) authorizes the imposition of costs for a party's failure to attend a deposition that *he* scheduled.

5. Contempt Power

a. Defiance of prior court order [§1591]

Failure to comply with a party-initiated discovery notice (*e.g.,* failure to answer an interrogatory to a party) is not in itself a basis for contempt. Contempt is an appropriate sanction only if the party or witness refuses to make disclosure in defiance of a *prior court order.*

> **Example:** A deponent who fails to submit to a deposition after having been *ordered* to do so, or who does not comply with a subpoena, may be held in contempt of court. [Fed. R. Civ. P. 37(b)(1), 45(e)]

b. Civil contempt [§1592]

The contempt sanction may be civil, and thus coercive in effect (*i.e.*, the witness may "purge" himself of the contempt at any time by providing the information sought). [**International Business Machines Corp. v. United States,** 493 F.2d 112 (2d Cir. 1975)]

c. Criminal contempt [§1593]

In a flagrant case, it may also be proper to impose punishment on a contumacious witness, even if he is now willing to submit. [*See* **Gompers v. Bucks Stove & Range Co.,** 221 U.S. 418 (1911)]

d. Limitation—no contempt to compel medical examination [§1594]

In deference to the personal rights of parties, the contempt power may not be used to compel medical examination. [Fed. R. Civ. P. 37(b)(2)(D)]

6. Compare—Sanctions for Improper Certification [§1595]

Federal Rule 26(g) makes the signature of an attorney on a discovery paper a certificate with respect to the following matters, and directs that if a paper is signed in violation of this requirement the court shall impose a sanction on the person signing the paper and/or the party on whose behalf it was submitted.

a. Supported by law [§1596]

The signature certifies that the request or response is consistent with the Federal Rules and warranted by existing law or a good faith argument for the extension, modification, or reversal of existing law.

b. Proper purpose [§1597]

The signature also certifies that the request or response was not interposed for any improper purpose, such as to harass or to cause unnecessary delay or needless increase in the cost of litigation.

c. Reasonable [§1598]

Finally, the signature certifies that the request or response is not unreasonable or unduly burdensome or expensive, given the needs of the case, the discovery already had in the case, the amount in controversy, and the importance of the issues at stake in the litigation.

F. Appellate Review of Discovery Orders

1. Orders Usually Not Appealable

a. Discovery orders not final [§1599]

To further the interest of judicial economy, generally only final orders are appealable. Orders concerning discovery are not final judgments, and hence are not appealable in most jurisdictions.

(1) Not collateral [§1600]

Despite the prohibition against appealing non-final orders, many jurisdictions allow immediate appeal of orders that are collateral (*i.e.*, not directly in issue) to the main case. Discovery orders are *not* regarded as "collateral" to the main action and so are not immediately appealable under this principle. (*See infra*, §§2119-2134). [**Cunningham v. Hamilton County**, 527 U.S. 198 (1999)—Rule 37 sanctions orders are not collateral to the merits]

b. Not injunctions [§1601]

Likewise, discovery orders are not injunctions within the meaning of statutes authorizing immediate appeals from orders granting or denying injunctions. [28 U.S.C. §1292(a); **International Products Corp. v. Koons**, 325 F.2d 403 (2d Cir. 1963)]

c. Appealable in some states [§1602]

In some states, discovery orders *are* appealable orders—*i.e.*, in those states, no "final decision" requirement is imposed as a condition of appellate jurisdiction. [*See* **Boser v. Uniroyal**, 39 App. Div. 2d 632 (1972)]

2. Modes of Review

a. Certified appeal (federal practice) [§1603]

If the discovery motion raises an important question about the controlling discovery rule, the trial court may *certify* the question to the appellate court if appropriate certification legislation has been enacted in the jurisdiction (*e.g.*, where the jurisdiction has adopted a statute allowing lower courts to certify important and unsettled issues to the state supreme court). [*See, e.g.*, **American Express Warehousing Ltd. v. TransAmerica Insurance Co.**, 380 F.2d 277 (2d Cir. 1967)]

b. Mandamus or prohibition (state and federal practice) [§1604]

An extraordinary writ such as a writ of mandamus (which orders a court to perform an act) may be issued by an appellate court to correct or prevent an *abuse of discretion* by the trial judge in exercising power over the discovery process. [28 U.S.C. §1651; **Schlagenhauf v. Holder**, *supra*, §1404; **Greyhound Corp. v. Superior Court**, 56 Cal. 2d 355 (1961)] Such writs usually are issued only in *extraordinary situations*.

c. Review after judgment [§1605]

If the trial court fails to compel effective disclosure, the appellate court *may* reverse the judgment on this basis. However, the discovery ruling must be shown to have been "prejudicial" (*i.e.*, likely to have affected the *outcome* of the case), or there is little likelihood of reversal. [*See* **Burns v. Thiokol Chemical Corp.**, 483 F.2d 300 (5th Cir. 1973)]

d. Sanction as final [§1606]

If the discovery sanction takes the form of a final disposition, such as a judgment of dismissal or any entry of judgment by default, that judgment is final and appealable. [**Brennan v. Engineered Products, Inc.**, 506 F.2d 299 (8th Cir. 1974)]

e. Review of contempt order [§1607]

An order of civil contempt is not final and hence is not generally appealable until final judgment is entered. [**International Business Machines Corp. v. United States,** *supra,* §1592] However, a conviction of criminal contempt is final and appealable. [**Union Tool Co. v. Wilson**, 259 U.S. 107 (1922)] *Caution:* Sometimes the distinction between civil and criminal contempt is difficult to discern. [*See* **United Mine Workers v. Bagwell**, 512 U.S. 821 (1994)—for purposes of right to jury trial, contempt order was criminal, although court announced penalty for violation in advance]

G. Use of Discovery at Trial

1. Statements of Adversary

a. Admissions [§1608]

A party's admissions (*i.e.*, statements detrimental to his case) in a deposition or in response to an interrogatory are admissible just like any other admission. However, such admissions are not conclusive, as they may be shown to have been inadvertent. [Fed. R. Civ. P. 32(a); Cal. Civ. Proc. Code §2025(u)]

(1) But note

An admission in a response to a request for admission under Federal Rule 36 is conclusive proof of the facts admitted. [Fed. R. Civ. P. 36(b); *see supra,* §§1364-1383]

b. Right to object [§1609]

The party whose statement is being used may object at trial on the basis of its irrelevance or impropriety and is not barred by her failure to interpose objections at the time of discovery. [Fed. R. Civ. P. 32(b), (d)]

2. Statements of Other Witnesses

a. Prior inconsistent statement [§1610]

Depositions may be admitted at trial for impeachment—*i.e.*, to prove a prior inconsistent statement of a witness who testifies at trial. [Fed. R. Civ. P. 32(a)(1); Cal. Civ. Proc. Code §2025(u)(1)]

b. Unavailability [§1611]

In addition, depositions may be admitted to prove the facts testified to at the deposition if the deponent is "unavailable" at trial (*e.g.*, witness out of state, too ill to testify, deceased, etc.). [Fed. R. Civ. P. 32(a)(3); Cal. Civ. Proc. Code §2025(u)(3)]

c. Party's own deposition [§1612]

A party may use her own deposition in lieu of personal testimony if she is "unavailable" for trial (*see* above), *provided* that she has not procured her own absence (*i.e.*, leaving the jurisdiction to avoid being called as a witness by the adversary). [Fed. R. Civ. P. 32(d)(3); *see supra*, §1347]

H. Private Investigation

1. Formal Discovery Not Obligatory [§1613]

Civil litigants are entitled to conduct their own private investigation of the facts and are not obliged to use the discovery process to secure information. [**IBM v. Edelstein,** 526 F.2d 37 (2d Cir. 1975)]

a. Exception—contact with opposing party [§1614]

However, ethical rules forbid a lawyer from contacting an opposing party known to be represented by counsel without the permission of that party's attorney.

2. Admissibility of Proof Privately Obtained [§1615]

Under the Fourth Amendment, the government may not use evidence in criminal trials that was obtained through improper means. Private parties, however, are not subject to the Fourth Amendment limitations on searches or exclusionary rules intended to enforce such constitutional restraints. Thus, at least in the absence of egregious wrongdoing, civil litigants may use material as proof even if it was obtained by tortious means. [**Sackler v. Sackler,** 15 N.Y.2d 40 (1964)]

Chapter Seven:
Summary Judgment

CONTENTS

Chapter Approach

Chapter Approach

Summary judgment is a pretrial device that permits the court to look outside of the pleadings to determine whether there is an issue of fact to be tried. In law school examinations, summary judgment issues are sometimes raised in connection with disputes about discovery that may bear on the issues raised by the summary judgment motion. When presented with a motion for summary judgment, ask yourself the following questions:

1. **Has the moving party made a sufficient initial showing?**

    If the moving party would have the burden of proof on the issue at trial, he must initially produce enough evidence to show that no reasonable jury could find for his opponent. If the moving party would not have the burden of proof, he still must make an initial showing of his opponent's lack of proof. If the initial showing is insufficient, the opposing party need not submit any opposing proof, and the motion should be denied.

2. **Was the opposing party given notice and an opportunity to respond?**

    If the initial showing was sufficient, summary judgment would still be improper unless the opposing party was given notice of the motion and an *opportunity to respond*. Note that the circumstances sometimes justify delay in the decision in order to give the opposing party an opportunity to gather evidence, especially if the motion is made early in the case or before there has been substantial discovery.

3. **Is there a triable issue?**

    Assuming the moving party's initial burden was met and the nonmoving party was given an opportunity to respond, the court must look at the evidence in the light most favorable to the nonmoving party to determine whether there is a genuine issue of fact to be tried. If the moving party would have the burden of proof at trial, the motion should be granted only if the evidence is so strong that a reasonable jury could find only for the moving party. If the moving party would not have the burden of proof at trial, the court should grant the motion only if the opposing party fails to come forward with sufficient evidence to support a verdict in his favor.

Also note that summary judgment may be partial (*i.e.,* only as to some issues or some parties). **Denial** of summary judgment is not immediately appealable. **Grant** of summary judgment, however, may be immediately appealable if it results in a final judgment. On review the appellate court has plenary power; it need not give deference to the trial judge's decision.

A. Introduction

1. Purpose [§1616]

Summary judgment is a method for getting beyond the allegations of the pleadings and examining evidentiary material without holding a full-dress trial. If the evidentiary material shows that there is actually no genuine controversy that requires a trial, summary judgment can avoid unnecessary delay and expense in deciding the case.

e.g. Example: In the complaint, plaintiff alleges that defendant made defamatory statements about him to two people. Defendant moves for summary judgment with affidavits from both people saying that defendant never made such statements to them, and his own affidavit denying that he ever made such a statement to either. This evidentiary material shows that there is no factual dispute warranting a trial because there was never a "publication," a required element of defamation. [**Dyer v. MacDougall,** 201 F.2d 265 (2d Cir. 1952)]

2. Pleadings Motions Compared [§1617]

Summary judgment differs from pleadings motions attacking the sufficiency of a claim or defense in that *summary judgment allows the court to look at evidentiary material.* Recall that pleadings motions look only at the face of the pleading and test only its legal sufficiency. (*See supra,* §§701, 756.) Usually, it is said that consideration of any material beyond the face of the complaint is forbidden on a pleadings motion, or such consideration may convert the motion into a motion for summary judgment. [*See, e.g.,* Fed. R. Civ. P. 12(b)—on motion to dismiss for failure to state a claim, if materials outside pleadings are presented and not excluded by court, motion is to be treated as one for summary judgment]

a. Relevance of pleadings to summary judgment [§1618]

The pleadings delineate what is in controversy in the case. Thus, if certain allegations have been admitted, those admissions may form part of the basis for summary judgment.

b. Reliance on pleadings in response to summary judgment motion [§1619]

An opposing party may not rely on the allegations in her pleadings to defeat a summary judgment motion. [Fed. R. Civ. P. 56(e)]

3. Judgment as a Matter of Law Compared [§1620]

Judgment as a matter of law (*infra,* §§1865-1882) is similar to summary judgment in that it uses essentially the same standard to determine whether there is a triable issue. However, there are some important differences.

a. Timing [§1621]

The summary judgment motion can be, and normally is, decided *before trial.*

A defendant may move for summary judgment at any time and a plaintiff may do so 20 days after commencement of the action. [Fed. R. Civ. P. 56(a), (b)] A motion for judgment as a matter of law usually is made at the close of evidence at trial and it may be renewed after a verdict is returned (*see infra,* §§1960-1967).

b. **Nature of material considered [§1622]**

The summary judgment motion is based essentially on pretrial written submissions, whereas a motion for judgment as a matter of law is based on live testimony and other evidence presented during the trial. However, note that summary judgment may be based on live testimony from depositions, which is usually recorded in a deposition transcript or by videotape.

c. **Burden of proof—initial showing requirement [§1623]**

Summary judgment also differs from judgment as a matter of law in that on summary judgment the moving party must make an initial showing to justify scrutiny of the evidence, which is not required for the motions at or after trial if the moving party does not have the burden of proof.

(1) **Opposing party with burden [§1624]**

If the moving party would not have the burden of proof at trial, to obtain judgment as a matter of law, he could allow the opposing party to put on her case and then point out the insufficiencies of that case. To obtain summary judgment, such a moving party would have to make an *initial showing* of the insufficiency of the evidence of his opponent's case. (*See infra,* §§1646-1661, for discussion of the initial burden.) Only if such an initial showing is made does the opponent then have the burden of bringing forth sufficient evidence to show that there is a genuine issue for trial.

(2) **Distinguish—moving party with burden [§1625]**

If the moving party has the burden of proof on the issue raised at the summary judgment stage, making that showing before trial does not represent an additional burden on the party because the party would have to put on such evidence at trial to justify a directed verdict. However, such a party must make a compelling case for entry of summary judgment, because a trial should be held if a reasonable jury could disbelieve the moving party's proof.

d. **Summary judgment may be more difficult to obtain [§1626]**

In many courts, it is said that summary judgment is more difficult to obtain than judgment as a matter of law—*i.e.,* it must be clearer to the court that the case can reasonably be decided only one way. However, it appears that courts are gradually becoming more accepting of summary judgment. (*See infra,* §1628.)

	PLEADINGS MOTIONS	SUMMARY JUDGMENT MOTION	MOTION FOR JUDGMENT AS A MATTER OF LAW
PLEADINGS MOTIONS, SUMMARY JUDGMENT, AND JUDGMENT AS A MATTER OF LAW COMPARED **gilbert**			
CAN COURT LOOK TO EVIDENTIARY MATERIAL?	No	Yes	Yes
WHEN MADE?	Before trial; often before answer	Before trial	Usually at close of evidence at trial
BASIS FOR DECISION?	The pleadings	Pretrial written submissions including affidavits, documents, and testimony from depositions	Live testimony and other evidence presented during trial

4. Impact on Right to Trial [§1627]

The traditional reluctance to grant summary judgment resulted in part from the belief that a litigant has a right to have her claims tested at trial. Nevertheless, there is no right to a trial where there is no genuine dispute about the facts, and the Supreme Court early upheld the validity of summary judgment against arguments that it violated the right to jury trial. [**Fidelity & Deposit Co. v. United States,** 187 U.S. 135 (1902)]

5. Trend Favoring Use of Summary Judgment [§1628]

For more than a decade, it has seemed that the courts have become more receptive to deciding cases on summary judgment. The Supreme Court has observed that "[s]ummary judgment is properly regarded not as a disfavored procedural short-cut, but rather as an integral part of the Federal Rules as a whole" and noted that it has an important role: "with the advent of 'notice pleading,' the motion to dismiss seldom fulfills this function [isolating factually insufficient claims or defenses] anymore, and its place must be taken by the motion for summary judgment." [**Celotex Corp. v. Catrett,** 477 U.S. 317 (1986)]

B. Standard for Grant of Summary Judgment

1. Basic Standard [§1629]

The court is to grant summary judgment when it determines that "there is no genuine issue as to any material fact" [Fed. R. Civ. P. 56(c)], or that there is "no triable issue as to any material fact" [Cal. Civ. Proc. Code §437c(c)].

2. Relation to Standard for Judgment as a Matter of Law [§1630]

The United States Supreme Court has stated that in federal court the standard for entry of judgment is the same at the summary judgment stage as at the judgment as a matter of law stage. [**Anderson v. Liberty Lobby, Inc.**, 477 U.S. 242 (1986)] This makes it appropriate to focus on whether the moving party has the burden of proof on the issue raised by the summary judgment motion.

EXAM TIP   **gilbert**

Recall that the burden of pleading various issues depends on whether they are considered *elements of the claim* or *affirmative defenses*. (*See supra*, §§833-838.) Usually, the party who must raise an issue in the pleadings must also prove it. Accordingly, you should be alert to the question of who has the burden of proof on the specific issue raised by the summary judgment motion.

---

a. Moving party with burden of proof [§1631]

If the party moving for summary judgment has the burden of proof on the issue raised by the motion, summary judgment should be granted only if the evidence favoring the moving party is of such strength that the jury could not reasonably disbelieve the moving party's evidence.

b. Opposing party with burden [§1632]

If the party moving for summary judgment does *not* have the burden of proof on the issue raised by the motion, summary judgment should be granted only if the opposing party fails to present sufficient evidence to permit a jury reasonably to find for him. Put differently, unless the opposing party comes forward with sufficient evidence to support a verdict in her favor, summary judgment should be entered in favor of the moving party.

3. Case-by-Case Determination [§1633]

The court's evaluation process must be made on a case-by-case basis. As with judgment as a matter of law, therefore, it is difficult to generalize "rules" for making summary judgment decisions, but there are a number of general principles that are helpful in approaching problems.

a. All reasonable inferences indulged in favor of opposing party [§1634]

The court is to make all reasonable inferences in favor of the opposing party, and to view the evidence in the light most favorable to that party.

b. Court may not "weigh" evidence [§1635]

The court is to determine whether there is a genuine dispute; if there is, it may not choose between two versions of events and grant summary judgment to the party whose version seems more persuasive.

c. Role of higher burden of proof [§1636]

The Supreme Court has held that when a party will bear a heightened burden of proof at trial, the court should use that higher standard in scrutinizing the evidence at the summary judgment stage. [**Anderson v. Liberty Lobby, Inc.,** *supra*, §1630—"clear and convincing" required] *Criticism:* It is difficult to know how the court is to give effect to the higher standard of proof without "weighing" the evidence.

d. Witness credibility [§1637]

Ordinarily, the credibility of witnesses cannot be assessed on summary judgment because that assessment is left to the jury at trial.

(1) Uncontradicted interested witness [§1638]

The testimony of an uncontradicted interested witness is usually said not to be sufficient to support summary judgment in favor of a party with the burden of proof. *Rationale:* Even an uncontradicted witness might be disbelieved if he has an interest in the litigation.

(2) Disinterested witness [§1639]

In some cases, courts suggest that an uncontradicted affidavit of a disinterested witness is sufficient to support summary judgment for a party with the burden of proof. [*See, e.g.,* **Lundeen v. Cordner,** 354 F.2d 401 (8th Cir. 1966)—affidavit of disinterested witness accepted in absence of a "positive showing that this witness's testimony could be impeached"]

(3) Sham affidavit doctrine [§1640]

If the deposition of a party or an interested witness is used as the basis for a summary judgment motion by the other side, and that witness submits an affidavit in opposition to summary judgment repudiating the deposition testimony, the court may disregard the affidavit. [**Perma Research & Development Co. v. Singer Co.,** 410 F.2d 572 (2d Cir. 1968)— "If a party who has been examined at length on deposition could raise an issue of fact simply by submitting an affidavit contradicting his own prior testimony, this would greatly diminish the utility of summary judgment as a procedure for screening out sham issues of fact"]

e. "Disbelief" evidence [§1641]

Although the jury may ordinarily disbelieve even an uncontradicted witness (*see supra,* §1638), the logical possibility that this disbelief would persuade the jury that the truth is actually the opposite of what the witness claims is *irrelevant* on a motion for summary judgment or a motion for judgment as a matter of law. [*See* **Dyer v. MacDougall,** 201 F.2d 265 (2d Cir. 1952)] *Rationale:* Allowing such credibility determinations to satisfy the burden of proof at trial would immunize the trial court's ruling on judgment as a matter of law from appellate review since demeanor of witnesses is usually not preserved in the record on appeal. In addition, it would mean that summary judgment could never be granted against a party with the burden of proof—

even though that party could point to no supporting evidence—when the moving party relied on a witness.

f. Motive, intent, and state of mind [§1642]

If issues of motive, intent, or state of mind are presented, it is said that summary judgment is peculiarly inappropriate. [**Cross v. United States**, 336 F.2d 431 (2d Cir. 1964)] *Rationale:* Assessments of a person's motive are best made on the basis of observing her demeanor while testifying, and the pertinent facts are peculiarly within her knowledge.

g. Cross-motions for summary judgment [§1643]

If both the plaintiff and the defendant move for summary judgment, it might seem that the court should grant the motion of one or the other, but that is not so. Instead, *the showing made by each party must be evaluated independently*. It would be entirely consistent to deny both motions if neither party made a sufficient showing; that would only mean that an issue of fact remains and a trial is necessary to decide the case.

EXAM TIP **gilbert**

Don't be fooled by an exam question in which two opponents move for summary judgment. If you lose sight of the purpose of summary judgment, you might think that the court must deny one party's motion and grant the other party's, but this is not so. Summary judgment is appropriate *only if there is no genuine issue of material fact* to be decided, and it is possible, maybe even likely, that *neither* party has presented a sufficient case to obtain summary judgment in its favor.

---

h. Complex cases [§1644]

For a time, a number of cases suggested that in complex cases (particularly antitrust cases) summary judgment was to be avoided. [*See, e.g.,* **Poller v. Columbia Broadcasting System, Inc.**, 368 U.S. 464 (1962)] Recently, however, courts have evinced more willingness to entertain summary judgment in such cases. [*See, e.g.,* **Matsushita Electric Industries Co. v. Zenith Radio Corp.**, 475 U.S. 574 (1986)]

i. "Slightest doubt" standard contrasted [§1645]

Under a line of Second Circuit cases, summary judgment was said to be inappropriate whenever there was the "slightest doubt" about the outcome at trial. [*See, e.g.,* **Arnstein v. Porter**, 154 F.2d 464 (2d Cir. 1946)] However, this approach has been repudiated. [*See, e.g.,* **Beal v. Lindsay**, 468 F.2d 287 (2d Cir. 1972)]

C. Procedure

1. Initial Showing [§1646]

Analytically, the court should not reach the question whether there is a genuine dispute until it has evaluated the moving party's showing to determine whether it suffices to justify pretrial scrutiny of the evidence.

a. Moving party's burden [§1647]

The moving party is to demonstrate "that there is no genuine issue as to any material fact and that the moving party is entitled to judgment as a matter of law." [Fed. R. Civ. P. 56(c)]

(1) Moving party with burden of proof [§1648]

If the moving party has the burden of proof, he must produce evidence of such strength that *no reasonable jury could find for the opposing party*.

(2) Moving party without burden of proof [§1649]

If the moving party does not have the burden of proof, the matter is more complicated.

(a) Early view [§1650]

Relying on a decision of the Supreme Court [**Adickes v. S.H. Kress & Co.**, *supra*, §582], some lower courts took the position that a moving party without the burden of proof had to make as strong a showing as one with the burden of proof (*supra*) to invoke summary judgment.

(b) Current view [§1651]

Celotex Corp. (*supra*, §1628), rejected the early view. However, the exact requirements in this circumstance are unclear, owing to disagreement within the Court on the proper formulation.

1) Mere conclusory assertion [§1652]

It appears that a bald assertion that the opposing party lacks sufficient evidence to support his case is not sufficient. [*See* **Celotex Corp. v. Catrett**, *supra* (White, J., concurring)—"It is not enough to move for summary judgment . . . with the conclusory assertion that the plaintiff has no evidence to prove his case"] *Rationale:* "Such a 'burden' of production is no burden at all and would simply permit summary judgment procedure to be converted into a tool for harassment." [**Celotex Corp. v. Catrett**, *supra* (Brennan, J., dissenting)]

2) Initial responsibility of informing court of basis for motion [§1653]

The majority in *Celotex* stated that the moving party has the initial responsibility of informing the court of the basis for its motion; the party must identify those portions of the record which it believes demonstrate the absence of a genuine issue of material fact. However, it is unclear how much more than a conclusory assertion this is designed to require.

3) Prima facie showing [§1654]

Justice Brennan, dissenting in *Celotex*, urged that the moving party should have to "make a prima facie showing that it is entitled to summary judgment."

(c) Method of making showing

1) Affirmative evidence [§1655]

The moving party can offer affirmative evidence that negates an essential element of the opposing party's case.

2) Preview of opposing party's case [§1656]

If the thrust of the motion is that the opposing party has no evidence, however, the showing should reliably indicate that. Thus, the moving party should be able to point to discovery calculated to elicit from the opposing party any evidence he had to support his case and then demonstrate that this evidence is inadequate. Such a showing invites the argument that the opposing party needs more time to gather facts. (*See infra*, §1680.)

3) Possible role for initial disclosure [§1657]

As amended in 2000, Rule 26(a)(1) requires each party to disclose witnesses and documents that it "may use to support" its claims or defenses. (*See supra*, §1291.) In some cases, the content (or absence) of such disclosures may be used to satisfy the initial showing requirement.

b. Opposing party's burden

(1) Initial showing not made [§1658]

If the moving party has not made the required initial showing, there technically is *no burden* on the opposing party to make any showing in response to the motion, which should be denied.

(a) No advance determination of sufficiency of initial showing [§1659]

However, the opposing party is not entitled to advance notice of the court's attitude toward the sufficiency of the moving party's showing. Thus, to be prudent, the opposing party should submit opposing evidence unless he is absolutely sure of the insufficiency.

(b) Attacking showing [§1660]

The opposing party can call the court's attention to other material in the record that demonstrates the existence of a genuine issue.

Example: In *Celotex*, plaintiff claimed that her husband died due to exposure to asbestos that defendant manufactured. Defendant moved for summary judgment on ground that there was no evidence in the record linking its products to plaintiff's husband's death. The court held that summary judgment should not be granted because plaintiff was able to point to material in the record that indicated that at trial she would have a witness to support her claim—a letter from an official of a former employer of plaintiff's husband indicating that company records showed that plaintiff's husband had been exposed to defendant's products. [**Catrett v. Celotex Corp.**, 826 F.2d 23 (D.C. Cir. 1987)]

---

(2) Initial showing made [§1661]

If the moving party has made the initial showing, the burden is on the opposing party to *come forward with evidentiary material* that establishes the existence of a triable issue, *i.e., sufficient evidence to support a jury verdict in his favor*.

2. Notice [§1662]

The opposing party is entitled to notice of the motion for summary judgment and an opportunity to submit opposing materials. [Fed. R. Civ. P. 56(c)—10 days; Cal. Civ. Proc. Code §437c(a)—28 days]

a. Notice of possibility of summary judgment against moving party [§1663]

The courts are divided on whether summary judgment can be entered against the *moving* party without prior notice that this result might occur. [*See* **Coach Leatherware Co. v. Ann Taylor, Inc.**, 933 F.2d 162 (2d Cir. 1991)—"a court need not give notice of its intention to enter summary judgment against the moving party"; *compare* **American Flint Glass Workers Union v. Beaumont Glass Co.**, 62 F.3d 572 (3d Cir. 1995)—court may not grant summary judgment sua sponte against the moving party unless the court gives notice and an opportunity to oppose summary judgment]

(1) Distinguish—cross-motions for summary judgment [§1664]

This situation is different from a case in which there are cross-motions for summary judgment. (*See supra*, §1643.) In that situation, each side is on notice that the other side is seeking summary judgment.

b. Contrast—notice of need to submit opposing material [§1665]

The opposing party generally is *not* entitled to notice of the need to submit opposing material to avoid summary judgment, even if there is a question about the sufficiency of the moving party's initial showing. However, some courts require that pro se litigants be advised, either by the court or by the moving party, about the general requirements of Rule 56 regarding the submission of materials to support their claims in response to summary judgment motions. [*See* **Vital v. Interfaith Medical Center,** 168 F.3d 615 (2d Cir. 1999)—pro se plaintiff must be given such notice; **Rand v. Rowland,** 154 F.3d 952 (9th Cir. 1998)—pro se prisoner litigants must be given notice]

3. Time for Motion [§1666]

The earliest moment for filing motions for summary judgment varies, and some effort is made to protect defendants against having to respond to such motions before they have a reasonable time to obtain representation and investigate the case. In federal court, the plaintiff must wait until 20 days after the commencement of the action, while the defendant can move for summary judgment at any time. [Fed. R. Civ. P. 56(a), (b)] In California, by way of contrast, the motion is not allowed until 60 days after the general appearance in the action of each party against whom it is directed. [Cal. Civ. Proc. Code §437c(a)]

4. Materials Considered on Motion

a. Pleadings [§1667]

Admissions contained in the pleadings may be used to decide summary judgment motions, but otherwise the pleadings do not bear on the summary judgment decision except to identify the issues in contention in the lawsuit. [*See* Fed. R. Civ. P. 56(e)—opposing party may not rest on allegations of pleadings in response to motion]

b. Affidavits [§1668]

Affidavits made on *personal knowledge* of facts, showing that the affiant would be competent to testify to these facts in court, may form the basis of a ruling on a motion for summary judgment. It is probably true that affidavits are the most common materials submitted in support of (or opposition to) motions for summary judgment. However, *the moving party is not required to submit affidavits.* [**Celotex Corp. v. Catrett,** *supra,* §1651]

c. Discovery materials [§1669]

Material developed through discovery, whether by interrogatory, document request, deposition, or request for admissions, may be used in connection with a summary judgment motion. Often, affidavits of attorneys are used as vehicles to bring such materials to the attention of the court by "authenticating" true copies of the discovery materials.

(1) Distinguish—materials improperly withheld from discovery or disclosure [§1670]

Materials that should have been disclosed or turned over through discovery, or to supplement prior disclosures or discovery responses, may not be used as evidence on a motion for summary judgment. [Fed. R. Civ. P. 37(c)(1); *see supra,* §§1304-1305] Thus, if either party submits such material, the opposing party may argue that the material should be disregarded in ruling on summary judgment for this reason.

d. Oral testimony [§1671]

Oral testimony may be heard on a motion for summary judgment, but only very rarely, since the objective is to decide the case without holding a trial, and hearing oral testimony might defeat that purpose. Moreover, the need to present matters orally may suggest that a credibility determination is necessary.

EXAM TIP   **gilbert**

Summary judgment issues often appear in law school exams. Be sure that your answer notes the basics. A court will grant summary judgment only if there is *no issue of material fact*. In determining whether there is an issue of material fact, the court should consider any admissions that were made; affidavits based on personal knowledge of relevant facts; and relevant material obtained through discovery (*e.g.,* copies of relevant documents, such as the contract in a contract case). Generally oral testimony is not taken.

---

e. Admissibility [§1672]

Materials considered in connection with a motion for summary judgment must generally be capable of admission into evidence. [Fed. R. Civ. P. 56(e); Cal. Civ. Proc. Code §437c(d)]

(1) Possible relaxation for opposing party [§1673]

Although the moving party must present material that would be admissible, it may be that the opposing party is not held to such requirements, as long as he can show that he will have admissible evidence at trial. For example, after remand in **Celotex Corp. v. Catrett**, *supra*, a dissenting judge pointed out that the court denied summary judgment based on a letter from an official, even though there was no showing that this official had personal knowledge on the subject or that there was admissible evidence to support the assertions in the letter.

(a) Criticism

Relaxing the requirement that the opposing party present admissible evidence may erode the value of summary judgment in weeding out groundless claims and defenses.

(b) Material need not be in admissible form [§1674]

Affidavits are usually not admissible at trial because they are hearsay, but they clearly suffice to oppose a motion for summary judgment when they indicate that the affiant would be able to testify to the facts recited. Thus, the nonmoving party need not produce evidence in a form that would be admissible at trial in order to avoid summary judgment.

(2) Determination of admissibility [§1675]

Before evaluating the evidentiary materials to determine whether summary judgment should be granted, the court can entertain objections to the admissibility of some of the materials and exclude them from consideration if they are not admissible. [*See, e.g.,* **In re Japanese Products Antitrust Litigation**, 723 F.2d 238 (3d Cir. 1983), *rev'd on other grounds sub nom.* **Matsushita Electric Industries Co. v. Zenith Radio Corp.**, *supra*, §1644—Court commended district court's hearing on evidentiary objections because it would afford fuller consideration of them than would be possible at trial]

(3) Waiver of evidentiary objections [§1676]

Evidentiary objections not made in connection with summary judgment proceedings may be waived, at least as to the summary judgment proceedings. [Cal. Civ. Proc. Code §437c(b)]

5. Partial Summary Judgment [§1677]

When only some of the claims or defenses are ripe for summary judgment, it can be granted as to some but not all the claims or defenses before the court.

EXAM TIP   **gilbert**

On your exam, it is important to remember that summary judgment can be directed to *individual claims*, even if it is not appropriate for the entire case. Thus, if a plaintiff's complaint alleges three causes of action (*e.g.*, unfair competition, trademark infringement, and breach of contract), the defendant may move for summary judgment on any one or more of the claims. If the defendant moves for summary judgment on all claims, the court may grant the motion as to all claims or fewer than all.

---

6. Order Establishing Material Facts [§1678]

If the summary judgment motion cannot be entirely granted, the court may enter an order determining that certain facts are established, and this order will govern the further course of the action. [Fed. R. Civ. P. 56(d); Cal. Civ. Proc. Code §427c(g)]

a. Statement of undisputed facts [§1679]

In some jurisdictions, the court requires that each party to a summary judgment motion list all facts it claims are undisputed. [*See, e.g.,* Cal. Civ. Proc. Code §437c(b)]

7. Inability to Provide Responsive Materials [§1680]

When the opposing party is unable to provide opposing materials, *the court may continue the hearing* to allow materials to be obtained. [Fed. R. Civ. P. 56(f); Cal. Civ. Proc. Code §437c(h)] *Rationale:* The Supreme Court identified the concerns behind this option in *Celotex* (*supra*, §1668): "no serious claim can be made that respondent was in any sense 'railroaded' by a premature motion for summary judgment. Any potential problem with such premature motions can be adequately dealt with under Rule 56(f)."

a. Showing required [§1681]

The opposing party is said to be required to make a showing that continuance is appropriate. For example, Federal Rule 56(f) permits a continuance for "reasons stated" in the opposing party's affidavits. *Note:* In practice, courts may be liberal in treating contentions about the need for more discovery as sufficient to justify continuances.

b. Facts material and important [§1682]

A continuance is appropriate only if the additional facts appear important to the disposition of the summary judgment motion.

---

e.g. **Example:** In an action for damages for personal injuries, defendant's need to do more discovery on the issue of damages would not be a reason for deferring ruling on plaintiff's motion for partial summary judgment on the question of liability.

---

c. Facts can be obtained [§1683]

A continuance is appropriate only if there is some reasonable possibility that the additional facts the opposing party wishes to present can be obtained.

---

e.g. **Example:** In an action growing out of an accident where the issue is whether the light was red for defendant and the only two witnesses known to the parties both have testified that the light was green for defendant, plaintiff's hope that another witness will be discovered may be insufficient to justify delaying a ruling on summary judgment. [*See* **Dyer v. MacDougall,** *supra,* §1641—all alleged witnesses to slander assert that statement was never made by defendant]

---

d. Prior opportunity [§1684]

If the opposing party has had a reasonable opportunity to obtain the facts but has not done so, that may cause the court to refuse the continuance.

---

e.g. **Example:** In an action where intervenor moved for summary judgment on the basis of affidavits by a disinterested witness, the court noted that plaintiff had not taken the opportunity to take the deposition of this witness. [**Lundeen v. Cordner,** *supra,* §1639]

---

8. Effect of Summary Judgment Decision [§1685]

If the motion is granted, judgment is entered for the prevailing party. If the motion is denied, the litigation continues.

9. Appellate Review

a. Standard [§1686]

The appellate court uses a plenary standard of review, and gives no deference to the trial court's decision.

b. Timing [§1687]

Unless summary judgment is entered as to the entire case, appellate review of the summary judgment decision may be delayed until the final decision of the case. (*See infra,* §§2094-2134, for discussion of the final judgment rule.)

c. Order denying motion [§1688]

If summary judgment is denied, no judgment results, so the order is not reviewable until after the trial. By that time, a mistaken denial of summary judgment may be treated as *harmless error* if the trial was properly conducted and the judgment after the trial is supported by the evidence at trial.

SUMMARY JUDGMENT—A SUMMARY	**gilbert**	
CIRCUMSTANCES	No genuine issue of material fact and moving party is entitled to judgment as a matter of law.	
SUPPORT FOR MOTION	Pleadings, affidavits, discovery materials, oral testimony (rare).	
TIMING	Defendant:	Anytime.
	Plaintiff:	Anytime after 20 days from commencement of the action or after receiving service of motion for summary judgment by adverse party.

Chapter Eight: Managerial Judging, Pretrial Conference, and Settlement Promotion

---

CONTENTS

Chapter Approach

Chapter Approach

Until recently, pretrial conference and settlement promotion were considered beyond the scope of a first year course, and they still are more likely to be given intense attention in an advanced course on complex litigation. Nevertheless, they have increasingly been covered in the basic first year civil procedure course. Moreover, they may play an increasing role in examinations involving challenges to actions by judges that fall outside the traditional realm of judicial activity. In connection with such examination questions, there are two basic questions to be asked:

1. **Did the court have authority to take the action it took?**

   Except for "inherent authority," a slippery idea, courts must usually ground their right to take nontraditional actions in some statute or court rule. Many jurisdictions allow or require scheduling conferences and orders to set time limits for joining parties, amending pleadings, limiting discovery, etc. Status conferences and final pretrial conferences are also allowed to discuss issue simplification and promote settlement. Courts have also been given some power to use mandatory nonbinding arbitration and summary jury trials to promote settlement without trial.

2. **Did the court abuse its discretion?**

   Assuming that there was authority, an appellate court could still reverse on the ground that under the circumstances this authority was abused. The main point to remember is that the court cannot club a party into submission.

In addition, examination questions may ask for evaluation of the *policy questions* that surround the innovations that are discussed in this chapter. Indeed, an examination question may ask the student to evaluate a proposed new program of expediting litigation by comparing it to current practices and considering the arguments for and against adopting the new regime. The main arguments for most procedures are that they streamline cases by simplifying issues and make trial results less uncertain and therefore promote early settlement. The main disadvantages are that the procedures: (i) take some control away from the parties over their own cases; (ii) may force important decisions early, before the parties have had a chance to fully investigate issues; and (iii) often force judges to "prejudge" a case or issue, before all the facts are in.

A. Pretrial Conferences and Managerial Judging

1. Historical Background

a. Federal Rule 16 [§1689]

The original Federal Rule 16 authorized a pretrial conference to be held shortly before trial in order to organize the trial. However, concern arose that the relaxed pleading requirements and broadened discovery of the Federal Rules (and the state systems that emulated the Federal Rules) had led to amorphous lawsuits involving excessive discovery expense because they were not focused. In response, and due to rising case-load pressures, federal judges in metropolitan districts began, during the 1970s, to experiment with more active pretrial control of litigation. Sometimes this control was handled on a judge-by-judge basis, and sometimes it was implemented by district-wide local rules. This expanded judicial role in the pretrial process was explicitly built into the Federal Rules, which provide for mandatory conferences among the parties [Fed. R. Civ. P. 26(f)], numerous pretrial conferences [Fed. R. Civ. P. 16(a) - (c)], and a final pretrial conference [Fed. R. Civ. P. 16(d)].

b. State court practices [§1690]

In state courts, such pretrial control was less prominent, in part because in many states, cases were not assigned to a single judge for all purposes. Nevertheless, some added emphasis on pretrial supervision has emerged. [*See, e.g.,* Cal. Civ. Proc. Code §§575-76—regarding pretrial conferences for judicial management]

2. Scheduling [§1691]

Under Rule 16, federal district court judges have an expanded pretrial role in the control and development of civil cases.

a. Mandatory scheduling order [§1692]

Except in categories of cases exempted by local rule, federal district courts are *required* to enter a "*scheduling order*" within 90 days after a defendant's appearance and within 120 days after service of the complaint. This order is to set time limits for joining parties, amending pleadings, completing discovery, and filing motions. [Fed. R. Civ. P. 16(b)]

b. Conference [§1693]

The scheduling order is to be preceded by consultation with the parties by telephone, mail, or other suitable means.

c. Other scheduling limitations [§1694]

Beyond the mandatory scheduling limitations, the court may impose much more specific scheduling requirements regarding a variety of matters as part of its pretrial management of a case. These orders can come at periodic pretrial or status conferences.

TIMING OF PRETRIAL SCHEDULING EVENTS

CONFERENCE OF PARTIES

At least 14 days before court's conference with parties or scheduling order; parties discuss nature and basis of claims and defenses

SCHEDULING ORDER

Within 90 days after defendant's initial appearance and 120 days after service of complaint; sets time limits for joining parties, completing discovery, and filing motions

FINAL PRETRIAL ORDER

Order regarding matters covered at conference; controls issues at trial

CONFERENCE WITH PARTIES

Some time before scheduling order is given, court contacts parties to discuss issues; may be by phone, mail, etc.

FINAL PRETRIAL CONFERENCE

After discovery is completed, court meets with parties to streamline case; gives both parties notice of subjects to be considered at trial

d. Significance [§1695]

Limitations on timing of discovery and other matters can be extremely significant to the parties, because they can no longer exercise unilateral control over the sequence and timing of pretrial litigation activities. In particular, this control may be especially significant where the parties wish to defer formal litigation activities for some reason (*e.g.,* to discuss settlement), but the court's schedule prevents this.

e. Exempted categories of cases [§1696]

A district court may, by local rule, exempt categories of cases from the scheduling order requirements on the ground that those requirements would be inappropriate in such cases. [Fed. R. Civ. P. 16(b)]

3. Discovery Control [§1697]

The Federal Rules affirmatively direct judges to limit discovery if it is cumulative, if the party seeking discovery has had ample opportunity already, or when the discovery sought is "unduly burdensome," given the needs of the case. [Fed. R. Civ. P. 26(b)(2)]

a. Conference by parties [§1698]

At least 14 days before the Rule 16(b) scheduling conference or order, the parties are to confer regarding "the nature and basis of their claims and defenses" and to develop a discovery plan. [Fed. R. Civ. P. 26(f)] Within 10 days after this meeting, they are to submit a written report to the court of their plan. [*See* Official Form 35]

(1) Exempted categories of cases

Cases falling in categories exempted from the initial disclosure requirements by Rule 26(a)(1) are also exempt from the conference requirement. [Fed. R. Civ. P. 26(a)(1)(E); 26(f) *see supra*, §1294] Recall, however, that courts may not exempt categories of cases from the initial disclosure requirements by local rule. (*See supra*, §1308.)

b. Court's pretrial order [§1699]

Based on the parties' report under Rule 26(f), the court is to enter an order that should limit the time to complete discovery [Fed. R. Civ. P. 16(b)(3)] and may include provisions regarding "the control and scheduling of discovery" [Fed. R. Civ. P. 16(c)(6)].

(1) Criticism

Such precise discovery limitations further impinge on the parties' freedom to control the lawsuit. Moreover, the task of designing such limitations requires the judge to develop a much greater familiarity with the action than would otherwise be necessary, and raises the risk that the judge may misapprehend what is important (and therefore worthy of pursuit through discovery).

4. Issue Simplification [§1700]

At a pretrial or status conference, the court can discuss *simplification of the issues* and seek to obtain *stipulations and admissions of fact* to simplify the case.

a. Rationale

By the time the matters are raised in the pretrial conference, it is said that the parties know more about their case and that, therefore, it is fair to pressure them to commit to binding positions for purpose of the litigation. However, there is concern that early pressure toward issue simplification may undermine the supposed benefits of relaxed pleading and unduly constrict cases before the facts are out.

b. Compelled admissions [§1701]

The court may not compel admissions from an unwilling party, but the court does have the right to pressure parties to abandon positions that seem unsupported. *Criticism:* Again, the court may not adequately appreciate the circumstances of the case based on the explanation given at the pretrial conference and may unjustifiably curtail legitimate litigation opportunities.

5. Settlement Promotion [§1702]

It has long been recognized that more active judicial involvement in pretrial activities could have an effect on settlement of cases, but for some time many judges were reluctant to become overtly involved in settlement discussions, because that might seem to erode their impartiality. This reluctance has waned, and Rule 16(c)(9) now explicitly authorizes discussion of the possibility of settlement.

a. Tactics [§1703]

Judges use a variety of tactics to foster settlement, including meeting separately with each side, requiring attendance of clients at settlement conferences, and meeting with clients outside the presence of their lawyers.

b. Mandatory attendance [§1704]

Rule 16(c) authorizes the court to require that a party or its representative be present or reasonably available by telephone to consider settlement.

c. No power to dictate terms of settlement [§1705]

The court is not authorized to dictate the terms of the settlement. [**Kothe v. Smith**, 771 F.2d 667 (2d Cir. 1985)—Rule 16 "was not designed as a means for clubbing the parties—or one of them—into an involuntary compromise"] Nevertheless, the court may suggest terms for a settlement that the parties may follow.

d. Ambiguity of judicial role [§1706]

The judge's role in settlement is hard to square with the traditional notion that the judge decides disputed matters according to standards set out by the law.

(1) Evaluation of terms of settlement [§1707]

It is unclear whether the judge should promote *any* agreement that seems likely to obtain the consent of the parties, or insist that the agreement correspond, somehow, to the strengths and weaknesses of the merits of the parties' positions.

(2) Absence of trial [§1708]

The judge would usually reach conclusions about the strengths and weaknesses of the parties' positions on the merits only after a trial. To the extent that the judge is to rely on her opinion about the strength of the case in suggesting proper parameters for settlement, involvement in settlement seems to circumvent the normal decisionmaking process.

---

e.g. **Example—the weak case for plaintiff:** If the case for the plaintiff appears weak, the judge's role becomes difficult to comprehend in traditional terms of decisions according to the law. For example, if the plaintiff has a strong case on liability, but little in the way of provable damages, the judge may be able to suggest a reasonable compromise based on the rules governing damages and her experience with awards in similar cases. However, when the plaintiff's case is weak on liability, it is hard to identify any benchmarks. There is no legal standard or reference point in decided cases for determining the "right" settlement amount in a case where the plaintiff has a small chance of success on liability, but large provable damages, since the result at trial would essentially be all or nothing for the plaintiff.

---

e. Promotion of alternative dispute resolution [§1709]

The judge may also explore the "use of special procedures (*e.g.,* mini-trials, summary jury trials, mediation, etc.) to assist in resolving the dispute" during pretrial conferences. [Fed. R. Civ. P. 16(c)(9)]

6. Final Pretrial Conference

a. Purpose [§1710]

The final pretrial conference is intended to simplify and streamline the trial and resolve as much as possible before trial. In addition, it serves to give both sides advance notice of the subjects to be covered at trial, so that they can be prepared.

b. Required pretrial disclosures [§1711]

The final pretrial conference will ordinarily follow the pretrial disclosures. At least 30 days before trial, each party is to make further disclosures regarding *evidence the party may present at trial.* [Fed. R. Civ. P. 26(a)(3)]

(1) Matters to be disclosed [§1712]

The following types of evidence should be disclosed, *except for evidence used solely to impeach witness testimony:*

(a) The *names of the witnesses* the party "expects to present" and those it "may call if the need arises" [Fed. R. Civ. P. 26(a)(3)(A)];

(b) The *witnesses whose testimony will be presented by deposition* [Fed. R. Civ. P. 26(a)(3)(B)]; and

(c) The *documents or other exhibits* the party expects to offer or which it may offer if the need arises [Fed. R. Civ. P. 26(a)(3)(C)].

(2) Waiver of objections [§1713]

As to the indicated exhibits, the other parties must object within 14 days or waive most objections to the admissibility of the exhibits or to the presentation of a witness by deposition in lieu of live testimony.

(3) Additional local requirements [§1714]

A number of courts, as a matter of local rule, require more detailed pretrial submissions.

c. Topics covered [§1715]

Local requirements vary, but courts may require delineation of a variety of matters, including the following.

(1) Undisputed facts [§1716]

The parties may be required to list all undisputed facts relevant to the case in pretrial filings.

(2) Disputed facts [§1717]

Similarly, the parties may have to list all facts that need to be resolved at the trial.

(3) Witness lists [§1718]

The parties are usually required to identify all witnesses they will call during their direct cases. (*See supra,* §1712.) In some instances, they are required also to provide a summary of the substance of the testimony that each witness will give.

(a) Direct testimony in writing—court trials

Some courts require that in cases to be tried to the court, the entire direct testimony of witnesses be submitted in writing in advance of trial.

(4) Legal issues [§1719]

The parties are often required to identify and brief all legal issues that are likely to arise in the case.

d. Final pretrial order [§1720]

Following the final pretrial conference, the court will usually enter a final pretrial order with regard to the matters covered at the conference. This order is to control the trial, and can be ***modified only "to prevent manifest injustice."*** [Fed. R. Civ. P. 16(e)]

(1) Exclusion of evidence and witnesses

The consequence of failure to list a witness or piece of evidence in the pretrial order can, therefore, be that the evidence will not be allowed in at the trial.

(2) Distinguish—amending pleadings

Ordinarily, the courts take a liberal attitude toward amendment of the pleadings, and it is uncertain how much more restrictive Rule 16 is than Rule 15 (dealing with pleading amendments). [*See* **Wallin v. Fuller**, 476 F.2d 1204 (5th Cir. 1973)—"It is unlikely that the pretrial order under Rule 16 was intended to make the pleadings, and therefore Rule 15, obsolete"; *compare* **United States v. First National Bank of Circle**, 652 F.2d 882 (9th Cir. 1981)—"Unless pretrial orders are honored and enforced, the objectives of the pretrial conference . . . will be jeopardized if not entirely nullified"]

7. Sanctions [§1721]

The federal courts have explicit authority to use sanctions to enforce their authority with regard to pretrial supervision of cases. [Fed. R. Civ. P. 16(f)]

a. Failure to appear [§1722]

If a party fails to appear through counsel at a pretrial conference, sanctions may be imposed. In some instances, the court may be able to require that the party appear personally. (*See supra*, §1704.)

b. Appearing substantially unprepared [§1723]

If a party or lawyer appears, but is not prepared to participate meaningfully in the conference, sanctions are appropriate.

c. Failure to participate in good faith [§1724]

A party can also be sanctioned for failure to participate in good faith. It is unclear whether the determination of good faith can be based on the court's disagreement with the party's views about proposed settlement terms or stipulations. (*See supra*, §§1705-1708, regarding absence of judicial power to require stipulations or impose terms of settlement.)

d. Sanctions available [§1725]

The court can impose the sanctions available for violation of discovery orders [Fed. R. Civ. P. 37(b)(2); *see supra*, §§1567-1594] and also impose expenses, including attorneys' fees, resulting from the failure to comply with responsibilities.

8. Effect on Work Product Protection [§1726]

Information such as the identity of witnesses and the subject matter of their testimony would ordinarily be protected work product, yet courts routinely require revelation of this material as part of the final pretrial process. It has been held that work product protection does not limit the power of the court to require revelation of pertinent information in pretrial preparation under Rule 16. [*In re* **San Juan Dupont Plaza Hotel Fire Litigation**, 859 F.2d 1007 (1st Cir. 1988)]

B. Court-Annexed Settlement Devices

1. Introduction [§1727]

Because informal settlement promotion seemed not to exhaust the potential for judicial promotion of settlement, judges began to experiment with other ways of facilitating settlement. Such efforts usually involved some simulation of a trial as a method of predicting the outcome of trial.

a. Rationale

A primary rationale for this form of judicial activity is that uncertainty about the outcome of a trial is a major impediment to settlement. Simulated substitutes, therefore, could erase much doubt and give the parties a more reliable format for negotiations. In addition, there are reports that such proceedings enhance litigant satisfaction and permit prompt resolution of cases.

b. Initial development at local level

In the federal court system, court-annexed programs initially developed at the local level as various districts experimented with different methods. The eventual federal statute (*see* below) built on and validated these methods.

2. Mandated Alternative Dispute Resolution in Federal Court [§1728]

Under the Alternative Dispute Resolution ("ADR") Act of 1998, district courts are directed to mandate in their local rules that, subject to certain exceptions, litigants in *all civil cases* "consider the use of an alternative dispute resolution process at an appropriate state in the litigation." [28 U.S.C. §652(a)] The Act further directs that each district devise and implement its own ADR program, and that it *"encourage and promote the use of alternative dispute resolution in its district."* [28 U.S.C. §651(b)] Because these activities occur in connection with cases proceeding in court, and under the auspices of the court, they are often referred to as *court-annexed ADR*.

a. ADR methods [§1729]

The Act authorizes use of *mediation, early neutral evaluation, summary jury trial, and, subject to certain limitations, arbitration.* All of these devices will be discussed in detail below.

b. Exempted categories of cases [§1730]

Each district court may exempt categories of cases from the ADR requirements. [28 U.S.C. §652(b)]

c. Panel of neutrals [§1731]

Each district is to maintain, and arrange for the training and evaluation of, a panel of neutrals to serve in ADR proceedings in the district. [28 U.S.C. §653] A neutral is usually a lawyer experienced in the legal field giving rise to the case.

d. Confidentiality [§1732]

Each district must, by local rule, provide for confidentiality in ADR proceedings conducted pursuant to the Act. [28 U.S.C. §652]

3. Mediation [§1733]

Mediation involves a neutral third party who attempts to find common ground on which the parties can reach an agreement and resolve their dispute. This role is very different from that of a judge or other person who "decides" a dispute.

a. Formal legal rules not binding [§1734]

Because the goal is to reach an agreement, the legal rules that might apply in court are not binding in mediation. They may, however, cast a "shadow" over the mediation and influence the result.

b. Creativity in devising solutions [§1735]

Because formal legal rules limiting court awards do not apply in mediation, the mediator can attempt to devise a solution that would not be available in an action litigated to judgment.

c. Goal is agreement of the parties [§1736]

If the mediator is successful, the parties will reach an agreement that should be *embodied in a contract between them*. These agreements are usually legally binding in accordance with principles of contract law.

d. Separate meetings with parties [§1737]

Mediators may often find it helpful to meet separately with the contending parties to try to develop solutions that warrant discussion. Separate meetings are permitted.

e. Mediation in state courts [§1738]

Mediation occurs in connection with state court actions as well as in federal court cases. In some states, there are statutory provisions authorizing court-annexed mediation. [*See* Cal. Civ. Proc. Code §§1775-1775.15]

4. Early Neutral Evaluation [§1739]

Early neutral evaluation originated in the United States District Court for the Northern District of California, and it relies on an experienced neutral lawyer (the neutral) to advise the parties on their prospects in the case after both sides have presented their positions. The parties get the advantage of an early, frank, and thoughtful assessment of their positions.

a. Experienced lawyer [§1740]
The neutral should be a lawyer with substantial experience in the field of law that gave rise to the suit.

b. Evaluative orientation [§1741]
The neutral is to bring a critical eye to the positions of the parties and offer them her assessment of the likely success of those positions. The goal is that this third-party assessment will *encourage the parties to be realistic about their chances of success.* This effort may include an indication by the neutral of her expectation of an award in the case.

c. Occurs early in case [§1742]
As suggested by the title of this ADR device, early neutral evaluation should occur early in the case, and before the parties have expended substantial resources on litigation.

d. Suggestions for future conduct of case [§1743]
Beyond assessing the likely outcome of the case, the neutral may offer the parties suggestions about the future conduct of the case to prepare it for trial should it not settle. These suggestions are conveyed only to the parties and are *not conveyed to the court.*

5. Summary Jury Trial [§1744]
The summary jury trial ("SJT") was invented in 1980 by a federal district judge in Cleveland.

a. Timing [§1745]
The SJT is normally deferred until all normal pretrial activities have been completed. All motions in limine (*i.e.,* motions seeking a protective order against prejudicial questions) and other similar pretrial matters should be disposed of and a final pretrial order entered.

b. Nature of hearing [§1746]
The specifics on summary jury trials may vary from place to place, but generally they have similar procedures:

(1) In courthouse [§1747]
The proceedings occur in the courthouse, in a regular courtroom, with a judge (or magistrate) presiding.

(2) Before jury [§1748]
The case is presented to a jury summoned to appear in the normal manner for juries.

(3) Lawyer presentations [§1749]

The bulk of the case is based on summaries by the lawyers of the evidence developed in the pretrial phase.

(a) Limitations on content [§1750]

Some guidelines will apply to limit the content of the summaries. The presentations may have to be based on material developed during discovery, or upon the attorney's representation that she has talked to the witness and that the witness would testify as described.

(b) Live testimony [§1751]

In some courts, limited live testimony may be allowed.

(4) Instructions by court [§1752]

After the lawyers have completed their summaries, the court gives the jury abbreviated instructions on the law applicable to the case.

(5) Verdict [§1753]

The jury is to render a consensus verdict, if possible, and if not, to report on reactions to the case on a juror-by-juror basis.

(6) Effort to settle [§1754]

With the added information provided by the jury verdict, the parties try to settle the case.

c. Secrecy [§1755]

Generally, the SJT is held in secret, and the public is not allowed to attend.

Example: In a suit claiming that builders of a nuclear power plant were liable for poor design because the facility leaked radioactive steam, a newspaper was denied access to the SJT on the ground that it was merely a settlement procedure. [**Cincinnati Gas & Electric Co. v. General Electric Co.,** 854 F.2d 900 (6th Cir. 1988)]

---

d. Binding effect [§1756]

In some instances, the parties can stipulate that the summary jury trial will be binding.

e. Compulsory participation [§1757]

There has been a split among the courts on whether an unwilling party can be compelled to participate in a SJT before being afforded an opportunity to have a regular trial in court. [*Compare* **Strandell v. Jackson County**, 838 F.2d 884 (7th Cir. 1987)—no power to compel—*with* **Arabian American Oil Co. v. Scarfone**, 119 F.R.D. 448 (M.D. Fla. 1988)—court has power to compel] However, a 1993 amendment to Rule 16 may have signaled a resolution of this split in favor of such judicial power, at least in districts that provide for SJT by local rule. [Fed. R. Civ. P. 16(c)(9)—court authority at pretrial conferences to take action with respect to "the use of special procedures to assist in resolving the dispute when authorized by statute or local rule"]

6. Court-Annexed Arbitration [§1758]

In the late 1970s, federal courts in some districts began experimenting with *mandatory nonbinding arbitration* in some cases. In 1988, Congress expressly sanctioned these experiments in 10 districts where such experiments had begun and authorized further experiments in 10 other districts. [28 U.S.C. §§651 *et seq.*] This authorization was further extended until Congress included arbitration in the 1998 Act, subject to certain limitations. States have authorized similar procedures in their courts. [*See, e.g.,* Cal. Civ. Proc. Code §§1141.10 *et seq.*]

a. Cases affected

(1) Federal court [§1759]

With the consent of the parties, a federal court may allow the referral for nonbinding arbitration of *any civil action* before it *except* cases involving *civil rights claims*, alleged *violations of constitutional rights*, or *damages* relief sought in an amount *exceeding $150,000*. [28 U.S.C. §654(a)]

(a) Safeguards on giving of consent [§1760]

District courts that authorize arbitration as an ADR device are required to adopt safeguards (*e.g.,* that the district court judge be informed of the identity of who consented) to ensure that parties who are asked to consent do so freely and knowingly. [28 U.S.C. §654(b)]

(b) Presumption regarding damages sought [§1761]

Unless counsel certifies that more than $150,000 is involved, the court may presume that damages do not exceed that amount. [28 U.S.C. §654(c)]

(2) State courts [§1762]

In state courts where arbitration is provided for, eligibility may turn on the amount claimed, as in federal courts. In California superior courts, for example, all civil actions where the amount in controversy in the opinion of the court will not exceed $50,000 are subject to arbitration. [Cal. Civ. Proc. Code §1141.11(a)]

(a) Dispute about amount claimed [§1763]

Under the California approach, there can be disputes about whether over $50,000 is really in controversy. [*See* Cal. Civ. Proc. Code §1141.16(a)—conference to be held to determine whether over $50,000 is actually in controversy]

(b) Equitable relief [§1764]

In California, arbitration may not be compelled if equitable relief is sought, unless the prayer for equitable relief is frivolous. [Cal. Civ. Proc. Code §1141.13]

b. Timing [§1765]

Arbitration generally occurs early in the litigation process.

c. Hearing [§1766]

The arbitration decision is based on a hearing, which resembles a trial, but may be more relaxed. The rules of evidence might not be applied with full force, and relaxed rules about the form of presentation of evidence (*e.g.,* narrative answers) may be allowed.

(1) Subpoena for witnesses [§1767]

Subpoenas under Federal Rule 45 are available to compel attendance of witnesses and production of documentary evidence for arbitration hearings. [28 U.S.C. §656]

(2) Oaths of witnesses [§1768]

Arbitrators may administer oaths and affirmations. [28 U.S.C. §655(a)(2)]

d. Award [§1769]

After the hearing, the arbitrator is to enter an award, which briefly identifies the prevailing party and (if necessary) the amount of damages. This award is filed in court and *becomes the judgment* of the court *unless a trial de novo is demanded.* [28 U.S.C. §657(a); Cal. Civ. Proc. Code §1141.20]

e. Trial de novo [§1770]

On timely demand, any party may insist that the case be restored to the regular trial calendar for trial de novo, which is conducted as a regular trial, unaffected by the arbitration proceedings. [28 U.S.C. §657(c); Cal. Civ. Proc. Code §1141.20]

(1) Less favorable result

In some jurisdictions, if the party who demands a trial de novo does not obtain a more favorable result in the trial de novo, it can be required to *reimburse the opposing party for certain costs.* [Cal. Civ. Proc. Code §1141.21]

f. Refusal to participate [§1771]

If a party refuses to participate in the arbitration or fails to participate in good faith, the court may have authority to deny a trial de novo. [*Compare* **New England Merchants National Bank v. Hughes**, 556 F. Supp. 712 (E.D. Pa. 1983)—trial de novo denied—*with* **Lyons v. Wickhorst**, 42 Cal. 3d 911 (1986)—no authority to deny trial de novo under California statute]

COURT-ANNEXED SETTLEMENT PROMOTION DEVICES **gilbert**

MEDIATION	EARLY NEUTRAL EVALUATION	SUMMARY JURY TRIAL	NONBINDING ARBITRATION
- Neutral third party helps parties find common ground on which to resolve a dispute - Formal rules of evidence and procedure not binding - Third party may meet with parties together or separately	- Neutral lawyer experienced in the type of case between the parties advises the parties on their chances of success in the case after hearing both sides present their positions	- Trial-like hearing before a jury; public not allowed - Lawyers present evidence to jury in a summary form based on discovery - Parties may try to settle based on information learned from jury verdict, or parties may stipulate that verdict is binding	- Trial-like hearing before an arbitrator - Available in civil actions where damages are less than $150,000, except civil rights or constitutional claims - Rules of evidence and procedure are relaxed - Arbitrator's award will be entered as a court order unless a trial de novo is timely demanded

Chapter Nine:
Trial

CONTENTS

Chapter Approach

This chapter covers a variety of topics pertaining to a trial. Some topics are important *before* trial: disqualification of the judge, right to trial by jury, and the selection of jurors. Some topics are relevant *during* trial: presentation of evidence, motions at the close of proof, arguments and instructions to the jury, and jury deliberations. Finally, some topics become important at the *end* of the trial, such as the motions after the verdict. Of these topics, the most likely to appear on your exam are:

1. **Right to Jury Trial**

    Consider whether there is a right to a trial by jury, normally because the case is at least in part *legal* (as opposed to equitable). If this right exists, has there been a *timely demand* for jury trial?

2. **Disqualification of the Judge**

    Look for facts showing *bias, personal knowledge* of the facts of the case, *financial interest* in the outcome, or a *relationship* with a party or counsel.

3. **Pre-Verdict Motions**

    Think about whether the side with the burden of producing the evidence has shown enough to create an issue for the jury. If not, the court may grant a motion for *judgment as a matter of law*. This was formerly called "directed verdict" in federal courts, and still is in most state court systems. Remember that the judge may *reserve ruling* on the motion and, if the jury verdict is not adequately supported by the evidence, grant a *judgment as a matter of law* or *new trial*.

4. **Jury Issues**

    Did the judge give the jury *proper instructions* as to the applicable law? Was there any *misconduct* of the jury that may provide a basis for *impeachment of the verdict*?

5. **Post-Verdict Motions**

    Besides *judgment n.o.v.* or post-verdict *judgment as a matter of law* in federal court (both of which are granted when the verdict is not adequately supported by the evidence), consider whether there are grounds for a *new trial* (*e.g.*, prejudicial misconduct, unfair surprise, improper evidence, etc.); a motion to *amend the judgment* (errors of law); or a motion for *relief from the judgment* (for clerical errors, fraud, newly discovered evidence).

A. Right to Trial by Jury

1. **Source of Right**

   a. **Federal courts**

      (1) **Federal Constitution [§1772]**

      The Seventh Amendment of the United States Constitution provides: "In suits at common law, where the value in controversy shall exceed twenty dollars, the right of trial by the jury shall be preserved." This requirement applies to diversity cases regardless of whether there would have been a jury trial if the case had been in state court. [**Simler v. Connor,** 372 U.S. 221 (1963)]

      (2) **Legislation [§1773]**

      In matters not covered by this constitutional provision, there may also be a statutory right to trial by jury where Congress has so provided.

   b. **State courts**

      (1) **No federal constitutional right [§1774]**

      Unlike many other Bill of Rights guarantees, the Seventh Amendment right to trial by jury in civil cases has not been held "incorporated" in the Due Process Clause of the Fourteenth Amendment. Hence, the federal Constitution does not assure such a right in state court proceedings. [**Walker v. Sauvinet,** 92 U.S. 90 (1875); **Minneapolis & St. Louis Railroad v. Bombolis,** 241 U.S. 211 (1916)]

      (2) **Federal legislation [§1775]**

      However, there may be a federal right to a jury trial in state court actions involving matters governed by federal law, where Congress has so provided.

      > **Example:** State court civil action based on claim under Federal Employers Liability Act. [*See* **Dice v. Akron, Canton & Youngstown Railroad,** 342 U.S. 359 (1952)]

      (3) **State constitutions [§1776]**

      Also, most state constitutions have provisions similar to the Seventh Amendment that apply to civil actions in state courts. [*See, e.g.,* Cal. Const. art. 1, §16]

2. **Cases Where Right Exists**

   a. **Basic historical test [§1777]**

   Because the Seventh Amendment and many state constitutional jury guarantees refer to "preserv[ing]" the right to a civil jury trial, a major factor in applying the guarantees is historical inquiry into practice at the time of their adoption. The right to jury trial existed in the English law courts but **not** in Chancery, where the system of equity was administered. Accordingly, with a traditional type of claim a federal court will consider whether the claim is *"legal"* or *"equitable"* as such terms were understood in 1791 (the year in which the Seventh Amendment became effective). [**Dimick v. Schiedt**, 293 U.S. 474 (1934)]

(1) Jury right after "merger" of law and equity [§1778]

With the abolition of separate law and equity court systems in the federal courts and nearly all states, the availability of a jury can no longer depend on the system in which a case is heard. Generally speaking (although with many qualifications), today if a claim would have gone before the law courts before merger, the constitutional jury right applies; if a claim would have been within equitable jurisdiction, there is no constitutional right to trial by jury.

(2) Criticism—vague distinction [§1779]

The line between "law" and "equity" was somewhat vague and shifting, and depended on the evolution of early English court systems. The main distinction related to the **remedy** sought. **Equity** generally afforded remedies such as **injunctions** that imposed duties directly on the parties, subjecting them to contempt sanctions in the event of disobedience. **Law courts,** on the other hand, usually afforded **monetary damages** and other remedies (*e.g.*, ejectment, replevin) that could be enforced by court officers with or without the cooperation of the parties.

RIGHT TO JURY TRIAL—EXAMPLES **gilbert**

RIGHT EXISTS		NO RIGHT EXISTS
Tort action seeking money damages for personal injury	⟷	Tort action seeking injunction against defendant's misconduct
Contract claim seeking money damages for breach	⟷	Contract claim seeking specific performance
Property action seeking replevin or ejectment	⟷	Property action seeking foreclosure of a mortgage

---

b. Present standards for right to jury trial

(1) Counterparts to actions at law—right to jury [§1780]

Modern actions that are counterparts to actions at law, such as personal injury damage claims or claims to recover damages for breach of contract, are triable to a jury.

(2) Counterparts to suits in equity—no right [§1781]

However, there is no right to a jury in actions that are counterparts to suits in equity—*e.g.*, actions to foreclose mortgages, to enjoin misconduct, or for specific performance of a contract.

(3) Statutory remedies [§1782]

With types of claims that existed when a constitutional guarantee was adopted, the historical inquiry is usually easy and determinative. Legislatures, however, regularly redefine common law rights, replace traditional claims with new forms, and create novel statutory rights. A simple historical test usually cannot resolve the jury right question in such cases, although historical analogies to traditional claims remain a significant factor.

(a) Statutory substitutes for actions at law [§1783]

Legislation cannot impair the right to jury trial in federal court when the right and remedy afforded fit the historical pattern of a judicial proceeding at law.

> **Example:** An action to evict a tenant for nonpayment of rent is triable to a jury, even where legislation has substituted a statutory remedy for the old common law remedy of ejectment. [**Pernell v. Southall Realty**, 416 U.S. 363 (1974)]

> **Example:** Suits by bankruptcy trustees to recover fraudulent conveyances from parties who had not submitted claims against the bankruptcy estate are "quintessentially suits at common law" and Congress could not remove the right to jury trial by assigning jurisdiction over such actions to bankruptcy courts. [**Granfinanciera, S.A. v. Nordberg**, 492 U.S. 33 (1989)]

1) Note

Federal bankruptcy judges (who lack Article III status) may conduct jury trials in proceedings within their authority, but only if they are "specially designated to exercise such jurisdiction by the district court and with the express consent of all the parties." [28 U.S.C. §157(e)]

2) But note

Proceedings under the federal Bankruptcy Code are mostly equitable, and a creditor who files a claim against the bankruptcy estate submits to the jurisdiction of the bankruptcy court. Such a creditor cannot insist on a jury trial should the trustee assert a claim to recover a preferential transfer. [**Langenkamp v. Culp**, 498 U.S. 42 (1990)]

(b) When "new right" involved [§1784]

Congress may provide for nonjury trials when the right to be enforced is one *not known* at common law and practical considerations justify withholding the right to a jury in order to assure efficient disposition, especially if initial adjudication and enforcement of the right are assigned to a *federal administrative agency* rather than an Article III court. When an action on a new statutory right can be initiated in *federal court,* the approach in such cases requires examining "both the nature of the issues involved and the remedy sought." There is to be a comparison of the statutory action to 18th-century, pre-merger English actions, and an examination of whether the remedy sought is legal or equitable in nature. The second *remedial inquiry is more important.* [**Chauffeurs, Teamsters & Helpers Local 391 v. Terry,** 494 U.S. 558 (1990)]

Example: Congress could create new duties of employers regarding employee safety and assign disputes to an administrative agency with which a jury trial would be incompatible. [**Atlas Roofing Co. v. Occupational Safety & Health Review Commission,** 430 U.S. 442 (1977)]

Compare: Proceedings to enforce new statutory rights *in federal court* are triable to a jury when the *remedy* sought is a legal remedy, such as damages (*e.g.,* claims under federal copyright or civil rights statutes). [**City of Monterey v. Del Monte Dunes at Monterey, Ltd.,** 526 U.S. 687 (1999); **Feltner v. Columbia Pictures Television, Inc.,** 523 U.S. 340 (1998); **Curtis v. Loether,** 415 U.S. 189 (1974)] Similarly, an employee who seeks back wages for a union's alleged breach of its duty of fair representation has a Seventh Amendment right to trial by jury in federal court. [**Chauffeurs, Teamsters & Helpers Local 391 v. Terry,** *supra*]

1) Civil penalty [§1785]

When a statute provides a civil penalty for violation (*e.g.,* a certain amount per day of violation), that is sufficient to create a right to jury trial in an action for a civil penalty. [**Tull v. United States,** 481 U.S. 412 (1987)—action for civil penalties for violation of Clean Water Act]

2) Distinguish—amount of penalty [§1786]

While holding that there is a right to jury trial *with regard to liability* for a civil penalty, the Supreme Court has held that there is no right to a jury trial on the *amount* of the penalty. [**Tull v. United States,** *supra*]

If you see a question on your exam in which Congress creates a new cause of action enforceable in court and provides that a jury trial shall not be available, chances are good that your professor wants you to discuss the Seventh Amendment right to a jury trial. Remember that the right is preserved *only as it existed in the 18th century;* if an 18th century citizen would not have had a right to a jury trial for a similar action, then Congress doesn't have to provide one now. A good rule of thumb to determine whether a right to a jury would have existed in the 18th century is to *look at the remedy sought.* If it is payment of money, there probably would have been a right to a jury. If it was a court order, there probably would not have been a jury trial right.

(4) Actions for declaratory relief [§1787]

Actions for declaratory judgments pose special problems because declaratory relief is a *statutorily created remedy* unknown to early English law or equity and thus neither legal nor equitable in nature. In general, the federal courts look to what the underlying nondeclaratory claim would have been and determine the jury right accordingly. [*See, e.g.,* **Terrell v. DeConna,** 877 F.2d 1267 (5th Cir. 1989)—declaratory judgment plaintiff's insurance coverage claim if brought for nondeclaratory coercive relief would have been equitable garnishment action, so no jury trial right existed]

(a) But note

Issues in declaratory judgment actions will often be questions of law for the court rather than of fact for the trier of fact, so no jury right may exist whether the action would be classified as legal or equitable.

3. Proceedings in Which Right to Jury Applies in Part

a. Actions joining legal and equitable claims [§1788]

Determining whether the right to trial by jury exists on a *claim* may be only part of the problem, for some cases involve both legal and equitable claims (*e.g.,* a contract action in which plaintiff seeks damages at law for past breach and an equitable order compelling future specific performance). In general, federal courts are to structure their proceedings to preserve a jury trial on issues common to the legal and equitable aspects of a case. [**Beacon Theatres v. Westover,** 359 U.S. 500 (1959)] This is usually true even if the equitable aspects of the case predominate [**Dairy Queen, Inc. v. Wood,** 369 U.S. 469 (1962)], which entirely or virtually eliminates in federal court any modern effect of the old equitable "clean-up" doctrine that allowed nonjury disposition of minor legal matters in a mainly equitable case. However, the clean-up doctrine survives in some states.

Remember that in federal courts, the right to a jury trial is paramount. Thus, if some issues in a case are jury triable and others are not, a jury trial should be granted *for the jury-triable issues*, even if those issues are minor in comparison to the nonjury-triable issues. This is not true in many states, however, which follow the equitable clean-up doctrine. The doctrine allows an equity court (not a jury) to hear minor jury-triable issues that are tied up with a case that is predominately equitable.

(1) Priority of issues at trial [§1789]

It may make a great deal of difference which issues in a case are tried first, since adjudication of the equitable claim may render meaningless the claim for legal relief, or vice versa. For example, suppose the plaintiff sues for rescission of a contract for fraud, while the defendant counter-sues for damages for breach of contract. If the court tries the rescission claim first and holds the contract unenforceable, it thereby disposes of any claim for damages by the defendant.

(a) State practice [§1790]

In state courts, the order of trial is usually within the *discretion* of the trial judge, who may order either the equitable or legal aspects tried first.

(b) Federal practice [§1791]

In federal courts, however, all issues affecting the claim for legal relief must ordinarily be tried *first* to the jury. The possibility of irreparable harm to a party from delay in granting an injunction can usually be handled by grant of *interlocutory injunctive relief* (*i.e.*, a temporary restraining order ("TRO") or preliminary injunction), which requires only provisional findings that will not bind the jury or dispose formally of the legal claims.

Example: The federal court was not to try equitable causes first in an antitrust case involving a complaint for declaratory judgment and injunction, and a counterclaim and cross-claim for antitrust treble damages, when final determination of common issues between the legal and equitable aspects of the case might prevent the jury trial of the counterclaim and cross-claim. [*See* **Beacon Theatres v. Westover**, *supra*]

1) Erroneous dismissal of legal claims [§1792]

The Seventh Amendment bars giving preclusive effect to a district court's determinations of issues common to legal and equitable claims when the court resolves the equitable claims first solely because it wrongly dismissed the legal claims. [**Lytle v. Household Manufacturing, Inc.**, 494 U.S. 545 (1990)]

b. Equitable proceedings seeking legal relief [§1793]

One historical role of equity was to provide procedural mechanisms for the resolution of complex disputes. Thus interpleader, class actions, and shareholder derivative suits were "inventions" of equity. However, in determining the right to jury trial, federal practice now focuses on the *nature of the underlying claim* rather than the procedural mechanism by which the claim is to be adjudicated.

(1) Shareholder actions [§1794]

In a shareholder derivative action in federal court, there is a right to jury trial on all issues that would have been tried by jury if the claim had been brought by the corporation itself. [**Ross v. Bernhard,** 396 U.S. 531 (1970)]

(2) Interpleader [§1795]

Similarly, an interpleader action would be triable to a jury when the underlying claims against the stakeholder would have been actions at law if brought by the interpleader claimants. [**Hyde Properties, Inc. v. McCoy,** 507 F.2d 301 (6th Cir. 1974)]

c. Issues of law and fact bearing on same claim [§1796]

Even when the right to trial by jury applies, some *issues* in a case may be questions of law for the judge while others are issues of fact for the jury. And if the issue of law is dispositive, the case is not decided by the jury. [**Markman v. Westview Instruments, Inc.,** 517 U.S. 370 (1996)—in a patent infringement case, construction of the patent is a question of law for the judge and may result in judgment as a matter of law against the patent holder, even though whether infringement occurred would be an issue of fact for the jury]

4. Right to Jury Trial Depends on Timely Demand [§1797]

Various rules govern the manner in which the right to jury trial must be asserted. Failure to comply with these rules operates as a waiver of the constitutional right.

a. State practice [§1798]

In state court proceedings, the right to jury trial usually must be exercised by a demand in writing at the time the case is set for trial. Otherwise, the right is waived.

(1) Note

If cases are set for trial by request of the parties (*e.g.,* in a motion for trial setting), the demand must be made as part of that request. Where cases are set for trial automatically by the court, the parties ordinarily have a limited period of time after receipt of the notice of trial setting within which to file the written demand for jury trial. [Cal. Civ. Proc. Code §631]

(2) And note

Frequently, a deposit of jury fees is required at the time of jury trial demand. Failure to make the deposit likewise waives the right (although the other party may "pick up the tab" to preserve a jury trial).

b. Federal practice [§1799]

In federal actions when the right to jury trial applies, a party must demand a jury trial in writing with regard to any issue within 10 days of the service of the last pleading directed to that issue. [Fed. R. Civ. P. 38(b)] Ordinarily, parties include the demand as an addendum to their pleadings: "Plaintiff demands a trial by jury of all issues triable by jury herein."

Example: If D's answer contains a counterclaim denominated as such, P must file a reply to the counterclaim. [Fed. R. Civ. P. 7(a)] If the counterclaim and reply deal with issues as to which a jury trial is available, either party has until 10 days following the filing of P's reply to demand a jury trial.

---

(1) Note

The filing of amended or supplemental pleadings does *not* revive the right to a jury trial if no demand was made when the original pleadings were filed (unless the amended or supplemental pleadings raise *new issues* that are triable to a jury).

(2) Withdrawal of demand [§1800]

Once a party has timely and properly demanded a jury, the case is to be tried to a jury unless all parties stipulate to trial to the court. [Fed. R. Civ. P. 39(a)]

5. Jury Trials Discretionary with Court

a. Where jury previously waived [§1801]

The court may order a jury trial on any or all issues in a case in which the right has been waived (*e.g.*, by failure to make timely demand therefor). [Fed. R. Civ. P. 39(b)]

b. By consent [§1802]

Even when no right to a jury exists, the court may order a binding jury trial with the consent of both parties. [Fed. R. Civ. P. 39(c)]

c. Advisory jury [§1803]

And the judge may order a trial by jury for the purpose of obtaining an "advisory" verdict. [Fed. R. Civ. P. 39(c); *see* **Cutter Labs v. R.W. Ogle & Co.**, 151 Cal. App. 2d 410 (1957)]

B. Selection of the Jury

1. Summons of the Venire [§1804]

Trial juries are selected from a larger panel of citizens, commonly known as the *venire*. Prospective jurors are summoned by the court.

a. Historical background on selection [§1805]

In earlier times, the clerk or jury commissioner selected veniremen by personal contact; the officer of the court was charged with identifying citizens of good repute to serve as jurors.

(1) The "key man" [§1806]

Members of the clergy and other professional people known favorably to the clerk or commissioner would frequently be asked to serve as "key men" to identify appropriate prospective jurors.

(2) Talesmen [§1807]

If the court was short of veniremen, the clerk or commissioner might go into the corridors of the courthouse for willing volunteers, known as *"talesmen."*

b. Constitutional requirements

(1) Systematic exclusion prohibited [§1808]

The systematic exclusion from jury panels of any religious, racial, ethnic, or political group is an unlawful denial of equal protection of the laws. [**Eubanks v. Louisiana,** 356 U.S. 584 (1957); *and see* Constitutional Law Summary]

(2) Cross section not required [§1809]

On the other hand, the Constitution does ***not*** require that juries be strictly representative. Jury service may be confined to persons meeting certain standards of education, intelligence, judgment, and character, as long as the standards are not administered in a discriminatory manner. [**Carter v. Jury Commission of Greene County,** 396 U.S. 320 (1970)]

(3) "Blue ribbon" juries [§1810]

Neither does the Constitution proscribe the use of "blue ribbon" juries selected on the basis of special intelligence or experience to handle complicated cases. [**Fay v. New York,** 332 U.S. 261 (1947)]

c. Contemporary selection practice

(1) Federal courts

(a) **Local plans [§1811]**

Jury selection methods in federal courts now conform to plans promulgated by local district courts in conformity with national standards. [28 U.S.C. §1863]

(b) **Fair cross section required [§1812]**

The national policy requires that juries be "selected at random from a fair cross section of the community." [28 U.S.C. §1861]

(c) **Use of voter registration lists [§1813]**

Every district uses voter registration lists as the basic source from which potential jurors are summoned. Some districts supplement these lists when necessary to foster the national policy (above). [28 U.S.C. §1863(b)(2)]

1) **When supplementation required [§1814]**

The voter registration list *must* be supplemented if it underrepresents any group identified by race, color, religion, sex, national origin, or economic status. [28 U.S.C. §§1862, 1863(b)(2)]

(d) **Challenge to array [§1815]**

If the venire has not been selected in strict compliance with statute and the local plan, either party may challenge the array (the whole group of prospective jurors) and require that a new venire be summoned. [28 U.S.C. §1867(c); *and see* **Thiel v. Southern Pacific Co.,** 328 U.S. 217 (1946)]

1) **Single nonrepresentative panel [§1816]**

It is not a basis for challenging the array that a single panel or venire is not cross-sectional, as long as the *method* by which the group was selected is random.

2) **Nonrepresentative system [§1817]**

However, if it can be shown that the system regularly produces panels or venires that are substantially nonrepresentative in the same way, this is an adequate basis for challenge.

(2) **State courts [§1818]**

Many state courts select juries in a manner similar to the federal system, others retain vestiges of the traditional practice, and some states continue the use of "blue ribbon" jury panels (*supra*).

2. Qualifications of Prospective Jurors

a. Exclusions [§1819]

Statutes generally provide that certain classes of citizens shall be excluded from juries. Categories typically excluded include minors, felons, aliens, and illiterates. [28 U.S.C. §1865; Cal. Civ. Proc. Code §203]

b. Excuses [§1820]

A prospective juror may be excused for good cause, such as extraordinary financial loss from service.

c. One-day or one-trial service [§1821]

Some courts are now summoning jurors to serve only one day or one trial. Where this practice is used, exemptions and excuses are likely to be more sparingly recognized.

3. Number of Jurors Required

a. Typical size of venire [§1822]

The venire usually consists of at least two or three times the number of persons who will be selected to serve as jurors.

b. Traditional jury of twelve [§1823]

Common law juries were composed of 12 members, and for some time it was assumed that this number was required in federal courts by the Seventh Amendment. [**Capital Traction Co. v. Hof,** 174 U.S. 1 (1899)]

c. Twelve not required by due process [§1824]

The common law requirement of 12 jurors has been held not to be required by the Due Process Clause. [**Williams v. Florida,** 399 U.S. 78 (1970)—criminal case] However, due process requires at least six jurors in a criminal case. [**Ballew v. Georgia,** 435 U.S. 223 (1978)]

(1) Civil cases [§1825]

The minimum number of jurors required in federal civil cases has not been finally resolved. Local district rules providing for *six-member* juries in civil cases have been upheld—on the rationale that the outcome of the verdict is not likely to be affected substantially by the number of jurors (at least as between 12 and six). [**Colgrove v. Battin,** 413 U.S. 149 (1973)]

(2) State practice [§1826]

Since the U.S. Constitution does not require states to provide jury trials at all, the number of jurors in state civil trials depends entirely on state law. Many states have long used juries with fewer than 12 members in civil cases, particularly where the amount in controversy is small.

d. Jury size in federal civil cases [§1827]

Federal Rule 48 provides that the court shall seat a jury of not fewer than six nor more than 12 jurors.

e. Appointment of alternate jurors [§1828]

Traditionally courts appointed alternate jurors in addition to regular jurors to provide for the possibility that a regular juror may be unable to serve for the full term of the trial. Alternates would sit through the trial, but would be excused before the commencement of jury deliberations unless needed to take the place of incapacitated jurors. However, the institution of the alternate juror was abolished by amendment of Rule 47 in 1991. Instead, the court may seat from six to 12 jurors, and may excuse some for good cause during trial or deliberations, as long as *at least six* remain (unless the parties agree otherwise).

EXAM TIP   **gilbert**

If an exam question involves the number of jurors in a federal case, be sure to point out that the Constitution does *not require a jury of 12*—juries of six have been upheld, and the Federal Rules provide for juries of between six and 12. Alternate jurors are no longer appointed; instead the court may excuse some jurors for good cause, as long as at least six remain.

---

4. Voir Dire Examination of Jurors [§1829]

After the venire has been screened by the court for persons who should be excluded, exempt, or excused, the prospective jurors are generally subject to further interrogation about their possible biases. This examination is known as *voir dire*.

a. Challenge for cause [§1830]

A party may challenge a prospective juror if it appears that the juror has a financial stake in the case or in similar litigation, if members of the juror's immediate family have such an interest, or if there is other sufficient reason to believe that the juror may be unable to render impartial service. [28 U.S.C. §1866(c)] There is *no limit* to the number of challenges for cause.

b. Peremptory challenge [§1831]

Each "side" is also entitled to a limited number of challenges *without* a showing of cause—*i.e.*, a peremptory challenge. *Rationale:* The purpose of the peremptory challenge is to give each side the opportunity to act upon intimations of bias that may not be demonstrable or even rationally explainable. In this way, those persons most distrusted by either side are removed from the jury.

(1) Number in federal courts [§1832]

In federal courts, each side is entitled to three peremptory challenges. [28 U.S.C. §1870]

(2) Number in state courts [§1833]

The number of peremptory challenges allowed in state court proceedings varies. In California, six challenges are allowed, with more permitted in multiparty litigation. [Cal. Civ. Proc. Code §231(c)]

(3) Racial grounds for exercise [§1834]

The Supreme Court has held that the equal protection component of the Fifth Amendment Due Process Clause precludes a private party in federal civil litigation from using peremptory challenges to excuse potential jurors on grounds of their race. [**Edmonson v. Leesville Concrete Co.,** 500 U.S. 614 (1991)] The same rule would apply to state court actions under the Fourteenth Amendment's Equal Protection Clause.

(4) Gender grounds for exercise [§1835]

The Supreme Court has also held that the Equal Protection Clause forbids use of peremptory strikes to remove jurors on the basis of their gender. [**J.E.B. v. Alabama** *ex rel.* **T.B.,** 511 U.S. 127 (1994)]

c. Questioning by court [§1836]

In most jurisdictions, the judge may control the voir dire examination by asking all questions of the jurors. [**Perry v. Allegheny Airlines, Inc.,** 489 F.2d 1349 (2d Cir. 1974)] However, the judge must ask all proper questions submitted by counsel, in order to enable them to make good use of their peremptory challenges. [**Kiernan v. Van Schaik,** 347 F.2d 775 (3d Cir. 1965)]

(1) Limited to grounds for challenge for cause [§1837]

In most jurisdictions the inquiry on voir dire examination of jurors is limited to grounds that might provide a basis for excusing jurors for cause. (*See supra,* §1830.) In some jurisdictions, however, in criminal cases counsel are allowed to inquire into any matter that may bear on their exercise of peremptory challenges.

d. Questioning by counsel [§1838]

Some courts permit counsel to ask questions directly, and in some states (*e.g.,* Texas), counsel have a right to do so. In other states (*e.g.,* New York), the examination may be conducted by counsel outside the courtroom, with the judge called in only to rule on objections.

(1) Improper questioning [§1839]

It is not proper to use the voir dire examination to put comments or hypothetical evidence before jurors which would not be admissible at trial. If such questioning has been allowed, a new trial should be ordered.

Example: Where P is not allowed to offer proof of D's insurance at trial, P's counsel should not be allowed to interrogate prospective jurors about the subject of insurance.

---

(2) Tactic [§1840]

Counsel may use the voir dire examination as an occasion to preview the case by asking prospective jurors whether they "could believe" proof of the sort described, or "could in good conscience award" damages of the amount or type being sought.

C. Disqualification of Judge

1. Grounds for Disqualification [§1841]

The judge assigned to a trial proceeding may be disqualified if her impartiality might reasonably be questioned. Bases for disqualification would therefore include the following. [*See generally* 28 U.S.C. §455; Cal. Civ. Proc. Code §170.1]

a. Personal bias [§1842]

If the judge has a personal bias or personal prejudice concerning a party, she may be disqualified.

b. Personal knowledge of the facts [§1843]

If the judge has personal knowledge of disputed evidentiary facts, she may be disqualified.

c. Previous involvement as lawyer [§1844]

If the judge served as counsel in connection with the controversy, or a lawyer with whom she practiced so served during the period of their association, she may be disqualified.

d. Financial interest [§1845]

A judge may be disqualified if she knows that she, her spouse, or her minor child has a financial stake in the controversy or an interest that could be substantially affected by the outcome.

e. Family relationship [§1846]

If the judge's spouse (or a relative of the judge or the judge's spouse) is a party, an officer of a party, or a lawyer for a party or is known to have a financial interest, or is likely to be a material witness, she may be disqualified.

f. Disqualification must be based on extrajudicial matters [§1847]

The judge's adverse reaction or hostility to the parties or the evidence generally is *not* a basis for disqualification. [**Liteky v. United States**, 510 U.S. 540 (1994)]

2. Duty of Judge [§1848]

The judge has a duty to be informed about possible bases for disqualification and to disqualify herself on her own motion if adequate grounds for disqualification exist.

3. Procedure for Disqualification

a. Federal practice [§1849]

In federal court, a party seeking to disqualify a judge must do so by filing an affidavit of bias—*i.e.*, a sworn statement setting forth the facts that are the basis for disqualification. [28 U.S.C. §144] Factual averments in such an affidavit are *not* open to challenge (except in a criminal proceeding to punish the affiant for perjury). If the facts set forth are legally sufficient to disqualify the judge, she *must* excuse herself and assign the case to another judge.

b. State practice [§1850]

State procedures vary greatly.

(1) Traditional rule [§1851]

Most states require an actual showing by affidavit of grounds for disqualification, as in federal practice.

(2) Peremptory challenge [§1852]

In some states, each party has an absolute right to disqualify *one* judge simply by filing an affidavit that he believes he cannot obtain a fair trial before that judge. As to any subsequent judge, a party may make a motion to disqualify and is entitled to a hearing on the facts in front of still another judge, who must determine whether the second should be disqualified. [*See, e.g.*, Cal. Civ. Proc. Code §170.6]

(a) Note

This system has been criticized as permitting too free an attack on judges and as a source of delay.

EXAM TIP   **gilbert**

It is important to remember that not only can a litigant seek to have jurors disqualified for bias or prejudice, a litigant can also seek to have a *judge* disqualified for these reasons as well. Actually, the judge should disqualify herself if she knows a reason why she should be disqualified. If the judge does not disqualify herself, some states give a litigant an absolute right to disqualify one judge. The federal courts require the party seeking disqualification to file an affidavit alleging bias, and the judge cannot challenge the affidavit; she must excuse herself. The only protection against lying on such an affidavit is the threat of a perjury charge.

D. Order of Trial

1. Right to Speak First and Last

a. General rule [§1853]

Ordinarily, the party opening and closing each phase of a trial is the party who has the *burden of proof* with respect to the principal issues. This usually will be the plaintiff—but it may be the defendant if the plaintiff's prima facie case has been established by the pleadings and pretrial order.

b. Discretion of court [§1854]

The decision to accord the right to speak first and last is ultimately one for the discretion of the trial judge. [Cal. Civ. Proc. Code §607—court may order different order of presentation for "special reasons"]

2. Stages of Jury Trial [§1855]

The normal sequence of a civil jury trial is as follows:

a. Opening statement of plaintiff;

b. Opening statement of defendant;

c. Presentation of direct evidence by plaintiff, with cross-examination of each witness by defendant, followed by re-direct and re-cross-examination (*plaintiff rests*);

d. Presentation of direct evidence by the defendant, with cross-examination, re-direct, and re-cross-examination (*defendant rests*);

e. Presentation of rebuttal evidence by plaintiff;

f. Presentation of rebuttal evidence by defendant;

g. Argument of plaintiff to jury;

h. Argument of defendant to jury;

i. Final closing argument of plaintiff to jury;

j. Instructions to jury by judge;

k. Verdict of jury.

3. Nonjury Trial [§1856]

The order of a nonjury trial is essentially the same up to the point at which all evidence has been presented. Prior to the presentation of argument, or in the course of argument, the parties may propose specific findings of fact and conclusions of law to the court. At the close of arguments, the judge will render his decision, which will take the form of specific findings of fact and conclusions of law. [Fed. R. Civ. P. 52(a)]

E. Presentation of Evidence

1. Control Over Presentation [§1857]

Ordinarily, presentation of the evidence at trial is the responsibility of the parties and their counsel, subject to control by the court. [Fed. R. Evid. 611(a)] Even so, most jurisdictions acknowledge the discretionary power of the trial judge to call witnesses on his own motion. [**Citizens State Bank v. Castro,** 105 Cal. App. 284 (1930)]

2. Rules of Evidence [§1858]

Proceedings in federal court are governed by the Federal Rules of Evidence. In some respects, these rules incorporate provisions of state law (*e.g.,* what privileges are recognized). Many states have adopted evidence rules that follow the Federal Rules. Some states, like California, have evidence codes, while others rely in varying degrees on common law rules. (*See* detailed discussion in Evidence Summary.)

3. Objections and Exceptions

a. Failure to object [§1859]

Failure to object to the admission of an item of evidence generally waives the ground for objection.

b. Amendment by proof [§1860]

If no objection is made to evidence that goes beyond the pleadings or the pre-trial order to raise new issues, the pleadings or the order will be treated as if they had been amended to allege the facts proved by the evidence admitted. [Fed. R. Civ. P. 15(b), 16] (*See supra,* §§937-952.)

c. Exceptions unnecessary [§1861]

In modern practice, it is sufficient to state an objection to the admission of evidence and the basis for the objection. It is not necessary, in order to preserve the issue for appeal, to take exception to rulings on such objections. [Fed. R. Civ. P. 46]

4. Burden of Producing Evidence [§1862]

The plaintiff must produce some evidence tending to prove each element of the *prima facie* case. If the plaintiff fails to do so, the defendant is entitled to a dismissal or a judgment as a matter of law at the close of the plaintiff's evidence. Similarly, if a defense is to be considered by the trier of fact, the defendant must produce some evidence tending to prove each element of his defense. *Note:* A party may be relieved of this burden by the adversary's admissions in pleadings, discovery proceedings, or at pretrial. (*See* Evidence Summary.)

5. Judicial Notice [§1863]

It is unnecessary to plead or prove facts that are not subject to reasonable dispute; the court must take judicial notice of such facts. (*See* Evidence Summary.)

F. Motions at Close of Proof

1. In General [§1864]

At the close of proof, motions may be used to determine whether a party has carried the burden of producing evidence, *e.g.*, motion for judgment as a matter of law, for nonsuit, or for involuntary dismissal.

2. Jury Trial—Motion for Judgment as a Matter of Law (Directed Verdict) [§1865]

In a jury trial, either party may move for judgment as a matter of law when the adversary has been fully heard with respect to the issue in question. [Fed. R. Civ. P. 50(a)] Some courts have developed acronyms for this motion. [*See, e.g.*, **Weese v. Schukman**, 98 F.3d 542 (10th Cir. 1996)—JML; **McKeel v. City of Pine Bluff**, 73 F.3d 207 (8th Cir. 1996)—JAML]

a. New terminology [§1866]

Before Federal Rule 50(a) was amended in 1991, what is now called a "motion for judgment as a matter of law" was called a "motion for a directed verdict." *State courts* usually still refer to such a motion as a *"motion for directed verdict."*

b. Standard for grant [§1867]

The general standard for whether to grant a motion for judgment as a matter of law looks to whether there is a *legally sufficient evidentiary basis* on which the jury could find for the nonmoving party. The application of this standard depends on whether the moving party has the burden of proof on the issue raised.

(1) Moving party with burden of proof [§1868]

If the moving party has the burden of proof, judgment as a matter of law is appropriate only if the evidence favoring the moving party is of such *compelling strength* that the jury could not reasonably find for the opposing party. Accordingly, to defeat the motion it is sufficient that the jury could reasonably disbelieve the witnesses upon whom the moving party relies.

(a) State court view [§1869]

In some states, a directed verdict cannot be entered if the movant has the burden of proof unless the facts are totally uncontroverted or the parties agree to them. [**Allstate Insurance Co. v. Miller**, 553 A.2d 1268 (Md. 1989)]

(2) Opposing party with burden [§1870]

If the party moving for judgment as a matter of law does not have the burden of proof, the motion should be granted only if the opposing party has *no substantial evidence* to permit a jury reasonably to find in its favor.

(a) Scintilla rule contrasted [§1871]

In some jurisdictions the "scintilla rule" still is invoked. Under this rule, a party with a scintilla of evidence would be allowed to have her case presented to the jury. The federal courts have rejected the scintilla rule. [**Galloway v. United States,** 319 U.S. 372 (1943)]

c. Case-by-case determination [§1872]

The court's evaluation process must be made on a case-by-case basis, and discussion of given cases should involve careful examination of the facts presented and inferences from them. As a consequence, it is difficult to present "rules" governing judgment as a matter of law. There are, however, a number of governing principles that are helpful in analysis, and these are discussed below.

(1) All reasonable inferences indulged in favor of opposing party [§1873]

The court is to make all reasonable inferences in favor of the opposing party, and to view the evidence *in the light most favorable to that party.*

(2) Court may not "weigh" evidence [§1874]

The court is to determine whether there is a genuine issue to present to the jury; it may not choose between two versions of events and grant summary judgment to the party whose version seems more persuasive.

(a) Role of speculation [§1875]

Within limits, the fact that the jury's decision will involve some speculation is not a ground for taking the case from the jury. If facts are in dispute or reasonable people may draw different inferences from the evidence, the jury may use speculation and conjecture to settle the dispute by choosing what seems to be the most reasonable inference. [**Lavender v. Kurn,** 327 U.S. 645 (1946)]

(b) "Equal possibilities" analysis [§1876]

It is sometimes said that the case should be taken from the jury when the evidence presented on any essential fact by the party with the burden of proof shows only an equal possibility of the existence of that fact. [*See, e.g.,* **Pennsylvania Railroad v. Chamberlain,** 288 U.S. 333 (1933)] This analysis has been *rejected* in most jurisdictions, as long as there is some basis on which the jury could choose between conflicting versions of events.

(3) Evidence to be considered

(a) Only opposing party's evidence [§1877]

Some courts limit their examination to the evidence offered by the opposing party, at least in cases where the opposing party has the burden of proof, and the courts may say that the moving party's evidence is irrelevant. [**Lavender v. Kurn,** *supra*—defendant's evidence was "irrelevant upon appeal, there being a reasonable basis in the record" to support the jury's verdict for plaintiff]

(b) All evidence presented in light most favorable to opposing party [§1878]

The *majority rule* is that the court should "consider all of the evidence—not just that evidence which supports the non-movant's case—but in the light and with all reasonable inferences most favorable to the party opposed to the motion." [**Boeing Co. v. Shipman,** 411 F.2d 365 (5th Cir. 1969)]

(4) Demeanor evidence [§1879]

The jury has observed the witnesses while testifying, and may draw conclusions about their truthfulness from their demeanor.

(a) Moving party with burden of proof [§1880]

If the moving party has the burden of proof and relies on witnesses whom the jury could disbelieve, it is not entitled to a directed verdict, even if there is no conflicting evidence offered. (*See supra*, §1868.)

1) Possible exception—disinterested, unimpeached witness [§1881]

The above rule may not apply if the witness relied upon is disinterested and has not been impeached. Under these circumstances, there may be no reasonable basis for disbelieving the witness. [*See* **Lundeen v. Cordner,** *supra*, §1684]

---

e.g. **Example:** Plaintiff, the executor of X's estate, sues defendant, the executor of Y's estate, to recover for X's injuries in the head-on automobile collision in which both were killed. The physical evidence at the scene of the accident does not show who drove over the center line and caused the accident, but Plaintiff charges that Y drove over the line and must prove this fact to collect. Plaintiff relies on the testimony of a highway patrol officer that she was driving behind Y's car and observed Y drive across the center line and collide with the car driven by X. There are no other witnesses and no other evidence, and the officer is not impeached in any way. Plaintiff should be granted a directed verdict.

---

2) Opposing party with burden of proof [§1882]

Demeanor evidence, sometimes called *disbelief evidence,* is not sufficient to satisfy the opposing party's burden of producing evidence. [**Dyer v. MacDougall,** *supra*, §1641]

(5) Compare—renewed motion for judgment as a matter of law (judgment n.o.v.) [§1883]

If a motion for judgment as a matter of law is made before a verdict is rendered but is denied and the verdict goes against the moving party, the party may make a "renewed motion for judgment as a matter of law" (formerly called a judgment n.o.v.). (*See infra*, §§1960-1972.) Whether resolved before or after the verdict, the motion uses the *same standard* and thus asks the same question at different times—whether the case should be (or should have been) submitted to the jury.

(a) Pre-verdict motion as predicate for renewed motion [§1884]

In federal court, a party may not make a renewed motion unless she moved for a judgment as a matter of law *at the close of all the evidence*. [Fed. R. Civ. P. 50(b)]

1) Constitutional justification [§1885]

This requirement is a result of the Supreme Court's early decision that the judgment n.o.v. (renewed motion) violated the right to jury trial [**Slocum v. New York Life Insurance Co.**, 228 U.S. 364 (1913)], which the Court modified to permit a renewed motion if there was first a directed verdict motion on which the judge "reserved" ruling. [**Baltimore & Carolina Line v. Redman**, 295 U.S. 654 (1935)] Thus, Rule 50(b) states that whenever there is a motion for judgment as a matter of law, the judge will be deemed to have reserved later ruling on it to satisfy *Redman*.

2) Opportunity to cure deficiencies in proof [§1886]

Some argue that the requirement of a predicate motion for a directed verdict permits parties to cure omissions from their proof before the case is submitted to the jury, and that there is good reason to give parties an incentive to call such problems to the attention of the other side.

(b) Deferring decision until after verdict [§1887]

Judges presented with directed verdict motions may consider a variety of factors, including the following, in deciding whether to defer decision where they find the motions persuasive.

1) Jury will agree [§1888]

If the judge feels that one side's case is so weak that judgment as a matter of law is proper, it is likely that the jury will also feel that way, and a jury verdict to that effect will be *harder to overturn on appeal*.

2) Judge may be wrong [§1889]

If the judge grants judgment as a matter of law and is reversed on appeal, it will be necessary to hold a *second trial,* whereas the appellate court may be able to reinstate the jury verdict if it reverses a post-verdict decision to grant judgment as a matter of law, and avoid thereby the need for a retrial.

3) Time savings [§1890]

By granting the pre-verdict motion, the judge will save the time occupied by instructions to the jury and jury deliberations. If the defendant moves for a directed verdict at the close of the plaintiff's case, the time needed for presentation of the defendant's case could also be saved.

3. Jury Trial—Motion for Nonsuit [§1891]

In some states, the defendant may move for a nonsuit at the close of the plaintiff's opening statement (or at the close of plaintiff's proof).

a. Test applied [§1892]

Such a motion should be granted if the opening statement or proof reveals the plaintiff's case to be *legally insufficient.* For example, the plaintiff's failure to offer any credible evidence of damages might justify a nonsuit in a negligence case. [**Seivell v. Hines,** 116 A. 919 (Pa. 1922)]

b. Judgment on merits [§1893]

Historically, a judgment of nonsuit was not a judgment on the merits, and thus did not bar a new action on the same cause. [**Oscanyon v. Arms Co.,** 103 U.S. 261 (1880)] However, this rule has been changed in most states by legislation or court rule. [Cal. Civ. Proc. Code §581(e)]

4. Nonjury Trial—Motion for Judgment as a Matter of Law [§1894]

In a nonjury trial, after any party has been fully heard with respect to an issue, the court may enter judgment as a matter of law against that party on that issue. [Fed. R. Civ. P. 52(c)]

a. Early common law treatment [§1895]

The historical analogue to this motion was a *demurrer to the evidence,* which required the trial judge to accept all of the plaintiff's evidence as true for the purpose of ruling on the demurrer.

b. State practice [§1896]

Nomenclature for this motion varies among the states. In some, it is referred to as a *motion to dismiss;* while in others it is a *motion for judgment.* [Cal. Civ. Proc. Code §631.8—motion for judgment]

c. Test applied [§1897]

Under modern practice, the court may grant the motion if it finds that the plaintiff's proof is *unpersuasive* on issues as to which plaintiff had the burden of persuasion. [**Huber v. American President Lines,** 240 F.2d 778 (2d Cir. 1957)] The rationale is that, in a nonjury trial, the judge is the ultimate trier of fact; and if she is already convinced, there is no reason to require further proof by the defendant.

MOTIONS AT CLOSE OF PROOF		gilbert
MOTION	**GROUNDS**	**TIMING**
Motion for Judgment as a Matter of Law	Evidence viewed in light most favorable to motion's opponent leads reasonable person to conclusion in favor of moving party	After opponent has presented case but before submission of case to jury
Motion for Nonsuit	Opening statement or proof reveals plaintiff's case to be legally insufficient	At close of plaintiff's opening statement or proof

G. Argument to Jury

1. Time for Argument [§1898]

In federal and most state courts, counsel's argument to the jury takes place at the close of the evidence and *before* the jury is instructed by the judge (so that the last words the jurors hear are those of the judge, rather than the impassioned pleas of counsel). [Fed. R. Civ. P. 51]

2. Right to Argue [§1899]

Counsel have an absolute right to argument in a jury trial. [**Shippy v. Peninsula Rapid Transit Co.,** 197 Cal. 290 (1925)]

3. Control of Argument by Court [§1900]

However, the trial judge in his discretion may control the duration and manner of argument.

4. Limitations on Argument [§1901]

In arguing to the jury, counsel is subject to the following constraints:

a. *Comment must be based on the evidence,* and counsel may not distort the facts or assume facts not in evidence.

b. *Argument must be within the limits of the substantive law* governing the action. Thus, for example, counsel may not argue for the use of an improper method of calculating damages (*e.g.*, to "punish" a defendant in an ordinary negligence case).

c. *Counsel may not appeal to the passions or prejudices of the jurors.* [**Pingatore v. Montgomery Ward & Co.**, 419 F.2d 1138 (6th Cir. 1969)] However, less restraint is imposed on counsel where the dispute is one fraught with emotion (such as a defamation trial). [**Curtis Publishing Co. v. Butts**, 351 F.2d 702 (5th Cir. 1965)]

5. Effect of Improper Argument [§1902]

Not every improper argument requires a reversal of the judgment obtained and a new trial. A new trial is in order only if the argument is not adequately corrected by the judge, so that an incorrect verdict is likely to have resulted.

H. Instructions to Jury

1. In General [§1903]

Before a case is submitted to the jury for a verdict, the trial judge instructs the jury on certain relevant matters.

2. Issues of Fact [§1904]

The jury's role is to decide *issues of fact* identified by the judge in the instructions, whereas the judge must decide questions of law (such as the meaning of statutes and documents).

a. "Law" vs. "fact" [§1905]

Issues of law can be said to be general and to pertain to interpretation of the controlling law, while issues of fact are specific and pertain to past events. However, the boundary between the two may be unclear at times—in which case the matter must be resolved by reference to historic policy regarding the role of the jury.

Example: The law of negligence is usually expressed in general terms (*e.g.*, "a failure to exercise reasonable care") that minimize the role of the judge in defining the issues and maximize the role of the jury in deciding cases.

Compare: If a decision necessarily requires that some additional meaning be attributed to the legal standard by the jury applying it, a law issue is inevitably intertwined with the fact issue, and such matters are sometimes said to present a *mixed issue* of law and fact. [*See* Wiener, *The Civil Jury Trial and the Law-Fact Distinction*, 54 Cal. L. Rev. 1867 (1966)]

b. **Jury decides disputed facts only [§1906]**

There is an issue of fact for the jury only if there is a genuine dispute about past events or the interpretation of those events.

(1) **Facts not in dispute [§1907]**

If only one reasonable inference can be drawn with respect to a matter, the judge should give instructions that *assume* the necessarily inferred fact. Thus, in a contract dispute in which a written contract is proved and the evidence presented by the defense bears only on the amount of damages, the court should not ask the jury to decide whether there was mutual assent.

(2) **Disputed facts [§1908]**

The judge may not give an instruction that assumes a fact in *dispute*. Each party is entitled to have the jury instructed to consider her version of matters that have been disputed. For example, if the defendant in a contract dispute offers proof tending to show that the written contract presented by the plaintiff was not signed by the defendant, the court must put the issue of mutual assent to the jury, however much the judge may doubt the denial.

3. **Burden of Persuasion**

a. **Assigning the burden [§1909]**

The judge must explain to the jury which party has the burden of persuasion in regard to each issue of fact that the jury must decide. The burden of persuasion will generally be assigned to the party having the burden of producing the evidence in regard to that issue; but this may not be the case if there is an applicable legal *presumption*. (*See* Evidence Summary.)

b. **Degree of persuasion**

(1) **Preponderance of the evidence [§1910]**

In a *civil* case, the trier of fact usually must be persuaded that a fact is more probable than not in order to resolve an issue in favor of the party bearing the burden of persuasion. [**Sullivan v. Nesbit,** 117 A. 502 (Conn. 1922)]

(2) **Clear and convincing proof [§1911]**

In regard to issues of *fraud, duress, or undue influence,* however, the trier of fact generally is instructed to find for the party having the burden of persuasion only if the evidence is "clear and convincing."

(a) **Comment**

This rule evolved in equity, which was said to *presume* honesty and fair dealing, thus requiring a greater amount of evidence to overcome the presumption.

(b) Note

Some modern courts have rejected this principle, holding that a mere preponderance is sufficient with respect to *any* issue in a civil case. [**Weiner v. Fleishman,** 54 Cal. 3d 476 (1991)]

EXAM TIP   **gilbert**

Students who have watched much television are probably very familiar with the standard of proof required in criminal cases—proof beyond a reasonable doubt. But TV shows usually give short shrift to the standard of proof *in civil cases*. If this issue comes up in an exam question, remember the general rule: The party with the burden of persuasion generally need only convince the trier of fact that his version of the facts is *more probable than not* (*i.e.,* just slightly more likely than any other version of the facts). For certain issues (*e.g.,* fraud, duress, or undue influence) some courts require a higher standard—*clear and convincing proof*—but even this higher civil standard is lower than that standard required in criminal cases.

---

4. Comment on the Evidence

a. Majority rule [§1912]

In most courts, the judge is allowed to comment on the quality of proof which bears on issues that the jury must decide, provided she informs the jury that it is the final decision maker. [**Trezza v. Dame,** 370 F.2d 1006 (5th Cir. 1967); Cal. Const. art. VI, §10]

b. Minority rule [§1913]

Some states do not permit *any* comment on the evidence, on the ground that a judge's comments are too likely to prejudice the jury.

5. Instructions Requested by Counsel

a. Responsibility for preparation [§1914]

While the ultimate responsibility for instructions rests with the judge, counsel has the duty of proposing instructions that present his theory of the case. [**Willden v. Washington National Insurance Co.,** 18 Cal. 3d 631 (1976)]

b. Form of requests [§1915]

Proposed instructions must be in writing and must be served on opposing counsel.

c. Time for filing [§1916]

The Federal Rules provide that requests for instructions must be filed at the close of the evidence or at such earlier time during the trial as the court reasonably requires. [Fed. R. Civ. P. 51] In a complex case, the judge often orders such proposals to be filed before trial (at the time of pretrial conference).

(1) State practice may vary [§1917]

In California, instructions covering the legal issues raised by the pleadings must be filed before the first witness is sworn. [Cal. Civ. Proc. Code §607a]

d. Objections [§1918]

Each party must be given the opportunity to object to instructions proposed by his adversary. Failure to make objection before the jury retires is generally a waiver of any error not pointed out to the judge. [Fed. R. Civ. P. 51]

e. Notice to counsel of court's action on requests [§1919]

Before counsel make their arguments to the jury, they are entitled to be informed of the judge's rulings on their requests for instructions. [Fed. R. Civ. P. 51] *Rationale:* Counsel need to know what the judge will say during instructions so that they can structure their closing arguments accordingly.

6. Appellate Review of Jury Instructions

a. Plain error [§1920]

Ordinarily, any error in the jury instructions is waived unless a timely objection was made in the trial court (*see* above). Traditionally, however, to prevent miscarriages of justice, many courts have held that an *egregious* ("plain") error in the instructions may require a reversal even if no timely objection was made. [**Thompson v. Paasche,** 950 F.2d 306 (6th Cir. 1991)] Some courts, though, read Rule 51 as allowing no or virtually no "plain error" exception. [**Deppe v. Tripp,** 863 F.2d 1356 (7th Cir. 1988)]

b. Harmless error [§1921]

On the other hand, if it appears unlikely that the jury was misled by a minor error in instructions, the error may be deemed harmless. [Fed. R. Civ. P. 61; Cal. Civ. Proc. Code §475] In applying this rule, the appellate court will consider the impact of the instructions as a whole. [**Marshall v. Ford Motor Co.,** 446 F.2d 712 (10th Cir. 1971)]

(1) Note

Where alternative theories are advanced, the instructions given are correct as to one theory but incorrect as to the other, and the jury returns a *general verdict* (with no indication as to which theory was accepted), reversal is generally required, because there is no certainty that the error was harmless. [**Pacific Greyhound Lines v. Zane,** 160 F.2d 731 (9th Cir. 1947)]

(2) But note

A minority of courts adheres to the principle that a jury should be presumed to have based its verdict on the correct portion of the instruction. [**State v. Hills,** 113 N.E. 1045 (Ohio 1916)]

I. Jury Deliberation and Verdict

1. Types of Verdicts [§1922]

Verdicts may take several forms, depending on the form of jury instructions.

a. General verdict [§1923]

The traditional and still most common form of verdict is the general verdict, in which the jury simply makes a decision in favor of one party or the other. Such a verdict *implies* a finding in favor of the prevailing party *on every material issue of fact* submitted to the jury. [Cal. Civ. Proc. Code §624]

Example: In the typical negligence case, a general verdict for the plaintiff necessarily rests on finding that the defendant was negligent, that the negligence proximately caused harm to the plaintiff, and that the plaintiff was free of contributory negligence. [**Sassano v. Roullard,** 27 Cal. App. 2d 372 (1938)]

---

(1) Criticism

At the same time, a general verdict may conceal a misunderstanding of the instructions or even a disregard of them. It has been called "the great procedural opiate" because it "draws the curtain upon human errors and soothes us with the assurance we have attained the unattainable." [Sunderland, *Verdicts, General and Special,* 29 Yale L.J. 253 (1920)]

b. Special verdict [§1924]

A special verdict consists of the jury's answers to specific factual questions that it is instructed to decide. In this situation, the jury does not decide directly which party should prevail on the law. Instead, the special verdicts should resolve all the material issues so the court can enter judgment. [Fed. R. Civ. P. 49(a); Cal. Civ. Proc. Code §624]

(1) Verdicts required on all disputed issues [§1925]

To serve their purpose, special verdicts should usually be fashioned to cover *all disputed issues,* so that the judge can determine the proper judgment from them.

(2) Advantages [§1926]

A special verdict reduces the burden on the judge of instructing the jury on the law and reduces the jury's need to understand the law.

(3) Disadvantages [§1927]

If a special verdict is used, the jury may find it harder to reach a unanimous verdict. Moreover, *inconsistent* findings on a crucial issue may necessitate a new trial. However, the court has the power to interpret the jury's findings in order to "mold" them to a judgment. [**Gallick v. Baltimore & Ohio Railroad,** 372 U.S. 108 (1963)]

(4) Disclosure to counsel [§1928]

Some courts hold that counsel should be given access to the special verdicts and an opportunity to comment on them. [**Sakamoto v. N.A.B. Trucking Co.,** 717 F.2d 1000 (6th Cir. 1983); **Clegg v. Hardware Mutual Casualty Co.,** 264 F.2d 152 (5th Cir. 1959)]

(5) Advising jury of legal consequences of answers [§1929]

Since the judge is to draw the legal conclusions from the special verdicts, it is not necessary that the jury be instructed on them, and some courts have held that the jury should not be so instructed. [*See* **United States v. Kim,** 111 F.3d 1351 (7th Cir. 1997)] Because the use of this procedure is discretionary with the court, however, others have decided that the judge may so instruct. [*See* **Simms v. Village of Albion,** 115 F.3d 1098 (2d Cir. 1997)] *Rationale:* The jury is likely to deduce from the lawyers' arguments which party will be benefited from a particular resolution of an issue, and so the judge should have the right to make it clear to the jury.

c. General verdict with special interrogatories [§1930]

The trial judge may combine the two foregoing forms of verdict by instructing the jury to return a general decision as to which party should prevail on the law, while simultaneously answering specific questions of fact posed by the evidence. [Fed. R. Civ. P. 49(b); Cal. Civ. Proc. Code §625]

(1) Purpose [§1931]

The idea of this combined form of verdict is to permit the jury to decide the whole case, while obtaining a "cross-check" that the jury understood and adhered to the instructions on the law.

(2) Disadvantage [§1932]

Like special verdicts, the general verdict with special interrogatories carries the risk of inconsistency necessitating a new trial.

(a) Inconsistency between finding and verdict [§1933]

If there is an inconsistency between the special finding and the general verdict, the judge in her discretion may disregard the general verdict and enter judgment according to the special findings. [Fed. R. Civ. P. 49(b); Cal. Civ. Proc. Code §625]

(b) Inconsistency among findings [§1934]

However, if there are inconsistencies among *several* of the special findings, the judge must order a new trial unless she can reconcile the inconsistencies. In doing so, there is a presumption in favor of the general verdict; and special findings should be reconciled so as to support the general verdict, if possible. [**Law v. Northern Assurance Co.,** 165 Cal. 394 (1913)]

(3) Failure to respond [§1935]

Failure to respond to a special interrogatory is not necessarily fatal to the verdict. The court in its discretion may assume that the missing answer would be consistent with the general verdict. [**Gulf Refining Co. v. Fetschan,** 130 F.2d 129 (6th Cir. 1942), *cert. denied,* 318 U.S. 764 (1943)]

(4) Inability to agree on an issue [§1936]

And even where the jurors announce their inability to agree on a particular issue, the verdict may be sustained if there is agreement on an alternative finding sufficient to support the general verdict (*e.g.,* jurors could not agree on which among several negligent acts by defendant caused plaintiff's injury, but agreed that one of those acts was responsible).

TYPES OF VERDICTS—A SUMMARY	**gilbert**
GENERAL	Jury simply makes a *decision in favor of one party*; judge must instruct jury on how to apply law to facts; no guarantee that jury acted properly when reaching its decision.
SPECIAL	Jury is to resolve *all disputed fact issues* so court may apply law to facts; can eliminate need for jury to understand law, but can also lead to inconsistent fact findings.
GENERAL VERDICT WITH SPECIAL INTERROGATORIES	Combination of the two above, with jury giving general verdict *and* answering specific fact questions so judge can cross-check that jury understood and adhered to the instructions and the law; although inconsistencies are still possible.

2. Requirement of Unanimity

a. General rule [§1937]

In federal and most state courts, the jury must render a unanimous decision, unless the parties otherwise agree. [Fed. R. Civ. P. 48]

(1) Purpose [§1938]

This requirement forces the jurors to deliberate in any case in which one of the group has serious doubt about the outcome.

(2) "Dynamite charge" [§1939]

If the jurors, after deliberating, announce that they are unable to reach a verdict, it is not improper for the court to emphasize to the jury the expense of a new trial and the unlikelihood that another jury would reach a better verdict, and to ask each juror to make a renewed effort to reach unanimity. [**Allen v. United States,** 164 U.S. 492 (1896)] Such a charge is sometimes referred to as a "dynamite charge."

b. Minority rule [§1940]

Some states permit nonunanimous verdicts. In California, for example, only three-fourths of the jury in civil cases must concur. [Cal. Civ. Proc. Code §618]

c. Tactic [§1941]

The unanimity requirement generally favors the defense, at least insofar as the plaintiff has the burden of persuasion on the disputed issues. Thus, if nonunanimous verdicts are allowed in state court, the plaintiff may prefer to litigate there, whereas the defense may seek to remove to a federal court.

3. Jury Deliberation and Impeachment of Verdict

a. Standards of jury conduct

(1) Materials taken into jury room [§1942]

In its deliberations, a jury normally has access to exhibits or other papers received in evidence. [Cal. Civ. Proc. Code §612] The judge may allow jurors to take notes during the trial, and such notes may also be used during deliberations.

(2) Consideration of matters outside the record [§1943]

The jury is not permitted to receive any information that was not presented at trial and made a part of the record.

(a) *Any communication from the judge* must be received in court in the *presence of counsel.* [Cal. Civ. Proc. Code §614] For example, it is error for the judge to provide the jury with a dictionary in counsel's absence, where it appears that jurors may use the dictionary definition of important terms in arriving at their verdict. [**Palestroni v. Jacobs,** 77 A.2d 183 (N.J. 1950)]

(b) *It is improper for jurors to fraternize with counsel* during the trial or during deliberation.

(c) *And it is likewise improper for the jury to conduct its own investigation* of the facts by calling experts in the absence of counsel, conducting experiments with the exhibits, or independently taking a view of the premises of an accident.

(3) Each juror shares in decision [§1944]

Consistent with the requirement of unanimity, each juror must make up her own mind on the verdict.

(a) Chance verdicts [§1945]

Accordingly, the jury may not decide by lot or other method of chance. [Cal. Civ. Proc. Code §657(2)]

(b) Quotient verdicts [§1946]

Nor may the jury reach a decision by taking an average of several awards of the jurors. Such an average *may* be computed as a means of assisting each juror to appraise the appropriate award; but the jurors may not bind themselves in advance to the result of the computation. [*See* **McDonald v. Pless**, 238 U.S. 264 (1915)]

EXAM TIP   gilbert

On your exam, don't snap at bait. The facts of a question might tell you that the jurors were deadlocked in a case. They all agreed on defendant's liability, but each wanted to award the plaintiff a different amount. Eventually, the jury foreperson wrote down the 12 amounts, added them up, and divided the total by 12. She then asked the jurors if they all agreed to the quotient amount. They all agreed. An improper quotient verdict? *No!* That was a perfectly legitimate way for the jury to arrive at a damages figure. The verdict would have been an improper quotient verdict *if the jurors agreed beforehand* that they would add up the various amounts, divide by 12, and use the quotient as a verdict.

(c) Coercion by judge [§1947]

The judge may not coerce the jury to agree. In this regard, it may be reversible error to *repeat* a "dynamite charge" (*see supra*, §1939) urging unanimity. [**United States v. Seawell**, 550 F.2d 1159 (9th Cir. 1977), *cert. denied*, 439 U.S. 991 (1978)]

b. Impeachment of verdict for misconduct

(1) Common law rule [§1948]

The traditional common law rule was that a juror could not impeach his own verdict. Thus, any misconduct in the deliberation had to be established by the testimony of someone *other than* the jurors, such as a bailiff or court attendant.

(a) Rationale

This rule safeguarded the secrecy of jury deliberations and protected jurors from harassment by counsel urging repudiation of verdicts. [*See* **McDonald v. Pless,** *supra*]

(b) Criticism

At the same time, the rule made enforcement of the standards of conduct described above very difficult.

(2) Federal Rule [§1949]

The Federal Rules of Evidence now permit a juror to testify to any *"extraneous prejudicial information"* or *"outside influence"* that may have altered the verdict. [Fed. R. Evid. 606(b)]

(a) Scope [§1950]

This rule does *not* authorize the use of juror testimony to attack the deliberative process (matters occurring *inside* the jury room), as by showing a quotient verdict. [*See* **Scogin v. Century Fitness, Inc.,** 780 F.2d 1316 (8th Cir. 1985)] It is possible, however, to use juror testimony to show gross misconduct, such as taking of a bribe or fraternizing with a party. [*See, e.g.,* **Jorgensen v. York Ice Machinery Corp.,** 160 F.2d 432 (2d Cir. 1947)]

---

e.g. **Example—use of intoxicants:** Where jurors drank heavily during lunch, some smoked marijuana or took cocaine during the trial, and jurors generally approached their task as "one big party," juror affidavit was inadmissible to impeach the verdict on these grounds, because they were "internal" to the verdict. [**Tanner v. United States,** 483 U.S. 107 (1987)]

(b) Distinguish—determining what was decided for collateral estoppel purposes [§1951]

The rule of exclusion applies to challenges to the validity of a verdict, but does not forbid use of juror affidavits to determine what was actually decided in order to give proper collateral estoppel effect to verdict. (For discussion of collateral estoppel, *see infra,* §§2225 *et seq.*)

(3) State rules [§1952]

Some states are much more permissive than the federal courts with respect to use of juror testimony to attack verdicts. In California, for example, *any improper influence*—inside or outside the jury room—may be shown. [**People v. Huchinson,** 71 Cal. 2d 342 (1969)]

---

e.g. **Example:** Juror testimony may be used to show that jurors were coerced to change their views or that improper consideration was given to the fact of insurance.

(a) Rationale

Assuring the "purity" of a verdict is more important than protecting its stability.

(b) Limitation

However, affidavits may not be used merely to show that a juror's reasoning or mental process was faulty.

EXAM TIP	gilbert

If an exam question poses the possibility of challenging a verdict for juror misconduct, remember that while some states are receptive to such challenges, other states and the federal courts will allow a juror to testify **only to extraneous** prejudicial information (*e.g.,* some jurors made a visit to the accident site and told the others about it). The juror may not testify to matters occurring inside the jury room. Thus, for example, even if jurors improperly entered a quotient verdict (*see supra,* §1946), it could be difficult to have the verdict overturned on this ground because the jurors cannot testify to what went on in the jury room.

c. Impeachment of verdict for inaccurate response on voir dire [§1953]

A juror's failure to respond correctly to voir dire may be a ground for impeaching the verdict.

(1) Showing required [§1954]

The party challenging the verdict must show that the juror *refused to answer honestly* a material question and that a correct response would have *provided a valid basis for challenge* for cause. [**McDonough Power Equipment, Inc. v. Greenwood,** 464 U.S. 548 (1984)]

> **Example:** A juror in a personal injury case was asked whether any member of his family had suffered "injuries . . . that resulted in any disability or prolonged pain or suffering." He failed to answer that his son had once been injured due to explosion of a truck tire, but because the juror honestly did not understand that this event was called for by the question, his failure to answer did not provide a ground to set aside the verdict. [**McDonough Power Equipment, Inc. v. Greenwood,** *supra*]

(2) Contempt [§1955]

When a juror intentionally withholds disqualifying information, he may be held in contempt for doing so. [**Clark v. United States,** 289 U.S. 1 (1932)]

d. Announcement of verdict [§1956]

To help ensure that deliberations were proper, the jury verdict must be announced in open court.

(1) Polling the jury [§1957]

At the request of either party, the jury may be "polled"—*i.e.,* each juror may be asked if he concurred in the verdict. If a juror fails to concur, the jury must continue its deliberations or a new trial must be ordered. [**Fox v. United States,** 417 F.2d 84 (5th Cir. 1969)]

(2) Correction of verdict [§1958]

Likewise, if the verdict returned is insufficient or incomplete, the court may direct the jury to continue and complete its deliberations. [Cal. Civ. Proc. Code §619]

(a) But note

Once the jury is discharged, a defect in the verdict cannot be cured. [**Sparks v. Berntsen,** 19 Cal. 2d 308 (1942)]

e. Investigation of jury misconduct [§1959]

Counsel may question jurors after they have given their verdict in order to ascertain any possible bases for impeachment.

(1) Limitation

However, hostile interrogation of jurors may be enjoined [**Rakes v. United States,** 169 F.2d 739 (4th Cir. 1948)], and some courts routinely limit post-trial interrogation of jurors.

(2) And note

Jurors cannot be subpoenaed unless there is some reason to expect that their testimony may reveal a ground for impeachment. The rationale is that jurors should not routinely be subject to being "placed on trial by defeated litigants." [**Linhart v. Nelson,** 18 Cal. 3d 641 (1976)]

J. Motions After Verdict or Judgment

1. Renewed Motion for Judgment as a Matter of Law (Judgment Notwithstanding the Verdict) [§1960]

Judgment *non obstante verdicto* ("n.o.v." or "notwithstanding the verdict") is a traditional device for nullifying a jury verdict that is not supported by the evidence. In 1991, the name was changed in federal court to renewed motion for judgment as a matter of law. [Fed. R. Civ. P. 50(b)]

a. Test applied [§1961]

The standard applied for a renewed motion is the same as for such a motion at the close of all the evidence; *i.e.,* the motion should be granted only if there is *no substantial evidence to support the decision* of the jury. [**Montgomery Ward & Co. v. Duncan,** 311 U.S. 243 (1940)] (*See supra,* §§1857-1882, regarding standard on motion before the verdict.)

b. Procedural requirements

(1) Motion [§1962]

In federal court, a renewed motion for judgment as a matter of law may *not* be entered by the court on its own motion. If no motion is made, not even an appellate court has power to enter judgment for the losing party. [**Cone v. West Virginia Pulp & Paper Co.,** 330 U.S. 212 (1946)]

(a) Some states contra [§1963]

In at least some states, judgment *can* be entered *sua sponte*. [Cal. Civ. Proc. Code §629]

(2) Timeliness of motion

(a) Federal Rule [§1964]

In federal court, a renewed motion for judgment as a matter of law must be made within 10 days after the entry of judgment on the verdict. [Fed. R. Civ. P. 50(b)]

(b) State practice [§1965]

Time limits in state practice may vary. [Cal. Civ. Proc. Code §629—15 days following notice of entry of judgment]

(3) Prior motion for judgment as a matter of law [§1966]

In the federal court, a motion for renewed motion for judgment as a matter of law cannot be considered unless the moving party made a motion for directed verdict at the close of all the evidence. [Fed. R. Civ. P. 50(b)]

(a) Rationale

Judgment n.o.v. was not known at common law, and hence presumably was forbidden by the Seventh Amendment. But a directed verdict *was* permitted at common law; and since the judge can reserve his ruling on that motion, a motion for judgment n.o.v. can be viewed as a renewal of the motion for a directed verdict. [**Baltimore & Carolina Line v. Redman**, *supra*, §1885]

(b) State practice contra [§1967]

Most states do not require a prior motion for directed verdict in order to move for judgment n.o.v. [Cal. Civ. Proc. Code §629]

(4) Joined with motion for new trial [§1968]

A post-verdict motion for judgment as a matter of law may be joined with a motion for new trial.

(a) If judgment granted [§1969]

If judgment as a matter of law is granted, the trial court should nevertheless rule in the alternative on the motion for new trial. In that way, if there is an appeal, the appellate court will have full knowledge of the trial judge's decision. [Fed. R. Civ. P. 50(c)]

(b) If judgment denied

1) Appeal [§1970]

The party whose motion is denied may appeal from the judgment as entered (but not from denial of the motion, which is a non-appealable order; *see infra*, §§2094 *et seq.*).

2) Responding party's ground for new trial [§1971]

If the moving party does appeal, the party seeking to preserve the verdict should assert in the alternative any grounds he may have for a new trial. Otherwise, the issues may not be preserved for consideration by the appellate court, which might reverse and order entry of judgment contrary to the verdict. [Fed. R. Civ. P. 50(d); *and see* **Neely v. Martin K. Eby Construction Co.**, 386 U.S. 317 (1967)]

3) Appellate court may enter judgment for verdict loser [§1972]

If a federal appellate court determines that some trial evidence was erroneously admitted and that the remaining evidence did not suffice to put the case before the jury, it may direct entry of judgment as a matter of law for the verdict loser. [**Weisgram v. Marley Co.**, 528 U.S. 440 (2000)]

2. Motion for New Trial [§1973]

The trial judge has the power to order a new trial on all or part of the factual issues in dispute. [Fed. R. Civ. P. 59(a); Cal. Civ. Proc. Code §657]

a. Grounds for motion—jury trial [§1974]

A federal court may order a new trial in a jury case "for any of the reasons for which new trials have heretofore been granted in actions at law in the courts of the United States." [Fed. R. Civ. P. 59(a)] Some state statutes are more explicit in enumerating grounds. [Cal. Civ. Proc. Code §657] In any case, appropriate grounds would include the following:

(1) Prejudicial misconduct [§1975]

A new trial may be granted if the court, the jury, or the adversary engaged in misconduct that prevented a fair trial.

Example: *Counsel's improper jury argument* was a basis for granting a new trial. [**Minneapolis, St. Paul & Sault Ste. Marie Railway v. Moquin**, 283 U.S. 520 (1931)]

Example: *A false answer by juror on voir dire examination* allowed for a new trial. [**Estate of Mesner**, 77 Cal. App. 2d 667 (1947)]

Example: *An improper delay* or continuance for personal convenience of the trial judge was also a basis for a new trial. [**Citron v. Aro Corp.**, 377 F.2d 750 (3d Cir. 1967)]

(a) No new trial for harmless error [§1976]

A new trial should not be ordered for misconduct that was not prejudicial or was adequately corrected by appropriate instructions from the judge. [Fed. R. Civ. P. 61]

(b) Waiver of prejudicial error [§1977]

And a party moving for a new trial may not rely on misconduct known to him *prior* to the verdict, but which he did not point out to the court. *Rationale:* Allowing the party to gamble on the outcome of the verdict would impose an unfair risk on the adversary, who would be faced with the alternative of an adverse verdict or a new trial. [**Lindemann v. San Joaquin Cotton Oil Co.,** 5 Cal. 2d 480 (1936)]

(2) Accident or surprise [§1978]

A new trial may be granted where a party is unfairly surprised by the evidence presented at trial.

(a) Prejudicial effect [§1979]

The surprise must have had a *material* effect on the outcome of the trial. [**Union Electric Light & Power Co. v. Snyder Estate Co.,** 15 F. Supp. 379 (W.D. Mo. 1936)]

(b) Diligence [§1980]

The party also must have been *diligent* in guarding against the surprise.

---

e.g. Example: A party who relies on a witness's promise to appear voluntarily and who fails to subpoena the witness is *not* entitled to a new trial when the witness fails to appear. [**Rudin v. Luman,** 53 Cal. App. 212 (1921)]

---

1) Incompetent counsel [§1981]

A party is charged with the mistake of his counsel, so that a new trial generally will *not* be granted on the ground that counsel was negligent or incompetent. [**Everett v. Everett,** 29 N.W.2d 919 (Mich. 1947)]

(c) Timely application [§1982]

Where surprise occurs, counsel must move for a mistrial or continuance at the earliest opportunity. [**Kaufman v. DeMuths,** 31 Cal. 2d 429 (1948)]

(3) Newly discovered evidence [§1983]

A new trial also may be granted in order to consider evidence discovered after the trial.

(a) Requirements

1) *The new proof must pertain to facts in existence at the time of trial,* not facts occurring later. [**Schuyler v. United Air Lines,** 94 F. Supp. 472 (M.D. Pa. 1950)]

2) *The new proof must be highly significant,* not merely cumulative. [**Wulfsohn v. Russo-Asiatic Bank,** 11 F.2d 715 (9th Cir. 1926)]

3) *And the moving party must show* that the evidence *could not have been obtained by due diligence before trial.* [**Toledo Scale Co. v. Computering Scale Co.,** 261 U.S. 399 (1923)]

(b) But note

A new trial should *not* be ordered where the "discovery" results from the failure of counsel earlier to appreciate the significance of available proof. [**Slemons v. Paterson,** 14 Cal. 2d 612 (1939)]

(c) And note

Generally, "newly discovered evidence" is a *disfavored* ground for new trial; and parties should not withhold or fail to develop proof in hopes of getting a second chance at a favorable verdict. [**Estate of Emerson,** 170 Cal. 81 (1915)]

(4) Improper evidence [§1984]

A new trial may be granted to correct an erroneous ruling on the admissibility of evidence, provided the error was prejudicial and was the subject of timely objection.

(5) Verdict contrary to law [§1985]

A new trial likewise may be granted if the evidence is *not legally sufficient* to support the verdict. An order granting a judgment n.o.v. may also be appropriate if the procedural requirements for such a motion were met. (*See supra,* §1966.)

(6) Weight of the evidence [§1986]

Finally, a new trial may be ordered if the judge finds the verdict to be contrary to the manifest weight of the evidence. [**Aetna Casualty & Surety Co. v. Yeatts,** 122 F.2d 350 (4th Cir. 1941)]

(a) Standard for decision [§1987]

The standard for decision has been expressed in different ways. An underlying policy concern is that motions for new trials on this ground not undermine the right to jury trial; if the judge can invalidate a jury decision on the ground she does not like it, the right to jury trial becomes insignificant.

1) Directed verdict standard [§1988]

Some courts phrase the standard in terms of whether there was substantial evidence to support the verdict—the directed verdict standard. *Criticism:* This seems overly narrow because the motion for new trial on this ground is intended as an additional safety valve in the jury system. On the other hand, when a party has failed to produce substantial evidence at the first trial, it is difficult to understand why the court should give the party a second chance and impose the cost of a second trial on the winner at the first trial.

2) Thirteenth juror standard [§1989]

At the opposite extreme is the thirteenth juror standard: The judge may grant a new trial whenever she disagrees with the jury. *Criticism:* This seems too easy to satisfy. It would constrict the right to jury trial because a litigant must persuade the judge, as well as the jury, in order to prevail.

3) Majority rule—miscarriage of justice [§1990]

Between the thirteenth juror and directed verdict standards is the standard applied by most courts—the miscarriage of justice standard. Under this standard, the judge is to ask whether the jury has reached a seriously erroneous result. In answering this question, she may weigh the evidence, assess the credibility of witnesses, and draw inferences from the evidence.

a) Possible exception

It has been held that as to nontechnical matters, the court should not grant a new trial on the basis of *credibility determinations* because those are peculiarly within the province of the jury. [**Lind v. Schenley Industries, Inc.,** 278 F.2d 79 (3d Cir.), *cert. denied,* 364 U.S. 835 (1960)]

(b) Constitutionality [§1991]

Because the motion for a new trial on this ground existed at common law, there has been no serious challenge to its constitutionality, even though it may seem to erode the value of the right to jury trial. [*See* **Galloway v. United States,** 319 U.S. 372 (1943)—discussing existence of motion for new trial at common law]

EXAM TIP   **gilbert**

If the jury in a test question reaches a result that seems to be at odds with the facts, be sure to discuss the possibility of moving for a new trial on ground that the verdict was against the manifest weight of the evidence. Explain that such a motion should *not be granted lightly* because courts want to protect the jury trial right. Nevertheless, if after assessing the credibility of witnesses and weighing the evidence the judge believes the jury has reached a *seriously erroneous result* so that there has been a miscarriage of justice, a new trial may be ordered.

GROUNDS FOR NEW TRIAL IN JURY TRIALS

A NEW TRIAL MAY BE GRANTED AFTER A JURY VERDICT ON THE FOLLOWING GROUNDS:

- ☑ *Improper attorney argument to jury*.

- ☑ *False answer by juror* on voir dire.

- ☑ *Improper delay* or continuance for personal convenience of judge.

- ☑ *Incorrect rulings* during the trial *on admission or exclusion* of evidence.

- ☑ A party was *unfairly surprised* by evidence presented at trial that affected the outcome in a material way, despite the party's diligence in guarding against the surprise.

- ☑ *New evidence* is discovered that is highly significant, pertains to facts that existed at the time of trial, and could not have been obtained by due diligence before trial.

- ☑ Verdict was *contrary to law or weight of evidence*.

(c) Appellate review

1) Traditional rule [§1992]

The traditional rule was that the weight of the evidence was to be assessed only by the trial judge—*i.e.*, whether he granted or denied a new trial on this ground, his decision ordinarily was not reversible. The trial judge's ruling would be reversed only if a new trial was denied and there was *no* substantial evidence to support the verdict—*i.e.*, if there should have been a directed verdict. [*See* **Portman v. American Home Products Corp.**, 201 F.2d 847 (2d Cir. 1953)]

2) Modern rule [§1993]

Today, appellate courts may reverse the denial of a motion for new trial if it is determined that the refusal to grant the motion was an "abuse of discretion." This means that if the evidence was seriously arguable, the trial judge should not substitute his view of the evidence for that of the jury. [**Lind v. Schenley Industries, Inc.**, *supra*]

3) Review of grant of new trial [§1994]

An order granting a new trial is *not immediately appealable* because it is not a final judgment. On appeal from the final judgment following the second trial, however, the appellant may claim error in the grant of the new trial. If the appellate court agrees, it can *reinstate the verdict* from the first trial, although this rarely happens.

4) Excessive or inadequate damages [§1995]

The trial judge may find that the jury's award of damages is against the weight of the evidence. In such cases, a partial or conditional new trial may be ordered. (*See* discussion of remittitur and additur, *infra*, §§2014-2025.) Such rulings are generally reviewable only for abuse of discretion. State substantive law on the standard for review of excessiveness or inadequacy of damage awards by the trial court, however, may supplant federal decisional law on that issue in state-law cases in federal court. [**Gasperini v. Center for Humanities, Inc.**, *supra*, §555]

b. Grounds for motion—nonjury trial [§1996]

If the trial was conducted without a jury, a motion for new trial is essentially a motion for rehearing. Such a motion may be granted on the following grounds:

(1) *Newly discovered evidence;*

(2) *Erroneous findings of fact;* and/or

(3) *Error in the conduct of the trial* (*e.g.*, erroneous rulings on admissibility of evidence).

c. Procedural requirements for new trial motion

(1) Necessity for motion

(a) Federal Rule [§1997]
A federal court may grant a new trial on its own motion. [Fed. R. Civ. P. 59(d)]

(b) State courts [§1998]
In some states, the court may order a new trial only on motion by a party. [Cal. Civ. Proc. Code §659]

(2) Timeliness of motion

(a) Federal Rule [§1999]
In federal courts, motion for new trial must be served within 10 days after entry of the judgment. [Fed. R. Civ. P. 59(b)]

(b) State courts [§2000]
State court time limits vary. In California, for example, the motion must be made within 15 days after notice of entry of the judgment. [Cal. Civ. Proc. Code §659]

(3) Affidavits [§2001]
A motion for new trial may be accompanied by affidavits if proof is necessary to establish the grounds.

(a) Time for filing [§2002]
In federal court, the movant's affidavits must be filed at the time of filing the motion. [Fed. R. Civ. P. 59(c)] State rules may allow later filing. [Cal. Civ. Proc. Code §659a]

(b) No oral testimony [§2003]
Most courts refuse to accept oral testimony in support of a motion for new trial. [**Linhart v. Nelson,** 18 Cal. 3d 641 (1976)]

(4) Hearings [§2004]
A motion for new trial must be heard by the judge who conducted the trial, unless he is disabled.

(5) Time for decision [§2005]
There is no time limit for the judge's ruling on a motion for new trial, at least in federal practice.

(a) State laws [§2006]
Some state statutes impose a limit. [Cal. Civ. Proc. Code §660— failure to grant motion within 60 days after filing operates as a denial]

d. Order

(1) In nonjury cases [§2007]

In ruling on a motion for new trial in a nonjury case, the court may order a full retrial or only *partial* new trials (*i.e.*, it may order the reopening of the judgment for the taking of additional proof, after which it may amend its findings of fact and conclusions of law or make new findings and conclusions and direct the entry of a new judgment). [Fed. R. Civ. P. 59(a)]

(2) In jury cases [§2008]

In a jury case, the court must grant or deny the motion, but it may do so in parts or on conditions (*e.g.*, new trial on damages only).

(a) Specification of grounds

1) Federal practice [§2009]

A federal court need not specify the grounds on which new trial is granted.

2) State practice [§2010]

State rules on specifications of grounds vary. In California, if the ground is *insufficiency of the proof,* the judge must specify the respect in which the proof is deficient (and this specification is reviewable on appeal). [Cal. Civ. Proc. Code §657]

(b) Excessive or inadequate damages [§2011]

If the judge finds that the jury's damage award is inappropriate, there are several alternatives:

1) Full new trial [§2012]

The judge may order a full new trial. This would be the only appropriate order if the award is so excessive that the judge concludes that the verdict is the result of passion. [**New York Central Railroad v. Johnson,** 279 U.S. 310 (1929)]

2) Partial new trial [§2013]

As a *time-saving move,* the court may order that the new trial be limited to certain issues. However, such a limited new trial may be used only when "it clearly appears that the issue to be retried is so distinct and separable from the others that a trial of it alone may be had without injustice." [**Gasoline Products Co. v. Champlin Refining Co.,** 283 U.S. 494 (1931)]

Example: When the low verdict for plaintiff indicates that it was a compromise verdict in which jurors who favored exonerating defendant altogether went along with a low award to plaintiff, a new trial limited to the issue of damages would be unfair to defendant.

3) Conditional new trial

a) Remittitur [§2014]

A remittitur is an order for a new trial, subject to recall if the plaintiff consents to *reduction* of the damage award. If the plaintiff so consents, a new trial is denied.

1/ Note

Remittitur was recognized at common law and has been held consistent with the Seventh Amendment. [**Northern Pacific Railroad v. Herbert,** 116 U.S. 642 (1886)]

2/ Proper sum [§2015]

Courts vary in their approach to what is the proper sum for a remittitur.

a/ Fair amount [§2016]

Many courts hold that the verdict should be reduced to whatever amount the trial judge determines to be fair and reasonable (*i.e.*, her estimate of what a properly functioning jury would have found)—on the theory that this gives the plaintiff adequate incentive to avoid the costs and risks of a retrial. [**Powers v. Allstate Insurance Co.,** 102 N.W.2d 393 (Wis. 1960); Cal. Civ. Proc. Code §662.5(b)]

b/ Lowest amount [§2017]

However, some courts reduce the verdict to the lowest amount that an impartial jury reasonably could have awarded—on the theory that this best protects the defendant from an improper award and that plaintiff can always protect himself by accepting a new trial. [**Meissner v. Papas,** 35 F. Supp. 676 (E.D. Wis. 1940)]

c/ Highest amount [§2018]

Still other courts reduce the verdict to the *highest* amount deemed not excessive—on the theory that the jury's verdict should be upheld insofar as possible. [**Gorsalitz v. Olin Mathieson Chemical Corp.,** 429 F.2d 1033 (5th Cir. 1970)]

d/ Note—effect on plaintiff's election [§2019]

Note that remittitur gives the plaintiff the choice whether to proceed to a new trial or accept a reduced award. Using the lowest possible award standard (§2017, above) signals to the plaintiff that this amount is the worst he can do at the second trial if he prevails on liability. Using the highest possible award standard (§2018, above) signals to the plaintiff that he cannot expect to do better at the new trial and keep that result. Thus, adoption of the highest possible award standard will be more likely to induce plaintiffs to accept remittitur than the lowest possible award standard.

3/ Waiver [§2020]

If the plaintiff agrees to a remittitur, most courts hold that he waives the right to appeal the propriety of the remittitur (except that if defendant thereafter appeals, plaintiff may cross-appeal from the reduction of damages ordered by the trial judge). [**Donovan v. Penn Shipping Co.,** 429 U.S. 648 (1977)] *Exception:* It has been held that a plaintiff did not waive the right to appeal where a court reduced a punitive damage award pursuant to a constitutionally mandated reduction in such damages, and the plaintiff did not have a choice between consenting to the reduction or going to a new trial. [**Johansen v. Combustion Engineering, Inc.,** 170 F.3d 1320 (11th Cir.), *cert. denied,* 528 U.S. 931 (1999)]

4/ Appellate court [§2021]

A federal appellate court may review a district judge's denial of a motion seeking remittitur, but only for trial-court abuse of discretion in applying the governing standard. [**Gasperini v. Center for Humanities, Inc.,** *supra,* §1995] State practice varies. For example, California Appellate Rule 24(c) expressly recognizes remittitur and additur by appellate courts of the state.

a/ Constitutional right to retrial [§2022]

In federal court, if the appellate court directs recalculation of damages due to excessiveness, the plaintiff has a right under the Seventh

Amendment to reject the recalculated figures as too low and insist on a new trial. [**Hetzel v. Prince William County**, 523 U.S. 208 (1998)]

b) Additur [§2023]

An additur is an order granting a new trial unless the defendant consents to an *increase* in the amount of the verdict.

1/ Federal practice [§2024]

Additur was not known at common law and has therefore been held forbidden in federal courts by the Seventh Amendment (*i.e.*, as violating plaintiff's right to jury trial on the issue of damages.) [**Dimick v. Schiedt**, *supra*, §1777] The modern Court has hinted, however, that it might be willing to rethink sympathetically the constitutionality of additur. [**Gasperini v. Center for Humanities, Inc.**, *supra*]

2/ State practice [§2025]

Many state statutes and constitutions allow additur as well as remittitur. [*See, e.g.*, Cal. Civ. Proc. Code §662.5(a)]

4) Entry of reduced judgment [§2026]

Some jurisdictions limit the amount of punitive damages available in tort cases and give courts power to reduce excessive awards. In the special and limited circumstance of a constitutionally mandated reduction of excessive punitive damages, one circuit takes the view that a trial court may bypass the usual remittitur procedure of granting a conditional new trial if the plaintiff accepts a reduction in the damage award. Instead, the court may enter judgment for the amount of punitive damages it finds to be constitutionally permitted. [**Johansen v. Combustion Engineering, Inc.**, *supra*]

3. Motion to Alter or Amend Judgment [§2027]

A motion to alter or amend judgment may be used to reopen judgments in both jury and nonjury cases. [Fed. R. Civ. P. 59(e); Cal. Civ. Proc. Code §663]

a. Errors of law only [§2028]

The purpose of the motion is to correct errors of law, and it cannot be used to secure a retrial on the facts.

---

e.g. Examples: Vacation of a judgment would be proper: where the judgment rests on *erroneous conclusions of law*; where *necessary conclusions of law were omitted*; or where the court *erroneously asserted jurisdiction*.

---

b. Time limitations [§2029]

A motion to alter or amend judgment is subject to the same time limits as a motion for new trial. [Fed. R. Civ. P. 59(e); Cal. Civ. Proc. Code §663a; *see supra*, §§1999-2000]

4. Motion for Relief from Judgment

a. For clerical mistakes [§2030]

If the judgment as entered by the clerk differs from that ordered by the court, the mistake can be corrected. [Fed. R. Civ. P. 60(a); Cal. Civ. Proc. Code §473]

(1) Procedure [§2031]

Corrections can be made on motion or *sua sponte.*

(2) Timing [§2032]

There is no time limit on the power to correct.

(3) "Clerical" mistake [§2033]

Clerical mistakes subject to correction by this motion may be those of either clerk or counsel who drafted the order or judgment, but *not* those of the judge. Judicial errors should be attacked by a motion to alter or amend (above).

b. Other grounds [§2034]

The court likewise may relieve a party from judgment on the following grounds:

(1) Mistake, inadvertence, or surprise [§2035]

A judgment may be reopened for these reasons, but the circumstances must be extraordinary. The standard of care to which the moving party is held is much higher than would be applied in a motion for new trial. [Fed. R. Civ. P. 60(b)(1); **Bershad v. McDonough,** 469 F.2d 1333 (7th Cir. 1972); Cal. Civ. Proc. Code §473; **Martin v. Taylor,** 267 Cal. App. 2d 112 (1968)]

(2) Excusable neglect [§2036]

The court may reopen a default judgment for excusable neglect. However, neglect of counsel is *not* a sufficient ground for relief. [**Universal Film Exchanges, Inc. v. Lust,** 479 F.2d 573 (4th Cir. 1973)]

(3) Newly discovered evidence [§2037]

The court may reopen a judgment to receive additional proof, but it must be shown that the moving party, by reasonable diligence, could not have discovered the new evidence in time to move for a new trial under Federal Rule 59. And the proof must be more than cumulative; *i.e.*, it is not enough that the moving party has now devised a new factual theory to explain the proof. [*See* **Stilwell v. Travelers Insurance Co.,** 327 F.2d 931 (5th Cir. 1964)] The standard is essentially the same as that used on a motion for a new trial on this ground. (*See supra,* §1983.)

(4) Fraud or misconduct [§2038]

A judgment may be reopened for fraud or other misconduct (*e.g.,* a judgment obtained by the use of perjured testimony). [Fed. R. Civ. P. 60(b)(3); **Peacock Records, Inc. v. Checker Records, Inc.,** 365 F.2d 145 (7th Cir. 1966)]

(a) Burden on party guilty of fraud [§2039]

The responding party then has the burden of showing that the fraud did not affect the outcome. [**Hazel Atlas Glass Co. v. Hartford Empire Co.,** 322 U.S. 238 (1944)]

Example: When defendant in a products liability action failed to produce a document called for by an order compelling production of documents, its failure to do so constituted misconduct. Since production of the document might materially have affected plaintiff's presentation of the case, judgment for defendant was vacated. [**Rozier v. Ford Motor Co.,** 573 F.2d 1332 (5th Cir. 1978)]

---

(5) Void judgment [§2040]

A judgment may be reopened if it is void (as where no notice was given prior to the entry of a default). [**Bass v. Hoagland,** 172 F.2d 205 (5th Cir. 1949)]

(6) Change of circumstances (equitable relief) [§2041]

Where the judgment provides for continuing equitable relief, as where an injunction is granted, the court may reopen the proceedings to consider whether supervening events make the old decree inequitable. [Fed. R. Civ. P. 60(b)(5); **De Filippis v. United States,** 567 F.2d 341 (7th Cir. 1977)]

(a) Note

This ground is generally not applicable in the case of money judgments. [**Ryan v. United States Lines,** 303 F.2d 430 (2d Cir. 1962)]

(b) And note

The parties may not contract to bar the court from considering the continuing equity of a decree; it is an abuse of discretion to refuse to modify a decree that no longer fairly serves its original purpose. [**System Federation No. 91, Railway Employees Department v. Wright,** 364 U.S. 642 (1961)]

(7) Relief otherwise justified [§2042]

Under the Federal Rules, the court may also reopen a judgment for "any other reason justifying relief." [Fed. R. Civ. P. 60(b)(6)] However, this rule has been *sparingly* applied, and the courts have frequently emphasized that it is *not* an alternative to appeal. [**Ackerman v. United States**, 340 U.S. 193 (1950)]

Example: Subsequent state-court interpretation of state law different from a federal court's interpretation of the same state law in a federal case that has become final is *not* by itself an extraordinary circumstance justifying relief under Federal Rule 60(b). [*See, e.g.,* **Kansas Public Employees Retirement System v. Reimer & Koger Associates**, 194 F.3d 922 (8th Cir. 1999), *cert. denied,* 120 S. Ct. 1268 (2000)]

(a) Exception

A federal court interpreted a state law differently from the way the state supreme court subsequently interpreted the same state law in a case involving another claimant injured in the *same accident* as the plaintiff in the federal case. The need to correct the federal court's erroneous interpretation of the state law in this exceptional circumstance was held sufficient to justify overriding the usual rule that mere error does not warrant disturbing a final judgment. [**Pierce v. Cook & Co.**, 518 F.2d 720 (10th Cir. 1975), *cert. denied,* 423 U.S. 1079 (1976)]

c. Time limits

(1) Federal practice [§2043]

A motion for relief from judgment must be made within "reasonable" time. This cannot be more than one year from the entry of judgment if the ground asserted is mistake, inadvertence, surprise, excusable neglect, newly discovered evidence, or fraud. [Fed. R. Civ. P. 60(b)]

(a) But note

There is no outside time limit where the ground is that the judgment is void or satisfied, or that there are "other reasons justifying relief" (*see* above).

(2) State practice [§2044]

Time limits in state courts vary. In California, the period is six months from the entry of judgment. [Cal. Civ. Proc. Code §473]

d. Distinguish independent suit to set aside judgment [§2045]

A motion for relief from a judgment must be distinguished from an independent suit in equity based on similar grounds. The motion is addressed to the court that entered the judgment; whereas the independent suit may be addressed to a different court. In addition, the grounds for an independent suit in equity tend to be narrower and more strictly scrutinized than those for a motion for relief from judgment. [**Lapin v. Shulton, Inc.,** 333 F.2d 169 (9th Cir. 1964)]

(1) Grounds for independent action [§2046]

The two basic grounds for an independent equity suit for relief from judgment are:

(i) *Jurisdictional defects*; and

(ii) *Fraud*—as where plaintiff was induced not to appear or contest the case by a false promise of settlement. [*See* **United States v. Throckmorton,** 98 U.S. 61 (1878); **Kulchar v. Kulchar,** 1 Cal. 3d 467 (1969)]

(a) Former limitation [§2047]

At one time, relief through an independent suit could be obtained only if the fraud was *extrinsic,* as distinguished from fraud such as perjury. However, this distinction has now been repudiated by most courts. [**Publicker v. Shallcross,** 106 F.2d 949 (3d Cir. 1939)]

(b) Modern limitation [§2048]

Relief from a federal court judgment by an independent action is authorized only "*to prevent a grave miscarriage of justice.*" [**United States v. Beggerly,** 524 U.S. 38 (1998)—alleged failure of adversary to search its records thoroughly and to make a full disclosure did not provide sufficient basis for vacating the judgment]

(2) State-federal relations [§2049]

A federal court may refuse to entertain an independent action in equity to set aside a state court judgment. [**Maicobo Investment Corp. v. von der Heide,** 243 F. Supp. 885 (D. Md. 1965)]

(3) Relation to motion for relief [§2050]

Seeking relief by motion in the main action is *not* a prerequisite to the independent action. However, if such relief is still available in the main action, the equity court may choose not to act because there is an adequate direct remedy.

(a) Note

If the ground for relief asserted in the equity suit was previously presented to the court that entered judgment and was held insufficient to reopen the judgment, that decision is *res judicata.*

MOTION	CIRCUMSTANCES	TIMING
Renewed Motion for Judgment as a Matter of Law	The verdict returned could not have been reached by reasonable persons. Moving party must have previously sought judgment as a matter of law at close of evidence.	Within 10 days after entry of judgment.
Motion for New Trial	Prejudicial misconduct, accident, surprise, newly discovered evidence, improper evidence, verdict contrary to law, verdict contrary to weight of the evidence.	**Federal:** No later than 10 days after entry of judgment. **State:** Timing varies among state courts.
Motion to Alter or Amend Judgment	Corrects errors of law.	**Federal:** No later than 10 days after entry of judgment. **State:** Timing varies among state courts.
Motion for Relief from Judgment	Clerical mistakes, mistake, inadvertence, surprise, excusable neglect, newly discovered evidence, fraud, misconduct, void judgment, change of circumstances.	**Federal:** Within a reasonable time, but no more than one year from entry of judgment if the ground asserted is mistake, inadvertence, surprise, excusable neglect, newly discovered evidence, or fraud. **State:** Timing varies among state courts.

(4) Jurisdictional basis [§2051]

A federal court has subject matter jurisdiction to entertain an independent action to set aside a federal court judgment *ancillary* to its jurisdiction over the original action (*see supra*, §§409-417). [**United States v. Beggerly,** *supra*]

5. Coram Nobis

a. State practice [§2052]

In some states, the common law writ of coram nobis is still available. The purpose of the writ is "to declare as false a fact previously determined to be true . . . "—as where a witness recants perjury, or evidence previously concealed by a party comes to light.

(1) Cautiously applied [§2053]

Writs of coram nobis are granted only if no other remedy is available and it is absolutely clear that the evidence involved was crucial to the outcome of the case. [**Rollins v. City and County of San Francisco,** 37 Cal. App. 3d 145 (1974)]

b. Federal practice [§2054]

In federal practice, the writ of coram nobis has been *abolished.* [Fed. R. Civ. P. 60(b)]

Chapter Ten:
Appeal

CONTENTS

Chapter Approach

Chapter Approach

Procedural issues in connection with appeal mostly fall under one of two headings: appealability and reviewability. *Appealability* concerns whether the action of the lower court is one that permits the case to be taken to a court of appeals *at that point*. *Reviewability* deals with *what issues*, once a case is before an appellate court, the court may consider, and what *standard of review* (de novo or deferential) governs the appellate court's consideration of the trial court's rulings.

1. **Appealability**

   a.   In most court systems, the main question is whether the lower court has entered a *final judgment*. If not, a decision is usually not appealable at that time.

   b.   There are *exceptions* to the final judgment rule permitting *interlocutory review*:

   —   Has the lower court granted or denied a *preliminary injunction*?

   —   Has the lower court *certified* a ruling for discretionary interlocutory review?

   —   Has the lower court made a ruling that qualifies as a *collateral order*?

   —   Is the order being appealed a grant or denial of a *class certification*?

   —   Is there a basis for review by *extraordinary writ*, such as mandamus or prohibition (ordinarily for serious abuse of discretion by the trial court)?

2. **Reviewability**
   What may be considered by the appellate court depends on the issue involved:

   a.   Was the objection *properly preserved* or was it *waived*, as by failure of counsel to make timely objection? If proper objection was not made, is there nonetheless *plain error*?

   b.   Is the challenge to a ruling on a *question of law*? If so, review is *de novo*.

   c.   Is the challenge to a *finding of fact*? If so, the appellate court will generally accord a degree of deference to the trier of fact.

   d.   Is the action one committed to the *discretion of the trial judge*? If so, the trial court can usually be reversed *only* for abuse of discretion or failure to apply the correct legal standards.

e.   Was the alleged error one with *prejudicial effect,* or was it simply *harmless error?*

A. Right to Appeal

---

1. Appeal Reviews Lower Court Rulings [§2055]

An appeal is the usual procedure for obtaining review by a higher court. The function of the appeal is to assure that the trial has been conducted in a lawful manner and that judgments conform to the law. An appeal ordinarily does not involve a retrial of the case in the higher court (except in some systems that allow for "appeal" of inferior court decisions by providing trial de novo in a trial court of general jurisdiction), but rather is limited to a consideration of the rulings by the lower court in light of the record on which those rulings were made.

2. Status as Right [§2056]

The right to appeal in civil matters is a creature of statute.

a. Common law [§2057]

There was no right to an appeal at common law. A *writ of error* could issue from a higher court, but was discretionary with that court.

b. Constitution [§2058]

Similarly, the Due Process Clause does not guarantee a right of appeal—at least in civil cases. [**National Union of Marine Cooks v. Arnold,** 348 U.S. 37 (1954); **Cobbledick v. United States,** 309 U.S. 323 (1940)—"the right to a judgment from more than one court is a matter of grace and not a necessary ingredient of justice"]

c. Statutory foundation of right

(1) State law [§2059]

Legislation in every state creates a civil appellate jurisdiction in some court of the state.

(2) Federal law [§2060]

There is, likewise, a statutory right of appeal in civil proceedings in federal district court. [28 U.S.C. §§1291 *et seq.*]

3. Waiver of Right [§2061]

The statutory right of appeal may be lost through any of the following:

a.   *Express waiver;*

b. *Untimely assertion*;

c. *Voluntary compliance with judgment* (*e.g.*, a party who pays the amount of a judgment or performs the act ordered by a decree may be held to have waived the right to appeal). However, performance must be voluntary. Where a judgment is executed by officers of the court and thereby satisfied, the judgment debtor's right of appeal survives [**Reitano v. Yankwich,** 38 Cal. 2d 1 (1951)]; and

d. *Acceptance of benefits*—when the plaintiff recovers a judgment and voluntarily accepts payment of the amount recovered, he may not thereafter appeal (*e.g.*, on the ground that the award was inadequate) [**Schubert v. Reich,** 36 Cal. 2d 298 (1950)].

B. Courts of Review

1. The Federal System

a. United States Courts of Appeals [§2062]

There are 13 United States Courts of Appeals. Twelve have a territorial jurisdiction; in addition, the Federal Circuit, seated in Washington, D.C., has subject matter appellate jurisdiction in patent cases and tort and contract claims against the United States. Appeals to the courts of appeals come from:

(1) District courts [§2063]

Most appeals from district court decisions are taken to the courts of appeals.

(2) Administrative agencies [§2064]

Proceedings to review decisions by many federal administrative agencies must be taken to the courts of appeals.

b. Supreme Court of the United States [§2065]

The Supreme Court has a limited original jurisdiction, as authorized by Article III of the Constitution. However, the Court performs primarily an appellate function, as follows:

(1) Direct review of district courts [§2066]

There is a statutory right of appeal from a district court decision *directly* to the Supreme Court when an act of Congress requires the case to be heard and determined by a *three-judge district court* (a rare thing) and the court *granted or denied injunctive relief.* [28 U.S.C. §1253]

(2) Review of courts of appeals [§2067]

Decisions of the United States Courts of Appeals may be reviewed by the Supreme Court as follows:

(a) By certiorari [§2068]

The Supreme Court may grant a writ of certiorari before or after judgment is entered (although review before final judgment is extremely rare). [28 U.S.C. §1254(1)] The Court has *complete discretion* to deny review without explanation.

(b) By certification [§2069]

A court of appeals may certify a question of law to the Supreme Court. [28 U.S.C. §1254(2)] This route is used very rarely, the courts of appeals generally taking the view that they have the responsibility to decide issues of federal law themselves, without seeking the Supreme Court's assistance.

(3) Review of decisions of state courts [§2070]

The Supreme Court may also review decisions of state courts by certiorari. [28 U.S.C. §1257]

(a) Highest possible state court [§2071]

The Supreme Court will not review a state court decision while further review is still possible in the state court system. Thus, the litigant seeking Supreme Court review must first exhaust state court appeal procedures.

(b) Involving federal law [§2072]

The Supreme Court can review a state court decision only to the extent that it involves issues of federal law.

(c) Distinguish—state law issues [§2073]

The Supreme Court has *no authority* to review state court decisions of issues of state law. The state courts are the highest authorities on the meaning of state law, as long as state law does not infringe on matters protected by federal law.

EXAM TIP | **gilbert**

Remember that while the Supreme Court can hear appeals from a state's highest court, it may take the appeal only to adjudicate *federal law*. Thus, if an exam question involves a state law claim decided by the state's supreme court, your answer should not suggest that the decision can be appealed to the United States Supreme Court unless there is an argument that federal law, such as the Constitution, forbids the state court's reading of state law.

---

2. State Appellate Systems [§2074]

There are substantial differences in the organization of court systems among the various states, and no particular structure can be regarded as typical.

a. New York [§2075]

In New York, the principal trial court of general jurisdiction is the supreme court.

(1) Appeals

There is an appellate division of the supreme court, which hears appeals of right from proceedings and orders of the trial courts. The appellate division is divided into four departments, each serving a different area of the state.

(2) Highest court

The highest court is the Court of Appeals of New York. Appeals of right to this court may be taken in constitutional matters and pursuant to various statutes. In addition, the Court of Appeals has the power of discretionary review over many types of lower court decisions.

b. California [§2076]

In California, the trial court of general jurisdiction is the superior court, which also exercises appellate jurisdiction over the municipal courts. [Cal. Const. art. VI, §§10, 11]

(1) Appeals

The courts of appeal, which are six in number, each serve a separate area of the state called a district. Three of the six are further divided into divisions. The courts of appeal hear all appeals of right from superior court judgments. Also, the superior court may certify an appeal from a municipal court judgment to the court of appeal.

(2) Highest court

The Supreme Court of California exercises discretionary jurisdiction over proceedings in civil cases in the courts of appeal. A hearing in the supreme court may be granted on petition for hearing by a party or by the court on its own initiative.

(a) *If a case is heard in the supreme court*, the decision of the court of appeal is nullified.

(b) *The purpose of supreme court review* is to secure uniformity of decision among the courts of appeal or to settle important questions of law. [Cal. Rules of Court 29(a)]

c. Texas [§2077]

The Texas courts of general civil jurisdiction are district courts.

(1) Appeals

Appeals from district courts in civil cases are taken to the courts of appeals, which are 14 in number, each serving a different area and reviewing particular district courts.

(2) Highest court

Review of civil decisions of the courts of appeals is by the Supreme

Court of Texas, which exercises civil jurisdiction only. (Criminal appeals go to the Court of Criminal Appeals, a court of last resort, directly from trial courts in capital cases and from the courts of appeals in other cases.)

d. Michigan [§2078]

Michigan is typical of a number of states that have a unified intermediate court, the Court of Appeals, which is subject to review in the Supreme Court of Michigan.

e. South Dakota [§2079]

South Dakota is typical of states that have only one appellate court, the supreme court, to which all appeals are taken.

C. Appellate Procedure

1. Filing of Appeal [§2080]

An appeal is commenced by filing a *notice of appeal*. The notice is filed in the appellate court or trial court, depending on the specific court rules. The notice of appeal is a written statement that the appellant invokes the jurisdiction of the appellate court to review a specified judgment from the court below. Formality in the notice is not essential; and the instrument will be liberally construed to prevent waiver. Indeed, under Federal Rule of Appellate Procedure 3(c)(4), which provides that an appeal "must not be dismissed for informality of form or title of the notice of appeal," a document meant as an appellate brief can qualify as the notice of appeal if it is filed within the time for filing notice and if it contains the information required in a notice of appeal. [**Smith v. Barry,** 502 U.S. 244 (1992)]

a. But note—need to name all appellants [§2081]

However, if there are multiple appellants, each one must be named in the notice of appeal. An attorney representing multiple appellants may satisfy this requirement by using such terms as "all plaintiffs" or "the plaintiffs A, B, *et al.,*" but it must be clear which parties intended to appeal. [Fed. R. App. P. 3(c)] Mere use of "A *et al.,*" will not suffice, and the lower court's judgment will be final as to the unspecified parties even if it is reversed as to those specified with adequate clarity. [*See* **Torres v. Oakland Scavenger Co.,** 487 U.S. 312 (1988)]

2. Time Limits

a. Federal courts [§2082]

In federal court, a notice of appeal in a civil case must be filed within 30 days after entry of judgment (or within 60 days, if the United States is a party). The trial judge may extend this period for not more than 30 days, upon a showing of excusable neglect. [Fed. R. App. P. 4]

(1) Premature notice of appeal [§2083]

Under Federal Rule of Appellate Procedure 4(a)(2), a notice of appeal filed between announcement and entry of a judgment or order is treated as filed immediately after its entry. Under this rule, a premature notice of appeal ripens and becomes effective after eventual entry of judgment even if the notice is filed with respect to a ruling that is not appealable if the decision would have been appealable if followed immediately by entry of judgment, because the party filing the notice reasonably (though mistakenly) could have believed the decision to be final. [**FirsTier Mortgage Co. v. Investors Mortgage Insurance Co.**, 498 U.S. 469 (1990)]

b. State practice [§2084]

State time limits for noticing an appeal vary. In California, the notice must be filed within 60 days after notice of entry of judgment or 180 days after actual entry, whichever is later. The court has *no* power to extend the time. [Cal. Rules of Court 2(a)]

c. Limits affect jurisdiction [§2085]

The time limits for an appeal are often jurisdictional and ordinarily cannot be waived.

3. Appeal Bonds

a. Costs [§2086]

To perfect an appeal, the appellant generally must file a bond to secure the payment of his adversary's costs on appeal in the event the judgment is affirmed. [Fed. R. App. P. 7]

(1) Possible constitutional limitation [§2087]

In limited circumstances, due process and equal protection may forbid conditioning the right to appeal upon payment of charges such as record preparation fees. [**M.L.B. v. S.L.J.**, 519 U.S. 102 (1996)—state that allows appeal from decision terminating parental rights may not deny right of appeal because of appellant's inability to pay a $2,300 record preparation fee]

b. Supersedeas [§2088]

If the appellant wishes to stay execution of the judgment pending appeal, he must usually assure that the judgment will be satisfied if it is ultimately affirmed. This assurance may be given in the form of a *supersedeas* bond, which is generally executed by a surety company. [Fed. R. App. P. 8]

(1) Possible constitutional limitations [§2089]

There may be a constitutional requirement that it be possible to obtain a supersedeas bond. In **Pennzoil Co. v. Texaco, Inc.**, 481 U.S. 1 (1987), Texaco argued that the Texas requirement that it post such a bond to avoid execution of a judgment for more than $10 billion violated its due process rights, because such a bond could not be obtained. The Supreme Court held that the federal courts should not intervene in this matter, which should have been handled in the state courts.

4. Record on Appeal [§2090]

Review on appeal is limited to proceedings in the trial court.

a. Clerk's record [§2091]

It is the duty of the clerk of the trial court to assemble and transmit the record on appeal, which will include the pleadings, motions, orders, verdict, and judgment in the case. [Fed. R. App. P. 11]

b. Reporter's transcript [§2092]

At the request of a party, the record may also include a transcription of the testimony at trial or such portions of the testimony that the party seeks to place before the appellate court. [Fed. R. App. P. 10]

5. Stay of Proceedings Below [§2093]

The taking of an appeal ousts the trial court of jurisdiction. While the appeal is pending, the trial court generally has *no power* to alter or vacate its judgment, and limited power to make any other order or decree affecting rights of the parties with respect to the case on appeal. [Cal. Civ. Pro. Code §916(a)]

D. Rulings Subject to Appeal

1. Final Decision Requirement [§2094]

Generally speaking, only a final decision may be appealed.

a. General rule

(1) At common law [§2095]

At common law, a writ of error could be taken only from a "final" judgment—*i.e.*, a written order of the trial court, which stated the outcome of its proceedings and manifested that those proceedings were complete.

(a) Rationale

The purposes of the rule were:

1) *To avoid the cost and delay of multiple appeals* in the same action;

2) *To avoid needless effort by appellate courts in considering issues* that may be rendered moot by subsequent proceedings in the trial court; and

3) *To avoid the demeaning effect on the status of the trial judge* that results from excessive review of his decisions.

(2) Modern practice [§2096]

Today, the final decision rule is the basic rule, but it is subject to exceptions.

(a) Federal courts [§2097]

Appeals to the United States Courts of Appeals may generally be taken only from final decisions of the district courts. [28 U.S.C. §1291]

(b) State courts [§2098]

Similarly, all but a few states adhere to the final decision requirement. The notable exception is New York, which includes trial court actions "involv[ing] some part of the merits," or "affect[ing] a substantial right," among appealable orders. [N.Y. Civ. Prac. Law & Rules §5701(a)]

(c) Separate instrument rule [§2099]

The final decision must also be embodied in a separate instrument that unequivocally manifests that the trial court proceeding is complete and that a disposition has been made. [Fed. R. Civ. P. 58]

(3) Nonappealable orders [§2100]

As a result of the final decision requirement, no immediate appeal may be taken from most orders of trial courts—including such important rulings as discovery orders, pretrial orders, orders denying summary judgment, and the like.

(a) Orders after judgment

1) Orders granting new trial

a) Federal practice [§2101]

An order granting a new trial is *not* appealable in the federal courts—so that the case must proceed to retrial and a new judgment before an appeal is allowed.

b) State practice [§2102]

In some states, an order granting a new trial *is* an appealable order. [Cal. Civ. Proc. Code §904.1(a)(4)]

c) Review after second trial [§2103]

In those jurisdictions where an order granting a new trial is not immediately appealable, the issue may be raised on appeal after final judgment in the second trial. If the appellate court finds that the grant of new trial was improper, it can order that the first judgment be reinstated.

2) Orders denying new trial [§2104]

An order denying a new trial is not itself a final appealable order, but it leaves intact the final judgment from which an appeal can be taken.

3) Appealable orders [§2105]

An appeal may be taken from other orders made after judgment that have the effect of *vacating* the judgment or *staying* its execution.

(b) Extraordinary review [§2106]

In exceptional circumstances, nonappealable orders may be reviewed by means of *extraordinary writs* (*see infra*, §2168).

(c) Orders not immune from review [§2107]

The fact that an order is not immediately appealable does not mean that it is immune from review. If a judgment adverse to the party aggrieved is later entered, an appeal from the judgment can contest the correctness of the previous nonappealable order. As to some orders, such as discovery orders, it is unusual for an appellate court to find that they were sufficiently prejudicial to warrant reversal.

EXAM TIP | **gilbert**

Remember the basic rule in most jurisdictions is that appeals may be taken only from *final decisions*. Thus, most trial court orders regarding pretrial matters, discovery, denial of summary judgment, etc., are not immediately appealable. This does not mean that the orders can never be reviewed; it only means that review must wait until the entire case can be reviewed.

---

b. "Jurisdictional" character of rule [§2108]

The final decision requirement is jurisdictional in the sense that it cannot be waived by the appellee. Thus, an appeal taken from a nonappealable order will be dismissed by the appellate court *sua sponte*. [**Conney v. Erickson,** 317 F.2d 247 (7th Cir. 1963)]

2. Exceptions to Final Decision Requirement

a. Partial final decisions [§2109]

If multiple claims or parties are involved in the action, an order disposing of fewer than all of the claims ordinarily is not a final judgment and, hence, is not appealable until the remainder of the claims are disposed of. [Fed. R. Civ. P. 54(b)]

(1) Appeal at discretion of trial court [§2110]

However, if the trial judge finds that there is no just reason for delay, he may enter a partial final judgment, which is then appealable. [Fed. R. Civ. P. 54(b)] Generally, this power is exercised only when hardship would result if the appeal from the partial disposition were delayed. [**Cullen v. Margiotta,** 618 F.2d 226 (2d Cir. 1980)]

(2) State practice [§2111]

State rules often permit an appeal where the claims of a single party are severed and determined apart from the others. [Cal. Civ. Proc. Code §579]

b. Review of equitable remedies

(1) In chancery [§2112]

The final decision rule was not applied in early equity practice. One reason was that equity often issued personal orders to the parties which, if erroneous, might result in consequences that could not be corrected later by review. Therefore, immediate appellate review was permitted even as to "interlocutory" orders.

(2) Modern statutory exception [§2113]

Modern practice generally preserves the right to interlocutory review of equitable remedies that are not final orders but which might result in irreparable consequences. Thus, 28 U.S.C. section 1292(a) provides the following *exceptions* to the final decision requirement:

(a) Interlocutory orders *granting or denying injunctions*;

(b) Orders *appointing receivers*;

(c) Decisions in *patent infringement actions* that are final except for an *accounting*; and

(d) Certain orders in *admiralty proceedings*.

c. Discretionary review [§2114]

Interlocutory appeals may also be permitted by leave of court. Thus, 28 U.S.C. section 1292(b) permits an appeal if:

(i) *The trial court certifies* that a determination by the appellate court of a *controlling question of law* as to which there is *substantial ground for difference of opinion* would speed the ultimate resolution of the case; *and*

(ii) *The court of appeals grants leave to appeal.*

(1) Entirely discretionary [§2115]

The court of appeals may decline leave to appeal for any reason, including calendar congestion.

(2) Reexamination of propriety of certification by district court [§2116]

Some courts of appeals also feel bound to reexamine the determination of the district court that an immediate appeal is warranted under the statute. [*See, e.g.,* **Garner v. Wolfinbarger,** 433 F.2d 117 (5th Cir. 1970)]

(3) Rationale for review [§2117]

When the district court is genuinely uncertain about the correct interpretation of the law, and it would materially advance the conclusion of the litigation to have this uncertainty cleared up, deferring appellate review would not be desirable.

(4) Scope of appellate jurisdiction [§2118]

Appellate jurisdiction extends to any question included within the order certified for review, and is not limited to the particular question formulated by the district judge. [**Yamaha Motor Corp. v. Calhoun,** 516 U.S. 199 (1996)]

d. Orders regarding class certification [§2119]

Interlocutory orders granting or denying class certification may be reviewed immediately if application for review is made within 10 days. [Fed. R. Civ. P. 23(f)] Although this resembles the discretionary review available under 28 U.S.C. section 1292(b) (*see supra,* §§2114-2118), it differs in that *district court certification is not required.* The appellate court has complete discretion to determine whether to accept the application for immediate review. [*See* **Blair v. Equifax Check Services, Inc.,** 181 F.3d 832 (7th Cir. 1999)—immediate appeal usually warranted only in cases in which (i) denial of class status is "death knell" of suit because individual plaintiff's claim is very small, (ii) grant of class status raises the stakes so much that defendant will feel compelled to settle, or (iii) an immediate appeal will clarify a fundamental issue of law; *and see* **Waste Management Holdings, Inc. v. Mowbray,** 208 F.3d 288 (1st Cir. 2000)—restricting third category to cases in which an immediate appeal will resolve an unsettled legal issue important to other cases and likely to escape appellate review if deferred until final judgment]

e. Collateral orders [§2120]

A qualification established by case law in the federal courts allows an immediate appeal from orders that are final with respect to certain "collateral" matters. [**Cohen v. Beneficial Industrial Loan Corp.,** 337 U.S. 541 (1949)] For a collateral matter to be reviewed, the following requirements must be met:

(1) Important issue completely separate from the merits [§2121]

The issue resolved by the court's order must be an important one that is completely separate from the merits of the underlying case. *Rationale:* The proper time to review all decisions related to the merits is after final decision of the case, and unimportant matters do not justify circumvention of the finality requirement.

Example—requiring derivative suit plaintiff to post security for expenses: In a derivative action, the district court decided that federal rather than state law should apply to determine whether plaintiff must post a bond to secure defendant's costs of litigation. This decision was appealable because it raised issues of choice between state and federal law, which were completely separate from the merits of plaintiff's claims of misconduct by corporate officers. [**Cohen v. Beneficial Industrial Loan Corp.,** *supra*]

Compare—order refusing to certify class: The decision whether to certify a class is closely tied up with the merits of the case, in the sense that the court must make a decision whether there are common questions of law and fact and whether the common questions predominate (in a Rule 23(b)(3) class action). Thus, the decision was not immediately appealable as a collateral order. [**Coopers & Lybrand v. Livesay,** 437 U.S. 463 (1978)] However, the subsequent adoption of Rule 23(f), permitting immediate review of class certification orders in the discretion of the court of appeals (*see supra,* §2119) provides a new avenue for review of such orders.

---

(2) Order effectively unreviewable on appeal from final judgment [§2122]
Early review should be allowed only if deferring review until entry of final judgment would effectively destroy the appellant's claimed rights.

(a) Illustration—denial of official immunity [§2123]
An order rejecting a government official's claim of immunity from suit could not be reviewed effectively on appeal from a final judgment because the immunity is designed to protect defendant from having to stand trial. [**Mitchell v. Forsyth,** 472 U.S. 511 (1985)]

1) But note—inapplicable to denial based on finding of sufficient evidence [§2124]
When a defendant seeks summary judgment based on a *fact-related* official immunity defense asserting that the record shows insufficient evidence of a genuine issue for trial, as opposed to a *legal* basis, such as that given facts show no violation of clearly established law, denial of the motion is not appealable. [**Johnson v. Jones,** 515 U.S. 304 (1995)]

2) Multiple appeals allowed [§2125]
If a defendant's Rule 12 motion to dismiss based on official

immunity is denied, he may appeal that ruling and then appeal a second time if the district court later denies a Rule 56 motion for summary judgment on immunity grounds. [**Behrens v. Pelletier,** 516 U.S. 299 (1996)]

3) Not required in state court [§2126]

State courts need not follow the rule of *Mitchell, supra,* and thus may decline to allow interlocutory review of denials of qualified immunity. [**Johnson v. Fankell,** 520 U.S. 911 (1997)—state provisions regarding appellate review did not confer right to immediate review of denial of official immunity]

(b) Illustration—Eleventh Amendment objection [§2127]

An order rejecting a claim of immunity from suit under the Eleventh Amendment could not be effectively reviewed after final judgment because the value of the protection afforded by that amendment against suit in federal court would be lost if the litigation proceeded past the motion stage. [**Puerto Rico Aqueduct & Sewer Authority v. Metcalf & Eddy,** 506 U.S. 139 (1993)]

(c) Distinguish—order refusing to disqualify counsel [§2128]

An order refusing to disqualify counsel for an alleged conflict of interest can be reviewed after trial is completed, at which time the actual course of events will permit a better judgment of whether there was a conflict. [**Firestone Tire & Rubber Co. v. Risjord,** 449 U.S. 368 (1981)—whether counsel sacrificed interests of his client to earn business from defendant's insurer]

(d) Distinguish—refusal to enforce forum selection clause [§2129]

An order refusing to dismiss on the ground of a contractual forum selection clause could be reviewed effectively after final judgment, because defendant objected only to defending in a particular place and not to having to defend at all. [**Lauro Lines, Inc. v. Chasser,** 490 U.S. 495 (1989)]

(e) Distinguish—discovery sanction against counsel [§2130]

A Rule 37 discovery sanction against counsel will often be inextricably intertwined with the merits of the action because review would require assessment of the completeness of the discovery responses in question. Thus, such an order can be reviewed after final judgment. [**Cunningham v. Hamilton County,** 527 U.S. 198 (1999)]

(3) Conclusively determines disputed issue [§2131]

The collateral order rule requires that the trial court have made its final decision on the issue challenged on the appeal. *Rationale:* If the trial court has not had its final say, the appellate court should not interfere.

> **e.g.** **Example—order imposing notice costs on defendant:** In a class action, an order imposing on defendant 90% of the cost of notifying class members of their right to opt out was held to be the trial court's final determination of this issue. [**Eisen v. Carlisle & Jacquelin**, *supra*, §1151]

EXAM TIP	gilbert

Remember that while orders as to collateral matters may be appealable before the whole case is resolved, such orders still *must be final* with respect to the issue involved. If they do not appear to be the court's final word on the issue, they are not appealable even though they involve a matter collateral to the main issue.

(4) Exception narrowly limited [§2132]

The Supreme Court has repeatedly emphasized that the collateral order exception applies to a *"small class" of cases* [**Cohen v. Beneficial Industrial Loan Corp.**, *supra*, §2121], and it has been used in a restrictive manner.

> **e.g.** **Example—discovery orders involving privileged material:** Discovery orders compelling disclosure of allegedly privileged material seem to satisfy the requirements of the rule, because they conclusively determine claims of privilege, which are separate from the merits, and which cannot effectively be reviewed after the materials are turned over to the opposition. Nevertheless, the Court has adamantly refused to entertain appeals from such orders, noting that the party resisting discovery could refuse to comply, be held in criminal contempt, and appeal immediately from the judgment of criminal contempt. (*See supra*, §§1599-1607 for discussion of appealability of discovery rulings.)

(5) No "pendent party" appellate jurisdiction [§2133]

An appellate court that has appellate jurisdiction over a collateral order against one party ordinarily may not exercise "pendent appellate jurisdiction" over otherwise unappealable interlocutory orders against other parties in the case, even though that might result in judicial efficiency. [**Swint v. Chambers County Commission**, 514 U.S. 35 (1995)]

f. Practical construction of "finality" [§2134]

The Supreme Court has stated that it will accord a "practical rather than a technical construction" to the finality requirement. [**Gillespie v. United States Steel**, 379 U.S. 148 (1964)] However, this does not cause a significant expansion of appealability.

> **e.g.** **Example—"death knell" doctrine:** The Supreme Court rejected a plaintiff's argument that refusal to certify a case as a class action is final (the "death knell") where the named plaintiff cannot afford to maintain the action alone. [**Coopers & Lybrand v. Livesay,** *supra,* §2121]

E. Scope of Appellate Review

1. In General [§2135]

Appellate review must be sufficiently broad to assure that the trial court properly applied the controlling substantive law and that the procedure conformed to the applicable standards. However, appellate review does not extend to retrying the facts or supplanting the trial judge's decision in matters committed to her discretion.

2. Findings of Fact Subject to Limited Review [§2136]

It is not the function of an appellate court to make factual determinations; yet the appellate court must examine factual determinations to assure that the trial court has not rested its decision on insupportable factual assumptions.

a. Jury verdicts [§2137]

When the findings below are embodied in a jury verdict, the role of the appellate court is essentially the same as that of the trial judge—*i.e.,* to oversee the jury's adherence to the law.

(1) Substantial evidence test [§2138]

The accepted test is that a jury verdict must be supported by substantial evidence, so that reasonable jurors could have found as they did—even if the reviewing judges think they would have found differently as triers of fact.

(2) Cases taken from jury [§2139]

When the trial judge has taken the fact-finding function away from the jury—*e.g.,* by granting a motion for judgment as a matter of law—the appellate court must examine the record to determine whether there is any substantial evidence to support a finding contrary to that of the trial judge. If it finds such evidence, the judgment will be reversed.

b. Judicial findings in nonjury trials

(1) Explicit findings required [§2140]

When a case is tried without a jury, the trial judge usually is required to make explicit findings of fact in order to facilitate review of her decision by the appellate court. [Fed. R. Civ. P. 52(a)]

(2) Clear error test [§2141]

A judge's finding of fact may not be set aside unless the appellate court finds that it is "clearly erroneous." To find clear error, it is not enough that the appellate court is convinced that it would have decided the case differently. [**Anderson v. City of Bessemer City**, 470 U.S. 564 (1985)] Rather, the reviewing court must be left "on the entire evidence . . . with the definite and firm conviction that a mistake has been committed." [**United States v. United States Gypsum**, 333 U.S. 364 (1948)] Due regard must be given to the opportunity of the trial court to appraise the credibility of the witnesses [Fed. R. Civ. P. 52(a)], although the requirement of deference is not limited to findings that rest on credibility determinations. [**Anderson v. City of Bessemer City**, *supra*]

(a) Distinguish—substantial evidence test [§2142]

The clear error test is less restrictive than the substantial evidence test, since a finding may be clearly erroneous even though there is substantial evidence to support it.

1) Rationale

A jury verdict is the product of a deliberative process and reflects democratic political values that assign special worth to the participation of lay decisionmakers. On the other hand, the findings of a trial judge are the product of a single mind, which may be more vulnerable to bias or idiosyncrasy. Still, considerable deference to trial judges' fact findings is due because of the judges' expertise in fact determinations and the costs of extensive review to the parties and to the system. [**Anderson v. City of Bessemer City**, *supra*]

c. "Fact" and "law" distinguished [§2143]

It is only findings of fact that are entitled to deference.

(1) Errors of law (jury trial) [§2144]

If the jury was erroneously instructed on the *law*, the verdict cannot stand, even if there is substantial evidence to support findings that could have been made pursuant to correct instructions.

(2) Erroneous conclusions (nonjury trial)

(a) Explicit conclusions required [§2145]

In a nonjury trial, the judge must state conclusions of law, either in a recorded oral statement or in writing, in order to facilitate appellate review. [Fed. R. Civ. P. 52(a)]

(b) Effect of erroneous conclusions [§2146]

If the conclusions are erroneous, so that the judge's findings rest on a false legal premise, the judgment cannot stand (even if the findings themselves are not clearly erroneous).

(3) Mixed issues of law and fact [§2147]

The distinction between a finding of fact and a conclusion of law is not always clear. Sophisticated observers have long noted a circularity in making this distinction for purposes of appellate review; *i.e.,* matters may tend to be treated as issues of fact if the appellate court feels less competent to resolve them and as issues of law if the court feels competent to resolve them without help from the lower court.

(a) Interpretation of legal documents [§2148]

The interpretation of a contract, deed, will, or other legal document is generally regarded as a question of law if the trial court interpreted the document without judging the credibility of extrinsic evidence. If so, the appellate court may disregard any conclusions reached by the trial judge as to the meaning or effect of the document and substitute its own interpretation. [**Estate of Platt,** 21 Cal. 2d 343 (1942)]

1) Distinguish—findings based on documentary evidence [§2149]

Note the difference between review of legal documents (*e.g.,* contracts, wills) and review of documentary evidence (*e.g.,* receipts, letters). Findings of fact based on documentary evidence (or on oral evidence) are reviewed under the clearly erroneous standard. [Fed. R. Civ. P. 52(a); **Anderson v. City of Bessemer City,** *supra,* §2142—disapproving the much-cited contrary case of **Orvis v. Higgins,** 180 F.2d 537 (2d Cir.), *cert. denied,* 340 U.S. 810 (1950)]

(b) Negligence [§2150]

It is arguable whether a finding of negligence represents a legal or factual conclusion. (*See supra,* §645, regarding pleading of negligence.) In either event, appellate courts generally defer to a jury determination on negligence—even when there is no dispute as to the basic events.

1) But note

In a nonjury trial, the judge's findings with respect to "negligence" are subject to the clear error test (*supra*).

(c) Other issues—suggested approach [§2151]

In other areas, a question usually will be treated as one of fact if it:

(i) *Pertains to the occurrence or nonoccurrence of a past event;*

(ii) *Is of specific interest* to the parties to the dispute and has no bearing on the rights or liabilities of others;

(iii) *Is determined on the basis of the testimony of witnesses*;

(iv) *Is not appropriately determined by reference to general policy*;

(v) *Is determined on the basis of intuitive instinct* about the application of some general morality to a specific event.

(e.g.) **Example:** One business person transfers a new automobile to another. Whether the transfer results in taxable income to the recipient, or instead is a "gift," is an issue of fact. [**Commissioner of Internal Revenue v. Duberstein,** 363 U.S. 278 (1960)]

---

1) Criticism

Reliance on the "intuition" of the trier of fact in such matters is the result of judicial unwillingness or inability to formulate explicit rules of decision to govern future like cases.

3. Review of Discretionary Rulings [§2152]

Especially with regard to procedural matters, many decisions by trial judges are entrusted by law to their discretion. In such cases, an appellate court will not substitute its discretion for that of the trial judge in the absence of clear abuse.

(e.g.) **Example:** Whether to *delay or continue a trial* on account of the unavailability of a witness is a matter for the discretion of the trial judge. [**Napolitano v. Compania Sud Americana de Vapores,** 421 F.2d 382 (2d Cir. 1970)] Likewise, *setting the amount of a security bond* to be required of a party seeking a preliminary injunction is a matter of discretion. [Fed. R. Civ. P. 65(c)] And whether to grant a new trial on the ground that the verdict is *contrary to the weight of the evidence* is within the sound discretion of the trial judge, although the modern trend is away from earlier rulings that the trial judge's discretion was virtually unlimited. [**Coffran v. Hitchcock Clinic, Inc.,** 683 F.2d 5 (1st Cir.), *cert. denied,* 459 U.S. 1087 (1982)]

---

a. Limitation [§2153]

The appellate court may properly review a discretionary ruling by a trial judge to determine whether he has *abused* his power. [**Allis-Chalmers Corp. v. Philadelphia Electric Co.,** 521 F.2d 360 (3d Cir. 1975)]

4. "Harmless Error" Standard

a. General rule [§2154]

The appellate court may not reverse a lower court judgment unless the trial court committed an error that was *prejudicial*—*i.e.,* one that affected the substantial rights of the parties. [Fed. R. Civ. P. 61; 28 U.S.C. §2111] State law is similar. For example, the California Constitution provides that: "No judgment shall be set aside . . . for any error as to any matter of pleading or procedure, unless after an examination of the entire cause, including the evidence, the appellate court shall be of the opinion that the error . . . resulted in a *miscarriage of justice.*" [Cal. Const. art. VI, §4-1/2]

e.g. **Example—harmless:** Erroneous rulings on the *pleadings or on matters of discovery* will rarely be sufficiently prejudicial in their effect on the trial that a reversal would be warranted.

e.g. **Example—harmless:** The admission of *improper evidence* in a *nonjury* trial is generally regarded as harmless, since it is assumed that a professional trial judge will discount the improper evidence and not permit it to influence his findings of fact. [**First American State Bank v. Continental Insurance Co.,** 897 F.2d 319 (8th Cir. 1990)]

b. **Burden [§2155]**

The burden of showing prejudice is usually on the party claiming it. There is no presumption of an impairment of substantial rights merely from the fact that error occurred.

c. **Distinguish—jury verdict [§2156]**

The rule is to the contrary in *jury* trials: It is assumed that jurors *will* be influenced by improper evidence, at least if they are not cautioned by the trial judge to disregard it.

d. **Limitation [§2157]**

The harmless error rule will not prevent reversal where the error is "egregious." In such cases, the appellate court may reverse as a means of disciplining the trial judge, even though his error would not likely have had an adverse effect on the rights of the appellant. [**Thiel v. Southern Pacific Co.,** 328 U.S. 217 (1946)—discrimination in selection of jury panel]

e. **Legal theory sustaining judgment [§2158]**

An appellate court may review a legal theory *not previously presented* to the trial court if considered for the purpose of sustaining the decision below. Thus, if the findings of fact below clearly support application of the correct legal principle to reach the result achieved below, the judgment will be affirmed even if the correct legal theory was never presented to the trial court. Any error in articulation of legal theory was *harmless.* [**Ward v. Taggart,** 51 Cal. 2d 736 (1959)]

5. **Waiver of Objections in Lower Court**

a. **General rule [§2159]**

An appellate court may not reverse a judgment below to correct an error that might have been avoided or corrected had the appellant made timely objection in the trial court. [**Security Pacific National Bank v. Geernaert,** 199 Cal. App. 3d 1425 (1988)] *Rationale:* The appellant should not be permitted to withhold objection and await the outcome of further proceedings before deciding whether to take advantage of a mistake by the court.

b. **Specific applications**

(1) **Jury instruction [§2160]**

An error in the instruction of the jury usually will not be the basis for reversal unless the appellant made a timely objection to the charge and proposed a correct instruction. [Fed. R. Civ. P. 51]

(2) **Admission of evidence [§2161]**

Similarly, an error in the admission of evidence generally will not be grounds for reversal unless the appellant made a timely and specific objection to the admission.

(3) **Invited error [§2162]**

If the aggrieved party *induced* the error of the trial court (*e.g.*, by proposing incorrect jury instructions or by offering inadmissible evidence), the case for waiver is strongest. [**Horsemen's Benevolent Association v. Valley Racing Association,** 4 Cal. App. 4th 1538 (1992)]

(4) **New matter [§2163]**

Newly discovered evidence, evidence of jury misconduct, or other matters coming to light *after trial* may not be presented directly to an appellate court. Such matters must be presented to the trial court by motion for a new trial or for relief from judgment. [*See* Fed. R. Civ. P. 60(b)(2)]

c. **Exceptions [§2164]**

An appellate court may review notwithstanding the failure of an appellant to make timely objection in the following situations:

(1) **Subject matter jurisdiction [§2165]**

When the court below lacked subject matter jurisdiction, no objection is necessary, since the jurisdictional issue can be raised belatedly or even *sua sponte.*

(2) **Clear and fundamental error [§2166]**

No objection is necessary when the error is so clear and fundamental that the trial court should have avoided it, even without timely objection, and it would be *unjust* to permit the judgment to stand.

> **Example:** In the course of a long trial, the judge took a long recess for his own vacation, causing a serious hiatus in the presentation of the case to the jury. Where the judge declared that under no circumstances would he consider a change in his plans, no objection was necessary to preserve the issue on appeal. [**Citron v. Aro Corp.**, 377 F.2d 750 (3d Cir.), *cert. denied*, 389 U.S. 973 (1967)]

6. Trial De Novo [§2167]

Legislation may sometimes authorize a trial *de novo*, which is in effect a new trial in a higher court. This form of review is generally limited to review of trial courts that exercise minor jurisdiction (*e.g.*, small claims courts) and that make no records of their proceedings.

STANDARDS OF REVIEW		gilbert
STANDARD	**USED TO REVIEW**	**TEST**
Substantial Evidence Test	Jury verdict	Verdict must be supported by substantial evidence, so that reasonable jurors could have found as the jury did
Clear Error Test	Judicial findings of fact in nonjury trials	On reviewing all the evidence, the appellate court is left with the definite and firm conviction that a mistake has been committed
Harmless Error Standard	Lower court judgment	Trial court judgment may be reversed only if the trial court committed an error that was prejudicial, *i.e.*, affected the substantial rights of the parties
Full Review	Lower court judgment	Trial court decision accorded no deference; appellate court decides how case should be resolved afresh

F. Appellate Review by Extraordinary Writ

1. **Prerogative Writs [§2168]**

   In exceptional cases, review of nonappealable orders may be had by means of a prerogative writ issued by the appellate court to direct the conduct of trial judges. The available writs, depending on the court system, are:

   a. *Mandamus*—an order directing the judge to perform her legal duty; and

   b. *Prohibition*—an order enjoining the judge from conduct that exceeds her lawful authority.

2. **Source of Power to Issue Writs**

   a. **State courts [§2169]**

      Writs in state court tend to be based on common law practice. In some states, statutes or constitutional provisions establish alternatives. In Michigan, for example, the appellate courts have power to issue "writs of superintending control."

   b. **Federal courts [§2170]**

      The United States Courts of Appeals have power to issue prerogative writs by reason of statute, which authorizes all federal courts to issue writs as necessary "in aid of their respective jurisdictions and agreeable to the usages and principles of law." [28 U.S.C. §1651(a)]

3. **Discretionary Character of Writ [§2171]**

   An important distinction between writs and an appeal is that the issuance of a prerogative writ is always discretionary with the appellate courts. The petitioner has *no right* to a hearing. [**Kerr v. United States District Court,** 426 U.S. 394 (1976)]

4. **Grounds for Issuance**

   a. **Conduct exceeding limits of power [§2172]**

      A prerogative writ may issue to prevent misuse of judicial power, such as:

      (1) *An abuse of discretion;*

      (2) *An excess of jurisdiction;* or

      (3) *A refusal to exercise jurisdiction.*

   b. **Necessity for immediate review [§2173]**

      Where the petitioner has no right to review by appeal at the present time, and would suffer undue hardship or substantial prejudice if appellate review was delayed until after a final judgment, a writ may properly issue.

      (1) **But note**

         Extraordinary writs will not issue where adequate review by appeal is available to the petitioner. [*In re* **McDonald,** 489 U.S. 180 (1989)]

5. Common Uses of Writ [§2174]

United States Courts of Appeals use discretionary writs:

a. *To correct the erroneous denial of a right to jury trial* [**Beacon Theatres, Inc. v. Westover,** 359 U.S. 500 (1959)];

b. *To prevent improper delegation of judicial power* with respect to special matters [**LaBuy v. Howes Leather Co.,** 352 U.S. 249 (1957)]; and

c. *To prevent unlawful remand to state court* of actions properly removed to federal court [**Thermtron Products, Inc. v. Hermansdorfer,** 423 U.S. 336 (1976)].

6. Supervisory Mandamus [§2175]

In rare circumstances, mandamus may be used to resolve *issues of first impression* that may be important in a significant number of cases.

Example: Where the question of the proper treatment of physical examinations of defendants under Federal Rule 35 was presented, mandamus was available to review an order requiring defendant to submit to a physical examination, because issue had never been resolved. [**Schlaugenhauf v. Holder,** 379 U.S. 104 (1964)]

---

a. Availability [§2176]

In a few jurisdictions, such as California, the grounds for issuing prerogative writs have been greatly expanded. In effect, the writ proceeding becomes a device for granting or refusing immediate appellate review of important interlocutory orders. [**Abelleira v. District Court,** 17 Cal. 2d 280 (1941)]

Chapter Eleven: Preclusive Effects of Judgments

CONTENTS

Chapter Approach

After a court has entered judgment, related matters may come up in later litigation involving the same or different parties. For several reasons—including economy, prevention of harassment, and avoidance of inconsistent rulings—doctrines of former adjudication sharply limit the extent to which *relitigation* is permitted. When relitigation is not permitted, parties cannot argue in a new proceeding that the prior ruling was erroneous; the point is taken as established in accord with the prior decision.

This field of law has two main components: (i) *claim preclusion* (or, in older terminology still in widespread use, *res judicata* in its narrow sense), which bars reassertion of the same claim; and (ii) *issue preclusion* (in the older terminology, direct or collateral estoppel), which bars relitigation of the same issue, whether it arises in connection with the same claim (*direct estoppel*) or a different claim (*collateral estoppel*).

1. Claim Preclusion

The questions are:

a. Is the judgment on the *same claim*? Most jurisdictions now define "claim" broadly to prevent the bringing of one aspect of a related matter in one action and another aspect in a second proceeding against the same party (rule against splitting claims).

b. Is the judgment *final*?

c. Is it *valid*—was it rendered by a court of competent jurisdiction, and was constitutionally adequate notice given?

d. Is it *on the merits*—did the court rule on the merits of the claim, dismiss with prejudice, or enter a default judgment?

e. Did the plaintiff in the prior action *prevail*? If so, the doctrine of *merger* precludes a second try—the original claim is merged in the judgment.

f. Did the plaintiff *lose* in the first action? If so, the doctrine of *bar* precludes the second suit, with the plaintiff's claim regarded as barred by the defeat.

2. Issue Preclusion

Key questions are:

a. Is the party against whom issue preclusion is sought to be invoked one who was a *party* to the prior litigation or in "*privity*" with such a party?

b. Was the issue *actually litigated and determined* and *necessary* to the judgment?

  c. Can *nonmutual estoppel* be applied?

    (1) Are the *stakes* so much higher in the present case that it would be unfair to apply estoppel?

    (2) Could the party asserting estoppel *easily have joined* in the earlier action?

    (3) Are *procedural opportunities* available to the party against whom estoppel is asserted in this action that were not available in the earlier action?

    (4) Have there been *inconsistent determinations* of the same issue in other cases?

A. Introduction

1. In General [§2177]

The res judicata doctrine has two components: (i) claim preclusion, and (ii) issue preclusion.

2. Claim Preclusion (Also Called Res Judicata) [§2178]

A final judgment on a claim or cause of action *precludes reassertion of that claim* or *cause of action* in a subsequent suit.

a. Merger [§2179]

If judgment was for the plaintiff on the claim, there is a *merger* of the claim in the judgment—*i.e.,* the prejudgment claim is transformed into the judgment claim.

b. Bar [§2180]

If judgment was for the defendant, it is a *bar* against the plaintiff's suing again on the claim.

3. Issue Preclusion (Also Called Collateral Estoppel) [§2181]

Preclusion prevents not only relitigation of a claim, but also, in some circumstances, relitigation of issues of fact resolved in a prior proceeding, even when the later case involves a different claim. A decision on an issue of fact may be binding in subsequent litigation between the same parties or, in some circumstances, between one of the parties and a different adversary.

4. Rationale [§2182]

The purposes of these doctrines are twofold: (i) to avoid the time and expense of multiple litigation over the same matter; and (ii) to give stability to the results of adjudication—to prevent inconsistent results.

B. Claim Preclusion

1. In General [§2183]

Before any judgment can have claim preclusive effect, it must be (i) final, (ii) "on the merits," and (iii) valid.

2. Policy Basis [§2184]

The basis for claim preclusion is that litigants should be compelled to litigate their entire claim on the first occasion they bring it before the courts. This can serve the following policy objectives.

a. Judicial efficiency [§2185]

Resolving all claims in a single lawsuit avoids waste of judicial resources on repeated litigation of the same claim.

b. Avoiding vexation of defendants [§2186]

Allowing plaintiffs to sue defendants repeatedly on the same claim by changing their legal theories would raise the risk of oppression of defendants. Defendants should be assured that they will not be forced to answer a given claim more than once.

c. Consistency [§2187]

Although it would often be legally consistent for a plaintiff to lose on one theory and then prevail on another with different elements, requiring litigation of all theories for a claim in a single action promotes the public appearance of consistency.

d. Effect—foreclosing matters that were never litigated [§2188]

The net effect of claim preclusion is, therefore, often to foreclose matters that were never litigated because they were never raised in the first litigation.

e.g. Example: Plaintiff sues defendant car salesperson for common law fraud in connection with defendant's sale of a used car to plaintiff. After judgment is entered in this action, plaintiff files a second suit against defendant, this time charging violation of the state Automobile Consumer Protection Act in connection with the sale of the same car. Even though the question of violation of the Act has never been litigated, the second suit is precluded by the first.

(1) Distinguish—issue preclusion [§2189]

Estoppel (particularly collateral estoppel) applies preclusion only to matters that were actually litigated and decided in the first lawsuit.

3. Meaning of Claim—Breadth of Preclusion [§2190]

Determining the scope of the claim in the first lawsuit is often difficult. Unless the claim in the second lawsuit is the "same," claim preclusion does not apply (although issue preclusion may).

a.   Traditional tests [§2191]

The traditional tests were derived from the code pleading concept of the cause of action. The idea was that the first litigation was res judicata only as to the same cause of action. The courts developed tests to give effect to this concept:

(1)   Same primary right and duty [§2192]

If the plaintiff asserted a violation of the same basic right in the second case as in the first, preclusion applied. *Criticism:* Distinguishing between differences in the law that mattered (in terms of the elements of the second claim compared to those of the first claim) made it hard to determine if the second suit involved the same "primary right."

(2)   Same evidence [§2193]

If the second claim turned on essentially the same evidence as the first claim, preclusion was said to apply. *Criticism:* Because there was usually some difference in the evidence that could be presented, this test was also difficult to apply.

(3)   Mere change of legal theory [§2194]

If the second suit merely changed the legal theory upon which the earlier suit relied, preclusion applied. *Criticism:* Although this test accurately portrays one concern of preclusion doctrine, it provides little guidance in determining whether something more than the legal theory has changed.

b.   Modern approach—transactional test [§2195]

The Restatement (Second) of Judgments adopts a transactional approach to the scope of claim preclusion: Claim preclusion applies to "all or any part of the transaction, or series of connected transactions, out of which the action arose." [Restatement (Second) of Judgments §24(1)]

(1)   Flexible definition [§2196]

The definition is flexible: "What factual grouping constitutes a 'transaction,' and what groupings constitute a 'series,' are to be determined pragmatically, giving weight to such considerations as whether the facts are related in time, space, origin, or motivation, whether they form a convenient trial unit, and whether their treatment as a unit conforms to the parties' expectations or business understanding or usage." [Restatement (Second) of Judgments §24(2)] This analysis requires an examination of the facts underlying the claim similar to that called for in assessing permissive joinder of parties under Federal Rule 20. (*See supra,* §§1031-1041.)

c.   Claims by or against different parties usually not foreclosed [§2197]

Ordinarily a claim by one plaintiff is considered a different claim for preclusion purposes from that of another plaintiff, and so is a claim against a different defendant. However, these rules may not apply if the parties are in privity (*see infra*, §§2241-2251), but closely similar claims can survive a final adjudication.

Example: In the first suit, plaintiff sought to recover for his own personal injuries in an auto accident but lost on a finding that defendant was not negligent. He then brought a second suit as representative for his wife and three minor children to recover for their injuries in the accident. He was allowed to pursue these claims because they were not the same as his personal claim. [**Freeman v. Lester Coggins Trucking, Inc.**, 771 F.2d 860 (5th Cir. 1985)]

---

(1) Successor in interest [§2198]

If the first plaintiff's claim is assigned to the second plaintiff, or passes by action of law, the second plaintiff is precluded. *Example*: If before death a victim of an accident sues the other driver and recovers for her injuries, the executor of her estate cannot file a second suit against the other driver to recover wrongful death damages for the estate. (*See infra*, §2049)

(2) Liability of one defendant depends on liability of another [§2199]

In some situations, one potential defendant may be held to be responsible for the conduct of another (*see infra*, §§2256-2257). In such cases, a judgment exonerating one potential defendant precludes an action on the same claim against the other.

4. "Final" [§2200]

A ruling at a pretrial hearing or the determination of an issue severed for trial does not decide a claim until judgment is rendered. However, if a claim has been separately determined in the course of an action, it may be treated as the equivalent of a final judgment for res judicata purposes, even if the action is still pending. The question for issue preclusion is whether the "prior adjudication of an issue in another action . . . is determined to be sufficiently firm to be accorded conclusive effect." The finality requirement is interpreted somewhat more strictly for purposes of merger and bar, since the question then is the creation of a new claim based on the judgment (merger) or the extinguishment of the claim (bar). [Restatement (Second) of Judgments §13, comment g]

a. Effect of appeal [§2201]

Whether a judgment on appeal is final for purposes of res judicata is determined by the *law of the jurisdiction in which the judgment was rendered*.

(1) Federal practice [§2202]

In federal practice, once a judgment is entered it is deemed to be final even though an appeal therefrom is pending. The judgment remains final and valid until reversed or modified by the appellate court. In such jurisdictions, preclusion attaches immediately upon entry of the judgment. [**United States v. Nysco Laboratories, Inc.**, 318 F.2d 817 (2d Cir. 1963)]

(a) Note

As a practical matter, however, any suit to enforce the judgment, or in which the res judicata issue is otherwise involved, is likely to be abated or continued until the pending appeal is determined.

(b) And note

Even courts that have somewhat expanded the notion of finality for preclusion purposes may look to whether there was an opportunity for appellate review. A partial summary judgment followed by a settlement that prevents appellate review, for example, will ordinarily not be given preclusive effect. [**American Casualty Corp. v. Sentry Federal Savings Bank**, 867 F. Supp. 50 (D. Mass. 1994)]

(2) State practice [§2203]

In many states, the taking of an appeal *automatically* postpones finality until the appeal is determined. Until then, no res judicata attaches. [Anno. 9 A.L.R.2d 984]

b. Modifiable judgments [§2204]

Many civil judgments are nonfinal in the sense that they are subject to modification (*e.g.,* alimony awards, child custody determination, and some kinds of injunctions). Such judgments do not prevent reconsideration of the relief granted, for example, when conditions have changed. But they are *res judicata until modified*. [Restatement (Second) of Judgments §13, comment c]

c. Conflicting judgments [§2205]

If two judgments are in conflict, the last in time controls. [Restatement (Second) of Judgments §15]

Example: If a judgment is rendered in action 1, but is not raised or established in action 2 (or the court in the second action holds that the earlier judgment is not entitled to res judicata), and both judgments are otherwise final, the second judgment is controlling. Hence, it (rather than the earlier judgment) is entitled to res judicata in any third proceeding on the same claim. [**Treinies v. Sunshine Mining Co.**, 308 U.S. 66 (1939)]

---

5. "On the Merits"

a. General rule [§2206]

A judgment is deemed to be "on the merits" if the claim has been tried and determined—*i.e.,* if the court has ruled that the *plaintiff has (or has not) established his claim*. This includes a determination by summary judgment,

judgment on the pleadings, nonsuit, and directed verdict, as well as a determination after trial and verdict.

(1) Note

Rulings not on the merits generally are preclusive only as to issues. If the court dismisses on a ground that *does not* relate to the merits (*e.g.,* for lack of jurisdiction, improper venue, or a dismissal expressly "without prejudice" to a new action), the judgment or dismissal usually does not bar a subsequent action. [Restatement (Second) of Judgments §20]

(2) But note

Such a judgment is determinative of *issues decided*. *Example:* A dismissal for improper venue because the defendant is not a resident of the county where sued is determinative of that *issue* in a subsequent suit (*see infra,* §§2223 *et seq.*). When the second suit is on the *same claim*, this relatively uncommon form of issue preclusion is known as *direct estoppel*.

b. Meaning of "on the merits" [§2207]

If an action is dismissed on a ground closely related to the merits, the following approaches apply:

(1) Dismissals [§2208]

If dismissal is for failure to state a claim, but it is possible that the complaint could be amended to state a valid claim, or if there was a dismissal for failure to diligently prosecute the action, earlier cases held that the judgment was not on the merits and hence not a bar.

(a) But note

Today, such a dismissal is *considered a bar*—on the theory that the plaintiff had a *fair opportunity* to get to the merits (by amending his pleading, appealing, etc.). [**Rinehart v. Locke**, 454 F.2d 313 (7th Cir. 1971)]

(2) Default and consent judgments [§2209]

Default and consent judgments terminate the cause of action and hence *have claim preclusion* effect (*i.e.,* result in merger or bar of the claim). Note, however, that a default judgment may be less effective in regard to issue preclusion. (*See infra,* §2228.)

(3) Punitive dismissals [§2210]

A punitive dismissal is a dismissal based on a party's refusal to obey trial court orders—*e.g.,* a dismissal of a plaintiff's action for failure to prosecute diligently, or a default judgment against a defendant for refusal to obey a discovery order. Because such judgments terminate the cause of action, they have claim preclusion effect; but they do not involve issue preclusion regarding issues going to the merits.

6. "Valid" [§2211]

The third requirement for claim preclusion is that the judgment be valid. A judgment is valid *unless*:

(i) The court lacked *subject matter jurisdiction* of the case (*see supra,* Chapter II.);

(ii) The notice given to the defendant failed to conform to *due process requirements,* or substantially departed from the requirements of statute or court rule concerning the *form of notice* (*see supra,* §§224 *et seq.*); *or*

(iii) The court lacked *personal jurisdiction* over the defendant (*see supra,* Chapter I.).

a. Determination of validity [§2212]

If the question of validity was *litigated* in the original action, that determination is itself res judicata. [**Baldwin v. Iowa State Travelling Men's Association,** 283 U.S. 522 (1931)] This is an example of direct estoppel (*see supra,* §2206).

Example: A court exercises jurisdiction in an action concerning land on the basis that the land is within the state, rejecting defendant's contention that the land is across the state boundary and hence in another state. This determination of jurisdiction is conclusive, and the judgment may not thereafter be attacked as invalid. [**Durfee v. Duke,** 375 U.S. 106 (1963)]

---

(1) And note

Res judicata also applies to decisions concerning the court's subject matter jurisdiction [**Stoll v. Gottleib,** 305 U.S. 165 (1938)] and the adequacy of notice [**Gordon v. Gordon,** 227 S.E.2d 53 (Ga. 1976)].

7. Claim Preclusion When Jurisdiction Is In Rem or Quasi In Rem

a. Definition [§2213]

Jurisdiction *in rem* or *quasi in rem* is based on the presence of the property about which the lawsuit is concerned (*see supra,* §60). For example, a state can exercise jurisdiction to determine rights under a mortgage pertaining to land in that state.

b. Res judicata effect [§2214]

If jurisdiction is exercised *in rem* or *quasi in rem*, the rules of claim and issue preclusion apply essentially as they do in *in personam* judgments, except that the preclusion is limited to claims in the property.

(1) Claim preclusion [§2215]

Suppose A brings a suit to foreclose a mortgage on property in State X, serving notice in State X on B, the mortgagor. A judgment for or against A is res judicata as to her claim to foreclose. However, if no jurisdiction was exercised to determine B's in personam indebtedness to A, that claim is not determined and still may be sued upon by A.

(2) Issue preclusion [§2216]

Any issues determined in the in rem proceeding (*e.g.,* the enforceability of the mortgage note) are conclusive in subsequent litigation.

8. Attachment Jurisdiction [§2217]

Attachment jurisdiction is exercised by seizing local property as a basis for collecting on an obligation allegedly due from its owner, the obligation being unrelated to the property.

a. Res judicata effect

(1) Claim preclusion [§2218]

A judgment based on attachment jurisdiction does *not* extinguish the claim, except to the extent of the property seized.

(2) Issue preclusion [§2219]

However, the issues actually litigated are conclusive on the parties if the amount of the property attached was large enough to give them a fair incentive to litigate.

b. Restriction [§2220]

Attachment jurisdiction has been considerably restricted by **Shaffer v. Heitner,** *supra,* §76, but it has not been eliminated.

9. Exceptions to Claim Preclusion [§2221]

Only under *extraordinary* circumstances may a party relitigate a claim that has been reduced to judgment. The losing party would have to establish grounds for setting aside the judgment (*e.g.,* fraud on the court) and that she has a good case on the merits. The policy is *very strongly against* relitigation. (*See supra,* §§2183-2188.)

Example: Seven consumers brought actions under the federal antitrust laws charging defendant department stores with conspiring to fix prices of women's clothing. The actions were dismissed on the ground that consumers had no standing to sue for price fixing. Five of the plaintiffs appealed and the other two filed new actions asserting claims under state antitrust law. The Supreme Court then held that consumers did have standing to sue, and the judgments against the five plaintiffs who appealed were reversed and remanded for further proceedings. In these circumstances, the Ninth Circuit created an exception to res judicata so that the other two plaintiffs could proceed with their actions. The Supreme Court reversed, stressing that res judicata serves the vital interest "that there be an end to litigation." [**Federated Department Stores, Inc. v. Moitie**, 452 U.S. 394 (1981)]

10. Defenses and Counterclaims

a. Effect of compulsory counterclaim rules [§2222]
A compulsory counterclaim rule or statute requires that the defendant set up any counterclaim she has against the plaintiff arising out of the same transaction as the plaintiff's claim. [Fed. R. Civ. P. 13(a)] If she fails to do so, she is barred from thereafter asserting the counterclaim, either as a defense or as the basis for affirmative relief in an independent action. Hence, the judgment in the former action is preclusive as to claims that were or should have been asserted as compulsory counterclaims in that action. [**Baker v. Gold Seal Liquors, Inc.**, 417 U.S. 467 (1974)]

b. Where no compulsory counterclaim rule involved [§2223]
If no compulsory counterclaim rule or statute applies, claim preclusion does not prevent the defendant from asserting the same matter first as a defense to the plaintiff's action, and later in a separate suit as a basis for independent relief against the former plaintiff.

---

e.g. Example: Contractor sues Owner for money due under a construction contract. Owner successfully defends by showing that the work was not properly done, but no counterclaim is asserted. Owner may subsequently file an independent damage action for the improper work (assuming no compulsory counterclaim statute is in effect).

---

(1) But note
Because of issue preclusion (below), the *issues actually litigated* and decided in the first action may not be relitigated.

(2) Exception—nullifying initial judgment [§2224]
If a former defendant seeks relief in a later suit based on a claim that could have been asserted as a counterclaim, and the relief sought would nullify the judgment entered in the earlier suit, the later action is barred even if there was no applicable compulsory counterclaim rule in the earlier action. [Restatement (Second) of Judgments §22(1)(b)]

Example: In the first action, McDonald's sued in a state court without a compulsory counterclaim rule to terminate its franchise agreement with plaintiff under a provision forbidding any member of plaintiff's family to acquire an interest in a competing fast food business. Plaintiff's son had bought a Burger Chef franchise in a nearby town. After judgment was entered in the first action finding a breach of the franchise agreement and directing sale of the franchise, plaintiff sued McDonald's, alleging that application of the noncompetition provision of the franchise agreement violated the antitrust laws. The court held the second action foreclosed because "its prosecution would nullify rights established by the prior action." [**Martino v. McDonald's Systems, Inc.,** 598 F.2d 1079 (7th Cir. 1979)]

C. Issue Preclusion

1. Direct Estoppel [§2225]

Issues actually litigated *between the parties* are binding on them in subsequent actions concerning the *same claim*. *Example:* In a child support suit in which several modification proceedings have been held, issues actually litigated and determined in an earlier proceeding (*e.g.*, legitimacy of the child) are binding on the parties in subsequent proceedings.

2. Collateral Estoppel [§2226]

If the second lawsuit involves a *different* claim (and hence no merger, bar, or direct estoppel), the first judgment may be invoked as to all matters *actually litigated and determined in the first action and essential to the judgment.* [**Cromwell v. County of Sac,** 94 U.S. 351 (1876); Restatement (Second) of Judgments §27] *Example:* A sues B to collect interest that has become due on a promissory note. B defends on the ground that she was induced by fraud to sign the note, and wins. If A later sues to collect the principal amount of the note after it matures, the prior determination on the question of fraud is conclusive against him.

a. "Actually litigated" [§2227]

The issue preclusive effect of a prior judgment applies to issues *actually litigated* in the former action, but not to those that merely *could* have been litigated therein.

Example: Landlord sues and recovers judgment against Tenant for rent owed. Later, Landlord sues again for additional rent owed under the same lease. Tenant now interposes the defense that the lease was invalid at all times. The earlier judgment is *not* collateral estoppel as to this issue, since the only thing litigated in the first action was the rental claim, and the court was not called upon to determine the validity of the lease.

(1) Default judgments [§2228]

There is a split of authority on whether a default judgment creates issue preclusion.

(a) Conclusive [§2229]

Many decisions hold that a default judgment is conclusive as to all issues that were necessarily involved in the former suit, even though the action went by default and there was no actual litigation thereof. [77 A.L.R.2d 1424]

(b) Not conclusive [§2230]

However, there is substantial authority contra, including Restatement (Second) of Judgments, holding that "actually litigated" requires evidence presented to, and a decision by, a trier of fact (so that default judgments do not qualify). [Restatement (Second) of Judgments §27, comment e]

1) Rationale

This is believed to be the better view, because a person defaulting to a complaint may not have foreseen that the admissions created thereby would return to haunt him in a subsequent, unrelated lawsuit.

(2) Stipulated judgments [§2231]

There is likewise a split of authority on whether a stipulated (consent) judgment is issue preclusive.

(a) Comment

Even if an issue conceded through a default or consent judgment is not treated as within the rule of issue preclusion, it will be admissible under the law of evidence as an *admission*. (*See* Evidence Summary.)

(3) Jury vs. nonjury trial [§2232]

The presence or absence of a jury in the first trial is a "neutral" factor—*i.e.,* matters actually litigated in action 1 may be held collaterally estopped in action 2, even if there was no right to a jury in the earlier action (*e.g.,* a suit in equity) and the present suit is jury triable (*e.g.,* action for damages). [**Parklane Hosiery Co. v. Shore**, 439 U.S. 322 (1979)]

b. "Essential to first judgment" [§2233]

Collateral estoppel applies only to those matters decided in the earlier lawsuit that were *essential to the court's determination—i.e.,* essential to the cause of action (or defense) established by the judgment therein. Other matters involved in the earlier lawsuit, even though "actually litigated," are not binding in a later action. [Restatement (Second) of Judgments §27]

e.g. Example: P sues D over personal injuries sustained in an auto accident. The court finds that: (i) P was contributorily negligent; and (ii) D was also negligent. The finding that D was negligent may not have been "necessary" (it would be immaterial if P's claim is barred by his own contributory negligence). Consequently, when D later sues P for his injuries in the same accident, the finding in the earlier action that D was negligent is not binding against D.

(1) Test [§2234]

An issue is "essential" to the court's determination in the former action only if it appears that the judgment could not have been reached without determining the issue. [**DeCourt v. Beckman Instruments**, 32 Cal. App. 3d 628 (1973)]

(2) Alternative findings [§2235]

There is a *split of authority* on whether alternative findings, either of which would have been sufficient to support the judgment, should create estoppel in other proceedings. [*Compare* **Halpern v. Schwartz**, 426 F.2d 102 (2d Cir. 1970), *and* Restatement (Second) of Judgments §27, comment i—no estoppel—*with* **In re Westgate-California Corp.**, 642 F.2d 1174 (9th Cir. 1981)—estoppel allowed]

e.g. Example: In an action to declare involuntary bankruptcy, debtor wife was found to have committed three acts of bankruptcy fraud, each of which would be sufficient to support the determination that involuntary bankruptcy was proper. In a subsequent action concerning her discharge, estoppel was asserted on the basis of one of the three findings because it involved fraud. The court held that estoppel should not apply because the finding was merely an alternative basis for the decision. [**Halpern v. Schwartz,** *supra*]

(a) Significance of appeal [§2236]

Some courts distinguish between cases in which the earlier judgment was appealed and those in which it was not. If no appeal was taken, they will hold that neither finding is preclusive. If an appeal is taken, however, there is preclusion with respect to those issues that the appellate court reaches that support its judgment. [Restatement (Second) of Judgments §27, comment o]

(3) "Ultimate" vs. "evidentiary" facts [§2237]

Some cases have held that the previous determination of an issue is conclusive when the "ultimate" facts in the two actions are the same, but not when the first finding is simply a step (*i.e.*, a "mediate or evidentiary fact") toward the ultimate fact in the second action. [**Evergreens v. Nunan**, 141 F.2d 927 (2d Cir. 1944)]

Example: In a personal injury action, a finding that D was "negligent" would clearly be an ultimate fact; whereas, a specific finding that D had failed to maintain or repair her vehicle in a safe condition might be treated as "evidentiary."

(a) Modern approach contrary [§2238]

This distinction generally is *not* accepted. [*See* **Synanon Church v. United States**, 820 F.2d 421 (D.C. Cir. 1987)—issue preclusion applies to *any* fact determination actually litigated and essential to the judgment, without any distinction between "ultimate" and "mediate" or "evidentiary" facts]

c. "Identical" issue [§2239]

The issue decided in the prior adjudication must be identical to the one presented in the instant action. Mere similarity of issues is not enough.

Example: When the first suit involved an alleged breach of contract by defendant, there was no collateral estoppel in a second action involving securities act violations because the issues were different, even though the same conduct by defendant was involved in both actions. [**Watson v. Roberts, Scott & Co.**, 466 F.2d 1348 (9th Cir. 1972)]

Example: In the first action, the court held that a worker could recover for injuries from defendant manufacturer of asbestos. This decision did not provide the basis for estoppel against the manufacturer in a later action brought by another worker, because issues raised in the later action were not identical and depended on the actual (and different) circumstances under which the later plaintiff was exposed to asbestos products. [**Hardy v. Johns-Manville Sales Corp.**, 681 F.2d 334 (5th Cir. 1982)]

d. Exceptions [§2240]

Issue preclusion is not as strictly applied as claim preclusion.

(1) *When the two actions involve the same parties*, under Restatement (Second) of Judgments section 28 the loser may be allowed to relitigate an issue in a subsequent action if, for example:

(a) As a matter of law, *appellate review* of the initial action was *unavailable*;

(b) Even if review was available, the *nature of the proceedings* in the court handling the first action was *informal or expedited*, as in a small-claims court;

(c) The *stakes involved* in the second suit are much larger, as when the first action was in small-claims court and the second involves a major personal injury claim;

(d)   The *issue is one of law* and the claims in the two actions are substantially unrelated [**American Casualty Co. v. Sentry Federal Savings Bank,** 867 F. Supp. 50 (D. Mass. 1994)];

(e)   The *burden of proof* is materially different or has shifted; or

(f)   There is a clear and convincing need for a new determination because, for instance, the party who lost on the issue *could not have been expected to foresee* that the issue would arise in a later action.

(2)   *When the second action involves a different party*, all these exceptions apply and, in addition, the loser may relitigate if there are other factors that justify allowing her to do so. (*See infra*, §2261.)

D. Persons Precluded By Judgments

1. Parties and Privies

a. Parties [§2241]

A party to a judgment is bound by *claim preclusion* (so that she cannot relitigate the claim) *and issue preclusion* (so that, ordinarily, she cannot relitigate an issue determined in the first action).

b. Privies [§2242]

A person in "privity" with a party is usually bound to the *same extent* as the party. "Privity" is a legal conclusion, indicating that the person in question has a relationship to the party such that he should be bound. Whether "privity" exists depends in part on the type of claims involved. There are two general categories of privity:

(1) Procedural privity [§2243]

If the party acted in the first action as the *representative* of the nonparty, the judgment therein binds the nonparty. [Restatement (Second) of Judgments §41]

Examples: A party appearing as the representative of a class in a class suit [**King v. International Union,** 114 Cal. App. 2d 159 (1952)]; a trustee or guardian representing a beneficiary or ward [**Armstrong v. Armstrong,** 15 Cal. 3d 942 (1976)—parent for child]; *or* a party whose interests are represented by an executor or administrator.

---

(2) Substantive privity [§2244]

Privity may also arise out of *substantive* legal relationships, with the nonparty bound because of a prior legal relationship to the party. [Restatement (Second) of Judgments §41] Examples include the following:

(a) Bailment [§2245]

Either the bailee or the bailor can sue a third party for injury to the bailed chattel; and an action by one precludes an action by the other. [**Anheuser-Busch, Inc. v. Starley**, 28 Cal. 2d 347 (1946)]

(b) Medical losses of child or spouse [§2246]

In most states, medical expenses (*e.g.*, hospital bills) paid by a parent or spouse can be recovered either by the injured person or by the parent or spouse who paid them. Hence an action by one of those who could recover the expenses precludes an action by any of the others. [Restatement (Second) of Judgments §48]

(c) Successor in interest [§2247]

A successor in interest to property is bound by a judgment to which his predecessor was a party. [**Kartheiser v. Superior Court**, 174 Cal. App. 2d 617 (1959)]

Example: A sues B, an adjoining landowner, to determine the boundary between the properties. After judgment, A transfers the property to C. C is bound by the prior determination of the boundary.

(d) Beneficiary of estate [§2248]

A beneficiary of an estate is bound by an action litigated on behalf of the estate by the trustee. [Restatement (Second) of Judgments §41(a)]

(e) Public official authorized by law to act on person's behalf [§2249]

If a public official is authorized by law to act on a person's behalf, the person is bound by the official's litigation on his behalf. [Restatement (Second) of Judgments §41(d)]

(f) "Virtual" representation [§2250]

In unusual circumstances, courts may say that even if there is no formal representational role, an earlier litigant was the "virtual" representative of the later litigant, and the later litigant is therefore bound. This doctrine is *narrowly interpreted* and available only in special circumstances. [**Tice v. American Airlines, Inc.**, 162 F.3d 966 (7th Cir. 1998)—criticizing "virtual representation" as a "catchy phrase" that has "cast more shadows than light on the problem to be decided," but recognizing that it may have validity in some "public law" cases]

Example: When a city had sued an airline to prevent it from using a certain airport in violation of a city ordinance and lost, other airlines could not file a second suit relying on the ordinance because private parties may not seek to enforce an ordinance after the governmental body that enacted the ordinance has tried unsuccessfully to enforce it. [**Southwest Airlines Co. v. Texas International Airlines**, 546 F.2d 84 (5th Cir. 1977)]

cf. **Compare:** The outcome in an antitrust suit brought by one company was not binding on another company making identical claims even though both companies had the same lawyer, and the president of the second company participated in strategy sessions before the trial of the first company's suit and voluntarily appeared as a witness for the first company at the trial of its case. [**Benson and Ford, Inc. v. Wanda Petroleum Co.**, 833 F.2d 1172 (5th Cir. 1985)]

(3) Distinguish—family relationships [§2251]

The fact that parties have a legal relationship with each other does not of itself make them "privies." Thus, a husband's lawsuit is not binding on his wife (unless, in a community property state, the husband represents the community in maintaining the suit); neither does a parent necessarily represent a child. Whether "privity" exists depends on whether there is a *representative* capacity arising out of the relationship.

e.g. **Example:** In a divorce action with wife, father litigated the question of whether he had given half ownership of the family farm to sons. Sons were not bound by the result, even though they testified as witnesses in the divorce action. [**Searle Brothers v. Searle**, 588 P.2d 689 (Utah 1978)]

e.g. **Example:** Parent and Child are both hurt in an automobile accident with D. If Parent sues D for his injuries and loses, that does not bar Child from suing D for Child's injuries.

cf. **Compare:** If Parent sues as Child's *guardian* for Child's injuries, that precludes a suit by Child (because she was represented in the first suit)—though it would not preclude a suit by Parent for *his own* injuries, because that is a different claim (*see supra,* §2197).

EXAM TIP   **gilbert**

Issue preclusion (*i.e.*, collateral estoppel) is a fairly common exam topic. Remember the basics: If an issue is actually litigated and determined in a proceeding, that determination is binding in any subsequent action between the parties, even if the subsequent action is unrelated to the first action. This preclusive effect applies only to issues that were **actually litigated** and only if the issue was **essential to the first judgment**. The preclusive effect extends to persons in privity with the parties. But also remember that issue preclusion will not apply if it would be unfair to do so because, for example, the stakes in the first suit were low (*e.g.*, a few hundred dollars) and the stakes in the second suit are much higher.

2. Nonparties

a. Nonparty not bound [§2252]

In general, a nonparty is **not bound** by judgment. Such a person has not had his day in court and, as a matter of **due process**, he cannot be denied a valuable interest (his right of action) without one. [**Parklane Hosiery Co. v. Shore**, *supra*, §2232] Instances of "privity" (above) are exceptions to the rule, justified on the ground that the nonparty's interests were adequately represented by the party to the first action.

---

e.g **Example—no binding effect on nonparties:** White firefighters, who had not been parties to a prior litigation between a city and civil rights claimants that resulted in consent decrees establishing minority hiring and promotion goals, were not precluded from bringing a discrimination suit against the city. It was immaterial whether the white firefighters could have intervened in the first litigation; the burden of joining additional parties to secure binding effect against them is on those already parties. [**Martin v. Wilks**, *supra*, §1070]

---

(1) Federal statutory exception [§2253]

For cases involving federal employment discrimination claims, Congress, in the Civil Rights Act of 1991, changed the ruling of *Martin, supra,* to give binding effect to a litigated or consent judgment or order when the nonparty had adequate notice and opportunity to present objections, or when the nonparty's specific interests had been adequately represented by another. [42 U.S.C. §2000e-2(n)]

(2) Due process limits on extreme application of state preclusion law [§2254]

Although states are generally free to decide the content of their own preclusion law, federal due process principles impose some limits on extreme applications to nonparties. [**Postal Telegraph Cable Co. v. City of Newport**, 247 U.S. 464 (1918)] Thus, individual taxpayers who sought to challenge a county occupation tax levied upon them could not be bound by a prior, unsuccessful nonclass action brought by a city against the county challenging the same tax, when the taxpayers received no notice of the first action and the court and parties had done nothing to assure adequate protection of their interests. [**Richards v. Jefferson County**, 517 U.S. 793 (1996); **South Central Bell Telephone Co. v. Alabama**, 526 U.S. 160 (1999); *compare* **Hansberry v. Lee**, *supra*, §1166]

b. Nonparty may benefit [§2255]

A nonparty may **benefit** from the judgment in an action to which he was not a party.

(1) Claim preclusion [§2256]

In a number of situations, two potential defendants will have a relationship such that one is responsible for the conduct of the other. Examples include master and servant (under the principle of respondeat superior) and insurer and insured (the insurer being liable, up to the policy limits, for acts of the insured). When this relationship of vicarious responsibility exists, a judgment *exonerating either* potential defendant precludes an action on the same claim against the other.

Example: P claims injuries as the result of negligence by Employee, who was acting in the course and scope of his employment for Employer. If P sues either Employee or Employer alone, a judgment *exonerating* that defendant (on a finding of no negligence by Employee) will preclude a claim against the other, since Employer's liability is derivative in nature.

(a) Not applicable to joint or concurrent liability [§2257]

This form of claim preclusion applies *only* in situations of *vicarious responsibility*, and not in cases of joint or concurrent tort liability. Thus, if A is injured by the *concurrent negligence* of B and C (each of whom operates his own car) and A sues B and loses, that judgment does not bar A from suing C. But if B was driving C's car, and A lost in an action against B, A could not sue C based on B's conduct.

(2) Issue preclusion

(a) Basic rule [§2258]

A party who litigates an issue against one party and loses may not relitigate that issue with another party.

Example: Driver A and passenger B are injured when A's car is hit by D's car. A sues D, contending that D was negligent, and wins. If B then sues D, D is bound by the first action and cannot relitigate whether he was negligent.

---

1) Rationale

If a party has had a *full and fair opportunity to litigate an issue* in one action, there is no reason to waste the time of the court and other persons in relitigating that issue. [**Blonder-Tongue Laboratories, Inc. v. University of Illinois Foundation**, 402 U.S. 313 (1971); **Bernhard v. Bank of America**, 19 Cal. 2d 807 (1942)] The rule is often referred to as the *"Bernhard"* rule.

(b) Background—mutuality rule [§2259]

Before *Bernhard, supra,* the mutuality rule prevented a nonparty from having the benefit of issue preclusion in his favor. The theory was that an estoppel should apply only if it was mutual—*i.e.,* since the nonparty would not have been bound by the issue had it been decided the other way (because he had not had his day in court), he should not be able to invoke an estoppel in his favor based on the earlier judgment. *Bernhard,* which rejected this mutuality rule, is now the majority view. [Restatement (Second) of Judgments §29]

(c) Offensive vs. defensive use of prior judgment [§2260]

Earlier decisions held that issue preclusion could be used defensively against a plaintiff, but not offensively against a defendant (to block defendant's attempt to relitigate issues on which he had lost in the earlier trial). However, the Supreme Court has held that this is *not* a critical distinction. [**Parklane Hosiery Co. v. Shore**, *supra,* §2252]

---

e.g. **Example—defensive use:** P claims to have been injured by the concurrent acts of B and C. In an action by P against B, it is found that P suffered no actual injury. If P later sues C for the same loss, C can invoke issue preclusion defensively. [**Ponce v. Tractor Supply Co.**, 29 Cal. App. 3d 500 (1972)]

---

e.g. **Example—offensive use:** P-1 and P-2, passengers in a bus, are hurt when the bus collides with a train. P-1 wins in his suit against the railroad. The better decisions would permit P-2 to use the earlier judgment as conclusive proof against the railroad in a suit by P-2.

---

e.g. **Example—offensive use:** In action 1, the SEC files suit against Corporation for false statements in a proxy solicitation in connection with a proposed merger (*i.e.,* mailings to the shareholders seeking their votes to approve the merger). Judgment is rendered against Corporation. In action 2, shareholders file suit against Corporation seeking damages as a result of their reliance on the same proxy solicitation. The judgment rendered against Corporation in the SEC action may be held to bar Corporation from relitigating the issue of whether the solicitation was false and misleading. [*See* **Parklane Hosiery Co. v. Shore**, *supra*]

EXAM TIP	gilbert

Watch out for fact patterns relying on the old doctrine of mutuality—*i.e.,* prohibiting a nonparty from taking advantage of issue preclusion because the party would not be allowed to use issue preclusion against the nonparty. Under modern law, a nonparty *can often use* issue preclusion both defensively against a plaintiff and offensively against a defendant (to block defendant's attempt to relitigate issues on which he lost in an earlier trial).

(d) Limitations [§2261]

Although issue preclusion can be used offensively or defensively, the benefits of such estoppel may be denied under certain circumstances.

1) Issue would not be conclusive between parties [§2262]

If the issue would not be treated as conclusive between the *parties* to the first action (*see supra,* §2240), it cannot be conclusive in *favor of a third person* not a party to the first action.

Example: P is slightly injured while a passenger in A's car when it collides with B's car. P sues A for $300 in doctor's bills and wins on a finding that A was negligent. B then sues A for $50,000 in personal injuries. The finding in the first action does not preclude A from litigating the question of negligence against B, because the amount involved in the first case was so small that it would not be treated as conclusive even between P and A in a second action.

---

2) Unjust under circumstances [§2263]

In addition, a third person cannot have the benefit of issue preclusion against a party to the first action if it would be unjust in the circumstances. In deciding whether preclusion would be "unjust," the court may consider relevant factors such as the following: [*See* Restatement (Second) of Judgments §29]

a) Whether the person seeking the benefit of preclusion *could have joined in the prior action,* but decided instead to "sit it out";

b) Whether the prior determination was itself *inconsistent with an earlier determination* of the same issue;

c) Whether the consequences in the second action are *much more serious* than those in the first action [**Cochran v. Union Lumber Co.,** 26 Cal. App. 3d 423 (1972)];

d) Whether the party to be estopped has *procedural opportunities* (*e.g.,* broader discovery, ability to compel live testimony of important witnesses) that were not available in the earlier action;

e) Whether the prior finding was apparently a *compromise verdict*;

f) Whether the issue is one of law whose *reconsideration should not be foreclosed* [**United States v. Mendoza,** 464

U.S. 154 (1984)—federal government not subject to issue preclusion from prior determination in litigation with different party]; and

g) Whether *other compelling circumstances* justify relitigation.

REQUIREMENTS FOR PRECLUSION	**gilbert**
CLAIM PRECLUSION	**ISSUE PRECLUSION**
Judgment must be: ● On the same claim; ● Final; ● Valid; and ● On the merits; and Party against whom claim preclusion is sought was a party to the prior litigation or in privity with such a party.	Issue decided in prior action was: ● Actually litigated; ● Essential to the first judgment; and ● Identical to the issue presented in the instant action; and Party against whom issue preclusion is sought was a party to the prior litigation or in privity with such a party.

E. Interjurisdictional Preclusive Effects of Judgments

1. Introduction [§2264]

In the United States, there are 50 state court systems as well as the federal court system. Although preclusion issues often arise when the later case is in the same court system as the earlier case, it also happens frequently that the second case is in a different court system. When that occurs, the attitudes toward preclusion of the first court system and the second court system may differ, and a decision will have to be made about which principles to apply.

2. Basic Rule [§2265]

The basic rule regarding interjurisdictional preclusive effects of judgments is that the *preclusion principles of the court system that rendered the judgment* should be used to determine its preclusive effect.

a. State court judgments constitutionally entitled to effect in other state courts [§2266]

Under the Full Faith and Credit Clause, Article IV, section 1 of the federal

Constitution, "Full Faith and Credit shall be given in each State to the . . . judicial Proceedings of every other State."

b. **State court judgments given effect in federal and state court by statute [§2267]**

The *Full Faith and Credit statute*, 28 U.S.C. section 1738, directs that state court judgments "shall have *the same full faith and credit* in every court within the United States and its Territories and Possessions *as they have by law or usage in the courts* of such State, Territory or Possession *from which they are taken.*" This statute requires federal courts, and courts of other states, to give effect to state court judgments, and also directs that the preclusion principles of the rendering jurisdiction be applied.

Example: Plaintiffs filed suit in an Illinois state court, alleging a violation of a "common law right of association" resulting from denial of their applications to a professional group. Their suit was dismissed and plaintiffs thereafter sued in federal court asserting that there had been a federal antitrust violation. The state court could not have entertained the federal antitrust claim because it was subject to exclusive federal jurisdiction. The federal district court nevertheless did not inquire about whether claim preclusion would apply under Illinois preclusion law, and instead dismissed based on general preclusion principles. This was error because section 1738 requires the federal court to look to state preclusion law. [**Marrese v. American Academy of Orthopaedic Surgeons**, 470 U.S. 373 (1985)]

Example: Even though federal common law of preclusion permitted relitigation if an earlier case ended in default judgment, a California state court judgment was binding in a subsequent federal bankruptcy court proceeding because California law treated default judgments as binding. [**Bay Area Factors v. Calvert**, 105 F.3d 315 (9th Cir. 1997)]

(1) **Caution**

In practice some state courts seem unaware of the obligation to follow the preclusion law that would govern in the courts of the system that rendered a judgment, and they may apply their own preclusion principles instead. Because preclusion doctrines are often similar in different systems, however, such ignorance of the proper source of applicable preclusion law will usually make no practical difference.

c. **Federal court judgment generally given effect according to federal principles of preclusion [§2268]**

Even though there is no explicit constitutional or statutory provision to this effect, it is accepted that federal court judgments are entitled to preclusive effect, and that this effect is determined according to *federal common law* of preclusion. [**Stoll v. Gottlieb,** 305 U.S. 165 (1938)—judgment of a federal court in a federal question case entitled to preclusive effect as determined by federal common law of preclusion]

(1) Diversity cases [§2269]

Federal common law governs the preclusive effect of federal courts' judgments in diversity cases; but, because state substantive law is at issue, no uniform federal rule is needed. Hence, absent a federal interest such as enforcement of sanctions for discovery misconduct, the federal common law governing the preclusive effect of a federal court's diversity judgment is the law that would be followed by the courts of the state in which the federal diversity court sits. [**Semtek International Inc. v. Lockheed Martin Corp.**, *supra*, §551]

d. Scope of effect of first judgment [§2270]

Although the preclusive effect of a judgment is determined in the first instance by the preclusion law of the state that entered it, that effect cannot exceed the scope of what the judgment could legitimately conclude, *e.g.*, it could not bind persons not parties to the judgment. [**Baker v. General Motors Corp.**, 522 U.S. 222 (1998)—Michigan state court injunction that prohibited witness from testifying without GM's permission in later cases in which GM was a party did not preclude subpoenaed testimony of that witness in suit against GM by unrelated plaintiff in federal court in another state]

3. Prohibition Against Giving Broader Preclusive Effect than Required [§2271]

Ensuring that judgments of sister states are given due respect might seem to permit giving them more effect than would the courts of the state where the judgment was rendered. Nonetheless, the Supreme Court has interpreted the Full Faith and Credit Statute to forbid a federal court to give more effect to a state court judgment than is called for by the preclusion rules of that state. [**Marrese v. American Academy of Orthopaedic Surgeons**, *supra*]

4. Preclusion Regarding Claims Within Exclusive Federal Jurisdiction [§2272]

A frequent problem arises when a federal suit asserts a claim that could not have been raised in an earlier state court action because it was subject to exclusive federal jurisdiction, and a party argues that the federal claim is nevertheless precluded by the judgment in the state court case.

a. Rule of jurisdictional "competence" for claim preclusion [§2273]

The law of most states is that *claim preclusion* is not available with respect to a claim over which the court does not have subject matter jurisdiction. [Restatement (Second) of Judgments §26(1)(c)] *Rationale*: If the court cannot entertain the claim, it should not be able by its judgment to extinguish the claim.

b. Distinguish—issue preclusive effects [§2274]

If the state court decision of a state law claim resolves issues that are also presented by a federal claim, those determinations can be given effect in a later federal suit asserting the federal claim even if that claim is within exclusive federal jurisdiction. [**Kremer v. Chemical Construction Corp.**, 456 U.S. 461 (1982)—issue preclusion applicable to Title VII employment discrimination claim although unclear whether there is exclusive federal jurisdiction over such claims; **Becher v. Contoure Laboratories, Inc.**, 279 U.S. 388 (1929)—issue preclusion from state court suit bars subsequent federal patent suit]

c. **Possible argument for exception to full faith and credit statute [§2275]**

If state law indicates that a state court judgment should be given preclusive effect even with regard to a claim within exclusive federal jurisdiction, there may be a basis for finding an exception to section 1738 if the grounds for prohibiting state courts from adjudicating such claims support finding a *partial repeal* of the statute. But the Supreme Court has said that this is a "relatively stringent standard" for finding such a repeal, depending on an "irreconcilable conflict" between section 1738 and the Congressional grant of exclusive federal jurisdiction. [**Matsushita Electric Industrial Co. v. Epstein**, 516 U.S. 367 (1996)]

Review Questions
and Answers

Review Questions

Answer the following review questions "Yes" or "No" where you can, and if the law is not certain, answer "Probably" or "Probably Not," etc. In some instances you will be asked to select among various alternatives, or to choose the alternatives that are correct (*e.g.*, (b) and (c) are correct but (a) and (d) are not).

**FILL IN
ANSWER**

TERRITORIAL JURISDICTION

1. P is a resident of State A. D is a resident of State B. P files suit against D in an appropriate State A court, serving D personally while D is in an airplane flying over State A. D has no other contacts with State A. Should the court grant D's motion to dismiss for want of jurisdiction over his person? _____

2. P is a resident of State A. D is a doctor in State B. P commenced an action against D in the court of State A, alleging that he had been injured in an auto collision in State A caused by a loss of consciousness in a patient of D, which in turn had resulted from an act of professional malpractice committed in State B. D moved to dismiss the action for want of jurisdiction over his person. Should the motion be granted? _____

3. P is a resident of State A. D is a drug manufacturer in State B that sells its products in State A. P commenced an action against D in the court of State A, alleging injury from a defective drug purchased by P in State A. Pursuant to the law of State A, P served D by mail at its place of business in State B. D moved to dismiss the action for want of jurisdiction over its person. Should the motion be granted? _____

4. P is a resident of State A. D is a resident of State B and is not subject to service of process in State A. P brings an action against D in the court of State A for breach of contract. Process is served on Hand, a resident of State A, who was designated as D's agent for receipt of service in the contract made between P and D. D moves to quash the service of process and to dismiss for want of jurisdiction. Should the motion be granted? _____

5. P is a resident of State A. D is a resident of State B and is not subject to service of process in State A. P commenced an action against D in the court of State A. After a contested trial, the jury rendered a verdict for P. D then raised want of jurisdiction over his person and moved to dismiss. Should the court grant the motion? _____

6. P is a resident of State A. D is a resident of State B and is not subject to service of process in State A. P writes D offering to settle a dispute on very reasonable terms if D will meet P in State A to discuss it. D arrives and is met at the appointed place

by a process server in an action brought by P on the dispute. D moves to quash service of process and to dismiss for want of jurisdiction. Should the court grant the motion?

7. P files a diversity suit in federal court in New York, claiming damages arising out of an accident which occurred in New Jersey. P resides in Connecticut and D resides in Pennsylvania, but P chose to file in New York because most of the witnesses reside there. Is venue proper in New York?

8. Can the action in question 7, above, be transferred to New Jersey? If transferred to New Jersey, can the action be transferred back again to New York for the convenience of the parties and witnesses under 28 U.S.C. section 1404(a)?

9. If a transfer for convenience of witnesses was proper, could the transfer be made on the motion of *plaintiff*?

10. P, a resident of New York, wishes to sue D, a resident of New Jersey, for injuries suffered in an auto accident in Pennsylvania. Would venue be proper for a federal action in New Jersey and Pennsylvania?

11. P Co. is incorporated in Delaware and has its principal place of business there. Its employee, E, is a citizen of Pennsylvania. P and E wish to join as plaintiffs in a suit against D1 (a citizen of Florida) and D2 (a citizen of Georgia) for damage done in a ship collision that occurred in international waters. In what state would venue be proper in a federal action?

12. P and D are residents of the same state. P commenced an action against D for breach of contract. Unable to find D—who lives alone—in person, and unable to get D to waive service, P attached D's weekend cottage, recording the writ of attachment and posting notice on the door of the cottage. A default judgment was entered for P and a writ of execution issued. Before the execution sale, D moved for relief from the judgment on the ground that it is void. Should the motion be granted?

13. P is a resident of State A. D is a resident of State B. P files a diversity suit against D for $150,000 in the federal court located in State A. Copies of the summons and complaint are mailed to D in his home state of B. Has D been effectively served?

14. P is a resident of State A. D is a resident of State B. D is subject to service of process in State A and has a bank account in that state. P files an action against D in a court of State A and serves a writ of garnishment on D's bank, thereafter notifying D of the proceedings. D moves to quash the writ of garnishment and to dismiss for want of jurisdiction. Should the court grant the motion?

FEDERAL SUBJECT MATTER JURISDICTION

15. P, a citizen of Texas, files a diversity action in federal court against "XYZ, Inc."

a. Assume that "XYZ, Inc." is in fact a partnership, having its principal place of business in Oklahoma, and consisting of three partners (X, Y, and Z), one of whom resides in Texas. Does the requisite diversity of citizenship exist?

_____

b. Assume that "XYZ, Inc." is a corporation incorporated in Delaware, having its principal place of business in New York with branch offices nationwide, including one in Texas. Does the requisite diversity of citizenship exist?

_____

16. D, a citizen of Virginia, takes a vacation trip to Mexico City, where he negligently injures P. P sues D for $150,000 damages in the federal court in Virginia, claiming diversity jurisdiction. Which, if any, of the following factors would justify the court's dismissing the action for *lack* of diversity?

_____

(A) P is a Mexican national.

(B) P is a United States citizen living permanently in Mexico City.

(C) P is a citizen of Virginia, but has been mentally incompetent since birth, and his longtime guardian is a citizen of Maryland.

17. P files suit against D in federal court, claiming diversity of citizenship jurisdiction. Which, if any, of the following facts would justify the court's dismissal of the action for *lack* of diversity?

_____

(A) P and D were both citizens of State A at the time the claim arose. P moved to State B just before filing suit against D, for the apparent purpose of *creating* diversity of citizenship.

(B) P and D were citizens of different states at the time the claim arose. Just before P filed his suit, D moved into the state where P resided, for the apparent purpose of *preventing* diversity of citizenship.

(C) P and D were citizens of different states at the time the claim arose and at the time the suit was filed. Shortly thereafter, however, D moved into the state where P resided.

(D) P and D are citizens of different states at all times. However, neither of them resides in the state in which the federal court is located.

(E) P and D are citizens of different states at all times, but P is suing on a claim assigned to him for collection by a citizen of the state in which D resides.

18. P1, a citizen of State A, and P2, a citizen of State X, join in an action against D1, a citizen of State B, and D2, a citizen of State X. Federal jurisdiction is invoked on grounds of diversity of citizenship. D2 moves to dismiss for want of federal jurisdiction. Should the motion be granted?

_____

19. P is a citizen of State A. D is a citizen of State B, but is subject to service of process in State A. P brought an action against D in the federal court in State A, alleging diversity of citizenship, and a tort claim with damages in the amount of $25,000. After trial, the jury rendered a verdict for P in the amount of $10,000. D then moved to dismiss for want of subject matter jurisdiction. Should the court grant the motion? _____

20. P files a diversity suit against D, alleging $125,000 damages for invasion of privacy. The jury subsequently awards P only $500 damages. Does the federal court have jurisdiction to enter such a judgment? _____

21. P sues B in a diversity suit for $60,000 owed on a promissory note and $50,000 in personal injuries. Has the required jurisdictional amount for diversity purposes been met? _____

22. P sues D1 and D2 as co-defendants in a diversity suit. P alleges that D1 owes her $60,000 on one promissory note, that D2 owes her $50,000 on another promissory note, and that both promissory notes were executed at the same time and as part of the same transaction. Is the jurisdictional minimum requirement satisfied? _____

23. P1 and P2 join as plaintiffs to sue D in a diversity suit to recover for an auto accident in which P1 and P2 were both riding in a car hit by a car driven by D. P1 seeks to recover $60,000 and P2 seeks to recover $50,000. Is the jurisdictional minimum requirement satisfied? _____

24. P is a citizen of State A. D is a citizen of State B. P brought an action against D in the federal court in State B, praying for a decree of divorce. D moved to dismiss for want of federal jurisdiction. Should the motion be granted? _____

25. P and D were divorced pursuant to an agreement providing for alimony payments by D to P in fixed amounts "after taxes." P was held liable for federal income taxes on payments received. She now brings an action in federal court to recover on the promise of D to bear the income tax liability, alleging that it arises under federal law. D moves to dismiss for want of subject matter jurisdiction. Should the motion be granted? _____

26. P brought an action against D in federal court for defamation, alleging federal jurisdiction based on the federal question presented by D's defense that his speech was constitutionally protected by the First Amendment. D moved to dismiss for want of federal jurisdiction. Should the motion be granted? _____

27. P claims that his business has been damaged by monopolistic practices by D, which allegedly violate *both* the Sherman Act and a state "fair practices" act.

   a.   Can P file an action asserting both claims in either state or federal court? _____

b. If P files in federal court, can the federal court grant relief under the state act even if no violation of the Sherman Act is proved? _____

28. If there are *several* co-defendants in a state court action, must they *all* join in the notice of removal to the federal court in order to confer jurisdiction on the federal court? _____

29. Smith, a citizen of Nevada, sues Jones, a citizen of California, in a California state court to enforce a promissory note for $100,000. Jones files a counterclaim against Smith for $1 million.

   a. Can Smith remove the action to the federal court in California? _____

   b. Can Jones remove the action to the federal court in California? _____

30. Black, a citizen of New York, sues Brown, a citizen of New Jersey, in a state court in New York. The claim is for copyright infringement. Can Brown remove the action to the federal court in New York? _____

31. P is a citizen of State A. D is a citizen of State B. P files an action against D for violation of the federal civil rights laws in a state court of general jurisdiction in State A. Should the court grant D's motion to dismiss for want of jurisdiction over the subject matter of the claim? _____

RELATIONSHIP BETWEEN STATE AND FEDERAL LAW

32. On July 14, P files an action against D in federal court in State X, properly invoking diversity jurisdiction, to recover for injuries sustained in an automobile accident on the previous July 15. One week after the suit was filed, D was personally served with the summons and complaint. D defends on the ground that the action is barred under the applicable one-year statute of limitations, citing a provision of State X law that the limitations period continues to run until a defendant is personally served. Is D's defense valid? _____

33. P files a diversity action against D in federal court in State X. To prove her right to recover, P must rely on certain hearsay evidence that would be inadmissible in state court in State X, but which is admissible under the Federal Rules of Evidence, which provide a number of exceptions to the hearsay rule. Should the evidence be admitted? _____

34. In P's diversity suit against D in federal court in State X, D moves for judgment as a matter of law at the close of all the evidence on the ground that P has failed to produce substantial evidence as required by federal precedents. P responds by invoking the rule of the courts of State X that such a motion should be denied if plaintiff has produced a scintilla of evidence, a lower requirement. Should the court apply the federal requirement? _____

35. P files a diversity suit against D in federal court in State X. Under a 30-year-old decision of the intermediate appellate court of State X, D has an absolute defense to the case, but the more "modern" view is that this defense is no longer valid. D moves to dismiss, citing the state appellate court decision. Should the court grant the motion? _____

PLEADING

36. P files an action in a code pleading state against D Riding Stable to recover for injuries sustained when P was thrown from a horse rented from D. P's complaint is captioned "for breach of contract," and alleges that "D allowed P to ride an unruly horse without adequate warning." D moves to dismiss because the complaint nowhere alleges the existence of any contractual relationship. Should the court grant the motion? _____

37. P files a complaint against D, a restaurant owner, alleging that he suffered food poisoning as the result of consuming "improperly prepared" food in D's restaurant.

    a. Is this sufficient to state a claim for relief in federal court (apart from jurisdictional allegations)? _____

    b. Is this sufficient to state a claim for relief in a code pleading state? _____

38. P sues D to quiet title to certain real property. P alleges "on information and belief" that D has recorded a document that clouds P's title. Is such an allegation sufficient to state a claim for relief? _____

39. P files a diversity action against D in federal court, claiming $125,000 damages for a battery. In one paragraph of a verified complaint, P alleges that D himself struck and battered P; but in a later paragraph he alleges that D did not do it personally, but rather paid a third person to batter P. D files a motion to dismiss for failure to state a claim. Should the court grant the motion? _____

40. P sued D seeking to enjoin D's operation of an amusement park as a nuisance interfering with P's enjoyment of his property. D defaulted to P's complaint. At the hearing on entry of judgment, the court found that an injunction would be harsh and unnecessary, and instead awarded P $50,000 damages for interference with the use and enjoyment of his property. Can D successfully appeal this judgment, having defaulted in the trial court? _____

41. P files a personal injury action against D. P's complaint adequately pleads the elements of negligence, and then avers: "Immediately after the accident, D paid $1,000 to P in settlement of P's claim, but P was defrauded by D into accepting the settlement and thereafter returned the money to D." If the action is filed in federal court, and D moves to dismiss for failing to state a claim upon which relief can be granted, should the court grant the motion? _____

42. P files a defamation action against D in a code pleading state, alleging in substance the defamatory words used by D (rather than quoting them verbatim). Is the complaint subject to a demurrer for failing to state a cause of action? _____

43. P files suit against D for personal injuries. The complaint alleges that P "sustained personal injury to his damage in the amount of $125,000." Under such allegation, which of the following items of evidence are admissible at trial? _____

    (A) Proof that P broke his right arm in the accident.

    (B) Proof that P's broken arm was extremely painful.

    (C) Proof that P's broken arm will cause some permanent disability.

    (D) Proof of the hospital and medical expenses incurred in treating P's broken arm.

    (E) Proof that future medical expenses will have to be incurred in treating P's broken arm.

    (F) Proof that D acted intentionally and willfully to inflict such injury, entitling P to additional, punitive damages.

44. P has three separate and distinct claims against D: (i) for nonpayment of a promissory note; (ii) for personal injuries; and (iii) to quiet title to certain property.

    a. Can P join all three claims in a single action against D in federal court? _____

    b. Would the answer be the same if P named D's wife as a co-defendant on the promissory note claim alone? _____

45. P files a breach of contract action against D. D files a general denial and also alleges, "P is a millionaire, and is bringing this suit hoping to force D into bankruptcy, so that he can pick up all of D's assets for a pittance." P moves to strike this allegation from D's answer. Should the court grant the motion? _____

46. P files a diversity suit in a federal court not having proper venue. D does not file a motion to dismiss, but raises the improper venue in his answer. At the time of trial, he moves for change of venue. Is D's motion timely? _____

47. P files a diversity suit in a federal court not having venue. D files a motion to dismiss for failure to state a claim. When this motion is denied, D files an answer in which he raises the venue objection. P moves to strike this portion of the answer because the issue was not raised in D's earlier motion to dismiss. Should the court grant the motion? _____

48. P files a diversity suit in a federal court. D moves to dismiss for improper venue, but his motion is denied. D then files an answer in which he raises the objection

that P's complaint fails to state a claim upon which relief can be granted. P moves to strike this portion of D's answer because the issue was not raised in D's earlier motion to dismiss. Should the court grant this motion?

49. P's complaint in a federal action shows on its face that the action is barred by the statute of limitations, but otherwise sets forth all elements of the claim sued upon. D moves to dismiss for failure to state a claim upon which relief can be granted. P counters that the allegations of time were surplusage and asks the court to disregard them in ruling on D's motion. Should the court grant the motion?

50. P files a verified complaint in a state court action in a code pleading state. D's answer (also verified) contains a general denial. P moves to strike D's answer on the ground that a general denial to a verified complaint is improper. Should the court sustain the demurrer?

51. P sues D for nonpayment of a promissory note. D's answer contains only the following allegation: "D neither admits nor denies P's charge, and puts P to his proof at trial." P moves for a judgment on the pleadings on the ground that D has admitted liability. Should the court grant the motion?

52. P files a federal action against D for breach of contract, claiming $125,000 damages. D files an answer containing only a general denial. Is D's answer an admission that some other sum is owed P?

53. P files a defamation action against D. D's answer contains only a general denial. At trial, which, if any, of the following matters may be proved by D?

   (A)   That D's utterance was true.

   (B)   That no one in fact heard what D said about P.

   (C)   That P and D later entered into a contract settling the matter.

   (D)   That P's reputation was already so bad that no harm was done by the utterance.

54. P sues D for personal injuries in a federal action. D's answer contains only a general denial. Later, D seeks leave of court to amend his answer to object to improper venue. Does the court have the power to permit such an amendment?

55. In answer to P's complaint, seeking to recover for injuries allegedly caused by food improperly prepared by D's restaurant, D alleges: "Whatever food poisoning P suffered resulted from his consuming food elsewhere than at D's restaurant." What sort of pleading is now required from P in order to preserve the issue (as to where he consumed the food) for trial?

56. D files a counterclaim to P's complaint in a federal court action. Which, if any, of the following would be a valid ground for striking D's counterclaim?

(A) The counterclaim was pleaded as part of D's answer rather than as a separate pleading.

(B) P's complaint was for copyright infringement, while D's counterclaim was for personal injury; hence no subject matter relationship.

(C) P's complaint was for $125,000 damages for breach of contract, with federal jurisdiction based on diversity of citizenship. D's counterclaim was for $5,000 for personal injury. Hence, no federal jurisdiction on the counterclaim.

(D) Several other parties would have to be joined for a complete determination of D's counterclaim.

57. P filed a complaint against D on June 1 for back injuries arising out of a highway truck accident. D filed a counterclaim on July 1 for damages to his own truck arising out of the same accident. P moves to strike on the ground that the statute of limitations on D's counterclaim ran on June 15. Should the court grant the motion? _____

58. P has filed a personal injury action in federal court against D1 and D2, claiming they were jointly responsible for causing a traffic accident in which he was injured. On which, if any, of the following grounds would it be proper for D1 to *cross-claim* against D2? _____

(A) D1 claims that the accident was entirely the fault of D2.

(B) D1 claims that his car was damaged in the accident, and D2 was responsible therefor.

(C) D1 claims that if P recovers a judgment against him, it should be made payable against D2 jointly.

(D) D1 claims that D2 owes him $15,000 on a promissory note.

59. Same facts as in the previous question. Suppose D2 claimed that he lost control of his car due to defective repairs made by D3. Could D2 file a cross-claim for indemnification against D3? _____

60. P sues D for personal injuries resulting from D's alleged negligence in causing an auto accident. Shortly before trial, P discovers that D had been driving under the influence of alcohol, and had been performing an errand for XYZ Co. By this time, however, the statute of limitations has run on all claims arising out of the accident.

a. If P seeks leave to amend his complaint to allege that D was driving while intoxicated so as to entitle P to punitive damages, should the court grant the motion? _____

b.   If P seeks leave to amend his complaint to name XYZ Co. as a co-defendant, asserting liability against it on respondeat superior grounds, should the court grant the motion? _____

61. P sues D1 in state court in State X, and D1 properly removes to federal court on grounds of diversity. Three years later, P amends the complaint to add D2 as a defendant. D2 had no notice of the suit until it was served with the amended complaint, and it moves to dismiss on the ground the claims against it are barred by the applicable two-year statute of limitations. Under the law of State X, added defendants who are not on notice have no limitations defense if the plaintiff sues some defendant within the limitations period. Should the court grant D2's motion to dismiss? _____

62. P files suit against "Alfred A. Albertson," alleging that Albertson negligently operated a model airplane so as to cause it to fly through an open window of P's house, striking P in the head and causing serious injury.

a.   At trial, the evidence shows that the real name of the person sued as "Alfred A. Albertson" is "Albert T. Albrittson." P seeks leave to amend her complaint to conform to proof. D resists on the ground that the statute of limitations has run. Should the court grant the motion? _____

b.   The evidence also shows that the model airplane destroyed a valuable vase in P's home worth $10,000. P seeks leave to amend to conform to proof. D objects. What ruling? _____

c.   The evidence also shows that since the time the original complaint was filed, P's injuries have worsened, and she is now blind in one eye. P seeks leave to plead these additional facts. D objects. Should the motion be granted? _____

63. On the date set for trial in a federal diversity suit, P discovers that a crucial witness is unwilling to testify. P moves for a dismissal of the action, hoping to sue again later. D objects, wanting to obtain a judgment in his favor so as to bar any later suit. Can the court simply refuse to grant a dismissal and force P to go to trial? _____

PARTIES

64. Which of the following parties would be entitled to sue in his own name on the claim in question without joining any other party as plaintiff? _____

(A) A collection agency on a debt assigned to it for collection.

(B) The beneficiary of a trust on a claim against a third person for wrongs to the trust estate.

(C) A third-party beneficiary on a contract made expressly and primarily for his benefit.

(D) The promisee of a contract made expressly and primarily for the benefit of a third person.

(E) The undisclosed principal on a contract entered into on his behalf by an agent.

65. If someone other than the real party in interest files suit, and the defendant fails to raise a timely objection, can the resulting judgment be attacked?   _____

66. In a federal action by a partnership asserting a state law claim, does federal law determine the partnership's capacity to sue as an entity (rather than as an association of individual partners)?   _____

67. Samantha, a minor female, wants to play baseball in the Little League system. After being refused, she files suit against Little League for injunctive relief. Little League moves to dismiss, on the ground that Samantha's father is the real party in interest. Should the motion be granted?   _____

68. P went into the hospital for surgery. He claims that Surgeon was negligent in performing the operation, whereby he was damaged in the sum of $110,000. He also claims that the hospital was negligent in caring for him after surgery, for which he seeks $50,000 damages.

   a. Can P join both defendants in a single action?   _____

   b. Can P join these separate claims in a single action?   _____

   c. Assume that P cannot prove whether his injuries were attributable to improper surgery or to improper care after surgery. Is it permissible for him to join both defendants under such circumstances?   _____

69. P brought an action against D1 and D2 alleging that each had defrauded him in separate securities transactions. D2 moves to dismiss the action for improper joinder. Should the motion be granted?   _____

70. P brings an action against D1 on a promissory note signed by D1 and D2. D1 moves to dismiss the action for failure to join D2. Should the motion be granted?   _____

71. P brings an action as a holder in due course against D to collect a portion of D's liability on a note. The remainder of the obligation had been assigned by the payee to A, who has not joined in the action. On motion by D, should A be joined?   _____

72. P, a citizen of State A, brought a federal diversity action against D, a citizen of State B, to recover for alleged mismanagement of a corporation partially owned by P. The corporation is a citizen of State B. D moved to dismiss the action for failure to join the corporation. Should the motion be granted?   _____

73. P files a diversity suit in federal court against D, claiming damages for breach of contract. D claims that he was prevented from performing the contract by reason of tortious interference by TP.

    a.   Can D join TP as a party to the action? _____

    b.   Can the federal court retain the case if it appears that TP is a resident of the same state as P? _____

74. P files a diversity suit against Duchess Sandwich Co., alleging that he became violently ill after consuming a sandwich purchased from Duchess which he alleges contained impure ingredients, thereby sustaining damages exceeding $110,000.

    a.   T, a co-worker in P's office, purchased a similar sandwich from Duchess on the same day as did P, and also became violently ill. If T moves to intervene in P's lawsuit against Duchess, should the court grant the motion? _____

    b.   XYZ is the company that furnishes Duchess with all of its ingredients, and has contracted to indemnify Duchess for any loss due to impurities in the ingredients furnished. If XYZ moves to intervene in P's lawsuit against Duchess, should the court grant the motion? _____

75. Don's life was insured for $5,000 by Apex Insurance Co., which has its principal place of business in California. Don is now dead. Apex has received conflicting claims for the insurance benefits from Don's wife, Wilma, a citizen of California, and Don's brother, Bob, a citizen of New York.

    a.   If Apex pays the $5,000 into federal court, can the federal court exercise jurisdiction to determine who is entitled to it? _____

    b.   Can the federal court in California exercise jurisdiction even though Bob is not subject to personal service in California? _____

76. P sues on behalf of himself "and all other students paying nonresident rate tuition at State University" to enjoin collection of the higher tuition charged nonresidents, on equal protection grounds. Approximately 500 students are affected. May the case proceed as a class action? _____

77. P, a citizen of California, files suit in federal court against Victor Vacuum Co., incorporated and having its principal place of business in New York. P sues "on behalf of himself and all other customers of Victor Vacuum Co." alleging various deceptive advertising and sales practices, causing aggregate losses exceeding $110,000. Which, if any, of the following arguments justify granting Victor's motion to dismiss the action? _____

    (A)   No diversity of citizenship, because some of Victor's customers reside in New York.

(B) No diversity jurisdiction, because the individual claims involved are not more than $75,000 each.

(C) Improper as class suit because each customer has a separate contract with Victor, hence no common question "predominates."

78. In determining whether an action should proceed as a class action, is it proper for the court to consider the suit's likelihood of success on the merits? _____

79. Assume that federal class action status is granted on the ground that there is a "predominant common question."

   a. Is it mandatory that all members of the class who can be identified with reasonable effort be notified, no matter how many of them there are? _____

   b. Is it mandatory that the plaintiff initially pay the costs of giving such notice? _____

   c. Will a resulting judgment necessarily bind all members of the class? _____

80. P owns a Blizzo Snowmobile. P sues Blizzo in state court on behalf of herself and all other owners of Blizzo Snowmobiles, alleging that the vehicles have defective parts that make them unsafe to ride in and cause an unusually fast depreciation in value. Blizzo offers P $15,000 to settle the claim, and to put up a fund which will assure that any other owner can recover $100 if a claim is made within one year. P then consents to entry of judgment in favor of Blizzo. Several months later, another owner, T, sues Blizzo for the same kind of damages. Is T bound by the judgment in P's action against Blizzo? _____

DISCOVERY

81. Must a party to a federal civil action disclose to an adversary, without having received any discovery request, the contents of a document in the party's possession that is harmful to its case? _____

82. P files an action against XYZ, Inc. in federal court. P wishes to conduct discovery by deposition, but is unsure which of the XYZ employees has the information he seeks, and therefore does not know whose name to put on the notice of deposition. Is it necessary for P to file interrogatories to find out the employee's name before sending out the notice of deposition? _____

83. P sues XYZ, Inc. for personal injuries sustained in a traffic accident with a truck belonging to XYZ and driven by employee E (who is not a party to the action).

   a. P took E's deposition prior to trial and obtained some admissions of negligence. Can P introduce E's deposition as substantive evidence of negligence at the time of trial? _____

b.   P also took the deposition of X, the president of XYZ, Inc., who admitted that E was driving within the course and scope of his employment. Can P introduce X's deposition testimony at trial as substantive evidence of this fact? _____

84.   Which, if any, discovery procedure is available under the Federal Rules to obtain the information indicated in the following cases?

a.   P was involved in a traffic accident with D, but is in doubt whether D was at fault. Hence, *before* filing suit, she wants to obtain the testimony of eyewitness W, who has refused to talk to P about the matter. _____

b.   P sues D for personal injuries sustained in a traffic accident. P claims she was off work for several weeks. D wants to check P's time card maintained by P's employer, but the employer has refused to provide this information. _____

c.   An eyewitness to the P-D traffic accident claims to have observed the collision from his living room window. D wants to take photographs from inside the witness's living room to check the credibility of the witness's claimed observations. _____

d.   The same eyewitness was wearing thick lenses at the time in question. D has reason to doubt whether the witness's vision is sufficient to have seen what he claims to have seen. Therefore, D asks for a court order to have the witness submit to a reasonable eye examination by D's doctor. Should the court grant D's motion? _____

85.   P sues D to quiet title to certain land. After considerable investigation, D's attorney obtains an old deed, which tends to support P's claim of title and to undermine D's defense. Somehow, P finds out about the deed and serves a request to produce on D. Which, if any, of the following are valid grounds for objection under the Federal Rules? _____

(A)   D does not have possession of the document.

(B)   The document is privileged as attorney's work product.

(C)   The request is improper because it was served without prior court order or any showing of good cause.

86.   In a personal injury case, P is examined by D's doctor. P's attorney requests and obtains a copy of the report made by D's doctor. Is D now automatically entitled to copies of all medical reports by P's doctors? _____

87.   P filed action against D Restaurant for $75,000, claiming food poisoning from impure food prepared by D. P served on D the following interrogatories, to which D objected on the grounds stated. P now moves to compel answers. How should the court rule on the motion to compel regarding each of the following interrogatories and objections?

a. Interrogatory: "Have you obtained statements in writing from other customers in the restaurant concerning the food served on the night in question?" Objection: Such statements are hearsay and inadmissible at trial. _____

b. Interrogatory: "Do you claim that plaintiff's food poisoning resulted from consumption of food elsewhere on the date in question?" Objection: Calls for a conclusion. _____

c. Interrogatory: "Has any other customer ever filed a lawsuit against you claiming food poisoning as the result of food you served?" Objection: Irrelevant. _____

d. Interrogatory: "In the event P recovers a judgment for the full amount of his claim, do you have assets sufficient to pay such a judgment?" Objection: Irrelevant. _____

e. Interrogatory: "Has your attorney caused any tests to be performed on the food in question to determine its purity, and if so, what are the results of the tests?" Objection: Calls for nondiscoverable expert opinion. _____

88. P has served and filed a set of interrogatories on D and D's wife. Which, if any, of the following are valid grounds for objection under the Federal Rules? _____

    (A) The interrogatories were served concurrently with the summons and complaint, and without court order authorizing such service.

    (B) D's wife is not a party to the action.

    (C) This is the third set of interrogatories served on D, and many of the questions were answered in earlier interrogatories.

    (D) The set of interrogatories includes 40 questions.

89. P sues D in federal court for copyright infringement of P's musical composition. P sends D a request to admit that a designated portion of a song published by D is in fact identical to a designated portion of P's song. D makes no response to this request. Which, if any, of the following statements is true? _____

    (A) Upon motion, the court may adjudge D in contempt and order D's answer stricken.

    (B) D's failure to respond constitutes a binding admission that the designated portions are identical.

    (C) No admission or denial was required because whether the designated portions are "identical" is the ultimate fact in issue for the trier of fact to determine.

90. P brings an action against D for personal injury. D's lawyer goes to P's place of employment, without notice to P and without permission of the employer, and interrogates P's employer and co-workers about the extent of his physical impairment. Which, if any, of the following statements are true? _____

    (A)   The employer and co-workers may lawfully refuse to talk to D's lawyer.

    (B)   On motion, the court will order D to desist from this practice because the proper way to get the information is by deposition.

    (C)   On motion, the court will exclude any information secured because it was the product of an unlawful trespass.

    (D)   P is at least entitled to a copy of all statements signed by the informants.

SUMMARY JUDGMENT

91. P files an action against D for personal injuries arising out of a traffic accident. D files a motion for summary judgment on the ground that he was not negligent. D's motion is supported by affidavits signed by all the other eyewitnesses, and by the police officer who investigated the accident. The only opposing affidavit is that of P, who simply controverts everything the eyewitnesses and police officer say. Does the court have the power to grant D's motion? _____

92. P files an action to rescind a deed for fraudulent misstatements made by D. D files a motion for summary judgment supported by his own affidavit to the effect that he believed the statements were true at the time he made them. No opposing affidavit is filed by P. Should the court grant D's motion? _____

93. P sues D to quiet title to property. P files a motion for summary judgment, based on an affidavit by his attorney that he has examined all pertinent land records and these records show that the chain of title is in P. D files no opposing affidavit. Should the court grant P's motion? _____

94. P sues D for copyright infringement of his musical composition. D's answer contains general denials of P's allegations. In deposition testimony, however, D admits that a significant portion of his song is identical to P's.

    a.   Can the court grant P's motion for a summary judgment as to the issue of infringement only? _____

    b.   If D files an affidavit denying the similarity, could the court grant P's motion based on its own comparison of the songs? _____

MANAGERIAL JUDGING

95. P brings an action against D in a federal court.

a.   Thirty days after the complaint was served, the court directed the parties to appear for a pretrial conference at which it would set deadlines for completion of discovery and the filing of all motions. Does the court have authority to require the parties to attend such a conference and to impose such restrictions? _____

b.   At a later pretrial conference, the court determines that there is a possibility of settlement and orders both P and D to appear in person for a settlement conference. Are P and D required to attend if they are represented by counsel? _____

c.   At the final pretrial conference, the court directs P and D to submit their cases to a summary jury trial. P objects that such a proceeding would require revelation of trial strategy and that the parties are too far apart in their settlement negotiations to make it worthwhile. Is P required to attend and participate in the summary jury trial if the judge insists? _____

d.   After the final pretrial conference the court enters an order listing the issues in the case and witnesses for each party. At trial P calls a witness not listed in the final pretrial order. D objects. Should the court allow P's added witness to testify? _____

TRIAL

96.   In which, if any, of the following cases is there a right to a jury trial in federal courts? _____

   (A)   P sues D for damages for trespass to land.

   (B)   P sues D to enjoin future trespasses upon her land.

   (C)   P sues D to enjoin future trespasses and for damages for past trespasses.

   (D)   D sues P for declaratory relief that his past entries were privileged and not actionable trespasses.

97.   P files a federal suit to rescind a contract on the basis of fraudulent misrepresentations by D. D counterclaims for damages based on P's nonperformance of the same contract. P's reply alleges that D's fraud excused his performance under the contract. D demands a jury trial on the counterclaim and moves for an order that the counterclaim be tried first. Should the court grant the motion? _____

98.   P sues D for medical malpractice in federal court. At the close of P's case, D moves for a judgment as a matter of law. The trial judge recognizes that P has made out a prima facie case technically, but believes that P's witnesses are not worthy of belief and hence that the jurors should not hold D liable. Should the court grant D's motion for a judgment as a matter of law? _____

99. P sues D for medical malpractice in federal court. At the close of P's case, D's counsel recognizes that P's witnesses are not likely to be believed, and she rests her case without presenting evidence. P moves for a judgment as a matter of law. Should the court grant the motion? _____

100. The trial of P's medical malpractice lawsuit resulted in a verdict for D. Which, if any, of the following would be a valid ground for appeal? _____

    (A)   The trial judge on her own motion called a medical witness to testify as to the standard of care in the community, which testimony hurt P's case.

    (B)   At the close of the trial, the judge told the jury that while they were the triers of fact, she personally did not believe P's testimony as to damages.

    (C)   In instructing the jury, the judge stated: "In determining whether D is liable, you should use your own common sense, as well as the standard of care in the community." P made no objection to this instruction in the trial court.

101. P sues D for personal injuries arising out of an auto accident. D's answer raises several affirmative defenses: contributory negligence; assumption of the risk; and P's execution of a release. The case goes to trial and there is evidence to support each of D's defenses. The judge's instructions to the jury are correct, except that he defines contributory negligence in a manner which is overly favorable to D. The jury returns a general verdict for D. P appeals on the ground that the contributory negligence instruction was incorrect, even though the instructions on the other defenses admittedly were correct. Should the appellate court reverse? _____

102. A jury returns a general verdict in favor of P but also answers special interrogatories which are inconsistent with a verdict for P and consistent with a verdict for D. The court thereupon enters judgment in favor of D. P appeals. Should the appellate court reverse? _____

103. P sues Dr. D for medical malpractice. The jury returns a verdict for D. P files a motion for new trial, claiming jury misconduct. Which of the following evidence is admissible in support of P's motion? _____

    (A)   An affidavit by Juror 1 that Juror 2 admitted during the course of deliberations that he was a former patient of Dr. D. Juror 2 had denied knowing D during voir dire questioning.

    (B)   An affidavit by Juror 3 that Juror 4 had been belligerent throughout the deliberations and had badgered and bullied him into voting for D.

    (C)   An affidavit by the bailiff that he overheard the jurors say that in order to reach a unanimous verdict they would all vote for whomever the majority of them wanted.

104. P sued D for medical malpractice in a federal court action, and the jury returned a unanimous verdict for P for $100,000. D moves for a new trial. Which of the following evidence, if any, is sufficient to support the granting of D's motion?

   (A) An affidavit by D's attorney that during the course of the trial, he discovered that several of the jurors had lunched and visited with P's wife, although he did not mention it to the court at the time.

   (B) An affidavit by D that after the verdict had been returned, he overheard P admit that he had been faking his injuries all along.

   (C) An affidavit by noted physician, W, that he had been prepared to testify as a witness for D, but had been called out of town just before the trial.

105. P sued D for medical malpractice in federal court. Although the witnesses for P gave testimony which the judge found unlikely, the judge denied D's motion for judgment as a matter of law, and the jury rendered a verdict for P. D renews the motion for judgment as a matter of law and moves, in the alternative, for a new trial. What ruling should the court make?

106. The jury returned a $30,000 verdict for P in a medical malpractice case in federal court. This amount was considerably less than the special damages proved by P. P moved for a new trial on the ground of inadequate damages. Can the court grant the new trial on condition that if D consents to increase the verdict to $85,000, a new trial will be denied?

107. P filed a federal suit against D for personal injuries sustained in a traffic accident. D was ill and upset at the time and forgot to turn the pleadings over to his attorney. P obtained a default judgment against D for $120,000, but did nothing to enforce the judgment for over a year. It was only when P executed on the judgment that D remembered the matter; and he then moved promptly to set aside the judgment on the ground that he had a valid defense to P's action, and that he failed to answer only through inadvertence and excusable neglect. Should the trial court grant the motion?

108. P sues D in federal court claiming diversity of citizenship. D lacks the funds to employ an attorney, and files no answer. P obtains a default judgment against D for $125,000. Several years later, D decides he wants to attack the judgment on the ground that he and P were at all times citizens of the same state, and hence the federal court lacked jurisdiction. However, all time limits for appeal or relief in the trial court have now expired. Is there any remedy available to D?

APPEAL

109. If a party inadvertently fails to file a notice of appeal within the required time limit, can he obtain an extension of time to file from the appellate court?

110. P obtains a jury verdict for $10,000 in a medical malpractice case, in which he had proved special damages of over $50,000. If he accepts payment of the $10,000 from D, can he appeal the judgment on ground of inadequacy of damages (giving D credit for the $10,000)?

_____

111. P sues D for personal injuries. D makes a motion to compel P to submit to a physical examination, but the trial court erroneously denies the motion. In view of the importance of the exam, can D immediately appeal the trial court's order?

_____

112. After trial to the court, the court made findings of fact and conclusions of law, and entered judgment in favor of D. P appeals, arguing that the evidence supported findings favorable to him. Which of the following is the appropriate standard of review?

(A) The appellate court may reverse only if it finds that there is no substantial evidence to support the judgment below.

(B) The appellate court may reverse if it finds that the findings below were clearly erroneous.

(C) The appellate court may reverse if it determines that the findings were against the weight of the evidence.

_____

113. P sues D for copyright infringement. At the outset of the action, the federal court grants a preliminary injunction against any further publication by D of the material that allegedly infringes P's copyright, pending trial of the case. Can D appeal the order granting this injunction?

_____

114. P sues D to quiet title to certain real property. At a trial to the court, P introduces both hearsay and nonhearsay evidence to support his claim. D objects to the hearsay, but her objection is overruled. The court grants judgment for P. D appeals on the ground that the judgment rests as much on inadmissible hearsay as it does on nonhearsay. Should the appellate court reverse?

_____

PRECLUSIVE EFFECTS OF JUDGMENTS

115. P unreasonably delays prosecution of his lawsuit against D, resulting in the court's dismissing his action. If the statute of limitations has not run, can P file a new action against D on the same claim and obtain a judgment?

_____

116. A sued B for damages for breach of contract and obtained a judgment. Thereafter, B sued A for damages, alleging that A had fraudulently induced him to enter into the contract sued upon in the first case. A moves for summary judgment on ground of res judicata. Should the court grant the motion?

_____

117. W sued H for installments due under their divorce property settlement agreement. H defended on the ground that W was in breach of the agreement. However, the

court granted judgment for W. Later, W sues H for other installments coming due under the agreement. H now raises the defense that the agreement was void and illegal because of fraud perpetrated by W at the time it was signed. W moves to strike H's defense, claiming issue preclusion. Should the court grant the motion? _____

118. A sued B for $500 damage to his car sustained in a traffic accident. B defended on the ground that he was not negligent and that even if he were, A was contributorily negligent. The jury returned a general verdict for A. Meanwhile, B had filed a $50,000 suit against A in a superior court for personal injuries sustained in the same accident. When the judgment in the A-B action became final, A moved for summary judgment against B's suit on the ground of issue preclusion. Should the court grant the motion? _____

119. A bus owned and operated by Buslines, Inc., and driven by Driver was involved in a traffic accident. Several passengers were injured, including P and X.

    a.   P sued Driver for negligence, and the jury returned a verdict for Driver. P thereupon filed suit against Buslines, alleging that it was vicariously liable for Driver's negligence (respondeat superior) and was also negligent in hiring Driver. Buslines moves for summary judgment against P's suit. Should the court grant the motion? _____

    b.   Assume P sued Buslines first on the respondeat superior theory and lost. P then files suit against Driver for negligence. Driver claims P is precluded by the first suit. Should the court sustain the defense? _____

    c.   Assume P sued Driver and won a judgment. P now files suit against Buslines on a respondeat superior theory and moves for a ruling that Buslines's liability was established by the judgment against Driver. Should the court grant the motion? _____

    d.   Assume P sued Buslines on a respondeat superior theory and won. Now another passenger on the same bus, X, brings suit against Buslines on the same theory and moves to establish liability on the basis of P's judgment against Buslines. Should the court grant X's motion? _____

Answers to Review Questions

1. **PROBABLY NOT**   Tradition holds that personal service within the state is always adequate to sustain personal jurisdiction and the Supreme Court has upheld "transient jurisdiction" over a nonresident temporarily within a state (although there was no majority opinion and some Justices expressed doubt if the presence were not intentional or voluntary). [§8]

2. **PROBABLY**   The action of D's patient in driving to State A probably establishes no meaningful contact between D and State A. *See World-Wide Volkswagen v. Woodson,* in which plaintiffs drove a car purchased from one defendant in New York to Oklahoma, where they had an accident; the Supreme Court found there was no constitutional basis for jurisdiction in Oklahoma. [§29]

3. **NO**   Distribution of the drug in State A establishes a minimum contact between D and the forum state; and as long as the state has authorized the method of service of process used here through long arm legislation, there is no constitutional objection to the exercise of jurisdiction. [§31]

4. **PROBABLY NOT**   An agreement appointing an agent is a valid means of forum selection by contract unless, perhaps, the contract was an overreaching by a powerful party. [§94]

5. **NO**   Lack of jurisdiction over the person is a defense which is waived if not raised at the first opportunity. D appeared and defended at trial, and thereby waived the objection. [§§101, 105]

6. **PROBABLY YES**   If D was induced to enter the state by fraud, which seems to be the case here, the service of process is invalid. [§112]

7. **NO**   Defendant does not reside there, and it is not where a substantial part of the events or omissions giving rise to the claim occurred. [§§146-147, 152]

8. **YES, NO**   When an action is brought in a federal district court where venue is improper, under 28 U.S.C. section 1406(a), the court may either dismiss it or transfer it to a district where the action could have been brought. [§188] Transfers for the convenience of parties or witnesses can be made only to a district in which venue *would be proper originally* (and here, venue was never proper in New York). [§194]

9. **YES**   Unlike motions to transfer for improper venue, motions for convenience transfers can be made by *either* party. [§195]

10.	**YES**	In diversity suits, venue is proper *either* in the district where any defendant resides, if all defendants reside in the same state, *or* in a district where a substantial part of the acts or omissions giving rise to the claim occurred. [§§**146-147, 152**]
11.	**PROBABLY NONE**	There is no state in which *all* defendants reside, nor any judicial district in which a substantial part of the acts or omissions giving rise to the claim occurred. There might, however, be venue in a district where either ship involved in the collision has its home port, or perhaps where it is located, or (lacking any other basis for venue) in a district where a defendant was subject to personal jurisdiction when the action was commenced. [§§**146-164**]
12.	**PROBABLY NOT**	If defendant will not waive service, does not live with anyone who can be served, and cannot be found, and if state or federal law authorizes assertion of jurisdiction by seizure of property, service by seizure is permissible. The Constitution requires reasonable efforts at providing actual notice of the action and of the opportunity to be heard, which requirements could be satisfied if D used the cottage with some frequency. [§**225**]
13.	**POSSIBLY**	Service may be made by any method authorized by state law where the court is located or process is served. In some states, service by mail on nonresidents is allowed. Moreover, under Federal Rule 4, plaintiff may request waiver of service by mailing the request and complaint to the defendant, and defendant has a duty to waive to avoid costs. Thus, under either approach service might be proper or waived (although if defendant refuses to waive service and state law does not allow service by mail, plaintiff must serve defendant in person or by leaving a summons and complaint with a "person of suitable age and discretion" residing at the defendant's home). [§§**116, 239-250**]
14.	**PROBABLY**	D was constitutionally entitled to notice and hearing before the attachment of his property. This rule generally applies even when the attachment is for the purpose of establishing jurisdiction. Once the garnishment is quashed, there is no jurisdictional basis for the proceeding, although the lack of jurisdiction could be cured by service of process. [§§**269-272**]
15.a.	**NO**	Diversity jurisdiction is determined by the residence of the *members* of the partnership. [§**321**]
b.	**YES**	A corporation is a citizen of any state where it is incorporated, *and* of the state where it has its principal place of business, but not of every state in which it operates. [§§**317-318**]
16.	**(B) and (C)**	Diversity can be based on *alienage*—i.e., all citizens on one side and all aliens on the other (A). [§**310**] (B) is correct because a United States citizen living abroad permanently *cannot sue or be sued* on the basis of diversity of citizenship (no United States domicile). [§**315**] On causes of action belonging to an

incompetent person, diversity depends on the residence of the incompetent person. [§330]

17. **(B) and (E)**   As long as diversity exists *at the time suit is filed,* the federal court has diversity jurisdiction. Thus, it makes no difference that P moved into the state for the purpose of creating such jurisdiction as long as P genuinely changed citizenship (A) [§333] or that once the suit was filed, diversity terminated (C) [§334]. The fact that neither party resides in the state where the court is located (D) may be relevant as to *venue* [§§146-164], but has no effect on diversity jurisdiction. [§313] Where claims are *assigned* for collection (E), the residence of the *assignor* determines diversity. [§340]

18. **PERHAPS**   There is diversity, but it is not complete. The jurisdictional defect might be cured by dismissal of one of the diversity-destroying parties, if he is not necessary to disposition. But if all are "indispensable," dismissal must result. [§§348-349]

19. **YES**   The jurisdictional amount is lacking, and lack of subject matter jurisdiction can be raised at any time. [§§282, 351]

20. **YES**   As long as the claim was filed in good faith, jurisdiction is not affected by the fact that the judgment ultimately recovered does not exceed the jurisdictional minimum. (But in such a case the court has discretion to deny costs to the plaintiff.) [§§353, 355, 357]

21. **YES**   Claims by a single plaintiff against a single defendant *can* be aggregated. [§362]

22. **NO**   Claims against several defendants can be aggregated only if it is shown that they are *jointly* liable on each claim. [§363]

23. **NO**   Claims by multiple plaintiffs against a single defendant can be aggregated only when plaintiffs assert a *joint* right to relief. [§364]

24. **YES**   Although there is diversity of citizenship, under a decisional exception to diversity jurisdiction, the federal courts lack jurisdiction over divorce, alimony, child custody, and probate cases. [§369]

25. **YES**   The involvement of federal law is merely incidental to the claim, which is essentially one of simple contract arising under the common law of the state. [§389]

26. **YES**   To the extent that the federal issue is raised by the complaint, it is not "well pleaded," but anticipates a defense. Only the defense, not the claim, arises under federal law. [§§392-393]

27.a. **NO**   Antitrust claims under the Sherman Act are within the *exclusive* jurisdiction of federal courts. [§296]

b.	**YES**	Under supplemental jurisdiction. [§§426-434]
28.	**YES**	Where the right exists, it belongs to all defendants *jointly*, except in cases in which one defendant can remove on the ground that it is the subject of a "separate and independent claim." [§477]
29.a.	**NO**	A plaintiff is *never* entitled to removal. Having filed in the state court, he must remain there. [§476]
b.	**NO**	Removal is not allowed in diversity actions in which any properly joined and served defendant is a resident of the state in which the action is filed. [§464]
30.	**YES**	On removal, the federal court has jurisdiction even if the state court lacked subject matter jurisdiction; the federal court's jurisdiction is no longer viewed as "derivative." Brown could, however, move to dismiss in state court for lack of subject matter jurisdiction rather than removing. [§482]
31.	**NO**	Unless there is statutory provision for exclusive federal jurisdiction, state courts exercise concurrent jurisdiction over claims that are within the federal jurisdiction and must accept such cases. [§§293-294]
32.	**YES**	The Supreme Court has held that, although Federal Rule 3 says that an action is commenced by the filing of a complaint, it was not intended to provide thereby for "tolling" of the limitations period in a state law action. Because the duration of limitations is a matter of state law, the definition of the events that toll it is also governed by state law, which can coexist with Rule 3, because there is no conflict between the rule and the state law provisions. [§538]
33.	**YES**	There appears to be a clear conflict between the state and federal provisions. The Federal Rules of Evidence were passed by Congress, so they are valid if "arguably procedural." Determinations about the admissibility of hearsay evidence seem to be arguably procedural, so that under *Hanna* the federal rule should be applied. [§542] (Note, however, that with regard to issues of privilege, Federal Rule of Evidence 501 in fact directs that state law should be applied in federal court with regard to issues governed by state law.)
34.	**PROBABLY**	The federal rule is judge-made, and the cases are divided on whether federal or state law governs on the sufficiency of the evidence for a case to go to the jury. The emerging majority view, however, favors the federal standard, especially when the question goes to whether judge or jury should evaluate the sufficiency of the evidence, rather than to the elements of the claim or the definition of the persuasion burden. Relations between judge and jury in federal court are an appropriate subject for determination by federal law. [§547]
35.	**UNCLEAR**	The task for the federal court is to determine how the state supreme court would resolve the issue, not to select the "better" legal rule. But a court should not be blind to trends in the law, and if there is reason to believe that the state

supreme court would not adhere to the older rule, the federal court should not do so. On the other hand, state appellate decisions are, in general, good indications of the content of state law, and the court should have some reason grounded in more recent, analogous state court decisions for disregarding the earlier decision squarely on point. [§§555-559]

36. **NO**   The court looks to the *facts* alleged, not the caption of the complaint or even the pleader's apparent legal theory. The complaint sufficiently pleads negligence (failure to give warning of known danger), and hence sufficiently states a claim on which relief can be granted. [§582]

37.a. **PROBABLY**   The allegations are sufficient if they give D *notice* of the *general nature* of the claim against him. After the pleading stage, however, the federal courts would demand sufficient factual matter to satisfy all elements of the claim. [§593]

b. **NO**   The allegations are not of "ultimate facts"—*i.e.*, the word "improperly" does *not* present a legal issue (negligence, warranty, strict liability). [§§588-590]

38. **NO**   Allegations on information or belief are proper only if the pleader lacks personal knowledge. Where, as here, he has *constructive knowledge* (*i.e.*, matters of public record), the allegation is insufficient. [§§608-611]

39. **NO**   In federal courts, pleaders are entitled to state their claims or defenses "regardless of consistency." (*Compare:* The result is contra in many code pleading states, particularly if the complaint is verified.) Plaintiff might, however, face sanctions under Federal Rule 11 if the factual allegations were made without "evidentiary support." [§§612-615, 630-634, 768-806]

40. **YES**   In a default case, the relief granted cannot exceed or differ in kind from that prayed for in the complaint. [§621]

41. **YES**   Usually, of course, P need not anticipate defenses. But when he has done so (settlement as release of claim), he must also *plead around* the defense. Allegations that the settlement was a "fraud" are not enough, because fraud must always be *pleaded with particularity*, even under the Federal Rules. [§§648, 650] Dismissal on such facts would ordinarily be with leave to amend.

42. **YES**   In most code pleading states, the defamatory words must be set forth verbatim. (The rule is contra under notice pleading.) [§653]

43. **(A), (B) and (C)**   The complaint alleges "general damages," which is sufficient to cover pain, discomfort, and disability. However, medical expenses (past or future) are *special damages* and must be specially pleaded. Similarly, punitive damages must be specially pleaded. [§§667, 669-670]

44.a. **YES**   There is no requirement of subject matter relationship among the claims joined against a *single* defendant. (State rules are contra.) [§684]

b.	**YES**	If there are multiple parties, one claim by or against them must arise out of the same transaction and involve a common question of law or fact. [§685]
45.	**PROBABLY**	Some courts deny a motion to strike where *no responsive pleading* is due. But the better view is to strike immaterial allegations to prevent such matters from being read to the jury at trial. [§§743-744]
46.	**YES**	D is never compelled to file a motion to dismiss. Raising the venue objection in his answer sufficiently preserves it. [§§749-750] However, some courts treat failure to raise the defense by motion as a forfeiture of the defense. [§753]
47.	**YES**	When the defendant *does* make a motion to dismiss, he must raise certain defenses and objections which he could raise by the motion, including venue, or he waives them. [§§749-751]
48.	**NO**	Failure to state a claim can be raised at any time. [§§749, 751]
49.	**YES**	A court may grant a motion to dismiss premised on a defense that appears on the face of the complaint. [§756]
50.	**YES**	The rule in code pleading states is that defendant must file *specific* denials to a verified complaint, because there is usually something which ought to be admitted. (*Note:* The federal rule is contra.) [§§817-820]
51.	**YES**	A failure to deny constitutes an admission. [§830]
52.	**NO**	In *federal* actions, allegations of damages are deemed controverted even if not denied. *Compare:* The rule in *state* courts in code pleading states is usually contra—*i.e.*, where a sum of money is alleged to be due, it must be *specifically* denied. [§831]
53.	**(B) and (D)**	Truth (A) is an affirmative defense and must be specially pleaded as new matter. Likewise, as to any release or settlement (C). However, proof that no one heard (B) is admissible under the general denial, as it contradicts the element of publication, which is a part of P's case. Likewise, evidence as to the extent of damages (D) contradicts P's case and is admissible under the general denial. [§§833-838]
54.	**NO**	In federal actions, objections to venue are waived if not raised in the initial answer. Subsequent amendments to add such objections are *not* allowed. [§§185, 750]
55.	**NONE**	Allegations of D's answers are *deemed controverted.* No responsive pleading by P is required to preserve the issues raised thereby. [§865]
56.	**ONLY (C)**	(A) is wrong because the counterclaim *should be* a part of D's answer. [§868] (B) is wrong because no subject matter relationship is required. [§868] (C) is

right because when a counterclaim is only *permissive* (not arising out of same transaction as complaint), there must be an independent ground for federal jurisdiction (here the parties are diverse, but the claim is for only $5,000). [§870] (D) is wrong because other parties can be joined when necessary. [§§876-880]

57. **NO**   P's filing of a complaint *tolls* the statute of limitations for counterclaims arising out of the same transaction. For limitations purposes, D's counterclaim "relates back" to the time P filed his complaint and hence is timely. (A minority view allows *any* counterclaim to be used defensively, even after the statute has run.) [§§888-890]

58. **(B) and (C)**   (A) is wrong because no affirmative relief is sought; D's "claim" is merely a defense. (D) is wrong because there must be a subject matter relationship to P's complaint. (B) and (C) are proper because there is the requisite subject matter relationship; claims for indemnity or contribution are permissible. [§§893-894]

59. **NO**   Cross-claims lie only against co-defendants. Claims against an outside party must be asserted by *impleader*. (Most courts permit impleader only if indemnification or contribution is sought; under this view, D2 would be permitted to implead D3 only if there were a claim for indemnification, but might then be permitted also to seek affirmative relief—*i.e.*, to recover for damage to his car.) [§1072]

60.a. **YES**   Amendments relating to the same transaction "relate back" for limitations purposes. A change in the nature or theory of the action does not prejudice D. [§§923-924]

   b. **PROBABLY NOT**   Amendments to bring in *new parties* after the statute of limitations has run are permitted only in limited circumstances. This amendment involves adding a party, not changing a party or the naming of a party against whom a claim is asserted, and would probably be allowed only under a liberal state policy on relation back. [§§925-931]

61. **NO**   Federal Rule 15(c)(1) allows relation back when it is permitted by the law providing the applicable statute of limitations. [§924]

62.a. **PROBABLY**   Here, the defendant appears to have had notice of the pendency of the action, and probably knew or should have known of the naming mistake. [§925]

   b. **DISCRE-TIONARY**   Even though such an amendment would be freely allowed *before* trial, courts are more reluctant to permit such amendments at the time of trial. In state practice, they may find a "material variance" where the relief sought by the amendment differs significantly. Federal practice is more liberal, putting the burden on the objecting party to show *prejudice* (although a continuance to enable D to prepare would usually remedy such claims). [§§937-950]

c. **YES**		P should be permitted to file a *supplemental complaint* to allege occurrence of developments after the date of her original complaint, where no alteration of the basic claim is involved. [§§953-957]
63.	**PROBABLY NOT**	The federal court has *discretion* to refuse; but such a refusal here is likely to be an abuse of discretion, at least if P could not have known sooner about the witness's unwillingness. [§981]
64.	**ALL EXCEPT (B)**	The person having the *right to sue* (*i.e.*, legal title to the claim) is the "real party in interest." (B) is wrong because usually only the trustee has the right to sue third persons for wrongs to the trust estate. [§§986, 1003]
65.	**PROBABLY NOT**	Unless serious injustice would result, D may be estopped to raise the issue by direct or collateral attack. [§§1012-1013]
66.	**NO**	In a diversity action, capacity of such a party is determined by the law of the state in which the federal court is located. [§1021]
67.	**NO**	Samantha *is* the real party in interest. The correct challenge would be that she lacks capacity (as a minor). However, this challenge is *waived* if not timely made. [§§986, 1015-1016]
68.a.	**YES**	Under modern rules, joinder of claims against multiple parties is proper as long as the claims arise out of the same transaction, occurrence, or series of transactions or occurrences; there is a common question of fact or law; and the defendants may be jointly or severally liable (or liable "in the alternative"). [§§1033-1037]
b.	**YES**	Basically, as long as the rules on joinder of *parties* are satisfied (above), so are the rules on joinder of claims. [§1038]
c.	**YES**	By alleging the facts showing *why* he is "in doubt," P is entitled to join defendants and claims *in the alternative*. [§1035]
69.	**NO**	But the actions should be severed because there is no connection between the transactions. If the questions of law or fact are sufficiently common to the two cases, they might be reconsolidated for the purpose of trial. [§§1033, 1116]
70.	**PROBABLY NOT**	If D2 can be joined, she should be, in order to give effective protection to D1's right to contribution. However, the court can and should proceed to enforce P's right if the joinder of D2 is not feasible or if it would destroy the jurisdiction of the court. If the obstacle to joinder is incomplete diversity, some federal courts might dismiss, leaving P to sue both D1 and D2 in state court. [§§1047-1050]
71.	**YES**	In federal court, and in most states, partial assignees or subrogees are necessary but not indispensable parties who should be joined if feasible to prevent a multiplicity of actions or inconsistent results, and the court can compel joinder of A as an involuntary plaintiff. [§1054]

72.	**YES**	The corporation must be joined as a plaintiff, but its joinder destroys the basis for federal jurisdiction; and the action must therefore be dismissed for want of federal jurisdiction. [§§1060, 1063, 1067]
73.a.	**YES**	D should file a third-party complaint against TP showing why TP should be held liable on a theory of *indemnification* for whatever liability D has to P. [§§1071-1072]
b.	**YES**	Because the impleader claim is deemed ancillary to the P-D lawsuit, TP's residence has *no* effect on jurisdiction and venue. [§1087]
74.a.	**PROBABLY NOT**	There is clearly no *right* to intervene. Permissive intervention can be granted where there is a "common question of law or fact," but here, there is only an inference that T's illness was caused by the same condition that caused P's. [§§1089, 1105]
b.	**PROBABLY NOT**	In this situation, intervention is unnecessary because a finding that Duchess is liable to P for selling a sandwich containing impure ingredients would not be binding on XYZ or affect its ability to defend against Duchess's claim for indemnification in a separate action, if Duchess fails to implead XYZ in the suit brought by P. [§§1089, 1095]
75.a.	**YES**	The Federal Interpleader Act permits a stakeholder to deposit a disputed debt with the court if the amount is at least $500 and diversity exists between the adverse *claimants*. [§1125]
b.	**YES**	Nationwide service is authorized in statutory interpleader. [§1133]
76.	**YES**	A class action is appropriate, since the issues and relief are identical for all members of the class. The number of students involved (and possibly the small amount of their individual claims) also makes a class suit the most practical way of resolving the issue, because nothing would be gained by requiring each member to litigate the same issue separately; *i.e.*, common questions *predominate*. [§§1177-1181]
77.	**(B)**	In federal class actions, *each* claim must exceed the jurisdictional minimum. (A) is wrong because diversity is determined only from residence of the *representative* (P). (C) is wrong because the common sales practices, if proved, could be the requisite "common question," although that might be more difficult with oral representations. [§§1155-1159, 1198-1199]
78.	**NO**	It is reversible error for the court to premise its certification decision on the likelihood of plaintiffs' success on the merits. [§1210]
79.a.	**YES**	*See* Fed. R. Civ. P. 23(c)(2). [§1223]
b.	**YES**	This is the impact of the *Eisen* case. [§1230]

c. **NO** Those who opt out are not bound. [§1260]

80. **NO** Because (i) there is no showing that adequate *notice* of the pending settlement was given to the class members, and (ii) the special recovery obtained by P indicates that she did *not* adequately represent their interests. In federal courts, the court would have to decide whether to approve any settlement of the class suit. [§§1249-1254]

81. **NO** Prior to December 2000, the Rule 26(a)(1) obligation of disclosure applied only to disputed facts alleged with particularity, but did not distinguish between materials favorable to the disclosing party and those harmful to that party's position. Effective December 2000, the rule was revised to require disclosure only of materials the disclosing party *"may use to support its claims or defenses."* Although that could be true of a document that contained harmful information, it usually would not be, and in any event Rule 26(a)(1) does not require disclosure of the contents of documents; it requires only a listing of them. [§§1291, 1298]

82. **NO** In federal practice, P may serve notice on a corporate party stating the *matters* upon which the deposition will be based. It is then up to the corporation to produce employees having knowledge as to such matters. [§1323]

83.a. **DEPENDS** If E is *unavailable* to testify, his deposition is admissible; otherwise it is not. [§1347]

b. **YES** The deposition of the adverse party or the officer of an adverse corporate party is admissible as substantive evidence. [§1345]

84.a. **NONE** Depositions to perpetuate testimony are proper before filing suit only when P can show that she is *unable* to sue now. Such depositions cannot (in federal practice) be used simply to determine the merits of P's claim. Rule 11 does not pose an obstacle to P's ability to bring suit now if she can assert that allegations against D are likely to have evidentiary support after an opportunity for discovery. [§1310]

b. **SUBPOENA FOR PRODUCTION OR DEPOSITION** A *nonparty* cannot be required to produce documents by a *request* to produce under Rule 34, but he can be *subpoenaed* under Rule 45 to produce them or to attend a deposition and to bring with him evidence in his control. [§1401]

c. **SUBPOENA FOR INSPECTION** A nonparty may be subpoenaed to permit inspection of premises in his control. [§1401]

d. **NO** A motion to compel a physical examination applies only to *parties*. [§1406]

85. **NONE** (A) is wrong because a party is deemed in control of that which is in his attorney's possession. [§1396] (B) is wrong because the work-product privilege

does not apply to evidence unearthed by the attorney. [§1384] (C) is wrong because a request to produce requires neither a court order nor a showing of good cause. [§1387]

86.	**YES**	By so requesting, the examined party becomes bound to provide copies of his own medical reports on the condition at issue. [§§1412-1413]
87.a.	**MOTION GRANTED**	Discovery is proper as to information which may *lead* to admissible evidence; the information itself need not be admissible. [§1420]
b.	**MOTION GRANTED**	A party's factual contentions are usually discoverable in order to flush into the open all claims or defenses. [§1442]
c.	**MOTION DENIED**	The test for the outer limits of discovery relevancy is whether the information relates to the "subject matter of the action," and that is only on court order. Otherwise discovery must be relevant to the claim or defense of a party. Unless P can somehow show that an earlier lawsuit relates to *his* claim of food poisoning, the discovery appears to be improper. [§1434]
d.	**MOTION DENIED**	Even though many courts permit discovery of insurance coverage (and the federal courts require disclosure without a discovery request of insurance agreements), most do *not* permit discovery of a defendant's financial status except in connection with claims for punitive damages. [§§1437-1441]
e.	**MOTION DENIED**	The testing would probably be treated as opinions obtained from experts retained to advise counsel. Unless they are going to testify, discovery may be allowed only in extraordinary circumstances. No such circumstances have been stated, although it might be possible to justify discovery if the allegedly tainted food no longer exists, so that P cannot test it now. [§§1506-1511]
88.	**ALL EXCEPT (C)**	(A) is right because parties generally may not initiate discovery in federal court without meeting to discuss, among other matters, a discovery plan. [§1354] (B) is right; interrogatories can be served only on parties (though these need not be adverse parties). [§1351] Unless the 25-question limit has been reached, (C) is not a ground for objection, although it may be grounds for a protective order. [§1462] (D) is right because interrogatories, including discrete subparts, may not exceed 25 in number without leave of court. [§1356]
89.	**(B)**	(A) is wrong because no such sanction may be imposed when there has been no prior court order to answer. [§1591] (B) is correct. [§1382] (C) is wrong because in federal practice (*e.g.*, copyright case), requests can be directed even as to the ultimate issues in the case. [§1368]
90.	**ONLY (A)**	A nonparty is not required to answer questions unless subpoenaed. [§§1319, 1322] But D has the right to conduct an investigation [§1613], and the exclusionary rule has no application to this situation [§1615]. The statements are clearly work product and there is no apparent reason for requiring them to be

disclosed. [§§1479, 1496] *Note:* In federal practice, the witnesses themselves have a right to a copy of their own statements. [§1503]

91. **NO** A motion for summary judgment must be *denied* if the essential facts are controverted by a witness competent to testify. If P claims to have seen the accident, that should suffice. Credibility cannot be determined at this stage. [§§1635, 1637]

92. **PROBABLY NOT** Assuming P has the burden of proving D's knowing deceit at trial (at least a debatable issue if there is no question that the statements were in fact false), it is likely that the court would find the surrounding circumstances sufficient to support the inference that D knew of their falsity, despite D's protestations of innocence. [§1638] Nevertheless, P cannot rely entirely on the jury's disbelief of D's testimony to satisfy P's burden of producing evidence of D's knowledge. [§1641]

93. **NO** The affidavit in support of the motion must be based on facts within the *personal knowledge* of the affiant, not hearsay or opinions. [§1668]

94.a. **YES** *Partial* summary judgment can be granted as to certain claims or issues, reserving the balance for trial. [§1667]

  b. **YES** A summary judgment can be based on any admissible evidence, including comparison of the songs. [§§1669-1672]

95.a. **YES** The court not only has the power to set such deadlines, but under Rule 16, it is required to set such deadlines early in the action. [§1692]

  b. **YES** If the court so orders, under its authority to require that a party or its representative be present or reasonably available by telephone to discuss settlement. [§1704]

  c. **PROBABLY** Rule 16 authorizes trial judges to use "special procedures to assist in resolving the dispute when authorized by statute or local rule." [§1757]

  d. **PROBABLY NOT** The final pretrial order should be amended only to avoid "manifest injustice." Unless there is some justification for P's failure to list this witness in the final pretrial order, the court would be justified in excluding the witness unless he is essential to P's case. Because the matter is discretionary, however, the court would have the power to allow the witness to testify. [§1720]

96. **ALL EXCEPT (B)** The right to jury trial extends to all actions "at law." Historically, (A) was "at law," while (B) was in equity. Where legal and equitable claims are joined (C), the *federal* rule is that the jury right must be preserved as to the legal claims (damages). There is a jury right in (D) because the court looks to the basic substance of the relief sought—here, to prevent tort liability (damages) for past acts. [§§1772, 1788]

97.	**YES**	In federal practice, the claim for legal relief (damages) *must* be tried first, to preserve the right of jury trial on the fraud issue free of binding prior adjudication on the equitable claim. [§§1789, 1791]
98.	**NO**	As long as a prima facie case is made out, a motion for judgment as a matter of law *must* be denied. [§§1865-1890]
99.	**PROBABLY NOT**	To prevail on a motion for judgment as a matter of law, the party with the burden of proof must put on such a strong case that the jury could not reasonably disbelieve it. Ordinarily, the jury could disbelieve witnesses on the basis of their demeanor while testifying; given the fact that D's lawyer thinks the witnesses are not likely to be believed, this does not seem to be a case in which the jury would have to believe them. [§§1868, 1880]
100.	**NONE**	A trial judge may call and interrogate a witness on her own (A). [§1857] The judge may also comment on the evidence, including the credibility of a witness (B) in *most* states (minority contra). [§§1912-1913] Failure to object to a jury instruction (C) is usually considered a waiver of any objection thereto, unless the error is so fundamental that it deprives a party of a fair trial. The instruction here is somewhat confusing, but does not seem to be fundamental in the foregoing sense. [§1920]
101.	**PROBABLY**	Since the jury may have based its verdict solely on the one defense as to which the instructions were incorrect, most courts would reverse. [§§1920-1921]
102.	**NO**	When inconsistent with the verdict, the jury's answers to interrogatories may control over their general verdict. [§1933]
103.	**(A) and (C) (most courts)**	The modern rule is that concealed grounds for disqualification (A) may be proved by juror affidavit. [§§1953-1954] Few courts, however, would permit juror affidavits to attack the deliberations themselves (B). [§§1948-1949] On the other hand, affidavits by outsiders (C) are generally admissible to show improper deliberations, and an agreement to be bound by majority rule when unanimity is required is clearly improper. [§§1937, 1948]
104.	**NONE**	(A) does not establish "juror misconduct" because it was known to D *during* the trial and he chose to do nothing about it (such as a motion for mistrial). [§1977] (B) might amount to fraud on the court, but usually trial verdicts may not be set aside on the basis of allegedly false testimony. [§§1975-1983] (C) does not establish "accident or surprise" because it fails to show that D had done all he could to procure W's attendance—*i.e.*, subpoenaing him. [§§1978-1983]
105.	**NEW TRIAL GRANTED**	Judgment as a matter of law cannot be granted because there is some evidence to support the verdict. [§1961] But the trial judge may order a new trial if he finds that the verdict is contrary to the weight of the evidence. [§1986]

106.	**NO**	In federal practice the trial court does *not* have the power of "additur." [§§2023-2024]
107.	**NO**	There is a *one-year limitation period* in federal practice for a motion for relief from judgment. [§2043]
108.	**YES**	D can bring a separate suit in equity to set aside the judgment. [§2045]
109.	**NO**	Time limits for filing appeals are usually jurisdictional. The Federal Rules permit the *trial* court to extend time for 30 days, but the appellate court cannot do so. [§§2082-2085]
110.	**NO**	P's voluntary acceptance of the benefits of a judgment *waives* his right to appeal therefrom. [§2061]
111.	**NO**	The final judgment rule bars any appeal of most interlocutory orders, and interlocutory review of discovery orders is especially rare. (However, appellate review by extraordinary writ may be available.) [§§2094-2107]
112.	**(B)**	Clear error is the correct test. [§§2141-2142]
113.	**YES**	Review of preliminary injunctions is one of the generally recognized "exceptions" to the final judgment rule. However, appellate review is generally limited to whether the trial court abused its *discretion* in granting the injunction. [§§2113, 2152-2153]
114.	**PROBABLY NOT**	In *nonjury* cases (quiet title) it is presumed that the trial judge considered only the legally admissible evidence in arriving at his decision. [§§2154-2156]
115.	**NO**	An involuntary dismissal is usually treated as a judgment on the merits, so it bars any later action on the same claim. [§2209]
116.	**YES**	B's fraud claim would have been a *compulsory counterclaim* in most jurisdictions, and since it was not raised in the first suit, it is *barred.* [§2222]
117.	**NO**	The first judgment is a bar with respect to the installments then in question. But it is preclusive only as to the issues *"actually litigated."* Since the fraud issue was not litigated, it can be raised with respect to the *later* installments. [§§2226-2227]
118.	**YES**	The general verdict in the A-B action necessarily found that B was negligent and A was not. The issue preclusion effect of those findings is fatal to B's claims against A in the second action. [§2234]
119.a.	**YES**	Buslines's liability, if any, is *derivative, i.e.,* predicated on a showing that Driver was negligent. P litigated and lost this issue in the first action and, thus, is barred from relitigating it in the second action. [§2258]

b. **DEPENDS**   If the sole issue in the first suit was Driver's negligence, the first judgment should preclude P. However, if Buslines raised some other defense (*e.g.*, Driver was not acting in course and scope of employment), the result would be contra. [§2235]

c. **NO**   Buslines should not be bound because it had no opportunity to litigate in the first case. Driver may or may not have defended it properly. [§2252]

d. **PROBABLY**   Even offensive use of issue preclusion by a stranger to the prior action is usually permissible in most jurisdictions, absent any of several special circumstances (such as much smaller damage exposure in the first action) that might make it unfair to give issue preclusive effect to rulings in the first action. [§§2260-2261]

Exam Questions and Answers

QUESTION I

Mitsui Machinery Co., a Japanese manufacturer, makes high-temperature ovens for heating nonferrous metals. The ovens are shipped from Japan to Mitsui-American Co., a California corporation that is a wholly owned sales subsidiary based in Los Angeles. Mitsui-American sells the ovens to various metals fabricators in the United States, including Pot Line Co., a Delaware corporation, whose principal place of business is in Utah. John Worker, a citizen of Utah, is an employee of Equipment Service Co., a Utah corporation that services manufacturing equipment, including the equipment at Pot Line.

A. Worker is injured while engaged in repairing a Mitsui oven at the Pot Line plant. Under Utah law, Worker's only remedy against Equipment Service Co. is under the workers' compensation law. Under Utah law, it is also arguable that his only remedy against Pot Line is limited to the workers' compensation law. Apart from any claim that Worker might have against Mitsui and Mitsui-American, what proceedings should he initiate? Explain.

B. Worker wishes to sue on the basis that the oven was of defective design. Can he join Mitsui Machinery and Mitsui-American, and if so, in what court or courts? Explain.

C. Assume Worker named Mitsui Machinery and Mitsui-American as defendants in an action in Utah state or federal court, and in connection with that action filed a writ of attachment upon Pot Line, asserting attachment jurisdiction over $35,000 due from Pot Line to Mitsui in payment for the oven.

    1. Assuming that Utah has state rules modeled on the Federal Rules of Civil Procedure in relevant respects, by what procedure may Mitsui Machinery and Mitsui-American challenge the attachment?

    2. Would the challenge be sustained?

D. Assume that the First National Bank of Utah had financed Pot Line's purchase of the oven and, upon learning of the attachment, is concerned that its rights under a chattel mortgage on the oven may be jeopardized by the attachment. What procedures might the bank use to protect its interest?

E. Assume that Worker sued Pot Line for damages on the theory that the oven was defective and that Pot Line impleaded Mitsui for indemnity. While discovery was being conducted, Pot Line settled with Worker for $200,000 and Worker's action against Pot Line is dismissed "with prejudice." What effect does that judgment have on Pot Line's claim against Mitsui?

QUESTION II

The Republican Party is an unincorporated association with headquarters in Washington, D.C. Paul Buchan, a member of the Party who lives in Virginia, decides to run as the Reform Party candidate for President. The National Committee of the Republican Party expels Buchan. He brings suit for reinstatement in the United States District Court for the Eastern District of Virginia, alleging that the expulsion violates the First Amendment and also his rights under the common law governing unincorporated associations. He also asks for damages. Analyze whether and on what basis a damages award would be binding against the Republican Party as an organization and against individual members of the Party.

QUESTION III

John Moline is a citizen of Illinois; Harry Duffalo is a citizen of New York. They enter into a joint venture for buying machinery in the United States and selling it in various parts of the world, Moline doing the buying and Duffalo doing the selling. The venture has an office in Chicago, at which Moline works regularly and to which Duffalo visits from time to time. After the business has been going for a while, Moline becomes suspicious that Duffalo has been cheating him by holding back payments from sales. By September 1999, Moline has collected enough evidence to convince himself of Duffalo's cheating, but on September 15, 1999, he suddenly dies of a heart attack.

On May 1, 2000, Moline's widow, as executor of his estate, commences an action in U.S. district court in Chicago against Duffalo to recover $550,000 of payments allegedly held back. Process is served on Duffalo in New York on May 5, 2000. On May 15, 2000, Duffalo commences an action in New York state court for (i) $100,000 of profits from the business that he alleges are due him but unpaid and (ii) a declaratory judgment that no sums are owing out of the joint venture accounts except the $100,000 mentioned in his first cause of action. Duffalo serves process on Mrs. Moline in Illinois and also garnishes Allstate Life Insurance Co., which had issued a life insurance policy for $250,000 on John Moline's life.

A.   Does the Illinois court have jurisdiction of this action filed by Mrs. Moline?

B.   Does the New York court have jurisdiction of the action filed by Duffalo?

QUESTION IV

Plaintiff brought an action in a federal district court for (i) specific performance of a contract and incidental damages for defendant's failure to perform on time, or (ii) full damages in case the court refused to order specific performance. Defendant filed an answer denying plaintiff's material allegations and counterclaimed for damages arising out of the same contract dispute.

A.   If plaintiff demands jury trial, what issues, if any, should be tried by a jury?

B. Assume that plaintiff does not demand a jury trial, but defendant does. What issues, if any, should be tried by a jury?

C. Assume that the court strikes defendant's demand and sets all the issues of the case for a court trial. Is the order then reviewable? If so, by what means?

QUESTION V

The sole issue being tried by the jury in a condemnation action was the issue of just compensation. After lengthy deliberation, the jurors advised the court that they could not agree on a verdict. The judge then instructed them that each juror should write his or her valuation on a piece of paper, that they should then divide the total by 12, and that should be their verdict. After returning to the jury room, the jury shortly came in with a verdict of $37,500 in favor of the landowner. Was the instruction proper? Assume that neither the United States (the condemnor) nor the defendant landowner had objected to the court's instruction. On appeal by the defendant-landowner from the judgment entered on the verdict, may the appellant raise the giving of the instruction as error?

QUESTION VI

A Santa Fe railroad freight train hit a school bus at a grade crossing in Lumpe, Texas. The crossing had a sign but no light or gate. Two children were killed and three others and the bus driver were injured. The locomotive engineer was killed by flying debris. An action was brought in federal district court against Santa Fe, a Kansas corporation, on behalf of the children who were killed and injured. In discovery, the depositions were taken of the bus driver, the fireman on the locomotive, and the brakeman on the train.

The fireman said that the train was going "about normal speed, which at that place on the route would be 60 miles an hour." He said that he was at his regular seat in the front of the locomotive cab, looking ahead, when the bus "came up to the tracks and just kept going." He said there is a speedometer in the control panel at his seat but "can't recall" looking at the speedometer in the interval just before the crash.

The brakeman said the train was going "about usual speed, which is supposed to be 60 miles an hour." He did not see the bus until after the collision.

The bus driver says that he slowed down as he approached the grade crossing, did not see the train, and nearly got across the tracks before the train hit the rear of the bus. He admits he did not stop, as required by state law.

Also through discovery, the railroad was compelled to produce the paper tape from the train's speed recorder. This is an automatic device that records the speed at which the train is going at each moment of a run. The tape indicates that the train was going 80 miles per hour at the time of the collision.

Plaintiff moves for summary judgment on the issue of liability, requesting that its previous demand for jury trial be applicable only to the issue of damages. In support of the motion, plaintiff appends the depositions and speed tape described above.

The Texas Constitution provides that in actions at common law, "the jury shall be the judge of the facts and the law."

Should summary judgment be granted?

QUESTION VII

The following is a complaint filed in United States District Court for the District of Connecticut:

1. Plaintiff Jane Smith is a citizen of Connecticut. The amount in controversy herein exceeds $75,000, exclusive of interest and costs.

2. Defendant Electronics Institute, Inc. is a Delaware corporation with its principal place of business in New York. It operates an establishment in New Haven, Connecticut.

3. Defendant advertised a course in electronics technology at a tuition of $2,500. The advertisements claimed that "completion of the course could lead to big money in electronics." Plaintiff enrolled in and completed the course and paid $2,500 in tuition therefor.

4. Plaintiff has been unable to find any employment in electronics at a wage exceeding the minimum wage. Plaintiff is informed and believes and therefore alleges that there are no jobs paying more than $8 per hour in the New Haven area for which the training provided by defendant is necessary and useful.

5. Plaintiff was induced to believe that employment at a high wage would result from taking the course provided by defendant. As a result of thus being misled by defendant, plaintiff suffered embarrassment, humiliation, and loss of self respect, to her damage of $100,000.

6. The training provided by defendant was substantially worthless.

Wherefore, plaintiff prays for restitution in the amount of $2,500; for additional damages in the amount of $100,000; and for interest and costs.

You represent the defendant. Write a memorandum for the file, analyzing motions that you might have good basis for asserting by way of attack on the complaint.

QUESTION VIII

Sierra Club, Inc. is a nonprofit corporation incorporated in California, having its headquarters in San Francisco and an office in Washington, D.C. It has 25,000 members who pay annual dues varying from $25 to $500 and who elect its board of directors. The Club organizes hikes and treks, promotes conservation through public education, and lobbies in Washington and in various state capitals for environmental regulation. In 1999 the Club discovered that persons employed by oil and coal companies were joining in large numbers and suspected an "infiltration" intended to oppose its political activism. In January 2000, Nelson Oil Bunker, a citizen of Texas and a member of the Club and president of Gusher Oil Co., sent a letter to the board demanding that the Club cease lobbying efforts because those efforts could jeopardize the Club's status as a tax exempt organization under the Internal Revenue Code. In February, the Club board adopted a resolution that no person could become or continue as a member except by subscribing to a "statement of principles" that affirmed the Club's involvement in environmental regulation. Bunker refused to sign the statement and demanded a list of Club members to contest the next election of Club directors. In April 2000, the Club board voted to cancel Bunker's membership. Litigation is imminent.

A. If the Club wishes to bring suit against Bunker individually to determine the validity of the cancellation of his membership, in what court or courts could it effectively do so? Identify the court(s) and the legal basis for it (their) being proper court(s).

B. Assume that on April 15, 2000, the Club brought a class suit in California Superior Court, San Francisco County, against three members, one from Texas, one from Nevada, and one from Oklahoma, named individually and as representatives of a class constituting those members who object to the requirement of signing the "statement of principles." The suit asks for a declaratory judgment that the requirement is valid. State a legal argument for the proposition that a judgment for the Club would be binding on Bunker.

C. Assume that, in the situation described in B., Bunker wished to become an individual party to the action. State the basis or bases upon which he could do so, with a supporting legal argument, if he acted (i) while the action was pending in state court and (ii) after the action was removed to federal court.

D. Assume that the suit mentioned in B. was removed to federal court and that the question of giving notice to the members of the class was then presented. Must notice be given to all class members? State reasons. Should Sierra Club be required to pay the cost of giving such notice? State reasons.

QUESTION IX

Kopp, a police officer, attempted to arrest Strong, a young man of 25, in a bar. An altercation resulted in punches; finally Kopp knocked out Strong with her blackjack. Strong subsequently sued Kopp for damages for assault. All six other persons present in the bar testified that Kopp was the aggressor and that Strong tried to avoid the altercation. The jury returned a verdict for Kopp. Within 10 days, Strong moved for a new trial but the motion papers were lost in the mail until 25 days later.

A.   Under the Federal Rules, may the judge grant a new trial? Could he grant a post-verdict judgment as a matter of law in favor of Strong?

B.   Is the answer different under state practice?

ANSWER TO QUESTION I

A. Worker should bring a workers' compensation proceeding against Equipment Service, a remedy limited in amount but very sure of recovery. Worker should also sue Pot Line on the theory that he is not an employee of Pot Line and, therefore, is not limited to a workers' compensation remedy against it. If this theory loses, he may seek a workers' compensation remedy (*see* above). The tort suit should be in Utah state court, not in federal court, because Pot Line has its principal place of business in Utah and, hence, is a co-citizen of Worker, who is also a Utah citizen. Thus, there is no diversity, so the federal court would lack subject matter jurisdiction.

B. Multiple tortfeasors may be joined as defendants under Federal Rule 20 and analogous state rules. Presumably, Utah and California have such provisions.

Subject matter jurisdiction: If the action is to be against Pot Line as well as Mitsui-American and Mitsui Machinery, Worker must proceed in Utah state court because there is no diversity with Pot Line (*see* above), and Pot Line is apparently not amenable to suit in California (there being no apparent contact between Pot Line and California). There is a question of territorial jurisdiction against the Mitsui companies (*see* below). Diversity exists between Worker and Mitsui-American, because Mitsui-American is a California corporation and its principal place of business is not in Utah. Diversity also exists with Mitsui Machinery, because it is an alien corporation.

Territorial jurisdiction: Territorial jurisdiction over Mitsui-American can be established in Utah if Utah has a typical long-arm statute. *International Shoe* contacts of Mitsui-American are plainly sufficient. Hence, Mitsui-American is amenable to suit in Utah state or federal court. Mitsui Machinery is probably subject to Utah territorial jurisdiction by its own contacts or on the theory that contacts of its wholly owned subsidiary should be attributed to it. Hence, Mitsui Machinery should be amenable to suit in Utah state or federal court if the Utah long arm statute reaches the case. Federal venue is based on where a substantial part of the events giving rise to the claim occurred.

If jurisdiction cannot be obtained in Utah, California should be considered. Territorial jurisdiction over Mitsui-American clearly can be established in California, where it is incorporated. California territorial jurisdiction over Mitsui Machinery is more problematic: Mitsui Machinery's contacts with California are more intense than with Utah, but the tort involved here apparently did not occur in California. However, contacts seem sufficient, as Mitsui Machinery apparently ships all the ovens it exports to the United States to its California distributor. Worker could sue in California state court or in federal court in California, at least if Mitsui Machinery has no valid federal venue objection.

C. 1. Mitsui should challenge jurisdiction and service with a Rule 12(b) motion on the basis of *Shaffer v. Heitner*, the line of cases culminating in *Connecticut v. Doehr*, and the lack of necessity for using attachment procedures.

2. Generally, under *Shaffer*, attachment jurisdiction can be established only if in personam jurisdiction could be established. If analysis of territorial jurisdiction in part B. (above) is correct, the "contacts" requirement is satisfied. Hence, the motion to dismiss should be denied as far as *Shaffer* is concerned. However, that means attachment is not necessary to establish jurisdiction and hence a valid *Fuentes-Doehr* objection may exist: Seizure without notice has occurred without the possible justifying circumstance that it was necessary to establish jurisdiction, which also violates Rule 4(n)(2) on assertion of jurisdiction by seizing assets.

    If "contacts" are insufficient for in personam jurisdiction, attachment is permissible only under an exception that the *Shaffer* doctrine would recognize. No such exception appears as to Mitsui-American, which is a United States corporation clearly amenable to suit in California. As to Mitsui Machinery, the doubtfulness of its amenability to suit in California (*see* above) might justify attachment jurisdiction, to give an American injured party an American forum.

D. ***Intervention:*** The bank might seek intervention by arguing that its interest in securing Pot Line's indebtedness is jeopardized by the attachment of the debt, because that might give Mitsui-American cause to reclaim the oven. Were that to happen, the bank's security would certainly be impaired, and it is not clear how it could protect this interest absent intervention. On the other hand, it is not clear what role it would play in the suit itself, as it has no interest in the issues being litigated at present, nor is it clear that Pot Line would fail to represent the bank's interest adequately, as it can be expected to contest tort liability to Worker vigorously.

    Subject matter jurisdiction: If the case is in federal court, the bank's participation in the case might raise subject matter jurisdiction problems, depending on the identities of the other parties and how the bank is aligned as a party. If it is considered adverse to Worker, there is no diversity between them, but there is no bar to supplemental jurisdiction over the state law claims of a nondiverse intervenor-defendant in a diversity case.

E. The claim was settled without adjudication, so no issues were litigated and hence issue preclusion is inoperative. The judgment extinguishes Worker's claim against Pot Line, but not Pot Line's claim against Mitsui. Hence, there is no claim preclusion either. If Mitsui participated in the settlement or manifested acquiescence in the reasonableness of the amount, it could possibly be estopped from disputing the existence of Pot Line's liability to Worker or the amount of that liability, but that would result from Mitsui's stance in the negotiations and not from the judgment as such.

ANSWER TO QUESTION II

Buchan's first claim is based on federal law. Federal Rule 17 seems to say that an obligation created by federal law against an unincorporated association and members of such an association rests against the association as an entity. If so, and if the entity concept is applied consistently, Buchan's damages claim based on the First Amendment would be binding on the Republican Party as an entity if the expulsion was the act of the organization's management, as it appears to have been. The claim would not be binding on any member of the Party, except for officers or directors who might be found individually to be co-wrongdoers with the entity, in the same way that an officer of a corporation can be held personally liable for a wrong committed in the course of corporate employment.

The binding effect of the state law claim is determined by applicable state law, which could be Virginia or District of Columbia. If that law treats an unincorporated association as an entity, then the analysis above applies. Whether that law treats an association as an entity may depend on whether the claim is in tort (open-ended damages) or contract (limited damages). If the association is not treated as an entity, the situation is essentially a suit against a large number of joint wrongdoers, some of whom (the officers and board) acted personally and others of whom (the members at large) are chargeable only on principles of vicarious liability. Buchan would have to prove liability on one or the other such bases against individuals to bind them.

Procedurally Buchan should treat the "defendant" both as an entity and as an aggregate of individuals. That is, process under Federal Rule 4 and designation of the defendant under Federal Rule 23.2 should be modeled after both a suit against a corporation and a suit against a class under Federal Rule 23.

ANSWER TO QUESTION III

"Jurisdiction" can mean subject matter jurisdiction or jurisdiction over the person. Both will be analyzed.

A.   As for subject matter jurisdiction, the federal court in Illinois appears to have such jurisdiction. The amount in controversy exceeds $75,000. There appears to be diversity of citizenship: Duffalo is a citizen of New York and Moline was an Illinois citizen. Note that it is the decedent's citizenship (Mr. Moline's), and not that of his executor (Mrs. Moline), that controls diversity. Whether the federal court in Illinois has personal jurisdiction depends on whether Duffalo has "minimum contacts" with Illinois and whether Illinois has a long arm statute that reaches him. It appears that Duffalo's contacts with Illinois are sufficient. He had a continuous business relationship based in Illinois and the lawsuit arises out of that business. It may be assumed that Illinois has a typical long arm statute. If so, such a statute very likely extends jurisdiction to persons "doing" or "engaging in" business in the state or entering into contracts in the state. Any such provision would be a sufficient statutory basis for asserting territorial jurisdiction over this claim arising out of Duffalo's local business.

B. As for subject matter jurisdiction of the New York state court, there is no diversity requirement. The only possible question with regard to subject matter jurisdiction is whether the suit is filed in the proper court in New York. Given the size of the claim asserted by Duffalo, that would be the trial court of general jurisdiction. [In New York that happens to be the supreme court, but this is a fact that students outside New York would not ordinarily be expected to know.]

The problem of territorial jurisdiction in New York is much more problematic. It may be assumed that New York can extend process to the decedent's representative if and only if it could extend process to the decedent himself, because there is no indication that the executor, as such, had any contacts with New York. Mr. Moline had only very tenuous connections with New York: He was a joint venturer with Duffalo and Duffalo evidently conducted much of the venture's business from New York. On that basis, it could be said that Moline himself was engaged in business in New York and hence subject to its process. On the other hand, the venture had its headquarters outside New York and Moline himself does not appear to have gone regularly to New York in the course of the business. The question could also be affected by the precise terms of the New York long arm statute. If it required that the defendant have "done business" in New York, it might be said that Moline did not personally do business in New York and that it would be a bootstrapping maneuver to say that he did business in New York because Duffalo did. On balance, territorial jurisdiction probably would not be sustained.

As for the garnishment of Allstate, the problem is similar to, but not identical with, *Rush v. Savchuk*. In that case, the policy sought to be attached was a liability insurance policy in which the obligation of "debt" came into being only if the merits of the controversy at hand were resolved in favor of the plaintiff. Here the policy is a life insurance policy and is an existing debt, regardless of the outcome of the Duffalo-Moline litigation. Hence, the insurance proceeds can properly be considered "property" that might be subject to attachment.

However, even so, the attachment is probably improper in New York. The Allstate Company is subject to process in New York and the "debt follows the debtor," so that the property is "in" New York for purposes of attachment. Nevertheless, simple presence of property is not a sufficient basis for exercise of attachment jurisdiction, at least when the property is not real property. *Shaffer v. Heitner* requires, in general, that the principal defendant (Moline's executor in this case) have "minimum contacts" with the state in which the attachment is made. On the analysis above, such minimum contacts are missing. Other possibly justifying circumstances recognized in *Shaffer* are not present. (For example, there is no indication that Duffalo could not sue in Illinois to enforce his claim.) Thus, the attachment of the life insurance policy in New York would not meet the requirement of *Shaffer* and could not be sustained.

ANSWER TO QUESTION IV

A. Under *Beacon v. Westover* and related cases, for purposes of determining the right to jury trial, a pleading is read with attention to its "legal" claims and with a presumption in favor of jury trial. Viewed in this way, the complaint in this case is an action for damages (the second cause of action) with an alternative claim for specific performance (the equitable cause of action). On this analysis, plaintiff has an action for damages, which is therefore triable by jury as to all issues of liability and measures of damages. The only issue triable to the *court* would be the propriety of granting specific performance, and the terms upon which it is granted, if liability is found by the jury.

B. The foregoing applies whether the demand for jury trial is by plaintiff or by defendant. Hence, the issues of liability and damages should be tried by a jury regardless of which party made the demand for jury trial.

C. If the court rejected the defendant's demand for a jury, the order is reviewable. Most obviously, the order would be reviewable on appeal from a final judgment after the case had been tried to the court. The more important question is whether the order could be subject to appellate review before the case goes to trial. The order is not a final judgment, and hence an appeal does not lie from the order. However, the order is one that can be certified for interlocutory appellate review under 28 U.S.C. section 1292(b). To obtain review by this method, the trial judge would have to certify the question as warranting immediate review and the appellate court would have to agree to accept the case on that basis. If the trial judge refuses to certify the order, section 1292(b) review cannot be obtained.

Furthermore, defendant may be able to obtain immediate review of the order by means of extraordinary writ, specifically, mandamus to compel the judge to put the case on the jury calendar. Review by extraordinary writ is generally disfavored in the federal courts, although the attitude varies considerably from one circuit to another. Nevertheless, where there is a plain and serious error going to important procedural rights, the writ has often been granted. In the light of *Beacon v. Westover* (itself a mandamus proceeding), the error here is serious. Hence, review by extraordinary writ might well be afforded.

ANSWER TO QUESTION V

The instruction was plain error. The procedure adopted is known as a quotient verdict, *i.e.*, one in which the jury sums up the jurors' individual proposed awards and then divides the total by the number of jurors. It is error for a jury to do this on its own initiative, and clearly error for the court to instruct the jury to follow such a procedure. The vice of the quotient verdict is that the process of jury discussion and mutual consideration of the issue of damages is displaced by the simple averaging of individual views.

So far as raising the objection on appeal is concerned, it is the general rule that a party may not complain on appeal of a ruling or action of the trial court unless the party raised timely objection in the trial court. The crucial questions therefore are whether the parties knew of the special instruction by the court and, if so, whether the circumstances were such that they did not have fair opportunity to object. For example, if the instruction was given without counsel (forbidden in most courts), then the party is excused from the requirement of timely objection. Similarly, if the judge allowed no time for objection or had notified the parties but had made it clear that he would tolerate no objection, the "timely objection" requirement might be excused. And even if the parties had knowledge of the instruction and opportunity to object, in this exceptional case an appellate court might regard the instruction as "plain error" subject to review despite the parties' failure to object.

ANSWER TO QUESTION VI

The first question is whether federal law or state law should govern the question of granting or denying summary judgment. If state law is applied, it would be arguable that summary judgment should be denied. Summary judgment is proper only when there is no genuine issue of fact and, as a matter of law, the movant is entitled to judgment. Under Texas law, as stated, it would be for the jury to determine whether "as a matter of law" judgment should be granted. Hence, under state law, summary judgment could not be granted on these facts. It thus is necessary to analyze whether state law is applicable.

The argument for applying state law is as follows: This is a diversity case, governed by state law in its substantive aspects. *Erie*, as construed in such cases as *Guaranty Trust v. York,* requires that a federal court, when not applying governing federal law, apply not only state "substantive" law, but also "outcome determinative" state law. Since the Texas rule on scope of jury authority could have "outcome" effect in this case, it could be argued that the state rule should be applied in determining whether there is an issue for trial.

Although this argument has support in some of the cases, the Supreme Court in *Hanna v. Plumer* and other decisions has established approaches that make it likely federal law should govern. If the source of the potentially applicable federal rule of law is regarded as being the "no genuine issue as to any material fact" language of Federal Rule 56 itself, then the test for the validity and governing force of the federal standard is provided by the Rules Enabling Act [28 U.S.C. §2072]. The federal rule qualifies as procedural within the terms of the Act, especially give the Supreme Court's broad definition of federal court rulemaking authority as including even "arguably procedural" rules in the border area between substance and procedure. And the Court's tolerance for "incidental" substantive impacts of Federal Rules makes it highly probable that the Court would not regard the summary judgment rule here as impermissibly abridging, enlarging, or modifying any substantive right.

More likely, the federal standard for sufficiency of the evidence to go to the jury would be regarded as purely decisional, and thus subject to the "twin aims" approach articulated in *Hanna* for the "relatively unguided *Erie* choice" between a federal decisional rule affecting federal court procedure and a conflicting state rule.

Lower federal courts have split over whether federal or state standards for sufficiency of the evidence to go to the jury govern on a motion for judgment as a matter of law on a state law claim, and the same problem should carry over to the summary judgment context. The question would be whether the federal court's following of the federal rule would be likely to lead to forum shopping and inequitable administration of the laws. Some forum shopping might result from plaintiffs' seeking to stay in state court for a better chance at getting to the jury in weak cases. There does not, however, appear to be great inequity or undermining of Texas policy if the federal courts in state law actions in Texas have the same substantive state law issues decided by a judge on summary judgment motion in a few cases that would get to the jury in Texas state court, and the amount of forum shopping would probably be small. The majority of federal courts that have considered the question of federal or state standard on sufficiency of the evidence have chosen the federal rule. *Gasperini v. Center for Humanities, Inc.,* 518 U.S. 415 (1996), does not change this result because the Supreme Court held federal law to be governing on the aspect of that case involving relations among federal court decisionmakers such as trial and appellate courts, applying state law only as to the standard governing the court's review of a jury verdict for excessiveness or inadequacy.

Applying the federal standard, a "genuine issue of fact" exists if, given the material presented in the summary judgment motion, it can be reasonably foreseen that a sufficient evidentiary basis will exist at trial for the case to go to the jury. Here the case looks very strong against the railroad, but there remains a "genuine issue." First, it has not been established in the affidavits that the speed recorder was operating properly. If it was not working properly, the indicated speed of 80 miles per hour may not have been the actual speed. Second, even if the train had been going 80, it is a question for the jury whether that speed was excessive under the circumstances. Third, even if the train was going at an excessive speed, that would not have been the proximate cause of the accident if the bus driver's conduct is regarded as a supervening cause. Although the bus driver's testimony in deposition is not contradicted, he is so situated that his testimony is self-serving. The jurors therefore could disbelieve the testimony. If they did, they could find the railroad was not responsible for the collision.

ANSWER TO QUESTION VII

Since the action is in federal court, the Federal Rules of Civil Procedure apply. There is no demurrer under the Federal Rules, so the question becomes what kind of motion should be prepared.

Possibly, a motion for more definite statement would be effective, but such motions are disfavored and rarely granted under the "notice pleading" approach of the Federal Rules. The complaint is very vague as to the details of the alleged advertisement. The gist of the claim seems to be fraud, which must be alleged with particularity under Rule 9. The pleading does not meet this standard. Furthermore, the allegations as to the availability of jobs in the field of electronics are also very vague. Even if a motion to make them more definite and certain were to be granted, however, it would provide only a temporary respite, because plaintiff would probably file a more definite pleading. There is little chance the suit would be dismissed on the ground that the complaint is uncertain, for under the Federal Rules an action may be dismissed only where it appears to a certainty that plaintiff could state no claim at all.

A motion to dismiss for failure to state a claim would probably not be effective. While there is grave doubt whether plaintiff states a claim entitling her to $100,000 damage, the claim for restitution of $2,500 does not seem substantively baseless. Since the plaintiff states a valid claim to this extent, the complaint would not be vulnerable to a motion to dismiss for failure to state a claim.

The most promising motion would be to dismiss for want of subject matter jurisdiction. There seems to be no basis at all for an argument on the part of plaintiff that her action is based on federal law. (If there were a valid federal claim, the amount in controversy requirement would not be applicable.) The amount in controversy in a diversity action in the federal courts must exceed $75,000. To meet the $75,000 amount in controversy requirement, the pleader must have a good faith basis upon which she might conceivably recover a judgment exceeding $75,000, exclusive of interest and costs. Although plaintiff may state a valid claim for restitution of $2,500, the defendant has a strong argument that no basis exists for recovery in excess of that amount. The allegations of fraud, which could lead to punitive damages, are insufficient. In particular, there is no allegation that defendant knew that employment of the type advertised would be virtually impossible to obtain by a graduate of the Institute. If the action is regarded as one for breach of contract, as opposed to fraud, the measure of damages under generally prevailing law does not include "embarrassment, humiliation," etc. The damage recoverable by plaintiff on a contract claim would be limited to the difference between the amount paid and the value of the education actually received. That could not exceed $2,500, and therefore the amount in controversy requirement is not met, and the court does not have jurisdiction of the action.

ANSWER TO QUESTION VIII

A. A suit individually against Bunker would seek to cancel his membership on the ground that he refused to abide by the rules governing membership. This claim is based essentially on the common law of unincorporated associations. A federal question might arise in the case, but it would be a defensive contention by Bunker that the Club rule requiring subscription to the "statement of principles" is a violation of his First Amendment rights. The fact that a federal question may arise defensively does not make the case one that "arises under" federal law. Therefore, the claim in an action by the Club to terminate Bunker's membership would be a state law claim.

Such a claim could be brought in federal court only if the requirements for diversity jurisdiction could be met, since the federal question basis of jurisdiction does not exist. There is diversity between the Club and Bunker. Bunker is a citizen of Texas, while Sierra Club is a citizen of California, where it is incorporated. (It does not appear that Sierra Club is also a citizen of the District of Columbia, because its principal place of business is in San Francisco.) However, diversity jurisdiction requires that the amount in controversy exceed $75,000. There is nothing to indicate that the value of the membership to Bunker is of that amount, nor that the value to the Sierra Club of excluding Bunker from membership would be in that amount. Possibly, the Club could meet the amount in controversy requirement by allegations that Bunker threatens disruption of the Club and that the disruption would damage it to the extent of more than $75,000. However, on the facts given, there seems no basis for making nonfrivolous allegations to this effect. Accordingly, the action could not be brought in federal district court.

The action could be brought in a state court where personal jurisdiction could be obtained over Bunker. That would include an appropriate state court in Texas, where presumably Bunker is subject to service of process. Possibly the action could also be brought in California on the ground that Bunker is subject to service of process there for any claim concerning his membership in the Club. His joining the Club was a voluntary action and he knew the Club was headquartered in California. With regard to a claim arising out of the membership activity itself, Bunker's "contact" with California seems sufficient to meet the constitutional standard applied in such cases as *International Shoe* and *Burger King Corp. v. Rudzewicz*. Because California's long arm statute goes to the limits of due process, service of process on Bunker is authorized by the statute.

There seems to be no basis upon which Bunker could be subject to process in the District of Columbia. There is no indication that he had any contact with the District or that he carried on activities relating to membership there. The simple fact that the Club has an office in the District is not a sufficient basis for subjecting members of the Club to jurisdiction.

B.   The class suit names as defendants individuals who object to the requirement of signing the "statement of principles." Such individuals would adequately represent the class if they can defend the litigation with reasonable competence and diligence. On that assumption, the litigation would meet the requirements for a binding class suit: The group of affected individuals is so large that it is impractical to join all those who are similarly situated; the individuals actually named are representative of the class; they appear to be able to defend the litigation on behalf of the class.

Under the principles of *Hansberry v. Lee*, they can represent the class as a whole. There does not seem to be a problem under *Phillips Petroleum Co. v. Shutts* with the California state court's exercising jurisdiction over out-of-state defendant class members, because of the members' voluntary contact with California. All this being so, the judgment would be binding on all members of the class, including Bunker.

C. If Bunker sought to become a party to the action as an individual, the proper procedure under either federal or state practice is to seek to intervene. If the action was pending in state court, his petition for intervention should state the essentials of intervention. These are that the pending action will or may determine his legal rights; that there is risk that the action will be defended by the class less effectively than Bunker could defend his own interest individually; that his petition is timely and his becoming a party will not unduly delay the progress of the litigation.

If the action were removed to federal court, the procedure would be essentially the same. However, Bunker should frame his petition in the alternative, first as a petition for intervention of right, and second as a petition for permissive intervention. There is no fundamental distinction between the two, except that intervention of right is permitted when the proposed intervenor stands in risk that his rights will be legally or practically affected by the judgment, whereas permissive intervention requires only that the petitioner show that his claim and the claims already pending in the action involve a common question of law and fact, although allowing permissive intervention is a discretionary decision for the trial court. The allegations outlined above establish that the judgment in the pending action may affect Bunker's interest. They also show that his claim involves a common question of law and fact with the claim pending in the existing action.

D. When a class action is pending in federal court, the question of notice to the class is determined under the Federal Rules. Under Rule 23, individual notice to each member of the class is required when the class suit is of the (b)(3) or damages type, where each individual member has the right to opt out. However, individual notice may not be required in other types of class suits, including those in which an injunction or declaratory judgment is sought regarding the rights and duties of the class as a whole. The present suit falls into the latter category and, therefore, individual notice is probably not required. It would be within the discretion of the court to require individual notice even in this type of class suit, but to do so might be regarded as an abuse of discretion in this case. The question involved is a legal issue common to all members of the class. Published notice to the class as a whole, plus perhaps individual notice to members known to oppose the "statement of principles," might be sufficient.

With regard to the cost of giving notice, the party opposing the class is not required to pay that cost in a "damages" type of class suit. [*See* Eisen v. Carlisle & Jacquelin] However, this is not a damages class suit so the court has broader discretion in determining whether the party opposing the class should be required to pay the cost of notice. And because this case involves a plaintiff seeking to invoke the class action procedure to sue a defendant class, it should not be a problem to make the plaintiff at least initially bear the notice costs.

ANSWER TO QUESTION IX

A. Following the jury verdict, Strong moved for a new trial. Apparently Strong sought to file the motion by mail rather than following the usual practice of filing the papers directly with the clerk of the court. While "service" of papers may be accomplished by depositing the papers timely in the mail, the same is not true of filing. Filing may be accomplished by depositing papers in the mail only if the mailing is actually received within the time limit. It seems unlikely that the filing was timely here, since the filing was not received until 25 days after the verdict. However, the 10-day time limit is measured from the time the judgment is entered (rather than from the time of the verdict), and it is possible that the court did not enter judgment until 15 days after the jury verdict.

If filing was not timely, a new trial could be granted if the court timely so decided. Under the Federal Rules, the court may act on its own motion to grant a new trial if it does so not later than 10 days after entry of the judgment. Note that the court could not grant a judgment as a matter of law under the Federal Rules, because that relief may be granted only on motion of a party specifically requesting it, and here Strong's motion sought only a new trial.

On the merits of the motion, a new trial may be granted only if the verdict is against the weight of the evidence. The cases are divided in regard to problems of witness credibility. Some decisions suggest that the trial judge can grant a new trial even if there is some testimonial evidence to support the verdict if, in the judge's opinion, that evidence is inherently incredible. Under that interpretation, the court could grant a new trial. Otherwise, the basic issue is credibility and Kopp's testimony constitutes "substantial evidence."

B. Under state practice, in some states the judge lacks power to grant a new trial on his own motion, but has power to grant a judgment n.o.v. (the term still used in most state systems for the federal post-verdict motion for judgment as a matter of law) on his own motion. The question of timeliness under state practice depends on the time periods allowed for post-verdict motions and whether deposit in the mail constitutes "filing" for purposes of compliance with the timeliness requirement. As for the merits of the motion, the standards for post-verdict motions under state practice vary. However, in most states the judge has at least the broader authority indicated above. In some states, the judge is authorized to weigh the evidence (the "thirteenth juror" approach) in determining whether to grant a new trial. Under the latter standard, the judge would clearly have authority to grant Strong a new trial.

Table of Citations

CITATIONS TO FEDERAL RULES OF CIVIL PROCEDURE (Fed. R. Civ. P.)

Rule	Text Reference	Rule	Text Reference	Rule	Text Reference
1	§583	11(b)(2)	§785	15(c)(2)	§§924, 926
2	§582	11(b)(3)	§776	15(c)(3)	§926
3	§§160, 540, 594	11(b)(4)	§§779, 858	15(d)	§§954, 956, 957
4	§§250, 542	11(c)	§798	16	§§1288, 1689, 1691,
4(a)	§160	11(c)(1)	§§807, 808		1720, 1860
4(d)	§244	11(c)(1)(A)	§§803, 806	16(a)	§1689
4(d)(1)	§§527, 541	11(c)(1)(B)	§810	16(b)	§§1689, 1692, 1696
4(e)(1)	§243	11(c)(2)	§800	16(b)(3)	§1699
4(e)(2)	§242	11(c)(2)(A)	§§792, 805	16(c)	§1689
4(f)	§245	11(c)(2)(B)	§§810, 979	16(c)(6)	§1699
4(k)(1)(A)	§128	11(c)(3)	§811	16(c)(9)	§§1702, 1709, 1757
4(k)(1)(B)	§129	12	§§749, 875,1062	16(d)	§1689
4(k)(1)(C)	§130	12(a)(3)	§862	16(e)	§§951, 1720
4(k)(1)(D)	§130	12(a)(1)(A)	§860	16(f)	§1721
4(k)(2)	§§131, 136	12(a)(1)(B)	§861	17	§§985, 1002
4(n)(2)	§135	12(b)	§§104, 640, 716,	17(a)	§989
7	§736		758, 851, 860	17(b)	§§1016, 1021,1025
7(a)	§§619, 734, 874,	12(b)(6)	§§592, 718, 741,	17(c)	§§1016, 1017
	896, 1199		747, 765, 967,	18	§1038
7(b)(1)	§746		1009, 1212	18(a)	§684
8(a)	§736	12(c)	§§968, 970	19	§§129, 417, 436, 441,
8(a)(1)	§§283, 600	12(d)	§§852, 971		1042, 1102, 1103
8(a)(2)	§§593, 720, 726	12(e)	§§734, 739	19(a)	§§880, 1064
8(b)	§§609, 822, 827	12(f)	§743	19(a)(1)	§1047
8(c)	§§835-836, 844, 846,	12(g)	§749	19(a)(2)(i)	§§1047, 1101
	874	12(h)(1)	§§105, 185, 750, 855	19(a)(2)(ii)	§1047
8(d)	§§831, 865, 875	12(h)(2)	§§751, 1069	19(b)	§§879,1048
8(e)	§§604, 615	13(a)	§§410, 873, 883, 2222	19(c)	§1061
8(f)	§598	13(b)	§§410, 868	20	§§436, 437, 2196
9(b)	§§652, 725, 726, 727,	13(g)	§§415, 893	20(a)	§§685, 1033, 1106
	733	13(h)	§§877, 897	20(b)	§§686, 1039
9(c)	§661	14	§§129, 411, 436, 441,	21	§1040
9(g)	§666		1071, 1083	22	§§1118, 1126, 1127,
10	§596	14(a)	§1085		1131-1133, 1137
10(b)	§603	15	§1720	23	§§439, 1142, 1146,
10(c)	§§606, 960	15(a)	§§913, 917, 972		1180, 1210, 1216,
11	§§549, 608, 627, 628, 769,	15(a)(1)	§935		1226, 1240, 1260
	771, 777, 781, 782, 784,	15(b)	§§944, 946, 948,	23(a)	§1239
	795, 797, 799, 802, 803,		952, 1860	23(a)(1)	§1148
	812, 814, 818, 983	15(c)	§§547, 934	23(a)(2)	§§1148, 1155, 1156

Rule	Text Reference	Rule	Text Reference	Rule	Text Reference
23(a)(3)	§1148	26(b)(4)(C)	§1508	37(a)(4)	§1588
23(a)(4)	§1148	26(c)	§§1532, 1544	37(b)	§§1306, 1337, 1589
23(b)	§§1148, 1173	26(c)(7)	§1533	37(b)(1)	§1591
23(b)(1)	§§1174, 1204, 1222, 1235	26(d)	§§1289, 1312, 1354, 1371, 1389	37(b)(2)	§§1360, 1573, 1725
23(b)(1)(A)	§1175	26(e)	§1414	37(b)(2)(A)	§1574
23(b)(1)(B)	§1176	26(e)(1)	§§1303, 1523, 1525, 1570	37(b)(2)(D)	§1594
23(b)(2)	§§1154, 1177, 1179, 1196, 1204, 1222, 1235, 1266	26(e)(2)	§1570	37(c)(1)	§§1304, 1570, 1670
		26(f)	§§1287, 1295, 1296, 1311, 1371, 1389, 1689, 1698	37(c)(2)	§1374
23(b)(3)	§§1152, 1180, 1181, 1192, 1195, 1196, 1223, 1229, 1232, 2121			37(d)	§1569
		26(g)	§1283	38(b)	§1799
		26(g)(1)	§1302	39(a)	§1800
23(c)	§1230	30(a)(2)(A)	§1314	39(b)	§1801
23(c)(1)	§1206	30(a)(2)(B)	§1316	39(c)	§§1802, 1803
23(c)(2)	§§1223, 1228	30(a)(3)(C)	§1290	41(a)	§977
23(c)(4)(A)	§1184	30(b)	§§1325, 1326	41(a)(1)(i)	§975
23(d)(2)	§1222	30(b)(2)	§1342	41(a)(2)	§§881, 976, 980, 981, 983, 984
23(e)	§§1224, 1249, 1251	30(b)(5)	§§1327, 1328		
23(f)	§§1215, 2119, 2121	30(b)(6)	§1323	42	§1116
24	§§416, 436, 437, 441, 1090	30(b)(7)	§1333	42(a)	§686
		30(d)(1)	§1335	42(b)	§§86, 88, 1086
24(a)	§1239	30(d)(2)	§1318	45	§1767
24(a)(1)	§1091	30(d)(3)	§§1338, 1563	45(a)	§1319
24(a)(2)	§1092	30(e)	§1341	45(a)(1)(C)	§1401
24(b)	§§1105, 1107	30(g)	§1540	45(b)(1)	§1320
25(c)	§995	31	§1331	45(c)(3)(A)(ii)	§1321
26(a)	§§1286, 1570	32(a)	§1608	45(c)(3)(B)	§1529
26(a)(1)	§§1304, 1392, 1657, 1698	32(a)(1)	§§1346, 1610	45(e)	§1591
		32(a)(2)	§1345	46	§1861
26(a)(1)(A)	§1297	32(a)(3)	§§1347, 1611	48	§1937
26(a)(1)(B)	§1298	32(b)	§§1339, 1348, 1609	49(a)	§1924
26(a)(1)(C)	§§672, 1299	32(d)	§§1348, 1609	49(b)	§§1930, 1933
26(a)(1)(D)	§§1300, 1437	32(d)(3)	§§1340, 1612	50(a)	§1865
26(a)(1)(E)	§§1294, 1698	33(a)	§§1349, 1353, 1356	50(b)	§§1884, 1960, 1964, 1966
26(a)(2)(A)	§1513	33(b)(3)	§1357		
26(a)(2)(B)	§1516	33(d)	§1359	50(c)	§1969
26(a)(2)(C)	§1514	34(a)	§1385	50(d)	§1971
26(a)(3)	§1711	34(b)	§§1393, 1394, 1397	51	§§1898, 1916, 1918, 1919, 2160
26(a)(3)(A)	§1712	35	§§1405, 2175		
26(a)(3)(B)	§1712	35(a)	§§1406, 1407	52(a)	§§1856, 2140, 2141, 2145, 2149
26(a)(3)(C)	§1712	35(b)	§§1412, 1413		
26(b)	§1435	36	§1382	52(c)	§1894
26(b)(1)	§§1420, 1421, 1422, 1424	36(a)	§§1364, 1365, 1367, 1368, 1371, 1372	54(b)	§§2109-2110
				54(c)	§§621, 622
26(b)(2)	§§1283, 1425, 1697	36(b)	§§1373, 1383, 1608	55(a)	§958
26(b)(3)	§§1479, 1481, 1488, 1491-1493, 1503, 1504	37	§1600	55(b)	§960
		37(a)	§§1310, 1336, 1360, 1566, 1567	55(c)	§964
				56	§§1165, 2125
26(b)(4)	§1413	37(a)(2)	§1363	56(a)	§§1621, 1666
26(b)(5)	§1478	37(a)(2)(d)	§1572	56(b)	§§1621, 1666
26(b)(4)(A)	§1524	37(a)(2)(A)	§1572	56(c)	§§1629, 1647, 1662
26(b)(4)(B)	§§1507, 1509, 1511	37(a)(3)	§1568	56(d)	§1628
				56(e)	§§1619, 1667, 1672
				56(f)	§1680
				58	§2099

Rule	Text Reference	Rule	Text Reference	Rule	Text Reference
59	§2037	60(b)	§§964, 2042, 2043, 2054	61	§§1921, 1976, 2154
59(a)	§§1973-1974, 2007			65(c)	§2152
59(b)	§1999	60(b)(1)	§2035	84	§676
59(c)	§2002	60(b)(2)	§2163	501	§§1461, 1462
59(d)	§1997	60(b)(3)	§2038	606(b)	§1948
59(e)	§§2027, 2029	60(b)(5)	§2041	611(a)	§1837
60(a)	§2030	60(b)(6)	§2042		

Table of Cases

Beggerly, United States v. - §§**2048, 2051**

Behrens v. Pelletier - §**2125**

Belcher v. Bassett Furniture - §**1388**

Bell v. Hood - §**400**

Bendictin Litigation, *In re* - §**400**

Benson and Ford, Inc. v. Wanda Petroleum Co. - §**2250**

Bensusan Restaurant Corp. v. King - §§**56, 58**

Berk v. Alperin - §**675**

Bernhard v. Bank of America - §§**2258, 2259**

Bershad v. McDonough - §**2035**

Black & White Taxicab Co. v. Brown & Yellow Taxicab Co. - §**497**

Blackstone v. Miller - §**63**

Blair v. Equifax Check Services, Inc. - §**2119**

Blonder-Tongue Laboratories, Inc. v. University of Illinois Foundation - §**258**

Blue Chip Stamps v. Manor Drug Stores - §**732**

Blumenthal v. Drudge, §§**55, 56**

Board of Harbor Commissioners, United States v. - §**741**

Boeing Co. v. Shipman - §**1876**

Borough of - *see* name of borough

Bosch, Estate of, v. Commissioner - §**562**

Boser v. Uniroyal - §**1602**

Bradford Trust Co. v. Wright - §**1176**

Brakhage v. Graff - §**1498**

Breier v. Northern California Bowling Proprietors' Association - §**972**

Bremen, The v. Zapata Off-Shore Co. - §**221**

Brennan v. Engineered Products, Inc. - §**1006**

Brennan v. Midwestern United Life Insurance Co. - §**1242**

Brewster v. Boston Herald-Traveler - §**638**

Brisco v. Reader's Digest - §§**582, 653**

Bristol Convalescent Hospital v. Sone - §**705**

Brockton Savings Bank v. Peat, Marwick, Mitchell & Co. - §**1580**

Brown v. North Ventura Road Co. - §**624**

Bryant v. Finnish National Airline - §**87**

Buckeye Boiler Co. v. Superior Court - §**39**

Burger King Corp. v. Rudzewicz - §§**27, 30, 39, 40, 42, 49, 79**

Burlington Coat Factory Securities Litigation, *In re* - §**765**

Burlington Northern Railroad v. Ford - §**184**

Burlington Northern Railroad v. Woods - §**547**

Burnham v. Superior Court - §§**10, 64, 111, 238**

Burns v. Thiokol Chemical Corp. - §**1605**

Business Guides, Inc. v. Chromatic Communications Enterprises, Inc. - §§**549, 781**

Byrd v. Blue Ridge Electric Cooperative, Inc. - §§**482, 488-490, 492-496, 512, 518-520, 522, 524-526, 551, 554, 555**

C

Calder v. Jones - §§**36, 51, 55**

Capital Traction Co. v. Hof - §**1823**

Carden v. Arkoma Associates - §**322**

Carnegie-Mellon University v. Cohill - §**486**

Carnival Cruise Lines, Inc. v. Shute - §**1221**

Carolina Power & Light Co. v. Uranex - §**74**

Carter v. Jury Commissioner of Green County - §**1809**

Cash Energy, Inc. v. Weiner - §**730**

Castano v. The American Tobacco Co. - §§**1151, 1160, 1185**

Caterpillar, Inc. v. Lewis - §§**484, 489**

Catrett v. Celotex Corp. (1987) - §**1660**

Celotex Corp. v. Catrett (1986) - §§**1628, 1651-1655, 1660, 1668, 1673, 1680**

Certain Interested Underwriters at Lloyd's of London v. Layne - §**325**

Chambers v. NASCO, Inc. - §§**554, 555, 814**

Chauffeurs, Teamsters & Helpers Local 391 v. Terry - §**1784**

Chesa International, Ltd. v. Fashion Associates, Inc. - §**1536**

Chicago, City of v. International College of Surgeons - §§**387, 461**

Chicago Rock Island & Pacific Railroad v. Igoe - §**195**

Chicago Rock Island & Pacific Railroad v. Martin - §**477**

Chiron Corp. v. Abbott Laboratories - §**730**

Cianci v. New Times Publishing Co. - §**1550**

Cincinnati Gas & Electric Co. v. General Electric Co. - §**1755**

Cine Forty-Second Street Theatre Corp. v. Allied Artists - §§**1575, 1584, 1587**

Cipollone v. Ligget Group, Inc. - §**1557**

Citizens State Bank v. Castro - §**1857**

Citron v. Aro Corp. - §§**1975, 2166**

City of - *see* name of city

Clark v. United States - §**1955**

Clearfield Trust Co. v. United States - §**571**

Clegg v. Hardware Mutual Casualty Co. - §**1928**

Cobbledick v. United States - §**2058**

Cochran v. Union Lumber Co. - §**2263**

Coffran v. Hitchcock Clinic, Inc. - §**2152**

Cohen v. Beneficial Industrial Loan Corp. - §§**2120, 2121, 2132**

Colgrove v. Battin - §**1825**

Collins v. Rocha - §**853**

Commercial Air Charters v. Sundorph - §**114**

Commissioner of Internal Revenue v. Duberstein - §**2150**

CompuServe, Inc. v. Patterson - §**54**

Cone v. West Virginia Pulp & Paper Co. - §**1962**

Conley v. Gibson - §§**593, 640, 721, 722, 728**

Connecticut v. Doehr - §§**269, 275**

Conney v. Erickson - §**2108**

Consolidation Coal Co. v. Bucyrus-Erie Co. - §**1469**

Continental Nut Co. v. Robert L. Berner Co. - §**669**

Contract Engineers, Inc. v. California-Dorian Co. - §**933**

Cooper v. American Savings & Loan Association - §**1225**

Cooper v. Leslie Salt Co. - §**707**

Cooper Industries, Inc. v. British Aerospace, Inc. - §**1396**

Inset Systems, Inc. v. Instruction Set, Inc. - **§57**

Insurance Corp. of Ireland v. Compagnie des Bauxites de Guinee - **§§43, 106, 140**

International Business Machines Corp. v. United States (1975) - **§§1592, 1607**

International Products Corp. v. Koons - **§1601**

International Shoe v. Washington - **§§21, 22, 25, 26, 64, 80, 111, 119**

J

J.E.B. v. Alabama *ex rel.* T.B. - **§1835**

J.I. Case v. Borak - **§386**

Jaffee v. Redmond - **§1475**

Jairath v. Dyer - **§390**

James Daniel Good Real Property, United States v. - **§273**

Japanese Products Antitrust Litigation, *In re* - **§1675**

Jenkins v. General Motors Corp. - **§§1162, 1163**

Jenkins v. Raymark Industry, Inc. - **§1185**

Jenkins v. Reneau - **§1053**

Jett v. Phillips & Associates - **§1050**

Jetty v. Craco - **§854**

Johansen v. Combustion Engineering, Inc. - **§§2020, 2026**

Johnson v. Fankell - **§2126**

Johnson v. Jones - **§2124**

Jordan v. Jackson - **§733**

Jorgensen v. York Ice Machinery Corp. - **§1950**

K

Kamen v. Kemper Financial Services, Inc. - **§569**

Kansas Public Employees Retirement System v. Reimer & Koger Associates - **§2042**

Kartheiser v. Superior Court - **§2247**

Kaufman v. DeMuths - **§1982**

Keckley v. Payton - **§888**

Keeton v. Hustler Magazine, Inc. - **§§48, 49**

Kerr v. United States District Court - **§2171**

Kiernan v. Van Schaik - **§1836**

Kilpatrick v. Texas & Pacific Railway - **§976**

Kim, United States v. - **§1929**

Klaxon Co. v. Stentor Electric Manufacturing Co. - **§§203, 557, 578, 559**

Kleiner v. First National Bank of Atlanta - **§1246**

Klotz v. Superior Electric Products Corp. - **§1081**

Kokkonen v. Guardian Life Insurance Co. - **§984**

Korean Air Lines Disaster of Sept. 1, 1983, *In re* - **§206**

Kothe v. Smith - **§1705**

Kramer v. Caribbean Mills, Inc. - **§340**

Kremer v. Chemical Construction Corp. - **§2274**

Kulchar v. Kulchar - **§2046**

Kulko v. Superior Court - **§§37, 40, 41**

L

LASA Per L'Industria del Marmo Societa per Azioni v. Alexander - **§§415, 894**

LaBuy v. Howes Leather Co. - **§2175**

Laddon v. Superior Court - **§1437**

LaFollette v. Herron - **§887**

La Mar v. H & B Novelty & Loan Co. - **§1268**

Landau v. Salam - **§1036**

Lane v. Sullivan - **§2269**

Langenkamp v. Culp - **§1783**

Lapenna v. Upjohn Co. - **§1324**

Lapin v. Shulton, Inc. - **§2045**

Larionoff v. United States - **§1172**

Lauro Lines, Inc. v. Chasser - **§2129**

Lavender v. Kurn - **§§1875, 1877**

Law v. Northern Assurance Co. - **§1934**

Lear, Inc. v. Adkins - **§295**

Leatherman v. Tarrant County Narcotics Intelligence and Coordination Unit - **§733**

Lee v. Hensley - **§763**

Lehman Bros. v. Schein - **§565**

Lelsz v. Kavanagh - **§1240**

Leroy v. Great Western United Corp. - **§153**

Lexecon, Inc. v. Milberg Weiss Bershad Hynes & Lerach - **§201**

Liberty Mutual Insurance Co. v. Fales - **§889**

Licht & Semonoff, Appeal of - **§794**

Lind v. Schenley Industries, Inc. - **§§1990, 1993**

Lindemann v. San Joaquin Cotton Oil Co. - **§1977**

Lindy Brothers Builders, Inc. v. American Radiator Corp. - **§1257**

Linhart v. Nelson - **§§1959, 2003**

Link v. Wabash Railroad - **§1586**

Liteky v. United States - **§1847**

Livingston v. Jefferson - **§175**

Louisville & Nashville Railroad v. Mottley (1911) - **§399**

Louisville & Nashville Railroad v. Mottley (1908) - **§§286, 393, 398**

Lovern v. General Motors Corp. - **§480**

Lumbermen's Mutual Insurance Co. v. Massachusetts Bonding and Insurance Co. - **§893**

Lundeen v. Cordner - **§§1639, 1684, 1881**

Lundy v. Adamar of New Jersey, Inc. - **§930**

Lyons v. Wickhorst - **§1771**

Lytle v. Household Manufacturing, Inc. - **§1792**

M

M.L.B. v. S.L.J. - **§2087**

McCormick v. Kopmann - **§§614, 616**

McDonald, *In re* - **§2173**

McDonald v. Pless - **§§1946, 1948**

McDonnell Douglas Corp. v. District Court - **§1175**

McDonough Power Equipment, Inc. v. Greenwood - §1954

McGee v. International Life Insurance Co. - §§23, 32, 48, 59

McHenry v. Renne - §742

McKeel v. City of Pine Bluff - §1865

McKenna v. Ortho Pharmaceutical Corp. - §563

McKnight v. General Motors Corp. - §788

McPherson v. Hoffman - §1076

Macheras v. Center Art Galleries - §332

Mack Trucks, Inc. v. Arrow Aluminum Castings Co. - §123

Mahoney v. Coralejo - §648

Maicobo Investment Corp. v. von der Heide - §2049

Marcera v. Chinlund - §§1264, 1266, 1270

Markman v. Westview Instruments, Inc. - §1796

Marrese v. American Academy of Orthopaedic Surgeons - §§2267, 2271

Marshall v. Ford Motor Co. - §1921

Marshall v. Mulrenin - §§547, 550

Martin v. Taylor - §2035

Martin v. Wilks - §§1070, 2252, 2253

Martino v. McDonald's Systems, Inc. - §2224

Mather Construction Co. v. United States - §1019

Mathews v. Eldridge - §266

Matsushita Electric Industrial Co. v. Epstein - §2275

Matsushita Electric Industries Co. v. Zenith Radio Corp. - §§1644, 1675

Mayer v. Gary Partners & Co. - §552

Megarry v. Norton - §653

Meissner v. Papas - §2017

Mendoza, United States v. - §2263

Mennonite Board of Missions v. Adams - §222

Merrell Dow Pharmaceuticals, Inc. v. Thompson - §§387, 388, 390, 400

Mertens v. Abbott Laboratories - §1183

Mesner, Estate of - §1975

Metropolitan Life Insurance Co. v. Robertson-Ceco Corp. - §92

Metropolitan Life Insurance Co. v. Taylor - §§396, 460

Millenium Enterprises, Inc. v. Millenium Music, L.P. - §58

Miller & Miller Auctioneers, Inc. v. G.W. Murphy Industries, Inc. - §1120

Milliken v. Meyer - §81

Mills v. Electric Auto Lite Co. - §1257

Minneapolis & St. Louis Railroad v. Bombalis - §1774

Minneapolis, St. Paul & Sault Ste. Marie Railway v. Moquin - §1975

Mitchell v. Forsyth - §§2123, 2126

Mitchell v. W.T. Grant Co. - §§262, 263, 265, 266, 267

Mobile, City of, In re - §472

Monterey, City of v. Del Monte Dunes at Monterey, Ltd. - §1784

Montgomery Ward & Co. v. Duncan - §1961

Moore v. Chesapeake & Ohio Railway - §§387, 390

Mova Pharmaceuticals Corp. v. Shalala - §1094

Mullane v. Central Hanover Bank & Trust Co. - §§73, 225, 227, 229, 233

Murphy Brothers, Inc. v. Michetti Pipe Stringing, Inc. - §479

Myers v. Stephens - §665

N

Napolitano v. Compania Sud Americana de Vapores - §2152

National American Corp. v. Federal Republic of Nigeria - §1054

National Association of Government Employees, Inc. v. National Federation of Federal Employees - §795

National Equipment Rental Co. v. Szukhent - §94

National Hockey League v. Metropolitan Hockey Club, Inc. - §1580

National Mutual Insurance Co. v. Tidewater Transfer Co. - §316

National Union Electric Co. v. Matsushita Electric Industrial Co. - §1385

National Union of Marine Cooks v. Arnold - §2058

Natural Resources Defense Council v. United States Nuclear Regulatory Commission - §1095

Navarro Savings Association v. Lee - §326

Neely v. Martin K. Eby Construction Co. - §1971

Nelson v. County of Allegheny - §1217

Nelson v. Miller - §§125, 126

Nemeth v. Hair - §996

New England Merchants National Bank v. Hughes - §1771

New Orleans Public Service, Inc. v. United Gas Pipe Line Co. - §1093

New York Central Railroad v. Johnson - §2012

Newing v. Cheatham - §645

Newman-Green, Inc. v. Alfonzo-Larrain - §348

Nichols v. G.D. Searle & Co. - §§80, 88, 191

Noonan v. Cunard Steamship Co. - §981

North Georgia Finishing, Inc. v. Di-Chem, Inc. - §§266, 267

Northern District of California "Dalkon Shield" IUD Products Liability Litigation, In re - §1176

Northern Pacific Railroad v. Herbert - §2014

Nysco Laboratories, Inc., United States v. - §2202

O

Oklahoma Tax Commission v. Graham - §456

Omni Capital International v. Rudolf Wolff & Co., Ltd. - §§117, 136

Oppenheimer Fund, Inc. v. Sanders - §1231

Orcutt v. Ferranini - §1008

Ortiz v. Fibreboard Corp. - §§1177, 1195

Orvis v. Higgins - §2149

Osborn v. Bank of the United States - §§376, 389, 405

Oscanyon v. Arms Co. - §1893

Samuelson v. Honeywell - **§163**

San Juan Dupont Plaza Hotel Fire Litigation, *In re* - **§1726**

Sanders v. Superior Court - **§1418**

Sandobal v. Armour & Co. - **§1058**

Santoro v. Carbone - **§840**

Sassano v. Roullard - **§1923**

Savage v. Van Marle - **§613**

Schiavone v. Fortune - **§928**

Schlagenhauf v. Holder - **§§1404, 1604, 2175**

School Asbestos Litigation, *In re* - **§1160**

Schubert v. Reich - **§2061**

Schultea v. Wood - **§736**

Schuyler v. United Air Lines - **§1983**

Scogin v. Century Fitness, Inc. - **§1950**

Searle & Co. v. Superior Court - **§652**

Searle Brothers v. Searle - **§2251**

Seattle Times Co. v. Rhinehart - **§§1547, 1556**

Seawell, United States v. - **§1947**

Security Pacific National Bank v. Geernaert - **§2159**

Seider v. Roth - **§14**

Seinfeld v. Austen - **§390**

Seivell v. Hines - **§1892**

Shaffer v. Heitner - **§§10, 63, 64, 65, 72, 73, 74, 75, 76, 78, 111, 135, 2230**

Shamrock Oil Co. v. Sheets - **§476**

Shea v. Donohoe Construction Co. - **§1587**

Shelton v. Pargo, Inc. - **§1254**

Sherman v. Hallbauer - **§920**

Shields v. Barrow - **§1045**

Shippy v. Peninsula Rapid Transit Co. - **§1899**

Shook v. Pearson - **§666**

Siler v. Louisville & Nashville Railroad - **§407**

Silicon Graphics, Inc., Securities Litigation - **§652**

Simler v. Connor - **§1772**

Simms v. Village of Albion - **§1929**

Singh v. Daimler-Benz AG - **§328**

Sirota v. Solitron Devices, Inc. - **§1210**

Skelly Oil Co. v. Phillips Petroleum Co. - **§398**

Skidmore v. Syntex Laboratories, Inc. - **§934**

Skolnick v. Hallett - **§744**

Slemons v. Paterson - **§1983**

Slocum v. New York Life Insurance Co. - **§1885**

Smith v. Barry - **§2080**

Smith v. Circle P Ranch Co. - **§1375**

Smith v. Kansas City Title & Trust Co. - **§§387, 390**

Smith v. Los Angeles Bookbinders Union - **§668**

Smith v. Sperling - **§338**

Smoot v. Fox - **§983**

Sniadach v. Family Finance Corp. - **§256**

Societe Internationale v. Rogers - **§1583**

Sosna v. Iowa - **§§1164, 1177**

Sosnow v. Storatti Corp. - **§1001**

South Central Bell Telephone Co. v. Alabama - **§2254**

Southern Leasing Partners, Ltd. v. McMullan - **§780**

Southern Methodist University Association of Women Law Students v. Wynne & Jaffe - **§987**

Southwest Airlines Co. v. Texas International Airlines - **§2250**

Spangler v. United States - **§1112**

Sparks v. Berntsen - **§1958**

Spectacor Managment Group v. Brown - **§367**

State v. - *see name of party*

State Farm Fire & Casualty Co. v. Tashire - **§§311, 1122, 1129**

Steel Co. v. Citizens for Better Environment - **§§287, 400**

Stewart v. Winter - **§1208**

Stewart Organization, Inc. v. Ricoh Corp. - **§§197, 222, 223, 546, 554**

Stilwell v. Travelers Insurance Co. - **§2037**

Stoll v. Gottlieb - **§§212, 2268**

Strandell v. Jackson County - **§1757**

Strawbridge v. Curtiss - **§313**

Stringfellow v. Concerned Neighbors in Action - **§1104**

Stromberg Metal Works, Inc. v. Press Mechanical, Inc. - **§438**

Sullivan v. Nesbit - **§1910**

Supreme Tribe of Ben-Hur v. Cauble - **§§330, 1198**

Sussman v. Bank of Israel - **§795**

Sutliff, Inc. v. Donovan Companies - **§722**

Swartz v. Gold Dust Casino, Inc. - **§927**

Swift v. Tyson - **§§493, 494, 495, 496, 497, 504, 505, 506, 508, 509, 566**

Swint v. Chambers County Commission - **§2133**

Swiss American Bank, United States v. - **§134**

Synanon Church v. United States - **§2238**

System Federation No. 91, Railway Employees Department v. Wright - **§2041**

Szabo Food Service, Inc. v. Canteen Corp. - **§794**

T

TMJ Implants Products Liability Litigation, *In re* - **§206**

Tanner v. United States - **§1950**

Tele-Views News Co. v. S.R.B. TV Publishing Co. - **§976**

Temple v. Synthes Corp. - **§1051**

Terrell v. DeConna - **§1787**

Textile Workers Union v. Lincoln Mills - **§§378, 570**

Thermtron Products, Inc. v. Hermansdorfer - **§§487, 489, 2174**

Thiel v. Southern Pacific Co. - **§§815, 2157**

Thillens, Inc. v. Community Currency Exchange Association - **§1265**

Things Remembered, Inc. v. Petrarca - **§489**

Thompson v. Paasche - **§1920**

Thornton v. Wahl - **§§790, 796**

Throckmorton, United States v. - **§2045**

Tice v. American Airlines, Inc. - **§2250**

Tidewater Marine Towing, Inc. v. Dow Chemical Co. - **§931**

Tiller v. Atlantic Coast Line - **§924**

Toledo Scale v. Computing Scale Co. - **§1983**

Tomera v. Galt - **§726**

Torres v. Oakland Scavenger Co. - **§2081**

Trans World Airlines, Inc. v. Civil Aeronautics Board - **§1111**

Travel Agents Malpractice Action Corps. v. Regal Cultural Society - **§1027**

Trbovich v. United Mine Workers - **§1098**

Treinies v. Sunshine Mining Co. - **§2205**

Trezza v. Dame - **§1912**

Triodyne, Inc. v. Superior Court - **§669**

Triplett v. Williams - **§1003**

Tull v. United States - **§§1785, 1786**

Tulsa Professional Collection Services, Inc. v. Pope - **§222**

U

Union Carbide Corp. Gas Plant Disaster at Bhopal, India, *In re* - **§209**

Union Electric Light & Power Co. v. Snyder Estate Co. - **§1929**

Union Pacific Railroad, United States v. - **§116**

Union Tool Co. v. Wilson - **§1607**

United Mine Workers v. Bagwell - **§1607**

United Mine Workers v. Gibbs - **§§406, 418, 425, 426, 432, 442, 444, 445, 448, 449**

United States v. - *see* name of party

United States Gypsum, United States v. - **§2141**

United States Parole Commission v. Geraghty - **§1164**

United Steelworkers v. R.H. Bouligny, Inc. - **§324**

Universal Film Exchanges, Inc. v. Lust - **§2036**

University of Pennsylvania v. E.E.O.C. - **§1477**

Upjohn Co. v. United States - **§§1452, 1465, 1488**

V

Valley Bank v. Superior Court - **§1441**

Van Dusen v. Barrack - **§204**

Vasquez v. Superior Court - **§1147**

Verlinden B.V. v. Central Bank of Nigeria - **§377**

Vesley v. Sager - **§758**

Vital v. Interfaith Medical Center - **§1665**

W

Walker v. Armco Steel Co. - **§§540, 541**

Walker v. City of Hutchinson - **§226**

Walker v. Sauvinet - **§1774**

Wallin v. Fuller - **§1720**

Ward v. Taggart - **§2158**

Warren Insurance Agency v. Surpur Timber Co. - **§1007**

Waste Management Holdings, Inc. v. Mowbray - **§2119**

Watson v. Cannon Shoe Co. - **§950**

Watson v. Employers Liability Assurance Corp. - **§1079**

Watson v. Roberts, Scott & Co. - **§2239**

Watterson v. Page - **§765**

Weese v. Schukman - **§1865**

Weiner v. Fleishman - **§1911**

Weisgram v. Marley Co. - **§1972**

West Mifflin, Borough of v. Lancaster - **§472**

Western Union Telegraph Co. v. Pennsylvania - **§63**

Westgate-California Corp., *In re* - **§2235**

Wetzel v. Liberty Mutual Insurance Co. - **§1222**

White Lighting Co. v. Wolfson - **§675**

Willden v. Washington National Insurance Co. - **§1914**

Williams v. Florida - **§1824**

Williams v. United States - **§931**

Wisconsin Department of Corrections v. Schacht - **§462**

Wisland v. Admiral Beverage Corp. - **§205**

Withers v. Tucker - **§1018**

Wolpe v. Poretsky - **§1105**

Woolen v. Surtran Taxicabs, Inc. - **§1239**

World-Wide Volkswagen Corp. v. Woodson - **§§27, 28, 29, 31, 33, 34, 35, 39, 43, 44, 126**

Worthington v. Kaiser Health Plan - **§1055**

Worthington v. Wilson - **§929**

Wright v. Arkansas Activities Association - **§1024**

Wulfsohn v. Russo-Asiatic Bank - **§1983**

Wyman v. Newhouse - **§§9, 112**

X

Xerox v. IBM - **§1502**

Y

Yaffe v. Powers - **§1154**

Yamaha Motor Corp. v. Calhoun - **§2118**

Yorty v. Chandler - **§653**

Z

Zahn v. International Paper Co. - **§§422, 1199, 1202**

Zenith Radio Corp. v. Matsushita Electric Industrial Co. - **§§1545, 1552**

Zielinski v. Philadelphia Piers, Inc. - **§822**

Zuk v. Eastern Pennsylvania Psychiatric Institute - **§§789, 813**

Index

waiver of, **§2061**

Rule 11 orders, **§812**

separate instrument rule, **§2099**

state court decisions, **§§2070-2073**

stay of proceedings below, **§2093**

substantial evidence test, **§§2138, 2142**

summary judgment, **§§1686-1688**

time limits, **§§2082-2085**

trial de novo, **§2167**

waiver of objections, **§§2159-2166**

weight of evidence, **§§1986-1995**. *See also* New trial, motion for

APPEARANCE

See also Territorial jurisdiction

in personam jurisdiction, **§§102-109**

limited, **§139**

special appearance rule, **§§103-104**

APPELLATE PROCEDURE

See Appeal

ARBITRATION, §§1758-1771

See also Pretrial conferences and managerial judging

ARGUMENT TO JURY

See Jury

ASSIGNMENT OF CLAIM

diversity jurisdiction, **§340**

ASSIGNMENTS

partial, **§§997-998, 1054**

real party in interest rule, **§§992-999**. *See also* Real party in interest rule

ATTACHMENT JURISDICTION, §§252-279, 2218-2220

ATTORNEYS' FEES

class actions, **§1257**

B

"BLUE RIBBON" JURY, §1810

See also Jury

C

CAPACITY TO BE SUED

capacity defined, **§1015**

corporations, **§1019**

guardian, **§1017**

incompetents, **§§1017-1018**

individuals, **§§1016-1018**

lack of, **§§1028-1029**

partnerships, **§§1020-1022**

representative parties, **§989**

unincorporated associations, **§§1023-1027**

CERTIFICATION BY ATTORNEYS, §§768-814, 1595-1599

See also Pleadings; Subscriptions

CERTIFIED FINALITY, §§2110, 2114

See also Final decision rule

CHOICE OF LAW, §§550-559

See also Erie doctrine

venue and, **§§203-206**

CITIZENS LIVING ABROAD, §315

CITIZENSHIP

See Diversity jurisdiction; Territorial jurisdiction

CLAIM PRECLUSION, §§2178-2180, 2183-2224

See also Res judicata

CLAIMS, JOINDER OF

See Class actions; Joinder

CLAIMS, SPLITTING OF, §§677-679

See also Complaint

CLASS ACTIONS

See also Shareholders' derivative actions

adequate representation, **§§1165-1172, 1239, 1262**

appeal of certification decisions, **§1215**

attorneys' fees, **§1257**

bilateral class action, **§§1268-1270**

certification, **§§1206-1215**

    partial, **§1196**

certification for settlement only, **§§1193-1195**

common predominant question, **§§1180-1192**

common question, **§§1155-1160**

communications with class members, **§§1243-1248**

consent to class, **§100**

decertification, **§1171**

defendant class actions, **§§1261-1270**

discovery, **§1242**

dismissal and compromise, **§§1249-1254**

distribution of proceeds, **§§1255-1256**

diversity jurisdiction, **§§330, 1198**

employment discrimination cases, **§1179**

Federal Rules, **§§1142-1146**

grounds for, **§§1173-1196**

historical background, **§§1139-1146**

"hybrid," **§1144**

intervention, **§§1238-1241**

joinder, **§§1140-1158**

judgment, effect of, **§§1258-1260**

jurisdictional amount, **§§422, 439, 1198-1202**

manageability, **§§1187-1191**

mass tort actions, **§§1185, 1192**

notice requirements, **§§1153, 1222-1231**

    contents, **§§1226-1229**

    costs of, **§§1230-1231**

    effect of, **§1229**

    when mandatory, **§§1223-1225**

numerous parties, **§§1149-1154**

    ascertainable class, **§1154**

opting out, **§§1204, 1218, 1232-1237**

pendent jurisdiction, **§§422, 429**

personal jurisdiction, **§§1203-1205, 1267**

"cross-demands deemed compensated," **§891**
joinder, **§§876-880**
jurisdiction, **§§869-870**
permissive, **§882**
pleading, **§§872-875**
statute of limitations, **§§888-892**
supplemental jurisdiction, **§§410, 414**
venue, **§871**
voluntary dismissal, **§881**

CROSS-CLAIMS
counterclaims compared, **§898**
generally, **§893**
impleader compared, **§899**
jurisdiction, **§894**
parties, **§897**
pleading, **§§895-896**
supplemental jurisdiction, **§415**

CROSS-COMPLAINTS—STATE PRACTICE, §§900-911
form, **§§901-903**
generally, **§900**
indemnification, **§911**
joinder of claims, **§§905-907**
joinder of parties, **§904**
responsive pleading, **§§908-911**

CROSS-DEMANDS
See Counterclaims

D

DAMAGES
See Complaint

DECLARATORY RELIEF
amount in diversity cases, **§359**
class actions, **§1266**
federal question, **§398**
right to jury trial, **§1787**

DEFAMATION ACTIONS
See Complaint

DEFAULT
See Pleadings; Res judicata

DEFENSES, AFFIRMATIVE
See Answer

DEFENSES, ANTICIPATORY
See Anticipatory defenses

DEMEANOR EVIDENCE, §§1879-1882

DEMURRER
common law, **§§693-695**
criticism of, **§711**
cross-complaints, **§909**
failure to raise grounds for, **§§708-710**
general, **§§694, 700**
grounds for, **§699**
overruled, **§705**

procedure, **§§702-703**
rulings on, **§§704-707**
"speaking," **§759**
special, **§§695, 700**
state practice, **§§696-711**
sustained, **§§706-707**

DENIALS
See Answer

DEPOSITIONS
See also Discovery
by telephone, **§1333**
compulsory appearance of witness, **§§1319-1324**
corporations, **§§1323-1324**
defined, **§1309**
documents, production of, **§1318**
durational limit, **§§1327-1340**
interrogatories compared, **§1350**. *See also* Interrogatories
motion to compel, **§1336**
notice, **§§1325-1326**
numerical limits, **§§1314-1317**
objections, **§§1334-1340**
optional, **§1313**
protective orders. *See also* Discovery
    inconvenient place, **§§1558-1562**
    unduly burdensome, **§1564**
    unreasonable conduct of deposition, **§§1338, 1563**
place of, **§§1321, 1558-1562**
questioning, **§§1329-1340**
real evidence, subpoena for inspection of, **§§1401-1402**
supplement, when necessary, **§§1414-1419**
timeliness, **§§1310-1312**
transcription, **§§1341-1343**
use at trial, **§§1343-1348**
videotape, **§1342**
written, **§§1331-1332**

DILATORY PLEAS
See Answer

DIRECT ESTOPPEL, §2225
See also Res judicata

DIRECTED VERDICT, §§1865-1890, 1894-1897
See also Judgment as a matter of law

DISCOVERY
appeal of discovery orders, **§§1599-1607**
bank records, **§1441**
class actions, **§1242**
collateral purpose, **§§1282-1284**
common law, **§1271**
cost to litigants, **§1280**
depositions, **§§1309-1348**. *See also* Depositions
documents, **§§1327-1328, 1384-1402**
duty to supplement, **§§1414-1419**
expert reports, **§§1505-1530**
    as fact witness, **§1530**
    nontestifying, **§§1506-1511**

G

GENERAL DEMURRER
See Demurrer

GENERAL DENIAL
See Answer

GENERAL JURISDICTION, §§79-92
See also Territorial jurisdiction

GOVERNMENT RECORDS
See Discovery

GUARDIANS
capacity to be sued, §1017
diversity jurisdiction, §331

H

HARMLESS ERROR, §§1976, 2154-2158
See also Appeal

"HYBRID" CLASS ACTIONS
See Class actions

I

IDENTICAL ISSUES, §2239
See also Res judicata

IMPLEADER
cross-claims compared, §§899, 1088
defined, §1071
indemnification, limited to, §§1072-1082
    contribution among tortfeasors, §1076
    insurers, §§1078-1080
    supplemental jurisdiction, §1082
jurisdiction, §1087
pleadings, §§1083-1085
potential liability, §§996-1000
separate trials, §1086
supplemental jurisdiction, §§411-414
venue, §1087

IN PERSONAM JURISDICTION
See Territorial jurisdiction

IN REM JURISDICTION
See Territorial jurisdiction

INCOMPETENTS
capacity to be sued, §§1017-1018
right to disaffirm judgment, §1018

INDEMNIFICATION, §§1072-1082
See also Impleader

INDEPENDENT SUIT TO SET ASIDE JUDGMENT,
    §§2045-2051

INDISPENSABLE PARTY
joinder, §§1045, 1053
supplemental jurisdiction, §417

INSURANCE
direct actions against insurer, §§1078-1079
discovery, §§1300, 1437
impleading insurer, §1080
in rem, §§14, 63, 77

INTERPLEADER
See also Joinder
cross-claims and counterclaims, §§1134-1136
defined, §1117
deposit "stake," §1120
diversity jurisdiction, §§1128-1131
Erie doctrine, §1138
federal, §§1124-1126
jurisdictional amount, §1132
jury trial, §1795
procedural matter, §1138
process, §§1133, 1136
Rule 22, §§1045-1056
statutory
    diversity jurisdiction, §§1047-1050
    generally, §1044
    venue, §1137

INTERROGATORIES
See also Discovery
burdensome, §1564. *See also* Discovery, protective
    orders
corporations, §1353
costs, §1363
defined, §1349
depositions compared, §1350
duty to investigate, §§1358-1359
duty to respond, §§1357-1359
expert witness lists, §1419
extensive search, §1359
failure to respond, §§1360-1363
motion to compel response, §§1360-1363
numerical limit, §1356
objections to, §1362
time for response, §1357
when served, §§1354-1355
who must answer, §§1351-1353

INTERVENTION
See also Supplemental jurisdiction
by right, §§1091-1104
    compulsory joinder compared, §§1101-1103
    standing compared, §1094
class actions, §§1238-1241
effect of, §§1110-1112
generally, §1089
permissive
    common question, §1105
    generally, §§1105-1108
    supplemental jurisdiction, §416
state practice, §§1113-1115
supplemental jurisdiction, §§416, 437

timeliness, **§1109**

venue, **§1111**

INVESTIGATION, PRIVATE, §§1613-1615

See also Discovery

INVITED ERROR, §2162

See also Appeal

ISSUE PRECLUSION, §§2181, 2189, 2225-2240

See also Res judicata

J

JOINDER

claims, **§§680-687, 905-907**

    no compulsory, **§680**

    permissive, **§§681-687**

    separate trials, **§686**

class actions, **§§1140, 1158**

collusive, **§339**

compulsory, **§§1042-1070, 1101-1103**

    dismissal, **§1067**

    diversity jurisdiction, **§1067**

    intervention compared, **§§1101-1103**

    modern approach, **§§1046-1060**

    nonjoinder, effect of, **§1048**

    practical consequences, **§1046**

    procedure, **§§1061-1067**

    venue, **§1066**

    waiver of, **§§1068-1070**

consolidation of actions, **§1116**

co-owners of property, **§§1055-1057**

counterclaims, **§§876-880**

cross-complaints, **§§904, 907**

diversity jurisdiction

    collusive joinder, **§339**

impleader, **§§1052, 1071-1088.** *See also* Impleader

improper, **§1040**

indispensable parties, **§1045**

interpleader, **§§1117-1138.** *See also* Interpleader

intervention, **§§1089-1115.** *See also* Intervention

joint obligees, **§1053**

joint obligors, **§1050**

necessary parties, **§1044**

partial assignees or subrogees, **§1054**

permissive, **§§1031-1041**

    additional unrelated claims, **§1038**

    common question, **§1037**

    improper joinder, **§1040**

    relief sought **§§1034-1035**

    same transaction, **§1036**

    separate trials, **§1039**

    subject matter jurisdiction, **§1041**

procedure for compelling, **§§1061-1067**

shareholders' derivative suits, **§1060**

supplemental jurisdiction, **§1041**

third-party beneficiaries, **§§1058-1059**

tortfeasors, **§§1051-1052**

JOINT OBLIGEES, §1053

JOINT OBLIGORS, §1050

JUDGE, DISQUALIFICATION OF, §§1841-1852

JUDGMENT AS A MATTER OF LAW, §§1865-1890, 1894-1897

and renewed motion, **§§1883-1890, 1966-1967**

burden of proof, **§§1864, 1867-1871**

case-by-case determination, **§§1872-1882**

demeanor evidence, **§§1879-1882**

nonjury trial, **§§1894-1897**

renewed motion, **§§1960-1973**

    joined with motion for new trial, **§§1968-1972**

    procedure, **§§1962-1973**

    test, **§1961**

    timeliness, **§§1964-1965**

scintilla rule, **§1871**

standard for grant, **§§1867-1871**

JUDGMENT N.O.V., §§1960-1973. *See also* Judgment as a matter of law

and motion for directed verdict, **§§1966-1967**

and motion for new trial, **§§1968-1972**

timeliness, **§§1964-1965**

JUDGMENT NOTWITHSTANDING THE VERDICT

See Judgment n.o.v.

JUDGMENTS

alternative. *See* Res judicata

modifiable. *See* Res judicata

on pleadings, **§§967-972**

relief from. *See* Motions

stipulated. *See* Res judicata

JUDICIAL NOTICE, §1863

JURISDICTION

See Diversity jurisdiction; Federal question jurisdiction;
                Subject matter jurisdiction;
                Territorial jurisdiction

JURISDICTIONAL AMOUNT

See also Diversity jurisdiction

aggregation of claims, **§§361-367**

class actions, **§§1199-1202**

diversity jurisdiction, **§§351-367**

federal question jurisdiction, **§404**

"good faith" limitation, **§355**

interpleader, **§1132**

removed actions, **§§356, 467**

JURY

advisory, **§1803**

alternate jurors, **§1828**

argument to, **§§1898-1902**

"blue-ribbon," **§1810**

coercion by judge, **§1947**

instructions, **§§1903-1921, 2160**

VOIR DIRE

See Jury

VOLUNTARY DISMISSAL

See Dismissal

WXYZ

WELL-PLEADED COMPLAINT RULE

See Federal question jurisdiction

WITNESS'S STATEMENTS

See Discovery

WITNESSES

See Discovery; Interrogatories

WORK PRODUCT

See Discovery

Notes

Notes

Notes

Notes